Steiner's Diary

Über Architektur
seit 1959

STEINER'S DIARY

About Architecture
Since 1959

Linzer Vorlesungen
Hg. / Ed. Kunstuniversität Linz
Roland Gnaiger | die architektur

 PARK BOOKS

CONTENTS

- 7   Linz Lectures – Reinhard Kannonier
- 8   Why This Book?
- 11   Start: Jacques Herzog and Dietmar Steiner

1st DAY — The 1960s

- 30   Experimental Architecture in Austria
- 36   Coop HausRucker – Wolf Prix and Laurids Ortner
- 50   Milan Towers – Velasca versus Pirelli
- 54   Brutalism

2nd DAY — The 1970s

- 66   Every Detail Is a Story
- 70   Ticino 1978
- 72   My Barcelona
- 82   Mies van der Rohe Award Winners
- 84   On Rob Krier
- 88   Arena 1976
- 89   The Year 1979

3rd DAY — The 1980s

- 92   Biennale 1980
- 94   Moscow and Leningrad 1982
- 96   Architecture Is Background – Hermann Czech
- 108   Blade Runner: In the Jungle of the Future
- 110   Futuristic Plagiarisms in an Apocalyptic Mood
- 112   Staatsgalerie Stuttgart: Everything Is Living Dead
- 114   IBA Berlin: Islands in the City
- 116   Rudolf Olgiati: The White Crystals of Laax
- 118   Letter to Martin Steinmann – archithese
- 128   Meat and Bones Architecture
- 142   The City – Networks and Bodies
- 154   The Heavy Dress
- 160   Analogous Architecture

4th DAY — The 1990s

- 166   Of Whores and Saints
- 182   There Is No Escape
- 194   Hollein – The Sketch of a Name
- 210   A Diary of Disney's Celebration

5th DAY — The 2000s

- 226   9/11
- 234   Promotional Architecture
- 242   Interview Jacques Herzog
- 256   Interview Rem Koolhaas
- 260   Lacaton & Vassal: Turkish Café
- 270   Jon Jerde
- 280   Rural Studio: Sweet Home Alabama
- 294   Loisium
- 298   Iceland 2008

6th DAY — The 2010s

- 314   Vienna Housing
- 328   Architecture: Reset
- 346   Amateur Architecture Studio
- 350   A Day with Alexander Brodsky
- 354   The Kornati Memorial
- 360   BUS:STOP Krumbach

7th DAY — Sunday

- 376   By the Wayside
- 382   The End: Anna Heringer and Dietmar Steiner

- 393   Biography Dietmar Steiner
- 394   Index
- 399   Imprint

INHALT

....

- 7   Linzer Vorlesungen – Reinhard Kannonier
- 8   Warum dieses Buch?
- 11   Anfang: Jacques Herzog und Dietmar Steiner

1. TAG — Die 1960er

- 28   Experimentelle Architektur in Österreich
- 37   Coop HausRucker – Wolf Prix und Laurids Ortner
- 50   Milano Torri – Velasca gegen Pirelli
- 54   Brutalismus

2. TAG — Die 1970er

- 58   Jedes Detail eine Geschichte
- 70   Tessin 1978
- 72   Mein Barcelona
- 82   Mies van der Rohe Award Preisträger
- 84   Über Rob Krier
- 88   Arena 1976
- 89   Das Jahr 1979

3. TAG — Die 1980er

- 92   Biennale 1980
- 94   Moskau und Leningrad 1982
- 96   Architektur ist Hintergrund – Hermann Czech
- 108   Blade Runner: Im Dschungel der Zukunft
- 110   London: Futuristische Plagiate in Endzeitstimmung
- 112   Staatsgalerie Stuttgart: Alles ist lebend tot
- 114   IBA Berlin: Inseln in der Stadt
- 116   Rudolf Olgiati: Die weißen Kristalle von Laax
- 119   Brief an Martin Steinmann – archithese
- 128   Fleisch- und Knochen-Architektur
- 142   Die Stadt – Netze und Körper
- 154   The Heavy Dress
- 160   Analoge Architektur

4. TAG — Die 1990er

- 167   Von Huren und Heiligen
- 182   Es gibt kein Entrinnen
- 194   Hollein – Die Skizze eines Namens
- 210   Ein Tagebuch des Disney Jubiläums

5. TAG — Die 2000er

- 226   9/11
- 234   Architektur als Werbung
- 242   Interview Jacques Herzog
- 250   Interview Rem Koolhaas
- 260   Lacaton & Vassal: Türkisches Café
- 270   Jon Jerde
- 280   Rural Studio: Sweet Home Alabama
- 294   Loisium
- 298   Island 2008

6. TAG — Die 2010er

- 314   Wiener Wohnbau
- 328   Architektur: Neustart
- 346   Amateur Architecture Studio
- 350   Ein Tag mit Alexander Brodsky
- 354   Memorial Kornati
- 360   BUS:STOP Krumbach

7. TAG — Sonntag

- 376   Am Wegesrand

- 382   Ende: Anna Heringer und Dietmar Steiner

- 393   Biografie Dietmar Steiner
- 394   Register
- 399   Impressum

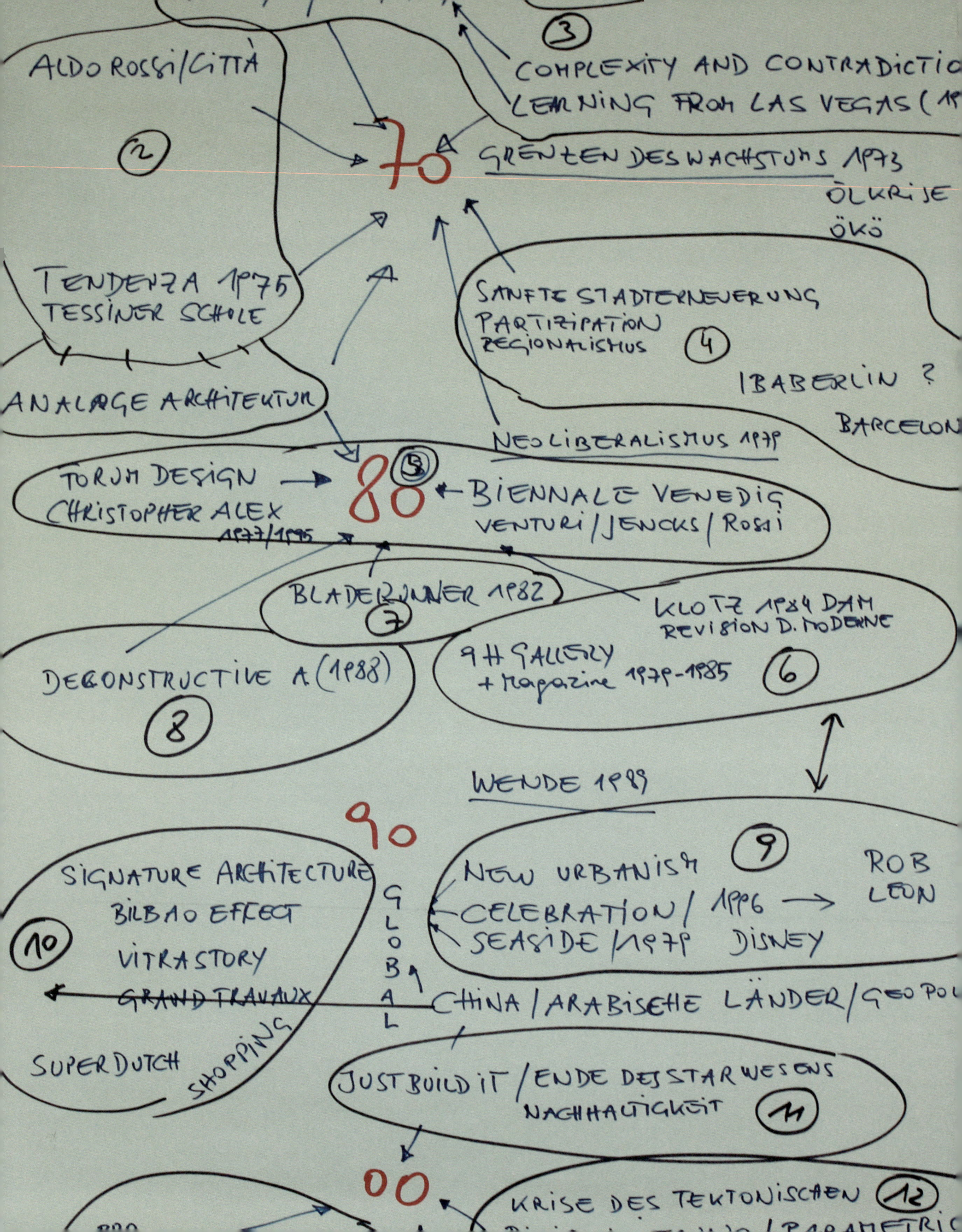

Linzer Vorlesungen

Linz Lectures

Dietmar Steiners „Verhältnis mit der Architektur" gleicht tatsächlich einer erotisch-intellektuellen Langzeitaffäre. Der chaotisch-penible Rechercheur, Lehrer an der Angewandten, Redakteur von *domus* (Milano), langjährige Leiter des Architekturzentrums Wien und vieles andere mehr verfügt über eine beispiellose inhaltliche Bandbreite und zugleich über eine unbeirrbare Schärfe des Blicks in die Tiefe und hinter die Kulissen. Es ist das Verdienst von Roland Gnaiger, Dietmar Steiner zu einer Vorlesungsreihe und auch als Mitglied einer Prüfungskommission an die Kunstuniversität Linz verführt zu haben – an eine (Aus-)Bildungsstätte für Architektur, die ihrerseits den mittlerweile inflationär gebrauchten Begriff „exzellent" tatsächlich verdient.

In gewisser Weise schließt sich mit dieser imposanten Publikation ein kleiner Kreis: Den großen Friedrich Achleitner, an dessen Institut Dietmar Steiner einst gearbeitet hat, holte Gnaiger nach Linz – das Resultat in Buchform, *Achleitners Blick auf Österreichs Architektur nach 1945,* erschien 2015 als erster Band der „Linzer Vorlesungen". Und nun also Dietmar Steiner: Besser und prominenter im schönsten Wortsinn könnte die Fortsetzung einer kleinen Reihe gar nicht erfolgen. Für die Studienrichtung architektur und darüber hinaus selbstverständlich für die gesamte Kunstuniversität Linz ist es eine große Freude und Ehre, dieses Buch edieren zu können.

REINHARD KANNONIER, Rektor

Dietmar Steiner's "relationship with architecture" actually equates to a long-term erotic-intellectual affair. The chaotic-fastidious researcher, instructor at the Academy of Applied Arts, editor of *domus* (Milan), long-time director of the Architekturzentrum Wien and many other things possesses an unparalleled bandwidth in terms of content and at the same time an imperturbable sharpness of sight into the depths and behind the scenes. It is Roland Gnaiger's credit to have beguiled Dietmar Steiner into holding a lecture series and becoming a member of an examination board at the University of Art and Design in Linz—at an educational and training institution for architecture, which for its part has indeed earned the meanwhile overused term "excellent."

In a certain way, a small circle closes with this impressive publication: The great Friedrich Achleitner, in whose institute Dietmar Steiner once worked, called Gnaiger to Linz—the result in book form, *Achleitners Blick auf Österreichs Architektur nach 1945* (A Survey of Austrian Architecture Post 1945), appeared in 2015 as the first volume of the "Linz Lectures." And now Dietmar Steiner: The continuation of a small series could not be carried out better and more prominently in the most beautiful sense of the word. For the architecture studies program and, beyond that, naturally for the entire University of Art and Design Linz, it is a great joy and honor to be able to edit this book.

REINHARD KANNONIER, *Dean*

Konzeptskizze für die Ausstellung · Concept sketch for the exhibition · *Am Ende: Architektur. Zeitreisen von 1959–2019* / *At the End: Architecture. Time Travels from 1959–2019* von · by Gabriele Kaiser, Karoline Mayer, Sonja Pisarik, Katharina Ritter. Archive Az W

Warum dieses Buch?

Why This Book?

I have long dreamt of making a book about my relationship with architecture. Various topics have emerged in the course of the last decades, but were also handled then by other already called authors or I was kept from pursuing these by professional commitments. It was not until Roland Gnaiger from the architectural faculty of the University of Art and Design in Linz invited me for a lecture series on the past decades of international architectural development that I first fleshed out the possibility to examine my experiences and observations in the 'world of architecture.'

I initially failed at the lectures. That was always the case. Often invited (exclusively outside of Vienna) to hold lectures at universities, I respectively accumulated material on the topic in order to ultimately sink into my chaos that I had not thought through to the end. My complete archive is a collection of coincidental depositions. There is no catalog raisonné of my texts and activities. I was neither interested nor involved in academic operations that demanded well-founded, reflected and therefore standardized lectures in terms of content. Therefore, I was always missing the necessary academic apparatus, as well as the freedom to occupy myself over a long period of time researching a specific topic.

Schon lange träume ich davon, über mein Verhältnis mit der Architektur ein Buch zu machen.

Verschiedene Themen sind im Laufe der letzten Jahrzehnte aufgetaucht, wurden aber dann von anderen, ohnehin berufeneren Autoren behandelt, oder ich wurde durch berufliche Verpflichtungen abgehalten, sie weiter zu verfolgen. Erst als mich Roland Gnaiger von der Architekturfakultät der Linzer Universität für künstlerische und industrielle Gestaltung zu einer Vorlesungsreihe über die letzten Jahrzehnte der internationalen Architekturentwicklung einlud, konkretisierte sich erstmals die Möglichkeit, meine Erfahrungen und Beobachtungen in der ‚Welt der Architektur' zu sichten.

An den Vorlesungen bin ich zunächst gescheitert. Das war schon immer so. Oftmals (ausschließlich außerhalb Wiens) eingeladen, an Universitäten Vorlesungen zu halten, akkumulierte ich jeweils Material zum Thema, um schließlich in meinem nicht zu Ende gedachten Chaos zu versinken. Mein ganzes Archiv ist eine Ansammlung von zufälligen Ablagerungen. Es gibt kein Werkverzeichnis meiner Texte und Aktivitäten. Am akademischen Betrieb, der inhaltlich fundierte, reflektierte und dadurch auch standardisierte Vorträge verlangte, war ich weder interessiert noch in ihn eingebunden. Dadurch fehlten mir immer auch der dafür notwendige akademische Apparat sowie die Freiheit, mich über einen langen Zeitraum forschend mit einem Thema zu beschäftigen.

Out of my lonely necessity the "Linz Lectures" arose from very personal narratives, experiences and stories. I rummaged through my jumbled archive, came upon texts, interviews, pictures, relicts of events, projects and data, as well as fragments of occurrences that had shaped my thought and view of international architecture of the past decades. It was odd and appealing at the same time to conduct archaeology in one's own architectonic image of the world. What has been assembled here conveys an initial insight into this archive. The selection of articles does not follow any recognizable system. I surfed in the digital archive and paged through the analog one and attempted to find those pieces that, as commentary on the respective era of the previous decades, can also contribute to their understanding.

Avoiding any analytical objectivity, the succinct title *Steiner's Diary* resulted from the selection of subjective perceptions, as did the subtitle *About* (and not *The*) *Architecture Since 1959*. Following the course of the decades, the book is structured into six days; the seventh day is then dedicated to the Biblical day of rest.

Not only are Professor Roland Gnaiger, Dean Reinhard Kannonier and the University of Art and Design Linz to be thanked that this book now exists. I would have never dared it if Eva Guttmann from Park Books, Claudia Mazanek as the critical copy editor in regards to content, Tom Kussin as the conceptual advisor in all not only graphic decisions hadn't formed a fantastic team who encouraged me, also critically observed by Gabriele Kaiser, to publish my accumulations from several decades. Brian Dorsey is also to be thanked for the translations and for checking the articles that had only been published in English up to now.

Aus dieser meiner einsamen Not heraus entstanden dann die „Linzer Vorlesungen" aus sehr persönlichen Erzählungen, Erlebnissen, Geschichten. Dazu stöberte ich in meinem ungeordneten Archiv, stieß auf Texte, Interviews, Bilder, Relikte von Veranstaltungen, Projekte und Daten sowie Fragmente von Ereignissen, die mein Denken und meine Sicht der internationalen Architektur der letzten Jahrzehnte geprägt hatten. Es war seltsam und reizvoll zugleich, im eigenen architektonischen Weltbild Archäologie zu betreiben. Was hier versammelt ist, vermittelt einen ersten Einblick in dieses Archiv. Die Auswahl der Beiträge folgt keinem erkennbaren System. Ich surfte im digitalen und blätterte im analogen Archiv und versuchte jene Beiträge zu finden, die als Kommentar zur jeweiligen Epoche der letzten Jahrzehnte auch zu deren Verständnis beitragen können.

Aus der nun vorliegenden Auswahl subjektiver Wahrnehmungen ergab sich der jede analytische Objektivität vermeidende lapidare Titel *Steiner's Diary* – sowie im Untertitel *Über* (und nicht *Die*) *Architektur seit 1959*. Dem Lauf der Jahrzehnte folgend ist das Buch in sechs Tage gegliedert, der siebente Tag dann der biblischen Ruhe gewidmet.

Dass es nun dieses Buch gibt, ist nicht nur Professor Roland Gnaiger, Rektor Reinhard Kannonier und der Linzer Universität zu verdanken. Ich hätte es nie gewagt, wenn nicht Eva Guttmann von Park Books, Claudia Mazanek als auch inhaltlich kritische Lektorin, Tom Kussin als konzeptueller Berater in allen, nicht nur grafischen Entscheidungen ein phantastisches Team gebildet hätten, das mich, kritisch beobachtet auch von Gabriele Kaiser, ermutigte, diese Ablagerungen aus mehreren Jahrzehnten zu publizieren. Sehr zu danken ist auch Brian Dorsey für die Übersetzungen und die Kontrolle der bislang nur auf Englisch erschienenen Beiträge.

The book also appears as my personal contribution to the final exhibition of my time as the director at the Architekturzentrum Wien, conceptualized by the curators Katharina Ritter, Karoline Mayer and Sonja Pisarik, advised by Anh-Linh Ngo and Gabriele Kaiser, and designed by BWM Architekten: *In the End: Architecture. Journeys through Time 1959–2019*, as well as the 20th Vienna Architecture Congress at the Az W, which is dedicated with the international involvement of many of my friends and companions to these past decades of architecture. Because the dialog with these actors and thinkers who are most meaningful for me has characterized the contents and positions of *Steiner's Diary*.

I ask for understanding that my observations on the international development of architecture since 1959 were carried out from a Central European fringe area. I was not really involved in the discourses of Western Europe or the American West and East Coast. Seen from Vienna, the 'East' was always closer to me than the 'West.' This could also be the contribution of this book to architectural history that goes beyond the personal.

Steiner's Diary does not bestow the appropriate appreciation upon the many publicized spectacles of architecture of the last decades. After all, it has always been the remote and the resistive, the mundane and the societal aspects that interested me. But I always felt at home where architecture manifested itself as intellectual endeavor. I am grateful for having been allowed to explore and witness this wonderful cosmos of architecture.

DIETMAR STEINER

Das Buch erscheint auch als mein persönlicher Beitrag zur letzten Ausstellung meiner Zeit als Direktor im Architekturzentrum Wien, die von den Kuratorinnen Katharina Ritter, Karoline Mayer und Sonja Pisarik konzipiert, beraten von Anh-Linh Ngo und Gabriele Kaiser, und von BWM Architekten gestaltet wird: *Am Ende: Architektur. Zeitreisen 1959–2019*, sowie zum 20. Wiener Architekturkongress im Az W, der sich mit internationaler Beteiligung vieler meiner Freunde und Wegbegleiter diesen letzten Jahrzehnten der Architektur widmet. Denn der Dialog mit diesen für mich bedeutendsten Akteuren und Denkern hat die Inhalte und Positionen von *Steiner's Diary* geprägt.

Um Verständnis bitte ich, dass meine Beobachtungen der internationalen Entwicklung der Architektur seit 1959 aus einer mitteleuropäischen Randlage erfolgten. In die Diskurse Westeuropas oder der amerikanischen West- und Ostküste war ich nicht wirklich eingebunden. Von Wien aus gesehen war mir immer der ‚Osten' näher als der ‚Westen'. Das könnte auch der über das Persönliche hinausgehende Beitrag dieses Buches zur Architekturgeschichte sein.

Steiner's Diary erweist vielen publizierten Spektakeln der Architektur der letzten Jahrzehnte nicht die entsprechende Würdigung. Es war eben immer mehr das Abseitige und das Widerständige, das Alltägliche und das Gesellschaftliche, das mich interessierte. Aber dort, wo sich Architektur als intellektuelle Anstrengung manifestierte, dort fühlte ich mich zuhause. Ich bin dankbar dafür, dass ich diesen wunderbaren Kosmos der Architektur erkunden und miterleben durfte.

DIETMAR STEINER

Start: Jacques Herzog and Dietmar Steiner on June 9, 2016 in Basel

Anfang: Jacques Herzog und Dietmar Steiner am 9.6.2016 in Basel

JH: We are conducting a conversation for an introduction to your book, which will be a type of retrospective on your involvement with architecture. It is the end of a chapter in your life in which you committed yourself very intensively to architecture and its international orientation. Throughout this stage of life our paths crossed again and again, offering many opportunities to exchange views on how the world of architecture and the world in general are changing and to what extent architecture is suited to perceive and express such changes. Is it possible, then, for you to say goodbye to this everyday reality, which is so strongly shaped by architecture, from one day of the next?

DS: I now have to pause once; my archive and my library are waiting for an overhaul. The past decades were characterized by an enormous workload and after 25 years at the Architekturzentrum it is simply time to make room for the next generation. I also have to admit that the current business architecture doesn't interest me anymore. In the last decades the universities have produced too many architects who only want to be successful on the market as service providers. The competition pressure is big; the conditions for the classic role model of the architect are becoming increasingly worse. For this reason my focus rather lies on the small, committed buildings and projects that move away from the mainstream. One of the guiding ideas of my book addresses the question of how architects can influence architectural critics. When reflecting upon it, it became apparent that Herzog & de Meuron is one of the architecture offices that has caused my 'antennas' to vibrate the strongest and most continually.

JH: Wir führen dieses Gespräch als Einleitung zu deinem Buch, das eine Art Rückblick auf deine Beschäftigung mit Architektur sein wird. Es ist das Ende eines Lebensabschnitts, in dem du dich sehr intensiv für die Architektur und ihre internationale Ausrichtung engagiert hast. Im Verlauf dieses Lebensabschnitts haben sich unsere Wege immer wieder gekreuzt, so dass sich viele Gelegenheiten ergaben, sich auszutauschen darüber, wie sich die Welt der Architektur und die Welt überhaupt verändert und inwiefern Architektur geeignet ist, solche Veränderung wahrzunehmen und auszudrücken. Ist es denn möglich, dass du dich von einem Tag auf den anderen von dieser so stark von der Architektur geprägten Alltagsrealität verabschiedest?

DS: Ich muss jetzt einmal innehalten, mein Archiv und meine Bibliothek warten auf die Aufarbeitung. Die letzten Jahrzehnte waren von einem gewaltigen Arbeitspensum gekennzeichnet und nach 25 Jahren im Architekturzentrum ist es einfach Zeit, den Platz für die nächste Generation freizumachen. Ich muss auch bekennen, dass mich die gegenwärtige Business-Architektur nicht mehr interessiert. In den letzten Jahrzehnten haben die Universitäten zu viele Architekten produziert, die nur mehr als Dienstleister am

JH: Naturally I'm very pleased about that. Basel is our home, with its proximity to Germany and France. Very soon we put our feelers out from there into all directions. Austria, however, was then our first real adventure abroad. In Vienna we had the opportunity with Adolf Krischanitz and you to dive into a world still foreign to us. Back then, Austria was outside of Tendenza. Architects such as Adolf Krischanitz, Otto Kapfinger, Luigi Blau and Hermann Czech were among the Austrians who advocated exciting positions and interested us in terms of generation and mentality. Besides, Tendenza was a parallel development towards rational architecture, which Aldo Rossi propagated. Rossi was our teacher and therefore certainly an important influence. But the Austrian movements (Loos, Wagner, Jugendstil, the rich architectural tradition) interested us very much, too. And you—as Spiritus Rector—were the moderator who published, exhibited and communicated differing positions. These were the beginnings through which we got to know each other.

DS: When thinking about this time, I have also realized that I had a hand in the background during many projects. Mediating, finding a common language between the architect and the client, always was an exciting as well as important task for me. For example, the project development for the Loisium would have nearly come to a stop, since the clients had the feeling that the architect—Steven Holl—wasn't taking their conceptual formulations into consideration. The diverging views could only be resolved through my facilitation.

Markt erfolgreich sein wollen. Der Konkurrenzdruck ist groß, die Bedingungen für das klassische Rollenbild des Architekten werden immer schlechter. Aus diesem Grunde liegt mein Augenmerk eher auf den kleinen, engagierten Bauten und Projekten, die sich abseits des Mainstreams bewegen. Einer der Leitgedanken meines Buches geht der Frage nach, wie Architekten Architekturkritiker beeinflussen können. Im Nachdenken darüber zeichnete sich ab, dass Herzog & de Meuron eines der Architekturbüros ist, welches meine ‚Antennen' am stärksten und kontinuierlichsten zum Schwingen gebracht hat.

JH: Das freut mich natürlich sehr. Unser Zuhause ist Basel mit seiner Nachbarschaft zu Deutschland und Frankreich. Sehr bald haben wir unsere Fühler von da aus in alle Richtungen ausgestreckt. Österreich war dann aber wirklich unser erstes Abenteuer im Ausland. In Wien haben wir mit Adolf Krischanitz und dir die Möglichkeit erhalten, in eine uns noch fremde Welt einzutauchen. Österreich war damals außerhalb der Tendenza. Bei den Österreichern waren Architekten wie Adolf Krischanitz, Otto Kapfinger, Luigi Blau, Hermann Czech dabei, die spannende Positionen vertreten haben und uns generations- und mentalitätsmäßig interessierten. Daneben war die Tendenza eine Parallelentwicklung zur rationalen Architektur, die von Aldo Rossi propagiert wurde. Rossi war unser Lehrer und somit natürlich ein wichtiger Einfluss. Aber auch die österreichischen Strömungen (Loos, Wagner, Jugendstil, die reiche Architekturtradition) haben uns sehr interessiert. Und du – als Spiritus Rector – warst der Moderator, der die unterschiedlichen Positionen publiziert, ausgestellt und vermittelt hat. Dies waren die Anfänge, über die wir uns kennengelernt haben.

DS: Bei Überlegungen über diese Zeit habe auch ich festgestellt, dass ich bei vielen Projekten im Hintergrund die Hände im Spiel hatte. Für mich war die Vermittlung, das Finden einer gemeinsamen Sprache zwischen Architekt und Bauherr immer eine spannende und auch wichtige Aufgabe. Zum Beispiel wäre es beinahe zu einem Abbruch der Projektentwicklung des Loisiums gekommen, da die Bauherren das Gefühl hatten, dass der Architekt – Steven Holl – nicht ihre Aufgabenstellungen berücksichtigt. Die unterschiedlichen Ansichten konnten durch meine Moderation geklärt werden.

Jacques Herzog • Dietmar Steiner

Luftbild Siedlung Pilotengasse · Aerial photo of the Pilotengasse housing estate, **Wien** · Vienna
Adolf Krischanitz, Jacques Herzog & Pierre de Meuron, Otto Steidle, 1992. Archive DS

JH: Wie sind wir zum Projekt in Aspern gekommen?

DS: Das war sowohl die Idee von Adolf Krischanitz als auch von mir. Der Wiener Wohnbau ist bis heute stark parteigebunden und bis 1989 war Erhard Busek Landesparteiobmann der Wiener ÖVP und davor Vizebürgermeister. Gemeinsam mit Jörg Mauthe hatten sie eine Initiative gestartet, dass der Volkspartei nahestehende Bauträger Projekte mit Architekten entwickeln, um eine bessere Qualität zu schaffen. Bezüglich der Auswahl der Architekten wurde eine Dachorganisation gegründet, die u.a. auch die Auswahl für die Pilotengasse in Aspern traf. Weitere Pilotprojekte waren die Traviatagasse mit dem Masterplan von Raimund Abraham, die Brunner Straße von Helmut Richter oder der Biberhaufenweg von Heinz Tesar, Carl Pruscha, Otto Häuselmayer. Die SPÖ hat erst später mit guter Architektur im Wohnbau nachgezogen. Doch wie ist es euch mit dem Projekt in Wien ergangen?

JH: Im Zuge des Projekts Pilotengasse hatten wir viele kreative Auseinandersetzungen mit den beteiligten Architekten, die letztendlich zu langjährigen Freundschaften führten. Soweit ich mich erinnere, hast du die österreichischen Architekten im Rahmen der Vortragsveranstaltung „Emerging European Architects", an der auch wir teilgenommen haben, 1989 in Harvard vorgestellt. Kennengelernt hatten wir uns aber bereits früher...

DS: Es müsste bereits 1983 an der AA gewesen sein, als Zaha Hadid ihre erste Ausstellung hatte.

JH: How did we come to the project in Aspern?

DS: That was the idea of Adolf Krischanitz as well as of mine. To this day Viennese housing construction is strongly partisan and until 1989 Erhard Busek was the state party chairman of the Vienna People's Party (ÖVP) and Vice Mayor prior to that. Together with Jörg Mauthe they started an initiative that building contractors affiliated with the People's Party develop projects with architects in order to create a better quality. With regard to the selection of architects, an umbrella organization was founded, which, among other things, made the selection for the Pilotengasse in Aspern. Further pilot projects were the Traviatagasse with the master plan by Raimund Abraham, the Brunner Strasse by Helmut Richter or the Biberhaufenweg by Heinz Tesar, Carl Pruscha and Otto Häuselmayer. The Social Democratic Party (SPÖ) first followed later with good architecture in housing construction. But how did you fare with this project in Vienna?

JH: In the course of the Pilotengasse project we had creative disputes with the participating architects which ultimately led to long-standing friendships. As far as I can remember, you introduced the Austrian architects in 1989 at Harvard in the scope of the lecture event "Emerging European Architects," which we also took part in. But we had already become acquainted with each other earlier...

DS: It had to have been 1983 already at the AA, when Zaha Hadid held her first exhibition.

JH: Exactly, that was when Ricky Burdett and Wilfried Wang organized our exhibition at 9H and Zaha Hadid was acclaimed because of her contribution to the Peak in Hong Kong. It was a mystery to me why this neo-constructivist language Zaha displayed in the Hong Kong design proved popular at that time. Her world and ours: That was the unexpected and irreconcilable clashing of two completely different stances of a new generation of architects.

DS: Through the connection to Wilfried Wang I have written texts for *9H* time and again—especially about the Viennese scene (Czech, Loos reception, etc.). What I deem crucial for our mutual experience is the strongly politicized student days. In your case Lucius Burckhardt, who I also knew well, and in our case the political conflicts at the Academy. Furthermore the change—how rational architecture came into being. Léon Krier reasoned it in the 1970s from a leftist position. It was a mix of sociology and politicizing, on the one hand, and the permanence of the city, on the other hand. In order to make this clear: In the 1970s I attempted to compose an architectural theory in which I wanted to join architecture and politics together; I tried to justify the necessity of the design with Antonio Gramsci's theory. It disturbed me, for instance, that theoretical manifestoes were primarily being written as diploma theses at German universities. It was always important for me to also connect architecture with reality.

JH: At the beginning of the 1970s it was likewise totally impossible at the ETH in Zürich to do and draw architectural projects, because these were decried as reactionary. Projects had to consist of texts and statistics with a planning-based approach. Most of it was useless garbage, because it was neither theoretically interesting nor of any practical or aesthetic use. The luck of our generation of students came in the person of Aldo Rossi, who was welcomed like a Messiah because he succeeded in linking a politically leftist position to the tradition and history of architecture. It was no contradiction for

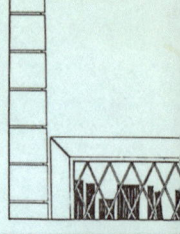

Architectural Association School, London, Veranstaltungsprogramm Herbst · Program of events autumn 1983. Archive DS

14

Jacques Herzog • Dietmar Steiner

JH: Genau, das war, als Ricky Burdett und Wilfried Wang unsere Ausstellung im 9H organisierten und Zaha Hadid wegen ihres Beitrags zum Peak in Hongkong gefeiert wurde. Mir war es schleierhaft, weshalb diese neo-konstruktivistische Sprache, die Zaha in dem Hongkong-Entwurf zur Schau stellte, damals derart Anklang fand. Ihre Welt und unsere: Das war ein unerwartetes und unversöhnliches Aufeinanderprallen von zwei grundverschiedenen Haltungen einer neuen Architektengeneration.

DS: Ich habe über die Verbindung zu Wilfried Wang immer wieder Texte für *9H* – vor allem über die Wiener Szene (Czech, Loos-Rezeption etc.) – geschrieben. Was ich für unsere gemeinsame Erfahrung für entscheidend halte, ist die stark politisierte Studienzeit. Bei euch Lucius Burckhardt, den ich auch gut kannte, und bei uns die politischen Auseinandersetzungen an der Akademie. Weiters der Wechsel – wie die rationale Architektur gekommen ist. Léon Krier hat sie in den 70er Jahren aus einer linken Position heraus argumentiert. Es war eine Mischung aus Soziologie und Politisierung auf der einen Seite und der Permanenz der Stadt auf der anderen. Um dies zu verdeutlichen: ich habe in den 70er Jahren versucht, eine Architekturtheorie zu verfassen, in der ich Architektur und Politik miteinander verbinden wollte, ich versuchte mit der Theorie von Antonio Gramsci die Notwendigkeit des Entwurfs zu begründen. Es hat mich gestört, dass z.B. auf deutschen Universitäten vor allem theoretische Manifeste als Diplomarbeiten geschrieben wurden. Für mich war es immer wichtig, die Architektur auch mit der Wirklichkeit in Verbindung zu bringen.

JH: An der ETH in Zürich war es zu Beginn der 1970er Jahre ebenfalls total unmöglich, Architekturprojekte zu machen und zu zeichnen, weil dies als reaktionär verschrien war. Projekte hatten aus Texten und Statistiken mit planungsmethodischem Ansatz zu bestehen. Das meiste war unbrauchbarer Mist, weil weder theoretisch interessant noch von irgendwelchem praktischen oder ästhetischen Nutzen. Das Glück unserer Studentengeneration kam in der Person von Aldo Rossi, der wie ein Messias empfangen wurde, weil es ihm gelang, eine politisch linke Position mit der Tradition und der Geschichte der Architektur zu verknüpfen. Für Rossi war es kein Widerspruch, einerseits Architektur anzuschauen, zu fotografieren, zu zeichnen, zu bauen und andererseits diese Erfahrungen mit einer linken Architekturtheorie der Stadt und der Gesell-

Rossi, on one hand, to look at, to photograph, to draw, to build architecture and, on the other hand, to combine these experiences with a leftist architectural theory of the city and the society. This was an important experience for us.
The other, extraordinary teacher at the ETH back then, the sociologist Lucius Burckhardt, followed and taught completely different contents which, however, likewise left a lasting mark on us. He was rather a thinker influenced by Basel Protestantism and a proponent of the sparse and the minimal intervention. Sharp observation was the basis for all of that.

As teachers, Rossi and Burckhardt represented totally divergent, ideological positions, but that was precisely so enriching for us.
When Pierre and I got to know each other, we had already realized several projects and above all submitted many competition designs. It was clear to us early on that we wanted to overcome such ideological positions in our own way: Sociology would not be able to replace architecture; rationalism and Rossi's analogous architecture were too confining for us, and we perceived postmodernism and neo-constructivism as mere gadgetry. We wanted to tackle each project separately and to let it emerge as something specific ensuing from the concrete location, the program and the contracting authorities. The most important prerequisite thereby was always the critical awareness and exact observation of all these factors, without a priori, without hidden preferences, without ideology. This conceptual approach always was the driving force for us and has remained so up to today.
During the best projects we succeeded in interweaving the physical expression in the conceptual considerations of the design in such a way that one cannot separate them from one another. Only in this way can architecture function at all and great architecture arise if need be. This is no different in literature or art.

DS: Yes, and that a project finds a design expression and does not get mired in theory. I had a good contact to Lucius Burckhardt at the time he was in Kassel. He even invited me to apply for his succession. In light of the level at the university in Kassel, however, I stopped my application lecture myself. I didn't want to teach in this provincial climate.

JH: You were certainly right in that case ... A university has to give you a certain backing, intellectually and politically, it should allow lecturers with different attitudes. Also in Switzerland there are cases again and again where lecturers are not supported because of an undesired political bent. Back then, Lucius was indeed veritably driven out of the ETH because he was such a radical and leftist thinker and such a provocative figure. It was perhaps better for you not to teach at a school. I don't see you as a lecturing theoretician. Starting from your socio-critical, but always pragmatic attitude, you were well-positioned at the interface between the academy and practice. On one hand, as a curator who is strongly connected with Vienna and a person who the Austrian essence is an important part of. On the other hand, you have been able to build up a relationship of trust to willing investors/clients because you have always attempted to bring the appropriate experts together and not to force any architecture merely because friends were involved. This form of mediation is a decidedly important task. Because the Viennese and all of us will miss you! You were perfect at the interface between theory and practice because of your independent thinking and mediating, and because of your love of architecture and the resulting friendships, some of which are life-long.

DS: I was also never really interested in the academic environment. Holding standardized lectures for uninterested students was never my intention. I was much more interested in placing committed architects with real building tasks.

schaft zu verbinden. Dies war für uns eine wichtige Erfahrung. Der andere, außergewöhnliche Lehrer an der damaligen ETH, der Soziologe Lucius Burckhardt, verfolgte und lehrte ganz andere Inhalte, die uns aber ebenfalls nachhaltig prägten. Er war eher ein vom Basler Protestantismus beeinflusster Denker und ein Verfechter des Kargen und des minimalen Eingriffs. Grundlage für das alles war scharfe Beobachtung. Rossi und Burckhardt vertraten als Lehrer völlig unterschiedliche, ideologische Positionen, aber das war gerade so bereichernd für uns.
Als Pierre und ich dich kennenlernten, hatten wir bereits einige Projekte realisiert und vor allem viele Wettbewerbsentwürfe vorgelegt. Uns war es früh klar, dass wir auf unserem eigenen Weg solch ideologische Positionen überwinden wollten: Soziologie würde Architektur nicht ersetzen können, der Rationalismus und die analoge Architektur von Rossi waren uns zu einengend und die Postmoderne und den Neo-Konstruktivismus empfanden wir als bloße Spielereien. Wir wollten jedes Projekt für sich angehen und es als etwas Spezifisches ausgehend vom konkreten Ort, dem Programm und den Auftraggebern entstehen lassen. Die wichtigste Voraussetzung war dabei stets die kritische Wahrnehmung und genaue Betrachtung all dieser Faktoren, ohne Apriori, ohne versteckte Vorlieben, ohne Ideologie. Diese konzeptuelle Vorgehensweise war für uns immer treibende Kraft und ist es bis heute geblieben.
Bei den besten Projekten ist es uns gelungen, den physischen Ausdruck und die konzeptuellen Überlegungen eines Entwurfs so miteinander zu verflechten, dass man sie nicht voneinander trennen kann. Nur so kann Architektur überhaupt funktionieren und allenfalls große Architektur entstehen. Dies ist nicht anders in Literatur oder Kunst.

DS: Ja, und dass ein Projekt zu einem Gestaltausdruck findet und nicht in der Theorie steckenbleibt. Ich hatte einen guten Kontakt mit Lucius Burckhardt zu jener Zeit, als er in Kassel war. Er hat mich sogar eingeladen, mich für seine Nachfolge zu bewerben. Aber angesichts des Milieus der Hochschule in Kassel habe ich selbst meinen Bewerbungsvortrag abgebrochen. Ich wollte in diesem provinziellen Klima nicht unterrichten.

JH: Da hattest du sicher recht... Eine Hochschule muss dir einen gewissen Rückhalt geben, intellektuell und politisch, sie sollte Dozenten mit unterschiedlicher Gesinnung zulassen. Auch in der Schweiz gibt es immer wieder Fälle, wo Dozenten nicht gestützt werden, wegen unerwünschter politischer Haltung. Lucius wurde ja damals von der ETH regelrecht vertrieben, weil er ein so radikaler und linker Denker und eine so provozierende Figur war.
Für dich war es vielleicht besser, nicht an einer Schule zu lehren. Ich sehe dich nicht als dozierenden Theoretiker. Ausgehend von deiner gesellschaftskritischen, aber stets pragmatischen Haltung, warst du gut positioniert an einer Schnittstelle zwischen Akademie und Praxis. Einerseits als Kurator, der stark mit Wien verbunden ist und bei dem das Österreichische einen wichtigen Teil darstellt. Anderseits hast du zu geneigten Investoren/Bauherren ein Vertrauensverhältnis aufbauen können, weil du immer versucht hast, die passenden Fachleute zusammenzubringen und keine Architektur zu erzwingen, bloß weil da Freunde im Spiel waren. Diese Form der Vermittlung ist eine ausgesprochen wichtige Aufgabe. Da wirst du den Wienern und uns allen fehlen! Du warst perfekt an dieser Schnittstelle zwischen Theorie und Praxis wegen deines eigenständigen Denkens und Vermittelns und wegen deiner Liebe zur Architektur und den daraus entstandenen, teilweise lebenslangen Freundschaften.

DS: Mich hat auch das akademische Milieu nie wirklich interessiert. Standardisierte Vorträge für uninteressierte Studenten zu halten war nie meine Absicht. Viel stärker hat mich die Vermittlung von engagierten Architekten mit realen Bauaufgaben interessiert.

JH: Aus welchen Teilen hat sich dein Gehalt in den letzten 25 Jahren zusammengesetzt?

DS: Typische Schweizer Frage. Natürlich aus dem moderaten Gehalt vom Architekturzentrum Wien. Aber ich wurde immer wieder zu Jurys, Beratungen etc. hinzugezogen. Am meisten Freude haben mir die Beratungen gemacht. Zum Beispiel die Auswahl der Architekten für Wettbewerbe wie das Liaunig Museum oder die Projektentwicklung für das Loisium mit Steven Holl. Ganz wichtig waren für meine Kenntnis der internationalen Architekturentwicklung auch die Jahre bei *domus* und insgesamt meine publizistische Tätigkeit. So war ich ständig gefordert, die neusten internationalen Entwicklungen zu beobachten und zu begleiten.

JH: So gesehen warst du immer auch dein eigenes Unternehmen, ein Freelancer.

JH: Which parts has your salary been made up of in the last 25 years?

DS: A typical Swiss question. Naturally of the moderate salary of the Architekturzentrum Wien. But I was repeatedly called into juries, consultations, etc. The consultations gave me the most pleasure. For example, the selection of architects for competitions such as the Liaunig Museum or the project development for the Loisium with Steven Holl. My years with *domus* and my journalistic activity altogether were also very important for my knowledge of the international advancement of architecture. In this way, I was constantly challenged to observe and accompany the latest international developments.

JH: Seen from this angle, you were always your own enterprise, a freelancer.

DS: Yes, I've always continued my free, international 'parallel existence,' even while heading the Az W in Vienna—to the benefit of the house. All the trips and encounters and interviews with international architects were paid by the respeceive media and could become effective for the Az W program.

JH: Were you only at *domus*?

DS: No, that was only the luxurious era of the 1990s. In addition, I have constantly reacted to inquiries of architectural magazines with essays. There are, however, many essays and commentaries for daily newspapers and lifestyle magazines as well.

JH: The media landscape has changed very much. Earlier at the architectural magazines there was the chief editor, who covered a certain point of view. These stances were strongly pronounced. Some architects were welcome there; others, on the contrary, had to have patience until a new editorial team took over the scepter. This doesn't exist today anymore in this form. The newspaper that probably has the largest global circulation and readership today is the *Financial Times*, more than the *Guardian*, *Daily Telegraph* or the *New York Times*, not to even mention the German and French dailies. Because it offers an interesting cultural and architectural section, the *FT* has thus become the extremely popular medium of globally active architects.

DS: I agree with you. At the beginning of the 1990s already I wrote an article on the topic "The End of Architectural Criticism" in *Baumeister*. It was about the postmodern condition that many things can stand next to each other equally and no sectarian wars and directional decisions (e.g., Behnisch versus Stirling, a glass façade is democratic, a closed façade is fascist) are fought out anymore. Criteria about what is right and wrong no longer existed. With this end of architectural criticism, the loss of common sense of how urban affairs are dealt with also reveals itself. An individualization then follows; the building as a grand spectacle and the urban context lost its meaning.

JH: You demonstrate this development in the 1990s. This development, however, actually already began after the war: Modernism had a strong phase in the 1960s, a type of 'cheerful,' liberated modernism, where very interesting architecture arose in Switzerland. But the scale of the existing city was thereby ignored. Modernism and not postmodernism demolished the typology of the old city. Originally—that means before the war—modernism had a fundamental concern: Not only the old city, but also the old bourgeois society was to be overcome in favor of a new, enlightened society. A mandatory aesthetic was to be found for it—namely through a new aesthetic that changes everything. That did not succeed. This is a failure of modernism and will lead to a conservative countermovement in architecture and urban planning, as architectonic postmodernism already indicated—in light of today's national conservative tendencies in politics worldwide probably now more than ever.

DS: I see this in differentiated stages. After postwar modernism (and this is very differently pronounced in the respective countries) comes brutalism. This movement is being strongly received by the current generation (Yugoslavian modernism, among others). This current still takes urban references very strongly into account. The question 'How do I build a city?' gains importance again (infrastructure, public space). These considerations, however, were then lost.
There is the famous sentence: Modernism never went over well with the people!

DS: Ja, ich habe meine freie internationale ‚Parallelexistenz' auch während der Leitung des Wiener Az W weitergeführt – zum Nutzen des Hauses. All die Reisen und Begegnungen und Interviews mit internationalen Architekten wurden von den jeweiligen Medien bezahlt und konnten für das Programm des Az W wirksam werden.

JH: Warst du nur bei *domus*?

DS: Nein, das war nur die luxuriöse Zeit der 1990er Jahre. Daneben habe ich ständig auf Anfragen anderer Architekturmagazine mit Essays reagiert. Es gibt aber auch viele Essays und Kommentare für Tageszeitungen und Lifestyle-Magazine.

JH: Die Medienlandschaft hat sich sehr verändert. Früher gab es bei den Architekturzeitschriften einen Redaktionsleiter, der eine bestimmte Ansicht abgedeckt hat. Diese Haltungen waren stark ausgeprägt. Da waren die einen Architekten willkommen, andere mussten hingegen Geduld haben, bis eine neue Redaktion das Zepter übernahm. Dies gibt es so heute nicht mehr. Die Zeitung, die heute wohl die größte globale Reichweite und Leserschaft hat, ist die *Financial Times*, mehr als der Londoner *Guardian*, *Daily Telegraph* oder die *New York Times*, ganz zu schweigen von den deutschen oder französischen Tageszeitungen. Weil sie einen interessanten Kultur- und Architekturteil anbietet, ist die *FT* deshalb bei den global tätigen Architekten zum äußerst beliebten Medium geworden.

DS: Da stimme ich zu. Ich habe schon am Beginn der 90er Jahre im *Baumeister* einen Artikel zum Thema „Das Ende der Architekturkritik" geschrieben. Darin ging es um den postmodernen Zustand, dass vieles gleichwertig nebeneinander stehen kann und keine Glaubenskämpfe und Richtungsentscheidungen (z.B. Behnisch gegen Stirling, eine Glasfassade ist demokratisch, eine geschlossene Fassade ist faschistisch) mehr ausgefochten werden. Es gab keine Kriterien mehr, was richtig und was falsch ist. Mit diesem Ende der Architekturkritik zeigt sich auch ein Verlust des Common Sense, wie mit dem Städtischen umgegangen wird, an. Es folgte dann eine Individualisierung, das Gebäude als großes Spektakel und der urbane Kontext verloren ihre Bedeutung.

JH: Du machst diese Entwicklung in den 90er Jahren fest. Aber eigentlich hat diese Bewegung schon nach dem Krieg begonnen: Die Moderne hatte in den 60er Jahren eine starke Phase: eine Art

Jacques Herzog • Dietmar Steiner

‚heitere', befreite Moderne, wo in der Schweiz sehr interessante Architektur entstand. Aber dabei wurde der Maßstab der vorhandenen Stadt ignoriert. Die Moderne und nicht die Postmoderne hat die Typologie der alten Stadt gesprengt. Die Moderne hatte ursprünglich – d.h. vor dem Krieg – ein Grundanliegen: Nicht nur die alte Stadt, sondern auch die alte bürgerliche Gesellschaft sollte zugunsten einer neuen, aufgeklärten Gesellschaft überwunden werden. Dafür sollte eine verbindliche Ästhetik gefunden werden – und zwar über eine alles verändernde neue Ästhetik. Das ist nicht gelungen. Dies ist ein Versagen der Moderne und wird in Architektur und Städtebau zu einer konservativen Gegenbewegung führen, wie sie die architektonische Postmoderne bereits andeutete – angesichts der heutigen nationalkonservativen Tendenzen weltweit in der Politik wohl jetzt erst recht.

DS: Ich sehe dies in differenzierteren Abschnitten. Nach der Nachkriegsmoderne (und diese ist in den jeweiligen Ländern sehr unterschiedlich ausgeprägt) kommt der Brutalismus. Diese Bewegung wird von der jetzigen Generation stark rezipiert (jugoslawische Moderne u.ä.). Diese Strömung berücksichtigte noch sehr stark urbane Bezüge. Die Frage „Wie baue ich Stadt?" bekommt wieder Bedeutung (Infrastruktur, öffentlicher Raum). Diese Überlegungen gingen dann allerdings verloren.
Es gibt ja den berühmten Satz: Die Moderne ist bei den Menschen nie angekommen!

JH: Ich denke, wir sind immer noch am Ringen mit diesem Prozess der Modernisierung. Gerade auch wenn du an die islamische Welt denkst, die sich diesem Prozess verweigert, oder wenn du siehst, wie gegenwärtig in der Türkei dies gar rückgängig gemacht wird. Architektur und Städtebau sind ja bloß Abbild, nicht Akteure dieser Prozesse.
Bei dem Versuch, die Begriffe Moderne oder Postmoderne zu differenzieren, geht es immer um das Bemühen, eine Form für eine sich ständig verändernde Welt zu finden. Obwohl das Thema des ‚Ikonischen' überwunden scheint, gibt es weiterhin keine Übereinkunft, wie man Stadt entwickeln kann, ob und wie man Agglomerationen verdichten soll oder neue Quartiere baut, die von den Menschen akzeptiert oder gar geliebt werden.
Deine Tätigkeit am Architekturzentrum war doch auch immer darauf ausgerichtet, neue Tendenzen aufzuzeigen, andere Regionen zu berücksichtigen, neue Generationen zu erreichen. Damit

JH: I think we are still grappling with this process of modernization. Precisely also if you think about the Islamic world, which is refusing this process, or if you see how this is even being rolled back currently in Turkey. Architecture and urban planning are merely a reflection, not actors, of these processes.
When attempting to differentiate the terms modernism or postmodernism, it always is a matter of first finding a mold for a constantly changing world. Although the issue of the 'iconic' appears to have been overcome, there continues to be no agreement on how one can develop city, whether and how one is to intensify agglomerations or build new quarters that are accepted or even loved by the people.
Your activity at the Architekturzentrum was, however, always aimed as well at pointing out new tendencies, taking other regions into consideration and reaching new generations. In this way you have ultimately tried to grasp what is happening in the world. To bring up for discussion whether the newly gained knowledge is suited for further developing the city theme. How do you perceive what is happening at the moment? Postwar modernism is now popular. But does it represent more than an aesthetic trend?

DS: I think we still have a postmodern condition, meaning that a lot is possible and allowed at the same time. This has nothing to do with a style or an attitude, but with an intellectual state of mind. For this reason there are no agreements, but isolated applications. Projects appear that make people ask whether they are from the 1920s, 1960s or 1990s. They have lost the signature of their era.

JH: I also see a tendency towards historicism. If the 60s are now en vogue again, that has nothing to do with the fact that the people like this. They simply take it up into their repertoire. Just like the mid-19th century when the architects were devoted to classicism, but did not shy away from using Gothic or Tudor style elements, too. The houses are made up of a cocktail of style

elements (medieval, baroque, classicistic). The Jugendstil trend, which moved in the direction of modernism, was new. Something really new was visible here. I think we still or again find ourselves in this process. The iconoclastic essence of modernism has something destructive and radical that not everyone loves and not everyone can deal with because values, habits and traditions were destroyed in the process. It would be wrong to believe that there was a development towards an ever-growing radicalization and towards constantly new forms. Instead, the history of architecture invariably shows that backwards movements or reversion exist. I see this neither with joy nor with chagrin. Our cities are the petrified expression of the psychological constitution of the society over the course of centuries. There is no Messiah constantly standing in front of the door, there is also not only an old or only a new world. Everything is in constant transformation. The notion and the excited anticipation that the end is approaching right now and that something new is coming is something eminently Austrian for me. I've never understood this attitude, but I've repeatedly encountered it in Austria: in Jugendstil, the Secession, in the art of actionism or also in architects like Hollein and especially Coop Himmelblau. Perhaps this mindset has something to do with the demise of the monarchy and the associated fear of the province. Maybe a type of defense against the fall into the provincial? Switzerland doesn't know this—Switzerland was always provincial.

DS: You are right, this connection exists. In order to elucidate it by means of an example: In Otto Wagner's Postsparkasse there is also a small exhibition about the building itself, which I supervised as a curator. During research further competition entries by other architects came to light. And when making this comparison it first became clear how revolutionary Wagner's design was. Austrian architects thus believe that it is possible to create something that is absolutely new.

JH: But you yourself were not only interested in the respectively new, but you have constantly followed various tendencies—also contrary positions. And outsiders also drew your attention. And you have worked with different people who hardly have an exchange among themselves, a veritable balancing act. Moreover, you have focused your view to the East. This

hast du letztlich versucht zu begreifen, was in der Welt passiert. Zur Diskussion zu stellen, ob die neu gewonnenen Erkenntnisse sich eignen, das Thema Stadt weiterzuentwickeln. Wie nimmst du das wahr, was im Moment passiert? Die Nachkriegsmoderne ist ja jetzt hoch im Kurs. Aber stellt sie mehr dar als einen ästhetischen Trend?

DS: Ich meine, wir haben nach wie vor einen postmodernen Zustand, das heißt, vieles ist gleichzeitig möglich und erlaubt. Dies hat nichts mit einem Stil oder einer Haltung zu tun, sondern mit einer intellektuellen Befindlichkeit. Aus diesem Grunde gibt es keine Vereinbarungen, sondern Insellösungen. Es tauchen Projekte auf, bei denen man sich fragt, ob sie aus den 20er, 60er oder 90er Jahren sind. Sie haben die Signatur ihrer Zeit verloren.

JH: Auch ich sehe eine Tendenz zum Historismus. Wenn jetzt die 60er Jahre wieder en vogue sind, hat das damit zu tun, dass dies den Leuten gefällt. Sie nehmen es einfach in ihr Repertoire auf. Ähnlich wie Mitte des 19. Jahrhunderts, als die Architekten zwar dem Klassizismus zugetan waren, sich aber nicht scheuten, auch gotische oder Tudor-Stil-Elemente zu verwenden. Die Häuser setzten sich aus einem Cocktail an Stilelementen (mittelalterliche, barocke, klassizistische) zusammen. Neu war die Strömung des Jugendstils, welcher sich in Richtung der Moderne bewegte. Hier wurde etwas wirklich Neues sichtbar. Ich denke, wir befinden uns noch immer oder erneut in diesem Prozess. Das Ikonoklastische der Moderne hat etwas Zerstörerisches, Radikales, das nicht alle lieben und mit dem nicht alle umgehen können, weil dabei eben auch Werte, Gewohnheiten und Traditionen zerstört wurden. Es wäre falsch zu glauben, es gäbe eine Entwicklung hin zu immer größerer Radikalisierung und zu stets neuer Form. Die Geschichte der Architektur zeigt vielmehr, dass es ständig auch Rückwärtsbewegungen oder Rückbesinnung gibt. Ich sehe dies weder mit Freude noch mit Verdruss. Unsere Städte sind der versteinerte Ausdruck der psychologischen Verfassung der Gesellschaft im Verlauf der Jahrhunderte. Es ist nicht stets ein Messias vor der Türe, es gibt auch nicht nur eine alte oder nur eine neue Welt. Alles ist in ständiger Transformation.
Die Vorstellung und aufgeregte Erwartung, dass gerade jetzt das Ende naht und dann etwas Neues kommt, ist für mich etwas eminent Österreichisches. Ich habe diese Haltung nie verstanden, bin

Jacques Herzog • Dietmar Steiner

Abril Jueves **23** April Thursday	10 h.	**Acto de Apertura** Colegio de Arquitectos de Cataluña. Pza. Nueva 5 08002 Barcelona. **Agustí Borrell** Decano del Colegio de Arquitectos de Cataluña. **Albert Broggi** Director de la UIMP en Barcelona. **Jordi Font** Coordinador del Area de Cultura Diputación de Barcelona.	10 hrs	**Opening ceremony** Professional Association of Architects of Catalonia. Plaza Nueva 5. 08002 Barcelona **Agustí Borrell** Dean of the Professional Association of Architects of Catalonia **Albert Broggi** Director of the UIMP in Barcelona **Jordi Font** Cultural Coordinator County Council of Barcelona
	11 h.	**Belleza y Verdad** **José Luis Mateo.** Barcelona. Arquitecto. ETSA de Barcelona. Director de QUADERNS d'Arquitectura i Urbanisme	11 hrs	**Belleza y Verdad** **José Luis Mateo.** Barcelona. Architect. ETSA, Barcelona. Editor of «QUADERNS d'Arquitectura i Urbanisme».
	13 h.	**Architecture and the democratic institutions** **Wilfried Wang.** Londres Arquitecto. Escuela de Arquitectura de Harward. Co-director de la revista *9H* y de la *Galería 9H*.	13 hrs	**Architecture and the Democratic Institutions** **Wilfried Wang.** London. Architect. Harward School of Architecture. Co-editor of *9H* and of the *9H Gallery*.
	16.30 h.	**Trop de choses, pas assez de formes** **Jacques Lucan.** París. Arquitecto. Escuela de Arquitectura de París-Belleville (U.P. 8). Redactor Jefe de A.M.C. (Architecture, Mouvement, Continuité).	16'30 hrs	**Trop des Choses, pas assez de Formes** **Jacques Lucan.** París. Architect. Architecture School of Paris-Belleville (U.P.8). Chief Editor of «A.M.C.» (Architecture, Mouvement, Continuité).
	18 h.	**The piece and the entirety** **Jacques Herzog.** Basilea. Arquitecto.	18 hrs	**The Piece and the Entirety** **Jacques Herzog.** Basel. Architect.
	20 h.	**Mesa Redonda**	20 hrs	**Open Discussion.**
Abril Viernes **24** April Friday	11 h.	**Arquitectura débil** **Ignasi de Solà-Morales.** Barcelona. Arquitecto. ETSA de Barcelona.	11 hrs	**Arquitectura Débil** **Ignasi de Solà-Morales.** Barcelona. Architect. ETSA, Barcelona.
	13 h.	**Architecture is now** **Wolf Prix (Coop. Himmelblau).** Viena. Arquitecto.	13 hrs	**Architecture is Now** **Wolf Prix (Coop Himmelblau).** Vienna. Architect.
	16.30 h.	**High rise in Europe** **Rem Koolhaas.** Rotterdam. Arquitecto. (Office for Metropolitan Architecture).	16.30 hrs	**High-Rise in Europe** **Rem Koolhaas.** Rotterdam. Architect. (Office for Metropolitan Architecture).
	18 h.	**Arquitectura e imaginación. Dos proyectos** **Alvaro Siza Vieira.** Oporto. Arquitecto. Facultad de Arquitectura de la Universidad de Oporto.	18 hrs	**Arquitectura e Imaginación. Dos Proyectos** **Alvaro Siza Vieira.** Oporto. Architect. Faculty of Architecture, Oporto.
Abril Sábado **25** April Saturday	11 h.	**Analogous Architecture** **Miroslav Sik.** Zurich. Arquitecto. ETH de Zurich.	11 hrs	**Analogous Architecture** **Miroslav Sik.** Zurich. Architect. ETH, Zurich.
	13 h.	**Abril** **Albert Viaplana. Helio Piñón.** Barcelona. Arquitectos. ETSA de Barcelona.	13 hrs	**Abril** **Albert Viaplana. Helio Piñón.** Barcelona. Architects. ETSA, Barcelona.
	16.30 h.	**Der peripherie des tempels** **Dietmar Steiner.** Viena. Arquitecto. Academia de Arquitectura de Viena. Redactor-Jefe de UM-BAU.	16'30 hrs	**Der Peripherie des Tempels** **Dietmar Steiner.** Vienna. Architect. Architectural Academy of Vienna. Chief Editor of UM-BAU.
	18 h.	**Teatri e antri Il ritorno del mondo soterraneo nella modernità** **Francesco Venezia.** Nápoles. Arquitecto. Facultad de Arquitectura de Nápoles.	18 hrs	**Teatri e Antri Il Ritorno del Mondo Soteraneo nella Modernità** **Francesco Venezia.** Naples. Architect. Faculty of Architecture, Naples.

Encuentro:

Arquitectura Europea Contemporánea

Director
José Luis Mateo

Secretario
Carmen Isasa

Seminar on:

Contemporary European Architecture

Director
José Luis Mateo

Secretary
Carmen Isasa

Programm des Seminars · Seminar on Arquitectura Europea Contemporáneo, Barcelona, 1987. Archive DS

Pierre de Meuron, Margarethe Cufer, Jacques Herzog, Dietmar Steiner, Restaurant 7 Portes, Barcelona, 1987. Archive Cufer

attempt not to forget the Eastern developments and to make their qualities visible is a very Viennese particularity. How do you see this relation to the culture or the architecture of the East today?

DS: The Czech Republic, Slovakia, Slovenia and Croatia were always very close to us in their traditions (Hungary somewhat less). We were very interested in the developments in these countries and with the fall of the Iron Curtain an open exchange was possible. I regard the architectural situation in Slovenia and Croatia as more exciting than that in Austria. For me personally, Zagreb is closer in the modes of behavior than Munich, for example.
The Az W was an entrance portal into the West for these countries in the East. Our exhibitions on Balkanology, Bogdan Bogdanović and Soviet Modernism established direct relationships. During my activity with the Mies van der Rohe Award it was also a great concern of mine to bring experts from the East into the juries or architects into the selection. After the opening, Croatia and Slovenia also very quickly managed to catch up with Western European standards, because they were able to connect to the very respectable building culture during the Tito era. Many Slovenians went to the AA or Croatians to the Berlage Institute, and in this way the architectural scene of both countries quickly connected to the modern developments. In Ljubljana as well as in Zagreb there is a scene with intellectual, self-conscious architects. But also since its accession to the EU, Poland has made an enormous advancement and is more important for me today than Spain.

JH: How did the Az W come into existence?

DS: At the beginning of the 1990s there was a cultural minister in Austria who was interested in architecture and diverted funds from the federal art budget for architecture. He wanted an architectural institution to be established in each federal state and I was asked to develop a concept for Vienna. More importantly, there were two city counselors in Vienna who were architecturally oriented, too. Since I knew already existing architectural institutions in Europe such as the DAM in Frankfurt or the AM in Basel, this posed an interesting challenge. The concept was accepted and I was asked to head the institution. After a year without a fixed location, the offer then came to precariously establish the Az W in the MuseumsQuartier. And in 2001 we then newly opened in the present size.

JH: How do you divide your work at the Architekturzentrum? Do you have to fight for money from the subsidy providers?

DS: The main task is not the curatorial activity, but the task of developing the political and economic frame conditions. But this is part of any cultural institution. In terms of content, I have to set the agenda, but when curating the individual activities I give very much freedom to internal and external collaborators. And there is a big problem in the funding, because the subsidies of the federal government have been frozen since 1995 and those of the City of Vienna since 2000. We were able to head off this real cutback over the years with sponsors and our own revenues; however, we remain precariously underfunded.

JH: Is there a collection?

DS: It was originally intended to establish Az W solely as a knowledge center. But in the mid-1990s we then saw that no institution was looking after the architectural heritage of the 20th and 21st centuries. And so we began with the acquisition of premortem bequests and estates, particularly of architects of the postwar era.

ihr aber in Österreich immer wieder begegnet: im Jugendstil, der Secession, in der Kunst des Aktionismus oder auch bei Architekten wie Hollein und besonders bei Coop Himmelblau. Vielleicht hat diese Einstellung mit dem Untergang der Monarchie zu tun und der damit verbundenen Angst vor der Provinz. Eine Art Abwehr gegen den Absturz ins Provinzielle vielleicht? Dies kennt die Schweiz nicht – die Schweiz war schon immer Provinz.

DS: Du hast recht, es gibt diesen Zusammenhang. Um ihn an einem Beispiel zu verdeutlichen. In der Postsparkasse von Otto Wagner gibt es auch eine kleine Ausstellung zum Bauwerk selbst, welche ich kuratorisch begleitet habe. Bei den Recherchen sind weitere Wettbewerbsbeiträge von anderen Architekten aufgetaucht. Und erst bei diesem Vergleich wird klar, wie revolutionär der Entwurf von Wagner war. So glauben österreichische Architekten, dass es möglich ist, das absolut Neue zu schaffen.

JH: Du selbst warst aber nicht nur am jeweils Neuen interessiert, sondern hast stets verschiedene Tendenzen verfolgt – auch konträre Positionen. Und auch Außenseiter interessierten dich. Und du hast mit verschiedenen Leuten gearbeitet, die untereinander kaum einen Austausch hatten, ein veritabler Spagat. Außerdem hast du deinen Blick in den Osten gerichtet. Dieser Versuch, die östlichen Entwicklungen nicht zu vergessen und ihre Qualitäten sichtbar zu machen, ist eine sehr wienerische Eigenart. Wie siehst du diesen Bezug zur Kultur oder der Architektur des Ostens heute?

DS: Tschechien, Slowakei, Slowenien, Kroatien waren uns in ihren Traditionen immer sehr nah (Ungarn etwas weniger). Wir waren an den Entwicklungen in diesen Ländern sehr interessiert und mit dem Fall des Eisernen Vorhangs war ein offener Austausch möglich. Ich halte die Architektursituation in Slowenien und Kroatien für spannender als jene in Österreich. Mir persönlich ist Zagreb näher in den Umgangsformen als zum Beispiel München. Das Az W war für diese Länder im Osten ein Eintrittsportal in den Westen. Unsere Ausstellungen zu Balkanology, Bogdan Bogdanović, Sowjetmoderne stellten direkte Bezüge her. Auch während meiner Tätigkeit beim Mies van der Rohe Award war es mir ein großes Anliegen, Experten aus dem Osten in die Jurys oder Architekten in die Auswahl zu bringen. Kroatien und Slowenien haben nach der Öffnung auch sehr rasch einen Anschluss an westeuro-

päische Standards geschafft, weil sie an die sehr respektable Baukultur unter der Tito-Ära anschließen konnten. Viele Slowenen sind ans AA oder Kroaten an das Berlage-Institut gegangen und so hat die Architekturszene beider Länder an die modernen Entwicklungen rasch angeschlossen. Sowohl in Ljubljana als auch in Zagreb gibt es eine Szene mit intellektuellen, reflektierten Architekten. Aber auch Polen hat seit dem EU-Beitritt eine enorme Entwicklung genommen und ist heute für mich wichtiger als Spanien.

JH: Wie ist das Az W entstanden?

DS: Es gab Anfang der 90er Jahre einen Kulturminister in Österreich, der architekturinteressiert war und dieser hat aus dem Kunstbudget des Bundes Mittel für die Architektur abgezweigt. Er wollte, dass in jedem Bundesland eine Architekturinstitution entsteht und für Wien wurde ich gefragt, ein Konzept zu entwickeln. Zudem gab es in Wien zwei Stadträte, die ebenfalls architekturaffin waren. Nachdem ich die in Europa bereits vorhandenen Architekturinstitutionen wie das DAM in Frankfurt oder das AM in Basel kannte, war dies eine interessante Herausforderung. Das Konzept wurde akzeptiert und ich wurde gebeten, die Institution zu leiten. Nach einem Jahr ohne festen Ort kam dann das Angebot, das Az W im Museumsquartier prekaristisch zu etablieren. Und 2001 wurden wir dann in der heutigen Größe neu eröffnet.

JH: Wie teilst du dir deine Arbeit im Architekturzentrum ein? Musst du um Gelder von den Subventionsgebern kämpfen?

DS: Die Hauptaufgabe ist nicht die kuratorische Aktivität, sondern die Aufgabe, die politischen und ökonomischen Rahmenbedingungen zu entwickeln. Aber dies gehört bei jeder kulturellen Institution dazu. Inhaltlich habe ich die Richtung vorgegeben, aber dann bei der Kuratierung der einzelnen Aktivitäten sehr viel Freiheit den internen und externen MitarbeiterInnen gegeben. Und bei der Finanzierung gibt es ein großes Problem, weil die Subventionen des Bundes seit 1995 und jene der Stadt Wien seit 2000 eingefroren sind. Diese reale Kürzung konnten wir über die Jahre mit Sponsoren und Eigeneinnahmen abfangen, aber wird sind nach wie vor prekär unterdotiert.

Az W-Archiv · The Az W archive Möllersdorf. © DS
Archive Herzog de Meuron Basel. © DS

JH: In the case of every estate, the question arises whether it makes sense to keep all the stuff. We have always carefully arranged and maintained our own archive holdings and stored plans, sketches, models, images, photos, etc., in sub-archives. A cabinet of considerable size consequently arose, which we built an individual storage building for. Last year we put it into service so that we can still work with it ourselves. One will now see if it is suited as a work instrument and as a place of research. Is something like this even needed today? And what is going to happen with it tomorrow? We are aware that a fine line exists between something valuable and garbage.

DS: The world of architecture collections has tremendously changed. The fact that large and important architectural offices keep their own collections in their own institutions today is a logical consequence of the development of the profession overall. Your decision, therefore, is groundbreaking. But in addition there are many estates that are simply valuable in terms of art history, which public institutions then have to care about.

JH: Art exhibitions attract a large audience; architecture exhibitions are much more difficult to communicate. I myself have a very critical attitude towards architecture exhibitions, because I've only seen very few that really were convincing. More exhibitions and debates on topical issues of urban development, which one could then respectively show the historic positions and architectural examples of, would be important. Today a disparity persists between the constantly advancing production of city, which indeed shapes our everyday life, and the quality of the engagement with this production. Architecture museums ought to position and distinguish themselves more strongly as places of dialog between planning, the builders and politics.

DS: One can surely say that among all arts architecture is still a somewhat secret science. The population does not perceive the built structure as architecture. Kevin A. Lynch's old theses from the 1960s about how urban perception functions are still valid for me. The perception of architecture does not occur by means of façades or buildings, but by means of everyday moments that recur.

JH: My experience is that many people do not really know their city at all, i.e., only perceive it very partially and often are astonished if a special detail, a figure on a fountain, a particular corner of a building or a special tree is pointed out to them. That is also okay, because every person decides for himself/herself how much attention he/she would like to devote to the perception of his/her environment. People have an unerring sense for the quality of public architecture, museums, stadiums, concert houses and pubs. Either they

JH: Gibt es eine Sammlung?

DS: Ursprünglich war gedacht, das Az W nur als Wissenszentrum aufzubauen. Aber Mitte der 90er Jahre haben wir dann gesehen, dass sich keine Institution um das architektonische Erbe des 20. und 21. Jahrhunderts kümmert. Und so begannen wir mit der Übernahme von Vor- und Nachlässen, speziell von Architekten der Nachkriegszeit.

JH: Es stellt sich bei jedem Nachlass die Frage, ob es Sinn macht, das ganze Zeug zu behalten.
Wir haben unseren eigenen Archivbestand stets sorgfältig geordnet und gepflegt und in Unterarchiven für Pläne, Skizzen, Modelle, Bilder und Fotos etc. aufbewahrt. Daraus ist ein Kabinett von beachtlicher Größe hervorgegangen, für das wir ein eigenes Lagergebäude bauten. Letztes Jahr haben wir es in Betrieb genommen, damit wir noch selbst damit arbeiten können. Man wird nun sehen, was es als Arbeitsinstrument und als Ort der Forschung taugt. Braucht es so etwas heute? Und was geschieht morgen damit? Wir sind uns bewusst, dass ein schmaler Grat besteht zwischen Wertvollem und Abfall.

DS: Die Welt der Architektursammlungen hat sich gewaltig verändert. Dass heute große und bedeutende Architekturbüros ihre eigenen Sammlungen in eigenen Institutionen bewahren, ist eine logische Folge der Entwicklung des Metiers insgesamt. Eure Entscheidung dafür ist bahnbrechend. Aber daneben gibt es viele Nachlässe, die einfach kulturgeschichtlich wertvoll sind, um die sich dann öffentliche Institutionen bemühen müssen.

JH: Kunstausstellungen ziehen ein großes Publikum an, Architekturausstellungen sind viel schwieriger zu vermitteln. Ich selbst habe eine sehr kritische Haltung zu Architekturausstellungen, weil ich nur sehr wenige sah, die überzeugten. Wichtig wären mehr Ausstellungen und Debatten zu aktuellen Themen der Stadtentwicklung, wozu man dann jeweils auch historische Positionen und Architekturbeispiele zeigen könnte. Es besteht heute ein Missverhältnis zwischen der ständig voranschreitenden Produktion von Stadt, die unseren Alltag ja prägt, und der Qualität der Auseinandersetzung mit dieser Produktion. Architekturmuseen sollten sich als Orte des Dialogs zwischen Planung, Bauherrschaft und Politik stärker positionieren und profilieren.

DS: Man kann sicher sagen, dass die Architektur unter allen Künsten nach wie vor eine gewisse Geheimwissenschaft ist. Die Bevölkerung nimmt das Gebaute nicht als Architektur wahr. Für mich gelten nach wie vor die alten Thesen von Kevin A. Lynch aus den 60er Jahren, wie Stadtwahrnehmung funktioniert. Die Wahrnehmung von Architektur erfolgt nicht anhand von Fassaden oder Gebäuden, sondern anhand von Alltagsmomenten, die wiederkehren.

JH: Meine Erfahrung ist, dass viele Menschen ihre Stadt gar nicht richtig kennen, d.h. sie nur sehr partiell wahrnehmen und oft staunen, wenn sie auf ein besonderes Detail, eine Brunnenfigur, eine besondere Gebäudeecke oder einen speziellen Baum hingewiesen werden. Das ist auch okay, weil jeder Mensch selbst entscheidet, wieviel Aufmerksamkeit er der Wahrnehmung seiner Umwelt widmen möchte. Für die Qualität von öffentlicher Architektur, Museen, Stadien, Konzerthäusern, Kneipen haben die Menschen ein untrügliches Gespür. Entweder sie funktioniert, sie wird akzeptiert und bevölkert, oder aber sie funktioniert nicht, was verschiedene Gründe haben kann, aber letztlich auf einen Mangel hinweist, der auch mit mangelnder Architekturqualität zu tun hat. Manchmal entstand solche Qualität erst über viele Jahre hinweg, ohne einen wirklichen, alleinverantwortlichen Autor. In meiner Generation war der Architekt als Autor notwendig und darum bemüht, urbane Qualität herzustellen, oft einzelne Bauwerke oder Plätze. Die Entwicklung der Bauwirtschaft hin zu einer Herrschaft der Investoren stellt dieses Modell des Autors auf breiter Basis in Frage. Wie nimmst du selbst diese Entwicklung am Ende deiner Amtszeit wahr?

DS: Was wir in den letzten Jahrzehnten erlebten, war zunächst die Entwicklung des Architekten zum singulären Autor, zum Star. Diese Autorschaft, die persönliche Signatur, hat sich durch die digitalen Planungsmöglichkeiten aufgelöst. Jeder kann alles, weil es ihm die Technologie der Planung (BIM) erlaubt. Das sinnlose Gewürm der autistischen freien Formen ist in Wahrheit voll in der Hand der sie ermöglichenden Bauindustrie. Und diese wird den Bauprozess in Zukunft noch stärker durchdringen und definieren. Es wird eine globale Business-Architektur geben, aber daneben immer noch die widerständigen und intensiv künstlerischen Manifestationen. Das inhaltlich und intellektuell spannende Einzelobjekt der Architektur wird es weiterhin geben. Aber eine Antwort auf die Konvention, die Kohärenz und Kontinuität der ‚Stadt' ist nicht zu finden.

Jacques Herzog beim Ricola Kräuterzentrum · at the Herb Center, Laufen bei Basel, 6.5.2014. © DS

function, they will be accepted and populated, or else they don't function, which can have various reasons, but ultimately points to a lack that also has to do with the lacking architectural quality. Sometimes such quality first emerged after many years, without a real, solely responsible author. In my generation, the architect was necessary as the author and therefore endeavored to create urban quality, often individual structures or squares. The development of the construction industry towards a domination of investors calls this model of the author into question on a broad basis. How do you yourself perceive this development at the end of your tenure?

DS: What we experienced in the last decades was initially the development of the architect into the singular author, into the star. This authorship, the personal signature, has dissolved through the digital planning possibilities. Everyone can do everything, because the technology of planning (Building Information Modeling) allows him/her to do it. The senseless vermin of autistic, free forms is, in truth, completely in the hands of the construction industry that enables it. And it will penetrate and define the building process in the future even more strongly. There will be global business architecture, but still the resistive and intensively cultural manifestations alongside it. Exciting intellectually and in terms of content, the single object of architecture will continue to exist. But an answer to the convention, the coherence and continuity of 'city' is not to be found.

1st DAY The 1960s

Der Knoten des · Nodes of the General Panel System von · by Wachsmann und · and Gropius, Hochbau-Skripten · civil engineering scripts · HTBLA · Higher Technical College for Civil Engineering Krems 1971. Archive DS

Coverentwurf der ersten Ausgabe der · Cover design of the first issue of · Auto Revue 1965. Archive Tom Kussin

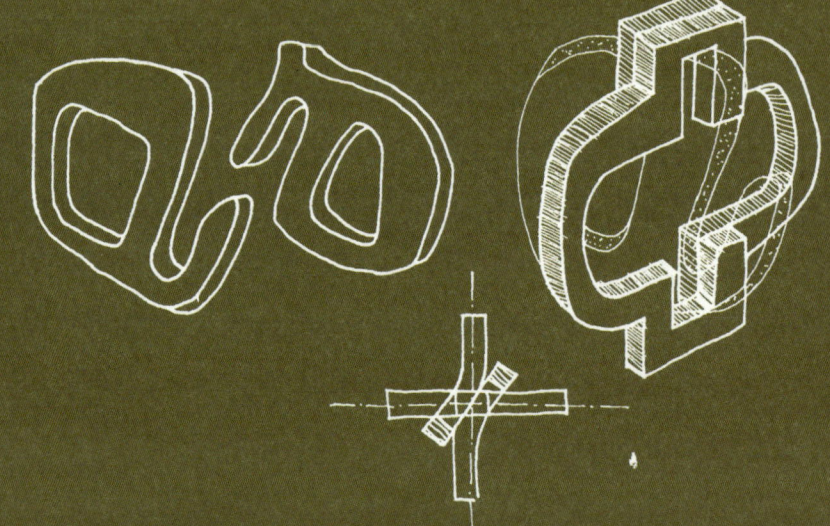

As a child and an adolescent I am not interested in architecture. Literature, pop music, cinema and theater make up my everyday life. When the first issues of the magazine *auto revue* appear, I want to become a design engineer of Formula One cars. But my stepfather, a mechanical engineer himself, decides that I am too sloppy for mechanical engineering and that I ought to turn to civil engineering instead. – +++ – At the Higher Technical College for Civil Engineering in Krems I have the fortune from 1966 to 1971 to have a class teacher who gets me enthused about architecture. Peter Schmid, a Holzmeister pupil with a curious biography, occupies us with the history of modernism. Details and stories of Jean Prouvé, Mies van der Rohe, Gropius and Wachsmann define the instruction. Architecture reveals itself to me as cultural history. The topic of my life is found. A charismatic German teacher, Alois Mahrer, a Communist, pushes my interest in literature. – +++ – From out of the province I observe the propaganda actions of the "Austrian Phenomenon" in the daily newspapers. Hollein, HausRucker-Co, Coop Himmelblau and Missing Link become my heroes. To me they are a promising architectonic expression in the realm of the new consumer culture, of the endless future, of pop culture, of space travel, of the conquest of the universe, of the 'blue planet,' of the flying nuclear-powered cars. – +++ – Decades later I was to first recognize the inner architectonic conflicts of this decade: that postwar modernism in Europe demanded a new urbanity, that the Team Ten revolted against the CIAM's separation of functions, that Rudofsky even called for a new way of living and that a remarkable 'style' of architecture had been created with brutalism, whose rediscovery began several years ago …

1. TAG Die 1960er

Prof. Peter Schmid, HTBLA · Higher Technical College
for Civil Engineering Krems 1971. © DS

Als Kind und Jugendlicher bin ich an Architektur nicht interessiert. Literatur, Pop-Musik, Kino, Theater sind mein Alltag. Als die ersten Nummern des Magazins *auto-revue* erscheinen, will ich Konstrukteur von Formel 1-Autos werden. Doch mein Stiefvater, selbst Maschinenbautechniker, entscheidet, dass ich für Maschinenbau zu schlampig sei und ich mich eher dem Hochbau zuwenden sollte – +++ – An der HTBLA für Hochbau in Krems habe ich das Glück, von 1966 bis 1971 einen Klassenvorstand zu haben, der mich für die Architektur begeistert. Peter Schmid, Holzmeister-Schüler mit kurioser Biografie, befasst uns mit der Geschichte der Moderne. Details und Geschichten von Jean Prouvé, Mies van der Rohe, Gropius und Wachsmann bestimmen den Unterricht. Für mich erschließt sich Architektur als Kulturgeschichte. Das Thema meines Lebens ist gefunden. Ein charismatischer Deutsch-Lehrer, Alois Mahrer, Kommunist, forciert mein Interesse an Literatur – +++ – Aus der Provinz beobachte ich in den Tageszeitungen die Propaganda-Aktionen des „Austrian Phenomenon". Hollein, HausRucker-Co, Coop Himmelblau, Missing Link, werden zu meinen Helden. Sie sind für mich ein vielversprechender architektonischer Ausdruck im Feld der neuen Konsumkultur, der unendlichen Zukunft, der Pop-Kultur, der Eroberung des Weltalls, des ‚Blauen Planeten', der fliegenden, atomgetriebenen Autos – +++ – Erst Jahrzehnte später sollte ich die innerarchitektonischen Konflikte dieses Jahrzehnts erkennen. Dass die Nachkriegsmoderne in Europa eine neue Urbanität forderte, dass das Team Ten gegen die Funktionstrennung von CIAM revoltierte, Rudofsky gar eine neue Lebensweise einforderte und mit dem Brutalismus ein bemerkenswerter ‚Stil' der Architektur geschaffen worden war, dessen Wiederentdeckung vor wenigen Jahren einsetzte…

Nach der »Genter Straße«

Obwohl sie in München leben und einen Schweizer Namen haben, sind Doris und Ralph Thut doch zum Teil der österreichischen Szene zuzurechnen. Sie ist Österreicherin, beide haben an der Akademie der bildenden Künste in Wien studiert. Die Wohnbebauung an der Genter Straße in München, die sie zusammen mit den Architekten O. Steidle und Partner realisierten, ist mit den in diesem Heft gezeigten österreichischen Projekten so nahe verwandt, daß es uns interessierte, wie sie die darin liegenden Gedanken weiterentwickelt haben. Hier ist ihr Bericht:

Ralph + Doris Thut
Jakob-Klar-Straße 7, 8000 München 40
Telefon (089) 3 78 12 13
Architekturstudium an der Akademie der bildenden Künste Wien und München.
Ab 1969 freiberufliche Architekten in München.

Wohnbebauung an der Genter Straße in München, zusammen mit den Architekten O. Steidle und Partner (Bauwelt 1/1972).

In unserer Arbeit hat sich eine zentrale Problemstellung herauskristallisiert, die nicht nur Gegenstand unserer theoretischen Überlegungen, sondern auch Anliegen unserer praktischen Tätigkeit ist.

Jede vom Architekten initiierte Wohnalternative scheitert in unserer Gesellschaft innerhalb der vorgegebenen Auftrags- und Planungsstruktur daran, daß

1. sie nicht nur vom Architekten initiiert, sondern von ihm auch umfassend als »Stellvertreter« geplant und strukturell festgelegt wird. Für Menschen, die sich als Subjekte in den Planungsprozeß nicht einbringen können und in diesem nur als klassifizierte Gruppen – Alte, Kinder, Ehepaare usw. – auftreten.

Der Planende denkt heute ausschließlich in verallgemeinerten Funktionen. In welcher Weise man heute auch versuchen mag, den Satz »Form folgt der Funktion« neu zu interpretieren, er baut in jedem Fall auf zum Teil fragwürdigen und abstrakt gefaßten Funktionen und führt zu ebensolchen Formen. In beiden spiegelt sich die Abwesenheit des Subjektes – und damit des Unterschiedes – und die Anwesenheit des eindimensionalen abstrakten Denkens.

In der Planung wird nicht nur der Bauprozeß abstrakt vorweggenommen, also der Bauende zum reinen Ausführungsorgan entmündigt, der Funktionalismus hat auch den Bewohner entmachtet und zum beliebig austauschbaren Objekt degradiert.

Das nach funktionalen Gesichtspunkten gebaute Haus läßt keine Interpretation, kein anderes als das vom Planer gedachte und fixierte Verhaltensmuster mehr zu.

Es zeigt sich, daß die Krise der Planung nicht nur eine politische ist. Sie widerspiegelt die Unbrauchbarkeit der abstrakten Logik, die den Planungsmethoden zugrunde gelegt ist, wenn es darum geht, das Subjekt mit seinen Bedürfnissen zu erfassen.

2. In unserer Gesellschaft hat *Repräsentation* die Herrschaft über den Gebrauch angetreten.

Repräsentation ist *Wertdarstellung*, Aufschub. Gebrauch ist *Verbrauch* und Zerstörung von Wert, Konsumtion.

Beide schließen einander aus. Das Besitzen und Zurschaustellen der Wertsymbole hat diese unserem unmittelbaren Gebrauch entzogen und damit auch unser Tun unter ihr Diktat gestellt.

Um dies zu verdeutlichen, wollen wir in Erinnerung rufen, was sich in jedem Haushalt abspielt. Generationen von Eltern zwingen ihre Kinder, für die alle Gegenstände nur eine unmittelbare Bedeutung im Erfahrungsprozeß haben, diese als Werte anzuerkennen. Sie entziehen damit systematisch den Kindern das Gebrauchen dieser Dinge – Gläser, Sofas usw. – und unterdrücken deren Bedürfnis nach Selbstverwirklichung in der kreativen Handlung. Für die Erwachsenen sind die angesammelten Reichtumssymbole Ersatz und Selbstdarstellung in der Kommunikation und Interaktion.

Mit der Wohnanlage in der Genter Straße wollten wir dazu auffordern, Leben an die Stelle von Repräsentation zu setzen.

Es hat sich aber gezeigt, daß diese Aufforderung über das Medium klassischer Planung und Architekturgestaltung, also über die Form nicht transportierbar und mitteilbar ist.

Statt das Haus in Gebrauch zu nehmen, es zu bewohnen, wird es wieder als Wertsymbol in Besitz genommen, weil es, unabhängig von seiner Form, Wert ist.

Zur Überwindung dieser Herrschaft ist ein Bewußtseinsprozeß Voraussetzung, dessen Ort der Prozeß des Wohnens und Hausbauens sein muß.

Eine neue Architektur, die nicht nur Stilvariante ist, kann nur und wird das Produkt eines *Prozesses* sein, der seine Bedeutung als Interaktions- und Kreativitätsprozeß zurückgewinnt.

Das Produkt, das Haus, die »Architektur« ist nur mehr Spur, die der abgelaufene Arbeitsprozeß hinterlassen hat. Von Bedeutung ist es nur mehr insoweit, als es die Hülle und Gegenstand für weitere darin und damit ablaufende Interaktionsprozesse sein wird.

Kriterien der »klassischen« Architektur wie: konstruktive Ehrlichkeit, formale Geschlossenheit usw. haben darin keinen Bestand mehr.

Wir arbeiten an einem Wohn-Experiment, das ein erster Schritt sein soll, Hausbauen und Wohnen als Prozeß der Selbstverwirklichung zu *ergreifen.*

Januar 1976, Doris Thut, Ralph Thut

Junge Architekten in Österreich

aus

Bauen+Wohnen 4_1976
„Experimentelle Architektur in Österreich"

Zur Situation des jungen Architekten

oder

Die Notwendigkeit, sich zu artikulieren

Es gibt wohl keinen zweiten Beruf, in dem man sich immer wieder verkaufen muß. Der Künstler arbeitet mit billigen Rohstoffen und produziert richtigerweise auf Vorrat. Der Spekulant handelt mit bereits bekannten Gegenständen und darf deshalb mit dem Verständnis des Publikums rechnen. Der kreative Architekt jedoch, der innovativ neue Lebensformen propagiert, hat nichts anderes vorzuzeigen als sich selbst. Für den jungen, der erst etwas werden muß, heißt das: Sich artikulieren, sichtbar machen, daß und was man ist.

In Österreich fällt dieser Prozeß mit den fünf Jahren zusammen, die ein junger Fachmann im Büro eines älteren Kollegen zubringen muß, um vom Staat zur Führung eines eigenen Büros zugelassen zu werden, um den – wie es im Jargon heißt – Vogel zu bekommen, der dann Aushängeschild und Briefkopf ziert. In diesen fünf Jahren, in denen man Frondienst für einen andern leistet, wird der Individuationsvorgang in andere Bahnen gelenkt, die nicht durch die staatliche Aufsicht verschlossen sind: Man schreibt, debattiert, reist, produziert sich und deklariert – um sich selbst treu zu bleiben – alles als Architektur.

Natürlich kann das »Österreichische Phänomen« nicht allein unter diesem Gesichtspunkt eines frustrierenden, von der älteren Generation verwalteten Milieus gesehen werden. Es hat seine Entsprechung im internationalen Geschehen: Es gab Anregungen und Kontakte. Der nachfolgende Artikel versucht zu klären, wie es entstand und ob es heute noch existiert. Die Leute, die es machten, gibt es jedenfalls noch. Sie haben schon lang ihren Vogel, zum Teil sind sie bereits Professoren. In die dadurch entstandene Leere stoßen die noch Jüngeren nach, stellen Neues in Frage, sind auf der Suche nach Positionen, die noch nicht durch jemanden besetzt sind – woraus schließlich ein solches Heft entsteht, eher zufällig, nicht als abschließendes, wertendes Dokument, aber als Abbild der Vielfalt, die im Dschungel der Selbstwerdung entsteht.

Ueli Schäfer
(mit der Bitte um Entschuldigung an alle jene, die auch in dieses Heft gehört hätten)

Sur la situation du jeune architecte

ou

La nécessité de s'articuler

Il n'y a sûrement pas une autre profession qui exige que l'on recommence sans cesse à prouver sa valeur. L'artiste travaille avec des matières premières bon marché et produit ses œuvres conséquemment à l'avance. Le spéculateur travaille sur des objets déjà connus et peut ainsi compter sur la compréhension du public. Par contre l'architecte créatif et innovateur qui propage de nouveaux modes de vie, n'a rien d'autre à montrer que lui-même. Pour le jeune qui doit d'abord se faire un nom, celà signifie: S'articuler, se montrer tel que l'on est et ce que l'on est.

En Autriche, ce processus correspond aux cinq années pendant lesquelles un jeune spécialiste doit rester dans le bureau d'un collègue plus ancien avant que l'Etat ne l'autorise à diriger son propre bureau; c'est à dire exprimé dans le jargon du métier «pour avoir son oiseau» qui décorera la plaque d'entrée du bureau et le papier à entête. Dans ces cinq années pendant lesquelles on est de corvée pour le compte d'un autre, le processus d'individualisation est dévié sur des tâches qui ne sont pas exclues par la surveillance officielle: On écrit, on discute, on voyage, on se produit et l'on déclare-afin de rester fidèle à soi même — on fait tout hormis de l'architecture.

Bien sûr on ne saurait voir ce «phénomène Autrichien» sous le seul aspect d'un milieu de frustration administré par la vieille génération. Ce phénomène a ses conséquences dans le contexte international où il a engondré des idées et des contacts. L'article qui suit cherche à expliquer comment ce phénomène s'est créé et s'il existe encore aujourd'hui. Ceux qui l'ont créé sont en tout cas encore présents. Ils ont leur «oiseau» depuis longtemps et certains sont même déjà professeurs. Dans le vide ainsi crée, il y a la poussée des plus jeunes qui remettent le tout en question dans leur recherche des positions qui ne sont pas encore occupées. Et finalement c'est le sujet d'un tel numéro composé plutôt par hasard et non pas comme un document définitif et valorisant; il s'agit du reflet de la multiplicité qui se crée dans la jungle de la réalisation de soi.

Ueli Schäfer
(en priant tous ceux qui auraient dû figurer eux-aussi dans ce volume de bien vouloir m'excuser)

The situation of the Young Architect

or

Self-expression as a necessity

The architect can probably claim to be unique in that he has always to put himself up for sale. The artist works with cheap raw-materials and goes on producing–rightly so–to pile up his stock of goods. The speculator deals in terms of objects that are already known and can therefore count on the understanding of his clients. The creative architect, however, propagates new constructional forms or designs and has nothing else to back them up with but himself. For the young architect who has still to earn his spurs this means: express yourself, make yourself seen, reveal what you are.

In Austria this phase coincides with the five years during which the young architect works in the offices of an older colleague. He becomes a full-fledged architect–with state approval–after this period of forced labour is over. He can then put up his sign and capture his own clients. But even before this happens his mind has been influenced by his surroundings, a process state control cannot prevent. The young architect writes, engages in discussion, travels, creates and declares, in order to remain true to himself, that everything he does or says is architecture. Of course the "Austrian phenomenon" cannot only be viewed from this angle, i. e. as an inhibiting process under the aegis of the older generation. It has its counterpart in the international sphere: it proved stimulating and led to new contacts. The following article purports to show how this came about and whether it still exists today. In any case the people responsible are still alive; they have got their piece of the cake and, in some cases, are already professors. The young follow on into the resulting vacuum, question that which is new on the look-out for vantage points that are still left vacant. This is how such an issue comes about, more by chance than otherwise. There is nothing final about it and it does not even attempt to establish values. It rather presents a many-sided picture that has come about in the process of self-development.

Ueli Schäfer–with apologies to those who should have appeared in this issue!

Dietmar Steiner, Wien

Experimentelle Architektur in Österreich

»... laßt uns die Gegenwart in hellerem Lichte sehen, der Zukunft aber laßt uns Blumen streuen...«
claude-nicolas ledoux

Versuch zur Klärung einer Situation

In den letzten zwei Jahrzehnten wurden in Österreich Gedanken zur modernen experimentellen Architektur entwickelt, die durch ihre Konzentration und Häufung dem Ausland erlaubten, von einem »österreichischen Phänomen« (Peter Cook in »experimental architecture«) zu sprechen. Verfänglich wäre es jedoch, eine einheitliche Richtung unter diesem Begriff zu verstehen. Es wird daher notwendig sein, Grundlagen und Ursprünge – auch die spezifische österreichische Situation – etwas zu beleuchten, um damit der Problematik näherzukommen. Unvollständig zwar, da die historische Distanz noch zu gering ist; das Abklingen der Bewegung erlaubt aber ein Zwischenresümee.

Bei der Entwicklung der modernen Architektur in Österreich sind in den zwanziger und dreißiger Jahren zwei wesentliche Schwerpunkte erkennbar. Die Schüler Otto Wagners bauten in

Translation by Brian Dorsey

"Experimental Architecture in Austria", 1976

" ... let us see the present in brighter light, but let us strew flowers to the future ..."

Claude-Nicolas Ledoux

In the last two decades thoughts on modern, experimental architecture were developed in Austria, which, through their concentration and frequency, allowed people abroad to speak of an "Austrian phenomenon" (Peter Cook in *Experimental Architecture in Austria*). It would be captious, however, to understand this term as a unified direction. Therefore, it is necessary to shine some light on the fundamentals and origins—of the specific Austrian situation, too—in order to approach the set of problems. Incomplete, to be sure, since the historical distance is still too small; but the fading of the movement allows an interim summary to be made.
In the development of modern architecture in Austria, two essential focuses are recognizable in the 1920s and 1930s. Otto Wagner's pupils built the manifestations of social democratic city administrations in Vienna as well as in several provincial cities, and the confrontation with nature led to considerable results in the alpine region. "The three years 1922, 1923 and 1924 were the most fruitful years of my life," Frederick Kiesler still said in 1964 about his years in Vienna (in a conversation with Raimund Abraham and Friedrich St. Florian in New York). But Austrofascism and the Nazi era created that intellectual and cultural vacuum which the young generation of architects found themselves in after the war.

They avidly started their search for the buried witnesses of modern architecture, accompanied by the skepticism of the postwar generation, which warned the social problems off the field of dispute. In 1955—in the year of the independence treaty—Giedion brought information about the new architectural developments; Konrad Wachsmann later wielded decisive influence as a teacher at the Salzburg Summer Academy. But in the autarchy of the Hohensalzburg Fortress and in the muses' temple of the Academy on Schillerplatz in Vienna, where the new building culture gradually began to take shape, one did not notice anything of the consolidation of capital, coddled up with Marshall Plan aid, which was happening around them. The last remainder of awareness and watchfulness was already driven out of the workers' heads in 1950 with the appeasement of the general strike. Powerless and defiant, the young architects in their field watched the wild goings-on of the communal politicians and construction trade, who did business with the politically and culturally submissive architects (meaning those who made no demands).

As one of the possible solutions back then, Hollein, Holzbauer and Uhl, among others, preferred the cultural emigration to America over an inner emigration. Returning from this excursion, Hollein brought the Austrians Rudolf M. Schindler and Frederick Kiesler back into their home country's awareness again. Kiesler's *Endless House* and his *City in Space*, created for the 1925 World Exposition in Paris upon Josef Hoffmann's invitation, of which van Doesburg said, "You have done what we all hoped one day to do," pointed to that visionary dimension which experimental architecture in Austria attempted to reconstruct. Hundertwasser's "Moldiness Manifesto" and Feuerstein's "Incidental Architecture" were reactions of the justified emotionality to a rationality based in the realistic situation that increasingly lost any sensual dimension. These artistic-individual protests ultimately land their home where individuality is still socially legitimized, where sensuality possesses its limited running area—in the art scene. The Galerie nächst St. Stephan constituted one of the most important of these homes of the "Austrian phenomenon." Here was the place, already back then, where an illustrious circle of those in the know, under the direction of Otto Mauer, discussed international art development, where the border of the provinciality of Austrian art was broken through. In the spring of 1963 the exhibition *Architektur* by Hans Hollein and Walter Pichler took place in its spaces and several years later it enabled the breakthrough of the next generation with the exhibition *Urban Fiction* by Günther Feuerstein's Clubseminar.

The international advancement of art, the connection to the visionary tradition also made the questioning of "form follows function" possible, allowing the replacement of "form is function." "Architecture is the art of making the unnecessary necessary; building is the art of making the necessary unnecessary," Frederick Kiesler wrote in 1965, and Schindler formulated: "The space architect uses the illumination of the room to shape it ..." (*Translucent House*, 1927). Projects, literary annotations to an architecture that apparently pursues no other purpose than itself, were now arising with high graphic effort. "The world am I and that's my business," Konrad Bayer wrote in his diary in 1963. Certainly the economic situation of Austria can now also be made responsible for the projects. Wachsmann's rational view of the modern technological possibilities collided with Austrian reality and unconsciously led to the ironizing collages of that time. An economic miracle with a certain reserve, contingent upon a high share of foreign capital and state-run industry, impeded any serious industrialization in the subsystem of the building sector. This technological deficiency did not exactly promote engagement with rational planning models. The "eternal makeshift solutions" resulted from the skillful juggling of creativity and political-economic power. Therefore, the traditional image of architects was also not called into question in architecture, and one could make thoughts about how it would be if everything suddenly became better.

The preparations for the "change of outlook, things are in order" (Konrad Bayer) now running in the cultural underground are also established in the cultural force field of Austrian tradition. Disdained, combated and yet effective. Austria's past grandness, the empire in which the sun never set, the Baroque's claim to universality and a landscape that draws attention to itself. They appear in the early projects, these geometrizing stagings which represent those illusionizations of reality that make concrete reality easier to grasp and allow Nestroy to say: "Reaction is a ghost, but ghosts don't exist. So stop being afraid and reaction will just cease to exist." (*Freedom in Krähwinkel*, 1849)
The "extension of the senses" (Marshall McLuhan) through the development of electronic technology ushered in a next phase of experimental architecture. In Feuerstein's 'Clubseminar' his tireless information work created that incubator of playful-cheerful projects with a strong emphasis on the psychological factors of environmental conditioning, which, in connection with the rather rational urban systems (primary and secondary structure), provided for the further development and spread of the "Austrian phenomenon." Co-initiated and journalistically supervised by the magazine *Bau*, which appeared as of 1965 in a new layout. With an international perspective, it drove the discussion on "environment" and the problem area of architecture all the way to the oft-quoted statement by Hans Hollein: "Everything is architecture." (John Cage: "Everything is music," Oswald Wiener: "Everything is literature.")

Now it's the end of "building." Space no longer defines itself solely through its material existence, but the intensity of media determines the degree of the experience. The libidinous freedom of the sensuality independent of the constructed space led to the living cells, aggregates and simulators that let the future appear "vanilla yellow" (HausRucker-Co) and open the way into the "inner space." The projects of this era certainly stood under the influence of the international youth movement. Timothy Leary legitimized drug consumption, William S. Burroughs postulated "You must learn to live alone in silence," Jack Kerouac sent the hippies "On the Road," the Rolling Stones sang "Street Fighting Man" and on the walls of Nanterre stood "Cours, camarade, le vieux monde est derrière toi." ("Run, comrade, the Old World is behind you.") And in Austria the groups made use of the drumming terminology of the advertising branch in order to hammer their products into the consciousness of citizens. Consumption, leisure time and the "endless growth" of the Western Hemisphere were the forces behind it.
The specific peculiarity of the "Austrian solutions" consists in their ambivalence. On the one hand, it is the playful irony, the charm that gathers its strength from the connection of unusual elements and, on the other hand, an apostrophization of loneliness almost plagued with self-destruction. In the reductions to minimal spaces there was nothing more left to notice of that collective sensuality of Lawrence Halprin's actions in California or the interpersonal theory of the Berlin-based "Kommune 2." One airily wafted away in intimate togetherness, plastic-wrapped in nature or was reduced to oneself and the media in a "portable living room," as if Hans Moser would be holding his dialog with the "grapevine louse."

Everything was too beautiful to be true. The dream ruled reality and, except for the verbal attacks against "those at the top," there was nothing to be noticed of politics. The abolishment of construction still documented itself in the clean framework of the culture and art scenes. The destruction of architecture, the destruction of art, the destruction of the state had to mean the next consequence. The escalation of the student movement and the Viennese actionists who were developing into martyrs of art molded the sphere of influence of those architectural actions that arose after 1968. H. C. Artmann proclaimed his "poetic act" in 1953 ("there is a sentence that is irrefutable, namely that one can also be a poet without having ever written or otherwise uttered a word.") The "literary cabarets" of the Wiener Gruppe broke through the consumption expectations of the cultural audience; the "Zockfest" (1967) and the event "Art and Revolution" (1968) ended with battles in the auditorium, court verdicts and an "Austrian exile government" in Berlin. These were stations of an art development that provided valuable stimuli to the student movement. Both were persecuted, endemic to the underground and chosen as the main thrust of the coercive mechanism of established power structures, and came together into a natural congruence.

Further causes of this awakening of architecture, which had shifted its starting point from the Academy of Fine Arts to the Technical University in Vienna, were also the academic tasks that hampered the scientificity and basic study, and sharply questioned the occupational profile in the disparity of complexity of the training and specialization in future practice. The cultural submarines of architecture, who had made a connection to the visionary tradition of the pre-war era two decades ago, were themselves established in the meantime and also constituted a target of new activities. In particular, they now made the suppression of the political dimension of architecture, which had been missing in the cultural agitation up to then, noticeable. This was now vigorously made up for and the actions laid claim to a degree of totalitarianism that pushed architecture to the fringe of events in favor of a societal rearrangement. There were no more "beautiful" solutions to the issues of the time. The destruction of everything that had to represent "social values" was the order of the day. "And the greater the contribution of destruction is, indeed if human work consists only of destruction, then it is truly human, natural and noble work" (Adolf Loos, 1926).
Pointing out all the fundamentals and origins of the "Austrian phenomenon" fails on account of the complexity and diverseness of the projects and Austria's border situation, which has always owed the specific idiosyncrasy of its cultural advancement to the influences of foreign countries. The dispute with the cultural ballast, the struggle with state art—which formally coerces one into resistance through its top-heaviness—is to be recognized as a continuous occurrence. In its tension field of conditioning and liberation, the psychological dimension points to an emotional cognizance of the meaning and effect of the constructed and non-constructed environment. The sensitization in respect to this environment, be it through form, through aggregate or the direct interpersonal action, are aspects of commonalities that allow us to speak of an "Austrian phenomenon" of architecture.

Wien und auch in einigen Provinzstädten die Manifestationen sozialdemokratischer Stadtverwaltungen, und im Alpinbereich führte die Auseinandersetzung mit der Natur zu bedeutenden Ergebnissen. »Die Jahre 1922, 23, 24 waren die fruchtbarsten meines Lebens«, sagte noch 1964 Frederick Kiesler über seine Jahre in Wien (in einem Gespräch mit R. Abraham und F. St. Florian in New York). Doch Austro-Faschismus und Nazi-Zeit schufen jenes geistige und kulturelle Vakuum, in dem sich die junge Architektengeneration nach dem Krieg vorfand.

Gierig machten sie sich auf die Suche nach den verschütteten Zeugnissen der modernen Architektur. Begleitet von der Skepsis der Kriegsgeneration, die die gesellschaftliche Problematik vom Feld der Auseinandersetzung wies. 1955 – im Jahr des Staatsvertrags – brachte Giedion Informationen über die neuen Architekturentwicklungen, Konrad Wachsmann übte als Lehrer der Salzburger Sommerakademie später einen entscheidenden Einfluß aus. Aber in der Autarkie der Festung Hohensalzburg und im Musentempel der Akademie am Schillerplatz in Wien, wo sich die neue Baukultur allmählich zu formulieren begann, bemerkte man von der rundum erfolgenden Konsolidierung des mit Marshallplanhilfe aufgepäppelten Kapitals nichts. Schon 1950 wurde der letzte Rest von Bewußtsein und Wachsamkeit mit der Abwiegelung des Generalstreiks aus den Köpfen der Arbeiter vertrieben. Machtlos und trotzig sahen die jungen Architekten in ihrem Bereich dem wilden Treiben von Kommunalpolitikern und Bauwirtschaft zu, die mit den politisch und kulturell (d. h. keine Ansprüche stellenden) willfährigen Architekten das Geschäft machten.

Hollein, Holzbauer, Uhl u. a. zogen die kulturelle Amerika-Emigration, als eine der damals möglichen Lösungen, einer inneren Emigration vor. Von diesem Ausflug brachte Hollein die Österreicher R. M. Schindler und F. Kiesler wieder ins Bewußtsein der Heimat. Kieslers »endless house« und seine auf Einladung von Josef Hoffmann für die Weltausstellung in Paris 1925 geschaffene »city in space«, von der van Doesburg sagte: »Sie taten, was wir alle einmal zu tun hofften, Sie haben es getan«, wiesen auf jene visionäre Dimension, die von der experimentellen Architektur in Österreich nachzuvollziehen versucht wurde. Hundertwassers »Verschimmelungsmanifest« und Feuersteins »Inzidente Architektur« waren Reaktionen der berechtigten Emotionalität auf eine in der realistischen Situation fußende Rationalität, die zunehmend jeder sinnlichen Dimension verlustig ging. Diese künstlerisch-individuellen Proteste fanden schließlich dort ihre Heimstatt, wo Individualität noch gesellschaftlich legitimiert ist, wo Sinnlichkeit ihren begrenzten Auslauf besitzt, im Kunstbetrieb.

Eine der wichtigsten dieser Heimstätten des »österreichischen Phänomens« bildete die Galerie nächst St. Stephan. Hier war schon damals der Ort, wo unter der Leitung von Otto Mauer ein illustrer Kreis von Eingeweihten die internationale Kunstentwicklung rezipierte, wo die Grenze der Provinzialität der österreichischen Kunst durchbrochen wurde. Im Frühjahr 1963 fand in ihren Räumen die Ausstellung »Architektur« von Hans Hollein und Walter Pichler statt, und einige Jahre später ermöglichte sie mit der Ausstellung »urban fiction« des clubseminars von Günter Feuerstein den Durchbruch der nächsten Generation.

Die internationale Kunstentwicklung, der Anschluß an die visionäre Tradition ermöglichten auch die Infragestellung von »form follows function«, erlaubten die Ersetzung von »form is function«. »Architektur ist die Kunst, das Überflüssige notwendig, Bauen die Kunst, das Notwendige überflüssig zu machen«, schrieb Frederick Kiesler 1965, und Schindler formulierte: »The space architect uses the illumination of the room to shape it ...« (translucent house, 1927). Nun entstanden mit hohem grafischen Aufwand Projekte, literarische Anmerkungen zu einer Architektur, die scheinbar keinen anderen Zweck verfolgt als sich selbst. »die welt bin ich, und das ist meine sache«, schrieb Konrad Bayer 1963 in sein Tagebuch.

Sicherlich läßt sich nun auch die ökonomische Situation Österreichs für die Projekte verantwortlich machen. Wachsmanns rationale Sicht der modernen technologischen Möglichkeiten kollidierten mit der österreichischen Wirklichkeit und führten unbewußt zu den ironisierenden Collagen jener Zeit. Ein schaumgebremstes Wirtschaftswunder, bedingt durch einen hohen Anteil an Auslandskapital und verstaatlichter Industrie, verhinderte im

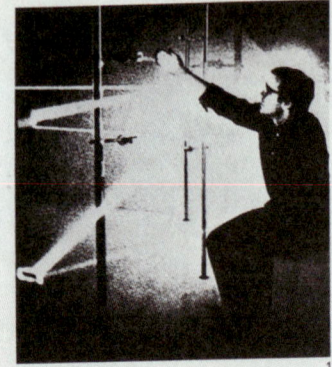

1
Friedrich St. Florian, »Imaginary space«, 1969.
Friedrich St. Florian, «Imaginary space», 1969.
Friedrich St. Florian, "Imaginary space", 1969.

2
Hans Hollein, »Erzeisenbahnwaggon«, 1963.
Hans Hollein, «Wagon de minerai», 1963.
Hans Hollein, "Ore car", 1963.

3
Hans Hollein, »Flugzeugträgerstadt«, 1964.
Hans Hollein, «Ville porte-avions», 1964.
Hans Hollein, "Aircraft-carrier city", 1964.

4
Walter Pichler, »Mündung einer unterirdischen Stadt«, 1963.
»Architektur bedient sich rückhaltslos der stärksten Mittel, die ihr jeweils zur Verfügung stehen.«
Walter Pichler, «Débouché d'une ville souterraine», 1963.
«L'architecture utilise toujours sans limite les moyens les plus forts qui sont disponibles.»
Walter Pichler, "Egress of a subterranean city", 1963.
"Architecture makes ruthless use of the strongest means available to it at any given time."

5
Rudolph M. Schindler, »Totenfeld für eine 5-Millionen-Stadt«, 1913.
»Die Architektur verwandelt sich in das einheitlich zu planende, unendliche Verlängerungen sozialer, technischer und organisatorischer Natur in sich bergende dynamische Feld.« (Otto A. Graf)
Rudolph M. Schindler, «Cimetière pour une ville de 5 millions d'habitants», 1913.
«L'architecture se transforme en un champ dynamique dissimulant une suite sans fin de prolongements concernant le social, le technique et l'organisation, qu'il s'agit de planifier en une unité.» (Otto A. Graf)
Rudolph M. Schindler, "Cemetery for a city of 5 million", 1913.
"Architecture becomes transformed into the dynamic field that is to be planned on a uniform basis and that includes endless extensions of a social, technical and organizational character." (Otto A. Graf)

6
Walter Pichler, »Kompakte Stadt«, 1963.
Walter Pichler, «Ville compacte», 1963.
Walter Pichler, "Compact city", 1963.

7
Haus Rucker-Co, »Ballon für Zwei«, 1967.
»Sie werden besser denken und besser lieben. Sie werden alles besser machen, weil sie ruhiger sind und entspannter. Sie können den Ballon bei sich zu Hause aufstellen. Neben dem Blumentischchen oder drüben beim Fernsehapparat. Er ist nicht anspruchsvoll.«
Maison Rucker-Co, «Ballon pour deux», 1967.
«Vous penserez mieux et aimerez mieux. Vous ferez tout mieux car vous êtes plus calmes et plus détendus. Vous pouvez placer le ballon chez vous à la maison, à côté du guéridon à fleurs ou là bas près de l'appareil de télé ... Il est peu exigeant.»
Rucker-Co House, "Balloon for two", 1967.
"You will think better and love better. You will do everything better, because you are calmer and more relaxed. You can set up the balloon at home. Next to the little flower stand or over there by the TV. It makes no demands."

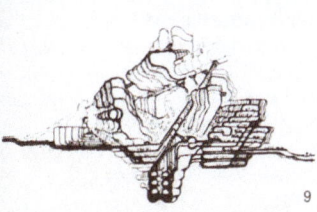
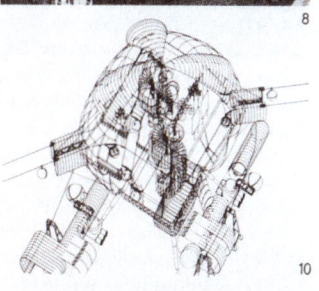
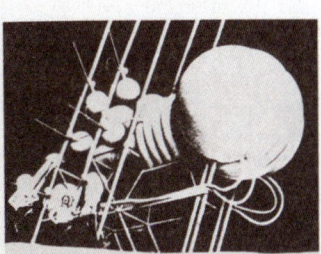

8
Bernhard Hafner, »Stadtstruktur«, 1964–66.
»... logistisch determinierte Formulierungen ordnender Möglichkeitsvorhaben ...«
Bernhard Hafner, «Structure urbaine», 1964–66.
«... expression logistique, déterminée des projets de mise en ordre envisageables ...»
Bernhard Hafner, ''Urban structure'', 1964–66.
"... logistically determined formulations of ordering potentialities ..."

9
Franco Fonatti, »Sensomobile Architektur«, 1967–68.
»... eine Architektur, die keine Spaltung zwischen rational denkenden und emotionalen Individuen hervorruft, ... größtmöglichen Spielraum läßt und dies in einem Ausmaß, das es ermöglicht, von einer regelrechten Architekturanarchie zu sprechen.« (Peter Pongratz)
Franco Fonatti, «Architecture sensomobile», 1967–68.
«... une architecture qui ne suscite pas de rupture entre les individus dont la pensée est rationnelle et ceux chez qui elle est intuitive, ... qui laisse la plus grande latitude possible et ceci de manière telle que l'on puisse parler d'une véritable anarchie de l'architecture.» (Peter Pongratz)
Franco Fonatti, ''Sensomobile architecture'', 1967–68.
"... an architecture that does not create any gap between rationally and emotionally oriented individuals, ... leaves a maximum free space, enough to permit one to speak of an architectural anarchy." (Peter Pongratz)

10
Missing Link, »Goldenes Wiener Herz«, 1970.
Ein transportables Vielzweckgerät zur Veränderung einer Nachbarschaft.
Missing Link, «Goldenes Wiener Herz», 1970.
Un appareil transportable polyvalent destiné à transformer un voisinage.
Missing Link, ''Goldenes Wiener Herz'', 1970.
A transportable multi-purpose apparatus for transforming a neighbourhood.

11
Coop Himmelblau, »Villa Rosa«, 1968.
»... Architekturmaschine mit drei Wohnprogrammen.«
Coop bleu azur, «Villa Rosa», 1968.
«... machine architecturale avec 3 programmes d'habitation.»
Sky Blue Coop, ''Villa Rosa'', 1968.
"... architecture machine with three living programmes."

12
Coop Himmelblau, »Das Haus mit fliegendem Dach«, 1973.
»Dieses Projekt war nicht nur als ›Ausstellung‹ gedacht, sondern als Werbung gegen die Schleifung ganzer Wohnbezirke ...«
Coop bleu azur, «La maison au toit volant», 1973.
«Ce projet n'était pas seulement pensé comme une ‹exposition›, mais voulait aussi être une publicité s'opposant à la destruction de quartiers résidentiels entiers ...»
Sky Blue Coop. "The house with the flying roof", 1973.
"This project was not conceived merely as an 'exhibition', but as publicity against the razing of entire residential districts ..."

Subsystem der Bauwirtschaft jede ernst zu nehmende Industrialisierung. Dieser technologische Mißstand förderte bei den Kommunalverwaltungen nicht gerade die Auseinandersetzung mit rationalen Planungsmodellen. Die »ewigen Provisorien« entstanden aus dem geschickten Jonglieren von Kreativität und politisch-ökonomischer Macht. In der Architektur wurde daher auch das traditionelle Architektenbild nicht in Frage gestellt, und man konnte sich Gedanken machen über das, was wäre, wenn alles einmal besser werden würde.

Die nun im kulturellen Untergrund laufenden Vorbereitungen zur »veränderung der anschauung, die dinge sind in ordnung« (Konrad Bayer) sind auch im kulturellen Kraftfeld der österreichischen Tradition angesiedelt. Geleugnet, bekämpft und doch wirksam. Österreichs vergangene Größe, das Reich, in dem die Sonne nie unterging, der Universalitätsanspruch des Barock und die Landschaft, die sich selbst in Szene setzt. In den frühen Projekten treten sie auf, diese geometrisierenden Inszenierungen, die jene Illusionierungen der Realität darstellen, die die konkrete Realität leichter faßbar macht und Nestroy sagen läßt: »Die Reaktion ist ein Gespenst, aber Gespenster gibt's gar nicht. Drum sich nicht fürchten davor, dann gibt's gar keine Reaktion.« (Freiheit in Krähwinkel, 1849.)

Die »Ausweitung der Sinne« (Marshall McLuhan) durch die Entwicklung der elektronischen Technologie leitete eine nächste Phase der experimentellen Architektur ein. In Feuersteins »Clubseminar« schuf seine unermüdliche Informationsarbeit eine Brutstätte spielerisch-fröhlicher Projekte mit einem Schwergewicht auf den psychischen Faktoren der Umweltkonditionierung, die in Verbindung mit den eher rationalen Stadtsystemen (Primär- und Sekundärstruktur) für die weitere Entwicklung und Verbreitung des »österreichischen Phänomens« sorgten. Mitinitiiert und publizistisch betreut von der ab 1965 in neuer Aufmachung erschienenen Zeitschrift »Bau«. Mit internationaler Blickrichtung trieb sie die Diskussion über »Umwelt« und den Problembereich der Architektur bis zur vielzitierten Aussage von Hans Hollein: »Alles ist Architektur.« (John Cage: »Alles ist Musik«, Oswald Wiener: »Alles ist Literatur.«)

Nun ist Schluß mit dem »Bauen«. Raum definiert sich nicht mehr allein durch seine materiale Existenz, sondern die Intensität der Medien bestimmt den Grad des Erlebnisses. Die lustvolle Freiheit einer vom gebauten Raum unabhängigen Sinnlichkeit führte zu den Wohnzellen, Aggregaten und Simulatoren, die die Zukunft »Vanille-Gelb« (Haus-Rucker-Co) erscheinen lassen und den Weg in den »inner-space« freimachen. Sicherlich standen die Projekte dieser Zeit unter dem Einfluß der internationalen Jugendbewegung. Timothy Leary legitimierte den Drogenkonsum, William S. Burroughs postulierte »You must have to learn to live in silence«, Jack Kerouac schickte die Hippies »On the road«, die Rolling Stones sangen »Street fighting man«, und an den Wänden von Nanterre stand »Cours camarade, le vieux monde est derrière toi«. Und in Österreich bedienten sich die Gruppen der trommelnden Terminologie der Werbebranche um ihre Produkte ins Bewußtsein der Bürger zu hämmern. Konsum, Freizeit und das »unendliche Wachstum« der westlichen Hemisphäre standen Pate.

Die spezifische Eigenart der »österreichischen Lösungen« besteht in ihrer Zwiespältigkeit. Einerseits ist es die spielerische Ironie, der Charme, der seine Stärke aus der Verbindung ungewöhnlicher Elemente empfängt, und andrerseits eine fast von Selbstvernichtung geplagte Apostrophierung der Einsamkeit. In den Reduktionen auf Minimalräume war nichts mehr zu bemerken von jener kollektiven Sinnlichkeit der Aktionen Lawrence Halprins in Kalifornien oder der zwischenmenschlichen Theorie der Berliner »Kommune 2«. Luftig entschwebte man in trauter Zweisamkeit plastikgehüllt in die Natur oder wurde in einem »tragbaren Wohnzimmer« auf sich selbst und die Medien reduziert, so als ob Hans Moser seinen Dialog mit der »Reblaus« halten würde.

Es war alles zu schön, um wahr zu sein. Der Traum regierte die Wirklichkeit und von Politik war außer den verbalen Attacken gegen »die da oben« nichts zu bemerken. Die Abschaffung des Bauens dokumentierte sich immer noch im sauberen Rahmen des Kultur- und Kunstbetriebs. Die Zerstörung der Architektur,

13

14

15

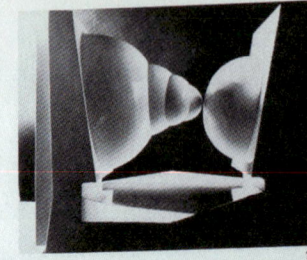

16

17

18

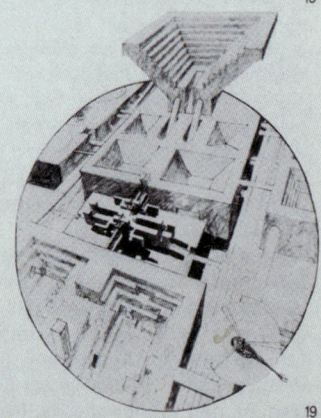

19

die Zerstörung der Kunst, die Zerstörung des Staates mußte die nächste Konsequenz bedeuten. Die Eskalation der Studentenbewegung und die sich zu Märtyrern der Kunst entwickelnden Wiener Aktionisten bildeten die Einflußsphäre für jene Architektur-Aktionen, die nach 1968 entstanden. 1953 proklamierte H. C. Artmann seinen »poetischen act« (»es gibt einen satz, der unangreifbar ist, nämlich der, daß man dichter sein kann, ohne auch nur irgend jemals ein wort gesprochen oder geschrieben zu haben«). Die »literarischen cabarets« der Wiener Gruppe durchbrachen die Konsumerwartungen des Kulturpublikums, das »zockfest« (1967) und die Veranstaltung »Kunst und Revolution« (1968) endeten mit Saalschlachten, Gerichtsurteilen und einer »österreichischen Exilregierung« in Berlin. Stationen einer Kunstentwicklung, die der Studentenbewegung wertvolle Anregungen vermittelte. Verfolgt wurden sie beide, im Untergrund beheimatet und als Stoßrichtung die Zwangsmechanismen etablierter Machtstrukturen auskoren, fanden sie zu einer natürlichen Kongruenz. Weitere Ursachen diesen Aufbruchs der Architektur, der seinen Ausgangspunkt von der Akademie der bildenden Künste auf die technische Hochschule in Wien verlagert hatte, waren auch die akademischen Aufgabenstellungen, die Wissenschaftlichkeit und Grundlagenstudium verhinderten und in der Disparität von Komplexität der Ausbildung und Spezialisierung in der künftigen Praxis das Berufsbild mit aller Schärfe in Frage stellten. Die kulturellen U-Boote der Architektur, die vor zwei Dezennien den Anschluß an die visionäre Tradition der Vorkriegszeit herstellten, waren inzwischen selbst etabliert und bildeten mit ein Angriffsziel der neuen Aktivitäten. Vor allem machte sich nun die Ausschaltung der politischen Dimension der Architektur, die bisher in der kulturellen Agitation versäumt wurde, bemerkbar. Dies wurde nun kräftig nachgeholt, und die Aktionen beanspruchten einen Totalitätsgehalt, der die Architektur zugunsten einer gesellschaftlichen Umgestaltung an den Rand des Geschehens drängte. Da gab es keine »schönen« Lösungen mehr auf die Fragen der Zeit. Die Zerstörung all dessen, was »gesellschaftliche Werte« zu repräsentieren hatte, stand auf der Tagesordnung. »Und je größer der anteil der zerstörung ist, ja, wenn die menschliche arbeit nur aus der zerstörung besteht, dann ist es wirklich menschliche, natürliche, edle arbeit« (Adolf Loos, 1926).

Sämtliche Grundlagen und Ursprünge des »österreichischen Phänomens« aufzuzeigen scheitert an der Komplexität und Verschiedenartigkeit der Projekte und an der Grenzsituation Österreichs, die immer schon den Einflüssen des Auslands die spezifische Eigenart seiner kulturellen Entwicklung verdankt. Die Auseinandersetzung mit dem Kulturballast, der Kampf mit der Staatskunst – die durch ihre Kopflastigkeit förmlich zum Widerstand zwingt – ist als durchgängige Erscheinung zu erkennen. Die psychische Dimension in ihrem Spannungsfeld von Konditionierung und Befreiung weist auf eine emotionale Kenntnis der Bedeutung und Wirkung gebauter und nicht gebauter Umwelt hin. Die Sensibilisierung gegenüber dieser Umwelt, sei es durch Form, durch Aggregate oder die direkte zwischenmenschliche Aktion, sind Aspekte der Gemeinsamkeiten, die es erlauben, von einem »österreichischen Phänomen« der Architektur zu sprechen.

13, 14
Missing Link, »Der Läufer«, »Der Pulk«.
TV-Film »16. November – Utopie in 9 wirklichen Bildern«, ein Tagesablauf, reduziert auf stilisiertes Rollenverhalten, der Mensch als Requisitenträger. »Selbst wenn wir uns völlig frei wähnen, tragen wir immer ein Bezugssystem mit uns, das in sein vorbestimmtes Ziel paßt.«

Missink Link, «Le marcheur».
Téléfilm «Utopie du 16 novembre en 9 tableaux réels», un déroulement journalier réduit à des rôles stylisés; l'Homme comme porteur de thèmes traditionnels. «Même si nous nous pensons totalement libres, nous portons toujours un système de référence qui correspond à son objectif préétabli.»

Missing Link, "The man on foot".
TV film: "November 16 utopia in 9 real scenes", the course of a day reduced to stylized role behaviour, man as a carrier of props. "Even when we think we are wholly free, we are always carrying around with us a system of references that fits into its predetermined slot."

15
Salz der Erde, »Hitl-Kripl-Taferl«, 1970.
Aktion zu Beendigung der Salzburger Festspiele. Ein Protest gegen jahrhundertealten Kulturfetischismus.

Sel de la terre, «Hitl-Kripl-Taferl», 1970.
Action à l'occasion de la clôture du festival de Salzburg. Une protestation contre un fétichisme culturel séculaire.

Salt of the earth, "Hitl-Kripl-Taferl", 1970.
Campaign to end the Salzburg Festival. A protest against immemorial culture fetishism.

16
Heinz Tesar, »Kontaktarchitektur«, 1967–70.
»... menschliche Situationen in spezifische Raumformen umsetzen.« (Prader–Fehringer)

Heinz Tesar, «Architecture de contact», 1967–70.
«... transformer des situations humaines en formes spatiales spécifiques.» (Prader–Fehringer)

Heinz Tesar, "Contact Architecture", 1967–70.
"... to convert human situations into specific spatial shapes." (Prader–Fehringer)

17
*H. Prader, F. Fehringer, »Lineare Stadteinheit«, »Städtebau ohne ›Megastrukturen‹, auf der Basis fabrikmäßig gefertigter Raumzellen.«

*H. Prader, F. Fehringer, «Unité urbaine linéaire», «Urbanisme sans ›mégastructures‹, à base de cellules spatiales fabriquées industriellement».

*H. Prader, F. Fehringer, "Linear Urban Unit", "Urbanization without 'megastructures', on the basis of industrially fabricated space cells."

18
Hans Hollein, »Stadt«, 1957–60.
Hans Hollein, «Ville», 1957–60.
Hans Hollein, "City", 1957–60.

19
Hans Hollein, »Stadt«, 1962–64.
»Architektur ist elementar, sinnlich, primitiv, brutal, schrecklich, gewaltig, herrschend. Sie ist aber auch Verkörperung subtilster Emotionen, sensitive Aufzeichnung feinster Erregungen, Materialisation des Spirituellen.«

Hans Hollein, «Ville», 1962–64.
«L'architecture est élémentaire, sensuelle, primitive, brutale, terrible, violante, dominante. Mais elle est aussi la concrétisation des émotions les plus subtiles et l'expression sensible des excitations les plus fines, matérialisation du spirituel.»

Hans Hollein, "City", 1962–64.
"Architecture is elementary, sensuous, crude, brutal, horrible, violent, dominating. But it is also the incorporation of the most subtle emotions, the delicate recording of the finest urges, materialization of the spiritual."

Alles ist Architektur

Tout est architecture
Everything is architecture

Hans Hollein, Wien

Le «phénomène autrichien» personnifié. Lauréat du prix de la Ville de Vienne 1974, un bureau à Vienne et des commandes de l'étranger.

The "Austrian Phenomenon" personified – awarded the Municipality of Vienna Prize in 1974, with office in Vienna and commissions from abroad.

tudium an der Akademie der Bildenen Künste Wien, Meisterklasse Prof. lemens Holzmeister, Diplom 1956. raduate Studies: Illinois Institute of echnology, Chicago; Architektur und tädtebau, 1958–1959; University of alifornia, Berkeley; College of Enronmental Design, 1959–1960; Master Architecture (M. Arch.) 1960. Tätigeit bei Ahlgren-Olson-Silow, Archikter SAR, Stockholm, und Franz Kieer, Wien. Seit 1964 freischaffender Architekt. 8 bis 12 Mitarbeiter (Hochchulabsolventen).
rofessor an der Staatlichen Kunstkademie in Düsseldorf seit 1967, ab 975/76 o. Professor an der Hochschule r angewandte Kunst in Wien und orstand des Instituts für Design. 1964 s 1970 Redakteur »Bau«, Wien chrift für Architektur und Städtebau. itglied der Kunstjury des Bundesinisteriums für Unterricht und Kunst, ien. Präsidialmitglied des Österreihischen Instituts für Formgebung.

2
igmund-Freud-Museum, Projekt 1969, ben Behandlungszimmer, ursprüngcher Zustand.
usée Sigmund Freud, projet 1969, en aut salle de soins dans l'état original.
gmund Freud Museum, project 1969, bove, consulting-room, original state.

Ich wurde gebeten, kurz meine Architektentätigkeit in und für Wien darzustellen, anhand des Freud-Museums, unter dem Titel »Alles ist Architektur«.

3
Rathausplatz Wien, Projekt, 1971.
Place de l'hôtel de ville, Vienne, projet, 1971.
City Hall Square, Vienna, project 1971.

4
Städtebauliche Studie Wollzeile-Landstraße, 1971/72.
Etude urbanistique Wollzeile-Landstrasse, 1971/72.
Urbanistic study, Wollzeile-Landstrasse, 1971/72.

5
Media-Linien, Olympisches Dorf, München 1972.
Lignes média, village olympique, Munich 1972.
Media lines, Olympic Village, Munich 1972.

6
Städtisches Museum Abteiberg, Mönchengladbach; Baubeginn 1976.
Musée municipal Abteiberg, Mönchengladbach; début des travaux 1976.
Municipal Museum, Abteiberg, Mönchengladbach; construction begun 1976.

7
Biennale Venedig, 1972.
Biennale de Venise, 1972.
Biennale, Venice, 1972.

Diese meine Feststellung, vor etwa 10 Jahren gemacht und inzwischen weitgehend zitiert, charakterisiert Haltung und Methode meiner Arbeit. Insofern, als eben viele Bereiche – auch nichtbaulicher Natur – Teil der Bemühungen der Architekten sind, daß eine Vielzahl von Medien unsere Umwelt bestimmen. Insofern aber auch, daß nur ein komplexer und vielschichtiger, widersprüchlicher Architekturbegriff adäquat ist, wiewohl manchmal (siehe obigen Titel, siehe »Flugzeugträgerstadt«) in simpler – aber assoziationsreicher – Feststellung präsentiert.

Haltung und Methode einer Stadt ist charakterisiert durch die Verleihung – »in Anerkennung seiner künstlerischen Leistungen« – eines Preises der Stadt Wien für das Jahr 1974 an Hans Hollein, »um damit zum Ausdruck zu bringen, wie sehr seine verdienstvolle Lebensarbeit auf dem Gebiete der Architektur dazu beigetragen hat, das kulturelle Ansehen Wiens zu mehren«.

Seit 1956 bin ich in Wien Architekt. Es wurden unzählige Wohnbauten, Kindergärten, Schulen, Hallen, Theater, Museen etc. von dieser Stadt, dieser mich ehrenden Gemeinde, errichtet; keiner dieser Bauten stammt aber von mir. Geehrte Architekten sollen zum Ansehen, nicht aber zum Aussehen ihrer Heimatstadt beitragen.

Das untenstehende Sigmund-Freud-Museum wurde nicht verwirklicht, Lehnstuhl und Couch des Begründers der Psychoanalyse nicht aufgestellt. Sollte es sein, daß es keinen Bedarf für eine Couch gibt?

Soweit zum Österreichheft. Mehr über meine Arbeit im nächsten US-, Deutschland-, Italien- oder Rußlandheft. H. H.

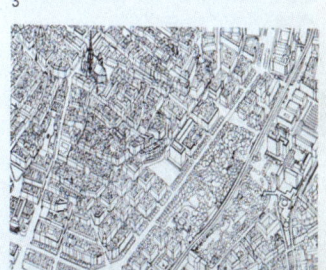

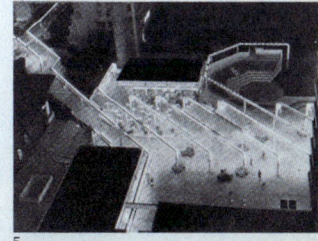

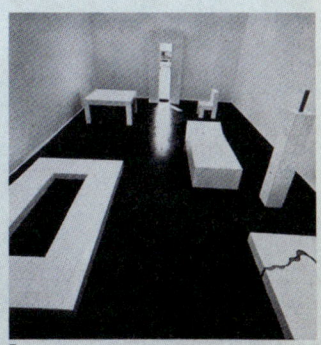

Erster Tag • Day One

Coop HausRucker

Young architecture in Austria today, at the end of this century, is recognizable in the media through two features in particular. The young architects are rarely lone fighters, but rather organize themselves in groups and frequently give themselves cryptic names. And, superficially speaking, many conceptual and formal approaches that recall the avant-garde endeavors of the late 1960s and early 1970s are to be seen. This is quite surely a bias, but should therefore be a reason to interview two of the pioneers from back then together for the first time. At the end of the 1960s, HausRucker-Co and Coop Himmelblau were the first groups of the "Austrian phenomenon" (Peter Cook), who internationally joined the ranks of a movement that was also shaped by other groups such as Archigram in London, Antfarm in the US, as well as Archizoom and Superstudio in Italy.

Today, almost exactly thirty years later, both these pioneers represent almost contrary positions on architecture. Prix and Swiczinsky were Coop Himmelblau at that time and are Coop Himmelb(l)au today. HausRuckerCo were Laurids and Manfred Ortner, Günter Zamp Kelp and Klaus Pinter back then, decidedly disbanded as a group in the mid-1980s, and are working today as architects. Wolf Prix and Laurids Ortner face the conversation about old times, the era of development, the position today and their view of today's young architecture; after all, they have all become professors in the meantime.

HausRucker-Co – Günter Zamp Kelp,
Manfred Ortner, Laurids Ortner. © Archive HRC
Coop Himmelblau – Helmut Swiczinsky, Wolf D. Prix.
© Michael Horowitz

aus · from

architektur aktuell 07/08_1999
Interview Wolf Prix – Laurids Ortner
Translation by Brian Dorsey

Coop HausRucker

Junge Architektur in Österreich heute, am Ende dieses Jahrhunderts, ist medial vor allem durch zwei Merkmale erkennbar. Die jungen ArchitektInnen sind selten Einzelkämpfer, sondern organisieren sich in Gruppen und geben sich häufig kryptische Namen. Und oberflächlich betrachtet sind viele konzeptive und formale Ansätze zu sehen, die an die avantgardistischen Bemühungen der späten sechziger und frühen siebziger Jahre erinnern. Dies ist ziemlich sicher ein Vorurteil, sollte aber deshalb ein Anlass sein, erstmals zwei der Pioniere von damals gemeinsam zu befragen. HausRucker-Co und Coop Himmelblau waren Ende der sechziger Jahre die ersten Gruppen des Austrian Phenomenon (Peter Cook), die sich international in eine Bewegung einreihten, die auch von anderen Gruppen wie beispielsweise Archigram in London, Antfarm in den USA, Archizoom und Superstudio in Italien geprägt war.

Heute, ziemlich genau dreißig Jahre später, vertreten diese beiden Pioniere geradezu konträre Position zur Architektur. Prix und Swiczinsky waren damals Coop Himmelblau und sind heute Coop Himmelb(l)au. HausRucker-Co waren damals Laurids und Manfred Ortner, Günter Zamp Kelp und Klaus Pinter, haben sich als Gruppe Mitte der achtziger Jahre dezidiert aufgelöst und arbeiten heute als Architekten. Wolf Prix und Laurids Ortner stellen sich dem Gespräch über alte Zeiten, die Zeit der Entwicklung, die Position heute und ihre Sicht der heute jungen Architektur, sind sie alle doch inzwischen auch Professoren geworden.

DMS: Coop Himmelb(l)au and Ortner+Ortner started with provocative projects and today are building proper houses. I'm now asking you to take a leap in time. Back then, at the end of the 1960s, when you founded yourselves, did you actually want to build proper houses someday?

PRIX: If we had wanted to do that, we wouldn't have called ourselves Coop Himmelblau, but Prix+Swiczinsky.

DMS: So why didn't you want to build any houses?

ORTNER: We saw a certain necessity in response to the situation to go as quickly as possible from zero to one hundred. Building was the worst method for that. But in general what we were doing was very market-oriented from our side. What we understood as market were the pop groups emerging at the time, the Beatles, the Rolling Stones, naturally that was totally attractive. The rapid fame, the fast money, to have just as many girls as them; that would have been attractive. Then it took some time until we found out that this doesn't quite work that way. So we indeed acted in a market-oriented way as far the PR and the appearances were concerned, but the product to actually market didn't exist then and was always more than iffy.

DMS: Why did you want to get out of the established architecture of the sixties at all? Why the change from the reference of architectural history to that of pop history?

PRIX: I wouldn't see it like that. Pop history and the groups were not the role model alone. It was the expanding of boundaries at all levels of culture. The Stones and Jimi Hendrix were innovators on the market of pop history. They extended the borders. And we wanted to likewise radically change architecture back then. The fact that this was, in retrospect, a total overestimation of the construction industry, of politics, of architecture, too, can now indeed be asserted. Nonetheless, at that time we wanted to do everything differently and much better.

ORTNER: Well, today I see in it much less a renewal than the possibility to be able to do something different. The architecture of the postwar era had certainly consolidated itself back then. The result was solitary buildings that stood around in the city like crooked teeth and had nothing to do with the surroundings. So in our case it was less the awareness of being able to do something totally new than to not want to go on any more as usual. In contrast to what the Coops were doing very playfully and sensually back then, for us it was rather sharply in response to the situation. Flower power, Timothy Leary, drugs, as a positive chance to expand consciousness without side effects. It was a sensuous time which was first brought down in the seventies to that which one called critical awareness.

DMS: The Viennese projects of this era differ, however, very strongly in international comparison with the others. The projects were more emotional, more sensual, sought a conditioning of emotional worlds.

PRIX: Above all there was, even if Viennese, nonetheless humor present, which allowed it to make fun of itself. If I choose the name 'Himmel-Blau,' (sky blue), that was also in contrast to 'Wüsten-Rot' (desert red, which is also the name of an insurance company). Also with the HausRuckers, moving the house around (in German: das Haus rucken) had also definitely been an emotional process. The focus on pleasure in architecture played a big role. Even if Laurids places emphasis on marketing now, it was more funnily and more subversively applied than what the young Dutchmen, who work in a totally market-oriented manner, are doing now.

ORTNER: That's right. Especially the works of Coop and HausRucker, with this sensuous direction, stood completely in contrast to similar works of this era, by Pichler, for instance. He indeed transported an artificial cynicism, a certain haughtiness or pride, to treat the whole thing 'critically.' That wasn't meant, at least by us. We wanted something that is to be produced in large quantities, that is obtainable; we racked our brains again and again to produce something that people would snatch out of our hands, like others snatch the records.

DMS: Coop Himmelb(l)au und Ortner+Ortner sind mit provokativen Projekten gestartet und bauen heute richtige Häuser. Ich fordere euch jetzt zu einem Zeitsprung auf. Wolltet ihr damals, Ende der sechziger Jahre, als ihr euch gegründet hattet, eigentlich irgendwann einmal richtige Häuser bauen?

PRIX: Wenn wir das gewollt hätten, hätten wir uns nicht Coop Himmelblau, sondern Prix+Swiczinsky genannt.

DMS: Also warum wolltet ihr keine Häuser bauen?

ORTNER: Wir sahen eine gewisse Notwendigkeit, aus der Situation heraus so rasch als möglich von null auf hundert zu kommen. Da war das Bauen dafür die schlechteste Methode. Aber generell war das was wir machten von unserer Seite sehr marktorientiert. Unter Markt verstanden wir die damals entstandenen Pop-Gruppen, die Beatles, Rolling Stones, das war natürlich total attraktiv. Der rasche Ruhm, das rasche Geld, ebensoviel Mädchen zu haben wie die, das wäre attraktiv gewesen. Es hat dann eine Zeit gedauert, bis wir dahinterkamen, dass dies nicht ganz so läuft. So haben wir uns zwar marktorientiert verhalten, was die PR und die Auftritte betraf, aber das eigentlich zu vermarktende Produkt gab es dann nicht und war immer mehr als ob.

DMS: Warum wolltet ihr überhaupt raus aus der etablierten Architektur der sechziger Jahre? Warum der Wechsel von der Referenz der Architekturgeschichte zu jener der Pop-Geschichte?

PRIX: So würde ich das nicht sehen. Die Pop-Geschichte und die Gruppen waren ja nicht allein das Vorbild. Es war die Grenzerweiterung auf allen Ebenen der Kultur. Die Stones und der Jimi Hendrix waren Erneuerer auf dem Markt der Pop-Geschichte. Sie haben die Grenzen erweitert. Und wir wollten damals ebenso die Architektur radikal verändern. Dass dies rückblickend gesehen eine totale Überschätzung der Bauindustrie, der Politik, auch der Architektur war, das kann man jetzt wohl feststellen. Trotzdem, damals wollten wir alles anders und viel besser machen.

ORTNER: Also ich sehe heute darin weniger eine Erneuerung als die Möglichkeit, etwas anders machen zu können. Die Architektur der Nachkriegszeit hatte sich ja damals konsolidiert gehabt. Das Ergebnis waren solitäre Bauten, die wie steile Zähne in der Stadt herumstanden und nichts mit der Umgebung zu tun hatten. So war bei uns weniger das Bewusstsein da, etwas total neu machen zu können, sondern so wie gehabt nicht mehr weitermachen zu wollen. Im Gegensatz zu dem, was die Coops damals sehr spiele-

risch und lustbetont machten, war es für uns ziemlich scharf aus der Situation heraus. Flower Power, Timothy Leary, Drogen als positive Chance Bewusstsein zu erweitern ohne Nebenwirkung. Es war eine sinnenfreudige Zeit, die erst in den siebziger Jahren heruntergebracht wurde auf das, was man kritisches Bewusstsein nannte.

DMS: Die Wiener Projekte dieser Zeit unterschieden sich im internationalen Vergleich doch sehr stark von den anderen. Die Projekte waren emotionaler, sinnlicher, suchten eine Konditionierung von Gefühlswelten.

PRIX: Vor allem war, wenn auch wienerischer, aber doch Humor dabei, der es erlaubt hat, sich über sich selbst lustig zu machen. Wenn ich den Namen ‚Himmel-Blau' wähle, so war das auch im Gegensatz zu ‚Wüsten-Rot'. Auch bei den HausRuckern ist das Haus rucken ja durchaus ein emotioneller Vorgang gewesen. Die Lustbetontheit in der Architektur hat eine große Rolle gespielt. Auch wenn Laurids das Vermarkten jetzt in den Vordergrund stellt, so war das um Dimensionen lustiger und subversiver angelegt als das, was jetzt die jungen Holländer tun, die total marktorientiert arbeiten.

ORTNER: Stimmt. Speziell die Arbeiten von Coop und HausRucker standen mit dieser lustbetonten Richtung ganz im Gegensatz zu ähnlichen Arbeiten dieser Zeit, von Pichler beispielsweise. Er hat ja einen artifiziellen Zynismus mittransportiert, einen gewissen Hochmut oder Stolz, das ganze ‚kritisch' zu behandeln. Zumindest von uns war das nicht gemeint. Wir wollten etwas, was in großen Stückzahlen zu produzieren ist, das erwerbbar ist, wir haben uns immer wieder den Kopf zerbrochen, etwas zu produzieren, das uns die Leute aus der Hand reißen wie anderen die Schallplatten.

PRIX: Ein typisches Linzer Phänomen. Alle Linzer haben damals von der Produktion großer Stückzahlen geträumt, um immens viel Geld zu verdienen, das man dann mit tollen Frauen ausgeben kann.

ORTNER: Wenn das ein Linzer Phänomen sein soll, dann war und ist es bis heute ein weltweit gut funktionierendes. Weil im Grunde genommen hat sich für mich bis heute an dieser Mentalität nicht sehr viel geändert. Diese Marktgerechtheit erscheint mir nach wie vor eine unerhörte Herausforderung zu sein. Der Markt ist hochintelligent, hochflexibel, und da intelligent etwas anzubieten, ist immer die Herausforderung.

Herzstadt · Heart City, Installation, Coop Himmelblau, 1969. Archive DS

PRIX: A typical Linz phenomenon. Back then all the Linzers dreamed of producing large quantities in order to make immensely much money that could then be spent with gorgeous women.

ORTNER: If that is supposed to be a Linz phenomenon, then it was and is up to today one that functions well worldwide. Because for me not much about this mentality has essentially changed up to today. This market conformity still seems to me to be a tremendous challenge. The market is highly intelligent, highly flexible and to intelligently offer something there is always the challenge.

PRIX: *(Laughs)* That really has to be noted: Laurids describes the market as highly intelligent.

ORTNER: Absolutely.

PRIX: Laurids! The market as a person doesn't exist. You mean those who make the market are highly intelligent.

ORTNER: No, precisely not. Rather the market as a figure and metaphor—as the sum of influencing factors, as the wholeness of a social and political wanting, the market is an existence.

PRIX: Bullshit.

DMS: I see, fundamental inconsistencies exist in the point. As suspenseful as it would be to talk that out now, I would nevertheless like to let the positions stand as they are in order to continue in the story. The sensuous euphoria of the sixties ended quite drastically with the beginning of the seventies. The criticism of modernism escalates, the notion of eternal progress is seized by a fundamental paradigm shift; the postmodern recollection looms. How did you experience this time, which was rather contrary to your initial goals?

ORTNER: After the endless progress, the reach for the stars, the reflection upon the problems of the Earth suddenly came with a completely new term: environmental pollution. Our own confrontation with the city theme also began there. All of the makeshift objects we made there for the city were always for us ourselves primarily pieces to clarify something for us. With a certain didactic character which I no longer find likeable at all today, but which resulted from the trivial aspect: What is today, how can I intervene here with the means of art or action and set something against the mainstream, the massiveness of constructed everyday life, which makes sense? At that time the airdome in Krefeld over Mies van der Rohe's Haus Lange was an important experience. What was interesting about it, however, was not the project idea—survival in a polluted environment by means of artificial conditioning—, but the aspect that this Mies dissolved and diffused within it. Suddenly this rulebook of construction disintegrated. In this peculiar light under the cover this house lost its proportions, it atomized itself inside there. In hindsight it was a beautiful lesson, although it wasn't meant to be one at all.

DMS: And at Coop there are projects in the mid-1970s such as the Straßenzimmer (Street Room)—likewise commentaries on urban situations.

PRIX: Those were attempts during this time when society canceled the contract with the youth after it had drawn attention to them in the preceding decade. For us these were unsatisfying attempts to find a new position. Despite all the sensuousness, the sixties were very serious for us. Against all laws of the market, authenticity was important for us. That totally fell apart in the seventies, because society had stripped the basis from us. We really stood around clueless back then and

PRIX: *(lacht)* Das muss man wirklich festhalten: Laurids bezeichnet den Markt als hochintelligent.

ORTNER: Absolut.

PRIX: Laurids! Den Markt als Person gibt es nicht. Du meinst die, die den Markt machen, sind hochintelligent.

ORTNER: Nein, eben nicht. Sondern der Markt als Figur und Metapher – als Summe von Einflussfaktoren, als Ganzheit eines gesellschaftlich und politischen Wollens, ist der Markt eine Existenz.

PRIX: Schwachsinn.

DMS: Ich sehe, an diesem Punkt sind grundsätzliche Unvereinbarkeiten vorhanden. So spannend es wäre, das jetzt auszudiskutieren, möchte ich dennoch die Positionen, so wie sie sind, einmal stehenlassen, um in der Geschichte fortzufahren. Die lustbetonte Euphorie der sechziger Jahre endet ziemlich drastisch mit dem Beginn der siebziger Jahre. Die Kritik an der Moderne eskaliert, die Idee des ewigen Fortschritts wird von einem grundsätzlichen Paradigmenwechsel erfasst, die postmoderne Rückbesinnung bahnt sich an. Wie habt ihr diese für eure anfänglichen Ziele doch konträre Zeit durchlebt?

ORTNER: Nach dem unendlichen Fortschritt, dem Griff nach den Sternen, kam plötzlich die Besinnung auf die Probleme der Erde, mit einem völlig neuen Wort: Umweltverschmutzung. Da setzte auch unsere eigene Konfrontation mit dem Thema Stadt ein. Alles was wir da an provisorischen Objekten für die Stadt gemacht haben, waren immer primär für uns selbst Stücke, um uns etwas zu verdeutlichen. Mit einem gewissen didaktischen Charakter, der mir heute gar nicht mehr so sympathisch ist, aber der aus dem trivialen Aspekt heraus kam: was ist das Heute, wie kann ich hier eingreifen mit den Mitteln der Kunst oder der Aktion, und dem Mainstream, der Massivität des gebauten Alltags etwas entgegensetzen, das Sinn macht. Da war die Traglufthalle in Krefeld über dem Haus Lange von Mies van der Rohe eine wichtige Erfahrung.

Villa Rosa, Prototyp · prototype M 1:1, Coop Himmelblau, 1968. Archive DS

Interessant daran war dann aber nicht die Projektidee – Überleben in verschmutzter Umwelt durch künstliche Konditionierung –, sondern der Aspekt, dass dieser Mies darin zergangen, diffundiert ist. Plötzlich ist dieses Regelwerk des Gebauten zerfallen. In diesem eigenartigen Licht unter der Hülle hat dieses Haus seine Proportionen verloren, hat sich da drinnen atomisiert. Es war im Nachhinein ein schönes Lehrstück, obwohl es gar nicht darauf ausgelegt war.

DMS: Und bei Coop gibt es Mitte der siebziger Jahre Projekte wie das Straßenzimmer – ebenso Kommentare zu urbanen Situationen.

PRIX: Das waren Versuche in dieser Zeit, in der die Gesellschaft den Vertrag mit der Jugend aufkündigte, nachdem sie ihn im Jahrzehnt davor in Szene gesetzt hatte. Da waren das für uns unbefriedigende Versuche, eine neue Position zu finden. Die sechziger Jahre waren für uns trotz aller Lustbetontheit sehr ernst. Gegen alle Gesetze des Marktes war uns die Authentizität wichtig. Das ist in den siebziger Jahren total zusammengebrochen, weil uns die Gesellschaft die Basis entzogen hatte. Wir sind wirklich damals ratlos in der Gegend herumgestanden und haben verschiedene Versuche gestartet, die aber dann abrupt in einer Verweigerungshaltung endeten, und wir weder veröffentlichen noch irgendwelche Projekte machen konnten. Wir haben uns zurückgezogen, um irgendwie was Neues zu finden, mit dem wir wieder leben konnten. Denn die Unbefriedigtheit mit dem nicht geglückten Experiment war einfach vorhanden. Wir haben damals oft die HausRucker in Düsseldorf besucht, um zu sehen, wie es in dieser Zeit doch geht, aber wir haben nie das Herz gehabt, diesen Weg zu gehen. Es war ein Rückzug, um den Punkt zu finden, von dem aus man die Welt der Architektur doch noch aus den Angeln heben kann.

DMS: Es war also eine kritische Situation, eine Zeit der Dürre für Coop Himmelblau. Trotzdem habt ihr in dieser Zeit die Reiß-Bar und den Roten Engel gemacht. Und auch das Atelier Baumann am Börseplatz, der sich mir gegenüber übrigens in den achtziger Jahren sehr kritisch über diese Phase eures Versuchs, eine Sprachlichkeit der Architektur zu erlangen, geäußert hat. Der echte Riß in der Reiß-Bar, die Moby Dick-Geschichte zum Roten Engel ...

Live, Riesenbillard · Giant Billards, Museum des 20. Jahrhunderts Wien, HausRucker-Co, 1970. Archive DS

started various attempts which, however, abruptly ended in an attitude of denial and we neither published, nor could do any projects. We withdrew in order to somehow find something new that we could live with again. Because the dissatisfaction with the unsuccessful experiment was simply existent. Back then we often visited the HausRuckers in Dusseldorf in order to see how it nonetheless worked at this time, but we never had the heart to go this way. It was a retreat in order to find the point from which one can still set the world of architecture on fire.

DMS: It was therefore a critical situation, a time of drought for Coop Himmelblau. Nevertheless, at that time we did the Reiß-Bar and the Roter Engel. And also Atelier Baumann on Börseplatz, who, by the way, spoke very critically to me about this phase of your attempt to attain a linguisticality of architecture. The real rift in the Reiß-Bar, the Moby Dick story about the Roter Engel ...

PRIX: Those were humoristic aperçus that remained strange to us even while we were making them. That's true, pieces that brought us further are to first be found again in the Baumann Atelier.

Ausstellung · Exhibition Cover / Museum Haus Lange, HausRucker-Co, 1971. Archive DS

ORTNER: But these pieces were, and I would see that exactly with Himmelblau as with us, attempts in this barren time to nonetheless disassemble architecture into usable parts.

PRIX: That was you; you took a stance on the issue of the era and indeed in an ad hoc way. Environmental pollution = HausRucker has an answer. The city = HausRucker has the backdrop.

ORTNER: At this time, however, there were also our projects *Half House*, *Linear House*, etc. From a present-day perspective, these were truly exemplary precursors of the pulling apart, the deconstruction of the building, which originally once had a completely fixed character. We deconstructed it in order to examine what could be redefined there. But we very quickly came to an end and these examinations were finished as of a certain point. Apparently where it first began for Himmelblau.

PRIX: Yes, because you approached the issue differently. You took on the issue in a straightforward manner. Here is the question, there is the answer. We didn't know the answer. And that's why many attempts were made, and first later, with these installations and projects, it once again had something to do with architecture.

DMS: It can thus be said that there was a new beginning for both in the eighties. HausRucker quits and Himmelblau comes into the project stage again.

PRIX: For us it was the *Flammenflügel (The Blazing Wing)* in 1981. That project was consciously positioned in that way: We are here again, we are making architecture again, we are going public again. HausRucker, in contrast, have continuously been working in the public all these years. We had withdrawn.

PRIX: Das waren humoristische Aperçus, die uns beim Machen selbst fremd geblieben sind. Es stimmt, erst beim Baumann-Atelier sind wieder Stücke zu finden, die uns selbst weitergebracht haben.

ORTNER: Diese Stücke aber waren, und ich würde das bei Himmelblau genauso sehen wie bei uns, Versuche in dieser dürren Zeit, doch Architektur auf verwertbare Teile zu zerlegen.

PRIX: Das wart ihr, ihr habt zum Thema der Zeit Stellung bezogen, und zwar ad hoc. Umweltverschmutzung = HausRucker hat eine Antwort. Die Stadt = HausRucker haben die Kulisse.

ORTNER: Es gab in dieser Zeit von uns aber auch die Projekte *Halbes Haus*, *Lineares Haus* etc. Das waren, aus heutiger Sicht, wirklich exemplarische Vorläufer des Auseinanderziehens, des Dekonstruierens des Gebauten, das ursprünglich einmal einen vollkommen fixen Charakter hatte. Das haben wir dekonstruiert, um zu überprüfen, was man da neu definieren könnte. Aber da kamen wir sehr rasch zu einem Ende und diese Überprüfungen waren ab einem bestimmten Punkt erledigt. Offenbar dort, wo es für die Himmelblau erst begonnen hat.

PRIX: Ja, weil ihr das Thema anders angegangen seid. Ihr habt das Thema straight forward angenommen. Hier ist die Frage, da ist die Antwort. Wir haben die Antworten nicht gewusst. Und deswegen hat es viele Versuche gegeben, und erst später, bei diesen Installationen und Projekten hat es dann wieder etwas mit Architektur zu tun bekommen.

DMS: Man kann also sagen, dass es in den achtziger Jahren für beide einen Neubeginn gegeben hat. HausRucker hört auf, und Himmelblau kommt wieder ins Projektstadium.

PRIX: Für uns war es der *Flammenflügel* 1981. Das Projekt war bewusst so positioniert: Wir sind wieder da, wir machen wieder Architektur, wir gehen wieder an die Öffentlichkeit. Dagegen haben die HausRucker all die Jahre dauernd an der Öffentlichkeit gearbeitet. Wir hatten uns zurückgezogen.

ORTNER: Jawohl, wir haben durchgearbeitet, es gab die verschiedenen Projekte, die *Nike* Mitte der siebziger Jahre, das *Halbe Haus*, und dann mit *Forum Design* in den achtziger Jahren das Zurückfinden zu einer Neudefinition von Alltag, von Alltagskultur. Das war dann auf einmal auch ein bestimmendes Thema. Da haben

wir auf einmal auch keine Probleme mehr gehabt uns hier einzuschleusen, ganz handfest auch daran wieder mitzuwirken. In dem Maße ist auch das Interesse am Bauen an tatsächlichen Aufgabenstellungen, an konkreten Bauaufgaben gewachsen.

PRIX: Das ist auch der tatsächliche Unterschied zu anderen Gruppen der sechziger Jahre. Das war immer schon impliziert. Wir haben uns am Anfang kurz Bau-Cooperative genannt. Weil wir immer die Sachen 1:1 machen wollten, die wir uns gedacht hatten. Alle anderen haben gezeichnet und Modelle gebaut, wir wollten die Bauten 1:1. Prototypen. Wenn wir sagten, der Herzschlag füllt den Raum, wollten wir das 1:1 auch sehen. Das ist ein Unterschied zu der italienischen Szene, die kritische Blätter gezeichnet haben, Superstudio, oder Archizoom, auch zur englischen Szene, wie Archigram.

ORTNER: Richtig. Zunächst war sicher Archigram der auslösende Impuls. Das gezeichnete Projekt allein erlangte damals internationale Gültigkeit. Mit ein paar guten Zeichnungen konntest du dir einen Namen verschaffen. Das ist heute vollkommen undenkbar. Wenn du es nicht 1:1 realisierst, kräht kein Hahn danach. Wichtig ist die Direktheit, die sich an der Schmutzigkeit des Alltags bewährt.

DMS: Ab Mitte der achtziger Jahre ist es also ganz klar, dass ihr verschiedene Wege geht.

ORTNER: Es hat sich einigermaßen dahingezogen. Es waren zunächst ganz spezifische Bauaufgaben, um die man sich beworben hat. Pavillons, Ausstellungen. Der Versuch, das Besondere mit dem Bauwerk zu verknüpfen, das hat uns lange gefesselt. Und es war eine schwierige Übung diesen Anspruch abzustreifen, dass irgend etwas besonders sein müsse.

ORTNER: Yes, we worked through, there were various projects, the *Nike* in the mid-seventies, the *Half House* and then, with *Forum Design* in the eighties, the finding back to a new definition of everyday life, of everyday culture. That was all of the sudden a determining issue then. Suddenly we didn't have any more problems smuggling ourselves in here, to also very concretely play a part in it. The interest in building on actual tasks, on concrete construction projects, also grew to that extent.

PRIX: That is also the actual difference to other groups of the sixties. That had always been implied. At the beginning we briefly called ourselves 'Bau-Cooperative.' Because we always wanted to do the things we had thought about 1:1. All the others drew and constructed models; we wanted the buildings 1:1. If we said the heartbeat fills the space, we also wanted to see that 1:1. That is the difference to the Italian scene, which drew critical sheets, Superstudio, or Archizoom, also to the English scene, like Archigram.

ORTNER: Right. Initially, Archigram was surely the triggering impulse. The drawn project alone gained international validity back then. With a few good drawings you could make a name for yourself. That is completely unthinkable today. If you don't realize it 1:1, nobody cares two hoots about it. What is important is the directness that proves itself in the filthiness of the daily grind.

DMS: As of the mid-eighties it is therefore clear that you go different ways.

ORTNER: It sort of dragged on somewhat. First there were quite specific construction projects that one competed for. Pavilions, exhibitions. The attempt to link the particular with the building had enamored us for a long time. And it was a difficult lesson to cast off this aspiration that anything had to be special.

PRIX: That is the major difference where our aspiration goes apart. Apparently already in the approaches in the

Nike, Forum Metall, Kunsthochschule · Art College Linz, HausRucker-Co, 1977. Archive DS

43

sixties. We've always asked ourselves how one can still change architecture after all. We began at the point where architecture is the most vulnerable and therefore also changeable. We started experimenting with the design process. Things then emerged that were surprising for us ourselves and which we then attempted to implement in the usual manner. That did not succeed for a long time, until it was finally so far that we could realize certain things which I still see as statements and not as things to repeat. That naturally brings a positioning that cannot be as powerful at the beginning as the market-oriented affair. One can see that now in the young architects who work entirely differently, who avoid these statements or only allow them insofar as they are market-compliant.

So while HausRucker, as the name already says, turned towards the houses, we tried to find new forms and ways of approach for architecture through the design process experiment.

ORTNER: That is perhaps also the most interesting point about it. The experiment! The decisive point might sit there. While Himmelblau really first developed the experiment into an ideology ...

PRIX: ... No, it is no ideology ...

ORTNER: ... then the experiment as an end in itself had actually been called more and more into question by us. It could formally have no more use for us. The vocabulary was already run through from A to Z; we discovered a whole lot in the process and also learned a lot for ourselves. But there was no reason for us anymore to continue this type of experiment in the present manner of urban interventions and statements. What resulted was the very clear and initially very arduous decision to step out of the 'academic league' with its self-created laws and its own scenarios and auditoriums. We wanted to quite brutally maneuver ourselves into a professional league that obeys the market laws.

DMS: It is interesting that both of your positions were actually quite fundamentally different from the beginning, although they looked so similar and were also gathered in a 'movement.' It probably had to take thirty years then to really clearly recognize the differences. That makes me a little cautious if I now ask you

PRIX: Das ist der große Unterschied, wo sich unser Anspruch trennt. Offenbar schon in den Ansätzen in den sechziger Jahren. Wir haben uns immer gefragt, wie man die Architektur doch noch verändern kann. Wir haben begonnen an dem Punkt, wo die Architektur am verletzlichsten und daher auch veränderbar ist. Wir haben begonnen, mit dem Entwurfsprozess zu experimentieren. Da sind dann neue Sachen entstanden, die für uns selber überraschend waren und die wir dann versucht haben in gewohnter Manier durchzusetzen. Das ist lange nicht geglückt, bis es endlich soweit war, dass wir gewisse Dinge realisieren konnten, die ich nach wie vor als Statements sehe und nicht als zu wiederholende Dinge. Das bringt natürlich eine Positionierung, die am Beginn nicht so kräftig sein kann wie eine marktorientierte Geschichte. Das sieht man jetzt an den Jungen, die ganz anders arbeiten, die diese Statements vermeiden oder nur soweit zulassen, als sie marktkonform sind.

Also während sich die HausRucker, wie der Name schon sagt, den Häusern zugewandt haben, haben wir versucht, über das Experiment Entwurfsprozess neue Formen und Zugangsweisen für die Architektur zu finden.

ORTNER: Das ist vielleicht auch der interessanteste Punkt daran. Das Experiment! Da dürfte der Scheidepunkt sitzen. Während die Himmelblau das Experiment da erst richtig zur Ideologie entwickelt haben ...

PRIX: ... Nein, Ideologie ist es keine ...

ORTNER: ... dann ist für uns eigentlich das Experiment als Selbstzweck immer mehr in Frage zu stellen gewesen. Für uns hat es formal nichts mehr Neues bringen können. Das Vokabular war für uns durchdekliniert, wir haben eine ganze Menge dabei entdeckt und für uns auch gelernt. Aber es gab für uns keinen Grund mehr, diese Art von Experiment weiter fortzusetzen, in der bisherigen Art und Weise der urbanen Interventionen und Statements. Daraus resultierte der sehr klare und anfänglich sehr mühevolle Entschluss, aus der ‚akademischen Liga' auszusteigen, mit ihren selbstgeschaffenen Gesetzen und ihren eigenen Szenarien und Auditorien. Wir wollten uns nun ganz brutal hineinmanövrieren in eine professionelle Liga, die den Marktgesetzen gehorcht.

DMS: Es ist interessant, dass eure beiden Positionen eigentlich von Anfang an geradezu grundsätzlich different waren, obwohl sie so ähnlich aussahen, und auch in einer ‚Bewegung' versammelt wurden. Es hat dann wohl dreißig Jahre dauern müssen, um die Unterschiede wirklich klar zu erkennen. Das macht mich ein wenig vorsichtig, wenn ich euch jetzt nach eurer Einschätzung der ‚Jungen' frage. Vielleicht machen wir auch hier den Fehler, ähnliche Erscheinungen in einen Topf zu werfen, die doch höchst different sind. Trotzdem: Mein Eindruck bei zeitgenössischen jungen Projekten ist, dass sehr vieles heute – auch sprachlich so holprig wie eure Erklärungen damals – was ‚jung' projektiert wird, in den Sechzigern angedacht wurde und jetzt wieder neu da ist. Ebenso auch jetzt wieder die Gruppennamen: poor boys enterprise, propeller z etc.

PRIX: Wen bezeichnest du als jung. Denn die Jungen haben ein ganz schönes Alter, die sind alle bereits an die 40, und von unserer Jugend damals wirklich weit entfernt. Wir waren damals unter dreißig, also wirklich noch blauäugigst, als wir hinausgetreten sind in die Weltöffentlichkeit.

DMS: Allerdings ist auch die Ausbildungssituation heute anders, die Jungen kommen viel später als ihr überhaupt mit Architektur in Berührung, es beginnt alles viel später.

PRIX: Es ist zunächst eine jeweils andere lokale Situation. Es ist in Wien anders als in Holland, in Spanien, in England, in Amerika. Wenn wir von Österreich reden, dann gibt es einige, die definieren sich total anders als wir damals, weil die Zeiten und das Umfeld nicht zu vergleichen sind. Sie haben ohne Zweifel momentan mehr Chancen, in den Markt zu kommen, das Blut früher zu lecken als wir damals. Was ein Vorteil ist, aber auch ein Nachteil sein kann.

ORTNER: Ich sehe die Problematik der jungen Gruppen in ihrer Konzentration auf formale Themen und wenig Anspruch, aus dieser Formalität herauszukommen und zu versuchen, zwischen den Schichten Dinge herauszupressen. Ich habe immer wieder das Gefühl bei den Jungen, bei den jungen Holländern, aber auch hier, dass man versucht, etwas sperrigere Formen, aber trotzdem sehr ins Auge stechende Dinge zu kreieren. Aber mir fehlt, dass man nicht aufsetzt auf das Thema der beruhigten äußeren Form, die aber zulässt, dass man sich mehr mit Atmosphäre, Fluidum, Duft beschäftigt, was total interessant wäre, auch als Ergänzung und Weiterentwicklung zu der Geschichte, die wir bisher selber durch-

Haus mit fliegendem Dach · House with the Flying Roof, **Coop Himmelblau**, London, 1973. Archive DS

for your estimation of the 'young.' Maybe we are also making the same mistake here, throwing similar appearances, which are highly different after all, into one pot. Nonetheless: My impression in the case of contemporary young projects is that very much today—also as linguistically clumsy as your explanations back then—that is projected as 'young,' was envisaged in the sixties and is now new again here. Just like the group names now again as well: poor boys enterprise, propeller z, etc.

PRIX: Who do you label as young? Because the young have reached a ripe age; they are all around 40 already and far removed from our youth back then. We were under thirty at that time, that is, still really as blue-eyed as could be when we stepped out into the global public.

Erster Tag • Day One

BMW Protoyp · prototype, Chris Bangle. Archive DS
BMW-Welt · BMW World, München · Munich, Coop Himmelb(l)au, Baustelle · construction site, 2006. © DS
Ansicht · view, 2007. Archive DS

DMS: The educational situation, however, is also different today, the young come much later than you into contact with architecture at all, everything begins much later.

PRIX: It is primarily a respectively different local situation. It is different in Vienna than in Holland, in Spain, in England, in America. If we speak of Austria, then there are several who define themselves totally differently than we did back then, because the times and the environment are not to be compared. Without a doubt they momentarily have more chances to come into the market, to taste blood earlier than us at that time. Which is an advantage, but can also be a disadvantage.

ORTNER: I see the problem of the young groups in their concentration on formal issues and less demand to come out of this formality and to try to press things out between the layers. I always have that feeling again and again with the young ones, with the young Dutchmen, but also here, that one tries to create somewhat more bulky forms, but things that catch the eye very much. But what I'm missing is that one doesn't put the calmed outer form on the theme, which, however, allows one to deal more with atmosphere, fluidity, bouquet, which would be totally interesting, also as an addition and further development to the story that we have experienced ourselves up to now. We all had created a formally very clear and provocative work, which, however, from my perspective today didn't do one thing, namely, to dare the attempt to regain the juice that makes architecture what it ultimately is. And that is not only what you see with the eyes, but is a complete three-dimensional impression. It is quite simply the characteristic of the medium. No other medium can do that: to be physically so universally tangible. I still see too few approaches to it there.

gemacht haben. Wir hatten ja alle ein formal sehr deutliches und provokantes Werk geschaffen, das aber aus meiner Sicht heute eines nicht getan hat, nämlich den Versuch zu wagen, den Saft wiederzugewinnen, der Architektur letztlich ausmacht. Und das ist nicht nur das, was du mit den Augen siehst, sondern das ist eine totale dreidimensionale Beeindruckung. Die ist das Charakteristikum des Mediums schlechthin. Das kann kein anderes Medium: physisch so universell erfahrbar zu sein. Da sehe ich nach wie vor zu wenige Ansätze dazu.

DMS: Ich möchte mich jetzt nicht auf die lokalen Szenen einlassen, sondern eine spezifische Entwicklung ansprechen. Das betrifft die Rolle des Computers, die Enträumlichung, die technische Konditionierung von Räumen und Erfahrungen. Bei diesen Projekten müsst ihr doch auch gewisse Déjà-vu-Erlebnisse haben. Das haben wir doch schon vor dreißig Jahren probiert, oder nicht?

PRIX: Das wäre total ungerecht, wenn wir angesichts dessen sagen würden, das haben wir alles schon einmal gemacht. Das stimmt vielleicht bei den Ansätzen von Entwicklungen, dass man da Ähnlichkeiten sehen könnte, aber das ist legitim und im Entwicklungsprozess normal. Lars Spuybroek beispielsweise weiß natürlich, dass viele seiner Überlegungen schon bei Kiesler intendiert und angedacht waren. Er ist nicht angepasst und irgendwann baut er etwas, was nicht angepasst und sehr sehr präzis und einflussreich sein wird. Es wäre deshalb zu diskutieren, wieweit sich die Jungen für eine Weiterentwicklung der Architektur zuständig fühlen.

DMS: Aber erfolgt derzeit nicht eine Angleichung der Formen durch die für jeden verfügbare Technologie. Und von wem wurde sie entwickelt? Karl S. Chu hat am SYNWORLD-Symposium im Architekturzentrum Wien die These vertreten, dass die Programme heute ganz stark von der Ideologie der Hippie-Kultur beeinflusst sind, dass hier durch die handelnden Personen, die Programmierer, eine durchgehende Ästhetik vorhanden ist.

PRIX: Es gibt ein Bild von den Doors, die in einem Raum sitzen, der ausschaut wie ein Raum heute von NOX oder Greg Lynn. Die Frage ist nach wie vor, wie werden sie es bauen?

DMS: I would not like to get involved with the local scenes now, but address a specific development. That concerns the role of the computer, the despatialization, the technical conditioning of spaces and experiences. In these projects you must have certain déjà vu experiences after all. We already tried that out thirty years ago, didn't we?

PRIX: That would be totally unfair if we would say in view of the fact that we already did that once. That is perhaps right in the approaches of developments that one could see similarities there, but that is legitimate and normal in the development process. Lars Spuybroek, for instance, naturally knows that many of his considerations were already planned and envisaged by Kiesler. He is not assimilated and he eventually builds something that will be unassimilated and very, very precise and influential. It would therefore have to be discussed to what extent the young feel responsible for a further development of architecture.

DMS: But isn't an assimilation of forms through the technology available to everyone currently taking place? And who was it developed by? At the SYNWORLD Symposium at the Architekturzentrum Wien, Karl Chu argued that the programs today are very strongly influenced by the ideology of the hippie culture, that here, through the acting persons, the programmers, a continuous aesthetic exists.

PRIX: There is a picture of The Doors, who are sitting in a space that looks like a space today by NOX or Greg Lynn. The question is still how will they build it?

ORTNER: But what is really so interesting about it? It is the 27th rehash, it may be a certain form of advancement, but our problem is, after all, that we have run through everything in the last fifty years; there is nothing about formal and intellectual attempts that wouldn't have been fit onto the previous ones, a craft room of the century. And now it appears much more interesting for me to demand from the medium of architecture what it could really accomplish. That is very tenacious and very long-term. But as the only medium, it can really be physically experienced from all dimensions. Because defining new social forms through the form already

existed in the classic modernism period. And that has been modified up to today. But someday I have to learn something from this lesson after all. And I ask myself today whether this permanent race for the new form is right and whether something is there, between the layers, some thing that we have been continuously running past for fifty years and would let itself be grabbed in one go if we knew where we can grab.

PRIX: Then do it.

ORTNER: I'll try.

PRIX: Do it. That is just as interesting as everything else. What I find so fascinating today is the simultaneity of the systems. That is the fundamental difference to back then. This simultaneity is over and done with.

ORTNER: But isn't the homogeneity of the field of competitors, of all competitors in every field who are suddenly effortlessly able to catch up again to any runaway, much more interesting today than the simultaneity of the systems that you are addressing? That wasn't always the case. It is one of the characteristics today that the differences are getting smaller and smaller. It is a nearly homogenous field that only defines itself still through the tiniest differences. If you want to belong to the top of any field today, you have to be quite intelligent. That has nothing to do with the world view and the culture, but with the basic approach to the métier. That is the simultaneity of the systems that I see. And it fascinates me how these people come nearer and nearer.

ORTNER: Aber was ist daran wirklich so interessant. Es ist der 27ste Aufguss, es mag eine gewisse Form der Weiterentwicklung sein, aber unser Problem ist doch, dass wir in den letzten fünfzig Jahren alles durchdekliniert haben, es gibt doch nichts an formalen und intellektuellen Versuchen, die nicht an die vorangegangenen gefügt gewesen wären, eine Bastelstube des Jahrhunderts. Und jetzt erschiene es mir doch viel interessanter, dem Medium der Architektur das abzuverlangen, was es wirklich leisten könnte. Das ist sehr zäh und sehr langfristig. Aber als einziges Medium kann sie wirklich aus allen Dimensionen körperlich erlebt werden. Denn über die Form neue Gesellschaftsformen zu definieren, das gab es schon in der klassischen Moderne. Und das ist bis heute modifiziert abgewandelt worden. Aber aus dieser Lektion muss ich doch irgendwann etwas lernen. Und ich frage mich heute, ob dieses permanente Rennen nach der neuen Form richtig ist, und ob nicht da etwas ist, zwischen den Schichten, irgend etwas, an dem wir fünfzig Jahre lang ununterbrochen vorbeigelaufen sind und das sich mit einem Griff herausgreifen ließe, wenn wir wüssten, wo wir zugreifen können.

PRIX: Dann mach mal.

ORTNER: Ich versuch's mal.

PRIX: Mach mal. Das ist genauso interessant wie alles andere. Was ich heute so faszinierend finde, ist die Gleichzeitigkeit der Systeme. Das ist der grundsätzliche Unterschied zu damals. Diese Gleichzeitigkeit ist gegessen.

ORTNER: Aber ist nicht noch viel interessanter als die Gleichzeitigkeit der Systeme, die du ansprichst, eigentlich heute die Homogenität des Feldes der Mitbewerber, aller Mitbewerber auf jedem Gebiet, die plötzlich spielend in der Lage sind, jeden Ausreißer wieder einzuholen. Das war nicht immer so. Es ist eines der Merkmale heute, dass die Unterschiede immer kleiner werden. Es ist ein fast homogenes Feld, das sich nur noch durch winzigste Unterschiede definiert. Wenn du heute auf irgendeinem Gebiet zur Spitze gehören willst, musst du ziemlich intelligent sein. Das hat nichts mit dem Weltbild und der Kultur zu tun, sondern mit der grundlegenden Herangehensweise an das Metier. Das ist die Gleichzeitigkeit der Systeme, die ich sehe. Und es fasziniert mich, wie sich diese Leute immer näher kommen.

Bene Büromöbel, Unternehmenszentrale · Headquarters, Waidhofen/Ybbs, Ortner & Ortner, 1988. © Ortner & Ortner

Landesarchiv · State Archive Nordrhein-
Westfalen, Duisburg, Ortner+Ortner Baukunst, 2013.
© Ortner & Ortner

PRIX: Es muss aber auch erlaubt sein, in einer extremen Form anders zu denken. Dazu müssen die Jungen Substanz entwickeln, um gewisse Widerstände aufbauen zu können, um sich gewisser Dinge zu erwehren. Man muss Widerstände leisten, das ist auch die Herausforderung an die Jungen, dass sie sich nicht zu früh aalglatt abschleifen zu lassen.

ORTNER: Aber das tut doch heute keiner mehr.

PRIX: *(nennt einige Namen junger holländischer, deutscher und österreichischer Architekten.)*

ORTNER: Wer heute in den Markt geht, geht mit allen Kriterien hinein, die du forderst. Härte zu zeigen, ist ein wichtiger Bestandteil. Aber es kommt eine ganze Reihe von Bedingungen, die ich ständig intelligent neu verknüpfen muss. Ich erfinde nichts Neues, aber ich versuche mit den schlechten Gegebenheiten etwas zu tun.

PRIX: Es ist wie in der Popmusik. Shooting-Stars, die nicht die ständige Bewährung im Lifekonzert bewältigen, werden zwar kurz gepusht, aber dann schnell wieder ausgespuckt.

So gibt es, am Ende des Gesprächs, also doch eine gemeinsame Position und Botschaft für die jungen Architekten. Im Laufe einer dreißigjährigen Karriere gibt es Entwicklungen, Erkenntnisse, Durststrecken, Veränderungen. Ein einmal erfolgreiches Thema kann und darf nicht perpetuiert werden. Denn die eigene Position muss immer wieder neu hinterfragt werden.

PRIX: But thinking differently in an extreme form must also be allowed. To do that the young have to develop substance in order to be able to build up certain resistances, in order to fend off certain things. One has to put up resistances, that is also the challenge to the young, that they don't let themselves be ground down too smoothly too early.

ORTNER: But nobody does that anymore.

PRIX: *(Calls off several names of young Dutch, German, and Austrian architects)*

ORTNER: Whoever goes into the market goes in with all the criteria you demand. To show toughness is an important component. But a whole series of conditions comes, which I have to constantly and intelligently re-link. I invent nothing new, but I try to do something with the worst circumstances.

PRIX: It's like in pop music. Shooting stars who don't manage the constant testing in live concerts are briefly pushed, but then quickly spit out again.

So at the end of the conversation there is a common position and message for the young architects. In the course of a thirty-year career there are developments, insights, lean periods, changes. A once-successful theme can and may not be perpetuated. Because one's own position has to repeatedly be questioned anew.

aus · from

Ö1 diagonal 19_1997
„Milano Torri: Velasca gegen Pirelli"
Translation by Brian Dorsey

Torri

Mailand, die Stadt und die zeitgenössische Architektur. Jedem einigermaßen aufmerksamen Beobachter fallen dabei vor allem zwei Türme ein: Die Torre Velasca und die Torre Pirelli. Beide sind rund vierzig Jahre alt und von außerordentlich plakativer Prägnanz. Und sie könnten unterschiedlicher nicht sein, kraftvolle und großartige Statements, fast Kampfansagen zweier Architekturrichtungen. Sie treten gegeneinander an. Warum zur selben Zeit in derselben Stadt? Versuchen wir dem Rätsel auf die Spur zu kommen.

Die Stadt und die Architektur haben in Mailand eine eigenartige Beziehung. Sucht man nach international bedeutenden Beispielen zeitgenössischer Architektur, dann wäre Mailand in etwa mit Düsseldorf oder Oslo vergleichbar. Es gibt verstreute Monumente der Nachkriegsarchitektur, wie die beiden Türme oder das Viertel Gallaratese, die internationale Bedeutung erlangten. Aber es gibt keinen Bau der letzten Jahre, der über ein provinziell lokales Interesse hinausragen würde. Selbst das demnächst eröffnende neue Piccolo Teatro von Marco Zanuso, dank Giorgio Strehler ein kulturelles Symbolbauwerk von europäischer Bedeutung, ist in der Maschine der Mailänder Baubürokratie bis zur Unkenntlichkeit vernichtet worden.

Towers

Milan, the city and contemporary architecture. Two towers in particular catch the eye of every somewhat attentive observer: Torre Velasca and Torre Pirelli. Both are around forty years old and of extraordinarily striking conciseness. And they could not be any more different, powerful and grand statements, almost the war declarations of two architectural directions. They compete against each other. Why at the same time in the same city? Let us try to unravel this mystery.

The city and architecture have a unique relationship in Milan. If one is searching for internationally prominent examples of contemporary architecture, then Milan would be approximately comparable to Dusseldorf or Oslo. There are scattered monuments of postwar architecture, like the two aforementioned towers or the Gallaratese district, which have attained international importance. But there are no structures of recent years that would project beyond a provincial, local interest. Even the soon-opening new Piccolo Teatro by Marco Zanuso, a cultural symbolic building of European significance thanks to Giorgio Strehler, has been destroyed beyond recognition in the machinery of Milanese construction bureaucracy.

In return, Milan is probably the only truly international metropolis of media architecture. So despite catastrophic organizational and political conditions, the Triennale di Milano is still a prime address. And, most notably, all relevant Italian and international architecture magazines have their editorial office address in Milan. Titles such as *Modo, Abitare, ottagono* are well-known far beyond Italy. Magazines like *Lotus international, Casabella* and *domus* have been determining the direction and themes of architectural debate for years and are world-leading today.

Torre Pirelli, Gio Ponti, Milano, 1955–58. © DS

Dafür ist Mailand wahrscheinlich die einzige wirklich internationale Metropole der medialen Architektur. So ist trotz katastrophaler organisatorischer und politischer Verhältnisse die Triennale di Milano noch immer eine erste Adresse. Und vor allem alle relevanten italienischen und internationalen Architekturmagazine haben ihre Redaktionsadresse in Mailand. Titel wie *Modo, Abitare, ottagono* sind weit über Italien hinaus bekannt, und Magazine wie *Lotus international, Casabella* und *domus* bestimmen seit Jahren und heute weltweit führend die Richtung und Themen der Architekturdebatte.

Jeder Architekt oder Designer, der weltweite Bedeutung und letztlich Weltruhm erlangen will, ist deshalb auf die Wahrnehmung durch den unkalkulierbaren Dschungel der Mailänder Medien angewiesen. Das bedeutet auch, dass die jeweiligen Positionen der Mailänder Architekturmedien Architekturgeschichte geschrieben haben und auch weiterhin schreiben.

So wird es wohl kein Zufall sein, dass die Torre Velasca ebenso wie die Torre Pirelli auch eine gebaute Illustration der Position der Mailänder Architekturmedien ist.

Die Daten: Die Torre Velasca wurde 1956–58 erbaut, vom Architektenteam BBPR, Ludovico Belgiojoso, Gian Luigi Banfi, Enrico Peressutti und Ernesto Nathan Rogers. Rogers war zu dieser Zeit Chefredakteur der Zeitschrift *Casabella*. Die Torre Pirelli, 1955–58 folgt einem Konzept und Entwurf von Gio Ponti, dem legendären Direktor der Zeitschrift *domus*.

Every architect or designer who wants to gain worldwide importance and ultimately global fame is therefore dependent on the perception through the incalculable jungle of Milanese media. This also means that the respective positions of the Milanese architectural media have written and also continue to write architectural history.

So it will probably not be a coincidence that Torre Velasca and Torre Pirelli are also a built illustration of the position of Milanese architectural media.

The data: Torre Velasca was erected from 1956 to 1958 by the architect team BBPR, Gian Luigi Banfi, Lodovico Belgiojoso, Enrico Peressutti and Ernesto Nathan Rogers. At that time Rogers was the chief editor of the magazine *Casabella*. Torre Pirelli, 1955–58, followed a concept and design by Gio Ponti, the legendary director of the magazine *domus*.

Torre Velasca, BBPR, Milano, 1956–58.
© CEphoto, Uwe Aranas

Also *domus* gegen *Casabella*, Ponti gegen Rogers, und die beiden Türme als Symbole eines Kampfes, oder besser zweier Wege der modernen Architektur, die damals, am Ende der fünfziger Jahre, so deutliche Markierungen setzten.

Pontis Torre Pirelli symbolisiert den Traum einer aufgeklärten, internationalen, einer eigentlich ortlosen technologischen Moderne. Der große italienische Statiker Pier Luigi Nervi half ihm dabei, die dünne Scheibe, die sich an den Schmalseiten verjüngt, zu realisieren. Wie ein elegant geschliffenes Schwert steht die Torre Pirelli da, verspiegelt und unnahbar, die monumentalisierte Entmaterialisierung ist ihr Versprechen.

Well, *domus* versus *Casabella*, Ponti versus Rogers, and both towers as symbols of a fight, or better two ways of modern architecture, which back then, at the end of the fifties, placed such distinct markings.

Ponti's Torre Pirelli symbolized the dream of an enlightened, international, actually placeless technological modernism. The great Italian structural engineer Pier Luigi Nervi helped him realize the thin slab, which tapers upwards on its narrow side. Torre Pirelli stands there like an elegantly sharpened sword, mirrored and unapproachable; its promise is the monumentalized dematerialization.

domus gegen *Casabella*, Ponti gegen Rogers, und die beiden Türme als Symbole eines Kampfes.

Demgegenüber nannte Ponti die Torre Velasca eine „creazione ambientale". Weil ihre auskragend abgespreizten Obergeschosse so direkt sprachlich auf das Castello Sforzesco motivisch antworten, dessen Sprache und Erscheinungsbild aufnehmen, dem Genius Loci so Referenz erweisend, Bezüge zur Tradition herstellend.

Deshalb ist die Torre Velasca ein erster Vorbote der sogenannten Postmoderne, die eigentlich erst zwanzig Jahre später so richtig plakativ aufbrechen wird, die Torre Pirelli hingegen im alten und heute wieder neuen Sinn modern zu nennen.

Seit eineinhalb Jahren bin ich zweimal im Monat in Mailand, fahre in meine Redaktion, um aus einem Stapel neuer Projekte der Weltarchitektur auszuwählen, welchem die Ehre zuteil wird, in einer der nächsten Ausgaben der inzwischen weltgrößten Architekturfachzeitschrift, in *domus*, zu erscheinen. Und allenthalben denke ich an Gio Ponti, an Ernesto Rogers, und bin ihnen dankbar dafür, dass es diese beiden Torri gibt. Schließlich helfen sie mir bei der unbeantwortbaren Entscheidung, ob nicht inzwischen die Postmoderne modern ist oder die Moderne postmodern. Oder ob beide Torri zu ihrer Zeit modern und deshalb schon postmodern waren.

Jedenfalls hat keine andere Stadt der Welt zwei derart exzellente singuläre Monumente des unauflöslichen architektonischen Konflikts dieses Jahrhunderts. Vielleicht ist Mailand doch eine Stadt der Architektur.

In contrast, Ponti called the Torre Velasca a "creazione ambientale." Because its protrudingly strutted upper floors motivically reply in such a direct linguistic manner to the Castello Sforzesco, taking up its language and appearance, bestowing its reference upon the genius loci, establishing references to tradition.

That is why the Torre Velasca is the first harbinger of so-called postmodernism, which actually will break open so boldly twenty years later, whereas the Torre Pirelli is to be called modern in the old and today once again new sense.

For one-and-a-half years I've been in Milan twice a month, travelling to my editorial office in order to select from a pile of new projects of world architecture which will be accorded the honor to appear in one of the next issues of the meanwhile world's largest architecture specialist magazine, in *domus*. And everywhere I think about Gio Ponti, about Ernesto Rogers, and I am grateful to them that both these *torri* exist. In the end, they help me in the unanswerable decision whether postmodernism is not modern in the meantime, or modernism postmodern. Or whether both *torri* were modern at their time and therefore already postmodern.

At any rate, no other city of the world has two such excellent singular models of the insoluble architectonic conflict of this century. Perhaps Milan is a city of architecture after all.

Brutalism Brutalismus

Seit dem neuen Jahrtausend gibt es eine Wiederentdeckung der brutalistischen Architektur der Nachkriegszeit des 20. Jahrhunderts. Jahrzehntelang wurde sie angefeindet und ignoriert, jetzt ist sie in technischer und kultureller Bedrängnis. Doch diese Bauten geben ein baugeschichtlich wertvolles Zeugnis für eine Epoche, in der staatliche und kommunale Planung noch gesellschaftlicher und politischer Auftrag war, bevor der neoliberale Städtebau die Macht übernahm.

Since the new millennium there has been a rediscovery of the brutalist architecture of the post-war era of the 20th century. For decades it was met with hostility and ignored; now it is in technical and cultural distress. These buildings nonetheless bear valuable witness in a construction historical sense to an era in which state and communal planning was still a social and political mandate, before neo-liberal urban development took power.

Alle Bilder All images © DS

Barbican, London, Chamberlin, Powell and Bon, 1982

Habitat, Montreal, Moshe Safdie, 1967

Transportministerium · Transport Ministry, Tbilisi, G. Tschachawa, Z. Dschalagania, T. Tchilawa, W. Kimberg, 1974

Krematorium · Crematorium, Kiew, A. Milezkyj, W. Melnytschenko, A. Rybatschuk, 1968–80

Busbahnhof · Bus terminal, Hrazdan, H. Arakeljan, 1978

Habitat, Montreal, Moshe Safdie, 1967

Sanatorium Druschba, Jalta · Sanatorium Druzba, Yalta, I. Wasylewskyj, J. Stefantschuk, W. Diwnow, L. Kesler, 1985

Erholungsheim der Schriftstellervereinigung · Guest house for the Armenian Writers' Union, Sewan-Halbinsel · Sevan Peninsula, G. Kotschar, 1969

Busbahnhof · Bus terminal, Hrazdan, H. Arakeljan, 1978

Stadtteil · City district, Split 3, Slowenisches Institut für Städtebau · Slovenian Institute for Urban Planning, V. Mušič, Architektur Ivo Radič 1979

Wohnkomplex · Housing, Jadwiga Grabowska-Hawrylak, Wroclav, 1968–78

Markthalle · Market hall, Schytnij, Kiew Kiev, W. Schtolko, O. Monina, 1982

Studentenheim · Students' hostel „Goce Delcev", Skopje, G. Konstantinovsky

Stadt Slawutytsch – als Ersatz für die durch das Tschernobyl-Unglück verlassene Stadt Pripjat gebaut. Die letzte Stadt der Sowjetunion · The city of Slavutych – built to replace the city of Pripyat, which was abandoned after the nuclear accident in Chernobyl. The last city of the Soviet Union, 1986–90

Stadtteil · City district Split 3, Slowenisches Institut für Städtebau · Slovenian Institute for Urban Planning, V. Mušič, Architektur Ivo Radič 1979

Schewtschenko Universität · Shevchenko University, Kiew · Kiev, W. Landyj, M. Budilowskyj, W. Kolomijez, 1990

Zirkus · Circus, Bischkek · Bishkek, L. Segal, I. Schadrin, D. Leontjew, W. Mironowitsch, A. Netschurin, 1976

Lenin-Sportpalast · Lenin Sports Palace, Bischkek · Bishkek, W. Kostin, W. Marukow, 1974

Stadtteil · City district Split 3, Slowenisches Institut für Städtebau · Slovenian Institute for Urban Planning, V. Mušič, Architektur Ivo Radič 1979

Hotel Salut, Kiew · Kiev, A. Milezkyj, N. Slogozka, W. Schwetschenko, 1984

2ⁿᵈ DAY The 1970s

Streik an der Akademie der bildenden Künste Wien ·
Strike at the Academy of Fine Arts Vienna, 1973.
© Gerhard Heller

The *documenta 5* curated by Harald Szeemann fundamentally expands my view of the world. – +++ – The study at the Academy of Fine Arts Vienna in the 1970s is characterized by the politicization of this era. We go on strike and lock in a team of professors. – +++ – The first project with E. A. Plischke, a representative of Viennese modernism who had returned from exile in New Zealand, is a single-family house. This old-fashioned task and Plischke's romantic position of a pure architecture of poetic function seems completely outdated to me in an architectural and socio-political sense. I design a structuralistic building for a house-sharing community – +++ – I find myself in a productive conflict with Plischke's successor Gustav Peichl. His view of architecture is too flat for me: "Just simply say I, as the architect, want it that way!" However, he successfully teaches us to defend designs in front of lay people; the presentation and publication of projects is trained. – +++ – The politicized German debate appeals to me in terms of content. I attend many conferences on the critical theory of architecture. The magazine *ARCH+* becomes the leading medium. – +++ – In the mid-1970s, the discussion in the German-speaking world is characterized by Aldo Rossi, Robert Venturi and *Tendenza*. – +++ – Rob Krier is called to the Technical University of Vienna in 1976 and I help him with the texts for his book *Architectural Composition*. – +++ – That same year I participate in the occupation of the "Arena" in Vienna's "Auslandsschlachthof" ("Overseas Slaughterhouse"). The "Arena" is to become a new alternative cultural center. – +++ – With a stipend for the German Democratic Republic I visit the Bauhaus in Weimar and Dessau. – +++ – As a guest student at the Swiss Federal Institute of Technology (ETH) in Zurich I discover Swiss modernism and my lasting, intimate relationship with the city of Barcelona begins. – +++ – In Vienna I get involved in the Austrian Society for Architecture (ÖGFA), become secretary and co-publisher of the magazine *UM BAU* …

2. TAG Die 1970er

Rob Krier, Dietmar Steiner, Berlin. © Margarethe Cufer

Die *documenta 5* von Harald Szeemann erweitert grundlegend meine Sicht der Welt – +++ – Das Studium an der Wiener Akademie in den 1970er Jahren ist von der Politisierung dieser Zeit geprägt. Wir streiken und sperren das Professoren-Kollegium ein – +++ – Das erste Projekt bei E. A. Plischke, einem aus dem Exil in Neuseeland zurückgekehrten Vertreter der Wiener Moderne, ist ein Einfamilienhaus. Diese altmodische Aufgabe und Plischkes romantische Position einer reinen Architektur der poetischen Funktion erscheint mir architektonisch und gesellschaftspolitisch völlig aus der Zeit gefallen. Ich entwerfe ein strukturalistisches Haus für eine Wohngemeinschaft – +++ – Mit Plischkes Nachfolger Gustav Peichl befinde ich mich in einem produktiven Konflikt. Seine Sicht der Architektur ist mir zu flach: „Sagen Sie einfach, ich als Architekt will das so!" Erfolgreich aber lehrt er uns Entwürfe vor Laien zu vertreten, die Präsentation und Publikation von Projekten wird trainiert – +++ – Inhaltlich reizt mich die politisierte deutsche Debatte. Ich besuche viele Konferenzen zur kritischen Theorie der Architektur. Die Zeitschrift *ARCH+* wird zum Leitmedium – +++ – Mitte der 1970er Jahre wird im deutschsprachigen Raum die Debatte von Aldo Rossi, Robert Venturi und der „Tendenza" geprägt – +++ – Rob Krier wird 1976 an die TU Wien berufen und ich helfe ihm bei den Texten zu seinem Buch *Über Architektonische Komposition* – +++ – Im selben Jahr wirke ich an der Besetzung des Wiener Auslandsschlachthofs mit. Die „Arena" sollte ein neues alternatives Kulturzentrum werden – +++ – Mit einem Stipendium für die DDR besuche ich das Bauhaus in Weimar und Dessau – +++ – Als Gaststudent an der ETH Zürich entdecke ich die Schweizer Moderne, und mein anhaltendes intimes Verhältnis mit der Stadt Barcelona beginnt – +++ – In Wien engagiere ich mich in der Österreichischen Gesellschaft für Architektur (ÖGFA), werde Sekretär und Mitherausgeber der Zeitschrift *UM BAU*…

Konzeption und Form

In den Tagen, in denen wir das vorliegende Heft 4 abschliessen, gelangt ein Text von Gregotti auf unseren Tisch, der sich mit dem Detail als Teil der sich verändernden architektonischen Sprache auseinandersetzt.* Der Text enthält Gedanken, die uns bei der Vorbereitung leiteten.

Gregotti geht von der zunehmenden Abstraktion des Details aus, die schon in der Einleitung von *archithese* 3 angesprochen wurde. In der Tat hängen die Hefte 3 und 4 darin zusammen, dass sie beide von der Beziehung von Konzeption und Form handeln. Diese wird im Detail sichtbar.

Wie Gregotti schreibt, wird das Detail mehr und mehr von der Konzeption bestimmt:

«Das hat zwei Folgen. Im einen Fall wird die Bedeutung der Konstruktion für den architektonischen Ausdruck negiert, was zu einer zunehmenden Abstraktion des Details führt (...). Im anderen Fall wird weniger die Ausdruckskraft des Details in Frage gestellt als der Umstand, dass es eine eigene Ausdruckskraft hat. Dies steht in Beziehung zur Krise der architektonischen Sprache als einer Objektsprache.»

In beiden Fällen wird versucht, die Sprachlosigkeit, die sich daraus ergibt, durch Zitieren von «anderen» Formen zu beseitigen. Aber:

«Es ist eine Täuschung, dass eine solche Form das Detail ersetzen könne bei der Artikulation der architektonischen Sprache, wie es auch, eine Täuschung ist, dass eine Konzeption den Entwurf in allen seinen Teilen beherrschen könne, ohne dass die Abwesenheit des Details, dies unterstreicht in polemischer Weise die Bedeutungslosigkeit der Konstruktion als Teil des druckes.»

Was gemacht wird hat eine die in der Sprache der Arch sagt, wie es gemacht ist. schreibt Gregotti, ist es wich Statut dieser Form zu untersu

«Das Detail (...) ist nich dazu da, allgemeine Entsch abzuwandeln, sondern es p Form, und macht ihren Sin kennbar.»

Aber es macht den Sin meinen Entscheidungen – h tion – in seinen eigenen Be kennbar: Darin liegt die tikulation der architekton che.

* Vittorio Gregotti: L'mentio Casabella 482, Juni 1982, Se

Conception et forme

aus

archithese 4_83
„Jedes Detail eine Geschichte"

Plötzlich hört es auf zu gähnen, macht seine Augen weit auf und streckt Willie seine große rote Zunge heraus. (So kommt es Willie jedenfalls vor – aber, wißt ihr, es ist nur ein roter Teepich, den Bridget zum Lüften aus dem Fenster gehängt hat.)

1

DIETMAR STEINER

Jedes Detail eine Geschichte

Wee Willie Winkie's World in Wien

«Da jetzt Ihre Arbeiten auf meinem Bau dem Ende zugehen, ist es mir Pflicht & Bedürfnis, Ihnen Dank & Anerkennung für Ihre hervorragende Leistung auszusprechen. Ich kann sagen, dass es ohne Ihre Arbeit unmöglich gewesen wäre, den Bau in der, dieser Bauart notwendigen, Präzision & Sachgemässheit herzustellen. Es ist meine Überzeugung, dass keine Firma in Wien imstande gewesen wäre, das was ich fordern musste, in ähnlicher Weise zu erfüllen.»[1]
Ludwig Wittgenstein an die Schlosserfirma Weber im November 1928

Dort wo die Architektur auf den Punkt kommt, verdichtet sich das Werk zu einer Miniatur seiner selbst. Details gleichen Akkumulatoren, die mit der Energie der architektonischen Arbeit, der Biographie des Architekten, seiner Philosophie und seinem Verhältnis zu den Dingen aufgeladen sind. Es ist selbstverständlich, dass uns diese Dinge und Gegenstände Geschichten erzählen können. Ähnlich der Werbung, die uns tagtäglich mit sprechenden Kochplatten und zufrieden seufzenden weil frisch gereinigten Kacheln überrascht. Aus diesen neuen und alten Mythen, Märchen und Sagen kennen wir die «beseelten Dinge». Man muss mit den Dingen ins Gespräch kommen, um die Angst vor der feindlichen Aussenwelt abwehren zu können.

In diesem Sinne entwirft Lyonel Feininger 1906 die Comic-Serie «Wee Willie Winkie's World» für die Sonntagsbeilage der «Chicago Tribune». Aufgeweckt unterhält sich der kleine Held mit Häusern, Wolken, Bäumen, mit Heuschobern, Windmühlen und Strassenbahnen. Adolf Loos wird 16 Jahre später derselben Zeitung seine «gebaute Columne» widmen. Dass dieser Entwurf auf die Lektüre der Comic-Seite der «Tribune» zurückzuführen sei, darf in diesem Zusammenhang ruhig als unzulässige Erfindung einer Geschichte bezeichnet werden...

Willie Winkie's Dialoge mit den Dingen finden meist im ungewissen Licht der Dämmerung statt. Einem Licht, wo die Welt nicht mehr eindeutig erkennbar ist, wo die Dinge von einer aufgerührten Phantasie leicht in lebende Gestalten verwandelt werden können. Auch Träume, als Form der Wirklichkeit, spielen bei Feiningers Geschichten eine Rolle. Aber immer folgt als letztes Bild der Story die Auflösung: «Und jetzt sieht man, was es wirklich ist...». Nach dem Aufwachen behalten Zweck- und Funktionsbestimmungen wieder die Oberhand.

Analog zu Wee Willie Winkie's World möchte ich diesen Beitrag verstehen: Die nicht immer deutlich lesba-

---
1 Lyonel Feininger: *Wee Willie Winkie's World Or How Things Looked to Wee Willie Winkie*; aus / de The Chicago Sunday Tribune, 19. August 1906 (Reprint Darmstadt 1975)

2 Ludwig Wittgenstein: Der Radiator / Le radiateur

ren Geschichten aus den Dingen hervorlocken, sie gesprächsbereit und -fähig machen. Details, die zuerst und zuletzt durch ihre Brauchbarkeit, Nützlichkeit und Funktionalität bestimmt sind, eine pränatale Botschaft auf den Weg geben. Das Detail, pars pro toto, gar als Fetisch einer abhanden gekommenen Architektur?

Das bedarf einer zusätzlichen Erläuterung: Ich erinnere mich noch an die schweisstreibende Gedächtnisarbeit in der Schule, um den Hakenverschluss des General-Panel-Systems von Gropius und Wachsmann auswendig zu lernen. Heute noch habe ich dieses sonderbar gekröpfte Aluminium-Gebilde vor Augen. Niemals machten wir uns damals darüber Gedanken, wie denn ein mit diesem System gebautes Haus aussehen könnte. Es war und ist auch weitgehend gleichgültig. Das Anschlussdetail der Elemente beinhaltet die gesamte Geschichte der Idee, es war die Erklärung der Methode, die Tendenz und der eigentliche Kern des Entwurfs. Wenn man einmal diese Aluminiumtrümmer finden wird und ihr Rätsel zu lösen imstande ist, dann wird man anhand dieses Superzeichens auch alles über diese Architektur wissen.

Auffallend an dieser Geschichte ist ihre Allgemeingültigkeit. Ist eigentlich schon jemandem aufgefallen, dass es immer die Details sind, die das Gebäude überleben? Nur in ihnen kann das Werk Umbauten und Zerstörungen überdauern. (In Wien kann die Toilette des Cafe Museum als Beispiel dienen, wo Reste der Loos'schen Einrichtung in devastiertem Zustand auf Archäologen warten.) Müssen wir nicht vielleicht überhaupt davon ausgehen, dass über – und mit (!) – Architektur zu sprechen, auf fragmentierte Einzelpunkte angewiesen ist. Die «grosse Form» ist unglaubwürdig geworden, im Netz unkontrollierbarer Bedingungen verloren. Verlässliche Auskünfte geben weder der impressionistische «Raum an sich», noch in sich selbst verstrickte kunsthistorisch-stilistische Vergleiche; die «Trümmer» werden zum eigentlichen Träger der Geschichten, und damit auch von Geschichte, «Geschichtetem», wie Heinz Tesar sagen würde.

Detailgeschichten vorzulegen, verlangt demnach einen Wechsel der Optik: Den Raum und das Haus hintanzustellen zugunsten einer isolierten, in sich stimmigen Geschichte, mit Anfang und Ende (Und wenn sie nicht gestorben sind, so ...). «Ich bin nicht sonderlich an Architektur interessiert» (Aldo Rossi); nicht an den Stimmungen und Gefühlen, die sie zu vermitteln imstande ist, und nicht an den sogenannten Analysen. Erst eine «schöne Geschichte» ermöglicht mir die Aneignung; daran bestimmt sich doch die Bedeutung und der Wert aller uns umgebenden Gegenstände. Oder?

Der Radiator

Es wird Zeit, auf die Funktionsbestimmung des Details zurückzukommen. Details sind richtig oder falsch, bedingungslos den Gesetzen funktioneller Logik unterworfen. Was liegt näher, als die Erzählungen mit Ludwig Wittgenstein zu beginnen: «Das Bild stimmt mit der Wirklichkeit überein oder nicht; es ist richtig oder unrichtig, wahr oder falsch» (Tractatus, 2.21)[2]

Betrachtet man die Geschichte der Radiatoren im Palais Wittgenstein, so muss sich die Frage stellen, ob hier jene, von Wittgenstein im Tractatus geforderten, aber nie formulierten Elementarsätze gebaut verwirklicht wurden? Hermine Wittgenstein schreibt in ihren Erinnerungen:

«Die Radiatoren selbst sind so tadellos in den Massen und in ihrer präzisen glatten schlanken Form, dass es nicht auffiel, wenn Gretl (die Bauherrin, d. Verf.) sie ausserhalb der Heizperiode als Sockel für einen ihrer schönen kunstgewerblichen Gegenstände benützte, ... Jeder dieser Eck-Radiatoren besteht aus zwei Teilen, die haargenau im rechten Winkel zueinander stehen und zwischen denen ein kleiner, auf den Millimeter fixierter Zwischenraum frei gelassen ist, und sie ruhen auf Füssen, auf die sie genau passen mussten. Es wurden erst einige Modelle gegossen, doch zeigte es sich, dass das, was Ludwig vorschwebte, in Österreich gar nicht gegossen werden konnte; man nahm dann für einzelne Teilstücke fertige Gussware aus dem Ausland, mit dieser schien es aber zuerst unmöglich, die von Ludwig geforderte Präzision zu erreichen. Ganze Partien von Rohrstücken mussten als un-

3 Luigi Blau: Schriften / Ecritures

4 Appelt-Kneissl-Prochazka: Die Posttrompete / La trompete de la poste

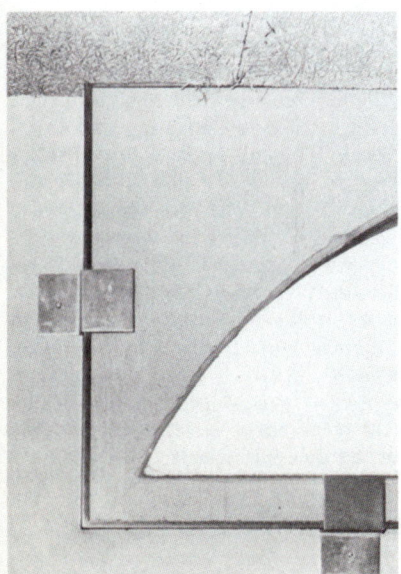

5 Appelt-Kneissl-Prochazka: Das Lewerentz-Fenster / La fenêtre Lewerentz

6 Hermann Czech: Die Medaillons / Les médaillons

brauchbar ausgeschieden, die anderen auf den halben Millimeter genau zugeschliffen werden. Auch die Anbringung der glatten Verschlussstücke, die (...) nach Ludwigs Zeichnungen hergestellt waren, machte grosse Schwierigkeiten; die Versuche wurden oft bis in die Nacht hinein unter Ludwigs Leitung fortgesetzt, bis endlich alles stimmte, und tatsächlich verging zwischen dem Entwurf der scheinbar so einfachen Radiatoren und ihrer Lieferung ein ganzes Jahr».[3]

Das industrielle Produkt wurde also handwerklich hergestellt, weil der Gedanke als logisches Bild der Tatsachen im Vorgegebenen nicht auszudrücken war. Betrachtet man die industriellen Teile als «Umgangssprache» im Wittgensteinschen Sinn, dann ist deren Umformung im Dienst der Philosphie notwendig.

«Es ist menschenunmöglich, die Sprachlogik aus ihr (– der Umgangssprache, d. Verf.) unmittelbar zu entnehmen. Die Sprache verkleidet den Gedanken. Und zwar so, dass man nach der äusseren Form des Kleides, nicht auf die Form des bekleideten Gedankens schliessen kann; weil die äussere Form des Kleides nach ganz anderen Zwecken gebildet ist als danach, die Form des Körpers erkennen zu lassen» (Tractatus, 4.002).[4]

Schwedische Souvenirs

Seitdem Architekten reisen, bringen sie Souvenirs mit nach Hause, die sie gerne in ihren Werken verwenden. Mario Botta schraubte Bolzen an die Wand der Bank in Freiburg und will das als «explizite Hommage» an Otto Wagner verstanden wissen. Das ist das Gesetz des Souvenirs: Eine Wiederholung des Originals wirkt am Ort des Verkaufs immer etwas deplaziert, dafür entfaltet es seine Pracht in der Fremde. Elsa Prochazka und Eberhard Kneissl erhielten einmal das Josef-Frank-Stipendium, verbunden mit einer Reise nach Schweden. Sie brachten das «Sigurd-Lewerentz-Fenster» nach Wien mit und bauten es als exquisites Einzelstück bei der Mehrzweckhalle am Rennbahnweg ein: Eine nackte Verbundglasscheibe ohne Rahmen wird mit Aluminiumwinkeln an die Wand geschraubt. Weiter sahen sie in Schweden viele Wohnhäuser mit dem billigen und widerstandsfähigen Trapezblech verkleidet. Die Dächer aller drei Mehrzweckhallen wurden dann mit diesem Material eingedeckt. Getreu der Devise, dass ein industrielles Programm durch verschiedene Möglichkeiten der ästhetischen Verarbeitung auch verschiedene Botschaften senden kann, wurden mit dem Trapezblech drei verschiedene Dachdeckungsmaterialien simuliert: Rot = Ziegel, Grün = Gras, Gelb = Stroh. Gleichermassen wurden die echten Garagenfalttore, die als Raumtrenner in den Mehrzweckhallen eingebaut sind, dreifach verschieden behandelt: lackiert und durch Holzrahmen in Felder eingeteilt; furniert, um einmal besonders «edel» auszusehen; mit Resopalplatten verkleidet, die ein durchgehendes Muster bilden, um die Fläche als Ganzes zu erproben. – Der Monteur erzählte mir verwundert, dass er bisher nicht ahnte, welch «schöne Tore» seine Firma herstellt...

Schreibarbeiten

Als Luigi Blau vor der Aufgabe stand, ein Schreibwarengeschäft zu beschriften, stand er zunächst vor dem verschlossenen Briefkuvert an der Eingangstüre. Da dieses Geschäft am Wiener Graben etabliert, eingesessen, ein Geschäft mit Geschichte ist, könnte eine kleine Geschichte des Schreibens, des Schildermalens, ein kleiner Aus-

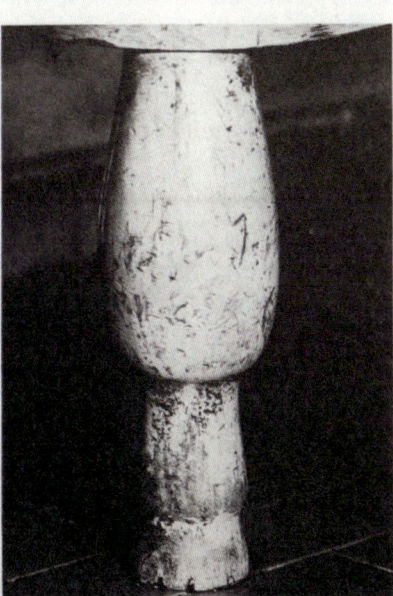

7 Hermann Czech: Der männliche Fuss / Le pied masculin

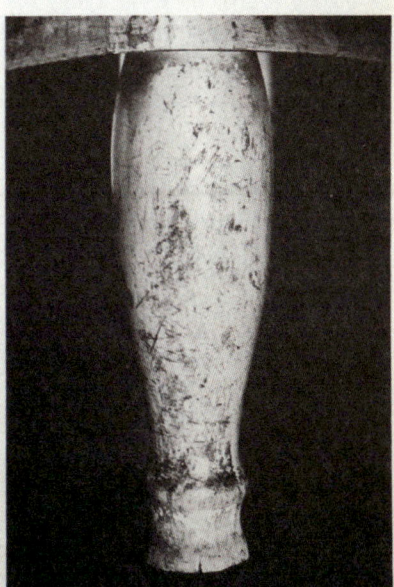

8 Herman Czech: Der weibliche Fuss / Le pied féminin

9 Hans Hollein: Die gereinigten Säulen / Les colonnes ravalées

flug in die Welt der Buchstaben ganz nützlich sein. So steht «Papier u. Schreibwaren» in Schreibschrift, ein weiteres Wort in Antiqua, und eines in einer anderen Schreibschrift, und eines in Blockschrift; – wir finden vier verschiedene Schriften, bis endlich die vollständige Geschäftsbezeichnung zu lesen ist. Aber nun geht die Geschichte weiter: Links davon ein Geschäft mit wieder anderen Schriften, und rechts davon ein Geschäft ... und so weiter; und letztendlich auf dem «Plakat» des Schreibwarengeschäftes selbst noch eine weitere Schrift als Bezeichnung für eine Füllfedermarke. Wie viele Schriften gibt es eigentlich?

Echt oder Falsch?

Ist das Briefkuvert bei Blaus Schreibwarengeschäft ein falsches, mit Holzfurnieren nachempfundenes, so ist das Posthorn bei einer Poststelle Perchtoldsdorf zwar kein schön verschlungenes «klassisches» Horn, aber dafür eine echte Trompete. Eigentlich aber sind es zwei Trompetenstücke, die Appelt-Kneissl-Prochazka in einer Musikalienhandlung kauften und mit Messingschellen an der Wand über dem Eingang befestigten. Deshalb hängt auch das Postschild als Sinn- und Funktionszeichen daran.

Echt sind ebenfalls die Medaillons in den Heizkörperverkleidungen der Galerie Hummel von Hermann Czech. Die gelegentlich eingehängten Schillingstücke bilden eine zarte Erinnerung daran, dass Kunst und Handel in einer Galerie auch mit Geld zu tun haben. «Die Wirkung des Anblicks von ‹echtem› Geld wird etwas durch den geringen Wert der Einzelstücke abgeschwächt», schreibt Czech dazu.

Falsch sind dafür wieder die Füsse der Sitzbänke in Czech's «Wunderbar». Sicher sind sie echt, aus Holz gedrechselt. Aber die Nachbildung männlicher und weiblicher Waden stimmt natürlich nur im Profil. Weniger Aufmerksamkeit wurde dabei der etwas verstärkten und durchtrainierten Männerwade gewidmet, weil Czech von den Versuchen «seiner» weiblichen Idealwade allzusehr in Anspruch genommen wurde. Dass die gotischen Rippen im selben Lokal aus Holz sind und eigentlich dem entsprechen, was die Neugotik in Wien auch tatsächlich machte, dürfte inzwischen allgemein bekannt sein.

Ebenso bekannt sind sicher die «Wiener Marmorspiele» von Krischanitz/Kapfinger, Hans Hollein und Appelt-Kneissl-Prochazka. Letztere haben kürzlich das bisherige Repertoire von Stuccolustro und Resopalmarmor durch die Verarbeitung von marmoriertem Fussbodenlinoleum zu einer exquisiten Wandverkleidung erweitert.

Den falschen Schein auf die (soziale) Spitze getrieben hat Hans Hollein beim neuen «Schullin»-Schmuckgeschäft. In einer kleinen Nische dieses sündteuren Geschäftes ist ein wirklich wunderschönes Muster eines Resopal-Marmors derart fein und kontrolliert verarbeitet, dass selbst dieses Spiels kundige Personen den Marmortempel erst aus nächster Nähe als Talmi entlarven können. Hollein wurde auch fast ein erstes Opfer dieses Spiels, weil nach der Eröffnungsparty des Schmuckgeschäftes die Reinigungsbrigade am nächsten Tag unbedingt die Schlieren von den Beleuchtungsstelen scheuern wollte. Sie konnte im letzten Moment davon überzeugt werden, dass sie im Begriff war, aus zartbuntem Stuccolustro reinweissen Alabaster zu machen. – Verlegen verstaute sie die Salzsäure wieder.

Begreifbare Türgriffe

Es lohnt sich, nochmals auf die Souveniers zurückzukommen – und deren Vorbilder. Die beiden Stossgriffe der Eingangstüre zum Reisebüro Kuoni von Krischanitz/Kapfinger sind Stäbe aus gedrechseltem Buchenholz. Ihre Form bezieht sich auf die Säulen im Erdgeschoss des gegenüberliegenden Kunsthistorischen Museums. Die typologische Säule ist natürlich kein Handgriff, sondern eine Stütze.

«Es wurde also etwas, das nie in der Hand lag und vornehmlich mit den Augen ‹begriffen› wurde -zigfach verkleinert und nun korrekt begreifbar. Gleichzeitig fand ein Wechsel des Materials statt, der an den Ursprung der Säule erinnert, an die hölzernen Zeltstangen und die körpernahen Tisch-, Bett- und Sesselfüsse und die Kandelaber, aus denen sich in der Antike die Steinsäulen

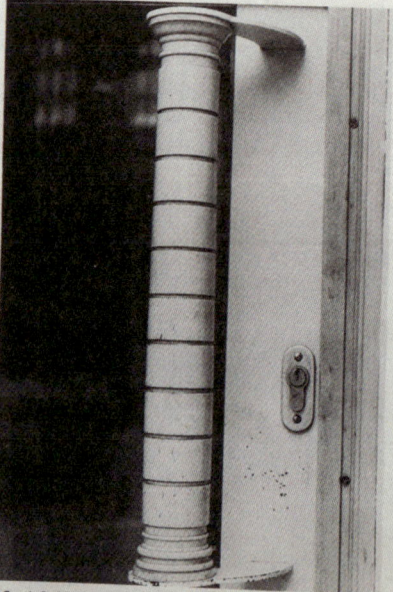

10 Adolf Krischanitz – Otto Kapfinger: Die Semper-Säule / La colonne de Semper

11 Hermann Czech: Die Vitrinen-Säule / La colonne de vitrine

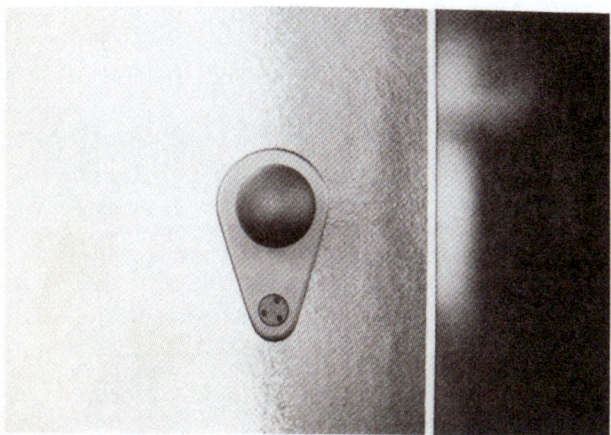

12 Helmut Richter und Heidulf Gerngross: Der Melnikow-Griff / La poignée Melnikow

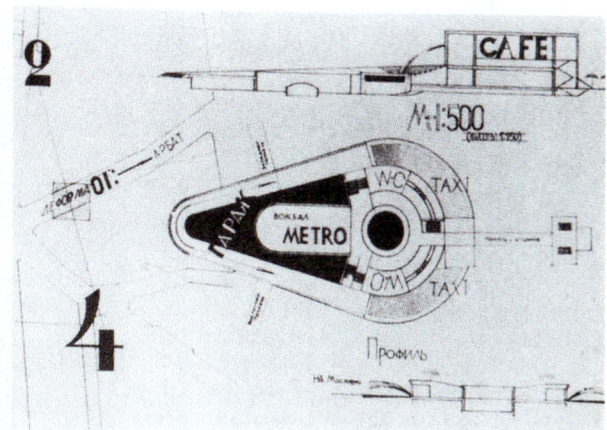

13 Konstantin Melnikow: Entwurf für den Arbat-Platz / La place Arbat (1931)

der Tempel entwickelten. Gottfried Semper – Mitautor des Kunsthistorischen Museums – hat diese Zusammenhänge anschaulich interpretiert. Dieser Türgriff ist nicht bloss Ornament für das Auge, sondern *der* funktionelle Teil des Eingangs, welcher Aussen und Innen vermittelt, der zunächst handfreundlich, griffig ist für den Tastsinn, und auf den zweiten Blick eine konkrete architektonische Beziehung und Erinnerung er-öffnen kann». (Kapfinger).

Noch kleiner als die Semper-Säule von Krischanitz/Kapfinger sind die Säulen des Vitrinentisches im Antiquariat Löcker von Hermann Czech. Ausgestattet mit Basis, Entasis (die der Tischler ursprünglich für eine Zeichnungenauigkeit hielt und deshalb nochmals drechseln musste), Kapitell und Abakus tragen sie die Glasplatte und bilden bei veränderter Optik eine vollkommene Säulenhalle, deren Abstände allerdings nicht griechische, sondern eher Wachsmannsche Dimensionen bezeichnen.

Etwas unpräziser haben Richter/Gerngross bei einem Türgriff auf das historische Vorbild geantwortet. Was macht man, wenn in einer Tür zwei übereinanderliegende Löcher für den Griff vorgesehen sind, und man irgendwo im Haus – versteckt zwar, aber doch – eine kleine Referenz an einen grossen Meister anbringen möchte? Der Entwurf für den Arbat-Platz, 1931 von Konstantin Melnikow gezeichnet, hat zwei Brennpunkte mit verschiedenen Kreisradien. Man nimmt also die Verhältniszahl dieser Radien und überträgt sie auf den Türgriff. Wesentlich dabei ist, dass diese konkrete Geste innerhalb der gesamten Arbeit berechtigt ist, aber auch soweit abstrahiert ist, dass sie unsichtbar bleibt – eine kleine moralische Rechtfertigung also, eine geheime Botschaft, der eingemauerten Urkunde einer Grundsteinlegung vergleichbar.

Der tödliche Boden

Ebenso unsichtbar für den Nichteingeweihten ist der Steinbelag eines Steh(!)-Cafes. Deshalb ist die tödliche Botschaft des Fussbodens im Kleinen Cafe mit seinem gesamten assoziativen Beziehungsgefüge erlaubt. Wirkliche Grabsteine von aufgelassenen Gräbern wurden verwendet. Hermann Czech hat die während und nach diesem Akt konkret möglichen Assoziationsfelder aufgezeichnet: Die Steine sind konisch, also ergeben sie, nebeneinandergelegt, eine Vulva. Zudem sind sie an ihrem schmalen, zueinander gerichteten Ende, zugespitzt. So wird die Restform zu einer bedrohlich beissenden *Vulva dentata*, – mit allen psychologischen Gefahren. Nachdem die geometrische Figur der Restform aber nüchtern betrachtet aus dem Langraum einen Zentralraum macht, ist eine extreme Vertikalität die Folge: Nach oben führt die Aufhebung der Geschlechter, nach unten der sexuelle Tod. Und Grabsteine eben flankieren das Begräbnis, wenn die Kenntnis dieser Geschichte einen illuminierten Besucher in den «offenen Erdspalt» hinunterzieht.

Recycling oder Auferstehung

Nach dem Tod durch die Vulva dentata darf Hoffnung an die Versuche zur Auferstehung verschwendet werden. Das geschieht in Wien durch das Stöbern im industriellen Müll, durch das Basteln von neuen Dingen aus den Resten. Es gilt, das thermodynamische System der Kultur aufrechtzuerhalten.

Appelt-Kneissl-Prochazka renovierten mit einem minimalen Budget ein Wiener Kino. Es stammte aus den 50er Jahren, und warum soll man den Stil wechseln, wenn doch keine andere Zeit mehr als diese mit dem *Kino* verbunden war. Um also neue Beleuchtungskörper für das Foyer zu suchen, fuhr man zum Lagerplatz der gemeindeeigenen Kinofirma. Dort fand man die passenden «Hirschgeweihe», beschwatzte einen Verwalter, um die Herausgabe aus dem Depot zu erwirken, brachte die Dinge zum Elektriker, der sich monatelang wehrte, in dieses Gerümpel neue Drähte einzuziehen. Auf der Baustelle war selbstverständlich niemand zuständig, weil umsonst geliefertes Altmaterial keinen Firmen-

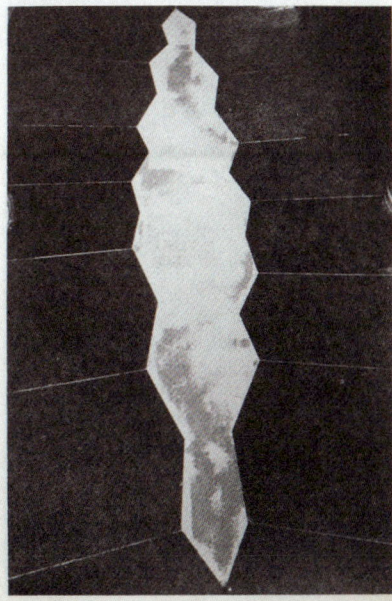

14 Hermann Czech: Die / La «vulva dentata»

lieferschein besass. Knapp bevor die Lampen endgültig auf den Müll wanderten, wurden sie doch montiert. Und das ist der Preis für Recycling: Obwohl die Lampen praktisch umsonst zu haben waren, stiegen die Kosten für Fahrten und Telefonate zu ihrer Rettung in ungeahnte Höhen.

Diese Kosten rechnen Krischanitz/Kapfinger beim Materialpreis von einem Franken pro Stück ihrer Lampenserie nicht ein. Die Leuchten werden innerhalb der Verwandschaft der Autoren aus handelsüblichen Teilen – Fassung, gelochte Stirnrosette und Spiralfeder zur Kabelführung, auf abgekantete, verchromte Blechstreifen montiert – zusammengesetzt. Bei der Ausweitung des Typenprogrammes verliessen sie aber auch das Sortiment verschwiegenster Eisenhandlungen. Der unbewachte Lagerplatz ausrangierter Lokomotiven und Eisenbahngeräte dient nun – bis auf weiteres – als Fundgrube von Industrieteilen für den Ausbau der Lampenserie.

Durch die gekonnte Wiederaufbereitung sieht man den Teilen ihre Herkunft nicht an. Ebenso beeindruckend ist das – inzwischen zum persönlichen Markenzeichen reüssierte – Bücherregal von Luigi Blau. In die Rohbaukosten eingerechnet werden die Wandvorsprünge aus Leichtbausteinen. Beim Verputzen werden Fächerträgerschienen eingelegt. Und warum sollen Bretter furniert, lackiert, ihre Kanten behandelt werden, – wenn handelsübliches Profilitglas nur auf die erfor-

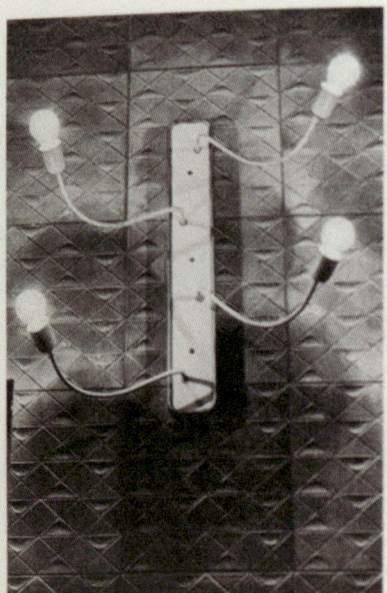

15 Appelt-Kneissl-Prochazka: Das Hirschgeweih / La ramure de cerf

16 Adolf Krischanitz-Otto Kapfinger: Lampe

derliche Länge zugeschnitten werden muss und ohne Nachbehandlung transparente Bücherbretter ergibt?

Es ist nicht nur eine geistige, private, architektonische «Substanzvariation», die diese Geschichten kennzeichnet. Wahre Meister im industriellen Maschinenbau, im Erfinden und Adaptieren von Details sind auch Richter/Gerngross und Boris Podrecca. Erstere fanden für die Einrichtung und Planung eines Badezimmers eine Nirosta-Wanne. Vier Stück lagerten bei einem Professionisten in Wien. Sie waren bei einem grossen Krankenhausauftrag

17,18 Adolf Krischanitz-Otto Kapfinger: Die Lampenserie / La série de lampes

übrig geblieben, weil sich die Kosten für die Polierung als zu hoch erwiesen. Nun sitzt das elegante Stück in einem Badezimmer, dem die Einmaligkeit nun gewiss ist. Bei einem Tisch erprobten Richter/Gerngross die statischen Fähigkeiten der Dichtungsmasse Silikon. Auf zwei Aluminiumschienen wurde damit eine Glasplatte geklebt. In die Schienen wurde ein Lochblech gebogen eingespannt, zwei Füsse schliesslich auf dieses Lochblech montiert, und der Tisch war fertig. Ihre Adaption der selbsttragenden Para-Schalen aus Aluminium vom Industriebau, diese nämlich bei der Errichtung normaler Einfamilienhäuser zu verwenden, ist schon aus früheren Publikationen bekannt. Dass diese konstruktivistischen Gebilde aber über höchst aufregende Detailzeichnungen verfügen, die unzweifelhaft einen selbständigen architektonischen Wert besitzen, soll an einem konkreten Beispiel dargestellt werden: Der Anschluss an einen Altbau erfolgt durch eine freie, daneben stehende Stahlsäule. Mit Blechtafeln und handelsüblichen Fensterprofilen wird diese Verbindung zu einem abstrakten Bild verwoben, das mit einem Punkt die Geschichte des ganzen Hauses erklärt. Wem dies noch zuwenig ist, der möge im Atelier von Richter/Gerngross die wiederverwerteten Reste der industriellen Produktion besichtigen. Die Musterteile aus Glas und Blech sind zu Büchertischen und Ablagen geworden. Ein in-

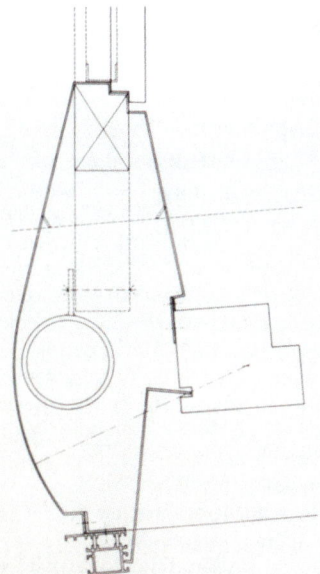

19 Helmut Richter-Heidulf Gerngross: Der Hausanschluss / Elément de liaison

stabiles System gewiss, aber: «Details müssen im Ansatz richtig sein, dann müssen sie nicht exakt sein» (Richter/Gerngross).

Bei Boris Podrecca wird schliesslich die Ahnung zur Gewissheit: Als oberflächliche Illustrierte entpuppen sich die handelsüblichen Bau- und Ausstattungskataloge, angesichts des weltweit verzweigten, und auch wieder ganz freundschaftlich-intimen Bezugsystems. Da werden Lampenschirme als Füsse eines Ausstellungsraumes verwendet, in Frankreich findet Podrecca Glasstäbe, um das Tageslicht eines Fensters einer gleichen Brechung auszusetzen, und den Restposten Wellblech bekommt er günstig bei einem Schlosser, um gleich die Innenausstattung mehrerer Aufgaben damit zu bewältigen.

Natürlich habe ich bei diesen gesammelten Erzählungen vieles ausser Acht gelassen, einige Namen nicht genannt, einige Geschichten aus privaten Rücksichten verschwiegen. Unerschöpflich ist das Mysterium der architektonischen Arbeit, auch ironische Kommentare zum Verhältnis Bauherr–Architekt warten auf ihre Entdeckung. Und um den Kreis zum Eingangszitat von Wittgenstein zu schliessen, sei verraten, dass alle erwähnten Architekten über eine erlesene Auswahl an Professionisten verfügen, deren Namen nur zu später Stunde unter dem Siegel strengster Verschwiegenheit weitergegeben werden. Diese «intime Situation» erleichtert die Kontinuität:

Oswald Haerdtl verwendete 1937 für den Kamin in der eigenen Wohnung den Skyros-Marmor des abgebrochenen Schmuckfederngeschäfts Steiner von Adolf Loos. Und Cipollino-Marmorplatten eines Loos-Kamins finden sich wieder auf der Bar und den Wandpulten in Czech's «Wunderbar».

Diese Geschichten resultieren aus «sprechenden Details». Sie setzen eine Obsession des Schöpfers voraus, die sich dieser nur als Flaneur erarbeiten kann. Er muss das Nebensächliche, am Strassenrand des Fortschritts Vergessene aufheben und mit seinen Geschichten versehen. Es sind die «stummen Details» des kanonisierten Angebots, die als fremdbestimmt gelten und durch eine bewusst- und drucklose Übergabe an den Ausführenden gekennzeichnet sind. – Weil aber bekanntlich der Teufel im Detail steckt, ist die Unterscheidung in sprechende und stumme Details auch eine moralische Kategorie der Architektur. So mancher Wiener Architekt, dem eine fehlende Obsession nachgewiesen werden konnte, leidet seither sämtliche Qualen einer Teufelsaustreibung. Und die Kriterien sind hart: Wem die Geschichten fehlen, dem ist das Fegefeuer gewiss. Wer hier nicht die feinen Regeln der Argumentation, den architektonischen Diskurs der Detailgeschichten erlernt, der wartet auf seine Erlösung bis zum Sanktnimmerleinstag.

20 Helmut Richter-Heidulf Gerngross: Der Silikon-Tisch / La table-silicone

Anmerkungen

[1] «Die Architektur von Ludwig Wittgenstein – Eine Dokumentation», Bernhard Leitner, Halifax, 1973, S. 122–124.
[2] Tractatus logico-philosophicus, Ludwig Wittgenstein, Frankfurt, 1969.
[3] wie 1, ergänzend dazu: «Wien, Kundmanngasse 19», Gebauer, Grünenwald, Ohme, Rentschler, Sperling, Uhl, München, 1982
[4] wie 2

Fotos: 2–5, 7–11, 14–18 von Margherita Krischanitz, Wien; 6 von Jerzy Surwillo, Wien

21 Adolf Loos: Schmuckfederngeschäft Steiner, Wien / Magasin de plumes Steiner, Vienne (1906/07)

22 Oswald Haerdtl: Haus Haerdtl, Kamin mit Marmor vom Schmuckfederngeschäft Steiner / Maison Haerdtl, cheminée avec marbre du magasin de plumes Steiner (1932)

Translation by Brian Dorsey

"Every Detail Is a Story", 1983

"Now that your work on my building is coming to an end, it is my duty and need to express my gratitude and appreciation for your excellent achievement. I can say that without your work it would have been impossible to build the structure with the precision and appropriateness necessary for this type of construction. It is my conviction that no company in Vienna would have been able to fulfill what I had to demand in a similar manner."[1]
Ludwig Wittgenstein's November 1928 letter to the metalworking shop M. Weber & Co

There where architecture comes to the point, the work condenses to a miniature of itself. Details resemble accumulators that are charged with the energy of the architectonic work, the biography of the architect, his philosophy and his relationship to the things. It is a matter of course that these things and objects can tell us stories. Similar to advertisement that surprises us day in, day out with talking cooking plates and tiles that are contently sighing because they have been freshly cleaned. We know the "animated things" from these new and old myths, fairy tales and sagas. One has to get into conversation with the things in order to be able to ward off the fear of the hostile outside world.

In this sense, Lyonel Feininger devises the comic series *Wee Willie Winkie's World* in 1906 for the Sunday supplement of the *Chicago Tribune*. The little hero alertly talks with houses, clouds, trees, haystacks, windmills and streetcars. Sixteen years later, Adolf Loos will dedicate his "built column" to the same newspaper. The fact that this design is to be attributed to the reading of the funny pages of the *Tribune* may by all means be referred to in this context as an unauthorized invention of a story ...

Willie Winkie's dialogs with the things mostly take place in uncertain twilight. A light in which the world is no longer clearly distinct, where the things can easily be transformed by a stirred up fantasy into living figures. Dreams, as a form of reality, also play a role in Feininger's stories. But the resolution always follows as the last picture of the story: "And now one sees what it really is ..." After awakening, the specific purposes and functions hold the upper hand again.

I would like to see this contribution on the analogy of Wee Willie Winkie's World: To entice not always clearly readable stories from the things, to make them ready and able to talk. Details that are firstly and lastly determined by their viability, usefulness and functionality, that give a prenatal message to take along. The detail, *pars pro toto*, even as a fetish of an architecture gone astray?

That necessitates an additional exposition. I can still remember the arduous mental work at school in order to memorize the hook closure of the General Panel System by Gropius and Wachsmann. Today I still clearly recall this peculiarly offset aluminum structure. We never made thoughts back then about how a house built with this system could look. It was and is also impervious to a large extent. The connection detail of the elements contains the entire story of the idea; it was the explanation of the method, the tendency and the actual core of the design. If one once finds this aluminum debris and is able to solve its riddle, then one will also know everything about this architecture on the basis of this super sign.

What is striking about this story is its universal validity. Has someone actually noticed already that it is always the details that survive the building? The work can only outlast conversions and destructions in them. (In Vienna, the toilet of the Café Museum can serve as an example, where vestiges of the Loosian appointments wait in a devastated condition for archaeologists.) Don't we perhaps have to assume altogether that talking about—and with (!)—architecture is dependent on fragmented specific points? The "grand form" has become non-credible, lost in the network of uncontrollable conditions. Neither the impressionistic "space in itself" nor art-historical-stylistic comparisons entangled in themselves provide reliable information. The "debris" becomes the actual bearer of the stories and hence of history, the "historicized one" as Heinz Tesar would say.

To present detailed stories accordingly requires a change of perspective: to put the space and the house aside in favor of an isolated, inherently consistent story with a beginning and an end (And they all lived happily ever after ...). "I'm not particularly interested in architecture" (Aldo Rossi); not in the moods and feelings they are able to communicate, and not in the so-called analyses. A "beautiful story" first makes the appropriation possible for me; the meaning and the value of all the objects surrounding us are to be determined by that after all. Right?

The Radiator

It is time to come back to determining the function of the detail. Details are right or wrong, unconditionally subject to the laws of functional logic. What is more obvious than beginning the tales with Ludwig Wittgenstein: "The picture agrees with reality or not; it is right or wrong, true or false" (Tractatus, 2.21).[2]

If one observes the story of radiators in Palais Wittgenstein, one has to pose the question here whether those elementary sentences, demanded by Wittgenstein in *Tractatus*, but never formulated, were realized in a built manner? Hermine Wittgenstein writes in her family recollections:

"The radiators themselves are so immaculate in their dimensions and in their precise, smooth, streamlined form that it did not strike one as unusual when, outside the periods when they were

needed for heating, Gretl (the client—author's note) used them as plinths for her beautiful artworks. ...
Each of these corner radiators comprises two elements that are arranged with absolute precision at right angles to one another. A small gap, specified down to the last millimeter, has been left between the two elements, and they had to fit exactly onto the legs that support them. Several models were cast to begin with, but it turned out that the design envisioned by Ludwig simply could not be cast in Austria; so ready-made cast-iron pieces from abroad were used for individual elements. However, it initially appeared to be impossible to achieve the precision that Ludwig demanded using these pieces. Entire batches of piping had to be discarded as unusable, while others had to be ground down to half-millimeter accuracy. Even installing the smooth seals, which [...] were manufactured following Ludwig's designs, created great difficulties; experimentation often continued into the night under Ludwig's instruction, until finally everything was just right, and it actually took a whole year after completing the design before the radiators, which appeared so simple, were finally finished."[3]

The industrial product was thus manufactured manually, because the thought of the logical image of the facts was not to be expressed in the prefabricated. If one considers the industrial components as "colloquial language" in the Wittgensteinian sense, then their deformation in the service of philosophy is necessary.

"It is not humanly possible to gather immediately from it (the colloquial language—author's note) what the logic of language is. Language disguises thought. So much so, that from the outward form of the clothing it is impossible to infer the form of the thought beneath it, because the outward form of the clothing is not designed to reveal the form of the body, but for entirely different purposes" (*Tractatus*, 4.002).[4]

Swedish Souvenirs

Ever since architects have been travelling, they have been bringing souvenirs home with them, which they gladly use in their work. Mario Botta screwed studs onto the wall of the bank in Freiburg and wants that to be interpreted as an "explicit homage" to Otto Wagner. That is the law of the souvenir: A repetition of the original always seems somewhat displaced at the point of sale, but it unfolds its splendor in foreign lands. Elsa Prochazka and Eberhard Kneissl once received the Josef-Frank-Stipendium, which included a trip to Sweden. They brought the "Sigurd Lewerentz window" to Vienna with them and built it as an exquisite single piece in the multipurpose hall on Rennbahnweg: a naked laminated glass panel without a frame is fastened to the wall with aluminum brackets. Moreover, in Sweden they saw many residential buildings clad with cheap and hard-wearing trapezoidal sheet metal. The roofs of all three multipurpose halls were then covered with this material. Faithful to the device that an industrial program can also send different messages through various possibility of aesthetic processing, three different roofing materials were simulated with the trapezoidal sheet metal: red = brick, green = grass, yellow = straw. Similarly, the real folding garage gates, which were fitted in the multipurpose halls as room dividers, were treated in three different ways: painted and divided into fields by wooden frames; veneered, to once look especially "noble"; clad with Resopal panels that form a continuous pattern, in order to test the surface as a whole. – The assembler told me in amazement that he had never sensed what "beautiful gates" his firm produces ...

Writing Work

When Luigi Blau faced the task of lettering a stationery shop, he first stood in front of the closed envelope on the entrance door. Since this shop, long-established on Vienna's Graben, is a shop with history, a little history of writing, of sign painting, a brief excursion into the world of letters could be quite useful. So "Paper and Stationery" stands in cursive, an additional word in Antiqua, one in a different cursive script and one in block letters;—we find four different scripts until the complete shop description can finally be read. But now the story continues: To the left there is a shop with different scripts again, and to the right a shop ... and so forth; and, finally, even on the "poster" of the stationery shop itself, a further script as the label of a fountain pen brand. How many scripts are there actually?

Real or False?

If the envelope at Blau's stationery store is a false one, recreated with wood veneers, then the post horn at the Perchtoldsdorf post office is indeed no beautifully serpentine "classical" horn, but rather a real trumpet. Actually, however, there are two trumpet pieces which Appelt-Kneissl-Prochazka bought at a music shop and fastened to the wall above the entrance with brass clamps. That's why the post office sign also hangs on it as a symbol of sense and function.

Likewise real are the medallions in the radiator coverings of Galerie Hummel by Hermann Czech. The occasionally mounted shilling coins form a tender reminder that art and commerce in a gallery also have to do with money. "The effect of the sight of 'real' money is mitigated somewhat by the low value of the single pieces," Czech writes.

False, on the other hand, are the legs of the benches in Czech's "Wunder-Bar." Surely they are real, made of turned wood. But the replications of masculine and feminine calves are naturally only correct in the profile. Less attention was devoted to the somewhat strengthened and well-toned man's calf, because

Czech was absorbed all too much in the attempts at "his" ideal female calf. The fact that the Gothic ribs in the same bar are made of wood and actually correspond to what Neo-Gothic indeed made in Vienna, may be common knowledge in the meantime.

Just as well-known are surely the "Viennese marble games" of Krischanitz/Kapfinger, Hans Hollein and Appelt-Kneissl-Prochazka. The latter have recently expanded the previous repertoire of stucco lustro and Resopal marble through the processing of marbleized floor linoleum into an exquisite wall covering. Hans Hollein has carried the false appearance to (social) extremes at the new "Schullin" jewelry shop. In a small niche of this outrageously expensive shop a really gorgeous pattern of a Resopal marble is processed in such a fine and controlled way that even people skillful at this game can first expose the marble temple as a Talmi at close range. Hollein also nearly became the first victim of this game, because after the opening party of the jewelry shop, the cleaning crew wanted to scrub the streaks from the lighting steles by all means. At the last moment they were able to be convinced that they were just about to make pure white alabaster out of soft-colored stucco lustro—embarrassed, they stowed the hydrochloric acid away again.

Graspable Door Handles

It pays to come back to the souvenirs—and their models. Both of the pull handles on the entrance doors to the Kuoni Travel Agency by Krischanitz/Kapfinger are rods made of turned beech wood. Their form refers to the columns on the ground floor of the Kunsthistorisches Museum opposite. The typological column is, of course, no handle, but rather a support.

"So it became something that never lay in one's hand and was primarily 'grasped' with the eyes, reduced umpteen times and now correctly comprehensible. At the same time, a change of material took place, recalling the origin of the columns, the wooden tent poles and the proximal table, bed and chair legs and the candelabras from which the stone pillars of the temples developed in antiquity. Gottfried Semper—co-author of the Kunsthistorisches Museum—vividly interpreted these coherences. This door handle is not merely ornamentation for the eye, but the functional component of the entrance, which communicates outside and inside, which is first hand-friendly, handy for the tactile sense and which, at second glance, can open up a concrete architectonic relationship and memory" (Kapfinger).

Even smaller than the Semper columns by Krischanitz/Kapfinger are the columns of the display case tables at Antiquariat Löcker by Hermann Czech. Equipped with the basis, entasis (which the joiner originally held as a drawing imprecision and therefore had to turn once again), capital and abacus, they support the glass plate and, when in an altered perspective, form a complete portico whose interspaces, however, do not constitute Greek dimensions, but rather those of Wachsmann.

Richter/Gerngross replied somewhat imprecisely to the historic model in the case of a door handle. What does one do if two holes, one above the other, are designed for the handle in a door and somewhere in the house one would like to place—hidden though, but nonetheless—a small reference to a grand master? The design for Arbat Square, drawn by Konstantin Melnikov in 1931, has two foci with different circle radii. One thus takes the ratio of these radii and transfers it to the door handle. What is essential, though, is that this concrete gesture is justified within the whole work, that it is also abstracted to the extent that it remains invisible—a small moral justification therefore, a secrete message, comparable to a bricked in document at the laying of the cornerstone.

The Deadly Ground

Equally invisible to the outsider is the stone floor of a stand-up (!) café. That's why the deadly message of the floor is allowed in the Kleines Café with its entire associative structure of relationships. Real gravestones from abandoned graves were used. Hermann Czech plotted the concretely possible association areas during and after the act: The stones are conical, so when laid next to each other they result in a vulva. Furthermore, they are tapered at their narrow end, where they are oriented toward each other. The remaining form thus becomes a threatening, biting vulva dentata,—with all of the psychological dangers. After the geometric figure of the remaining form, however, viewed soberly, makes a central space out of the long space, an extreme verticality is the consequence: Leading upwards is the dissolution of the genders, leading downwards is sexual death. And gravestones precisely flank the burial, if the knowledge of this story pulls an illuminated visitor down into the "open crevice."

Recycling or Resurrection

After death by the vulva dentata, hope may be wasted on the attempt at resurrection. That happens in Vienna by poking around in the industrial waste, by crafting new things out of remnants. It is imperative to keep up the thermodynamic system of culture. Appelt-Kneissl-Prochazka renovated a Viennese cinema with a minimal budget. It originated from the 1950s and why shall one change the style even though no other era was associated with the *cinema* more than this one. So, to look for new lighting fixtures for the foyer one drove to the storage yard of the public-owned cinema company. One found the fitting "deer antlers" there, conned an administrator into procuring their release from the depot, brought the things to an electrician, who refused for months to pull new wires in through this junk. Of course, no one was responsible on the building site, because old material delivered to no avail did not possess a company delivery note. Shortly before the lamps ultimately wandered into the trash, they were mounted after all. And that is the price for recycling: Although the lamps were to be had practically for free, the costs for the journeys and telephone calls to save them rose to unimagined heights.

Krischanitz/Kapfinger do not calculate these costs at the material price of one franc per piece into their lamp series. The lights will be assembled within the authors' relations out of commercially available parts—the socket, perforated star rosette and spiral spring for the cable conduit, mounted on bevel-edged, chrome-plated metal strips. During the expansion of the type program, however, they also left the assortment to the most discrete hardware shops. The unguarded storage area of scrapped locomotives and railroad equipment now serves—until further notice—as a treasure trove of industrial components for the expansion of the lamp series.

Through skillful reprocessing, one does not see the origin of the parts. Equally impressive is the book shelf —which has meanwhile becoming a personal trademark—by Luigi Blau. The wall projections made of lightweight blocks are included in the calculation of the shell construction costs. The truss support rails are inserted during plastering. And why should boards be veneered, painted and have their edges treated—if customary Profilit glass only has to be cut to the required length and results in transparent book boards without further processing?

It is not only a spiritual, private, architectonic "substance variation" that characterizes these stories. Richter/Gerngross and Boris Podrecca are also true masters in industrial mechanical engineering, in the invention and adaptation of details. The former found a stainless steel bathtub for the fitting and planning of a bathroom. Four pieces were available from a skilled craftsman in Vienna. They were left over from a large hospital project, because the costs for polishing proved to be too high. Now the elegant piece sits in a bathroom that is certain to become unique. Richter/Gerngross tested the static capabilities of the sealing material silicon on a table. A glass plate was glued to two aluminum rods with it. A perforated plate was clamped in a bent fashion into the rods; two legs were lastly mounted onto this perforated plate and the table was finished. Their adaptation of the self-supporting aluminum para-shells from industrial construction, to use these namely in the erection of normal single-family houses, is already known from earlier publications. But the fact that this constructive entity is equipped with highly exciting detail drawings that undoubtedly possess an independent architectonic value is to be illustrated by a concrete example: The connection of an old building is carried out by means of an open steel column standing next to it. This connection is interwoven with metal sheet panels and commercially available window profiles into an abstract image that explains the history of the whole house with one point. Those for whom this is still too little may inspect the recycled remnants of industrial production at the studio of Richter/Gerngross. The model parts made of glass and sheet metal have become book tables and shelves. An instable system sure enough, but: "If details are correct in the approach, then they do not have to be exact" (Richter/Gerngross).

In the case of Boris Podrecca, premonition ultimately becomes certainty: The customary construction and equipment catalogues turn out to be, given the globally branched and once again very friendly-intimate reference system, superficial magazines. Lampshades are used as the bases of an exhibition space; in France Podrecca finds glass rods to expose the daylight of a window to the same refraction; and he gets odd lots of corrugated sheet metal cheaply at a metal worker's shop, in order to manage the interior decoration of several projects right away.

Naturally I have left out much in these collected narratives, not mentioned several names, kept several stories secret out of private considerations. The mystery of architectural work is inexhaustible: ironic commentaries on the relationship between client and architect are also waiting for their discovery, in order to close the circle to the initial quote by Wittgenstein; it can be revealed that all of the mentioned architects have a select choice of skilled craftsmen at their command, whose names are passed on only at a late hour under the pledge of secrecy. This "intimate situation" facilitates the continuity:

In 1937, Oswald Haerdtl used the Skyros marble of the demolished Steiner Plume and Feather Shop by Adolf Loos for the fireplace of his own apartment. And the Cipollino marble plates of a Loos fireplace can be found again on the bar and the wall-mounted desks in Czech's "Wunder-Bar." These stories resulted from "speaking details." They presuppose an obsession of the creator which he/she can only earn as a flâneur. He has to remove the trivial, that which was forgotten on the roadside of progress, and furnish it with his stories. It is the "silent details" of the canonized offer that are considered heteronomous and are characterized by an unconscious and unpressured handover to the executors.—Because, as you know, the devil is in the detail, the difference in the speaking and silent details is also a moral category of architecture. Many a Viennese architect, who could be attested to having a lack of obsession, has thus been suffering all of the agonies of an exorcism since then. And the criteria are tough: Whoever is missing the stories is sure to end up in purgatory. Whoever does not master the fine rules of argumentation, the architectonic discourse of detail stories, will have to wait for his/her salvation until the cows come home.

Notes

[1] Bernhard Leitner, *The Architecture of Ludwig Wittgenstein – A Documentation* (Halifax/London: Nova Scotia College / Studio International Publications Ltd., 1973) 122–124.

[2] Ludwig Wittgenstein, *Tractatus logico-philosophicus* (Frankfurt: Suhrkamp, 1969). English translation by David Pears / Brian McGuiness (1961). Available at: http://people.umass.edu/phil335-klement-2/tlp/tlp.pdf

[3] Cf. 1, in addition, Gunter Gebauer, Alexander Grünenwald, Rüdiger Ohme et al., *Wien. Kundmanngasse 19: Bauplanerische, morphologische und philosophische Aspekte des Wittgenstein-Hauses* (Munich: Wilhelm Fink Verlag, 1982). English translation by A. Godfrey in Sebastian Sunday Grève and Jakub Mácha (eds.), *Wittgenstein and the Creativity of Language* (London: Palgrave MacMillan, 2016) vii.

[4] Cf. 2.

Ticino 1978 Tessin 1978

Als 1975 der Katalog *Tendenzen – Neue Architektur im Tessin* erschien, erlangte er als ‚blaue Bibel' internationale Bedeutung. Eine kleine Provinz der Schweiz produzierte eine Architektur widerständig und abseits des internationalen Mainstreams. Sie definierte den Ort und die Typologie des Bauens auf revolutionär neue Art. Als ich Friedrich Achleitner im Katalog die Casa Tonini zeigte, fragte er 1974 oder 1794? Daraus wurde eine lebenslange Freundschaft mit Bruno Reichlin. Bilder einer Studienreise damals.

When the catalog *Tendencies – New Architecture in Ticino* appeared in 1975, it gained international importance as the 'blue Bible.' A small Swiss province produced an architecture that is resistive and stands apart from the international mainstream. It defines the location and the typology of building in a revolutionarily new way. When I showed Friedrich Achleitner the Casa Tonini in the catalog, he asked, '1974 or 1794?' What resulted was a lifelong friendship with Bruno Reichlin. Pictures of a study trip back then.

Alle Bilder · All images © DS

Kantonales Gymnasium · Cantonal grammar school in Morbio Inferiore, Mario Botta, 1972–76

Kantonales Gymnasium · Cantonal grammar school in Morbio Inferiore, Mario Botta, 1972–76

Haus · House in Cadenazzo, Mario Botta, 1970–71

Casa Tonini in Torricella, Bruno Reichlin + Fabio Reinhart, 1972–74

Wohnbau · Residential building in Monte Carasso, Luigi Snozzi, 1974

Casa Sartori in Riveo, Bruno Reichlin + Fabio Reinhart, 1976

Casa Sartori in Riveo, Bruno Reichlin + Fabio Reinhart, 1976

Haus House in Riva San Vitale, Mario Botta, 1971–72

Haus House in Cadenazzo, Mario Botta, 1970–71

Wohnbau · Residential building in Gallaratese, Milano, Aldo Rossi, 1970

Casa Tonini in Torricella, Bruno Reichlin + Fabio Reinhart, 1972–74

Casa Tonini in Torricella, Bruno Reichlin + Fabio Reinhart, 1972–74

Wohnbau · Residential building in Gallaratese, Milano, Aldo Rossi, 1970

Casa Snider in Verscio, Luigi Snozzi, Livio Vacchini, 1966

Casa Kalman bei · near Minusio, Luigi Snozzi, 1974–76

Wohnbau · Residential building in Gallaratese, Milano, Aldo Rossi, 1970

Casa Kalman bei · near Minusio, Luigi Snozzi, 1974–76

Wohnbau · Residential building in Gallaratese, Milano, Aldo Rossi, 1970

Originalbeitrag · Original contribution

Translation by Brian Dorsey

My Barcelona

Mein Barcelona

Barcelona. Es gibt keine andere Stadt, zu der ich eine so lang anhaltende Beziehung habe. Ich habe dort nie gelebt, die Stadt immer nur besucht, in mindestens 30 verschiedenen Hotels gewohnt. Trotzdem wurde sie, neben Wien, meine zweite Heimatstadt. Es begann Mitte der 1970er Jahre – ich war noch Student an der Akademie der bildenden Künste in Wien – als mich der Kontakt mit der „Tessiner Schule" der Architektur in Verbindung mit den Aktivitäten der ETH Zürich brachte. Ich wurde als Gasthörer zu Seminaren an der ETH eingeladen. Aldo Rossi unterrichtete dort von 1972–1974 und übte großen Einfluss auf die Schweizer Architekturszene aus. Ihm folgte der Tessiner Architekt Mario Campi mit den von Rossi übernommenen Assistenten Bruno Reichlin, Fabio Reinhart, Eraldo Consolascio, Marie-Claude Bétrix. Aldo Rossi wiederum hatte in den 1970er Jahren auch großen Einfluss auf die Architekturdebatte in Barcelona. Von seiner Lehre der historischen Analyse der Typologie der Stadt war eine Gruppe junger Architekten in Barcelona stark beeinflusst. Dies zeigte sich in dem von ihnen publizierten Magazin *2c Construccion de la Ciudad*. Der Titel 2c referierte auf die Propaganda-Schrift der Moderne AC im Katalonien der Vorkriegszeit.

Barcelona. There is no other city that I have had such a long-lasting relationship to. I have never lived there, always only visited the city and stayed in at least 30 different hotels. Nonetheless, it became my second home city after Vienna. It began in the mid-1970s—I was still a student at the Academy of Fine Arts in Vienna—when the contact with the "Ticino School" of architecture led to a connection with the activities of the Swiss Federal Institute of Technology (ETH) in Zurich. I was invited as a guest student to seminars at the ETH. Aldo Rossi taught there from 1972 to 1974 and exerted great influence on the Swiss architectural scene. Mario Campi, a Ticino architect, succeeded him and took on Rossi's assistants Bruno Reichlin, Fabio Reinhart, Eraldo Consolascio and Marie-Claude Bétrix. In the 1970s, Aldo Rossi in turn also had considerable influence on the architectural debate in Barcelona. A group of young architects in Barcelona were strongly influenced by his teaching of the historical analysis of city typology. This was manifested in a magazine published by them, *2c Construcción de la Ciudad*. The title *2c* refers to the modernist propaganda magazine *AC* in pre-war Catalonia.

Headed by Salvador Tarragó Cid and Carlos Martí Arís, the 2c group supervised a 1976 study trip of the ETH Zurich to Barcelona, which I was invited to by the chair Mario Campi. A comprehensive basic course on the city history of Barcelona was taught, focusing on the architecturally revolutionary period up to Franco's seizure of power. Back then I learned everything about Barcelona.

Die 2c-Gruppe, angeführt von Salvador Tarragó Cid und Carlos Martí Arís, betreute 1976 eine Studienreise der ETH Zürich nach Barcelona, zu der ich vom Lehrstuhl Mario Campi mit eingeladen wurde. Dabei wurde in einem Grundkurs die Stadtgeschichte von Barcelona umfassend vermittelt, mit Schwerpunkt auf der architektonisch revolutionären Zeit bis zur Machtergreifung von Franco. Damals lernte ich alles über Barcelona.

1976, ein Jahr nach Francos Tod, befand sich Barcelona in einer auch politisch aufgeregten und instabilen Situation. Die Guardia Civil mit ihren Gummigeschossen war allgegenwärtig, und jede Ansammlung von mehr als drei Menschen im öffentlichen Raum wurde aufgelöst. Da Salvador Tarragó damals Sekretär der „Gesellschaft der Freunde Gaudís" war, hatte er Zugang zu allen, auch den privat bewohnten Bauten Gaudís. Allerdings nicht für die große Gruppe der ETH-Studenten. So erfand er eine Methode der Besichtigung für wenige. Wir starteten frühmorgens und Salvador führte uns mit zunehmender Beschleunigung zu Fuß durch die Altstadt. Dabei ‚verloren' wir alle nicht so interessierten Studenten, und so konnte dann die kleine Gruppe der Unentwegten mit drei bis vier Taxis die privaten Bauten von Gaudí besichtigen … Das war eine einzigartige und großartige Einführung in die Stadtgeschichte und Architektur Barcelonas. Doch von 2c und seinen sozialrevolutionär engagierten Akteuren habe ich niemals wieder etwas gehört.

*

In den 1980er Jahren kam es zu meiner zweiten Begegnung mit Barcelona. Josep Lluís Mateo und Marta Cervelló übernahmen die Redaktion von *quaderns*, dem Magazin der Architektenkammer von Barcelona. Nun ging es nicht mehr um die Vergewisserung der lokalen Tradition der Moderne, Aldo Rossi war vergessen, die neue Architektur Kataloniens verband sich in den 1980er Jahren mit der internationalen Debatte, und die Gruppe um *quaderns* war die Avantgarde. Auch Manuel Gausa und Vicente Guallart lernte ich damals kennen. In dieser Zeit begann sich Barcelona zum Zentrum der internationalen Architekturdiskussion zu entwickeln. Ich erinnere mich an eine engagierte

Cover des Magazins *2c*, Nummer 9, 1977. Ein Architekt aus Deutschland hatte angefragt, ob die Redaktion eine Nummer über sein Werk publizieren würde, wenn er diese bezahlt. Josef Paul Kleihues ist nicht der Schlechteste, meinte ich damals. Kann man machen. · Cover of the *2c* magazine, issue 9, 1977. A German architect had inquired whether the editorial team would publish an issue about his work if he paid for it. Josef Paul Kleihues is not the worst, I thought back then. One can do it. © Archive DS

In 1976, one year after Franco's death, Barcelona also found itself in a politically charged and unstable situation. The Guardia Civil with their rubber bullets were omnipresent and any gathering of more than three people in the public space was broken up. Since Salvador Tarragó Cid was the secretary of the "Society of Friends of Gaudí" at the time, he had access to all buildings by Gaudí, even the privately inhabited ones. However, not for the large group of ETH students. So he invented a tour method for just a few people. Starting in the early morning, Salvador guided us with increasing speed on foot through the old city. We "lost" all of the not so interested students and the small group of stalwarts could then visit the private Gaudí buildings with three to four taxis … That was the unique and great introduction to the city history and architecture of Barcelona. Yet I never heard anything again from 2c and its social-revolutionary committed actors.

*

und lebendige Konferenz, 1986 von *quaderns* organisiert, an der Jacques Herzog mit Jacques Lucan über dessen Diagnose der Architektur in heftigen Streit geriet, Miroslav Šik seine ‚analoge Architektur' vehement als einzige Alternative für die Zukunft propagierte und Wolf Prix ganz auf Pop-Star machte und bei seinem Vortrag, eine Cava-Flasche schwenkend und trinkend, den radikalen Individualismus forderte. Diese glorreiche Epoche von *quaderns* ging zu Ende, aber Barcelona blieb in der Architekturdebatte präsent.

Da war das große Programm für den öffentlichen Raum. Viele Plätze wurden von Architekten mit internationalen Künstlern neu gestaltet. Große urbane Investitionen wurden getätigt, neue Kulturinstitutionen gegründet. Und den großen Schub der Stadtentwicklung brachten die Olympischen Sommerspiele 1992. Eine gewagte Ringautobahn entlastete den Durchzugsverkehr. Mehrere Straßenverbindungen durch den Tibidabo ermöglichten neue große Stadtentwicklungen im Hinterland. Die gesamte Hafen- und Uferzone zum Meer wurde neu entwickelt. Barcelona, das sich historisch mit dem Rücken zum Meer entwickelt hatte, drehte sich förmlich um, und es eröffneten sich völlig neue Möglichkeiten, die in großem Stil umgesetzt wur-

I had my second encounter with Barcelona in the 1980s. Josep Lluís Mateo and Marta Cervelló took over as the editors of *quaderns*, the magazine published by the Barcelona Chamber of Architects. Now it no longer had anything to do with the reassurance of the local tradition of modernism, Aldo Rossi was forgotten, the new architecture of Catalonia coalesced with the international debate in the 1980s, and the group associated with *quaderns* was the avant-garde. Back then I also got to know Manuel Gausa and Vicente Guallart. At this time Barcelona began to develop into a center of international architectural discussion. I recall a committed and lively conference organized by *quaderns* in 1986, where Jacques Herzog got into a hefty argument with Jacques Lucan and his diagnosis of architecture, Miroslav Šik angrily propagated his "analogous architecture" as the only alternative for the future and Wolf Prix totally acted like a pop star during his lecture, swinging and drinking from a Cava bottle, calling for radical individualism. This glorious epoch of *quaderns* came to an end, but Barcelona remained present in architectural debate.

There was the grand program for the public space. Many squares were redesigned by architects with international artists. Major urban investments were made, new cultural institutions founded. And the 1992 Summer Olympic Games brought the large boost of urban development. A daring beltway relieved through traffic. Several road links through the Tibidabo enabled new, large urban developments in the hinterlands. The entire port and coast zone on the ocean was redeveloped. Barcelona, which had historically developed with its back to the sea, turned itself around formally, and it opened entirely new possibilities that were executed in grand style. The coast zone was redesigned as a large recreational area; residential buildings replaced the old industrial grounds. In the last forty years no other city in Europe has accomplished such an enormous transformation at a comparably high level of urban planning and architecture. The political authorities and mayors of this era who were conscious of this responsibility are to be especially thanked for this.

Öffentliche Räume in Barcelona in den 1980er Jahren · Public spaces in Barcelona in the 1980s. © DS

*

den. Die Uferzone wurde als großes Freizeitareal neu gestaltet, Wohnbauten ersetzten die alten Industrieareale. Keine andere Stadt in Europa hat in den letzten vierzig Jahren eine derart gewaltige Transformation auf vergleichbar hohem Niveau der Stadtplanung und Architektur geleistet. Zu danken ist dies vor allem den politischen Instanzen und Bürgermeistern, die sich dieser Verantwortung bewusst waren.

*

1996 fand eine bis heute unterschätzte Wende der Architekturdebatte in Barcelona statt, und zwar anlässlich des Weltkongresses der UIA, der Internationalen Architektenvereinigung. Normalerweise eine eher müde Versammlung von Funktionären der weltweiten Berufsvertretungen der Architekten. Doch Barcelona wollte mehr. Erstmals sollten alle erdenklichen international berühmten Architekten der Zeit Vorlesungen vor Publikum halten; dazu noch Workshops über die Rolle der Medien und den Stand der Theorie der Architektur, verstreut an vielen Orten der Stadt. Doch am ersten Tag des Kongresses war die Stadt von lautstarken Demonstrationen blockiert. Was war geschehen? Nach Ablauf der Anmeldefrist für den UIA-Kongress der Funktionäre, hatten sich angesichts des Staraufgebots rund 10.000 Architekturstudierende aus Südamerika auf den Weg gemacht und die Kapazitäten des vorgesehenen Programms gesprengt. Die Organisatoren reagierten flexibel. Peter Eisenman hielt seinen Vortrag vom Balkon des MACBA aus im Dress des FC Barcelona. Die anderen Vorträge wurden in das olympische Basketball-Stadion von Arata Isozaki verlegt, mit 6000 Besuchern. Zaha Hadid kämpfte sich Autogramme verteilend zur Bühne durch, Wiel Arets rief, „it's impossible to give a lecture, let's play basketball". Architektur, die Präsenz von Star-Architekten, wurde erstmals zu einem nie zuvor gekannten Pop-Event. Hatte die Strada Novissima der Architekturbiennale Venedig 1980 den ‚Star-Architekten' geboren, so katapultierte der UIA-Kongress Barcelona 1996 die Architektur endgültig in die massenmediale Kulturindustrie. Unvergesslich die private Party am Ende des Kongresses, wo das bestimmende Thema des Abends der allgemeine Schock über dieses Ereignis und die nun neue Bedeutung der Architektur wurde.

In 1996 the turning point in the architectural debate, one that has been underestimated to this very day, took place in Barcelona. It was the world congress of the UIA, the International Union of Architects. Normally a rather tired gathering of functionaries from worldwide professional associations of architects. But Barcelona wanted more. All imaginable internationally famous architects of the time were to hold lectures in front of an audience for the first time. Scattered around various locations in the city, workshops on the role of media and the status of architectural theory were additionally conducted. On the first day of the congress, however, the city was blocked by vociferous demonstrations. What was going on? After the end of the registration deadline for the UIA Congress of the functionaries, around 10,000 architecture students from South America headed for Barcelona because of the star-studded event and burst the capacities of the scheduled program. The organizers reacted flexibly. Dressed in an FC Barcelona uniform, Peter Eisenman held his speech from the balcony of the MACBA. The other lectures were relocated to the Olympic basketball stadium by Arata Isozaki, with 6,000 visitors. Signing autographs, Zaha Hadid fought her way to the stage; Wiel Arets shouted: "It's impossible to give a lecture, let's play basketball." For the first time, architecture and the presence of star architects became a pop event unknown prior to that. If the Strada Novissima of the 1980 Architecture Biennale in Venice had given birth to the "star architect," the 1996 UIA Congress in Barcelona conclusively transformed architecture into the mass media cultural industry. The private party at the end of the Congress, where the defining theme of the evening was the general shock about this event and the now new meaning of architecture, remains unforgettable.

Zweiter Tag • Day Two

In dieser Zeit lud mich die Mies van der Rohe Foundation in die Jury des Preises für 1996 ein. Der Preis war Teil der Initiative, die 1983–86 den Deutschen Pavillon der Weltausstellung von 1929 in Barcelona wiederrichtet hatte, und sollte biennal die besten Bauten Europas küren. Die Projekte werden von Experten aus ganz Europa nominiert und von einer Jury begutachtet. Über die Jahre bis heute haben sich Auswahl und Präsentation vor der Jury immer mehr professionalisiert. Das Prozedere ist aber seit 1988 gleich: Eine Jurysitzung in Barcelona, bei der die nominierten Projekte analysiert, selektiert und die Finalsten bestimmt werden. 1996 wurde aber erstmals auch eine Besichtigung der Objekte geplant. Das führte zu einer geradezu surrealen Reise, die Diane Gray, die langjährige Organisatorin des Awards, mit gigantischem Aufwand mit Einzeltickets auf Linienflügen für alle organisierte: Treffen der Jury in Trondheim, weiter mit einem Kleinbus ‚into the middle of nowhere', stundenlang durch verschneites Niemandsland zum Aukrust Centre von Sverre Fehn. Von Trondheim Flug nach London, am nächsten Tag zum Rowing Center von David Chipperfield – bemerkenswert, aber der Innenausbau hatte noch nicht begonnen. Dann Flug nach Lyon, per Bus zum European Archeological Center von Pierre-Louis Faloci und weiter nach Paris. Eingehende Führung durch die innere Logistik der Nationalbibliothek von Dominique Perrault. Übernachtung am Flughafen. Flug nach Zürich und mit dem Bus nach Vals zur Therme von Peter Zumthor. Zurück nach Zürich, Flug nach Athen, tags darauf nach Thessaloniki, der Kulturhauptstadt 1997, wo die Schluss-Jury stattfand. Den Preis bekam Dominique Perrault, weil sich die Nationalbibliothek am deutlichsten zu einer Entwicklung der europäischen Stadt bekannte.

Jury: Fritz Neumeyer (Chair), Andrej Hrausky, Toyo Ito, Jacques Lucan, Marja-Riitta Norri, Francesco Venezia, Dietmar Steiner, Elia Zenghelis

At this time, the Mies van der Rohe Foundation invited me to join the jury of the 1996 award. The prize was part of the initiative that had rebuilt the German Pavilion of the 1929 World Exposition in Barcelona from 1983 to 1986 and was to choose the best buildings in Europe biennially. The projects are nominated by experts from all over Europe and assessed by a jury. Over the years and up to today the selection and the presentation in front of the jury has become more and more professionalized. Since 1988, however, the procedure has been the same: a jury meeting in Barcelona, where the nominated projects are analyzed and selected, and the finalists determined. But in 1996, the viewing of the objects was planned for the first time. This led to an almost surreal journey which Diane Gray, the long-time organizer of the award, arranged for everyone with single tickets on scheduled flights with gigantic effort: a meeting of the jury in Trondheim, onwards in a small bus to the middle of nowhere, travelling for hours through snowy no-man's land to the Aukrust Centre by Sverre Fehn. A flight from Trondheim to London, on the next day to the Rowing Center by David Chipperfield—remarkable, but the interior fitting had not yet begun. Then a flight to Lyon, by bus to Pierre-Louis Faloci's European Archaeological Center, and further to Paris. An in-depth tour through the inner logistics of the National Library by Dominique Perrault. Overnight stay at the airport. Flight to Zurich and bus trip to Vals, to the thermal baths by Peter Zumthor. Back to Zurich, flight to Athens, the next day to Thessaloniki, the 1997 European cultural capital where the final jury took place. Dominique Perrault received the award, because the National Library most clearly professed to the development of the European city.

Jury: Fritz Neumeyer (Chair), Andrej Hrausky, Toyo Ito, Jacques Lucan, Marja-Riitta Norri, Francesco Venezia, Dietmar Steiner, Elia Zenghelis

Mein Barcelona • My Barcelona

Kunsthaus Bregenz, Peter Zumthor, 1990–97.
© Archive DS, Margherita Spiluttini

Villa in Bordeaux, Modell · model, OMA, 1994–
unvollendet · uncompleted. © Architekturzentrum Wien,
Sammlung · Collection

Eine dramatische Entscheidung war die Jurysitzung des Preises 1998. Wir besichtigten die Villa von OMA in Bordeaux, die Beyeler Foundation von Renzo Piano in Basel, das Appenzell Museum von Gigon und Guyer, das Kunsthaus Bregenz von Zumthor und das Jüdische Museum in Berlin von Libeskind. Vor der Reise war für die Jury das Jüdische Museum der absolute Favorit, doch die gebaute Wirklichkeit enttäuschte. Die Diskussion spitzte sich schließlich zu zwischen der Villa in Bordeaux und dem Kunsthaus Bregenz. Mehrere Abstimmungen führten immer zum gleichen Ergebnis: 4:4. Der Vorsitzende Vittorio Magnago Lampugnani enthielt sich dabei immer der Stimme. Von den Zumthor-Befürwortern wurde die Villa von OMA geradezu gehasst, wogegen das OMA-Lager durchaus die Leistung von Zumthor anerkannte. Irgendwann trat Erschöpfung ein, die Befürworter von OMA resignierten und gaben ihre Stimmen dem Kunsthaus Bregenz.

Jury: Vittorio Magnago Lampugnani (Chair), Wiel Arets, Oriol Bohigas, Andrej Hrausky, Marja-Riitta Norri, Dominique Perrault, Wilfried Wang, Dietmar Steiner, Elia Zenghelis

The jury session for the 1998 award ended in a dramatic decision. We viewed the villa by OMA in Bordeaux, the Beyeler Foundation by Renzo Piano in Basel, the Appenzell Museum Liner by Gigon and Guyer, the Kunsthaus Bregenz by Zumthor and the Jewish Museum in Berlin by Libeskind. Prior to the trip, the Jewish Museum was the jury's absolute favorite, but the constructed reality disappointed. The discussion ultimately came to a head between the villa in Bordeaux and Kunsthaus Bregenz. Several votes repeatedly led to the same result: 4:4. The jury chairman Vittorio Magnago Lampugnani always abstained from voting. The villa by OMA was downright hated by the Zumthor proponents, whereas the OMA camp definitely acknowledged Zumthor's accomplishment. Exhaustion eventually set in, the OMA advocates gave up and voted for the Kunsthaus Bregenz.

Jury: Vittorio Magnago Lampugnani (Chair), Wiel Arets, Oriol Bohigas, Andrej Hrausky, Marja-Riitta Norri, Dominique Perrault, Wilfried Wang, Dietmar Steiner, Elia Zenghelis

Ab 2000 wurde die Ausschreibung des Preises von der EU nicht nur beobachtet, sondern mitbestimmt, und die Organisation wurde europaweit neu ausgeschrieben. Das bedeutete zunächst eine kritische Situation für die Mies van der Rohe Foundation. Jede andere Institution in Europa hätte sich nämlich auch bewerben können. Die Expertise der Mies Foundation und das aufgebaute Archiv wären wertlos geworden. Da beschloss der Advisory Board – mit all seinen nationalen Institutionen – eine gemeinsame Bewerbung mit der Foundation. Somit konnte keine andere relevante Institution in Europa mehr mithalten. Zudem verfolgte die EU-Bürokratie die Abschaffung der traditionellen Entscheidungsfindung für das beste europäische Projekt und wollte nur mehr das erste Projekt eines europäischen Architekten, das nicht in seinem Land realisiert wurde, prämieren. Mit vielem Aufwand konnten wir die EU-Gremien davon überzeugen, dass dieses Vorhaben inhaltlich und logistisch unmöglich war. Es endete mit der Einführung des zusätzlichen, nicht genau definierten Preises für ‚Emerging Architects' (EA).

Durch diese Mitbestimmung der EU wurde aber ein anderes Probleme relevant. Zum Preis zugelassen waren zwar Länder, die nicht EU-Mitglied waren, aber über ein Kulturabkommen verfügten – seit damals ist auch die Türkei dabei. Doch ausgerechnet die Schweiz weigert sich bis heute, ein Kulturabkommen mit der EU zu ratifizieren. Deshalb sind alle Projekte von Schweizer Architekten in Europa und von europäischen Architekten in der Schweiz vom Mies-Preis ausgeschlossen. Diese Absurdität hat bis heute allein die Schweizer Kulturbürokratie zu verantworten.

Wiederum wieder war die Besichtigung der Finalisten eine eindrucksvolle Reise quer durch Europa: Besichtigung des Gerichtsgebäudes von Jean Nouvel in Nantes, am nächsten Tag nach Altamira zu Juan Navarro Baldewegs Museum mit seinen perfekten Replicas der Höhlenmalereien. Weiter nach San Sebastian zum neuen Kursaal von Rafael Moneo. Dann nach Kopenhagen zur Uni-Bank von Henning Larsen. Für einige Jurymitglieder was das eine überzeugende Lösung für

As of 2000, the competition was not only monitored by the EU, but co-determined, and the organization was newly tendered Europe-wide. That initially meant a critical situation for the Mies van der Rohe Foundation. Any other institution in Europe would have namely been also able to apply. The expertise of the Mies van der Rohe Foundation and the established archive would have become worthless. The Advisory Board—with all of its national institutions—decided on a joint application with the Foundation. As a result, no other relevant institution in Europe could keep up. Moreover, the EU bureaucracy pursued the abolishment of the traditional decision-making procedure for the best European project and only wanted to award the first project of a European architect that was not realized in his or her country. With much effort we were able to convince the EU committees that this undertaking was impossible logistically as well as in terms of content. It ended with the introduction of an additional, not precisely defined prize for "emerging architects" (EA).

However, a further problem became relevant through the EU's co-determination. Countries that were not EU member states, but had a cultural agreement, were now also authorized for the prize competition—since that time, Turkey has also been part of it. But Switzerland, of all countries, has refused up to today to ratify a cultural agreement with the EU. For that reason all projects by Swiss architects in Europe and by European architects in Switzerland are excluded from the Mies van der Rohe Award. To this day, the Swiss cultural bureaucracy alone has to answer for this absurdity.

Once again, however, the inspection of the finalists entailed an impressive journey all across Europe: viewing of the court building by Jean Nouvel in Nantes, on the next day to Altamira to Juan Navarro Baldeweg's Human Evolution Museum with its perfect replicas of the original cave paintings. Further on to San Sebastián

eine Corporate Architecture. Es wäre ein Zeichen gewesen, den Preis auch einmal einem Bürobau zu verleihen. Doch wir blieben in der Minderheit und Moneo gewann mit 4:3 Stimmen. Rein architektonisch gesehen, wäre die Tate Modern von Herzog & de Meuron oder das Kulturzentrum Luzern von Jean Nouvel die bessere Wahl gewesen. Aber die Schweiz hat dies verhindert.

<small>Jury: Vittorio Magnago Lampugnani (Chair), Wiel Arets, Esteve Bonell, David Chipperfield, (Kristin Feireiss), Luis Fernández-Galiano, Dominique Perrault, Dietmar Steiner, Elia Zenghelis</small>

Meine letzte Beteiligung an einer Jury fiel in das Jahr 2007. Nach der Auswahl der Finalisten war eigentlich klar, dass das Mercedes-Museum von UN Architects gewinnen müsste. Zur Besichtigung traf sich die Jury in Valencia, zum Americas Cup-Gebäude von David Chipperfield – eindrucksvoll in seiner konzeptionellen Klarheit. Weiter mit einem kleinen Charter-Flugzeug nach Lissabon, mit einem Bus nach Sines. Ein Kulturzentrum von Mateus Architects – die Bilder und Pläne waren besser als die gebaute Realität. Dann nach Léon: das MUSAC von Mansilla + Tuñón sah in den Unterlagen ziemlich unbedeutend aus, doch die realen Raumfolgen, die multifunktionalen Nutzungen überzeugten. Am gleichen Tag nach Bordeaux zur University of Management von Lacaton & Vassal – sehr konzeptionell, schöne Räume und Verschränkungen mit dem Außen, aber roh und spartanisch in der Ausführung. Weiter nach Marseille: Rudy Ricciottis Tanzzentrum in Aix-en-Provence ist trotz seiner skulpturalen Anmutung ein sehr gut durchdachter Bau. Danach Flug von Marseille nach Stuttgart, luxuriöse Betreuung zur Besichtigung des Mercedes-Museum. Es ist wirklich ein gigantischer Kraftakt. Am nächsten Tag in Wolfsburg das phæno von Zaha Hadid besichtigt – autistisch, mit schwachen Räumen, städtebaulich überhaupt nicht funktionierend. Sitzung: Ein etwas formalisierter Ab-

to the new Kursaal Congress Center and Auditorium by Rafael Moneo. Then to Copenhagen to the Uni-Bank by Henning Larsen. For several jury members that was a convincing solution for a corporate architecture. It would have been a signal to award the prize once to an office building as well. We remained in the minority, however, and Moneo won four votes to three. Seen from a purely architectonic perspective, the Tate Modern by Herzog & de Meuron or the Kulturzentrum Lucerne by Jean Nouvel would have been the better choice. But Switzerland prevented this.

<small>Jury: Vittorio Magnago Lampugnani (Chair), Wiel Arets, Esteve Bonell, David Chipperfield, (Kristin Feireiss), Luis Fernández-Galiano, Dominique Perrault, Dietmar Steiner, Elia Zenghelis</small>

America's Cup-Gebäude · building „Veles e Vents", Valencia, David Chipperfield, 2005–06. © DS

Zweiter Tag · Day Two

Mercedes Benz-Museum, Stuttgart, UN Studio, 2001–06. © DS

Jury Reise · Jury trip 2007, Lluís Hortet, Ricky Burdett, Mohsen Mostafavi, Peter Chachola Schmal, Luis Fernández-Galiano, Bettina Götz, Ellen van Loon, Diane Gray, Francis Rambert, Dietmar Steiner. © Mies van der Rohe Pavilion Foundation

Ben van Berkel still bombarded me days later with SMS questions and news and couldn't understand that the Mercedes-Benz Museum hadn't won …

My last participation in a jury was in 2007. After the selection of the finalists it was actually clear that the Mercedes-Benz Museum by UN Architects would have to win. The jury met in Valencia to take a tour of The America's Cup building by David Chipperfield—impressive in its conceptual clarity. Further onwards in a small charter airplane to Lisbon, by bus to Sines. A cultural center by Mateus Architects—the pictures of the plans were better than the constructed reality. Then on to Léon: the MUSAC by Mansilla + Tuñón looked rather insignificant in the documents, but the real spatial sequences and the multifunctional usages were convincing. On the same day to Bordeaux to the University of Management by Lacaton & Vassal—very conceptual, beautiful spaces and exterior interleaves, but raw and spartan in the execution. Further to Marseille: Despite its sculptural look and feel, Rudy Ricciotti's Centre Chorégraphique National in Aix-en-Provence is a very well-thought-out structure. Afterwards a flight from Marseille to Stuttgart, lavish attention during the inspection of the Mercedes-Benz Museum. It is really a gigantic feat. On the next day in Wolfsburg a visit to the phæno by Zaha Hadid—autistic, with weak spaces, it doesn't work at all in urban planning sense. Jury ses-

stimmungsritus diesmal, bei dem das MUSAC schlussendlich knapp gewann, auch aufgrund seines Beitrags zur Aufwertung der Umgebung und damit zur europäischen Stadt. Ben van Berkel belagerte mich noch Tage danach mit SMS-Fragen und Nachrichten und konnte nicht verstehen, dass das Mercedes-Museum nicht gewonnen hatte ...

<small>Jury: Ricky Burdett (Chair), Beth Galí, Luis Fernández-Galiano, Bettina Götz, Ellen van Loon, Mohsen Mostafavi, Francis Rambert, Peter Chachola Schmal, Dietmar Steiner</small>

Seit meinem ersten Kontakt mit der Mies-Foundation sind nun 20 Jahre verstrichen. Das waren, jenseits der Jurys, intensive Jahre der Zusammenarbeit, immer davon geprägt, die Logistik und die Popularität des Preises zu verbessern. Mit dem Ziel, die inhaltliche Qualität der Architektur zu befördern und ihren Beitrag zur Entwicklung einer zeitgenössischen europäischen Identität zu leisten. ‚Mein Barcelona' hat sich dafür als idealer Treffpunkt der Welt der Architektur etabliert.

Dazu kam, ab 2000, auch der „European Prize for Urban Public Space", der vom CCCB – Centre of Contemporary Culture of Barcelona – ausgelobt wird. Ausgehend von einer historischen Recherche über die öffentlichen Räume Europas, wird nun alle zwei Jahre ein Preis für den besten „urban public space" ausgeschrieben. Damit ergänzt das CCCB den Mies van der Rohe Preis um die Dimension des öffentlichen Raums. Seit 2002 ist in die Entwicklung und Jurierung dieses Preises eine ausgewählte Anzahl von europäischen Architekturinstitutionen, darunter das Az W, eingebunden.

‚Mein Barcelona' war im Lauf der Jahrzehnte zum inhaltlichen und diskursiven Zentrum der Zukunft der europäischen Architektur und Stadt geworden. Keine andere Stadt in Europa hat sich in den letzten 40 Jahren so sehr inhaltlich und konzeptionell mit seiner eigenen Zukunft beschäftigt. Hat vergleichbare inhaltliche Beiträge zur Entwicklung der europäischen Stadt geleistet. Wir alle können von Barcelona nur lernen ...

sion: a somewhat formalized voting ritual this time, in which the MUSAC narrowly wins in the end, also due to its contribution to the upgrading of the surroundings and thus to the European city. Ben van Berkel still bombarded me days later with SMS questions and news and couldn't understand that the Mercedes-Benz Museum hadn't won …

<small>Jury: Ricky Burdett (Chair), Beth Galí, Luis Fernández-Galiano, Bettina Götz, Ellen van Loon, Mohsen Mostafavi, Francis Rambert, Peter Chachola Schmal, Dietmar Steiner</small>

20 years have now passed since my first contact with the Mies van der Rohe Foundation. Beyond the juries these were intensive years of collaboration, always characterized by the effort to improve the logistics and popularity of the award. With the goal of promoting the quality of architecture in terms of content and making its contribution to the development of a contemporary European identity. "My Barcelona" has established itself as an ideal meeting point for the world of architecture.

From 2000 onwards the European Prize for Urban Public Space, awarded by the CCCB—the Centre of Contemporary Culture of Barcelona—was also added. Originating from historical research on the public spaces of Europe, a prize for the best urban public space is now tendered every two years. The CCCB thus complements the Mies van der Rohe Award by the dimension of public space. Since 2002 a selected number of European architectural institutions, among them the Architekturzentrum Wien (Az W), have been involved in the development and judging of this award.

Over the decades, "My Barcelona" had thus become the center of the future of European architecture and the city in regard to content and discourse. No other city in Europe has occupied itself so much with its own future in terms of content and conceptualization in the last 40 years. Or has made comparable contributions to the development of the European city content-wise. We all can only learn from Barcelona …

Mies van der Rohe Award – Winners Preisträger 1988–2015

Die Preisträger des Architekturpreises der Europäischen Union – Mies van der Rohe Pavilion Foundation werden von einer internationalen Jury ausgewählt. Die Projekte werden von einer großen Gruppe von Architektur-Experten und den Berufsvertretungen der Architekten der teilnehmenden Länder nominiert. Nach einer ersten Jurysitzung wird eine Shortlist für die Wanderausstellung und die Auswahl der Kandidaten erstellt. Dann besichtigt die gesamte Jury die fünf bis sechs Projekte und fällt die Entscheidung. Durch das aufwendige Nominierungsverfahren und die konkrete Auseinandersetzung mit den Objekten vor Ort, ist der Mies-Preis der wichtigste Architekturpreis Europas.

The prize winners of the Architectural Prize of the European Union – Mies van der Rohe Pavilion Foundation are chosen by an international jury. The projects are nominated by a large group of architectural experts and professional associations of the participating countries. After an initial jury meeting, a short list for the travelling exhibition and the selection of candidates is prepared. Then the entire jury inspects the five or six projects and makes the decision. Through the sophisticated nomination procedure and the concrete engagement with the objects on site, the Mies Award is one of Europe's most important architectural prizes.

Alle Preisträger bisher · All prize winners to date.
© Archive Mies van der Rohe Pavilion Foundation

1988: *Banco Borges e Irmão* Vila do Conde
Álvaro Siza Vieira

1990: *New Terminal Development Stansted Airport* London
Norman Foster + Partners

1992: *Municipal Sports Stadium* Badalona
Esteve Bonell, Francesc Rius

1994: *Waterloo International Station* London
Nicholas Grimshaw & Partners

1996: *French National Library* Paris
Dominique Perrault Architecture

1998: *Kunsthaus Bregenz*
Peter Zumthor

2001: *Kursaal Congress Centre and Auditorium* San Sebastián
Rafael Moneo

2003: *Car Park and Terminus Hoenheim North* Strasbourg
Zaha Hadid Architects

2005: *Netherlands Embassy Berlin*
Rem Koolhaas, Ellen van Loon, OMA

2007: *MUSAC Contemporary Art Museum of Castilla y León*, León
Mansilla + Tuñón Arquitectos

2009: *Norwegian National Opera & Ballet* Oslo
Kjetil Trædal Thorsen, Tarald Lundevall, Craig Dykers, SNØHETTA

2011: *Neues Museum*, Berlin
David Chipperfield Architects
in collaboration with Julian Harrap

2013: *Harpa Reykjavik*
Henning Larsen, Architects, Studio Olafur Eliasson, Batteríið Architects

2015: *Philharmonie Stettin*, Szczecin
Barozzi Veiga

aus · from

Hintergrund 42_2009
„Über Rob Krier"
Translation by Brian Dorsey

Über Rob Krier

On Rob Krier

Rob Kriers Zeit Wien? War da was? Warum redet niemand mehr davon?

Tatsächlich – als Zeitzeuge vergisst man das leicht – liegt heute ein seltsames Schweigen über dieser wesentlichen Epoche der jüngeren Architekturgeschichte. Rob Krier (geb. 1938 in Luxemburg) wurde 1976 als Professor für Gestaltungslehre an die TU Wien berufen. Nur ein Jahr zuvor hatte er mit seiner Publikation über die Stadtraumanalyse Stuttgarts, die eine Neukonzeption nach Regeln bewährter Stadtbaukunst forderte, für ziemliches publizistisches Aufsehen gesorgt. Ein plakatives Statement zur Theorie der Postmoderne, deren schiere Existenz man zu dieser Zeit nicht nur an der TU Wien wahrscheinlich nicht einmal zur Kenntnis nehmen wollte und konnte. (Es wäre deshalb, nebenbei gesagt, durchaus erhellend zu erforschen, wie es überhaupt zum ‚Irrtum' dieser Berufung kommen konnte.)

Rob Krier's time in Vienna. Was something going on there? Why doesn't anybody talk about it anymore?

As a matter of fact—one easily forgets that as a contemporary witness—an odd silence lies today over this crucial era of recent architectural history. Rob Krier (born in 1938 in Luxemburg) was appointed in 1976 as Professor of Design Theory at the Technical University of Vienna. Just one year earlier he had caused quite a media stir with his publication on the urban space analysis of Stuttgart, which called for a new concept according to the rules of proven urban architecture. A striking statement on the theory of postmodernism, whose sheer existence one probably could not and did not want to even take notice of at this time not only at the TU Vienna. (Incidentally. it would therefore be quite illuminating to explore how it could have even come to the "mistake" of this appointment.)

Gemeindewohnbau · Council housing estate Breitenfurter Straße, Wien · Vienna Rob Krier, 1981–87. © Architekturzentrum Wien, Sammlung · Collection, Margherita Spiluttini

Mit der Präsentation und Diskussionsveranstaltung zu Rob Kriers Wiener Zeit[1] sollte über die Würdigung seiner Person hinaus auch an eine Zeit erinnert werden, als man noch nach Positionen einer Theorie der Architektur suchte. Die siebziger Jahre waren eine – viele sagen heute die letzte – Zeit der Definition und Auseinandersetzung über eine Theorie der Architektur, die zwischen dem konkret alltäglich gelebten Leben und der gebauten Form einen Zusammenhang herstellen wollte. Ein paar Hinweise dazu: Das fröhliche Gewitter einer unendlichen Zukunft der Pop-Utopisten der späten sechziger Jahre wurde durch die „Energiekrise" 1972/73 beendet. Aber damit stieß auch die unaufhaltsame Gewalt des Nachkriegsfunktionalismus an ihre Grenzen und wurde durch das Paradigma der Rettung der noch bestehenden Stadt ersetzt. Theoretisch auch als Entwurfsthema begründet wurde die Permanenz und Wiederentdeckung der europäischen Stadt

[1] am 25 Februar 2009 im Architekturzentrum Wien

Beyond the appreciation of him personally, the presentation and discussion meeting on Rob Krier's Vienna period[1] should also recall the time when one was still searching for positions of a theory of architecture. The seventies were a—many today say the final—period of the definition of and dispute over a theory of architecture that wanted to establish a relationship between concretely daily-lived life and the constructed form.

Here are a few references: The cheerful tempest of an endless future of late-sixties pop utopians was ended by the "Energy Crisis" of 1972/73. But the relentless force of postwar functionalism was also stretched to its limits thereby and replaced by the paradigm of the saving of the still-existing city. The permanence and rediscovery of the European city were also theoretically grounded as a design theme through Aldo Rossi's *L'architettura della città* (already published in 1966, like Robert Venturi's *Complexity and Contradiction*, but both first appeared in German in the mid-seventies!). Venturi, in turn, opened up a completely new formal cosmos of dealing with the form stock of everyday life. Venturi and Rossi, and many others as well, showed the architecture students of the seventies new ways towards an

[1] On February 25, 2009 at the Architekturzentrum Wien

durch Aldo Rossis *L'architettura della città* (bereits 1966 erschienen, ebenso wie Robert Venturis *Complexity and Contradiction*, doch beide erst Mitte der siebziger Jahre auf deutsch publiziert!). Venturi wiederum eröffnete einen völlig neuen formalen Kosmos des Umgangs mit dem Formenfundus des Alltäglichen. Venturi und Rossi, und viele andere auch, zeigten den ArchitekturstudentInnen der siebziger Jahre neue Wege zu einer architektonisch gestaltbaren Wirklichkeit, der von den damaligen Professoren, die gerade den Schock der Provokationen der sechziger Jahre verdaut hatten, ahnungslos ignoriert wurde.

Es klingt heute paradox, aber in Rossis und Kriers *rationalismo* wurde ebenso wie in Venturis massenmedialer Alltagskultur ein formaler Widerstand gegen die herrschenden Baupraktiken gefunden, der sich in der Theorie mit den partizipatorischen Bewegungen zur Rettung der Stadt gegenüber den ahnungslos politisch Mächtigen verbinden konnte. Partizipation und die Permanenz der Form der Stadt waren kein Widerspruch. Dafür war das Jahr 1976 in Wien ein wichtiges Datum: Die „Arena" wurde besetzt, die Reichsbrücke stürzte ein, und Rob Krier kam an die TU. Sanft und leise traf er ein, doch seine Gestaltungslehre sollte eine Revolution werden. Friedrich Achleitner fand endlich wieder einen ‚Jungen', mit dem er auch über Architekturgeschichte reden konnte, Krischanitz und Kapfinger reizte an Krier die Debatte der Typologien, und ich hatte einen Gesprächspartner gefunden, der authentisch wusste, was sich ‚draußen' in der Architekturdebatte damals ereignete. Ein informeller Freundeskreis bildete sich, der mit ihm das nun eröffnete Tor zur Welt benutzte: Adolf Krischanitz organisierte 1980 die Ausstellung *A New Wave of Austrian Architecture* an Eisenmans legendärem Institute for Architecture and Urban Studies in New York. Rob Krier war dabei, aber auch Heinz Frank.

architectonically designable reality that was obliviously ignored by the professors at that time, who had just digested the shock of the provocations of the sixties.

It sounds paradoxical today, but a formal resistance against the prevailing building practices, which could be combined in theory with the participatory movements to save the city from the clueless political powers that be, was found in Rossi's and Krier's *rationalismo*, as well as in Venturi's mass media everyday culture. Participation and the permanence of the form of the city were no contradiction. For that reason the year 1976 was an important date in Vienna: The Arena was occupied, the Reichsbrücke collapsed and Rob Krier came to the TU. He arrived gently and quietly, but his design theory was to become a revolution. Friedrich Achleitner finally found a 'young one' again with whom he could also talk about architectural history. Krischanitz and Kapfinger were stimulated by Krier's debate on typologies and I had found a discussion partner who authentically knew what was happening 'outside' in the architectural debate back then. An informal circle of friends formed, which used the now-opened gateway to the world with him: In 1980 Adolf Krischanitz organized the exhibition *A New Wave of Austrian Architecture* at Eisenman's legendary Institute for Architecture and Urban Studies in New York. Rob Krier was involved, but also Heinz Frank.

What Rob accomplished in teaching at the TU largely remained a secret to me. But he also had his office at the TU. The projects for the IBA '84 in Berlin and the few Viennese residential buildings were designed here. After I completed my diploma I gratefully accepted his invitation to work on the editing of his opus magnum, *Über architektonische Komposition (Architectural Composition)*. Many notes on this work can be found in my archive. I was visibly searching at that time for a philosophic supplementation, from Georg Lukács' *Notion of Analogy* right up to the emancipatory justification of

Was Rob an der TU in der Lehre bewirkte, blieb mir weitgehend verschlossen. Er hatte aber auch sein Büro an der TU. Hier wurden die Projekte für die IBA 84 in Berlin und die wenigen Wiener Wohnbauten entworfen. Seine Einladung, nach meinem Diplom an der Redaktion seines Opus magnum, *Über architektonische Komposition*, mitzuarbeiten, nahm ich dankend an. In meinem Archiv befinden sich viele Notizen zu diesem Werk. Ich suchte sichtlich damals nach einer philosophischen Unterfütterung, von Georg Lukács' *Begriff der Analogie* bis zur politisch emanzipatorischen Begründung seiner Forderungen. Aber dafür reichte dann doch meine Bildung nicht, und es war auch nicht wirklich das Interesse von Rob. Er war Künstler, antizipierte naiv eine andere Welt, die sich heute wohlbegründet im ‚New Urbanism' ausformulierte.

Uns – Achleitner, Krischanitz, Kapfinger, vor allem – war Rob Krier in seiner Wiener Zeit ein beständiger Ansporn in der kritischen Rezeption aller postmodernen Positionen, von Amerika bis zum Tessin, die schließlich u. a. in der Gründung der Zeitschrift *UM BAU* mündete. Rob Kriers Architektur hat aber, jenseits seiner eigenen Bauten, kaum Nachfolger in Wien gefunden. Eine kurze Zeit in den achtziger Jahren war das Klima für sein Vokabular fruchtbar. Ernst Hoffmann und Eric Steiner für Heinz Neumann, haben eine Serie von Wettbewerbserfolgen mit ‚abgespeckten' Projekten à la Krier gefeiert.

Doch zehn Jahre nach Kriers Ankunft war in Wien seine Architektur wieder beendet. Als der Wohnbau Breitenfurter Straße eröffnet wurde, meinte der zuständige Beamte der Wohnbauabteilung der Stadt Wien, dass – kaum hätte er sich von den ‚alten Formen' überzeugen lassen – jetzt doch wieder Glas und Flachdächer angesagt wären. Womit eines der größten ungelösten Rätsel der jüngeren Architekturgeschichte illustriert wäre: Wer oder was hat, oder warum wurde die Postmoderne als Stil beendet?

Cité Judiciare · The Judiciary City, Luxemburg, Léon + Rob Krier, 1992–2008. © DS

his demands. However, my education was not adequate enough for that and it also really wasn't Rob's interest. He was an artist, naively anticipating a different world that was formulated today in a well-founded manner in 'New Urbanism.'

During his time in Vienna, Rob Krier was a constant stimulus for us—Achleitner, Krischanitz and Kapfinger above all—in the critical reception of all postmodern positions, from America to Ticino, which ultimately led to the founding of the magazine *UM BAU*. Beyond his own buildings, however, Rob Krier's architecture has hardly found successors in Vienna. The climate for his vocabulary was fertile for a short period in the eighties. Ernst Hoffmann and Eric Steiner, working for Heinz Neumann, celebrated a series of competition successes with "pared-down" projects à la Krier.

Ten years after Krier's arrival, however, his architecture was ended again in Vienna. When the housing development on Breitenfurter Strasse was opened, the responsible official of the Housing Department of the City of Vienna said—and he had just let himself be convinced by the "old forms"—that glass and flat roofs were now in again after all. Wherewith one of the greatest unsolved mysteries of recent architectural history would have been illustrated: Who or what ended postmodernism as a style, and why?

VERHINDERN WIR DIE NOTSCHLACHTUNG DES SCHLACHTHOFES

TREFFPUNKT: SAMSTAG 26. JUNI 1976 SCHLACHTHOFGELÄNDE 16ʰ

KOMMT ALLE

VORSICHT STEINSCHLAG

WO SIE SICH JETZT BEFINDEN RATTERN AB 10. JULI DIE BAUMASCHINEN!

DIE VERWALTER DIESES GEMEINEIGENTUMS HABEN ANDERE INTERESSEN ALS SEINE BENUTZER. DER VERKAUF AN DIE FA. „SCHÖPS" IST PROFITABLER ALS INVESTITIONEN FÜR GEMEINSCHAFTLICHE AKTIVITÄTEN. KULTURELLES LEBEN SOLL TEXTILEM KONSUM GEOPFERT WERDEN.

SCHAUN SIE SICH DAS AN! DIE OBJEKTE SIND IN GUTEM BAULICHEN ZUSTAND. HIER IST DIE MÖGLICHKEIT FÜR KREATIVE EXPERIMENTE. AUSGEHEND VON DEN BEDÜRFNISSEN UND INTERESSEN DER BEVÖLKERUNG KÖNNEN SIE DEN NOTWENDIGEN SCHWERPUNKT GEGENÜBER DER INSTITUTIONALISIERTEN BUNDESTHEATER-„KULTUR" BILDEN.

➡ FORDERN SIE MIT UNS:

EINE ARENA FÜR DAS GANZE JAHR AUF DEM GELÄNDE DES SCHLACHTHOFES

MIT ATELIERS, WOHNUNGEN, WERKSTÄTTEN, KINDERGÄRTEN; MIT FILM, THEATER, MUSIK, WORK-SHOPS, SEMINAREN UND AUSSTELLUNGEN.

INFORMIERT BEKANNTE UND KOLLEGEN, BETEILIGT EUCH AN DEN WEITEREN AKTIVITÄTEN BEVOR ES ZU SPÄT IST.

WENN IHR VON DER NOTWENDIGKEIT DIESER SACHE ÜBERZEUGT SEID, DANN HELFT MIT BEIM

KAMPF UM DIE ERHALTUNG DES SCHLACHTHOFES

DER SCHLACHTHOF DARF NICHT STERBEN

Mein Flugblatt für die Erhaltung des Auslandsschlachthofs in Wien als Kulturzentrum. Der Auftakt für die Besetzung 1976 · My flyer for the preservation of the Overseas Slaughterhouse in Vienna as a cultural center. The prelude to the 1976 occupation. © DS

1979

The New China
After 30 years of Mao Zedong begin 30 years of Deng Xiaoping. His capitalistic communism opens China's path to world power. The USA and China establish diplomatic relations for the first time.

Das neue China
Nach 30 Jahren Mao Zedong beginnen 30 Jahre Deng Xiaoping. Sein kapitalistischer Kommunismus eröffnet Chinas Weg zur Weltmacht. Die USA und China nehmen erstmals diplomatische Beziehungen auf.

Das Ende der Stadtplanung
Margaret Thatcher wird Premierministerin In Großbritannien, im folgenden Jahr Ronald Reagan in den USA. Beide erklären den Neoliberalismus zu ihrem politischen Programm. Die Privatisierung öffentlicher Aufgaben ist das Ende von kommunaler Stadtplanung und führt zur Herrschaft von privaten Investoren über die Stadt. Die Städte verlieren ihre lokale Identität und werden zum globalen Konsumgut.

The End of City Planning
Margaret Thatcher becomes prime minister in Great Britain; Ronald Reagan is elected US president the following year. Both declare neo-liberalism as their political program. The privatization of public services spells the end of communal city planning and leads to the rule of private investors over the city. The cities lose their local identity and become a global consumer good.

The Islamic Revolution
After the abdication of Reza Shah Pahlavi the Western powers decide to enthrone Ayatollah Ruhollah Khomeini in Iran. Western modernism thereby ends in all Islamic countries. They have unknowingly enabled the Islamic Revolution, which becomes a global political problem from now on. Saddam Hussein seizes power in Iraq.

Die islamische Revolution
Nach der Abdankung von Reza Schah Pahlavi beschließen die Westmächte im Iran Ajatollah Ruhollah Chomeini zu inthronisieren. Damit endet die westliche Moderne in allen islamischen Staaten. Ahnungslos haben sie die „Islamische Revolution" ermöglicht, die von nun an ein weltpolitisches Problem wird. Saddam Hussein erringt die Macht im Irak.

The New Culture
The first Pritzker Prize is awarded to Philip Johnson. It is endowed by the private Hyatt Foundation as a supplement to the Nobel Prize in terms of content. In Ridley Scott's film *Alien* a woman—Sigourney Weaver— becomes the main character of an action and science fiction film for the first time. The spaceships are no longer cleanly futuristic and technoid, but rather remind one of the junk at the end of the Industrial Age.

Die neue Kultur
Der erste Pritzker-Preis wird an Philip Johnson verliehen. Gestiftet von der privaten Hyatt-Foundation als inhaltliche Ergänzung zum Nobel-Preis. Im Film *Alien* von Ridley Scott wird erstmals eine Frau – Sigourney Weaver – zur Hauptdarstellerin eines Action- und Science-Fiction-Films. Die Raumschiffe sind nicht mehr sauber futuristisch und technoid, sondern erinnern eher an den Schrott am Ende des Industriezeitalters.

The First End of the Soviet Union
The ill-advised invasion of the Soviet Union into Afghanistan leads to a war that was not to be won, and fundamentally shatters the Soviet Union's confidence of victory. Pope John Paul II visits his home country Poland as the first communist country. In the Soviet Union's self-understanding, the doctrine of communism was basically challenged in a communist state by this professed Catholicism. Elton John is the first Western pop musician to give a concert tour in the Soviet Union.

Das erste Ende der Sowjetunion
Der unüberlegte Einmarsch der Sowjetunion in Afghanistan führt zu einem Krieg der nicht zu gewinnen war, und erschüttert die Siegesgewissheit der Sowjetunion grundlegend. Papst Johannes Paul II. besucht sein Heimatland Polen als erstes kommunistisches Land. Damit wurde im Selbstverständnis der Sowjetunion die Glaubenslehre des Kommunismus durch diesen bekennenden Katholizismus in einem kommunistischen Staat grundlegend infrage gestellt. Elton John gibt als erster westlicher Pop-Musiker eine Konzerttournee in der Sowjetunion.

Die Umwelt
In Genf findet die erste internationale Konferenz zum Welt-Klima-Problem statt.

The Environment
The first World Climate Conference takes place in Geneva.

3rd DAY The 1980s

Einige meiner Publikationen aus diesem Jahrzehnt ·
Some of my publications from this decade. Archive DS

The first Architecture Biennale in Venice. For me this signals the end of postmodernism as a socio-critical reading of the city and the beginning of individualistic star architecture. – +++ – Friedrich Achleitner brings me as his assistant to the new Institute of the Theory and History of Architecture at the University of Applied Arts Vienna. – +++ – Achleitner recommends Otto Kapfinger and me for regular architectural criticism in the daily newspaper *Die Presse*. It is the last decade of architectural criticism with distinct criteria and clear enemy stereotypes. – +++ – A trip to the Soviet Union enables me to examine the archive holdings and built incunabula of Soviet constructivism in Moscow and Leningrad. – +++ – Collaboration with the 9H group in London, which operates a subversive architectural gallery and publishes ambitious catalogs about *emerging architects*. – +++ – The topic of the decade is the International Building Exhibition in Berlin. A constructed world exposition on the architecture of this time. – +++ – An architectural reform takes place among the building contractors of the Austrian People's Party (ÖVP) in Viennese social housing construction. I am permitted to advise during these pilot projects. For the first time "cultural architects" can develop social housing construction. – +++ – With eichinger oder knechtl I design an exhibition on the architectural reform in Salzburg for Johannes Voggenhuber, a politician of the Salzburg Citizens' Initiative. – +++ – *Birth of a Capital City* is the title of a Lower Austrian State Exhibition in St. Pölten. Magnificent research into the question of a "capital city" is conducted with an international team. It is my greatest defeat. I go to court for two years because of unpaid fees …

3. TAG Die 1980er

Katalog · Catalog *The Architecture of Adolf Loos*,
Arts Council Exhibition, London, 1985. Archive DS

THE STRENGTH OF THE OLD MASTERS: ADOLF LOOS AND ANTIQUITY

Dietmar Steiner

'Behold, the time is at hand, fulfilment is awaiting us. Soon the streets of the cities will glow like white walls! Like Zion, the holy city, the capital of heaven. It is then that fulfilment will have come.'

Adolf Loos
'Ornament and Crime', 1908

There is in Adolf Loos a yearning which, in the end, also determines his polemic Modernism. This yearning ascribes to him the role of David, who fights against Goliath of the Philistines, against false teachings. Loos will enter Jerusalem, the daughter of Zion, victorious. The white walls of the eschatological capital of heaven

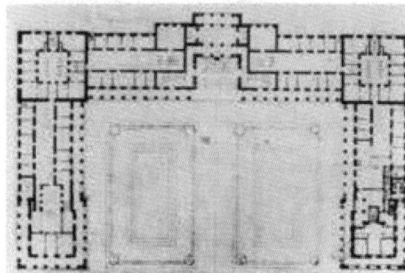

will then be aglow for Loos with the radiance of antiquity, which will at last have been reestablished...

To describe this thesis as Loos's mission does not mean robbing him of his cathartic Modernism. It is only to push one aspect of his thought and intention into the foreground, one that may only have become decipherable today: that Adolf Loos's Modernism did not follow a fashion without a past, but that, on the contrary, it consciously placed itself in relation to antiquity, and measured itself against it. It is a thesis which actually applies to a large part of twentieth century 'Classical Modernism' which, however, no one formulated so clearly as Adolf Loos. Jürgen Habermas' definition of the term is probably best suited to Loos's work, his writings and sketches, his designs and buildings: 'But while the merely fashionable becomes out-of-date as it is transposed into the past, the modern maintains a secret relationship to the classical'. There is one difference: the relationship to the classical is evident, not secret, in Loos's work.

For this purpose, we must turn our view from Loos's widely publicised icons – the 'naked' façades of the Steiner, Scheu, Moller and Müller Houses for instance – by taking a detour via illustrations from other projects so that these too may be seen in the light of classicism.

Let us assume that Loos had realised his project for the completion of the Gartenbau site (1917) with its *grand cour d'honneur* with colonnades of Ionic columns; or that he had built the Villa Konstandt (1919) with its caryatid hall as the gentlemen's room (!), or even one of his much larger projects, for instance, the various banks or office buildings, scarcely one of which managed without a tower crowned with a classical temple. The radiant white walls of his yearning should be seen, above all, as a reaction to meaningless, opulent historicism: the Potemkinesque City. His architectonic intention, however, would be secured in an awakening towards an antiquity aware of the *Last Days*. His polemic would acquire an apocalyptic dimension – for he, who does not follow Loos, his message and his teaching, does not only count as 'unmodern', but will also have to face the Last Judgment of architecture.

'The old and the new direction in the art of building'
The journal 'Der Architekt' announced a literary competition under the above title in 1898. In his entry Loos expressed his creed, which he was not to depart from until his death: 'The architect does not merely create for his time; posterity also has a right to enjoy his work. For this one needs a firm, unchanging standard, at present and in the future, until perhaps a great event calls for a complete revaluation: this is classical antiquity'. The great event, which would have called for a 'complete

Die erste Architektur Biennale in Venedig. Für mich das Fanal des Endes der Postmoderne als sozialkritischer Lektüre der Stadt und der Beginn der individualistischen Star-Architektur – +++ – Friedrich Achleitner holt mich als seinen Assistenten an das neue Institut für Geschichte und Theorie der Architektur an der Hochschule für angewandte Kunst – +++ – Achleitner empfiehlt Otto Kapfinger und mich für eine regelmäßige Architekturkritik in der Tageszeitung *Die Presse*. Es ist das letzte Jahrzehnt der Architekturkritik mit eindeutigen Kriterien und klaren Feindbildern – +++ – Eine Reise in die Sowjetunion erlaubt mir eine Sichtung der Archivbestände und gebauten Inkunabeln des sowjetischen Konstruktivismus in Moskau und Leningrad – +++ – Zusammenarbeit mit der Gruppe von 9H in London, die eine subversive Architekturgalerie betreibt und ambitionierte Kataloge über *emerging architects* publiziert – +++ – Das Thema des Jahrzehnts ist die „Internationale Bauausstellung" in Berlin. Eine gebaute Weltausstellung der Architektur dieser Zeit – +++ – Im Wiener Sozialen Wohnbau findet bei den Bauträgern der ÖVP eine Architekturreform statt. Ich darf bei diesen Pilotprojekten beraten. Damit können erstmals ‚Kulturarchitekten' Sozialen Wohnbau entwickeln – +++ – Für Johannes Voggenhuber, Politiker der Bürgerinitiative Salzburg, konzipiere ich mit eichinger oder knechtl eine Ausstellung zur Salzburger Architekturreform – +++ – *Geburt einer Hauptstadt* ist der Titel einer niederösterreichischen Landesausstellung in St. Pölten. Mit einem internationalen Team wird eine inhaltlich großartige Recherche zur Frage einer ‚Hauptstadt' geführt. Es ist meine größte Niederlage. Ich prozessiere zwei Jahre lang über ausstehende Honorare...

Biennale 1980

Die Architektur Biennale 1980 in Venedig, kuratiert von Paolo Portoghesi, mit dem Titel *Die Gegenwart der Vergangenheit* war das Fanal der Postmoderne. Sie stellte die Nachkriegsmoderne grundsätzlich infrage und forderte ein neues Bekenntnis zur ‚Stadt'. Die „Strada novissima" etablierte den Begriff des ‚Star-Architekten'. Viele Architekten der *Strada* gerieten in der Folge in mediale Vergessenheit, andere, wie Frank O. Gehry und OMA fanden am Ende des Jahrzehnts ihre Wiederauferstehung als „Deconstructivist Architects".

Entitled *The Presence of the Past* and curated by Paolo Portoghesi, the Architecture Biennale in 1980 in Venice was the beacon of postmodernism. It fundamentally challenged post-war modernism and called for a new acknowledgement of the 'city.' The *Strada novissima* established the term "star architect." Many architects of the *Strada* consequently faded into media obscurity. Others like Frank O. Gehry and OMA found their resurrection at the end of the decade as "deconstructivist architects."

Strada novissima im · in the Arsenale, Venedig · Venice. Archive DS

Entwurf Fassade · Façade design Josef Paul Kleihues. Archive DS

Entwurf Fassade · Façade design Charles Moore. Archive DS

Entwurf Fassade · Façade design Frank O. Gehry,
Archive DS

Entwurf Fassade · Façade design Purini+Thermes.
Archive DS

Entwurf Fassade · Façade design Allan Greenberg.
Archive DS

Entwurf Fassade · Façade design Léon Krier.
Archive DS

Entwurf Fassade · Façade design Robert A.M. Stern.
Archive DS

Entwurf Fassade · Façade design Studio Grau.
Archive DS

Entwurf Fassade · Façade design OMA.
Archive DS

Entwurf Fassade · Façade design Massimo Scolari.
Archive DS

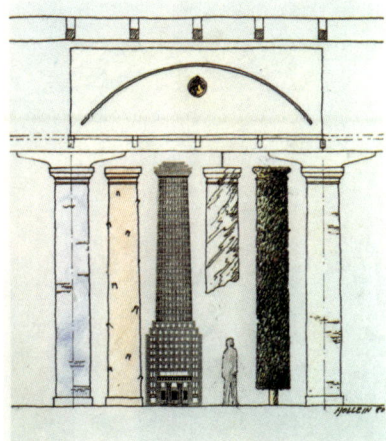

Entwurf Fassade · Façade design Hans Hollein.
Archive DS

Moscow and Leningrad Moskau und Leningrad 1982

Haus der Gesellschaft politisch Verbannter · House of the Society of Political Prisoners, Moskau · Moscow, Brüder Wesnin · Vesnin Brothers, 1930–32

Panzerkreuzer · Battleship Aurora – Symbol der Oktoberrevolution · Symbol of the October Revolution

Deutsche Botschaft · German embassy in Leningrad, Peter Behrens, 1911–12

Schreibplatz im Haus von · Writing space in the house of Konstantin Melnikow, Moskau · Moscow 1929

Sommerpavillon im Park im Peterhof · Summer pavilion in the park at Peterhof Palace, Leningrad

Sujew-Klub · Sujew Club, Moskau · Moscow, Ilja Golossow, 1926–28

Narkomfin-Dachterrasse · Narkomfin Roof Terrace, Nowinski-Boulevard, Moskau · Moscow, Moisei Ginsburg, Ignaty Milinis, 1928–30

Narkomfin-Wohnhaus · Narkomfin Communal House, Nowinski-Boulevard, Moskau · Moscow, Moisei Ginsburg, Ignaty Milinis, 1928–30

aus · from

Wiener, 10_1980
„Architektur ist Hintergrund – Hermann Czech"
Translation by Brian Dorsey

Hermann Czech, 1978. © Archive Löcker Verlag

Architecture Is Background – Hermann Czech

"No Need for Panic" is the title of a warning written by Hermann Czech in 1971, which explains one of his fundamental positions on architecture at the same time. "All public relations should be viewed with scepticism: all publicity that is not theory or design, all 'social engagement' that is not political action, all 'project architecture' and related witticisms, all obscenity that is not produced for its own sake—in short, all attempts to extort another role for architecture apart from standing there and keeping quiet. Architecture is not life. Architecture is *background*. Everything else is *not* architecture."

One year before that, Peter Cook gave the air bubbles and linear towns produced hereabouts in the 1960s the title "The Austrian Phenomenon" (Peter Cook *Experimental Architecture*, New York, 1970). Actionism cast its shadow on architecture and the group "Salz der Erde" ("Salt of the Earth") labeled their films and actions as political. The self-confidence and sense of

Architektur ist Hintergrund – Hermann Czech

„Nur keine Panik" ist der Titel einer von Hermann Czech im Jahr 1971 verfassten Warnung, die gleichzeitig eine seiner grundsätzlichen Positionen zur Architektur erklärt. „Ich schlage zur Beruhigung vor, alle Öffentlichkeitsarbeit für suspekt zu halten: alle Publizität, die nicht Entwurf oder Theorie vorstellt, alles ‚gesellschaftliche Engagement', das nicht politische Aktion ist, alle ‚Projektarchitektur' und dergleichen Schmunzelkunst, alle Obszönität, die nicht um ihrer selbst willen veranstaltet wird – kurz alle Versuche, der Architektur eine andere Rolle zu erpressen, als dazustehen und Ruhe zu geben. Architektur ist nicht das Leben. Architektur ist *Hintergrund*. Alles andere ist *nicht* Architektur."

Ein Jahr vorher gab Peter Cook den in den sechziger Jahren hierorts produzierten Luftblasen und Bandstädten den Titel „The Austrian Phenomenon" (Peter Cook, *Experimental Architecture*, New York, 1970). Der Aktionismus warf seine Schatten in die Architektur und die Gruppe Salz der Erde bezeichnete ihre Filme und Aktionen als politisch. Die Selbstsicherheit und das Sendungsbewusstsein der ‚jungen Wilden' strebten dem Höhepunkt zu. Hans Hollein, Walter Pichler und Günther Feuerstein hatten bereits die Kontrolle über ihre Zauberlehrlinge verloren. Holleins „fragmentarische Anmerkungen eines Beteiligten" (*Bau* 1971) wirkten in ihrem Versuch, eine historische Kontinuität der Nachkriegsdiskussion herzustellen, fast schon wie ein Griff nach der Notbremse.

mission of the 'young and wild' was heading for the climax. Hans Hollein, Walter Pichler and Günther Feuerstein had already lost control over their sorcerer's apprentices. In his attempt to establish a historical continuity of the postwar discussion, Hollein's "Fragmentarische Anmerkungen eines Beteiligtens" ("Fragmentary Notes of a Participant") (*Bau* 1971) nearly had the effect of a grab for the emergency brake.

And Hermann Czech is so brazen and writes about the good old architecture that only has to remain in the background after all. Actually, one would have to place him on a pedestal for doing that; because he knew everything back then already and because he is immune to fashionable streaks. Why I mention the 'pedestal' merely as a possibility, however, refers to the rather lonely and individual aspect of this statement. The successful persons namely looked indignantly away during all the experiments and the younger ones at the universities followed in quick succession in imitating what they found in the media. The fact that some of them have seamlessly become 'alternative' and 'participatory' in the meantime is only an indication that a whole generation missed out on architecture.

Czech and several others of the 'deferred generation,' who are on average ten years younger than the pioneers of Austrian postwar architecture who have predominantly been raised to the level of professors, all of a sudden found themselves between the fronts. The 'deferred' were animated by the heroes and driven into a Kafkaesque father-son relationship in order to ultimately be demoted to water boys or to be reprimanded in the case of possible independent achievements.

Und da ist Hermann Czech so frech und schreibt über die gute alte Architektur, die doch nur Hintergrund zu bleiben hat. Dafür müsste man ihn eigentlich nachträglich auf den Sockel heben; dass er alles damals schon gewusst hat und dass er vor modischen Anflügen gefeit ist. Warum ich aber den ‚Sockel' nur als Möglichkeit bezeichne, bezieht sich auf den eher einsamen und individuellen Aspekt dieser Aussage. Die Arrivierten schauten nämlich bei all den Experimenten indigniert weg und die Jüngeren an den Hochschulen überschlugen sich in der Nachahmung dessen, was sie in den Medien fanden. Dass einige von ihnen inzwischen nahtlos ‚alternativ' und ‚partizipatorisch' geworden sind, ist nur ein Indiz dafür, dass eine ganze Generation die Architektur versäumt hat.

Czech und einige andere der ‚verschobenen Generation', die im Schnitt zehn Jahre jünger sind als die mehrheitlich in den Professorenstand abgehobene Pioniergarde der österreichischen Nachkriegsarchitektur, fanden sich auf einmal zwischen den Fronten. Die ‚Verschobenen' wurden von den Helden animiert und in ein kafkaeskes Vater-Sohn-Verhältnis getrieben, um letztlich zu Wasserträgern degradiert oder bei eventuellen selbständigen Leistungen getadelt zu werden.

Wer also nicht das Brandzeichen der Holzmeister-Schule trug oder zumindest den Hochschuladel erlangte, blieb suspekt. Das führte soweit, dass Czechs *Zur Abwechslung* geschriebene Texte zur Architektur, die immerhin einen Zeitraum von 15 Jahren umfassen und 1978 herausgekommen sind (bei Löcker, Wien), entweder mit peinlichem Schweigen oder spöttischer Ironie bedacht wurden.

Warum ich das alles erzähle? Weil die Meister inzwischen als Lehrer an den Hochschulen sitzen und beseelt sind von der Multiplikation ihrer Lehre. Dort läuft es nicht so, wie sie es gerne hätten, da sich nach dem Interregnum der architektonischen Verweigerung eine neue Generation von Studenten herausgebildet hat. Diese ist unbelastet von den historisch gewordenen

Whoever did not carry the brand mark of the Holzmeister School or at least attain academic nobility remained suspicious. That led so far that Czech's texts on architecture, which he wrote *For a Change*, encompassing a time period of 15 years after all and published in 1978 (by Löcker, Vienna), were either met with embarrassing silence or deriding irony.

Why am I explaining all of this? Because the masters are meanwhile sitting as teachers at the universities and are impressed by the multiplication of their teaching. But it is not running there the way they would have liked to have it, because the architectural refusal of a new generation of students has evolved after the interregnum. This generation is unburdened by the now-historical achievements of the masters and, free of father conflicts, looks around in the landscape. And there, unexpectedly factual, the works of Hermann Czech, Boris Podrecca, Heinz Tesar, Luigi Blau and Missing Link will be taken as the benchmarks of one's own work. (I purposely name several names here, since these denote the current situation. New ones can already join in tomorrow and a monthly magazine is, after all, no Gotha of architecture).

What is essential thereby is that the point of view and the theoretical interest of the young have shifted. At this juncture I would maintain that the 'deferred generation' has not really noticed at all yet that it has advanced to become 'secret teachers'. Of course, there are still several among the old masters who they can congenially put on the shelf there. Strangely enough, they do not find themselves under the institutionalized pressure of the multiplication of their teaching. (Is it due to the state-supporting importance of universities, to bureaucracy or even to the calming granting of tenure?) I would thereby like to only point, for instance, to the talent pool of Gunther Wawrik and/or Hans Puchhammer, which one can almost label as a private school. Johann Georg Gsteu and Friedrich Achleitner have also

> And another weak point of Czech's is openly visible: His actual significance, which can be explained by the most unseemly connection that architecture knows: the simultaneity of historical research and the development of an architectonic theory.

Leistungen der Meister und schaut sich, frei von Vaterkonflikten, in der Landschaft um. Und da werden unerwartet sachlich die Arbeiten von Hermann Czech, Boris Podrecca, Heinz Tesar, Luigi Blau und Missing Link zum Maßstab der eigenen Arbeiten genommen. (Ich nenne hier absichtlich einige Namen, da diese die aktuelle Situation kennzeichnen. Schon morgen können neue dazutreten, und eine Monatszeitschrift ist schließlich kein Gotha der Architektur).

Wesentlich dabei ist, dass sich bei den Jungen der Blickwinkel und das theoretische Interesse verschoben haben. Ich würde an dieser Stelle behaupten, dass die ‚verschobene Generation' noch gar nicht richtig be-

succeeded in preventing the senescence through recognition. The most offensive among the secret teachers is, without a doubt, Hermann Czech. Writing about him equates to an expedition into the Viennese sewer system. The rats are lurking everywhere and the sardonically grinning swill of this city's self-proclaimed cultural scene washes around one's boots.

In the spring of this year, Czech was a participant in the much-noticed exhibition *A New Wave of Austrian Architecture*, which was organized by the Institute for Architecture and Urban Studies in New York and wandered through ten American universities. Shortly thereafter, a contribution to the otherwise conceptless *Forum Design* in Linz followed, and one will also be able to view Czech's work (together with Heinz Tesar's and Boris Podrecca's) at this year's Biennale in Venice. These are all signs that mark an escape attempt from the warm room of Viennese silence. A silence that hands down verdicts on the quiet: Hermann Czech's works are thus labeled as 'overstrung like secondary literature'; he is accused of 'penetrating obsession' and a 'Viennese provincial nostalgia.' All of them are verdicts that ultimately concern each one of those in this city who do not take up flight into refusal or seek refuge in meaninglessness.

And another weak point of Czech's is openly visible: His actual significance, which can be explained by the most unseemly connection that architecture knows: the simultaneity of historical research and the development of an architectonic theory. Seeing that he still builds in addition to that, he already exceeds the rules of the standstill agreement. Theory is measured on what is built and, moreover, it is still asked to what extent those he has devoted his explorer heart to look over his shoulder when he designs. A double inspection, therefore, which no one so quickly exposes himself/herself to.

merkt hat, dass sie zu ‚geheimen Lehrern' avanciert ist. Natürlich gibt es unter den Altmeistern noch einige, die sich da kongenial zur Seite stellen können. Eigenartigerweise befinden sie sich nicht unter dem institutionalisierten Druck der Multiplikation ihrer Lehre. (Liegt's an der staatstragenden Bedeutung der Hochschulen, am Bürokratismus oder gar an der beruhigenden Pragmatisierung?) Hinweisen möchte ich dabei nur zum Beispiel auf die Talenteschmiede von Gunther Wawrik und/oder Hans Puchhammer, die man fast als Privatschule bezeichnen kann. Auch Johann Georg Gsteu und Friedrich Achleitner ist die Hintanhaltung der Vergreisung durch Anerkennung gelungen. Am offensivsten unter den geheimen Lehrern ist zweifellos Hermann Czech. Über ihn zu schreiben gleicht damit einer Expedition ins Wiener Kanalsystem. Überall lauern die Ratten, und die hämisch grinsende Brühe der selbsternannten Kulturszene dieser Stadt umspült die Stiefel.

Czech war im Frühjahr dieses Jahres Teilnehmer der vielbeachteten Ausstellung *A New Wave of Austrian Architecture*, die vom New Yorker Institute for Architecture and Urban Studies veranstaltet wurde und durch zehn amerikanische Hochschulen wanderte. Kurz darauf folgte ein Beitrag beim ansonsten konzeptlosen *Forum Design* in Linz, und auch bei der diesjährigen Biennale von Venedig wird man Czechs Arbeiten (zusammen mit denen Heinz Tesars und Boris Podreccas) besichtigen können. Alles Zeichen, die einen Ausbruchsversuch aus der Wärmestube des Wiener Schweigens markieren. Ein Schweigen, das hinter vorgehaltener Hand die Urteile fällt: So werden die Arbeiten von Hermann Czech als ‚überkandidelt wie Sekundärliteratur' bezeichnet, ihm werden ‚penetrante Obsession' und eine ‚Wiener Provinznostalgie' vorgeworfen. Allesamt Urteile, die letztlich jeden betreffen, der in dieser Stadt nicht die Flucht in die Verweigerung antritt oder in der Bedeutungslosigkeit Zuflucht sucht.

Werbeinserat · Print ad Löcker Verlag. Archive DS

In collaboration with the ambitious publisher Löcker Verlag, he was able (together with Wolfgang Mistelbauer) to publish the study on the Looshaus (1976). I already mentioned his selected writings, and a three-volume work on Josef Frank, which Czech is likewise supervising, is to appear soon.

I have to point out these merits, since draining the swamp of ignorance will not succeed otherwise. An attempt at bending back snap judgments ought to therefore be allowed here. This is necessary in light of the saturated complacency of the masters and those young 'modernists,' who have laid their private parts in the beds of the large offices. A blink of the eye barely lets them know that the "New York Five" attained *Spiegel* honors and Aldo Rossi's Teatro del Mondo for Venice was announced in *Playboy*.

Surrounded by this ignorance, Hermann Czech sits in a devastated attic studio—not unlike Josef Frank—and tortures clients and craftsmen to the point of self-flagellation with nothing other than architecture.

Und noch ein Angriffspunkt liegt bei Czech offen zutage: Seine eigentliche Bedeutung, die sich aus der unschicklichsten Verbindung erklärt, die die Architektur kennt. Die Gleichzeitigkeit von historischer Forschung und der Entwicklung einer architektonischen Theorie. Da er zudem noch baut, überzieht er bereits die Regeln des Stillhalteabkommens. Die Theorie wird am Gebauten gemessen und zudem wird noch gefragt, inwieweit ihm jene, denen er sein Forscherherz gewidmet hat, beim Entwurf über die Schulter schauen. Eine doppelte Kontrolle also, der sich so schnell niemand aussetzt.

In Zusammenarbeit mit dem ambitionierten Löcker-Verlag konnte er (gemeinsam mit Wolfgang Mistelbauer) die Studie über das Looshaus veröffentlichen (1976). Seine ausgewählten Schriften habe ich schon erwähnt und demnächst soll ein dreibändiges Werk über Josef Frank erscheinen, das ebenfalls von Czech betreut wird.

Ich muss auf diese Verdienste hinweisen, da es ansonsten nicht gelingt, den Sumpf der Ignoranz trocken zu legen. Ein Versuch der Zurückbeugung von Blitzurteilen soll also hier erlaubt sein. Dies ist notwendig angesichts der saturierten Selbstzufriedenheit der Meister und jener jungen ‚Modernen', die ihre Weichteile in den Betten der Großbüros zur Ruhe gelegt haben. Ein kurzes Blinzeln mit den Wimpern teilt ihnen gerade noch mit, dass die „New York Five" zu *Spiegel*-Ehren gelangten und Aldo Rossis Teatro del Mondo für Venedig im *Playboy* angekündigt wurde.

Umgeben von dieser Ignoranz sitzt Hermann Czech in einem devastierten Dachatelier – Josef Frank nicht unähnlich – und quält Bauherren und Handwerker bis zur Selbstzerfleischung mit nichts anderem als Architektur.

Commitment to the Big City

The opposite standpoint to Hermann Czech's reproached obsession is most easily recognizable here. He demands from urban construction "… a convention that, like in the old city, creates a matter-of-fact framework, absent of 'ideas,' that can give variety to the individual building—and may even yield an architectural work of art." ("Towards a New City" in *Zur Abwechslung*)

A position that wasn't invented by Rob and Léon Krier in the mid-70s after all and is currently rearing its ugly head at the International Building Exhibition in Berlin (1984); —Czech wrote these lines in 1966.

In all the topicality of this self-evident idea, one thing ought not to be forgotten: In Hermann Czech's imagination—in contrast to the many restorative-evolutionary proposals common today—the technological contingency of the present and the experiences of 20th century architecture are always distinguishable as well. It is almost embarrassing to have to specially point this out, but too many unreflective and ahistorical reveries are currently dominating the market of architectural ideas. Whoever wants to convince oneself only needs to leaf through the respective international architecture magazines. In return, the Viennese deliberations on the big city, not only by Czech alone, have been lying around, disregarded, for nearly 20 years. And in their pragmatic reason they are nonetheless current as never before. Czech's truly splendid analysis of the Wagnerian big-city concept based on the Vienna Metropolitan Railway, written in the 1960s, and its continuation through the work of Missing Link in the past years, is not even acknowledged, as daily life proves. The self-sufficient city administration sees its once-in-a-century project in switching the venerable Metropolitan Railway to a subway operation, erecting VÖEST prefabricated houses as barriers against the exodus of potent classes, and lets urban renovation be managed over the car telephones of the building tycoons.

Bekenntnis zur Großstadt

Hier ist am leichtesten die Gegenposition zur vorgeworfenen Obsession von Hermann Czech erkennbar. Er fordert vom Bauen in der Stadt „… eine Konvention, die wie in der alten Großstadt ohne ‚Einfälle' einen selbstverständlichen Rahmen schafft, den das einzelne Haus – auch als architektonisches Kunstwerk – variieren kann."

Eine Position, die also nicht von Rob und Léon Krier Mitte der siebziger Jahre erfunden wurde und die derzeit bei der Internationalen Bauausstellung in Berlin (1984) fröhliche Urständ feiert; – Czech schrieb diese Zeilen 1966.

Bei aller Aktualität dieser selbstverständlichen Idee sollte auf eines nicht vergessen werden: Bei Hermann Czechs Vorstellung sind – und das zum Unterschied zu vielen heute gängigen restaurativ-revolutionären Vorschlägen – immer auch die technologische Bedingtheit der Gegenwart und die Erfahrungen der Architektur des 20. Jahrhunderts erkennbar. Es ist fast beschämend, dies extra anführen zu müssen, aber zu viele unreflektierte und geschichtslose Träumereien beherrschen derzeit den Markt der architektonischen Ideen. Wer sich davon überzeugen will, braucht nur in einschlägigen internationalen Architekturmagazinen nachblättern. Dafür liegen die Wiener Überlegungen zur Großstadt, nicht nur von Czech allein, seit fast zwanzig Jahren unbeachtet herum. Und sind trotzdem in ihrer pragmatischen Vernunft aktuell wie nie zuvor. Czechs wirklich prächtige Analyse der Wagner'schen Großstadtidee anhand der Wiener Stadtbahn, in den sechziger Jahren geschrieben, und deren Fortsetzung durch die Arbeiten von Missing Link in den letzten Jahren, all dies wird nicht einmal zur Kenntnis genommen, wie der Alltag beweist. Die selbstgenügsame Stadtverwaltung sieht ihr Jahrhundertwerk darin, dass sie die ehrwürdige Stadtbahn auf U-Bahn-Betrieb umstellt, VÖEST-Fertighäuser als Barriere gegen die Abwanderung potenter Schichten errichtet, und die Stadtsanierung über die Autotelefone der Baulöwen erledigen lässt.

Im Vorwort zu seinen Schriften klingt bei Hermann Czech die diesbezügliche Resignation durch:

In the preface to his writings, Hermann Czech's resignation in this respect comes through:

"My engagement with Vienna took a hypothetical big-city concept as a basis; now I doubt whether such an idea is viable at all and in Vienna of all places." There is nothing more to add to this. Hermann Czech's big-city concept is warmly recommended to students and historians. Too many officially missed chances can be read in it.

Marauders and impostors rule the city and the serious architects are migrating to the inner and outer periphery. Small installations, shops, galleries and cafés in the city and several objects on the outskirts. "Little architecture" in the cracks, which leave the big distributors to remain. Architecture as the culture of a minority. The trained and unerring sense of style of punching dolls and district mayors takes care of the huge remainder. Under these portents, architecture is better off in the media on the domestic politics pages after all.

The Effect of the Point

One of the Hermann Czech's father figures is undoubtedly Konrad Wachsmann. During his American emigration he worked together with Walter Gropius on problems of prefabrication and the industrialization of building. As of 1956 he was a teacher at the Salzburg Summer Academy for a few years and had a great influence on modern Austrian architecture after the war.

Wachsmann's rational methodology, in particular, is echoed in Hermann Czech. The solution to a problem is initially sought on the level of the quantifiability of the conditions and requirements. A rationality of the procedure that is missing in many of today's solutions; especially when architecture seeks refuge in private formalisms and only finds its comprehensibility in the

„Meiner Auseinandersetzung mit Wien lag eine hypothetische Großstadtidee zugrunde; nun bezweifle ich, ob eine solche Vorstellung überhaupt und gar in Wien tragfähig ist." Dem ist nichts mehr hinzuzufügen. Studenten und Historikern sei die Großstadtidee von Hermann Czech ans Herz gelegt. Zu viele offiziell verpasste Chancen sind daran ablesbar.

Plünderer und Gaukler beherrschen die Stadt und die seriösen Architekten wandern ab, in die innere und äußere Peripherie. Kleine Einbauten, Geschäfte, Galerien und Cafés in der Stadt und einige Objekte am Stadtrand. „Little architecture" in den Ritzen, die die großen Verteiler übrig lassen. Architektur als Kultur einer Minderheit. Den großen Rest besorgt das geschulte und untrügliche Stilempfinden von Watschenmännern und Bezirksvorstehern. Unter diesen Vorzeichen ist die Architektur in den Medien doch besser auf den Seiten der Innenpolitik aufgehoben.

Die Wirkung des Punktes

Eine der Vaterfiguren Hermann Czechs ist zweifellos Konrad Wachsmann. Dieser arbeitete in der amerikanischen Emigration mit Walter Gropius zusammen an Problemen der Vorfertigung und Industrialisierung des Bauwesens. Ab 1956 war er einige Jahre Lehrer an der Salzburger Sommerakademie und übte dadurch einen großen Einfluss auf die österreichische moderne Architektur nach dem Krieg aus.

Bei Hermann Czech findet sich vor allem die rationale Methodik Wachsmanns wieder. Die Lösung eines Problems wird zunächst auf der Ebene der Quantifizierbarkeit der Bedingungen und Anforderungen gesucht. Eine Rationalität des Verfahrens, die viele heutige Lösungen vermissen lassen; vor allem dann, wenn sich die Architektur in private Formalismen flüchtet und sich ihre Nachvollziehbarkeit nur mehr in den psychischen Komponenten des Entwerfers findet. Mit Wachsmann as a role model, Czech's intensive work method is also explainable. His optimization of details that frequently lose any actual scale in their importance and only serve to illustrate a principle of the solution. If one wants it that way, one can explain it with the notion of appropriateness: How much attention does a point, which only appears in an object perhaps a single time, deserve? Is it necessary then to dedicate so much energy and intensity of work to it as if it had to go into production? "… don't give every point the same attention and value …," Hollein once formulated. Which promptly brought him Czech's response: "Doing nothing somewhere over a long period of time is not possible with these jobs, because there are no long periods of time." Czech refers thereby to the 'little jobs' he had to deal with up to now. Naturally, the principal problem of architectural work is thus faced. The available potential is a constant size; the scale and magnitude of the jobs are variable.

Bar Palais Schwarzenberg, 1982–84. © Architekturzentrum Wien, Sammlung · Collection, Margherita Spiluttini

Wachsmann als Vorbild ist auch Czechs intensive Arbeitsmethode erklärbar. Seine Optimierung von Details, die oftmals in ihrer Bedeutung jeden tatsächlichen Maßstab verlieren und nur mehr zur Darstellung eines Prinzips der Lösung dienen. Man kann dies, wenn man so will, mit dem Begriff der Angemessenheit erklären: Wie viel Aufmerksamkeit verdient ein Punkt, der in einem Objekt vielleicht nur ein einziges Mal vorkommt. Ist es dann notwendig, ihm soviel Energie und Intensität der Arbeit widmen, als müsste er in Serie gehen? „… nicht jedem Punkt dieselbe Aufmerksamkeit und Wertigkeit geben …", hat es Hollein einmal formuliert. Was ihm prompt die Antwort von Czech einbrachte: „Irgendwo über eine weitere Strecke nichts zu tun, ist bei diesen Aufgaben nicht möglich, weil es keine weiteren Strecken gibt." Czech bezieht sich dabei auf die ‚kleinen Aufgaben', mit denen er bisher zu tun hatte. Natürlich stellt sich so das prinzipielle Problem der architektonischen Arbeit. Das zur Verfügung stehende Potenzial ist eine konstante Größe, Ausmaß und Größenordnung der Aufgaben sind variabel.

Womit einem Sessel die gleiche Intensität zur Verfügung steht wie einem städtebaulichen Problem. Eine natürliche Grenze der Leistungsfähigkeit, die den Vorwurf an bestimmte Dimensionen von Planungen beinhaltet? Auf dem Schreibtisch von Stadtrat Zilk steht das Modell der UNO-City als Briefbeschwerer. Das filigrane Ornament der Anlage zeigt in diesem Maßstab seine ganze Schwächlichkeit und formale Lächerlichkeit deutlich. Damit ist der Beweis erbracht, dass es auch im Maßstab 1:1 nicht besser wird. Es fehlt ihm einfach jene Zurückhaltung und städtebauliche Selbstverständlichkeit, die einem Bauwerk dieser Größenordnung angemessen wäre. Auf dieses Monster in Transdanubien trifft eben genau nicht zu, was Czech in einem Bonmot über die Ringstraße formulierte: „Von ihr kann man behaupten, dass es ein Fehler war, das Glacis zu bebauen. Aber wenn Fehler einmal diesen Maßstab einer Stadtentwicklung erreichen, dann sind es keine Fehler mehr, dann werden sie Geschichte."

"… to make a space in such a way as if it had always been like that."

Whereby a chair has the same intensity at its disposal as an urban planning problem. A natural limit of effectiveness that contains the reproach to certain dimensions of planning? The model of the UNO City stands on City Councilor Zilk's desk as a paperweight. At this scale, the filigree ornament of the complex clearly shows its entire weakness and formal ridiculousness. The proof is thus furnished that it also does not become better on a 1:1 scale. It is simply lacking that reservation and urbanistic implicitness which would be appropriate for a structure of this magnitude. What Czech formulated in a bon mot about the Ringstrasse precisely *does not* apply to this monster in Transdanubia: "One can argue that it was a mistake to develop the Glacis. But if mistakes once reach this scale of urban development, then they are no longer mistakes, they become history."

Wachsmann's method of the quantifiability of problems also appears in Czech's works in the calculation of their *effect*. The conditions for solving a problem listed by Wachsmann often remain mired in technological details. In Czech's case I assume that he has expanded this method by the elements of vision, meaning and effect.

Bar Palais Schwarzenberg, 1982–84. © Architekturzentrum Wien, Sammlung · Collection, Margherita Spiluttini

Wachsmanns Methode der Quantifizierbarkeit von Problemen tritt bei Czech auch in der Kalkulation der Wirkung seiner Arbeiten auf. Die von Wachsmann erfassten Bedingungen zur Lösung eines Problems bleiben oftmals im Technologischen stecken. Bei Czech vermute ich, dass er diese Methode um die Elemente der Anschauung, Bedeutung und Wirkung erweitert hat.

„Das was ich als Wirkung erreichen will, kann ich exakt zum Thema der architektonischen Erörterung machen." Die Konsequenz dieser Erörterung lautet bei Czech dann so, dass „… jedes Problem, das sich stellt, so gelöst werden muss, dass es überall auftreten kann …". Als Zielvorstellung gerinnt die Methode zum ästhetischen Programm und er wünscht sich „… einen Raum so zu machen, als wäre er immer schon so gewesen." Begriffe wie *immer* und *überall* verweisen auf einen universalen Standpunkt, dem jede marktschreierische Einmaligkeit fremd ist. Nicht elitär, sondern allgemein, nicht teuer, sondern arm, Beiläufigkeit und nicht Überraschung – so könnten die Werte des ästhetischen Ziels bezeichnet werden.

"What I want to achieve as an effect is what I can exactly make as the subject of architectonic consideration." The consequence of this consideration then sounds in the case of Czech that "… every problem that arises must be solved in such a fashion that it can appear everywhere …" As the objective, the method congeals into an aesthetic program and he wishes "… to make a space in such a way as if it had always been like that." Notions like *always* and *everywhere* point to the universal stance that is alien to any gimmicky uniqueness. Not elitist, but general; not expensive, but poor; casualness and not surprise—that's how the values of the aesthetic goal could be described.

At this point I would like to dare to make a hypothetical comparison to Hollein: The most beautiful stage set in his Schnitzler excursion at the Burgtheater was that brief moment towards the end of the first act, when the sterility and coldness, the staged demise, became a real

Galerie Hummel, 1978–80. © Architekturzentrum Wien, Sammlung · Collection, Margherita Spiluttini

Ich möchte an dieser Stelle einen hypothetischen Vergleich zu Hollein wagen: Das schönste Bühnenbild in seiner Schnitzler-Exkursion ans Burgtheater war jener kurze Moment gegen Ende des ersten Aktes, als die Sterilität und Kälte, der inszenierte Untergang, ein tatsächlicher wurde. Das alles bedeckende Zelt schwebte zu Boden. Die überrascht geöffneten Münder des Publikums schluckten den aufgewirbelten Staub und ein verhaltenes Hüsteln beantwortete diesen Akt der Zerstörung.

Das Gegenbeispiel: Der Eingangsstufe zur Galerie Hummel hat Hermann Czech unendliche Aufmerksamkeit und Arbeit gewidmet, damit sie den Zustand des Gebrauchs erreicht. Die abgeschliffene Stufe inszeniert diesen Zustand bevor dieser eigentlich eintritt.

Czechs Konzept einer „Architektur, die nur spricht, wenn sie gefragt wird", erfordert einen hohen Arbeitseinsatz des Architekten, damit eben diese Arbeit, die an

one. The tent that covered everything floated to the floor. The surprisingly open mouths of the audience swallowed the stirred up dust and a restrained coughing answered this act of destruction.

The counterexample: Hermann Czech devoted endless attention and work to the entry stairs to Galerie Hummel so that they reach the condition of usage. The polished stairs stage this condition before it actually occurs.

Czech's concept of "architecture that only speaks when it is asked" requires a high work effort of the architect so that precisely this work which was performed on an object is not recognizable at first glance and remains background. In contrast, Hollein's act of destruction has to be dramatized because its architecture "speaks to you also without being asked." It rams a hawker's tray full of images into your body and you can no longer choose between similarly clamoring sensa-

einem Objekt geleistet wurde, nicht auf den ersten Blick erkennbar ist, Hintergrund bleibt. Demgegenüber muss Holleins Akt der Zerstörung dramatisiert werden, weil seine Architektur „mit dir spricht, auch ohne gefragt zu werden". Sie rammt dir einen Bauchladen voller Bilder in den Leib und du kannst nur mehr zwischen gleichermaßen schreienden Sensationen wählen. Bei Hollein ein begriffsloses Staunen, das dich auf die Schubladen deiner Bildung festnagelt. Jede weitere Interpretation fordert den Marsch von Leistungsstufe zu Leistungsstufe, um den Zenit der Architektur zu erreichen – Sarastro wird dich dort gütig empfangen.

Ich würde nicht über Hermann Czech schreiben, wenn mir das beiläufige, zwanglose Gespräch seiner Architektur nicht lieber wäre. Seine Architektur erzählt Geschichten, die ich nicht hören muss. (So wie die Aussparungen in den Sitzen des *invisible cinema* von Peter Kubelka den Ellbogenkontakt mit dem Nachbarn ermöglichen, aber nicht vorschreiben.) Das *zwanglose Gespräch* ist *die* unaktuellste, aber menschlichste Sache schlechthin. Es entzieht sich dem Markt – auch dem Markt der Architektur – und wirft den architektonischen Zweck auf seinen eigentlichen Nutzer, den Menschen, zurück. Die Rücknahme gemachter Arbeit im Ergebnis, die dienende Funktion mit dem Ziel der Ableugnung des Urhebers. „Stille Architektur", um einen Begriff zu erfinden, die eine Auseinandersetzung auf den zweiten Blick verlangt und sich der gängigen und brüllenden Hysterie einer alles überbietenden Einmaligkeit entzieht.

Und wenn du an einem trostlosen Nachmittag in der noch nicht überfüllten Wunderbar sitzt, bewegen sich deine Gedanken langsam in den Garten der Lüste. Da entlockt dir der ‚kleine Unterschied' der männlichen und weiblichen Beine der Sitzbank gegenüber ein leichtes Schmunzeln. In diesem Augenblick hast du mit der Architektur gesprochen – sie war dein *Hintergrund*. Alles andere ist *nicht* Architektur.

tions. In Hollein's case an amazement devoid of notion, which nails you to the drawers of your education. Each further interpretation demands the march from achievement level to achievement level in order to reach the zenith of architecture—Sarastro will benevolently receive you there.

I would not write about Hermann Czech if I did not prefer the casual, relaxed conversation of his architecture. His architecture tells stories that I do not *have to* hear. (Just like the recesses in the seats of Peter Kubelka's *Invisible Cinema* enables, but does not prescribe elbow contact with the neighbor.) The *casual conversation* is *the* most un-current, but most human thing. It eludes the market—the market of architecture, too—and reflects the architectonic purpose back to its actual user, the human being. The revocation of done work in the result, the serving function with the goal of repudiating the originator. "Quiet architecture," in order to invent a term, which calls for an examination at second glance and evades the usual and screaming hysteria of an all-surpassing uniqueness.

And if you sit on a dreary afternoon in the not yet overfilled Wunderbar, your thoughts slowly move into the garden of earthly delights. The 'small difference' of the masculine and feminine legs of the bench seat across from you will elicit a slight smirk. At this instant you have spoken with the architecture—it was your *background*. Everything else is *not* architecture.

Film *Blade Runner*, DVD-Kassette mit allen Editionen des Films · DVD box set with all editions of the film. © Tom Kussin

Translation by Brian Dorsey

"In the Jungle of the Future"

We find ourselves approaching a big city, Los Angeles for example. Night-black sky. We are floating past billowing smokestacks in a machine that seems to have been rigged together. Appearing on the horizon are four-hundred-story-high building pyramids, shrouded in a web made of steel struts and installation cables. Deep below, in the streets of the cities, a humid and moist atmosphere surrounds us; we encounter people with glowing umbrellas rushing past the rubbish heap in a stop-and-go, beeping traffic chaos. In the houses we will find cast iron elevators and the halls of the 19th century, as well as halls with Egyptian palm columns in front of large glass walls with automatic blinds. We will be allowed to take a quick look at the façade of a Frank Lloyd Wright building, and old-fashioned propeller fans rotate above futuristic gadgetry.

Only by a few indications in the descriptions of these images is it recognizable that the film *Blade Runner* moves us into the year 2019 and accordingly wants to be understood as a so-called science-fiction film. A categorization that is just as unessential as the comic strip story of the simple-minded plot proclaiming American philosophical pragmatism. It is explained with one sentence: Artificial people, conceived by a highly developed genetic technology, embark on a search for their nonexistent past. *Blade Runner*, however, is one of the most important architecture films since Fritz Lang's *Metropolis* (the trained architect Lang shot it together with Otto Hunte, Erich Kettelhut and Karl Vollbrecht in 1926). Revolutionary in the almost scientific meticulousness with which our present-day appearance of the environment was "extrapolated" by approximately 40 years, *Blade Runner* makes references to many avant-garde designs of contemporary architects in the category of exerted, but anachronistic misspeculation.

The rather one-dimensionally oriented American film industry has had a cuckoo's egg laid into its nest by the English director Ridley Scott and the design specialists Douglas Trumbull and Syd Mead, one that merely misleads them to the succinct conclusion that it is a question here of "Hollywood's first realistic science-fiction film." In truth, Ridley Scott has packed an improbable number of messages about aesthetic and technological developments—including their societal use—in his cascade of images, and I even indeed contend that the conceptual design of the film constitutes an essential contribution to architectural-theoretical discussion.

With which intention and tendency Ridley Scott stylizes the "constructed story" of the film's main actor demands a closer inspection. In this film we do not find ourselves in any synthetic, futuristic environment in which everything glitters and flashes, in which everything was newly invented, in which there are no witnesses of the past and therefore no future as well. The street scenes already alluded to were shot on the Burbank Studios lot. This is the home of the famous "New York Street," built in 1929, which provided the backdrop for many film noir movies, the gangster flicks with Humphrey Bogart or James Cagney. Images of New York, Hong Kong, Tokyo's Ginza District, Milan's business center and, finally, elements of London's Piccadilly Circus were fitted into this street like found pieces, souvenirs of a journey around the world. With this production, Ridley Scott, on the one hand, pays his respects to a document of cinematic history, but, on the other hand, to the internationalization of Hollywood as well, which can only sell a product with references to reinvigorated "local" cultures.

Blade Runner provides the actual and primarily superficial evidence of the designation "architecture film" with the subjects of the exterior shots. Three buildings that actually exist in Los Angeles play along. Frank Lloyd Wright's Ennis-Brown House, erected in 1924, makes its façade available for the main character's apartment. Wright used the "textile block" here, an ornamental concrete block that is only cited in the design of the interior spaces and creates an archaic atmosphere that contrasts with the high-tech furnishing. The second building is the Union Station, a monument of American railroad architecture planned by John and Donald Parkinson and Herman Sacks in 1938: a type of cathedral of the machine age, featuring a bell tower and a main entrance, attributed to Art Deco, and its atmospheric, nearly sacred inner space functions as a reception hall of the special police operatives called "Blade Runners." The Bradbury Building, designed in 1893 by then-32-year-old George Wyman, a big city office tower of the 19th century with a glass-covered inner courtyard and delicate cast-iron constructions, ultimately plays a real main role. In the movie it is the residence of the "genetic designer," filled with quirky human inventions, and then again abandoned suites of rooms full of wistful nostalgia.

No doubt: *Blade Runner*, a science-fiction film, also plays in historical settings. This initially means nothing other than the fact that the designers assumed that a completely new world will not emerge before our very eyes in 40 years, but that many houses, cars and everyday things already—or still—existing today will be in use. The structures, monuments, of architectural history are, however, no synthetically maintained objects of study. Devastated at times, made to serve new functions.

Up to this point the film would merely be the "realistic, extrapolated" everyday life of the year 2019. The buildings, however, are

Dritter Tag · Day Three

Zur ersten Ausstellung von Zaha Hadid an der Architectural Association London erschien ein Katalog als Kassette eines LP-Albums – mit Bildern ihrer Air-Brush-Entwürfe und ihrem postmodernen Bekenntnis zur Architektur des sowjetischen Konstruktivismus · For Zaha Hadid's first exhibition at the Architectural Association London a catalog appeared as an LP album box—with images of her air-brush designs and her postmodern acknowledgement of Soviet constructivist architecture. © Tom Kussin

Translation by Brian Dorsey

"Futuristic Plagiarisms in an Apocalyptic Mood"

London in the fall of 1983 essentially presents itself no different than ten years before; one still finds the unobtrusive, self-evident and often merely banal architecture of simple residential buildings, checked off as "must-sees" by many architecture excursions in the seventies. A lot of dreamed architecture is still being drawn, more is being written, lectured and published about architecture than elsewhere. Everything has tradition here, even modernism, as soon as it is equated with quick zeitgeist interpretations. Fashion and music answer to this need probably more than the slow, built architecture. This is simply terribly normal or just as terribly rapid and superficial.

A report about contemporary new architecture in London thus unavoidably remains a conversation about fashion. And peculiar parallels result if one compares a T-shirt in the shop window of an exclusive London boutique with the huge new centers and office towers of this city: Both phenomena are morbid, brutal and angst-inducing. The London glitterati are processing the forms of punk and new Japanese fashion. They show themselves in artfully tattered, preferably black remnants of clothing, wear silver torture instruments as jewelry and loop stylized ammunition belts casually around their hips. On the other hand, the prevailing style of new London architecture—insofar as it sees itself as being professional—is regarded as a particularly extreme variant of "high tech." This is the abbreviation for high technology and wants to connote that the constructed outcomes have to possess a special "industrial" image.

This leads to the fact that Richard Rogers, for instance, is planning a supports-capsule-pipes-cocoon in the new construction of Lloyd's Insurance in Central London, whose support structure supposedly consists of steel columns encased in concrete that are again to be treated so that they look like steel columns. Because steel, wire and glass are the very modest repertoire of "high tech," where the proximity to technocratic rule is sought with obtrusive significance. In an all too blue-eyed manner the high-tech specialists are dreaming of calculable and projectable humans to whom they serve the machine-made kitsch from 1950s science fiction films. The pipe jungle of oil refineries is also gladly shown off as an emblematic background.

The cynical arrogance of these speculative buildings is especially absurd if one compares it with London fashion. Springing from a similar spirit, it is namely already a step farther than this architecture. Whoever sits in grey flannel in these fully air-conditioned glass cases doesn't know that it only takes a single angry and agitated punk who can throw the complete computerized façade energy program into the utmost state of confusion with one toss of a stone. The attire already tells of "The Day After;" when the survivors stagger through the destroyed city and brawl over the coal that still serves fashionable boutiques today as shop window decoration. Outrageously expensive paratrooper equipment, furnished as a survival kit with all hand-to-hand combat utensils, aesthetically spread that apocalyptic mood which is probably needed as the dialectic counterpart to an overly committed peace movement. The aggressiveness of fashion and speculative architecture carries itself forward in the once harmlessly burbling disco sound. Today one hears piercingly hard march sounds interrupted by machine gun salvos; and girls who are fitted out with sadomasochistic gear operate the control panels of the imposing spotlight batteries in these temples of decadence with their feet. Oddly fitting, Marinetti's futuristic manifesto could be declaimed at such places. The powerless anger of a street culture will be put on display by the glitterati in a cynically inflated way.

To die in beauty and to gain hope from the death wish seems to be an extremely current message. That's why it cannot be a coincidence that the culture of the Viennese fin-de-siècle finds such mindful attention in the whole world today. So a sincere and serious group of young architects and historians in London has surprisingly advanced into universally—also by the "building pros"—respected architectonic-moral authorities who possess a particularly exact knowledge of Viennese modernism and its themes. This group publishes a very theoretically-oriented magazine that carries the meaningfully title 9H: 9H is the designation for the hardest and therefore most precise pencil lead. The group advocates a rationality of architectonic experience, a general value system that does not shy away from realizing "big" messages in "small" solutions—whereby an affinity to new Viennese architecture, in turn, is given, which is very exactly followed in London. Beyond their own magazine, the people from 9H also enter into the current debate again and again with articles in other magazines, with talks, exhibitions and events.

The 9H team rightly sees the sense of architecture preserved in the realized object—and no matter how small it is—, so the hedonistic principle of the architectural drawing as an end in itself still prevails at the exclusive school of the Architectural Association. A large exhibition of the Iraqi architect Zaha Hadid, who lives in London, is currently taking place. Zaha Hadid studied at the Architectural Association and then worked at OMA—the Office of Metropolitan Architecture led by Rem Koolhaas and Elia Zenghelis. OMA was represented at the postmodern Biennale in Venice with a piece of the façade of the "strada novissima"

e, die die Ar-
undert einge-
de gegangene
denzen der
hat das noch
ist verspielt.
chitekten zwar
ber dem Lauf
tiker hat ein-
ittelalters die
s entgegenge-
. Jahrhundert
len zu wollen,
eit versanden.
t kann, führt
offenbar, was
uprüfen wäre,
neller Grund-
s Feststellung
ssen allzu eu-
enhofsiedlung,
vird Stuttgart
alismus erhal-
er Verhältnis-
des Schinkel-
arten mit dem
Dom, der zur
d.   gk

ander Freiherr
Martin Bruck-
n, Berlin (Vor-
Herbert Fecker,
tuttgart; Horst

Brawne, Lon-
Verner Krause,
lannheim; Karl

Additi...
Die klare Architektur de... ...en wird
durch Annexbauten (Störfaktoren) einerseits ge-
steigert, andererseits wird durch diese Elemente
der Anlage ein menschlicher Maßstab gegeben.
Der Entwurf wird mit seiner hohen architektonischen Qualität der gestellten Aufgabe für die
Staatsgalerie Stuttgart sowohl in formaler wie
auch in städtebaulicher Hinsicht überzeugend
gerecht..."

werte be...
nauer-Straße
die Gestaltung ...
Neubau-Anlage. Allerdi... ...ngs-
möglichkeit für Plastiken im Freien ...nt optimal gelöst...
Die innere Funktionsverteilung ist konsequent
... Das Projekt ist konstruktiv sehr klar aufgebaut. Die Gestaltung des Gebäudes ist bewußt
als ‚technisches Gerät, mit dem Museum und
Theater arbeiten können' vorgesehen."

3. Preis Wettbewerb Stuttgarter Staatsgalerie · 3rd prize of the Stuttgart State Gallery competition, Behnisch und Partner, Kammerer, Belz und Partner. © *Bauwelt* 40_1977

Translation by Brian Dorsey

"Everything Is Living Dead"

Since 1977, when the design competition was decided, James Stirling's project of the Neue Staatsgalerie Stuttgart has taken the center stage of a West German architectural debate in which the terms "democratic" or "fascist" architecture are to be clarified by simple formal attributions. The house has been opened. It has resolved the debate; ashamed are those who confused coming to terms with the past with suppression. Practically all of the neighboring country's media reported extensively, but these reports fluctuated between inhibited amusement and helplessly wondering ridicule.

What resulted was a gigantic popular success—one speaks of 25,000 visitors who storm the Neue Staatsgalerie on the weekends alone—, that cannot be explained solely by the outstanding collection and the free admission. The house itself certainly plays a role, and the uncertainty of the professional world, paired with the general attention, provokes the direct question about Big Jim Stirling's architectural "recipe." Let us briefly dwell on this term and search for the ingredients of this spicy feast for the eyes. Basically, one takes the classical museum type of the 19th century, a u-shaped complex with a rotunda at the center, and cites Schinkel's design for the Altes Museum in Berlin (1823-1830). One strips this of its base; the pointer to present-day reality is the underground garage with the installation rooms that forms the plinth. The rotunda now becomes "archeologized," grasses grow rampant in the exposed dome rim. Thinking back to the past, a portico is buried in its inner outdoor space; it may be Doric, even if its proportions are Egyptian. Then one takes a piece of modernism from the locality; a house of Le Corbusier in the Stuttgart Weissenhof Estate may appear reframed in a piece of the façade of the administration building. One could obtain the concrete mushroom columns from America, perhaps from Frank Lloyd Wright.

The unresolved German past—wherein the attack against Stirling is based—can be initially surveyed in the construction photos of the Nuremberg Reichsparteigelände (National Socialist Party Parade Grounds). Whereupon one definitively completes the—still?—anticipated ruin value; with a very thin natural stone facing, with open, cigarillo-wide joints. One then mixes in new brutalism in places. In exceptional cases with two opposing rainspouts in a narrow lane, instilling the architect with the fear of water. The flower power plastic world of "happy design," meanwhile banned by consumer protection, is not to be forgotten. With banging-red entrance drums, pink and bright blue balustrade hand rails and the bilious green rubber floor covering in the entrance foyer. And, finally, old and new constructivism in the mechanistic elevator monument and the oppressively oversized canopies may still be lent, for example, from the Centre Pompidou. Recent rationalistic super signs, the plaster façade with the square transom windows, are still added to the dish at the end as a current reference.

No cultural writer could previously elude passages such as these at the Stuttgart Staatsgalerie. Architectonic education can easily be put on parade here, the historic utilization of leftovers damned as substantial hopelessness or acclaimed as cheerful postmodernism.

Is Stirling's building set now really only a historic style game whose architectural quality is simply established in the virtuosic dealing with the signs? Here the cunning Englishman may know his critics; he directs the view towards the pictures and thereby offers endless writing material. He dedicates his actual game to the breaks in the scale, where inherently small details become big, condensed building elements and the dubiousness of those insignias, which would have had to mark the grandness and monumentality, are revealed. Here he is much finer and more intelligent than the Americans, than Michael Graves, Allan Greenberg or Charles Moore. In Stirling's case the architectonic value can still be recognized behind each "picture." The entire assemblage of the entrance foyer creates strongly differentiated places, whereas access to the arrangement of halls on the gallery floor is only provided via two inserted glass oriels.

The Stuttgart Staatsgalerie, however, is also a conclusive answer to the West German situation. The competition design was, as mentioned, also denounced as fascist. The counter-example was the design by Günter Behnisch, Hans Kammerer and Walter Belz. It wanted to be called democratic architecture; "no structure, but rather technical equipment," said its architects. In its anti-sensual enmity towards form, this ideology has the deadly German postwar reality to answer for. Stirling replies to its themes, its technocraticism, where a rubber dimpled floor covering and a colorful hand rail were already regarded as architecture.

In contrast, Stirling remembers that a museum is a museum, and not a department store. Precisely because sovereignty has meanwhile gathered in technoid reticence, it must be countered with sensual wit. A museum is and remains a monumental cultural task. The institution stays the same, even if it would hide behind a neutral, so-called democratic box. Monumentality per se, however, associates dignity and constancy, elucidates eternal values, regresses to a hierarchically closed, credible society that doesn't exist anymore, that cannot exist artistically. Therefore, this monumentality must be ironically refracted in its architectonic significance, if it doesn't want to fall victim to an unintentional comicality.

Dritter Tag · Day Three

IBA Neubau: „Wohnen am Berlin-Museum" · "Residential Park am Berlin Museum," Haus · House G, Berlin, Arata Isozaki, 1982–86. © DS

Translation by Brian Dorsey

"Islands in the City"

One cannot escape it, the IBA, the International Building Exhibition Berlin, and its Report Year 1984. At least the leaves are rustling in the autumn press. After all, there is no magazine dedicated to architecture, construction, habitation that would miss this event. "Berlin as a Model" is what the London *architectural review*, for instance, titled its special issue in order to then precisely name the gap between journalistic endeavor and constructed reality, between the visionary steps into the future of the city and the travail of everyday building problems "The milestone and the millstone."

IBA on site; that is what one program point in Berlin is called. A journey through the city shall show the concrete measures of the IBA. What can be seen, first of all, are the so-called "city signs"; these are colorful wooden frames decorated with peculiar symbols. One can read on an attached board what the IBA is planning here, at this location. The city signs can be encountered in Tegel, on Prager Platz in Schöneberg and then frequently in the southern Tiergarten quarter, in the southern Friedrichstadt district, in Luisenstadt and in Kreuzberg's SO36. An extensive review of all IBA locations fails on account of their sheer number. If one believes the recently published project overview, it has to be 158 in total. The thematic range is limitless; it spans from Gustav Peichl's "Phosphate Elimination Plant" in Tegel to the extension of a children's farm of the "Deutsche Schreberjugend e. V." on a field behind the baroque Berlin Museum, where metropolitan life once pulsated. The main theme of the "Inner City as a Place to Reside," however, is and remains residential housing.

The renovation, called "careful urban renewal" by the Altbau-IBA, takes place in Luisenstadt and in Kreuzberg, which is in danger of becoming a slum. Much was begun here, much is being built, apartment improvements invisible from outside are being made, many self-help groups are in the middle of their work, sights are set on residential streets and a placid idyll of green backyards. That was the trend reversal in 1979, because back then, when the IBA began to work, more than 3,000 apartments were still being torn town in one of their work areas, at Kottbusser Tor. Today one wouldn't even think about such a measure anymore, says the Berlin Senate employee in the modern high-capacity bus of the official IBA tour. But here in Kreuzberg a different reality already exists.

Not exactly friendly, but nonetheless colorful paint bombs are being thrown at the buses (acrylic lacquer, of course, which is particularly expensive to remove). And the opening festivities of the IBA Report Year at the Philharmonic, in the strict Berlin political ritual, were consequently met with whistles and boos. This energy, according to the challenge of Urban Development Senator Franke, ought to be better placed into the renovation of houses. A cynical demand, since considerable renovation funds were simply cancelled by the government in the middle of the work. The Altbau-IBA is finished, so one doesn't even hear from the parties affected. The speculators are already lurking about, waiting for their chance to thin out the jungle of the Kreuzberg mix with the tried and tested "clear-cut renovation." So in the sparkling clean tour bus there is more than one person who is ashamed to be driven through the "safari park," lulled by beautiful patter, shielded by sun protection glass in the well-tempered mini-climate, and then to let the helpless anger of the paint bombs carom off oneself. One reads "IBA out" on the house walls. The benevolent partner is thus beaten, because he is tangible, and yet what is meant by that is the government, the politicians who are capable of destroying so much hope with one stroke of the pen.

This foundering on reality is the fate of the IBA, because its concrete possibilities stand in no relation to the theoretical aspiration of the exhibitions and publications. "The Building Exhibition is an institution that conducts conceptual planning preparation, competitions and expert assessments, awards research contracts and carries out the associated public relations. Implementation decisions are prepared by the Building Exhibition with the respective architects, planning partners, the affected parties and Berlin institutions; public and private construction companies continue to build." That is how the official definition of the IBA reads. With its current staff of 90, the IBA is a brain trust, an advertising agency for the future of the city. If the client is not willing, even the most beautiful project is to no avail.

So the Neubau-IBA included 100 projects and problem areas in its propagandistic sphere of action. Today, five years after its founding, no more than four projects have been completed in the housing construction realm. The Neubau-IBA currently has a total of 350 apartments to offer, which is in no way sensational. Oswald Mathias Ungers planned quarters on Lützowplatz, but had to distance himself from the method of execution while construction was still going on. Five so-called "energy-saving houses" were realized by a team of German architects at the Landwehrkanal. Without considering the cardinal direction and the building fabric structure, the current theme was pushed through there with much effort. The "city houses" on Lützowufer, somewhat larger row houses with in-law apartments, are recommended at best as ambitious German average quality. Committed most strongly to the block idea propagated by the IBA,

R. OLGIATI   dipl. Architekt BSA   FLIMS-DORF GR   Tel. 081/39 12 56

7017 FLIMS-DORF, 27. November 1984

Herrn
Arch. Dietmar Steiner
Drorygasse 15/24
1030 W i e n

Sehr geehrter Herr Steiner,

Sie schreiben in Ihrem Buch "Häuser im Alpenraum" "dafür faltet er die dünne Aussenwand nach innen ...". Ich freue mich grenzenlos über diesen Satz, da ich sehe, dass Sie mir nicht zumuten, dass ich Massivität vortäuschen will, sondern nur die Schale optisch etwas üppiger machen will – und auch das überhelle Föhnlicht etwas bündeln will – um dadurch dem optisch aufgelösten Hintergrund (Weiden, Wiesen etc. oder im Tiefland dem Schlachtfeld von optischen Bravour-Stücken) widerstehen zu können.

Deshalb ist es mir umso peinlicher, dass ich auf Ihre Einladung nicht rechtzeitig geantwortet habe. Trotz meines Alters habe ich immer noch Hemmungen vor Unbekannten zu sprechen und dazu kommt, dass ich allerlei Hoffnungen auf unserem Gebiet aufgegeben habe. Dass heute nur ein Mensch begreift, was in Griechenland eine Säule, ein Pilaster oder ein Kubus war, ist sozusagen unmöglich. An Le Corbusier schätze ich am meisten, dass er – der Zerstörer der klassizistischen Architektur – die klassische griechische Architektur wieder entdeckt hat. Bei uns haben die deutsch- und romanischsprachigen Bauern (in Davos und im Münstertal) ihre Bauten in kubische oder kristalline Formen gebracht und diese nicht durch Fensterbänder zerstört, (wie es z.B. die Denkmalpflege in Zürich tut, wenn sie in gotischen Häusern dunkle Fenster + dunkle Fensterläden in ein Band bringt.) Dies alles taten die Bauern nicht aus hochkünstlerischem Empfinden, sondern – genau wie ein Hersteller von Verkehrssignalen diese in Quadrate oder Kreisflächen bringt – damit diese mehr optischen Bestand haben.

Ich bitte Sie nochmals herzlich, mein Verhalten zu entschuldigen. Kommen Sie nicht einmal in die Gegend von Flims, damit wir uns unterhalten können?

Mit herzlichem Gruss
R. Olgiati

Brief von Rudolf Olgiati, nachdem er mir zuvor den Kontakt zur Publikation im Buch *Häuser im Alpenraum* verweigert hatte · Letter from Rudolf Oligati after he had previously refused contact concerning the publication of the book *Houses in the Alps*. Archive DS

Translation by Brian Dorsey

"The White Crystals of Laax"

An odd purism accompanied academic architecture reception through the history of modernism. Everything that had success, that the public plainly and simply liked, was dubious. Architecture was art and this had to be suffered for. And the unknowing consumer had to first be educated towards social progress through better architecture. Now it appears that this front has fallen for some time; allowed is what is liked. If the strict hierarchy of architectonic values is thus no longer generally binding, one may nonetheless speak of parallel levels and reference systems that are fashionably called forms of discourse.

That means, seen once from the perspective of communication science, that every media network has its own value system, its own language forms and thus has evaluation criteria as well. There is the sophisticated discourse of the specialist magazines that is based on the science of art. There is the distinct language form in the home furnishing magazines with high circulation, with their different target groups. Right up to television, where the general validity of the statements is only to be reached with the most extreme simplification. What is now valued in a media network as a major positive accomplishment will be criticized in a different reference system or in reality not even noticed at all most of the time. The thesis to this: Except for approved historical architecture, there is no architecture that could succeed in being positively argued—across all types of discourse—in all media. An architecture that endures all linguistic forms of approach.

Perhaps, and that is an assumption, the media networks are only so densely interwoven that they cannot look curiously across their borders at all anymore. What the public likes in a "network" is merely suspicious in a different network. That's why it is a special joy to point once to an architect and his work, where all of the borders of media group languages have apparently fallen. An architecture whose suggestive power no one can elude. This is the architecture of Rudolf Olgiati, who will turn 75 this year and lives detached from the world in the Swiss canton of Grisons. I was first made aware of him at the end of the seventies by friends and through a catalog that the ETH Zurich published back then. A very sober and dry catalog of works which nonetheless was already in its third edition. About four years ago I saw many of the buildings by Rudolf Olgiati in Flims and Laax, and a little bit later I saw a film about him on German television. Subsequently, one of these colorful home furnishing magazines more and more frequently ended up in my hands. In the midst of renovated castles and farmhouses, of pathetically kitschy Hollywood villas, beclouded in the same flowery language, an Olgiati house appeared. The first Olgiati plagiarizers also emerged, who, as regionalistic (that is what the architectonic utilization label is called) motif seekers, all recognized the formula for success in Olgiati's structures.

And one was allowed to speak of success. Because Olgiati was plagued by a fate that made him suspicious for a certain architectonic form of discourse: He had happy and satisfied clients, yes, almost a sworn flock of pilgrims who, as was to be heard, for instance, in the television film, thank God and their architect each day anew that they were given such a divine and wonderful house.

And for exactly that reason I have placed such special emphasis on the forms of access, the circumstances of the reception and journalistic exploitation of Rudolf Olgiati's architecture. To also illustrate the ignorance of a certain networked system, which—stewing in its own discourse—does not want to acknowledge what success has in a different system. Since objectively, from its architectonic value, no reason is to be named to not discuss Olgiati's architecture just as extensively as that of Robert Venturi, for instance, even of Hans Hollein, too. Olgiati's disadvantage in this system is that he is no nattering self-professed architect, does not offer "theories," but—in a virtuosic and fascinating manner—simply builds.

As already said, he primarily builds in his own closer surroundings. And here mostly holiday houses. In an old rural cultural landscape that he has exactly studied, whose historical identity is his "material." To him, however, this regional reference applies equally as classical antiquity, as Le Corbusier and the history of modernism. This results in a relationship system that has preoccupied many "modern" architects of the postwar era up to today. Where, however, only motivic bastards have mostly arisen from it, but seldom an adequate architecture.

Olgiati's houses are white points in front of a dark landscape. They segregate this; formally isolate the private, the intimate realm. For Olgiati, an important means in this "localization" is the wall, addressed as skin. Skin, therefore, because it seems vulnerable like human skin in his structures, only permits limited and precisely placed openings. The space-confining skin of the walls now has to formally "bear" the roof. On the old houses in Grisons Olgiati experienced this appreciation that allowed him to lay simple, flat inclined double pitch roofs calmly in the wall frames. The fifth façade in Alpine architecture, but also in classic architecture was—Olgiati probably had thought—always committed to homogeneity, to calmness, to serenity. Instead he almost always pushes the gable surface over the real roof edge, symbolizes the silhouette as the image of the house in this way.

Dritter Tag • Day Three

Translation by Brian Dorsey

"To the Editorial Team of archithese"
February 1983

Esteemed Martin Steinmann,

Several weeks have now passed since we phoned about the new issue with the theme "Place and Context." I cannot listen to them anymore, these architectonic platitudes, I replied back then. This argumentative hit of the 70s has become powerless; used all too excessively, place and context has degenerated into an all-purpose metaphor. (The writers shouldn't use the word 'peace' anymore for some time, so that it can be given back its meaning after this pause, said the Austrian writer Barbara Frischmuth recently about this comparable problem.) So I also plead guilty to having shamelessly exploited place and context in everyday journalism. This 'contexting' was so awfully comfortable, an argument was somehow always found, which connected a good example with the place and could not be attested as a bad example of poor relationships. I thus wanted to expiate these sins; nothing comes to my mind concerning place, I said at that time; I cannot write such an article anymore.

Shortly after this phone call, I got into the car at midnight and drove directly from Bregenz to Vienna. It was a wonderful, long and lonely night. With all the 'Convoy' and truck driver sentimentalities, with a sunrise over the highway and hot coffee from a plastic cup. The world was black and white, like in the early 'borderland films' of Wim Wenders; Bruce Springsteen's *Nebraska* resounded out of the tape recorder into the steel skin:

"... Gotta hit the gas 'cause I'm runnin' late, this New Jersey in the mornin' like a lunar landscape..."

There they were then, all of a sudden, the images of places, stations of a line. Connected with meaning, with some kind of occurrences and stories of other trips. A gas station on Arlberg, which I rolled into with an empty tank, a garage that had repaired an alternator for me years ago on the way to Zurich, several distinctive houses, completely insignificant from an architectonic perspective, yet regular points of reference.
An absolutely unexceptional story that happens to everyone again and again. That's why I want to speak very egocentrically and ignorantly about my places here, which thereby become everyday-special architectonic places.

I found an arrow in the notes, along with the name Paul Virilio. A German edition of several of his writings carries the title *Fahren, fahren, fahren ... (Drive, Drive, Drive ...)*. He dedicated it to Sarah Krasnoff, "who for five months in 1971 crossed the Atlantic over 160 times in the planes of KLM without interruption while fleeing from psychiatrists before she died, ruined and totally exhausted, in Amsterdam in Room 103 of the Hotel Frommer."

Virilio writes about the increase of acceleration, the military power of speed, the way times fall over us, that we are all passengers and travelers. "The quick movement covered the experience of the crossed area with ice, the facts dissolved, like in the desert we have no reference point any more except ourselves, relativity misleads us—the continent of speed was hence the brutal intrusion of a *non-place* into history, the vehicle world would have finally dispersed the last enclave, and industry (the industrial revolution) only showed itself still as a fabrication of speed."

The non-places of speed are the unoccupied places. They are somewhere-and-everywhere-places. No antithesis, but a lucky punch against the certain, the defined order. In the case of the explained place and its context the 'losses'—isn't that remarkable?—are always lamented, where the 'rootedness' and the conventions have gone astray or are on the wane, where the search for 'identity' becomes the main problem. I leave it to your interpretation why this affliction of the occupied place, with all its regulations and rules precisely today, in this political situation, so generally affects us. Why the genius loci of Christian Norberg-Schulz has wandered into the amen corner of the support-seeking architect. A meaning is connoted to architecture here through the philosophical back door, rules are applied to it that it no longer has, cannot have. Architecture is no longer the Heideggerian 'the world as a collection of things' that can lend meaning to a place, because these places don't exist anymore. At the point where a social consensus can be found through a binding architectonic context, it concerns without exception places occupied by landscape preservation, historic building preservation, ensemble preservation. An architecture-theoretical genius loci can be pushed here, can be established; the legal impoundment will follow him straightaway.

Today there is no built structure that is architecture and at the same time can pay tribute to a social consensus. That would be, yes, that is also in reality an architecture of the dead 'metanarrative' which, according to Lyotard, has long gotten lost in parallel, private narratives. The occupied places belong to an anachronistic system that we, that architecture, have to escape from. Warning! You are now leaving the protected sector ...

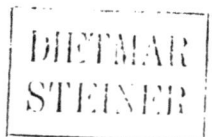

An die
Redaktion "archithese"
Grossmünsterplatz 2
CH - 8001 Zürich

Typoskript

Brief vom Februar 1983
an *archithese*
Grossmünsterplatz 2
CH-8001 Zurich

Verehrter Martin Steinmann,

es sind jetzt einige Wochen vergangen, seit wir über das neue Heft mit dem Thema "Ort und Kontext" telefoniert hatten. Ich kann sie nicht mehr hören, diese architektonische Plattitude, antwortete ich damals. Dieser argumentative Hit der siebziger Jahre ist kraftlos geworden, allzu inflationär verwendet ist Ort und Kontext zur Alleweltsmetapher verkommen. (Die Schriftsteller sollten einige Zeit das Wort "Frieden" nicht mehr verwenden, damit ihm nach diese Pause seine Bedeutung zurückgegeben werden kann, sagte kürzlich die österreichische Schriftstellerin Barbara Frischmuth zu diesem vergleichbaren Problem.) So bekenne auch ich mich schuldig, Ort und Kontext in der tagtäglichen Journalistik schamlos ausgebeutet zu haben. Das "kontexteln" war ja so furchtbar bequem, irgendwie fand sich immer ein Argument, das ein gutes Beispiel mit dem Ort verband und einem schlechten Beispiel mangelnde Beziehungen nachgewiesen werden konnten. Ich wollte also diese Sünden abbüssen, zum Ort fällt mir nichts ein, sagte ich damals, so einen Artikel kann ich nicht mehr schreiben.

Kurz nach diesem Telefonat, ~~ich führte es von einer Vorarlberger Telefonzelle,~~ setzte ich mich um Mitternacht ins Auto und fuhr direkt von Bregenz nach Wien. Es war eine wunderschöne lange und einsame Nacht. Mit all den "Convoy" und Truck-Driver-Sentimentalitäten, mit Sonnenaufgang über der Autobahn und heissem Kaffee aus dem Plastikbecher. Die Welt war schwarz-weiss, wie in den frühen "Grenzlandfilmen" von Wim Wenders, aus dem Recorder schallte Bruce Springsteens "Nebraska" in die Blechhaut:

"...Gotta hit the gas 'cause I'm runnin' late, this New Jersey
in the mornin' like a lunar landscape..."

Da waren sie dann auf einmal, die Bilder von Orten, Stationen eine Linie, mit Bedeutung, mit irgendwelchen zurückliegenden Ereignisse und Geschichten von anderen Fahrten verbunden. Eine Tankstelle am Arlberg, zu der ich einmal mit leerem Tank hinrollte, eine Werkstätte, die mir vor Jahren auf dem Weg nach Zürich die Lichtmaschi repariert hatte, einzelne markante Häuser, architektonisch völlig unbedeutend, dennoch regelmässige Orientierungspunkte.

Eine völlig alltägliche Geschichte, die jedem immer wieder passier Aber jetzt habe ich die Raststättennotizen von damals wieder gefunden, und "abgesehen vom Ort" steht hier als möglicher Titel für einen Artikel, den ich nicht schreiben werde. Ich will deshalb ~~in diesem Brief~~ hier ganz egozentrisch und ignorant von meinen Orten sprechen, die damit zu alltäglich-besonderen ~~nur selten auch~~ architektonischen Orte werden ~~sind~~. In den Notizen fand ich einen Pfeil, und dazu den Namen Paul Virillo. Eine deutsche Ausgabe einiger Schriften von ihm trägt den Titel "Fahren fahren, fahren...". Er hat sie Sarah Krasnoff gewidmet, "die 1971 auf der Flucht vor den Psychiatern praktisch ohne Unterbrechung fünf Monate lang in den Maschinen der KLM sass und über 160 mal den Atlantik überquerte, bevor sie ruiniert und am Ende ihrer Kräfte im Zimmer 103 des Hotel Frommer in Amsterdam starb".

Virillo schreibt über die Zunahme der Beschleunigung, die militärische Macht der Geschwindigkeit, das Ineinanderfallen von Zeite über uns, die wir alle Passagiere und Reisende sind. "Die schnelle Bewegung hat die Erfahrung des durchquerten Bereichs mit Eis überzogen, die Tatsachen haben sich aufgelöst, wie in der Wüste haben wir keinen Anhaltspunkt mehr ausser uns selbst, die Relativität führt uns in die Irre - der Kontinent der Geschwindigkeit wäre demnach der brutale Einbruch eines Nicht-Ortes in die Geschichte,

die Fahrzeugwelt hätte so schliesslich die letzte Enklave aufgelöst, und die Industrie (die industrielle Revolution) zeigte sich nur noch als Fabrikation von Geschwindigkeit."

Die Nicht-Orte der Geschwindigkeit sind die unbesetzten Orte. Sie sind die Irgendwo-und-überall-Orte. Keine Antithese, sondern ein lucky punch gegen den bestimmten, den definierten Ort. [SETZTEN SIE DAS WORT ORDNUNG STAT ORT] Beim erklärten Ort und seinem Kontext werden immer - ist das nicht auffalle: ? - "Verluste" beklagt, wo die "Verwurzelung" abhanden gekommen o [UND DIE KONVENTION] im Schwinden begriffen ist, wo die Suche nach "Identität" zum zentralen Problem wird. Ich überlasse es deiner Interpretation warum uns diese Heimsuchung des besetzten Ortes, mit all seinen Ordnungen und Regeln gerade heute, in dieser politischen Situatio so allgemein trifft. Warum der Genius loci von Christian Norberg-Schulz in den Herrgottswinkel des haltsuchenden Architekten gewandert ist. Durch die philosophische Hintertür wird hier der Architektur eine Bedeutung suggeriert, werden ihr Regeln auferlegt, die sie nicht mehr hat, nicht haben kann. Die Architektur ist nicht mehr das Heideggersche "die Welt versammelnde Ding" das einem Ort Bedeutung verleihen kann, weil es diese Orte nicht mehr gibt. Dort wo ein gesellschaftlicher Konsens über einen verbindlichen architektonischen Kontext gefunden werden kann, handelt es sich ausnahmslos um die von Landschaftsschutz, Denkmalschutz, Ensembleschu besetzten Orte. Hier kann ein architekturtheoretischer Genius lociert, festgeschrieben werden, ihm folgt auf der Stelle die juristische Exekution.

Es gibt heute kein Gebautes, das Architektur ist und gleichzeitig einem gesellschaftlichen Konsens Tribut leisten kann. Das wäre, ja das ist auch in Wirklichkeit, eine Architektur der toten "Metaerzählung", die sich laut Lyotard längst in parallele, private Erzählungen verlaufen hat. Die besetzten Orte gehören einem anachro-

nistischen System, dem wir uns, dem sich die Architektur entziehen muss. Warnung ! Nun verlassen Sie den geschützten Sektor....

Ich will ein Beispiel für den ungeschützten, den unbeobachteten Sektor geben. Es war schon eine Irritation des Ortes, dass ich in London einen Vortrag von Herzog/De Meuron sah. Die Gegend, der Ort ihres Fotostudios in Wyl erregte meine Aufmerksamkeit. Es war eine Gegend, die es überall gibt. Diese Nicht-Orte (Virillo) gibt es auch bei uns, im Wiener Becken, im Umfeld von Linz, an der Salzburger Alpenstrasse, in der Schlucht von Innsbruck. Die Gegend gibt es aber auch in Athen, in Barcelona, in London, überall wo man beispielsweise vom Flughafen in die Stadt fährt. Herzog/De Meuron haben aus dem "Material" dieser Gegend eine vom Ort befreite Architektur geschaffen. Sie haben den Geist des Nicht-Ortes auf phantastische Art und Weise "beschleunigt". So ist ein Manifest der Peripherie entstanden, keine kontextualistische sondern eine periphere Architektur, die Aldo Rossi und Gianni Braghieri in einem Projekt für eine Wohnsiedlung in Salzburg kürzlich zu höchster poetischer Kraft verdichteten. In einem agrarisch-industriellen Randbezirk, der folgende Merkmale aufweist: Kleingewerbe und Industrie, dazwischen Einfamilienhäuser, eine Schrebergartensiedlung, ein Schiesstand, ein Trabrennplatz, nahe der deutschen Grenze ein Flecken naturgeschütztes Gebiet. Sie haben einen Bezirk ausgegrenzt, bewohnbare Mauern errichtet, ein Wegenetz gelegt, Punkthäuser in die Felder gesetzt, eine Scheune als freien Ort vorgeschlagen. Ist es architektonisch unanständig, wenn ich mir wünschen würde, dieses Projekt würde ganz brutal von einem Bauspekulanten verwirklicht werden, und wäre dennoch die legitime Fortschreibung der sozialen und territorialen Eindrücke dieses unbesetzten Ortes ?

To the Editorial Team of archithese

I want to give an example of the unprotected, the unobserved sector. It already was an irritation of the place that I saw a lecture by Herzog & de Meuron in London. The area, the place of their photo studio in Wyl, aroused my attention. It was an area that exists everywhere. These non-places (Virilio) are also here in Austria, in the Vienna Basin, on the outskirts of Linz, along Alpenstrasse in Salzburg, in the Innsbruck Ravine. But the area also exists in Athens, in Barcelona, in London, everyplace where one, for instance, drives from the airport into the city. From the 'material' of this area Herzog & de Meuron have created an architecture liberated from place. They have 'accelerated' the spirit of the non-place in a fantastic way. A manifesto of the periphery has thus emerged, not a contextualistic architecture, but a peripheral one, which Aldo Rossi and Gianni Braghieri recently condensed into the highest poetic power in a project for a housing complex in Salzburg. In an agrarian-industrial outlying district that possesses the following features: small businesses and industry, there between single-family houses, an allotment garden settlement, a shooting range, a harness racing track, and a piece of nature reserve near the German border. They have excluded a district, erected inhabitable walls, laid a road network, placed tower blocks in the fields, proposed a barn as an open place.

It is architectonically indecent if I wished that this project would be quite brutally realized by a building speculator, and would nonetheless be the legitimate perpetuation of the social and territorial impressions of this unoccupied place?

The non-places of Herzog & de Meuron, of Aldo Rossi and Gianni Braghieri, of many others today sought as the last enclave of architecture and filled with private narratives,—these non-places are moveable places, 'irrespective of the place' after all. Their context consists of a network of social relationships and stories. They are initially movement places with only one direction: away from here. No places where someone drives to today. Getaway spots, way stations. But only here, where I am actually nowhere, I feel free, I begin to dream, intently listen to the minor and major stories.

That's why I thought about the places and the context on my nocturnal drive from Bregenz to Vienna, and only stories always came into my mind, very concrete, damned private narratives. In Fussach in Vorarlberg Wolfgang Juen built a house together with his housemates. 25 meters long, a rod in a no-man's land filled with huts. Plastered red with a steely glass veranda. And we stood there at the window and Wolfgang Juen pointed out to the shore of Lake Constance, talked about the canals that earlier led past the house here; he mentioned a storage building, the original house of what is today a large Vorarlberg freight forwarder, a decaying wall, a monument still dying. His house stands precisely in this context, although nothing 'adjusts,' 'fits in' architectonically. And into which system, too? But the stories of the past give the non-place meaning, just like the new narratives. We look to a non-descript single-family house; it is the bordello of Fussach. Wolfgang Juen's little son sees the nice cars of the pimps and customers in front of the house. He shows me his favorite toy. It is a sleek, silver-gray BMW M1 ...

All these peripheral narratives have nothing to do with the 'place,' which wants to communicate in such an ostensible architectonic manner. At the photo studio by Herzog & de Meuron one will probably not even notice its quite special everydayness when driving by; the Salzburg project of Rossi and Braghieri is—and I am tempted to say thank God—not politically executable today, and who among the architecture-theoretically, contextualistically planned place- and home-seekers is interested in the stories one tells at the house in Fussach.

Before this letter starts to become an article after all, I'd like to finish it. I only wanted to emphatically warn the editorial staff about a further perpetuation of the theory of the occupied place, which shows the way to the poetic melancholy of the periphery. The new (stay on the ground prophet!) architecture can only come from this no-man's land, this peripheral occurrence, divested of the powers of urban or rural design statutes. For that reason I prefer an anarchistic, an unlawful 'context' of refusal to the genius loci. He ought to remain reserved for those who use their privileged position in order to be able to bemoan the eternal 'loss' of culture, who seek the rooted identities and in the end merely tailor the emperor's new clothes.

Bruce Springsteen sings a song where he drives away at night, without a driver's license and without papers. But he has a clean conscience and he imploringly pleads: "Mister state trooper, please don't stop me ..." Which could mean to us, you, who call yourselves places and laws, who prescribes your adaptation, leave a few of them the freedom from all regulations, let them savor the adventure of the non-place. Let's take care of our beautiful 'God's own junkyard' so long until we are also driven out of this paradise.

Yours sincerely
completely irrespective of place,

Dietmar Steiner

Die Nicht-Orte von Herzog-De Meuron, von Aldo Rossi und Gianni Braghieri, von vielen anderen heute als letzte Enklave der Architektur gesucht und mit privaten Erzählungen gefüllt, - diese Nicht-Orte sind bewegliche Orte, eben "abgesehen vom Ort". Ihr Kontext besteht aus einem Netz von Sozialbeziehungen und Geschichten. Es sind zunächst Bewegungsorte mit nur einer Richtung: weg von hier. Keine Orte wo heute jemand hinfährt. Fluchtorte, Durchgangsstationen. Aber nur hier, wo ich eigentlich nirgendwo bin, fühle ich mich frei, beginne ich zu träumen, höre aufmerksam die kleinen unbedeutenden Geschichten.

Deshalb habe ich auf meiner nächtlichen Fahrt von Bregenz nach Wien über die Orte und den Kontext nachgedacht, und immer sind mir nur Geschichten in den Sinn gekommen, ganz konkrete, verdammt private Erzählungen. Da hat in Vorarlberg, in Fussach, Wolfgang Juen gemeinsam mit seinen Mitbewohnern ein Haus gebaut. 25 Meter lang, eine Stange in einem verhüttelten Niemandsland. Rot verputzt mit einer stählernen Glasveranda. Und da standen wir am Fenster und Wolfgang Juen zeigte hinaus auf das Ufer des Bodensees, erzählte von den Kanälen, die früher hier am Haus vorbei führten, er erwähnt ein Lagergebäude, das Heimathaus einer heute grossen Vorarlberger Spedition, ein verfallenes Gemäuer, Monument noch im Sterben. Sein Haus steht in genau diesem Kontext, obwohl sich architektonisch nichts "anpasst", "einfügt", in welches System auch ? Aber die Geschichten von früher geben dem Nicht-Ort Bedeutung, ebenso wie die neuen Erzählungen. Wir blicken auf ein unscheinbares Einfamilienhaus, es ist das Bordell von Fussach. Der kleine Sohn von Wolfgang Juen sieht vor diesem Haus die tollen Autos der Zuhälter und Kunden. Er zeigt mir sein Lieblingsspielzeug: Es ist ein schnittiger, silbergrauer BMW M1....

Alle diese peripheren Erzählungen haben nichts mit dem "Ort", der sich so vordergründig architektonisch mitteilen will, zu tun. Am Fotostudio von Herzog/De Meuron wird man seine ganz besondere Alltäglichkeit wahrscheinlich im Vorbeifahren gar nicht bemerken; das Salzburger Projekt von Rossi und Braghieri ist - und ich bin versucht Gottseidank zu sagen - politisch heute nicht durchsetzbar und wen von den architekturtheoretisch kontextualistisch disponierten Ort- und Heimatsuchenden interessieren schon die Geschichten, die man sich im Haus in Fussach erzählt.

Bevor dieser Brief nun doch ein Artikel zu werden beginnt, möchte ich ihn beenden. Ich wollte nur die Redaktion vor einer weiteren Fortschreibung der Theorie vom besetzten Ort nachdrücklich warnen, den Weg zur poetischen Melancholie der Peripherie zeigen. Die neue (- bleib am Boden Prophet!) Architektur kann nur aus diesem Niemandsland, diesem peripheren Ereignis, den Mächten städtischer oder dörflicher Gestaltsatzungen entzogen, kommen. Deshalb ziehe ich einen anarchischen, einen ungesetzlichen "Kontext" der Verweigerung dem Genius Loci vor. Der soll ruhig jenen vorbehalten bleiben, die ihre privilegierte Position benutzen um den ewigen "Verlust" der Kultur beklagen zu können, die verwurzelte Identitäten suchen und letztlich bloss dem Kaiser neue Kleider schneidern.

Bruce Springsteen singt ein Lied, wo er nachts im Regen losfährt, ohne Führerschein und ohne Papiere. Aber er hat ein reines Gewisse und inständig bittet er: "Mister state trooper, please don't stop me...". Was für uns heissen könnte, ihr, die ihr euch Orte und Gesetze nennt, die ihr Anpassung vorschreibt, lasst einigen wenige die Freiheit von allen Reglementen, lasst sie das Abenteuer der Nicht-Orte auskosten. Pflegen wir unseren schönen "Gods own junkyard" solange, bis wir auch aus diesem Paradies vertrieben werden.

MIT FREUNDLICHEN GRÜSSEN
GANZ ABGESEHEN VOM ORT

DIETMAR STEINER

Zugreise · Train journey, 1981. © Achitekturzentrum Wien, Sammlung · Collection, Margherita Spiluttini

Dritter Tag • Day Three

Frei Photographic Studio · Fotostudio Frei, Weil am Rhein, Herzog & de Meuron, 1981–82. Archive DS

aus · from

Ausstellungskatalog · Exhibition catalog
Herzog & de Meuron
Architekturmuseum Basel, 1988
Translation by Brian Dorsey

Fleisch- und Knochen- Architektur

Jacques Herzogs & Pierre de Meurons Projekte und Bauten sind nicht einfach ‚nur modern' im antipodischen Sinn herrschender Trends. Sie ermöglichen über die noch immer befreiende Funktionalität hinaus die ‚innere' Geschichte des Dialogs Mensch und Architektur in elementarer, ja körperlicher Hinsicht zu erleben. Über den unersetzlichen Zugang zur Architektur, der sich über Raumstimmungen, Temperaturen, Gerüche, Assoziationen, Erinnern und Wiedererkennen eröffnet. Ihre Bauten und immer gebaut gedachten Entwürfe sind in einer neuen Bedeutung den gotischen Kathedralen vergleichbare mnemonische Geräte. In gewisser Hinsicht Welterklärungen heutiger Zivilisation, wenn man in die Enzyklopädie ihrer Teile eintritt.

Meat and Bones Architecture

Jacques Herzog's and Pierre de Meuron's projects and buildings are not simply 'only modern' in the antipodal sense of prevailing trends. Beyond the still-liberating functionality, they enable the 'inner' history of the dialog between the human being and architecture to be experienced in an elementary, yes, physical respect. Through the indispensible access to architecture, which opens through room atmospheres, temperatures, smells, associations, memory and recognition. Their structures and designs, thought out always as built, are, in a new meaning, mnemonic devices comparable to the Gothic cathedrals. In a way, explanations of the world of present-day civilization, if one enters into the encyclopedia of their parts.

1. Die individuellen Landeflächen des gemeinsamen Flugfelds

Der Stand der Debatte 1988: Wir haben eigentlich fast alle möglichen und denkbaren Parameter der Architektur durchlebt und sind heute an jenem Punkt angelangt, an dem wir unser Feld neu abzustecken versuchen. Wer ist Wir? Eine Generation? Bitte nicht, Generationen gibt es nicht mehr. Eine kulturelle Minderheit dann? Vielleicht sind wir heute nur unterwegs, die Autonomie und Würde der Architektur zu suchen, ohne Heilige oder gar Propheten sein zu wollen.

Dieser Text ist – soll sein – ein fiktiver, ein fragender Dialog mit Jacques & Pierre, weil ich denke, dass unsere architektonische Sozialisation ähnlich verlief. (Also doch ‚Generation'?) Die Fakten dazu:

Wir haben uns am Beginn des Studiums mit der sozialen und politischen Dimension der Architektur gequält. Damals, in den späten sechziger Jahren hat uns die soziale Verantwortlichkeit gezeichneter Träume den Bleistift aus der Hand genommen, zu den Daten und Statistiken getrieben und eine agitatorische Sozialplanung abverlangt. In Wahrheit haben wir natürlich doch auch diese Zeit ‚durchgezeichnet'. (Zumindest in Wien waren die Künstler damals weiter als die Agitatoren.)

Diese Erfahrung haben wir dann hinübergerettet in die siebziger Jahre, in denen langsam, aber stetig die Architektur wiederentdeckt und anhand ihrer inneren Logik thematisiert wurde. Da konnte man dann die Produktion von Architektur, das was ich mit Bruno Reichlin als „architektonische Arbeit" diskutieren durfte, neu begründen, und es brach ein Staudamm in unseren Hirnen. All die sozialisierten ‚Bilder' wurden freigelegt. Aldo Rossi mit seinen Referenzen an Maurice Halbwachs – das Gedächtnis betreffend – war die ‚soziale Komponente'. Rossis Begriff der „Permanenz" gab uns zudem noch den Glauben an die Sinnhaftigkeit des architektonischen Entwurfs. Robert Venturi hingegen, mit seiner „complexity" und seinem „almost alright" war die Bestätigung für die heterogenen Bilderstürme, denen auch wir in Europa inzwischen ausgesetzt waren.

1. The Individual Landing Sites of the Common Airfield

The status of the debate in 1988: We have actually lived through nearly all possible and conceivable parameters of architecture and have reached that point today where we try to mark our field anew. Who is 'we'? A generation? Please don't, generations don't exist anymore. A cultural minority, then? Perhaps we are only on the move today to seek the autonomy and dignity of architecture without wanting to be a saint or even a prophet.

This text is—should be—a fictive, a questioning dialog with Jacques and Pierre, because I think that our architectonic socialization proceeded similarly. (A 'generation' after all?). Here are the facts:

At the beginning of our studies we struggled with the social and political dimension of architecture. Back then, in the late-sixties, the social responsibility of sketched dreams took the pencils out of our hands, drove us to the data and statistics, and demanded an agitational plan. In truth, however, we naturally 'drew through' this era as well. (At least in Vienna the artists were further than the agitators at that time.)

We then carried this experience over into the seventies, in which architecture was slowly but surely rediscovered and addressed on the basis of its internal logic. One could then reestablish the production of architecture, that which I was allowed to discuss with Bruno Reichlin as 'architectonic work,' and it broke a logjam in our brains. All of the socialist 'images' were uncovered. Aldo Rossi, with his references to Maurice Halbwachs—pertaining to memory—was the 'social component.' Rossi's concept of "permanence" gave us, more importantly still, the belief in the meaningfulness of the architectural design. Robert Venturi, in contrast, with his "complexity" and his "almost right," was the confirmation for the heterogeneous iconoclasms which we in Europe were meanwhile exposed to as well.

We were therefore sent into the archives, on one hand, to research the historical and archaeological layers of the location as the justification of the design. And schizophrenic as we postwar children were, we made a pilgrimage, on the other hand, into the cinemas at the same time still and loafed in front of the TV watching series in order to inhale the new aesthetic of everyday life. We analyzed the elements of historicity and we devoted ourselves to the appearances of constructed everyday life—still with a core of political emancipation. That is the 'cultural mood' which concerns us. Proven by you with the feverishly sensual notion of 'individual landing sites.'

"The specific gravity of architectures means *my own individual norm*, not a general one like the specific gravity of gold. The specific gravity is my idea of things, a substitution of things with *my images*." (*archithese* 2–82, "The Specific Gravity of Architectures")

A time slice and then the year 1980: Deep depression prevails behind the gleaming façades of an incipient boom of architecture. Portoghesi's postmodern Biennale in Venice unequivocally celebrated the end of a quite honorable movement. The cabins of the exhibitions were those 'garages' that a skier is familiar with: a dead end, only a radical turnaround is possible. No, we have no use for these 'images' anymore. That was a sweet late vintage, the excessive consumption of which only upset the stomach. (The reaction of today's student generation to it is now disconcerting. All Krierisms and Bofillades lie centuries in the past for them, and a-historical as students simply are, they venerate 'OMA's' images, which were already disembodied at the Biennale back then, too.)

> In any case, the prevailing mood at that time in Biennale shock was characterized by disappointed sadness, when I discovered the first project by Jacques and Pierre in Martin Steinmann's *archithese* with the suggestive title "Nachkriegsgeneration" ("Postwar Generation").

Dritter Tag • Day Three

> But it has to be images that are nonetheless able to reach out into an obligation of the general.

Da wurden wir also einerseits in die Archive geschickt, um die historischen und archäologischen Schichten des Ortes als Begründung des Entwurfs zu recherchieren. Und schizophren wie wir Nachkriegskinder waren, pilgerten wir andererseits zur selben Zeit immer noch in die Kinos und lungerten vor den Serials der TV-Programme, um die neue Alltagsästhetik zu inhalieren. Wir haben die Elemente der Geschichtlichkeit analysiert und wir haben uns den Erscheinungen des gebauten Alltags gewidmet – immer noch mit einem Kern der politischen Emanzipation. Das ist die ‚kulturelle Stimmung', die uns betrifft. Belegt von euch mit dem fiebrig sinnlichen Begriff der „individuellen Landeflächen".

„Unter dem spezifischen Gewicht der Architekturen verstehe ich *meine individuelle Norm*, keine allgemeine, wie z.B. das spezifische Gewicht von Gold. Das spezifische Gewicht ist meine Vorstellung von den Dingen durch *meine Bilder*." (*archithese* 2–82 „Das spezifische Gewicht der Architekturen")

Ein Zeitschnitt dann das Jahr 1980: Hinter den glänzenden Fassaden einer beginnenden Konjunktur der Architektur herrscht tiefe Depression. Portoghesis postmoderne Biennale in Venedig zelebrierte unmissverständlich das Ende einer durchaus ehrenwerten Bewegung. Die Kabinen der Ausstellung waren jene ‚Garagen', die einem Schifahrer geläufig sind: ausweglos, nur radikale Umkehr ist möglich. Nein, mit diesen ‚Bildern' konnten wir nichts mehr anfangen. Das war eine süße Spätlese, deren exzessiver Genuss nur den Magen verdarb. (Befremdlich ist nun die Reaktion der heutigen Studentengeneration darauf. Für sie liegen alle Krierismen und Bofilladen Jahrhunderte entfernt, und a-historisch wie Studenten nun einmal sind, verehren sie ‚OMAs' Bilder, die auch schon auf der damaligen Biennale entleibt wurden.)

In any case, the prevailing mood at that time in Biennale shock was characterized by disappointed sadness, when I discovered the first project by Jacques and Pierre in Martin Steinmann's *archithese* with the suggestive title "Nachkriegsgeneration" ("Postwar Generation"). My antennas were reactivated in a flash, an apprehension of the future, a possibility of continuing despite the fact opened up. I felt and sensed a parallelism of lived experience and attitude. All of the sudden they were there, the 'common images.'

"To me, the late '60s—an era I spent as a teenager in Basel going to high school—are closely linked with an idea of an expanding economy with many professional possibilities, with major highway construction, with the films of Jean-Luc Godard and Roman Polanski's *Knife in Water* shown in the Bon Film of the Royal cinema, with the first cigarettes and the first kisses." (*archithese* 2–82)

At the same time we were discussing these images in Vienna. A wonderful, theoretical chamber music piece by Krischanitz and Kapfinger about a stretch of the Vienna Belt Road already existed and Eberhard Kneissl was asked at the opening of one of his 'suburban churches' whether he knew Venturi and he pertly re-

Blaues Haus · Blue House, Oberwil,
Herzog & de Meuron, 1979–80. Archive DS

plied with yes, but he only corrected the name to Lino Ventura. Venturi himself, invited by Hollein—that is, from star to star—found Hermann Czech's "Kleines Café" to be "almost alright" and didn't discover a trace of an architecture in it. Others, in turn, criticized these 'Viennese investigations' for a historicity and formal playfulness that is nothing other than the authentic re-assurance of the existing 'material.'

But it already had to do with other things—and they were already hinted at in the discussions with you; it had to do with a different way of observing and processing the 'outer world.' Naturally it was again Aldo Rossi, who had published the famous "Pablo" text under the title "Realism as Education" in the old, 'little' archithese, where he superimposed his architectures with the impressions of neo-veristic film.

"I began to also think freely about architecture; therefore, Clara Calamai could pursue her love and sin in the movie *Ossessione* just as well in the corridors and halls of my designs."

Jedenfalls war die Grundstimmung damals im Biennale-Schock von enttäuschter Traurigkeit gezeichnet, als ich in Martin Steinmanns *archithese* mit dem beziehungsreichen Titel „Nachkriegsgeneration" die ersten Projekte von Jacques & Pierre entdeckte. Da wurden meine Antennen blitzartig neu aktiviert, eine Ahnung von Zukunft, eine Möglichkeit des Trotzdem-Weitermachens tat sich auf. Ich fühlte und spürte eine Parallelität der gelebten Erfahrung und der Haltung. Da waren sie auf einmal da, die ‚gemeinsamen Bilder'.

„Für mich sind die späten 60er Jahre – die ich als Teenager in Basel im Realgymnasium verbrachte – eng verbunden mit einer Vorstellung von Expansion der Wirtschaft, mit vielen beruflichen Möglichkeiten, mit dem Autobahnbau, mit den Filmen von Jean-Luc Godard und z.B. mit dem ‚Messer im Wasser' von Roman Polanski im Bon Film des Kino Royal, mit den ersten Zigaretten und den ersten Küssen." (*archithese* 2–82)

Diese Bilder diskutierten wir zur selben Zeit in Wien. Von Krischanitz und Kapfinger gab es bereits ein wunderbares theoretisches Kammermusikstück über einen Straßenabschnitt des Wiener Gürtels, und Eberhard Kneissl wurde anlässlich der Eröffnung einer seiner ‚Vorstadtkirchen' gefragt, ob er Venturi kenne und er antwortete keck mit ja, nur korrigierte er den Namen auf Lino Ventura. Venturi himself, von Hollein eingeladen – also von Star zu Star –, fand dafür Hermann Czechs „Kleines Café" „almost allright" und entdeckte nicht die Spur einer Architektur darin. Andere wiederum kritisierten an diesen ‚Wiener Recherchen' eine Historizität und formale Verspieltheit, die doch nichts anderes sei als die authentische Vergewisserung des vorhandenen ‚Materials'.

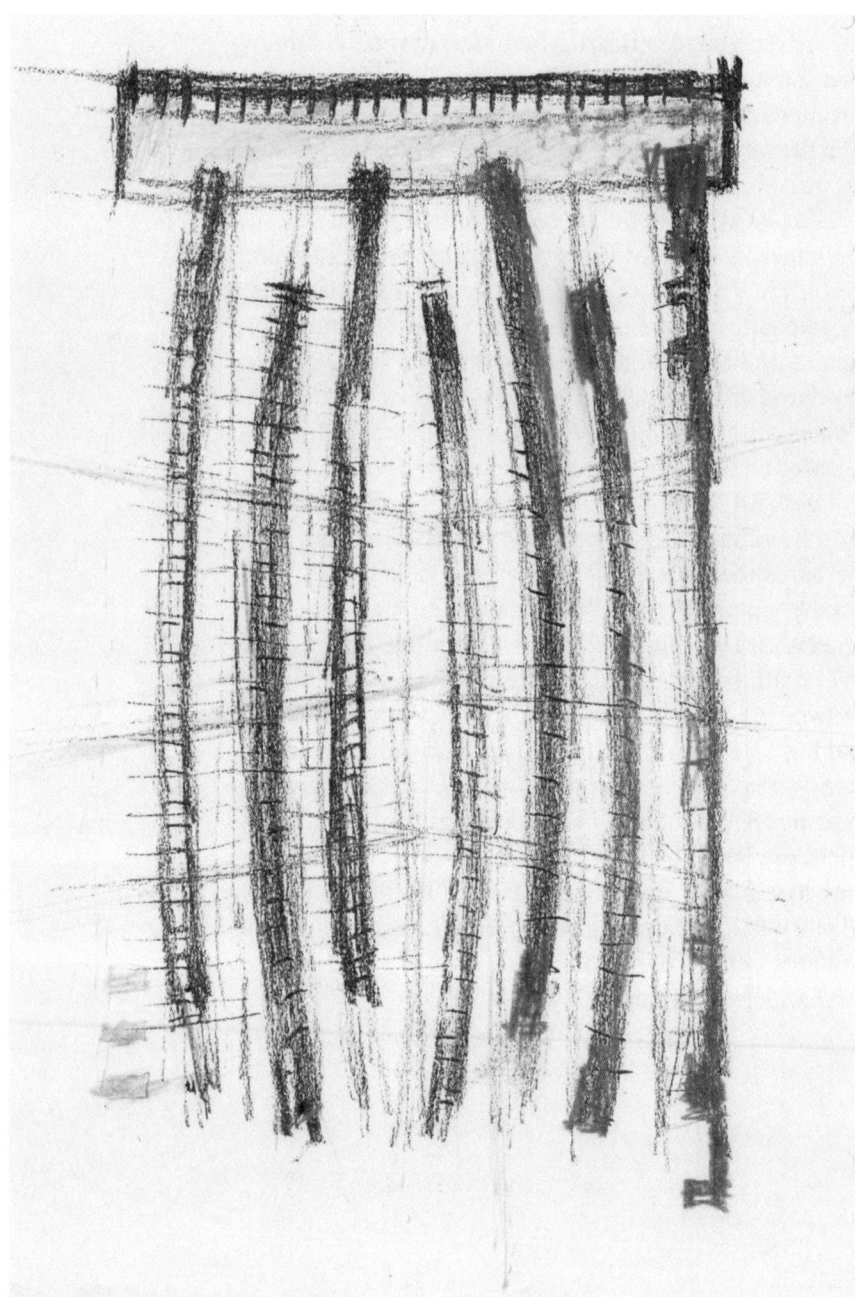

Aber es ging – und in den Gesprächen mit euch klangen sie bereits an – schon um andere Dinge; um eine andere Art der Beobachtung und Verarbeitung der ‚Außenwelt'. Natürlich war es wieder Aldo Rossi, der schon in der alten, der ‚kleinen' *archithese* den berühmten „Pablo"-Text unter dem Titel „Realismus als Erziehung" publiziert hatte, wo er seine Architekturen mit den Eindrücken des neoveristischen Films überlagerte.

„Ich fing an, auch über Architektur frei zu denken; so könnte Clara Calamai im Film *Ossessione* ihrer Liebe und Sünde genauso gut in den Gängen und Hallen meiner Entwürfe nachgehen."

Dazu gesellte sich dann Jacques' virtuose Betrachtung des grauen und des braunen Managers im Text „Das spezifische Gewicht der Architekturen":

„Das in den 60er Jahren so beliebte Grau wurde nun als kalt und ‚monoton' empfunden und verschwand. Sogar die Anzüge und der Manager waren nun vorwiegend braun und beige, die Hemdkragen breit, ebenso die Krawatte, sogar lange Haare, zuvor an Hippies und Künstlern indigniert abgelehnt, wurden selbstverständliches Attribut."

Imaginationen und Poetiken dieser Art waren auf einmal in der Lage, das Gebaute mit Erfahrenem zu verbinden. Das alles kulminierte zu einer Sicht der Architektur, die sich ‚jenseits des Bildes' versammelt. Keine Bilder der Architekturgeschichte mehr, aber auch keine individualistischen Eruptionen. Die Architektur, soll sie autonome künstlerische Disziplin sein und dialogfähig mit anderen Künsten bleiben, kann sich nicht mehr selbstreflexiv auf die Bilder nur ihrer akademischen Geschichte beziehen. Sie muss neue Felder der Verständigung eröffnen. „Bilder, die noch nicht kodiert sind durch die Architekturgeschichte", las ich bei Martin Steinmann einmal zu euren Projekten. Aber Bilder müssen es sein, die trotzdem hinauszureichen vermögen, in eine Verbindlichkeit des Allgemeinen.

Skizze zum Layout der Siedlung Pilotengasse · Sketch of the layout of the Pilotengasse housing estate, **Wien** · Vienna, **1987.** Archive DS

Then Jacques' virtuosic observation of the gray and the brown manager in the essay "The Specific Gravity of Architectures" accompanied it:

"The much-liked gray hue of the '60s was now thought to be cold and 'monotonous.' It disappeared. Even the managers' suits were mostly brown and beige; shirt collars were wide and so were the ties. And long hair, once disdainfully associated only with hippies and artists, had become a self-understood attribute."

Imaginations and poetics of this type were suddenly capable of combining the built structure with experience. All of this culminated in a new view of architecture that comes together 'beyond the image.' No more images of architectural history, but no individualistic eruptions either. The architecture, if is to be an autonomous artistic discipline and remain open to dialog with other arts, can no longer self-reflexively refer only its academic history to the images. "Images that are not yet coded by architectural history," I read from Martin Steinmann once about your projects. But it has to be images that are nonetheless able to reach out into an obligation of the general.

2. The Type of Settling

I can no longer recall the season, but it was wet and cold and we stomped through this field on the outskirts of Vienna. The inspection of the site with the builder, with Adolf Krischanitz and an associate of Otto Steidle, who was to be the third in the league of this design. Together—Germany, Switzerland, Austria—a housing estate was to be realized under the conditions of social housing construction in Vienna. This initial encounter with the concrete site is again and again a feverish, magical experience for me. In situations like these I remember the story that Uhl and Achleitner spread in their book about Lois Welzenbacher:

2. Die Art des Siedelns

Ich kann mich nicht mehr an die Jahreszeit erinnern, aber es war nass und kalt und wir stapften durch dieses Feld am Stadtrand von Wien. Das Begehen des Ortes mit dem Bauträger, mit Adolf Krischanitz und einem Mitarbeiter von Otto Steidle, der der dritte im Bunde dieses Entwurfs sein sollte. Gemeinsam – Deutschland, Schweiz, Österreich – sollte eine Siedlung unter den Bedingungen des sozialen Wohnbaus in Wien realisiert werden. Diese erste Begegnung mit dem konkreten Ort ist für mich immer wieder ein fiebriges, ein magisches Erlebnis. In Situationen wie dieser erinnere ich mich an die Geschichte, die Uhl und Achleitner in ihrem Buch über Lois Welzenbacher kolportierten:

„Ein fast ‚ritueller' Charakter kam dem ersten Besuch des Grundstückes zu. Es konnte geschehen, daß Welzenbacher auf Grund der Lage oder der baulichen Nachbarschaft einen Bauauftrag ablehnte. Die Beschäftigung mit der Lage eines Hauses währte oft (an Ort und Stelle) mehrere Tage, wobei der Bauplatz nach allen Richtungen hin abgeschritten und studiert wurde. Der Vergleich ist sicher weit hergeholt, aber es gibt in alten afrikanischen Kulturen den Brauch, daß der Bauende zuerst einige Tage und Nächte auf dem ausgewählten Bauplatz verbringt, um die positive und negative Reaktion der anwesenden (besitzenden) Geister zu erfahren und sie gegebenenfalls zu versöhnen. Diese magische Handlung hatte sicher auch den praktischen Zweck, den Bauplatz genau kennenzulernen, um seinen Gegebenheiten maximal entsprechen zu können. Welzenbacher hat dieses In-Kontakt-Treten als wesentlichen Teil der Entwurfsvorbereitung angesehen. Es wird sogar berichtet, daß er verschiedene Blicklinien ‚auf den Kopf gestellt' (also zwischen den gespreizten Beinen durchblickend) verfolgte. In dieses Geheimnis hat er jedoch niemanden eingeweiht."

Dritter Tag • Day Three

Haus eines Veterinär-Chirurgen · House of a veterinary surgeon, Dagmersellen, Herzog & de Meuron, 1983–84. Archive DS

Mag sein, dass es richtig ist, sich derart einem extremen Platz im ‚Gebirge' zu nähern, wenn man den Kampf aufzunehmen hat, mit einem territorial außerordentlichen Ort. Welzenbachers Begegnung mit dem Ort des Bauens war noch eine topologisch bestimmte. Damals konnte man noch von ‚Landschaften' sprechen. Aber welche Rolle kann heute noch ‚ein' Baum, ‚ein' Felsen, ‚eine' Mulde spielen, wenn alle Bäume in Gefahr sind, der Boden vergiftet ist. Zynisch und politisch dumm wäre es, unter all den sterbenden einem einzigen Baum Bedeutung zu geben. Dagegen muss klar gesagt werden: Ihr habt keine Bäume, keine Landschaften mehr, auf die ihr euch berufen könnt. Das was ihr seht sind die Bilder davon, die Masken. Befragt nach der Dynamik eurer Entwürfe im architekturhistorischen Vergleich am Beispiel des Foto-Studios in Wyl habt ihr geantwortet:

"The first visit to the lot took on a nearly 'ritual' character. It could happen that Welzenbacher refused a construction contract on account of the location or the built surroundings. The preoccupation with the location of a house often lasted (on site) several days, whereby the lot was paced off and studied in all directions. The comparison is surely far-fetched, but there is a custom in old African cultures that the builder first spends several days and nights on the chosen construction site in order to experience the positive and negative reactions of the present (possessing) spirits and to reconcile them if need be. This magical act certainly had the practical purpose as well of getting to know the building site exactly in order to be able to maximally conform to its conditions. Welzenbacher regarded this coming into contact as a crucial part of the design preparation. It was even reported that he traced various sightlines 'upside down' (that is, looking between his splayed legs). However, he never divulged this secret to anyone."

It may be that it is right to approach an extreme place in 'the mountains' in such a way if one has to take up the fight with a territorially extraordinary location. Welzenbacher's encounter with the location of construction was still a topologically determined one. One could still speak of 'landscapes' back then. But which role can 'one' tree, 'one' rock, 'one' hollow still play today if all trees are in danger, the ground is poisoned? It would be cynical and politically dumb to give meaning to a single tree among all the dying ones. It has to clearly be said in contrast: You no longer have any trees, any landscapes that you can refer to. What you see are the images of them, the masks. When asked about the dynamics of your designs in an architectural-historical comparison using the example of the photo studio in Wyl, you replied:

"We find Aalto's diverging of the movements very interesting. In his case, these movements always refer to the landscape, while in the photo studio the movement refers to nothing at all, and is rather an inner dynamic—we have a totally different situation geographically and culturally, and belong to a different generation. We find it absurd to point somewhere into our landscape." (*Werk, Bauen + Wohnen* 7/8_82)

That's why our inspection of the field for the new housing estate on the outskirts of Vienna had other impacts. The concrete situation is plain and inconsequential. Here is apparently nothing, but will soon be something. How do the images of what is to be built in the future develop then in one's head at such a place?

We drove out of the rain and mud of the lot to a restaurant in the Prater and warmed ourselves up with hot spiced wine. And the basis of the design emerged there. A unique, a rare situation of the 'architectonic discussion.' Everyone spilled out their images and ideas—and they were instantly communicable between you and Krischanitz. I listened attentively and 'my images' were confirmed by your sentences and sketches. The location came up for discussion, a level, nearly without a horizon, nothing is there, the thoughts fly. The 'middle' of the lot, the future estate, was addressed. How shall it be? An unsurfaced, an 'open' plaza, simply a lenticular, slightly sagging space? Where the cars do

„Das Divergieren der Bewegungen bei Aalto finden wir sehr interessant. Bei ihm beziehen sich diese Bewegungen immer auf die Landschaft, während im Foto-Studio die Bewegung sich auf überhaupt nichts bezieht, eher schon eine innere Dynamik ist – wir haben ja eine geographische und kulturell ganz andere Situation und gehören zu einer anderen Generation. Wir finden es absurd, irgendwohin zu zeigen in unsere Landschaft." (*Werk, Bauen+Wohnen* 7/8_82)

Deshalb hatte unsere Begehung des Feldes für die neue Siedlung am Stadtrand von Wien ganz andere Auswirkungen. Die konkrete Situation ist schlicht und belanglos. Hier ist scheinbar nichts, aber bald wird etwas sein. Wie entwickeln sich dann an einem derartigen Ort die Bilder des künftig Gebauten im Kopf?

Aus dem Regen und Schlamm des Grundstücks fuhren wir in ein Restaurant im Prater, wärmten uns bei Glühwein. Und da entstand die Grundlage des Entwurfs. Eine einmalige, eine seltene Situation des ‚architektonischen Gesprächs'. Jeder schüttete seine Bilder und Vorstellungen aus – und sie waren sofort kommunizierbar zwischen euch und Krischanitz. Ich hörte angespannt zu, und ‚meine Bilder' wurden durch eure Sätze und Skizzen bestätigt. Der Ort kam zur Sprache, eine Ebene, fast ohne Horizont, da ist nichts, die Gedanken fliegen. Die ‚Mitte' des Grundstücks, der künftigen Siedlung wurde angesprochen. Wie soll sie sein? Ein unbefestiger, ein ‚freier' Platz, einfach ein linsenförmiger, leicht durchhängender Raum? Wo die Autos nicht ‚parken', sondern zielbewusst kommunikativ abgestellt sind? Wie am Samstag Abend auf dem Parkplatz vor der Land-Disco, wo die Autos nach Ritualen geparkt werden, die schon das inszenierte Abfahren berücksichtigen. Der ‚unheimlich starke Abgang', das ist immer der letzte Test dafür, wer bei wem einsteigen

wird. Erotik im Staub und Wind am Rande der Stadt, die Erinnerung an James Dean, irgendwo hinfahren an einen „Nicht-Ort" des erotischen Erwachens. Der Mitarbeiter von Steidle meldete mitten in dieses kreative Gespräch hinein etwas von Einliegerwohnungen an, aber das Klima eines möglichen Entwurfs war längst schon bei Themen wie der „schwarzen Wand" am Rande des Grundstücks angelangt. Gedacht war damals eine Doppelmauer als Begrenzung der Siedlungsinsel, dazwischen Höfe, Häuser und Gärten.

Inzwischen ist das Projekt ausgereift, steht vor seiner Verwirklichung. Der ‚Halt' wurde jetzt an der Hauptstraße gefunden, letztlich logischer Ort dafür. Hier hängen die ‚Züge' der Zeilen, zur ‚Abfahrt' bereit. Leicht gebogen sind diese Zeilen, schaffen so virtuelle Grenzen, dehnen und verkürzen den Raum in der Bewegung. Und darüber liegt eine zweite Ordnung, die der Natur und der Wege, nach einem anderen geometrischen Prinzip. So entsteht eine informelle, eine räumliche Ordnung und Orientierung. Von selbst, im Laufe des Bewohnens der Menschen, werden sich hier die ‚Zeichen' des inneren Zusammenhangs einstellen.

Was ist die Sehnsucht?

Material, offen, frei.

3. Jenseits der Bilder
Material und Raum und Körper, Architektur als Kunst

Ich habe am Beginn die notwendige neue Positionsbestimmung der Architektur erwähnt; ohne dabei zu bedenken, dass damit jetzt die Karten auf den Tisch gelegt werden müssen. Was ist unser ‚Material' heute? Nach allem, was in den letzten Jahrzehnten mit der europäischen Stadt, mit der europäischen Landschaft geschehen ist, gibt es die konkreten Orte nicht mehr.

> That garbage which has determined and shaped the realms of experience of our "generation."

not 'park,' but are purposefully parked in a communicative manner? Like on Saturday night at the parking lot in front of a country disco, where the cars are parked according to rituals that already take the staged leaving into account. The 'incredibly strong departure,' that is always the final test for who will get in with whom. Eroticism in the dust and wind at the edge of the city, the memory of James Dean, driving somewhere, to a "non-place" of erotic awakening. In the middle of this creative discussion, Steidle's associate threw in something about 'granny apartments,' but the climate of a possible design had already long proceeded to issues such as the 'black wall' at the edge of the lot. At that time a double wall was conceived as a boundary to the settlement island, with courtyards, houses and gardens in-between.

The project has matured in the meantime and is about to be realized. The 'foothold' was then found on the main road, ultimately the logical location for it. Here the 'lines' of the rows hang ready for 'departure.' These rows are slightly curved, create virtual borders in this way, elongate and shorten the space in the movement. And a second order lies above, that of nature and of the paths, according to a different geometrical principle. An informal, spatial order and orientation thus arises. By themselves, in the course of being inhabited by people, the 'signs' of the inner context will appear here.

What is longing?

Material, open, free.

Sperrholz Haus · Plywood house, Bottmingen,
Herzog & de Meuron, 1984–85. Archive DS

3. Beyond the Images
*Material and Space and Body
Architecture as Art*

At the beginning I mentioned the necessary new position determination of architecture: without considering that the cards have to be laid on the table now. What is our 'material' today? After everything that happened in the last decades with the European city, with the European landscape, the concrete locations no longer exist.

All of them have been replaced by images; that architecture of the 'location' and its purported cultural tradition and stratification has lost its justification. But the opposite of that is also not true. I myself invented the term "non-place" years ago, Since then it has gladly been argued, if it is about loose 'simulation' theories or if the Americanization of Europe is meant, with the universally valid 'world location of the periphery.' But precisely this "non-place" is not empty, because it is filled with impressions, experiences, feelings and moods.

Alle sind durch Bilder ersetzt, jede Architektur des ‚Ortes' und seiner angeblichen kulturellen Tradition und Schichtung hat ihre Begründung verloren. Aber auch das Gegenteil davon stimmt nicht. Ich selbst habe vor Jahren den Begriff des „Nicht-Ortes" erfunden. Er wird seit damals gerne ins Treffen geführt, wenn es um lockere ‚Simulations'-Theorien geht oder wenn die Amerikanisierung Europas gemeint ist, mit dem allgemeingültigen „Weltort der Peripherie". Aber gerade dieser „Nicht-Ort" ist nicht leer, denn er ist gefüllt mit Eindrücken, Erlebnissen, Gefühlen und Stimmungen.

„Viele Architekten reagieren auf die ‚schlechte und belanglose Architektur' durch eine übertriebene Bezugnahme auf kunsthistorisch und städtebaulich bearbeitete und akzeptierte Perioden der Stadtentwicklung. Mich interessiert die Stadt hingegen in einem viel umfassenderen Sinn: In allem, was die Stadt ausmacht; die ganze räumliche Situation, Randsteine, Strassen, Häu-

ser, Tafeln, Gerüche und Menschen, die Stadt als architektonische Skulptur. Deshalb reagiere ich mit meiner Architektur nicht mit vermeintlich exaktem, historischem Bezug, sondern mit meinen Bildern und Räumen von der Stadt, innerhalb der Erfahrung meiner eigenen Geschichte. ... Diese Sehweise steht eher in der Tradition meiner eigenen Erfahrungen als in einer Tradition des Ortes im herkömmlichen Sinne. Dennoch sind meine Bilder immer auch Bilder meiner Generation, also innerhalb eines grösseren Zusammenhangs begreifbar." (*Werk, Bauen+Wohnen* 7/8_82)

Die ‚Generation' ist, so glaube ich, der Schlüssel der neuen Haltung der Architektur. Es erzählen die Bilder des Kinos, des Films, des Fernsehens, ja selbst der Werbung nicht mehr die ‚Geschichten', als die sie von einer ‚alten' Kulturkritik verstanden werden, die diese noch nach Inhalten kategorisierte. Sie sind aber auch nicht die verkürzenden ‚Logos', die Markenzeichen, die einzig ein Konsumverhalten vorschreiben. Natürlich sind alle Bilder falsch. Sie geben vor, Geschichten zu erzählen, und doch sind es nicht die Geschichten, die uns bedrängen. Es sind Bilder, die – in ihrem besten Sinn – alte Mythen neu beschwören.

Häuser sind Batterien, mediale Aggregate. Deshalb auch sind eure Architekturen für mich eigentlich ‚Installationen', Häuser, die nur auf Besuch sind auf dieser Erde, verschwinden können, nur dokumentiert als Gedanken eingeschrieben sind in das Gedächtnis. Objekte, die einen ‚Sachverhalt' verdeutlichen, ganz konkrete Realien erlebbar machen. Endlich wieder Gebautes auch. Das Material wirksam werden lassen. Jedes Ding, das uns umgibt, ist heute schon mit Bedeutung aufgeladen. Es gibt und gab niemals einen Nullpunkt der Erfahrung. Nichts kann uns wirklich überraschen. Alles was ist, deutet auf etwas anderes, das schon einmal war. Jeder denkbare Text ist schon gelesen, jedes denkbare

"Many architectures react to 'bad and trivial architecture' through an exaggerated reference to periods of urban development that are processed and accepted in an art-historical and urban planning sense. By contrast, I am interested in the city in a much more encompassing sense: In everything that makes the city what it is; the entire spatial situation, curbstones, streets, houses, signs, smells and people, the city as an architectonic sculpture. That's why I react with my architecture not with a purportedly exact, historical reference, but with my images and spaces of the city, within the experience of my own history. ... This point of view rather stands in the tradition of my own experiences than in the tradition of the location in the conventional sense. Nevertheless, my images are always images of my generation, too, and are therefore tangible within a larger context." (*Werk, Bauen + Wohnen* 7/8_82)

The 'generation' is, I believe, the key to the new stance of architecture. The images of the cinema, of film, of television, yes, even of advertising no longer tell the 'stories' as they are understood by an 'old' cultural criticism which still categorizes them according to content. But they are also not the abridging 'logos,' the trademarks that solely prescribe a consumer behavior. All images are naturally false. They pretend to tell stories and yet they are not the stories that oppress us. These are images that—in their best sense—re-invoke old myths.

Houses are batteries, media aggregates. That is why your architectures are also actually 'installations' to me, houses that are only on a visit on this earth, that can disappear, that can be documented as thoughts, that are inscribed in memory. Objects that clarify a 'set of facts,' make very concrete realities come to life. Again at last,

built structures, too. Letting the material take effect. Every object that surrounds us is already loaded with meaning today. There never is nor was a zero point of experience. Nothing can really surprise us. Everything that is, points to something else that already once was. Every conceivable text has already been read, every conceivable image has already been seen, and even the spaces which we can ever encounter: Didn't I see in this or that film, in this or that scene, fright, horror, wonder, overcoming—in the confrontation of a human with color, light, wind, cold, warmth, that is, space?

"It strikes us, however, as essential to differentiate between the various building materials, not to merely use them in a manner 'appropriate for the material involved' and 'suitable for production,' but to bring in their inherent physical properties into the theme of a house, to use affinities and contrasts of materials like concrete, lime, asphalt, eternit, iron, copper, gold, color as plastic elements." (*archithese* 1–80)

Only the assembly, most of the time it is translations of the experience from a different discipline into that of architecture, opens up a new purpose, breaks it up, the eminent weariness of our era. There is no bourgeois 'shock' anymore. Observing life itself: It is never again real, in the contemplating and visualizing sense. Fed from the experiences of the general, the geometry and materiality of architecture can again become a generator. My hope is tied to that. And I thereby risk a final exclusion and separation. In today's most advanced 'old' position of architecture, Libeskind and Hejduk and Abraham and others, too, flee in a poet and mythic approach beyond and in radical rejection of civilization's garbage. That garbage which has determined and shaped the realms of experience of our 'generation.' The experienced existence of this garbage makes us immune, but also against the claim of monumentality and of infinity, holds the contact of architecture to what is certainly still called life.

Bild ist schon gesehen, und selbst die Räume, denen wir jemals begegnen können: Sah ich nicht in diesem oder jenem Film, in dieser oder jener Szene, Erschrockenheit, Entsetzen, Verwunderung, Überwältigung – in der Konfrontation eines Menschen mit Farbe, Licht, Wind, Kälte, Wärme, also Raum?

„Uns erscheint es jedoch wesentlich, die verschiedenen Baumaterialien zu unterscheiden, nicht bloß ‚materialgerecht' und ‚fertigungsgerecht' zu verwenden, sondern ihre innewohnenden physikalischen Eigenschaften ins Thema eines Hauses einzubringen, Verwandtschaften und Gegensätze von Materialien wie Beton, Kalk, Asphalt, Eternit, Eisen, Kupfer, Gold, Farbe als plastische Elemente zu gebrauchen." (*archithese* 1–80)

Nur die Montage, meist sind es Übersetzungen der Erfahrung aus einer anderen Disziplin in jene der Architektur, eröffnet eine neue Bestimmung, bricht sie auf, die eminente Müdigkeit unsere Epoche. Es gibt keinen bürgerlichen ‚Schock' mehr. Das Leben selbst beobachtend: Nie mehr ist es wirklich, im betrachtenden und verbildlichenden Sinn. Die Geometrie und Materialität von Architektur kann wieder, gespeist aus den Erfahrungen eines Allgemeinen, zu einem Generator werden. Daran knüpft sich meine Hoffnung. Und ich wage dabei eine letzte Ausgrenzung und Scheidung. In der heute avanciertesten ‚alten' Position der Architektur fliehen Libeskind und Hejduk und Abraham und andere auch in einen poetischen und mythologischen Ansatz jenseits und in radikaler Ablehnung des zivilisatorischen Mülls. Jenes Mülls, der die Erfahrungswelten unserer ‚Generation' bestimmt und geprägt hat. Die erlebte Existenz dieses Mülls immunisiert uns aber auch gegen den Anspruch der Monumentalität und der Ewigkeit, hält den Kontakt der Architektur mit dem, was allemal noch Leben genannt wird.

Lecture · Vortrag

Architectural Association School of Architecture, London
January · Jänner 1989
Translation by Brian Dorsey

The City – Networks and Bodies

Die Stadt – Netze und Körper

Wenn ich hier von Stadt spreche, dann ist damit die europäische Stadt gemeint. Nicht über die Metropolen der Dritten Welt will ich sprechen, deren akute Probleme sicher mit Planung und Architektur nicht mehr zu lösen sind. Mein Thema soll die europäische Stadt sein, ihre Bedrohung heute und die Möglichkeit, ihrer Tradition und Botschaft neu zu begegnen.

Ich will mit der These beginnen, dass es die Stadt als kollektiven Begriff eigentlich nicht mehr gibt. Natürlich existiert die Stadt als gebaute und bildhafte Realität, als Ort, an dem wir leben.

Es ist etwas anderes mit ihr geschehen. Der Gegenstand, das Thema selbst scheint verloren gegangen zu sein. Es gibt keine Übereinstimmung mehr darüber, was die Stadt ist, welchen Bildern und Zielen, welchen Vorstellungen sie folgen soll. Wir beklagen das Fehlen der kollektiven Identität einer Architektur der Stadt, die zu einem planbaren Bild ihrer Zukunft gerinnen könnte.

If I speak of the city here, then the European city is meant. I do not want to speak about the metropolises of the Third World, whose acute problems are surely no longer to be solved with planning and architecture. My theme is to be the European city, its threat today and the possibility of encountering its tradition and message in a new way.

I want to begin with the thesis that the city, as a collective notion, actually doesn't exist anymore. Of course the city exists as constructed and pictorial reality, as a place where we live.

Something different happened to it. The object, the theme itself, appears to have gone lost. There is no consensus anymore about what the city is, which images and goals, which ideas it shall follow. We lament the absence of the collective identity of an architecture of the city, which could congeal into a plannable image of its future.

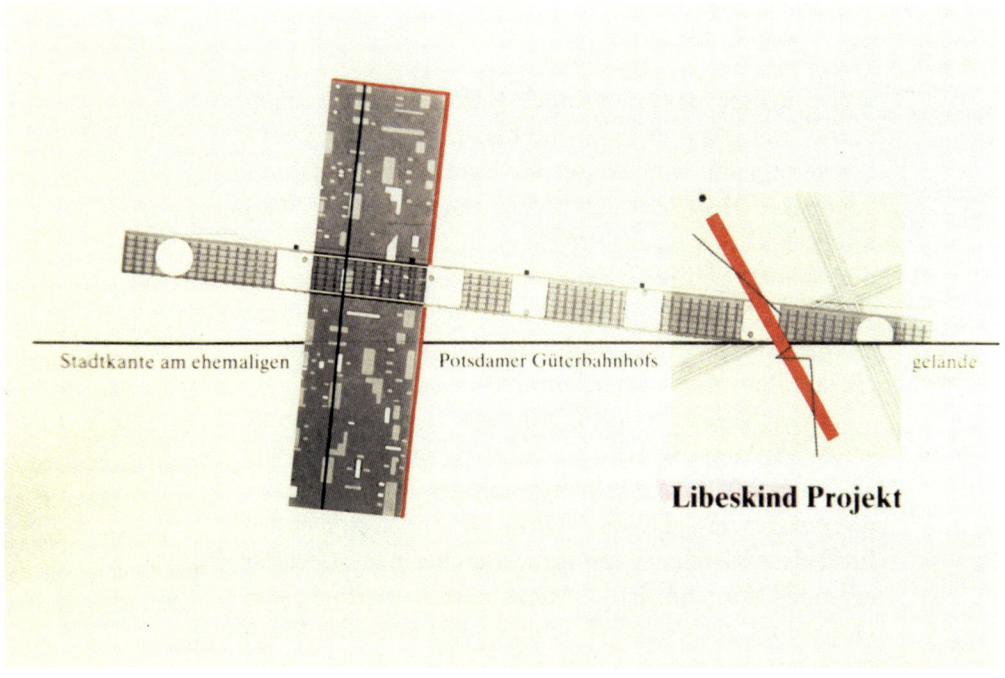

Letztes Projekt der IBA Berlin für Moabit von Daniel Libeskind – auf seiner Website nicht gelistet, ca. 1985 · Last project of the IBA Berlin for Moabit by Daniel Libeskind—not listed on his website, ca. 1985. Archive DS

Dieser Bruch, diese scheinbare Verwirrung, entstand durch die sich langsam entwickelnde Krise der Modernität, die erst in den siebziger Jahren zum endgültigen Ausbruch gelangte und die keineswegs, wie viele glauben mögen, durch die Architektur der Postmoderne abgelöst wurde. Die Postmoderne hat nur den Blick auf die Stadt verschoben, hat die leer und abstrakt gewordene Idee der Moderne durch ein ebenso leeres Bild der Stadt abgelöst. Keine Sprache der Architektur der Stadt wurde hier in Wahrheit wiederentdeckt, lediglich Signale, Zeichen, Werbebilder wurden verkündet, die rasch in einen massenmedialen Verwertungsprozess eingegliedert wurden.

Inzwischen hat der Stil der Postmoderne seinen Prozess der Sickerung in das Allgemeinverständnis abgeschlossen. Mit einem bemerkenswerten Ergebnis: Die Personalstile der Architektur-Stars werden heute in der Konkurrenz der Städte als Markenartikel gehandelt,

This breach, this apparent confusion, arose through the slowly developing crisis of modernity, which first came to a conclusive outbreak in the seventies and which was in no way replaced, as many like to believe, by the architecture of postmodernism. Postmodernism only shifted the view to the city, replaced the notion of modernism, which had become empty and abstract, by an equally empty image of the city. In actual fact, no language of the architecture of the city was rediscovered here; signals, signs, advertising images that were quickly incorporated into a mass media reutilization process were merely proclaimed.

Meanwhile, the style of postmodernism has completed its process of seeping into common understanding. With a remarkable result: The personal styles of the architecture stars are traded today in the competition of cities as branded products, which means that the customer (that is, the city) already knows beforehand

was bedeutet, dass der Kunde (also die Stadt) schon vorher weiß, was er (bzw. sie) bekommen wird: Darüber kann auch der Wechsel der Aktualität dieser Markenartikel nicht hinwegtäuschen. Es ist für die Stadt unerheblich, ob sie das Projekt einer „alten Stadt" nach dem Muster von Léon Krier, ob sie einen „Architekturunfall" von Coop Himmelblau, ob sie die schweigsame Archaik von Aldo Rossi oder die metropolische Rhetorik von Rem Koolhaas bekommt.

Vielleicht aber ist diese Strategie der architektonischen Markenartikel doch nicht so falsch? Nehmen wir als Beispiel Paris und seinen gewaltigen Ring von Satellitenstädten. Hier haben die Projekte – noch sind es nur Projekte – Größenordnungen, die eine neue Qualität erzeugen könnten. Es gibt dazu eine Bemerkung von Hermann Czech, der in Hinblick auf die Wiener Ringstraße meinte, dass es wohl ein Fehler war, das Glacis zu bebauen, doch werden Planungsfehler groß genug, dann nennt man sie im Rückblick Stadtentwicklung. Und zweifellos ‚Geschichte' geworden sind beispielsweise die Fertigteilklassizismen eines Ricardo Bofill. Immerhin konnte in ihren Räumen Terry Gilliam seinen Science-fiction-Film *Brazil* derart überzeugend inszenieren, dass auch schon eine mögliche Zukunft zu erahnen ist. Bofills Projekte sind aber nur eine Spielart der neuen Städte an der Pariser Peripherie. Im Vorjahr wurde ein Projekt von Coop Himmelblau ausgewählt. Und für eine andere Satellitenstadt, am Weg nach Marne-la-Vallée, wo bekanntlich das europäische Disneyland entstehen wird, kämpft Norman Foster gegen Rob Krier, als ob man nicht schon vorher gewusst hätte, welcher Art die Projekte der beiden sein würden. Somit könnten ganze Städte oder zumindest Stadtteile zu gestylten Markenartikeln werden, die für die Bewohner neue konsumistische Identitäten erzeugen: Ich fahre BMW und wohne in Krier, ich fahre Honda und wohne in Foster – so kann das weiter gespielt werden.

So können Stadtimages neu kreiert werden, die auch dem Stadtmarketing – das heute auch unsere alten europäischen Städte erfasst hat – fördernd zur Seite ste-

what he (resp., she) will get: The change in the currency of these branded products also cannot hide the fact. It is unimportant for the city whether it gets the project of an 'old city' according to the model of Léon Krier, an "architectural accident" of Coop Himmelblau, the taciturn archaic of Aldo Rossi, or the metropolitan rhetoric of Rem Koolhaas,

But perhaps this strategy of the architectonic branded product is not so wrong after all? Let us take Paris and its huge ring of satellite cites as an example. The projects here—they are still only projects—have dimensions that could create a new quality. There is a comment to this end by Hermann Czech who, in regard to the Vienna Ringstrasse, opined that it was probably a mistake to develop the Glacis, but if planning mistakes become large enough, they can then be called 'urban development' in retrospect. And the pre-fabricated classicisms of a Ricardo Bofill, for instance, have undoubtedly become 'history.' After all, Terry Gilliam was able to stage his science fiction film *Brazil* in its spaces so convincingly that a possible future is already to be surmised as well. Bofill's projects, however, are only a variation of new cities on the Paris outskirts. A project by Coop

Screenshot des Films · of the film *Brazil* von · by Terry Gilliam, 1985. Archive DS

hen. Und da jedermann einen bestimmten Begriff von Venedig, Wien oder London hat, werden die traditionellen Stadtplaner abgelöst von Dramaturgen und Regisseuren, die diese inszenierten Räume mit Leben füllen und betreuen müssen.

In der Folge aber wird es überflüssig sein, dabei von Architektur, von städtebaulicher Kultur zu sprechen, weil von diesem Marketing nicht nur die Werke der Star-Architekten betroffen sind, sondern dafür auch andere Bilder und Images herangezogen werden können. Müssen es denn ‚architektonische Bilder' sein, die vermarktet werden, warum sollte nicht die Disney-Corporation eine Stadt planen und bauen?

Diese Ablösung der Architektur der Stadt durch ihr Marketing habe ich selbst einmal versucht bis an die Grenze auszureizen. Das Projekt nannte sich *The Heavy Dress* und war eine Ausstellung von Skyscraper-Modellen, entworfen und gebaut von Matteo Thun.

Thun entwarf Türme für mächtige reale und imaginäre Institutionen. Für eine Fluglinie ebenso wie für eine vereinigte Weltkirche, für die Zentrale des Olympischen Komitees oder für ein Museum für moderne Kunst. Entscheidend dabei war, dass wir bei diesem Projekt bewusst nicht von ‚Architektur' sprachen, sondern die Türme unter dem Begriff der ‚Bekleidung' diskutiert wissen wollten. Die gebauten Modelle waren somit Models auf dem Laufsteg der Medien.

Eröffnet wurde die Ausstellung um Punkt Mitternacht im Museum für angewandte Kunst in Wien. Das Publikum strömte, wie im Kino, in einen dunklen Raum, der dann plötzlich von Spots erhellt wurde, und vom Tonband kam Funk-Musik unterbrochen von Werbeslogans für die Türme.

Zu diesem Zeitpunkt sprach man in den benachbarten Lokalen bereits davon, im Museum würde eine neue Pop-Gruppe mit dem Namen The Heavy Dress auftreten. Wir hatten somit eine Architekturausstel-

Antike Ruinen · Ancient ruins. © DS

Himmelblau was selected in the preceding year. And Norman Foster is fighting against Rob Krier for a different satellite city, on the way to Marne-la-Vallée, where, as everybody knows, the European Disneyland will arise, as if one already hadn't known beforehand what type of projects the two would develop. Whole cities or at least city districts could consequently become styled branded products that create new consumptive identities: I drive a BMW and live in a Krier, I drive a Honda and live in a Foster—that's how it can be played on.

City images can thus be newly created to promotionally support city marketing—which has also grabbed hold of our old European cities today. And since everyone has a certain idea of Venice, Vienna or London, the traditional city planners are replaced by dramatic advisors and directors who have to take care of these staged spaces and fill them with life.

Subsequently, however, it will be superfluous to speak of architecture, of urban planning culture, because not only are the works of star architects affected by this marketing, but other pictures and images can also be drawn upon for this purpose. Does it have to be 'architectonic images' that are marketed? Why shouldn't the Disney Corporation plan and build a city?

Dritter Tag • Day Three

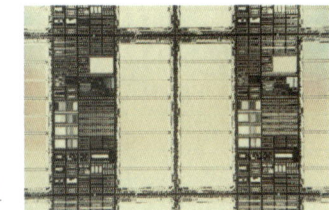

1   Ein Mikrochip könnte auch als Plan einer Stadt gelesen werden ·
    A microchip can also be read as a plan for a city. Archive DS

2   Spuren menschlicher Manifestationen, Pyramide in Ägypten,
    Maturareise · Traces of human manifestations, pyramids
    in Egypt, school graduation trip 1971. © DS

3   Skyline: La Defénsè (?), Die Stadt der isolierten Objekte,
    · The City of isolated Objects. © DS

4   Das war Telekommunikation Ende der 1980er Jahre: Fax,
    Schnurlostelefon, Anrufbeantworter mit Tonbandkassetten · This
    was telecommunications at the end of the 1980s: fax, cordless
    telephone, answering machine with audio tape cassettes. © DS

I once tried myself to push this replacement of the architecture of the city by its marketing to the limit. The project, an exhibition of skyscraper models designed and built by Matteo Thun, was named *The Heavy Dress*.

Thun designed towers for powerful, real and imaginary institutions. For an airline as well as for a united worldwide church, for the headquarters of the Olympic Committee or for a museum of modern art. Crucially important was the fact that we consciously didn't speak of 'architecture' during this project, but wanted the towers to be discussed under the concept of "clothing." The constructed models were thus models on the catwalk of the media.

The exhibition was opened at the stroke of midnight at the Museum of Applied Arts in Vienna. Like at the cinema, the audience flocked into a dark room that was suddenly illuminated by spots; funk music, interrupted by advertising slogans for the towers, came from an audiotape.

At this point word was already going around in the neighboring bars that a new pop group called The Heavy Dress would perform at the museum. We had thus opened an architecture exhibition discotheque. The first reports about *The Heavy Dress* also consequently appeared in lifestyle magazines. Reports about *The Heavy Dress* were first published in *domus*, *forum* and other professional architecture magazines a year

lungs-Diskothek eröffnet. Folgerichtig erschienen auch die ersten Berichte über *The Heavy Dress* in Lifestylemagazinen. Erst ein Jahr später erschienen die Berichte über *The Heavy Dress* in *domus*, *forum* und anderen sachkundigen Architekturmagazinen. Und den Brief mit den Glückwünschen zur „gelungenen Theorie" dieser Aktion vom Hitler-Verehrer Philip Johnson verwahre ich heute als Dokument dieses Experiments architektonischen Hedonismus.

Wenn wir von der Spitze dieser Entwicklung zurückkehren zur sogenannten ernsthaften Architektur der Stadt, dann können wir sie nur mehr als Spiegelung dieses massenmedialen Zustands wahrnehmen. Denn jedes Projekt, jede Architektur der Stadt wird durch die allgemeine Rezipierbarkeit zu einer simplen Unterscheidbarkeit gezwungen. Deshalb ist ein stilistisches Urteil bei neuen Projekten relativ einfach zu fällen: Geboten wird die Spannweite von der Rekonstruktion unter Aufsicht des Denkmalschutzes – unter dem Stichwort: altes Bauen in neuer Umgebung – bis zum singulären architektonisch-ästhetischen Artefakt – unter dem Stichwort: moderne Skulptur.

Beispielhaft dafür war die Entwicklung der Internationalen Bauausstellung in Berlin. Sie begann mit dem Thema „Rekonstruktion der Stadt", und eines der ersten Projekte war der Krier-Plan für die südliche Friedrichstadt (1978).

Ausgangspunkt dieses Projekts war der im Zweiten Weltkrieg vernichtete Stadtgrundriss Berlins. Und das architektonische Thema schlechthin war Mitte der siebziger Jahre ‚der Block' – ob unauffällig eingeflochten in das traditionelle Straßennetz des 19. Jahrhunderts bei Krier oder autonom in den Stadtinsel-Projekten von Oswald Matthias Ungers.

Aber erst die in Berlin gebauten Beispiele der folgenden Jahre zeigten die Unlösbarkeit einer ‚Rekonstruktion der Stadt'. Zuwenig bedachte man, dass ‚der Block' nur *ein* Baustein in dem großen und heterogenen Feld der Stadt war. Es blieb bei isolierten Schaustücken, bei im Maßstab verunglückten Kleinstadtidyllen. Und was in Berlin vor ziemlich genau zehn Jahren mit Krier begann, endet nun, als letztes Projekt der Internationalen Bauausstellung mit einem Bau von Daniel Libeskind.

later. And today I keep the letter from Hitler admirer Philip Johnson with congratulations on the "successful theory" of this action as a document of this experiment in architectural hedonism.

If we return from the apex of this development to the so-called serious architecture of the city, then we can only perceive it anymore as the reflection of this mass media condition. Because every project, every architecture of the city is forced into a simple discriminability by the way it is generally received. That's why a stylistic judgment is relatively easy to pass in new projects: What is offered is the range from reconstruction under the supervision of the monument protection agency— under the heading: old construction in a new surrounding—right up to the singular architectonic-aesthetic artifact—under the heading: modern sculpture.

The development of the International Building Exhibition in Berlin was exemplary for this. It began with the theme "Reconstruction of the City," and one of the first projects was the Krier plan for Southern Friedrichstadt (1978).

The starting point of this project was Berlin's city layout, which had been destroyed in the Second World War. And the architectonic theme per se was 'the block' in the mid-sixties—whether unobtrusively woven into the traditional street grid of the 19th century by Krier or autonomous in the *Stadtinsel* (urban island) projects of Oswald Mathias Ungers.

But the examples of the following years that were constructed in Berlin first showed the indissolubility of a "Reconstruction of the City." One considered too little that 'the block' was only *one* building block in the large and heterogeneous field of the city. It remained at isolated showpieces, at small town idylls that failed in scale. And what began in Berlin with Krier almost exactly ten years ago is now ending, as the last project of the International Building Exhibition, with a structure by Daniel Libeskind.

Der Weg von Krier zu Libeskind mag zufällig scheinen, doch ist er bedeutsam und vielsagend. Überraschend dabei ist, dass auch Libeskind in der Argumentation seines Projekts vom ‚Stadtgrundriss' ausgeht, aber inzwischen, nach einem Jahrzehnt, zu einer gänzlich anderen Definition kommt als Krier.

Entscheidend ist allein der Weg der architektonischen Kultur, der hier begangen wurde. Es ist der Weg vom Versuch einer artifiziellen Rekonstruktion der Stadt zur isolierten poetischen Skulptur, die letztlich als einzige noch zu einer künstlerischen Aussage über den verlorenen Ort der Stadt imstande ist. Einsam und ohne kollektive Identität und Kommunizierbarkeit. Ja nicht einmal der Versuch einer sinnstiftenden architektonischen Begründung der Stadt kann noch unternommen werden.

Die unsichtbare Stadt

Dieses Ergebnis erkennend, öffnet sich für uns nun ein neuer Blick auf die Architektur der Stadt. Die Stadt ist heute ein virtuelles Konstrukt, eine emotionale Sehnsucht, vielleicht eine Erinnerung, aber ohne eigentliches Programm. Die Stadt ist nur mehr ein einzelnes Haus in einem globalen Dorf.

Wir müssen, um überhaupt noch zu architektonischen Themen durchdringen zu können, andere kulturelle Medien und Erscheinungen rezipieren. Also mit ganz anderen als den bisher gelernten Methoden Stadt betrachten und beobachten. Es ist uns heute erlaubt zu sagen: Ich habe noch nie eine Stadt gesehen, und ich entwerfe meinen Traum von ihr.

Ich spreche also von einem neuen Blick auf die Stadt. Und hier gibt es gar keine andere Möglichkeit als mit den immateriellen Beziehungsmustern, diesen Netzen und Knoten, die von und zwischen den Menschen und den Dingen Kraftfelder eröffnen, um neu zu beginnen.

Plan der südlichen · Plan of southern Friedrichstadt für die · for the IBA Berlin, Rob Krier, 1977. Archive DS

The way from Krier to Libeskind may seem coincidental, yet it is meaningful and telling. What is surprising about it is that Libeskind, in the argumentation of his project, assumes a 'city layout,' but meanwhile, after a decade, has come to a completely different definition than Krier.

Solely decisive is the path of architectural culture that was taken here. It is the path from the attempt of an artificial reconstruction of the city to an isolated poetic sculpture, which is ultimately the only one still capable of making an artistic statement about the lost location of the city. Lonely and without collective identity or communicability. Not even the attempt at a meaningful, architectonic justification of the city can still be undertaken.

Wir müssen wieder hinein in den Alltag – das bleibt die bedenkenswerte Botschaft Venturis –, diesen Alltag aber auf eine andere Art rezipieren. Pop-Musik und Kino sind dabei als Material ebenso wichtig wie die realen sozialen Konflikte.

Die Entwicklung der Massenmedien und der Telekommunikation hat die reale Stadt nicht vernichtet, wie noch die sechziger Jahre voraussagten, sondern mit neuen Möglichkeiten überlagert. Neue räumliche Dispositionen geschaffen.

Einige Beispiele dazu: Ich sah einen Strotter in Los Angeles, der saß auf einer kleinen Mauer in einem Park, hinter ihm eine Säule mit einer Stromleitung. Diese hatte er angezapft und einen kleinen tragbaren Fernseher daran angeschlossen. Ob rund um ihn eine reale Stadt war, war nicht so wichtig wie seine künstliche, seine virtuelle Stadt auf dem Bildschirm.

Oder: Vor einigen Monaten gab mir ein junger englischer Designer in Wien seine Visitenkarte. Darauf stand nur zu lesen: Jasper Morrison, London, 7223512. London ist seine Stadt, ist genannt, aber er braucht keine Straße, kein Haus mehr, nur mehr eine Nummer für seine Identität. Möglicherweise ist an diese Nummer angeschlossen ein Funktelefon, ein Anrufbeantworter, ein Telefax, ein PC … Ich weiß es nicht. Klar ist nur, dass er an diesem Ort – gibt es überhaupt einen räumlichen Ort hinter dieser Nummer? – nicht einmal mehr als Person anwesend sein muss. Mit der Annullierung von Straße und Hausnummer ist auch die reale Stadt vernichtet worden. Es gibt keine möglichen Erinnerungen an einen Stadtgrundriss mehr. Jasper Morrison als Person ist nicht mehr verbunden mit einer gebauten Substanz. Man kann nur vermuten, dass sich hinter dieser Nummer zumindest ein Zimmer befindet.

Das sind kleine und unbedeutende Beispiele aus dem Alltag der realen Auswirkungen der Telekommunikation heute. Sie beweisen nichts mehr als die reale Existenz der Immaterialität, besser gesagt, die Existenz von virtuellen Räumen mit starker und gleichzeitiger, mit kommunikativer Dichte.

The Invisible City

Recognizing this result, a new view to the architecture of the city opens up for us. Today the city is a virtual construct, an emotional yearning, perhaps a memory, but without an actual program. The city is only a single house in a global village.

In order to still be able to get through to architectonic themes at all, we have to receive other cultural media and phenomena. That is, with totally different methods of contemplating and observing the city than those learned up to now. We are allowed to say today: I've never seen a city and I'm designing my dream of it.

I'm thus speaking about a new view to the city. And there is no other possibility whatsoever here than to begin anew with the immaterial patterns of relationships, these nets and knots that open force fields from and between the people and the things.

We have to go back into everyday life—that remains the thought-provoking message of Venturi—but receive this daily routine in a different way. Pop music and the cinema are just as important as material as the real social conflicts.

The advancement of mass media and telecommunications did not destroy the real city, as the 1960s still predicted, but overlaid it with new possibilities. Created new spatial dispositions.

Several examples of this: I saw a vagabond in Los Angeles sitting on a small wall in a park, behind him a pillar with a power line. He tapped it and connected a small portable television to it. Whether a real city was surrounding him wasn't as important as his artificial, his virtual city on the screen.

Or: A few months ago a young English designer in Vienna gave me his business card. The only thing to be read on it was: Jasper Morrison, London, 7223512. London is his city, is named, but he doesn't need a street, a house anymore, just a number for his identity. Perhaps a cellular phone, an answering machine, a telefax, a PC is connected to this number … I don't know. What is clear though is that he no longer even has to be present as a person at this location. Is there a spatial location behind this number at all? With the nullification of the street and house number, the real city has also been destroyed. No possible memories of a city layout exist anymore. Jasper Morrison, as a person, is no longer connected with a built substance. One can only presume that at least a room stands behind this number.

Deshalb werden wir klarer sehen, wenn wir die Stadt zunächst nur als ein Medium betrachten. Ein vorerst noch unsichtbares Netz aus Linien und Daten der Energien, des Transports, der Informationen. Dem Medium Stadt entspricht heute das Bild eines Mikrochips. Zur räumlichen Wirklichkeit wird die Stadt in dem Moment, wenn die Linien sich zu verknoten beginnen, wenn die Spuren des Netzes Punkte erzeugen, die sich zu Zeichen und Signalen verwandeln. Daraus entsteht, auch heute noch, immer auch ein gebauter Ort.

Es sind dann immer in irgendeiner Form die Umsteigestationen, die wieder eine Bedeutung erlangen. Sie sind die wahren Monumente unserer Zeit. Die Orte, wo im ‚Medium Stadt' von einem System zum anderen gewechselt werden muss. Diese Kreuzungen, diese Knoten erzeugen die sichtbare Stadt. Entscheidend dabei ist nun, dass in der europäischen Stadt dieser Ort immer schon vorhanden ist, ihm Geschichten und Traditionen bereits eingeschrieben sind. Entscheidend ist weiters, dass die neuen Technologien in Europa keine neue Stadt erzeugen, sondern dass sich diese einnisten in die Struktur der alten Stadt, sie überlagern und mit neuen Bedeutungen und Nutzungen füllen.

Knoten und Modelle

Wir haben also miterlebt, wie die avantgardistischen Ideen der sechziger Jahre – all die Walking Cities und Plug-in-Cities – als formale Ideen aus der Pop-Kultur kamen und auch dort wieder landeten und bestenfalls einige futuristische Geschäfte und Diskotheken beeinflussten. Diese Formen waren zwar in Übereinstimmung mit den Träumen und Wünschen der Menschen, aber weit entfernt vom Stand der tatsächlichen technologischen Entwicklung jener Zeit.

Wir haben dann gesehen, dass in den siebziger Jahren die Erinnerung an die Tradition der europäischen Stadt einsetzte. Diese Formen waren in Übereinstimmung mit der noch existierenden europäischen Stadt, hatten aber dafür die inzwischen stattgefundene soziale, kulturelle und technologische Entwicklung ignoriert.

These are small and insignificant examples of the everyday, real impacts of telecommunication today. They prove nothing more than the real existence of immateriality, better said, the existence of virtual spaces with strong and, at the same time, communicative density.

That's why we will see more clearly if we first consider the city solely as a medium. A network of lines and data of energies, of transport, of information, that is still invisible for the time being. The medium of the city corresponds today to the image of a microchip. The city becomes a spatial reality at the moment the lines begin to knot themselves together, the traces of the net begin to create points that transform into signs and signals. What comes out of it, even today, is always a constructed place.

It is the transfer stations, then, that always reacquire a meaning in any way, shape or form. They are the true monuments of our time. The places where, in the "medium of the city," a change from one system to another has to be made. These intersections, these knots create the visible city. What is now decisive is that this place always exists in the European city, is already inscribed in stories and traditions. Further decisive is the fact that the new technologies do not create a new city in Europe, but that they lodge themselves into the structure of the old city, superimpose and fill them with new meanings and uses.

Knots and Models

We have thus witnessed how the avant-garde ideas of the sixties—all the walking cities and plug-in cities—came out of pop culture as formal ideas and also landed there again and, at best, influenced several futuristic shops and discotheques. These forms were admittedly in accordance with the dreams and desires of the people, but far removed from the status of the actual technological development of that time.

We then saw that the memory of the tradition of the European city started in the seventies. These forms were in accordance with the still existing European city, but had ignored the social, cultural and technological development taking place in the meantime.

Wir müssen also jenseits einer technologischen Euphorie und jenseits einer historischen Schwermut dem Schicksal der europäischen Stadt produktiv begegnen können. Deren Schicksal ist nun einmal ihre Geschichte, die festgeschriebenen, weil fest gebauten Strukturen ihrer jahrhundertelangen Tradition und ihrer jahrtausendealten Gründungsmythen. Die europäische Stadt beruht auf ihrem Gedächtnis, ihrem Speicher.

Diese Stadt ist die Erinnerung der Orte. Die Orte und Bauten geben archäologisches Zeugnis über die Schichten der Stadt und ihrer Erinnerung. Sie erzählen uns Geschichten über die gebaute Geschichte. Die konkreten Tiefenschnitte an Ort und Stelle zeigen uns Veränderungen, die doch nur die Überlagerung von Bedeutungen belegen.

Dem massenmedialen Sturm auf die alte europäische Stadt können wir nur entkommen, wenn wir im einzelnen architektonischen Projekt für die Stadt eine poetische Kraft verankern. So wie die geheimnisvollen schwarzen Quader, die als Botschaft einer außerirdischen Intelligenz selbst den Supercomputer in Stanley Kubricks *2001 – Odyssee im Weltraum* außer Kontrolle brachten.

Derzeit befinden wir uns mit den postmodernen Megaprojekten in diesem Zustand der „Berauschung seltsamer Art, mitten in einer öden, matten, von Elend geschüttelten Zeit" (Bloch). Aber wir wissen ebenso, dass alles das nur Oberfläche ist, dass der Lack, das Styling die ersten Sprünge und Risse zeigt. Und die Frage ist zu stellen, ob dann, wenn die neu-historischen Fassaden der Projekte von ihren Stahlgerüsten herabrutschen, ob dann dahinter Substanz, ob materielle Qualitäten von Architektur sichtbar werden.

We therefore have to be able to productively respond to the fate of the European city beyond a technological euphoria and beyond a historical gloom. Its fate is now its history, the established, because solidly built structures of its centuries-long tradition and its millennia-old founding myths. The European city is based on its memory, its storage.

The city is the memory of places. The places and buildings provide archaeological evidence of the layers of the city and its memory. They tell us stories about the constructed history. The concrete depth sections on location show us the changes that only prove, however, the overlapping of meanings.

We can only escape the mass media storming of the old European city if we anchor a poetic power in single architectural projects for the city. Just like the mysterious black slabs which, as the message of an extraterrestrial intelligence, even knocked the supercomputer in Stanley Kubrick's *2001—A Space Odyssey* out of control.

We currently find ourselves with the postmodern megaprojects in this condition of "intoxication of a strange type, in the midst of a dull, dim era rocked by misery" (Bloch). But we also likewise know that all of that is only a surface, that the paint, the styling, is showing the first cracks and tears. And the question is to be asked if when the neo-historic facades of the projects slide down from their steel frameworks, if substance, if material qualities of architecture become visible behind them.

A European project of a new architecture of the city has to counter this situation of decadence created by the marketing of cities with a radical new realism. And realism here means nothing less than the difficult task of reconciling tradition with the immaterial technology

Der schwarze Monolith im Film *2001 – Odyssee im Weltraum* ·
Black monolith in the film *2001 – A Space Odyssey*.
© William Beutler, CC BY 2.0

Dritter Tag • Day Three

Ein europäisches Projekt einer neuen Architektur der Stadt muss dieser durch das Marketing der Städte geschaffenen Situation der Dekadenz mit einem radikalen neuen Realismus begegnen. Und Realismus hier bedeutet nichts weniger als die schwierige Aufgabe, die Tradition mit der immateriellen Technologie der Information zu versöhnen. Nach wie vor müssen wir mit dem Studium der gebaut vorhandenen Substanz der europäischen Stadt und ihren Dokumenten beginnen, aus ihnen die Botschaften, die seit damals der Alltag eingeschrieben hat, herauslesen.

Auf Stadtplänen und Landkarten findet man alte Ansichten von Städten und Gebäuden, Orte der Erinnerung, magische Namen – Stadtpläne und Landkarten sind die Gedächtnisbücher der Welt. Jeder Ort, jede Stätte erscheint in einer verschiedenen Farbe auf einem unterschiedlichen Hintergrund; doch jede Farbe kann der Reisende, dessen Ziel auf der Karte nicht zu finden ist, gegen eine andere Farbe austauschen.

„Eine Reise in das Innere einer Stadt und ihrer Architektur bringt es mit sich, dass zufällige Punkte, unterbrochene Linien und Namen außerhalb der Reihe entlang der Achse der ewigen Hoffnung neu einander zugeordnet werden."

Es ist diese Spurensuche, die der Arbeit von Libeskind Bedeutung gibt. Und es ist dieselbe Spurensuche, auf die sich John Hejduk in einem kurzen Text über die Stadt, konkret Mailand, bezieht:

"Among the documents I received from Milan were the Italian Touring Club plan and atlas. Their content obsesses me ... the maps and information regarding the city of Milan haunt me. I am constantly drawn in. I am a foreigner to Milan. I try to grasp Milan through the documents, which serve as cloudy x-rays. They are full ... with places and names. They require attention. ... I hold them in my hands. ... I am constantly reading. ... I remove them as a surgeon would the loose folded map. I open it and put myself into the task. ... I search. ... I probe. I twist my vision."

of information. We still have to begin with the study of the built, existing substance of the European city and its documents, to read out the messages from them that have inscribed everyday life since then.

On city plans and maps one finds old views of cities and buildings, places of memory, magical names—city plans and maps are the memory books of the world. Every place, every site appears in a different color on a different background; yet the traveler, whose destination is not to be found on the map, can exchange any color for a different one.

"A journey into the inner realm of a city and its architecture entails that coincidental points, interrupted lines and names outside of the row along the axis of eternal hope will be newly assigned to one another."

It is this search for traces that gives meaning to Libeskind's work. And it is the same search for traces that John Hejduk refers to in a short text about the city, concretely Milan:

"Among the documents I received from Milan were the Italian Touring Club plan and atlas. Their content obsesses me ... the maps and information regarding the city of Milan haunt me. I am constantly drawn in. I am a stranger to Milan. I try to grasp Milan through the documents, which serve as cloudy x-rays. They are full ... with places and names. They require attention. ... I hold them in my hands. ... I'm constantly reading. ... I remove them as a surgeon would the loosely folded map. I open it and put myself into the task. ... I search. ... I probe. I twist my vision."

And it is precisely this search for traces that Vitruvius wrote about in the preamble to Book VI of *de Architectura*:

"Aristippus, the Socratic philosopher, shipwrecked on the coast of Rhodes, perceiving some diagrams thereon, is reported to have exclaimed to his companions, 'Be of good courage, I see marks of civilization.'"

The traces of the city are inscribed in a ground, in an area that can also be referred to as our collective consciousness. It is to be understood in this way if Libes-

Und es ist eben diese Spurensuche, über die Vitruv in der Vorrede zum sechsten Buch geschrieben hat:

„Als der Philosoph Aristippos, durch Schiffbruch an die Gestade der Rodier geworfen, in den Sand gezeichnete geometrische Figuren bemerkt hatte, soll er seinen Begleitern gegenüber folgenden Ausruf getan haben: ‚Lasst uns guter Hoffnung sein! Ich sehe nämlich Spuren von Menschen!‘"

Die Spuren der Stadt sind eingeschrieben in einen Grund, in eine Fläche, die auch als unser kollektives Unbewusstes bezeichnet werden kann. So ist es zu verstehen, wenn Libeskind in seinem Text fortfährt mit einem Verweis auf das Papier, auf verschiedene Papiere mit verschiedenen Schriften und Bedeutungen, die im Wasser treiben wie Schiffe. Dieses Wasser schließlich ist die Substanz, die als Bewusstsein haften bleibt. Und er folgert daraus: „Auf diese Weise wird die Realität als Essenz der Hoffnung zum Beweis unsichtbarer Freuden – das Berlin des geöffneten Himmels. Untersucht man diesen Himmel, der sich permanent weigert, seine Identität zu offenbaren, so entdeckt man: alles, was vermessen, bezeichnet und eingeordnet ist, alles entgleist in die Dimensionen des Unbestimmten und des Sphärischen. Dieser Ort des Ungleichgewichts, von dem die Freiheit ewig ausgeht und zu dem sie ständig zurückkehrt, ohne heimzukommen, dieser Ort zeigt sich als Stätte, an der Architektur zu sich selbst findet als Anfang am Ende."

Wir nehmen sein Wort auf, von der Architektur, „die zu sich selbst findet als Anfang am Ende", und erkennen zum Schluss darin jene alte Sehnsucht der europäischen Moderne, die sich am erfüllten Ende der noch nicht begonnenen Aufklärung auf den Anfang der Kultur zurückgeworfen sieht. Dort wird dann die europäische Stadt nach den Gebäuden suchen, die den gotischen Kathedralen gleich, mnemonische Geräte, Bewusstseins-Maschinen und Gedächtnisspeicher sind. Und das neue architektonische Projekt für die europäische Stadt muss diese Dimension einer verschwiegenen poetischen Kraft erreichen, wenn es für die Zukunft Bedeutung haben will.

kind continues in this text with a reference to the paper, to different papers with different writings and meanings that float in water like ships. This water is ultimately the substance that lingers as consciousness. And he infers from this: "In this way reality, as the substance of things hoped for, becomes a proof of invisible joys—the Berlin of open skies. In exploring the shape of this sky, which continually refuses to come into identity or equivalence, one discovers that what has been marked, fixed, and measured nevertheless lapses in both the dimension of the indeterminate and the spherical. This space of non equilibrium—from which freedom eternally departs and toward which it moves without homecoming—constitutes a place in which architecture comes upon itself as beginning at the end."

We take up his word, about architecture "that comes upon itself as beginning at the end," and finally recognize in it that old yearning of European modernism which, at the fulfilled end of the not yet begun enlightenment, sees itself thrown back to the beginning of culture. The European city will then search for the buildings there, which, like the Gothic cathedrals, are mnemonic devices, awareness machines and memory storages. And the new architectonic project for the European city has to reach this dimension of a reticent poetic power if it wants to have meaning for the future.

Nachdenklicher Blick auf die Spuren der Zivilisation an ihrem Ende · Pensive view at the traces of civilization at its end Ägypten · Egypt, Maturareise · school graduation trip 1971. © DS

aus · from

The Heavy Dress
Falter Verlag Wien · Vienna 1986
Translation by Brian Dorsey

The Heavy Dress
The Surface as the Manifesto

The Heavy Dress
Die Oberfläche als Manifest

Die Bilder, die Sie sehen, sind Bilder von Modellen. Models auf dem Laufsteg der Medien und selbst Medium. Sie stellen sich vor, Hochhäuser zu sehen? Irrtum. Sie sehen nur deren Bilder, sie urteilen über Bekleidung, Sie sind mit Mode konfrontiert. Vergessen Sie sofort alles, was Sie an bedeutungsschweren und pathetischen Erklärungen über das ‚Gesamtkunstwerk' Architektur gehört haben mögen. All den vergeistigt überfrachteten Insiderquatsch über ‚Bedeutung' und ‚Absichten' von gebauten Räumen. Denn wirkliche Häuser stehen nicht mehr zur Debatte. Es gibt keine Häuser mehr, nichts Gebautes, das dieses Wort verdienen würde, wird noch wahrgenommen.

*

Alles was wir sehen, sind schemenhafte Silhouetten, das überanstrengte Auge ist konditioniert von der flimmernden Quadratur des ‚Schirms': langsames und Nichtssagendes wird reflexlos abgespeichert. Nur manchmal hält das Auge inne, bricht seine automatisierte Geschwindigkeit, beginnt zu SEHEN, stoppt vor dem SCHÖNEN KLEID! so ist es, wenn ein Skelett verhüllt seine Haut zu Markte trägt. Das ist „The Heavy Dress"!

*

The images you see are images of models. Models on the media catwalk, and a medium themselves. Do you imagine seeing high-rises? Wrong. You only see their images; they pass judgment on dress; you are confronted with fashion. Immediately forget all of the portentous and pathetic explanations about the 'Gesamtkunstwerk' of architecture you may have heard. All of the intellectualized, overloaded insider nonsense about 'meaning' and 'intentions' of constructed spaces. Because real houses are no longer open to debate. There are no houses anymore; nothing built that would deserve this word will still be perceived.

*

Everything we see is hazy silhouettes; the overstrained eye is conditioned by the flickering quadrature of the 'screen': slow things and things that say nothing are stored without a reflex. The eye only sometimes takes a pause, breaks its automatic speed, begins to SEE, stops in front of the BEAUTIFUL DRESS! That's the way it is if a skeleton risks its own covered skin. That is the "Heavy Dress!"

*

Dort stehen wir heute. Unmerklich fast hat sich diese Wandlung, diese Entleibung der Häuser vollzogen. Das geschieht mitten in einer einmaligen, bisher nicht für möglich gehaltenen Konjunktur der Architektur. Architektur ist IN! Die besten ihres Faches jonglieren mit Engagements und Terminplänen wie Opernstartenöre. Die Städte dürsten nach den großen Stadtbildmagiern, die eingebunden werden können in die Werbestrategien ‚interkommunaler Konkurrenzen'. Überall soll alles schöner werden, weil nichts mehr besser werden kann.

*

Die „Heavy Dress"-Kollektion von Matteo Thun ist die erste realistische Antwort auf die heutige und zukünftige Rolle von Bildern in der Stadt. Sie ist ein Bekenntnis zur MODE. Denn die Mode, die Manifestation der ‚Oberfläche' befreit die Bilder der möglichen Bauten aus ihrer einseitigen Verwendung und Bedeutung. Die Konzentration auf die Haut und ihr Bild ist eine Befreiung von allen funktionalen und technokratischen Zwängen. Endlich kann wieder neugierig über Zukunft, über neue Symbole, über das was die fortgeschrittenste Zivilisation in das kollektive Unbewusste eingeschrieben hat, geredet, gedacht, geforscht, erfunden und entworfen werden. Der „Heavy Dress" ist Oberfläche. Aber Oberfläche als Haut, glatt oder rau, bunt oder eindeutig, edel oder banal, teuer oder bescheiden – Glas, Keramik, Kunststoff, Metall, Licht und Farbe.

*

Noch einmal sollten wir erwähnen, dass die ‚Häuser' verschwunden sind. Häuser hatten Bauherren, die gibt es heute nicht mehr. Firmen und Institutionen, ja selbst ‚Private' sind nicht ästhetisch autonom, sondern ordnen sich erfundenen Bildern und gesellschaftlichen Rollen unter. Die Häuser sind verschwunden, an ihre, Stelle ist der NAME getreten. Der Markenname ist das Bild, das Image. Die Internationale Bauausstellung in Berlin ist ‚Stararchitektur': egal was sie konkret produ-

„Times Square". © Matteo Thun

That is where we stand today. This metamorphosis, this disembodiment of the houses, takes place almost imperceptibly. This is happening in the middle of a unique boom of architecture, one not considered possible up to now. Architecture is IN! The best of their profession juggle with commitments and appointment schedules like star opera tenors. The cities are thirsty for the grand cityscape magicians who can be integrated into the advertisement strategies of 'intercommunal competitors.' Everything is to get more beautiful everywhere, because nothing more can get better.

*

ziert, es ist auf jeden Fall auf mediale Vervielfältigung angelegt. ‚Architekturstars' sind auch die Vollzugsorgane des Frankfurter Museumsufers. Es ist medial eine Sensation lange vor der tatsächlichen Verwirklichung. Es gibt keine wirklichen Städte mehr, es gibt auch keine wirklichen Firmen, die eindeutige Produkte herstellen, mehr: Benetton ist ein Pullover und ein Formel-I-Auto, General Motors ist Auto oder Vorabendfernsehserie. Das Produktionskapital ist diversifiziertes Finanzkapital, die Firma ist ein NAME, ein Image, das ein Bild benötigt.

*

Die „Heavy Dress"-Kollektion von Matteo Thun ist deshalb imaginären Bauträgern gewidmet. Es sind Symbolproduzenten angesprochen, die in der Lage sind, die gesellschaftlichen Werte dieser Gesellschaft zu ‚zeigen'. Die neuen Herren sind: die Bank, das Hotel, das Museum, die Religion, die Printmedien, die Telekommunikation, der Sport, die Airline, die Mode selbst. Aus diesen Wertungen entwickeln sich die Superzeichen, die ein Beispiel geben von den visuellen Möglichkeiten der Bilder, die eine Andeutung geben von der rasanten Präsenz der Bekleidung, die einfach ‚starke Häute': eine „Heavy Dress"- Kollektion benötigen.

*

Matteo Thun's "Heavy Dress" collection is the first realistic answer to the present-day and future role of images in the city. It is a commitment to FASHION. Because fashion, the manifestation of the 'surface,' liberates the images of possible buildings from their one-sided use and meaning. The concentration on the skin and its image is a liberation from all functional and technocratic constraints. Finally people can once again curiously speak about, think of, seek, invent or design the future, new symbols and what the most progressive civilization has inscribed into its collective consciousness. The "Heavy Dress" is surface. But surface as skin, smooth or rough, colorful or distinct, noble or banal, expensive or modest—glass, ceramic, plastic, metal, light and color.

*

Once again we should mention that the 'houses' have disappeared. Houses had clients; they don't exist anymore today. Companies and institutions, even 'private people' are not aesthetically autonomous, but subordinate themselves to invented images and social roles. The houses have vanished; the NAME has appeared in their place. The brand name is the picture, the image. The International Building Exhibition in Berlin is 'star architecture': regardless of what it concretely produces, it is aimed in any case at media duplication. 'Architecture stars' are also the executing agents of the Frankfurt Museum Embankment. It is a media sensation long before the actual realization. There are no real cities anymore; there are also no real companies that make distinct products anymore: Benetton is a sweater and a Formula 1 car, General Motors is an automobile or an early evening television series. Production capital is diversified financial capital; the company is a NAME, an image that needs a picture.

*

li · l: „NASA Roofscape", re · r: „Olympic Games". © Matteo Thun

Wo führt das hin? Modellhäuser aus der Boutique? Oder noch ärger: Irgend etwas wird irgendwo irgendwie gebaut – dann kommt der Couturier mit seiner Musterkollektion, entwirft ein Modellkleid, passend für die ganz konkrete Gelegenheit. So sehen es die Pessimisten. Als das Endstadium einer Entwicklung, wo heute schon jeder halbwegs Informierte das passende Architekturmodell für seine Aufgabe aus den Personalstilen der Weltstars auswählen kann. Die nötige Beratung erhält man in den ‚Architekturausstellungen' und ausgestellten Architekturen von Frankfurt, Berlin oder Paris. You can get, what you want: einen herb-kühl quadratischen Ungers, einen goldschimmernd opulenten Hollein, einen blendend weißen Pappmacheebau von Richard Meier, stereometrische Stahlmonumentalität von Helmut Jahn, dem Bayern aus Chicago, oder einen kleinen Verkehrsunfall vom Kalifornier Frank Gehry … die Modelle stehen bereit. In diesem Feld der Beliebigkeit ist das Bekenntnis zur „Heavy Dress"-Kollektion die einzig radikale Erneuerung.

*

„Das Bedürfnis des Schutzes, der Deckung und der Raumschließung war einer der frühesten Antriebe zu industriellem Erfinden. Der Mensch lernte natürliche Decken, z.B. das zottige Fell der Tiere, die schützende Rinde der Bäume, in ihrem Wesen und ihrer Bestimmung erkennen, sie zu eigenen Zwecken noch ihrer richtig aufgefassten natürlichen Bestimmung benutzen, sie zuletzt durch künstliches Geflecht nachbilden. Der Gebrauch dieser Decken ist älter als die Sprache, der Begriff der Deckung, des Schutzes, des Abschlusses ist unauflöslich an jene natürlichen und künstlichen Decken und Bekleidungen geknüpft, die somit die sinnlichen Zeichen für jene Begriffe geworden sind und als solche vielleicht das wichtigste Element in der Symbolik der Baukunst bilden."

Gottfried Semper, *Der Stil*

*

li · l: „United Vatican", re · r: „All United Airlines". © Matteo Thun

The "Heavy Dress" collection of Matteo Thun is therefore dedicated to imaginary builders. Symbol producers are addressed, those who are capable of 'showing' the social values of a society. The new masters are: the bank, the hotel, the museum, the religion, the print media, the telecommunications, the sport, the airline, fashion itself. What develops out of these valuations are the super signs that give an example of the visual possibilities of images, that give an indication of the swift presence of dress that simply needs 'strong skins': a "Heavy Dress" collection.

*

Where does this lead to? Model houses from the boutique? Or even worse: Something will be built somewhere, somehow—then the couturier comes with his sample collection, designs a model dress, fitting for the whole concrete occasion. That's the way pessimists see it. As the final stage of a development where today every halfway-informed person can already choose the suitable architectural model for his task from the personal styles of the world stars. One receives the necessary consultation at the 'architecture exhibitions' and in the exhibited architectures of Frankfurt, Berlin or Paris. You can get what you want: an austere-cool, quadratic Ungers, a gold-shimmering, opulent Hollein, a dazzling white papier mâché structure by Richard Meier, stereometric steel monumentality by Helmut Jahn, the Bavarian from Chicago, or a minor car accident by the Californian Frank Gehry … the models stand ready. In this field of randomness, the commitment to the "Heavy Dress" collection is the only radical innovation.

*

Cover-Katalog der Ausstellung, Grafik · Catalog cover of the exhibition, graphics: eichinger oder knechtl, Falter Verlag. Archive DS

Alle Architektur beginnt mit Bekleidung. Skyscraper, Türme, sind eindeutige Zeichen, Machtsymbole. Austrainierte Stadtkämpfer für den einzigen Zweck des Triumphes. Skyscraper steigen in den Ring der Stadt, betonen schon vor dem Kampf ihre Einzigartigkeit, glitzern und glänzen in ihren Rüstungen. Aggressiv sind ihre Signale, die Schwerter sind Bilder. Die stärksten Bilder gewinnen.

*

Mit der Bekleidung beginnt die Zukunft. Vom Verlust des ‚Materiellen' ist die Rede. Die Maschinen sind normiert, austauschbar, mein Euromotor in allen Autos des Kontinents. Die Unterscheidbarkeit ist reduziert auf den Austausch von Zeichen, Symbolen, Signalen. Das eigentliche Problem ist die Karosserie. Diese Haut ist mehr als nur Oberfläche, ihre Signale führen zum Dialog, wortlos allerdings tauschen wir die Bilder aus. Wenig noch wissen wir über ihre Bedeutung, ihre Grammatik. Obwohl heute schon jedes Wahrnehmen von Wirklichkeit aus dem Erinnern an unbewusst eingeschriebene Bilder besteht.

*

"The need for protection, cover, and spatial enclosure supplied some of the earliest inspiration for industrial invention. Human beings first learned to recognize the essence and purpose of natural covers (shaggy animal skins, protective tree bark) and began to use them for their own needs according to their correctly perceived natural use. Later, they imitated them with synthetic weaving. The use of these covers is thus older than language. The concepts of covering, protecting, and enclosing are indissolubly connected with those natural and synthetic covers and dressings that have become the sensible sign for those concepts. As such they form perhaps the most important element in the symbolism of architecture."

Gottfried Semper, *Style*[1]

*

All architecture begins with dress. Skyscrapers, towers, are clear signs, symbols of power. Well-trained urban fighters for the sole purpose of triumph. Skyscrapers step into the battle ring of the city, already emphasizing their uniqueness before the bout, gleaming and shining in their armaments. Their signals are aggressive, the swords are images. The strongest images win.

*

The future begins with the dress. The talk is of the loss of the 'material' dimension. The machines are standardized, replaceable, my Euroengine in all of the continent's cars. The discriminability is reduced to the exchange of signs, symbols, signals. The actual problem is the body. This skin is more than just a surface; its signals lead to dialog; wordlessly, however, we substitute the images. We still know little about their meaning, their grammar. Even though every perception of reality today already consists of the memory of unconsciously inscribed images.

*

Die „Heavy Dress"-Kollektion ist ein Forschungsprojekt, ein Testprogramm. Im Bekenntnis zum Bild, zur Oberfläche, zur Mode, sucht es den Ausweg aus der absurden Situation, wo für das noch immer ‚gebaute Statement', das bereits unabhängig von Zweck, Funktion, Konstruktion und Verwendung ist, allein der Name des Erfinders, die sogenannte Bedeutung des Architekten, eine kuriose Authentizität einfordert. Dagegen führt die bewusste Produktion von Bildern, die Erarbeitung einer Kollektion von Haus-Häuten zur Eliminierung des ‚Autors', entzieht ihm die Möglichkeit der privaten maniera und des abstrusen Personalstils! – will endlich wieder zu einer zeithältigen Anonymität kollektiv oder öffentlich wirksamer Botschaften kommen. Deshalb sind die Skyscraper nur ein Vorwand: Sie sind einfach eine ‚hervorragende', eine ausgesetzte Situation, an ihr kann jene Reduktion erprobt werden, die sich allein auf das kalkulierte Spiel von Volumina und Außenhaut verlassen muss.

*

Nur vordergründig wird das Spiel der Beliebigkeit forciert. Dessen Überwindung ist das Bekenntnis zur Oberfläche der Haut. Ich weiß nicht, ob wir uns bereits jenseits der Postmoderne befinden … wenn wir nicht mehr von Architektur als Sprache sprechen, von Historizität, Ironie und Mehrfachkodierung. Jenseits der Postmoderne befinden wir uns, wenn die Stadt als Wüste gesehen werden muss – nicht mehr als Dschungel. Als Wüste von immergleichen, Hauskörnern, wo uns nur die Autonummern an eine konkrete Stadt erinnern. In dieser Wüste sind wir selbst die ersten Pfähle, die einen Ort fixieren. Wir sind die Skyscraper, in die Tierhäute, Baumrinden und Decken Gottfried Sempers gehüllt:

„Die Kunst des Bekleidens der Nacktheit des Leibes ist vermutlich eine jüngere Erfindung als die Benützung deckender Oberflächen zu Lagern und zu räumlichen Abschlüssen."

In der Wüste gibt es keinen Stadtraum mehr. Nur inszenierte, abgegrenzte Stammesräume. Der Clan lässt sich nieder, richtet als Begrenzung seine Zeichen auf, es ist Ereignisraum, oder gar kein Raum. Die erste Haut der Wiedergeburt muss ein „Heavy Dress" sein, ein starkes Kleid, ein Bild für das es kein Sprechen gibt, das aber alle verstehen.

The "Heavy Dress" collection is a research project, a test program. In the commitment to the image, to the surface, to the fashion, it seeks the escape from the absurd situation where the name of the inventor alone, the so-called significance of the architect, calls for a curious authenticity for the still 'built statement,' which is already independent of purpose, function, construction and usage. By contrast, the conscious production of images, the preparation of a collection of house skins for the elimination of the 'author,' deprives him/her the possibility of the private maniera and the abstruse personal style!—and wants to finally come again to a temporal anonymity of collectively or publically effective messages. That is why the skyscrapers are only a pretense: They are simply an 'outstanding,' an exposed situation; that reduction, which has to depend solely on the calculated play of volumes and outer skin, can be tried on it.

*

The game of arbitrariness is only expedited superficially. Its overcoming is the commitment to the surface of the skin. I don't know whether we already find ourselves beyond postmodernism … if we no longer speak of architecture as language, of historicity, irony and multiple coding. We find ourselves beyond postmodernism if the city has to be seen as a desert—no longer as a jungle. As a desert of always the same house grains, where only the license plate numbers remind us of a concrete city. In this desert we ourselves are the first stakes that secure a place. We are the skyscrapers, wrapped in Gottfried Semper's animal skins, tree bark and coverings:

"The art of dressing the body's nakedness is presumably a more recent invention than the use of coverings for encampments and spatial enclosures."[2]

In the desert there is no more urban space. Only staged, confined tribal spaces. The clan settles down, sets up its sign as a boundary; it is event space or no space at all. The first skin of rebirth has to be a "Heavy Dress," an image devoid of speech, but which everyone understands.

---

[1] English translation by Harry Francis Mallgrave and Michael Robinson in *Style in the Technical and Tectonic Arts; or, Practical Aesthetics* by Gottfried Semper (Los Angeles: The Getty Research Institute, 2004), p. 123.
[2] Ibid., p. 247.

Dritter Tag • Day Three

Wohnhaus · Apartment building in Zürich, Selnau 111, Miroslav Šik. © Thomas Boga, 1987

aus · from

Falter, Mai · May 1989
„Analoge Architektur"
Translation by Brian Dorsey

Analoge Architektur

Analogous Architecture

Bilder, akribisch filmisch, realistisch gezeichnet, die jeder schon irgendwann und irgendwo einmal gesehen hat, Stadtbilder, Architekturbilder, Raumbilder – wie Tapeten kleiden sie die Wände aus. Man findet sich in einer Ausstellung, die sich *Analoge Architektur* nennt. Die einzelnen Bilder sind jeweils auf den Punkt der intendierten Stimmung gebrachte Architekturprojekte. Entstanden sind sie in den letzten Jahren am Lehrstuhl von Fabio Reinhart an der ETH Zürich unter der Ägide von Miroslav Šik.

Die Ausstellung der analogen Architektur läuft – um nur ihren medialen Raum zu bestimmen – wie ein Film seit einiger Zeit durch die Städte Europas. Und sie gastiert überall als eine Art Aufführung im jeweiligen Programmkino.

Und es ist die derzeit wohl einprägsamste und markanteste Dokumentation einer neuen jungen, einer nächsten Generation der Architektur. Diese Projekte und ihre Bilder sind bereits die Reaktion auf die jetzt in Konjunktur befindliche Architektur der 1980er Jahre, entwickelt von Studenten, für die die Geschichte der Moderne nur mehr ‚Geschichte' ist und für die selbst die Geschichte der Postmoderne nur mehr eine ‚Geschichte' ist.

Images, meticulously cinematic, realistically drawn, which everyone has already seen sometime and somewhere, city images, architectural images, spatial images—they line the walls like wallpaper. One finds oneself in an exhibition entitled *Analogous Architecture*. The individual images are architectural projects respectively boiled down to the intended mood. They have emerged in the past years at the Fabio Reinhart chair at the Swiss Federal Institute of Technology (ETH) in Zurich under the aegis of Miroslav Šik.

The exhibition of analogous architecture has been running—to only determine its media space—like a film for some time through the cities of Europe. And everywhere it makes a guest appearance as a type of performance in the respective repertory cinema.

And at the moment it is probably the most memorable and distinctive documentation of a new, young, next generation of architecture. These projects and their images are already the reaction to the architecture of the 1980s, which now finds itself in great demand, developed by students for whom the history of modernism is merely 'history' and for whom the history of postmodernism is only a 'story' for they themselves.

So anverwandeln und einverleiben sich beispielsweise die analogen Architekten aus Zürich unbelastet die Reden der Traditionalisten vom Anfang des Jahrhunderts. Damit machen sie eine Parallele zum 19. Jahrhundert deutlich, wo ebenfalls die kathartischen Avantgardisten Ende ihres Jahrhunderts dessen biedermeierlichen Anfang neu entdeckten. Die Position dieser ‚analogen' Architektur hat eine sehr intime, kindliche Sehnsucht als Programm. Sie will die noch gelebte und erlebte Geschichte ihrer in den 1960er Jahren geborenen Erfinder, einfangen und erinnernd versiegeln. Das Alltägliche, Banale, das Liegengebliebene, das bald schon vom Verwertungsprozess des besinnungslos Neuen überrollt werden wird, soll davon gesichert und überliefert werden. In diesem Sinne bezeichnen sich die analogen Architekten als konservativ, idealistisch und sentimental. Ein Widerstandsmoment keimt hier, gegen die Sensationen des schnellen Blicks und gegen das Spektakel der originären Signatur des Meisterarchitekten. Eine gesamtkulturelle Verantwortung bildet demnach die Basis der analogen Architektur – ökologische Prämissen ganz grundsätzlich bedenkend und das formale Repertoire aus der Welt der sozial Schwachen schöpfend.

Hier deutet sich jene unabdingbar neue und grundsätzliche ‚Haltung' der Architektur an, die sich auch in ihrer Sprache der sozialen Verantwortung bewusst ist. Sie arbeitet, massenmedial überformt, notwendigerweise mit ‚Bildern', eröffnet mit diesen aber eine Wahrnehmung, die vom glatten Bauwirtschaftskarusell niemals berücksichtigt werden kann. So sentimental traditionell und konservativ die Bilder der analogen Architektur auch erscheinen mögen – in ihrer gedachten und gebauten Konsequenz sind sie angesichts der Verhältnisse einer geradezu revolutionären Aufklärung verpflichtet.

Unencumbered, the analogous architects from Zurich, for instance, appropriate and incorporate the speeches of the traditionalists from the beginning of the century. They thereby make a parallel to the 19th century clear, where the cathartic avant-gardes likewise rediscovered their Biedermeier origin at the end of the century. The position of this "analogous" architecture has a very intimate, childlike longing as its program. It wants to capture the still lived and already experienced history of its inventors who were born in the 1960s and seal it commemoratively. The everyday, the banal, the left behind, which will soon be rolled over by the exploitation process of the insensible new, ought to be saved and passed on. In this sense, the analogous architects describe themselves as conservative, idealistic and sentimental. A moment of resistance germinates here, against the sensations of the quick glance and against the spectacle of the distinct signature of the master architect. An all-encompassing cultural responsibility thus forms the basis of analogous architecture—considering ecological assumptions very fundamentally and drawing the formal repertoire from the world of the socially weak.

Indicated here is that indispensably new and basic "stance" of architecture which is also conscious of the social responsibility in its language. Reshaped by mass media, it inevitably works with "images," but opens up an awareness with these, which can never be taken into account by the slippery construction industry carousel. As sentimentally traditional and conservative as the images of analogous architecture may also appear—in their conceived and constructed consequence they are, in the face of the circumstances, indebted to a nothing less than revolutionary enlightenment.

Analoge Architektur · Analogous Architecture

Konsulat der BRD · Consulate of the FRG in Zürich,
Andreas Hild, © Thomas Boga, 1987

Wohnhaus · Apartment building in Zürich, Selnau 111,
Miroslav Šik, © Thomas Boga, 1987

Autohaus · Car dealership in Zürich Örlikon,
Christian Kerez, © Thomas Boga, 1987

Autohaus · Car dealership in Zürich Örlikon,
Andrea Deplazes, © Thomas Boga, 1987

4th DAY The 1990s

Cover by Jenny Holzer, *domus 784, 1997*

Midlife crisis, what can I do, who wants me, a new life chapter begins. I quit my assistant job at Achleitner's institute because I have too many other projects to supervise and the students' disinterest in architecture demotivates me. – +++ – The German art consulter Helge Achenbach hires me as a consultant for architecture. It is a new experience to recommend architects to German companies for construction projects. An exciting time in which I learn a lot about decision-making processes in large companies in regard to architecture. – +++ – An invitation from politicians to formulate a concept for an architecture center in Vienna comes. I do not anticipate that this will be the assignment of my life. For the first time I can link my local existence with my international one. – +++ – This is followed by my active membership in ICAM, the International Confederation of Architectural Museums. From 1998 onwards I am a board member, later the ICAM president for years. The conferences and tours to many places are enormously stimulating. – +++ – Involvement in the European Prize for Contemporary Architecture of the Mies van der Rohe Pavilion Foundation in Barcelona also begins. – +++ – Lucius Burckhardt invites me to become his successor at the University of Kassel; I abort my application lecture. – +++ – Guest professorship at MIT – +++ – Offers to be head of the Architectural Association in London and the Netherlands Architecture Institute in Rotterdam – +++ – François Burkhardt, the director of *Domus*, invites me to take over the magazine's editorial department for architecture. Peter Eisenman says to me: "You are now the new air traffic controller of world architecture." And this is indeed the zenith or the last gasp of magazine journalism. We have unlimited budgets for authors, photographers and trips. All architects in the world love me. – +++ – Jury member of the Architecture Biennale in Venice in 1996 …

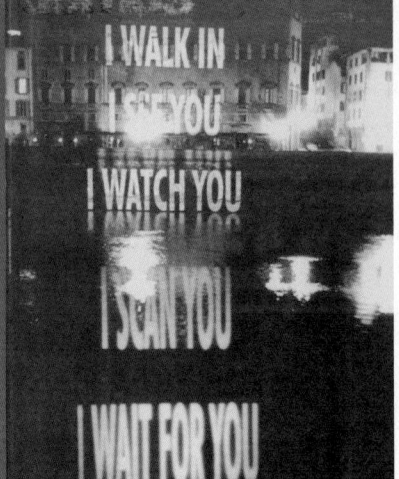

4. TAG Die 1990er

Pressekonferenz Eröffnung · Press conference for the opening of the Az W, Rudolf Scholten, Ursula Pasterk, Hannes Swoboda, 1993. © Archive Az W

Midlife-Crisis, was kann ich, wer will mich, es beginnt ein neuer Lebensabschnitt. Die Assistenz an Achleitners Institut kündige ich, weil ich zu viele andere Projekte zu betreuen habe und mich das Desinteresse der Studierenden an Architektur demotiviert – +++ – Der deutsche Kunst-Consulter Helge Achenbach engagiert mich als Berater für Architektur. Es ist eine neue Erfahrung, deutschen Unternehmen Architekten für Bauaufgaben vorzuschlagen. Eine spannende Zeit, in der ich viel über Entscheidungsprozesse in großen Unternehmen in Bezug auf Architektur lerne – +++ – Es kommt die Einladung aus der Politik, ein Konzept für ein Architekturzentrum in Wien zu formulieren. Ich ahne nicht, dass dies die Bestimmung meines Lebens sein wird. Erstmals kann ich meine lokale Existenz mit meiner internationalen verbinden – +++ – Dem folgt die aktive Mitgliedschaft bei ICAM, der internationalen Konföderation der Architekturmuseen. Ab 1998 bin ich Mitglied im Board, später jahrelang ICAM-Präsident. Die Konferenzen und Tours zu vielen Orten sind enorm anregend – +++ – Es beginnt auch die Mitwirkung am europäischen Architekturpreis der Mies van der Rohe Pavilion Foundation in Barcelona - +++ - Lucius Burckhardt lädt mich zu seiner Nachfolge an der Hochschule Kassel ein, ich breche den Bewerbungsvortrag ab – +++ – Gastprofessur am MIT – +++ – Angebote für die Direktion der AA in London und des NAi in Rotterdam – +++ – François Burkhardt als Direktor von *domus* lädt mich ein, die Architekturredaktion für die Zeitschrift zu übernehmen. Peter Eisenman sagt zu mir: „You are now the new air-controller of world architecture." Und tatsächlich ist dies die Hochblüte oder das letzte Aufbäumen des Magazin-Journalismus. Wir haben *unlimited budgets* für Autoren, Fotografen und Reisen. Alle Architekten der Welt lieben mich – +++ – Mitglied der Jury der Architektur Biennale Venedig 1996…

aus · from

werk, bauen+wohnen 6_1992
„Von Huren und Heiligen"
Translation by Brian Dorsey

Of Whores and Saints
Theses on the Practice of Future Architecture

Once upon a time there was "the modern architect." He was released from the rigid contextual objectives of princely builders. He was released from the degradations of the building trade. He was powerless, the "modern architect," but he was responsible for everything. The free partnership agreement, the cultural accord, allowed him to work, to fulfill himself, in the name of a higher order, generally called art. (The "modern artist," sculptor, painter, musician, etc., proceeded in like manner.) This system functioned for decades, was constitutive for "modernism" and is currently subject to a fundamental revision. The present transformation of the occupational profile has its basis in the status and in the development of the theory of architecture. This, however, is never autopoetic, but reacts to the changes of policy, of the economy, of culture. Since the cultural policy context of a project had always interested me stronger already as a critic than the analysis and criticism of the object in itself, I want to formulate this development as "Theses on the Practice of Future Architecture." The title "Of Whores and Saints" is thought of as a type of anticipation of the explication. The image of the whores and saints touches on a deep-seated pain among architects today. They have been trained as saints after all, at the academies and colleges that are not dissimilar to monastery schools in excluding the cold reality of building and conspiring towards "mindsets." Released from the monastery schools, the "saints" find themselves, as a rule, for want of family on the street as "whores." Who subsequently plays which role is not even a moral question, but rather not one at all. Because this question is not to decide, since it is already decided. Architecture is a service, and it is only a question of weighing up how much whoredom exists in every saintliness. Since the critic—the theoretician, the scribe, the publicist—is not to be excluded from this system, he (as well as I and this medium) is to consequently be referred to as a "pimp." Whereby every incorrigible "saint" who wants to enter into a publicly disclosed contact is to merely be made clear as to whose hands he is placing himself into (without paying the otherwise necessary tribute for it).

Von Huren und Heiligen

Thesen zur Praxis zukünftiger Architektur

Es war einmal der ‚moderne Architekt'. Er war entlassen aus der rigiden inhaltlichen Programmatik fürstlicher Bauherren. Er war entlassen aus den Niederungen des Baugewerbes. Er war machtlos, der ‚moderne Architekt', aber er war für alles zuständig. Der freie Gesellschaftsvertrag, die kulturelle Übereinkunft, erlaubte ihm zu arbeiten, sich zu verwirklichen, im Namen eines höheren Auftrags, gemeiniglich Kunst genannt. (Der ‚moderne Künstler', Bildhauer, Maler, Musiker etc. verfuhr ebenso.) Dieses System funktionierte nun jahrzehntelang, war konstitutiv für die ‚Moderne' und unterliegt derzeit einer grundsätzlichen Revision. Der nunmehrige Wandel des Berufsbildes hat seine Grundlage im Stand und in der Entwicklung der Theorie der Architektur. Diese aber ist nie autopoetisch, sondern reagiert auf die Veränderungen der Politik, der Wirtschaft, der Kultur. Da mich eigentlich auch schon als Kritiker immer das kulturpolitische Umfeld eines Projekts stärker interessiert hat als die Analyse und Kritik des Objekts an sich, will ich diese Entwicklung als „Thesen zur Praxis zukünftiger Architektur" formulieren. Als eine Art Vorwegnahme der Erläuterungen ist der Titel „Von Huren und Heiligen" gedacht. Das Bild von den Huren und den Heiligen, das berührt einen tiefsitzenden Schmerz bei den Architekten heute. Sind sie doch als Heilige ausgebildet worden, an den Akademien und Hochschulen, die in der Ausklammerung der kalten Wirklichkeit des Bauens und der Verschwörung auf ‚Gesinnungen' Klosterschulen nicht unähnlich sind. Aus den Klosterschulen entlassen, finden sich die ‚Heiligen' im Regelfall mangels Familie auf der Straße als ‚Huren' wieder. Wer in der Folge welche Rolle spielt, ist nicht einmal eine moralische, sondern gar keine Frage. Denn diese Frage ist nicht zu entscheiden, da sie schon entschieden ist. Architektur ist eine Dienstleistung, und es ist nur eine Frage der Abwägung, wieviel Hurerei in jeder Heiligkeit vorhanden ist. Nachdem der Kritiker – der Theoretiker, der Schreiber, der Publizist – aus diesem System nicht ausgenommen werden soll, soll er (und auch ich und dieses Medium) somit als ‚Zuhälter' bezeichnet werden. Womit jedem unverbesserlichen ‚Heiligen', der einen öffentlich veröffentlichten Kontakt eingehen will, nur klargemacht werden soll, in wessen Hände er sich begibt (ohne dafür den ansonsten notwendigen Tribut zu entrichten).

The Theory of Architecture

Apparently nothing has changed. Architecture magazines maintain the discourse chosen by the editorial staff and the editorial policy as always. Growing spirally, theory convulses into newer and newer concepts. It began with postmodernism, followed by critical regionalism, to which analogy was again held up against the regional, and finally, as a climax of postmodernism, an attempt was made to establish a deconstuctivism (yes, it is a true child of postmodernism!) in the media, which failed miserably due to the heterogeneity of its propenents' approaches. Only the term "crisis" (of architecture, of culture in the most general sense) has continuously survived, at least since the 1950s. Recently it was once again strained by Ignasi de Solà-Morales, that cultural pessimism which proclaims the last days of Western art and architecture because they have lost the binding values (*domus*, March 92). Solà-Morales, from whom the term "weak architecture" originates, once again replies to critical regionalism there. He links it with the notions of identity and difference and assigns it an "architecture of phantasm," that is, conjuring delusions of history. On the other hand, however, Solà-Morales locates an "architecture of the limit," an architecture that goes to the limit of invisibility, inspired by minimal art. Solà-Morales admittedly strikes the depth of the projects of the architects he cites here, but he nonetheless only scratches upon the surface of the conditions of contemporary architecture. As a matter of fact, the good old discipline of architecture currently endeavors more or less desperately to oscillate between the requirements of identity and the necessity of invisibility. The real background of this transitional stuation is a plain fact: The cubature that will be newly set into the landscape is steadily growing. Construction will be done, probably more than ever. Architects are involved in it, likewise more than ever. And in almost world-historical uniqueness, this new cubature creates a boom for architecture. The supposedly so "weak architecture" enables its most outstanding representatives access to construction projects in a magnitude that can only be found in distant history. In any case, the history of modernism cannot offer any comparison of this scale. What is meant is the connection of the artistic reputation of an architect with a contract volume, comparably purely economically structured architecture firms. Who would have thought at the end of the 1970s that insider heroes of the debate on theroretical architecture such as Aldo Rossi, Richard Meier, Frank Gehry, Peter Eisenman, Mario Botta, Norman Foster, O. M. Ungers and many others, today, at the beginning of the 1990s, possess worldwide, globally active architecture firms, without naturally understanding this as a fall of mankind.

Realism

Let us once note that the stylistic (not theoretic) waves of the 1980s have mainly thrown nameable styles onto the market. The ironic abbreviated references to this effect originate from Argentinean architecture students: "pomo"—post-modern, "deco"—deconstructivist, "nemo"—neo-modern. When I, in fundamental defense against these architectonic ornaments, dared to speak of a "realistic programmatic objective" for the future of architecture, this was ironically shortened into "repro" by Professor Prix (Coop Himmelb[l]au). However, this does not prevent observing that development which was not foreseeable for the theoretical debate of the sixties and seventies. It includes the development of the last decade, the

Die Theorie der Architektur

Scheinbar hat sich nichts geändert. Architekturzeitschriften pflegen den von der Redaktion und Blattlinie gewählten Diskurs wie eh und je. Die Theorie verkrampft sich spiralisch anwachsend in immer neue Begriffe. Es begann mit Postmoderne, es folgte der Kritische Regionalismus, dem wieder die Regionale Analogie entgegengehalten wurde, und schließlich wurde als Höhepunkt der Postmoderne versucht, einen Dekonstruktivismus (jawohl, er ist ein echtes Kind der Postmoderne!) medial zu etablieren, der an der Heterogenität der Ansätze seiner Proponenten kläglich scheiterte. Nur der Terminus der ‚Krise' (der Architektur, der Kultur ganz allgemein) hält sich durchgehend, zumindest seit den neunzehnfünfziger Jahren. Kürzlich wurde er wieder einmal von Ignasi y Solà-Morales strapaziert, jener Kulturpessimismus, der eine Endzeit der westlichen Kunst und Architektur verkündet, weil ihr die verbindlichen Werte abhanden gekommen seien (*domus*, März 92). Solà-Morales, von dem der Terminus der „weak architecture" stammt, repliziert da noch einmal auf den Kritischen Regionalismus. Er verknüpft ihn mit den Begriffen von Identität und Differenz, und weist diesen eine „Architektur des Phantasmas" zu, also Trugbilder der Geschichte beschwörend. Auf der anderen Seite aber ortet Solà-Morales eine „Architektur des Limits", eine Architektur, die an die Grenze der Unsichtbarkeit geht, inspiriert von der Minimal Art. Hier trifft Solà-Morales zwar die Tiefe der Projekte der von ihm zitierten Architekten, aber er kratzt dennoch nur an der Oberfläche der Bedingungen zeitgenössischer Architektur. Tatsächlich bemüht sich die gute alte Disziplin der Architektur derzeit mehr oder weniger verzweifelt auszupendeln zwischen den Anforderungen der Identität und der Notwendigkeit der Unsichtbarkeit. Der reale Hintergrund dieser Situation des Übergangs ist eine schlichte Tatsache: Stetig wächst die Kubatur, die neu in die Landschaft gesetzt wird. Es wird gebaut, wahrscheinlich mehr denn je. Architekten sind daran beteiligt, ebenfalls mehr denn je. Und in geradezu weltgeschichtlicher Einmaligkeit erzeugt diese neue Kubatur eine Konjunktur für Architektur. Die angeblich so ‚schwache Architektur' ermöglicht ihren hervorragendsten Vertretern den Zugang zu Bauaufgaben in einer Größenordnung, die nur in weit zurückliegender Geschichte gefunden werden kann. Auf jeden Fall hat die Geschichte der Moderne keinen Vergleich dieser Größenordnung anzubieten. Gemeint ist die Verbindung von künstlerischer Reputation eines Architekten mit einem Auftragsvolumen, vergleichbar rein ökonomisch strukturierten Architekturfirmen. Wer hätte Ende der siebziger Jahre gedacht, dass Insider-Helden der Debatte der theoretischen Architektur wie Aldo Rossi, Richard Meier, Frank Gehry, Peter Eisenman, Mario Botta, Norman Foster, O. M. Ungers und viele andere mehr, heute, am Beginn der neunziger Jahre, über weltumspannend global agierende Architekturfirmen verfügen, ohne dies selbstverständlich als Sündenfall zu verstehen.

Der Realismus

Halten wir einmal fest, dass die stilistischen (nicht theoretischen) Wellen der achtziger Jahre vor allem benennbare Stile auf den Markt geworfen haben. Von argentinischen Architekturstudenten stammen die diesbezüglichen, ironischen Kurzbezeichnungen: „pomo" – postmodern, „deko" – dekonstruktivistisch, „nemo" – neomodern. Als ich, in grundsätzlicher Abwehr dieser architektonischen Ornamente, von einer „realistischen Programmatik" für die Zukunft

eighties, and that of the future. The utopias of the 1960s were fulfilled. The utopias of the communication industry, of computer technology, architectonically planned ahead in the avant-garde, have now cashed themselves in technologically. The telecommunicative world village has become reality with the PC, cellular telephone and satellite television. Right up to the "walking cities" that now represent themselves as investment machines that destroy everything that no longer meets the requirements of a floating investment capital. But the "city" is also no longer that which critical regionalism committed itself to as hope. The city is divided into the protected area of identity, maintained by historic preservation and the interests of city tourism, coffined as an image and in the area of the periphery that is the same everywhere. That is the basis for insights such as those of Tzonis & Lefaivre, who replied to the critical regionalism of Kenneth Frampton with a simple word picture: re(gion)alism—and from this "realism" Liane Lefaivre distilled a "dirty realism" that deals architectonically with everyday life, indeed, with the reality of the new city that is the same everywhere. As representatives for this commitment she named: Rem Koolhaas, Nigel Coates, Jean Nouvel, Bernard Tschumi, Laurids Ortner, Hans Kollhoff … And we recall that we wanted to meld living, technology and work and that a strategic invisibleness resulted out of it, one that cannot offer any specific identity anymore on its own accord. A jungle of signs and spaces, like Nigel Coates already formulated this in 1983 with NATO (Narrative Architecture Today): to imagine that the building would be in use. And Rem Koolhaas supplied the hidden basic explanation for these new tasks of a "realistic objective" by redefining the architectonic object, the building: "Buildings have both an interior and an exterior. In Western architecture there has been the humanistic assumption that it is desirable to establish a moral relationship between the two, whereby the exterior makes certain revelations about the interior that the interior corroborates. The 'honest' facade speaks about the activities it conceals. But mathematically, the interior volume of three-dimensional objects increases in cubed leaps and the containing envelope only by squared increments: less and less surface has to represent more and more interior activity. Beyond a certain critical mass the relationship is stressed beyond the breaking point; this 'break' is the symptom of Automonumentality. [...] The architectural equivalent separates exterior and interior architecture. In this way the Monolith spares the outside world the agonies of the continuous changes raging inside it." That has opened the gate to the new tasks, the large volumes which—facelessly and functionally—create a new identity of invisibleness. These "automonuments" will be defined by the architects as the outcome of programs. Objects that consider themselves as concentrations and end points in an urbanized net. Because the old places themselves, the cities themselves are seeping away in sprawl. The large forms virtually provoke the emergence of a new "rhetoric of making" (according to the title of an issue of *Arch+*). A rhetoric of making does not invent any individualistic statements, but devotes itself to programmatic, realistic questions. Technological questions and problems of "intelligent buildings" are found among them as well as those of the cultural identity of a contracting authority for an administrative building. Hans Kollhoff formulated the action step belonging to a "realistic objective": "In this sense for me it is about sensitizing myself on all levels that have something to do with the program in order to filter out what actually urges towards form in the first priority. And one has to then give into it. The functional scenario thus means the translation process from a dead program to a living expression; to let the program come, well aware that the house will have a form in the end." Starting from the debate on the theory of architecture of the 1980s, the question of an appropriate

der Architektur zu sprechen wagte, wurde dies sofort von Professor Prix (Coop Himmelblau) ironisch auf „repro" verkürzt. Das hindert allerdings nicht, jene Entwicklung zu betrachten, die für die Theoriedebatte der sechziger und siebziger Jahre nicht vorhersehbar war. Es ist die Entwicklung des letzten Jahrzehnts, der achtziger Jahre, und jene der Zukunft miteingeschlossen. Es wurden die Utopien der sechziger Jahre erfüllt. Die Utopien der Kommunikationsindustrie, der Computertechnologie, architektonisch in der Avantgarde vorgedacht, haben sich nun technologisch eingelöst. Das telekommunikative Weltdorf ist mit PC, Funktelefon und Satellitenfernsehen Wirklichkeit geworden. ==Bis hin zu den „walking cities", die sich nun als Investitionsmaschinen darstellen, die alles vernichten, was nicht mehr den Anforderungen eines flottierenden Investitionskapitals entspricht.== Aber auch die ‚Stadt' ist nicht mehr das, worauf sich der kritische Regionalimus als Hoffnung verpflichtete. Die Stadt ist geteilt in den geschützten Bereich der Identität, betreut von der Denkmalpflege und den Interessen des Städtetourismus, eingesargt als Image und in den Bereich der überall gleichen Peripherie. Das ist die Grundlage für Einsichten wie jene von Tzonis & Lefaivre, die auf den Kritischen Regionalismus von Kenneth Frampton mit einem simplen Wortbild antworten: Re(gion)alism – und aus diesem „realism" destillierte Liane Lefaivre einen „dirty realism", der sich architektonisch mit dem Alltag, ja mit der überall gleichen Wirklichkeit der neuen Stadt beschäftigt. Sie nannte als Vertreter für dieses Engagement: Rem Koolhaas, Nigel Coates, Jean Nouvel, Bernard Tschumi, Laurids Ortner, Hans Kollhoff, … Und wir erinnern uns, dass wir Wohnen, Technologie und Arbeiten verschmelzen wollten und dass daraus eine strategische Unsichtbarkeit resultiert, die von sich aus keine spezifische Identität mehr anbieten kann. ==Ein Dschungel von Zeichen und Räumen, wie dies Nigel Coates mit NATO (Narrative Architecture today) bereits 1983 formuliert hat: sich vorzustellen, das Gebaute wäre im Gebrauch.== Und die versteckte grundsätzliche Erklärung für diese neuen Aufgaben einer ‚realistischen Programmatik' hat Rem Koolhaas geliefert, indem er das architektonische Objekt, das Gebäude, neu definierte: „Gebäude haben eine Innenseite und eine Außenseite. In der westlichen Architektur gab es das humanistische Ideal, nach dem zwischen den beiden eine moralische Beziehung hergestellt werden sollte, bei der das Äußere verlässliche Offenbarungen über das Innere machte, die vom Inneren bestätigt wurden. Die ‚ehrliche' Fassade spricht über die Aktivitäten, die sie verbirgt. Doch mathematisch gesehen vermehrt sich beim Wachsen eines dreidimensionalen Objekt das Volumen in kubischen Sprüngen und die umgebende Hülle nur in langsamer Oberflächenzunahme: Immer weniger Oberfläche muss immer mehr innere Aktivität repräsentieren. Jenseits eines kritischen Punktes zerbricht diese Beziehung, das Gebäude wird zum ‚Automonument'. Indem der Monolith die innere von der äußeren Architektur trennt, verschont er die Außenwelt von den Seelenqualen des ständigen Wechsels, der im Inneren tobt." ==Das hat das Tor geöffnet zu den neuen Aufgaben, den großen Volumen, die gesichtslos, multifunktional, eine neue Identität der Unsichtbarkeit schaffen.== Diese „Automonumente" werden von den Architekten definiert, als Ergebnis von Programmen. Objekte, die sich verstehen als Verdichtungen und Zielpunkte in einem urbanisierten Netz. Denn die alten Orte selbst, die Städte selbst versickern im Sprawl. Die großen Formen fordern geradezu heraus, dass eine neue „Rhetorik des Machens" entsteht (so der Titel einer Nummer von *Arch+*). Eine Rhetorik des Machens erfindet keine individualistischen Statements, sondern widmet sich programmatischen, realistischen Fragen. Darunter finden sich technologische Fragen und Probleme von ‚intelligent buildings' ebenso wie jene nach der kulturellen Identität eines Auftraggebers für ein Verwaltungsgebäude. Hans

practice is also raised. Can architecture still approach the complexity of problems and programs now stated by it with individual "objets trouvés"? Jean Nouvel explained in a debate that today an architect is more a composer than a director. He thus only watches how others perform his piece. That is not meant negatively, but outlines the actual architectonic scope of action today. Whoever composes wants to be performed; whoever draws wants to be built. The fact that the comparison with music is well chosen was proven by Ulrich Dibelius, who pointed to those developments in modern serious music that are comparable to architecture at the symposium *Wien modern* in 1988: "If, however, the demands of the composition, regardless of whether spiritual or technical, exceed the artists' power of composition, then the described transmission losses already occur before the music piece has even reached the listener." Consequently, Dibelius states, Schönberg founded his *Society for Private Musical Performances* back then. (To form a relationship out of the origination process of the Wittgenstein House would be interesting.) In the mentioned "dirty realism" issue of *archithese*, Fritz Neumeyer brought the contrastingly essential "urban architecture" to the point of "realistic objective": "In the greenhouse atmosphere of our present pluralism, architecture threatens to disappear into a type of semantic jungle. The 'art of building,' which requires a distinct sensibility for necessities, appears to be replaced by an 'art of interpretation' which, in the tectonics, sees little more than the pillar of the rhetoric levels of the narrative structure in order to effectively stage the play of the surfaces and signs. It would be worth a try to imagine an architecture that not only sets surfaces free with a new urban optimism, but also a body, which are given a metropolitan function and a metropolitan consciousness: as a provoking expression of reality and as a mediatory instrument of perception."

The Star System

There are architects who are already working on the execution of the position mentioned by Neumeyer, but architectural debate is still currently ruled by the much-celebrated soul sellers of identity. In the past years I already pointed several times to the change of those production conditions of architecture that are marked by cultural-industrial circumstances. The reference to the "star" system may thereby be ostensibly entertaining; it also comforts the souls of the upstanding and disadvantaged architects whose true inner values have simply not been discovered yet. However, it is only superficially about that. The "star" system is a necessary consequence of the change of the professional field in cultural-industrial conditions that are still largely unknown for architecture. Perhaps the problem can be grasped if one observes those cultural branches which are clearly produced and utilized in a cultural-industrial manner: film, music, opera and all the following union-protected areas of performance and interpretation such as theater, for instance. Dibelius again helps us along with his music diagnosis: "The always difficult judging of the artistic performance, which, under an array of experience, knowledge, possibilities of comparison and spontaneous responsiveness, is endeavored to comprehend the peculiarites of an object of art, is being increasingly supplanted by the nimble estimation and appraisal of the social prestige value. Simultaneously and quite consequently, the interest of the acutal art product in question shifts to the personality of the artist. His reputation and renown vouch for what he has brought forth. As a result, not only he himself—viewed soberly—becomes a serial producer whose latest

Kollhoff hat den einer ‚realistischen Programmatik' zugehörenden Handlungsschritt formuliert: „In diesem Sinn geht es mir darum, mich auf allen Ebenen, die etwas mit dem Programm zu tun haben, zu sensibilisieren, um herauszufiltern, was eigentlich in erster Priorität zur Form drängt. Und dem muss man dann nachgeben. Das funktionale Szenario meint also den Übersetzungsprozess von einem toten Programm zu einem lebendigen Ausdruck; das Programm kommen zu lassen, wohl wissend, dass das Haus am Ende eine Form haben wird." Es stellt sich also, ausgehend von der Debatte der Theorie der Architektur der achtziger Jahre auch die Frage nach einer entsprechenden Praxis. Kann sich die Architektur der nun von ihr konstatierten Komplexität der Probleme und Programme noch mit individuellen *objets trouvées* nähern? Jean Nouvel hat in einer Debatte erklärt, dass ein Architekt heute mehr ein Komponist ist als ein Regisseur. Er sieht also nur mehr zu, wie andere sein Stück aufführen. Das ist nicht negativ gemeint, sondern umreißt den eigentlichen architektonischen Handlungsspielraum heute. Wer komponiert, will aufgeführt werden, wer zeichnet, will gebaut werden. Dass der Vergleich mit der Musik gut gewählt ist, bewies Ulrich Dibelius, der beim Symposion *Wien modern* 1988 auf jene der Architektur vergleichbaren Entwicklungen bei der modernen E-Musik hingewiesen hat: „Wenn allerdings die Anforderungen der Komposition, einerlei, ob geistig oder spieltechnisch, das Darstellungsvermögen der Interpreten übersteigen, dann treten die geschilderten Transmissionsverluste schon ein, noch ehe das Musikstück den Hörer überhaupt erreicht hat." Konsequenterweise, konstatiert Dibelius, hat Schönberg damals seinen *Verein für musikalische Privataufführungen* gegründet. (Daraus eine Beziehung zum Entstehungsprozess des Wittgenstein-Hauses zu bilden, wäre interessant.) Die demgegenüber erforderliche „urbane Architektur" hat Fritz Neumeyer im erwähnten „dirty realism"-Heft auf den Punkt der „realistischen Programmatik" gebracht: „In der Treibhaus-Atmosphäre unseres gegenwärtigen Pluralismus droht die Architektur in einer Art semantischem Dschungel zu verschwinden. Die ‚Kunst des Bauens', die ausgeprägte Sensibilität für Notwendigkeiten verlangt, scheint durch eine ‚Kunst der Interpretation' abgelöst zu werden, die im Tektonischen kaum mehr als den Träger von rhetorischen Ebenen der Erzählstruktur sieht, um das Spiel der Oberflächen und Zeichen effektvoll zu inszenieren. Es wäre den Versuch wert, sich eine Architektur vorzustellen, die mit neuem urbanen Optimismus nicht nur Flächen, sondern auch einen Körper freisetzt, dem großstädtische Funktion und großstädtisches Bewusstsein gegeben sind: als provozierender Ausdruck von Realität und als vermittelndes Instrument der Wahrnehmung."

Das Star-System

Es gibt Architekten, die bereits an der Umsetzung der von Neumeyer erwähnten Position arbeiten, aber die Debatte der Architektur wird derzeit noch beherrscht von den vielgefeierten Seelenverkäufern der Identität. Dazu habe ich in den letzten Jahren schon mehrfach auf den Wandel jener Produktionsbedingungen von Architektur hingewiesen, die durch kulturindustrielle Verhältnisse gekennzeichnet sind. Der Hinweis auf das ‚Star'-System mag dabei vordergründig unterhaltend sein, er tröstet auch die Seelen der aufrechten und zu kurz gekommenen Architekten, deren wahre innere Werte eben noch nicht entdeckt sind. Darum aber geht es dabei nur vordergründig. Das ‚Star'-System ist eine notwendige Folge des Wandels des Berufsfeldes in kulturindustrielle Bedingungen, die für die Architektur noch reich-

work respectively feeds upon the accumulated fame of the older one, but at the same time the art judegment shifts from the individual responsibility of the critic to the anonymous 'one,' that undefinable social authority who attributes validity and assesses its current market value." (Ulrich Dibelius, „Von der Privataufführung zur Selbstdarstellung – Paradoxien im Verhältnis von Musik und Management", Symposion *Wien modern*, 1988) Dibelius called it the "as-if stance." The artists produce works as if it had to do with the works themselves. The critics form an opinion as if it would depend on their verdict. But behind this border wait the flock of exploiters, no matter whether it concerns spectacle music or spectacle architecture. And, naturally, the grail of uselessness, fine art, after its liberation from the objectives of the commissioner, is also caught in the new dependence on the culture industry. What distinguishes the cultural-industrial conditions is a closed system of task, product and exploitation. The creative subject and its creative product are surrounded by the entities and institutions of positioning and assessment. In the special case of architecture this system naturally existed earlier in a limited form, too. There were historians and critics, the natural agents of positioning, so to say. They "understood" the intention of the architects in the arthistorical sense, basing themselves on analyses of the work, on texts of the architects. The culture of architecture was only seldom observed under cultural-sociological aspects, that meaning the contractual relation that addresses the issue of relation of task, program and solution and thus included the role of the client. (A popular exception here was the book by Bentmann and Müller, *Die Villa als Herrschaftsarchitektur*. Frankfurt am Main, 1970.) In this regard, modern architecture was limited in essence to a circle of the initiated, of connoisseurs. It succeeded, however, in achieving a "stylistic penetration" of society by way of decision-making processes that were largely determined intradisciplinarily through public competitions. This position was basically shattered by the criticism of postwar architecture and later atomized just as fundamentally by postmodernism in a variety of stlye games that have now become legitimate. Seen from a cultural-sociological perspective, this atomiztion could only be absorbed by an artitstic equality of the most different contextual and formal architectonic approaches. Rob Krier had to be declared a star, just like Norman Foster … However, after our whole entertainment society negotiated its way within the existent cultural complexity only with the Pavlovian reflex to the star system, this was the logical development. We remind ourselves: The film industry has its Oscars, the opera its top fees as the distinguishing feature, science its Nobel Prizes, architecture its Pritzker Prize. Through the generally communicable star system, however, the access to architecture was also made possible to a considerably broader circle of the population and especially the clients. The star system offers the cultural assurance of having made the right choice. The media industry supplies proof of this to the client. The previous decade was also the decade of the lifestyle industry with the unavoidable name dropping of designer and architecture labels. The thesis on the practice of future architecture reads from this point of view: If the artistically discerning architect has seen the most creative part of his effort in the design up to now, and was and will still be trained to that effect, he has to question this self-understanding in a very basic way. The acquisition stands before the design. In this phase he has to make it comprehensible to the potential client why he can do what he was asked to do. The self-presentation, the accounting for previous accomplishments, it is no longer pulled off with a typewritten list of competition successes. Here it is essential to invest creative intelligence and to cultivate the art of personal presence. Because this is also a law of the culture industry.

lich unbekannt sind. Vielleicht lässt sich das Problem fassen, wenn man jene Kultursparten betrachtet, die eindeutig kulturindustriell produziert und verwertet werden: Film, Musik, Oper und all die folgenden gewerkschaftlich geschützten Bereiche der Aufführung und Interpretation wie Theater beispielsweise. Wieder hilft uns Dibelius mit seiner Musik-Diagnose weiter: „An die Stelle eines immer schwierigen Beurteilens der Kunstleistung, das sich unter Aufgebot von Erfahrung, Wissen, Vergleichsmöglichkeiten und spontaner Reaktionsbereitschaft um das Erfassen der Eigenheiten eines Kunstobjektes bemüht, ist mehr und mehr das behende Abschätzen und Taxieren des gesellschaftlichen Prestigewertes getreten. Gleichzeitig und durchaus konsequent verlagert sich das Interesse vom eigentlich infrage stehenden Kunstprodukt auf die Person des Künstlers. Sein Ruf und Renommée steht ein für das, was er hervorgebracht hat. Dadurch wird nicht nur er selbst – nüchtern betrachtet – zum Serienfabrikanten, dessen neuestes Werk jeweils vom angestauten Ruhm der älteren zehrt, sondern zugleich verlagert sich das Kunsturteil aus der Einzelverantwortung des Kritikers auf das anonyme ‚man', jene undefinierbare gesellschaftliche Autorität, die Geltung zumisst und ihren aktuellen Kurswert bemisst." (Ulrich Dibelius, „Von der Privataufführung zur Selbstdarstellung – Paradoxien im Verhältnis von Musik und Management", Symposion *Wien modern*, 1988) Dibelius nannte es die „Als-ob-Haltung". Die Künstler produzieren Werke, als ob es um diese ginge. Die Kritiker bilden sich eine Meinung, als ob es auf deren Urteil ankäme. Aber hinter dieser Grenze wartet die Schar der Verwerter, egal ob es sich um Erlebnismusik oder Erlebnisarchitektur handelt. Und selbstverständlich ist auch der Gral der Nutzlosigkeit, die bildende Kunst, nach ihrer Befreiung von der Programmatik des Auftraggebers in die neue Abhängigkeit von der Kulturindustrie geraten. Was die kulturindustriellen Bedingungen auszeichnet, ist ein geschlossenes System von Aufgabe, Produkt und Verwertung. Das kreative Subjekt und sein kreatives Produkt sind umgeben von den Instanzen und Institutionen der Positionierung und Bewertung. Im besonderen Fall der Architektur hat dieses System natürlich in eingeschränkter Form auch früher existiert. Es gab Historiker und Kritiker, sozusagen die natürlichen Agenten der Positionierung. Sie ‚verstanden' im kunsthistorischen Sinn die Intentionen der Architekten, stützen sich dabei auf Werkanalysen, auf Texte der Architekten. Nur selten wurde die Kultur der Architektur unter kultursoziologischen Aspekten betrachtet, das heißt das Auftragsverhältnis, das Verhältnis Aufgabe, Programm und Lösung thematisiert und damit die Rolle des Bauherrn einbezogen. (Ein populärer Sonderfall war hier das Buch von Bentmann/Müller, *Die Villa als Herrschaftsarchitektur*, FfM 1970) Die moderne Architektur war in dieser Hinsicht im Wesentlichen auf einen Kreis von Eingeweihten, von Kennern beschränkt. Es gelang ihr allerdings, im Wege weitgehend fachintern bestimmter Entscheidungsprozesse über öffentliche Wettbewerbe eine ‚stilistische Durchdringung' der Gesellschaft zu erreichen. Diese Position wurde durch die Kritik an der Nachkriegsarchitektur grundsätzlich erschüttert und später durch die Postmoderne ebenso grundsätzlich in eine Vielzahl nun legitim gewordener Stil-Spiele atomisiert. Diese Atomisierung konnte nur mehr, kultursoziologisch gesehen, durch eine künstlerische Gleichberechtigung unterschiedlichster inhaltlicher und formaler architektonischer Ansätze aufgefangen werden. Rob Krier musste zum Star erklärt werden, ebenso wie Norman Foster … Nachdem aber unsere ganze Entertainment-Gesellschaft sich innerhalb der nun vorhandenen kulturellen Unübersichtlichkeit nur mit dem Pawlow'schen Reflex auf das Star-System zurechtfindet, war dies die logische Entwicklung. Wir erinnern uns: Die Filmindustrie hat ihre Oscars, die Oper die Stargagen als Unterscheidungsmerkmal, die Wis-

"Stars" also cannot be made by the strongest media. They have to possess the necessary strength and intelligence to be able to assert themselves on the peak as well. And the utilization comes after the design. A project comes nowhere near to an end with its completion. It needs criticism, processing, publicity. In this sense, American conditions have also reached Europe. There is no renowned and successful American architect's office that does not have its own departments for the acqusition of contracts and for the public relations of completed buildings.

The Performance

The old architect, the universalist is dead; a new universalism is in demand. An architectonic object in the so-called professional setting has to face a fragmented, new situation. It is buffeted by experts and expertises for site analysis, functional planning, design concept, usage mix, economic viability, marketing concept, rental strategy, utilization management. These are only the specialist fields of creating and positioning an object, and the inner-architectural specialization with statics, building physics, in-house installations, light design, climate concept, supply and disposal, computer networking right up to an authorized ecological agent are only noted in the margin. That stands at the beginning of the second thesis. May the "cultural-industrial conditions" for many architects only affect the surface of their occupation, the end of universality already hits the core itself harder. Here is also the place to point to the problem of new production conditions of architecture. Architecture suffers worldwide from an explosive rise in the complexity of building. Excessive bureaucracy increasingly restricts the architectonic possibilities of the project. Standards and zoning laws are becoming more and more rigid; the armada of specialists is multiplying exponentially in ever-shorter intervals. The "expulsion of reason" is an obvious metaphor here. The fundamental question of where the architectonic decision is actually and responsibly located is posed here. In the course of the formation of a project, the architects today are mainly occupied with receiving any information at all about the influencing variables. Talk of the control, of the much-vaunted artistic overhead line only remains as an ornament at the edge of the process. New occupations and firms have emerged. Firms for project management, controlling, take over representative tasks for builders as well as for architects. There is no question that the architect retreats here to the design and is forced to give up all other activities. If architecture is to even become a part of the whole company strategy—which architecture always wanted—, then it also has to be aware of the participation of all departments of an enterprise. In the scope of a corporate design strategy, architectonic concerns have to be harmonized with the overall field of an enterprise (financing, real estate, construction, development, marketing, public relations, advertising). The occupational field of the architect today is the respective determination of his role in the process of the formation of objects.

senschaften ihre Nobel-Preise, die Architektur ihren Pritzker-Preis. Durch das allgemein kommunizierbare Star-System wurde aber auch der Zugang zur Architektur einem wesentlich breiteren Kreis der Bevölkerung und vor allem der Bauherren ermöglicht. Das Star-System bietet die kulturelle Sicherheit, die richtige Wahl getroffen zu haben. Den Beweis dafür lieferte dem Bauherrn die Medienindustrie. Das letzte Jahrzehnt war auch das Jahrzehnt der Lifestyle-Industrie, mit dem unvermeidlichen Namedropping von Designer- und Architektur-Labels. Die These zur Praxis künftiger Architektur lautet unter diesem Gesichtspunkt: Hat der künstlerisch anspruchsvolle Architekt bisher den kreativsten Teil seiner Leistung im Entwurf gesehen und wurde und wird noch immer dahingehend ausgebildet, so hat er dieses Selbstverständnis ganz grundsätzlich zu hinterfragen. Vor dem Entwurf steht die Akquisition. In dieser Phase hat er dem potenziellen Auftraggeber verständlich zu machen, warum er das kann, wozu er aufgefordert wurde. Die Selbstdarstellung, die Aufarbeitung bisheriger Leistungen, sie ist nicht mehr mit einer schreibmaschinengeschrieben Liste der Wettbewerbserfolge abgetan. Hier gilt es kreative Intelligenz zu investieren und die Kunst der persönlichen Präsenz zu kultivieren. Denn auch dies ist ein Gesetz der Kulturindustrie. ‚Stars' können auch nicht von den stärksten Medien gemacht werden. Sie müssen die nötige Kraft und Intelligenz besitzen, um sich am Gipfel auch behaupten zu können. Und nach dem Entwurf kommt die Verwertung. Ein Projekt ist mit seiner Fertigstellung noch lange nicht zu Ende. Es braucht die Kritik, die Aufbereitung, die Publizität. In diesem Sinne haben amerikanische Verhältnisse auch Europa erreicht. Es gibt kein renommiertes und erfolgreiches amerikanisches Architekturbüro, das nicht über eigene Abteilungen für die Akquisition von Aufträgen und für die Public Relation von fertigen Bauten verfügt.

Die Aufführung

Der alte Architekt, der Universalist ist tot; ein neuer Universalismus ist gefragt. Ein architektonisches Objekt in sogenannt professioneller Umgebung hat sich einer aufgesplitterten neuen Situation zu stellen. Es ist umtost von Experten und Expertisen für Standortanalyse, Funktionsplanung, Gestaltungskonzept, Nutzungsmix, Wirtschaftlichkeit, Marketingkonzept, Vermietungsstrategie, Nutzungsmanagement. Das sind nur die Fachbereiche der Erstellung und Positionierung eines Objekts, und dabei ist die architekturinterne Spezialisierung mit Statik, Bauphysik, Gebäudeinstallation, Lichtdesign, Klimakonzept, Ver- und Entsorgung, Computervernetzung bis hin zum Ökologiebeauftragten nur am Rande vermerkt. Das steht am Beginn der zweiten These. Mögen die ‚kulturindustriellen Bedingungen' für viele Architekten nur die Oberfläche ihres Berufs tangieren, so geht das Ende der Universalität schon stärker an die Substanz selbst. Hier ist auch die Stelle, auf die Problematik der neuen Produktionsbedingungen von Architektur hinzuweisen. Die Architektur leidet weltweit unter einer explosiven Zunahme der Komplexität des Bauens. Eine überbordende Bürokratie beengt zunehmend die architektonischen Möglichkeiten des Projekts. Normen und Baugesetze werden immer rigider, die Armada der Sonderfachleute multipliziert und potenziert sich in immer kürzeren Abständen. Die „Vertreibung der Vernunft" ist hier eine naheliegende Metapher. Hier stellt sich die grundsätzliche Frage, wo denn eigentlich verantwortlich die architektonische Entscheidung angesiedelt ist. Im Zuge der Gestaltwerdung eines Projekts sind die Architekten heute überwiegend damit beschäftigt, über die

Architecture Management

From the scenario up to now one sees very clearly that traditional strategies of architecture, indeed its very autonomy, is up for discussion here. Even the star system can no longer be responsibly carried out because the signature of globally active stars increasingly comes into conflict with the world of signs of the company it symbolizes. To bemoan a pending loss now is a glass bead game and only exacerbates the crisis. By contrast, an offensive strategy that makes the new influencing variables nameable and integrates them into the program of architecture is the order of the day. Let's call these strategies, for a start, architecture management (in this medium one can agree that it is a matter of camouflage.) Since the fact is that architectonic decisions in companies still possess a large symbolic power and are seldom able to fundamentally shape whole company philosophies. Several examples for this are named. Although still current at the present time, the "old strategy" is represented by builders like Vitra or Alessi. That is the relatively arbitrary collection of icons of international architecture. It may be that a certain touristic interest results out of it one day, commensurate with Bavaria's King Ludwig castles. The second strategy, already significantly more clever than the first, is that of Michael Eisner and the Disney Corporation. They have succeeded in committing the hired stars (Graves, Rossi, Gehry, Isozaki, Stern, Predock, etc.) to a "program," respectively formulated by the company, that filled them with delight and pleasure. The frame of the "sign world" and its reception is predefined, yet several realizations show that impressive architectonic accomplishments are also possible under these conditions. The third strategy, the only one prepared for the future of architecture, is only rudimentarily recognizable up to now. It penetrates into the innermost identity of a company and takes up the challenge of the existing paradigms of a corporate design. As simple as it first sounds, the binding determination of an architectonic "niveau" belongs to it, then the designation and integration of all interfaces of architectonic work to the other formative activities of a company (marketing, advertising, corporate identity, image factors, product development). The individual steps of this architecture management are familiar from the development of CI concepts (analysis, briefing, concept, development, guidelines, motivation, execution). Without strictly following these steps, an Austrian office furniture company has optimally realized this uniquely promising concept. There, at Bene Büromöbel, Laurids Ortner is, for instance, fully involved as the architect in product development and company strategy and thus also fully responsible for the architectonic appearance, in precisely those realistic objectives that are also theoretically secured. The architect as a player, as a fellow player in the realm of signs and signals. If he can fulfill this task, then no affliction of the profession exists in principle, either. He only has to know that he isn't the only one who is capable of creating signs and spaces.

Einflussgrößen überhaupt noch Informationen zu bekommen. Von der Kontrolle, der vielgerühmten künstlerischen Oberleitung, ist nur noch als Ornament am Rande des Prozesses die Rede. Neue Berufe und Firmen sind entstanden. Firmen für Projektmanagement, Controlling übernehmen stellvertretende Aufgaben für Bauherren ebenso wie für Architekten. Keine Frage, dass sich der Architekt hier zurückzieht auf den Entwurf und alle anderen Tätigkeiten abzugeben gezwungen ist. Wenn Architektur gar Teil einer ganzen Unternehmensstrategie wird – was die Architektur immer wollte –, dann muss sie sich auch der Mitsprache aller Abteilungen eines Unternehmens bewusst sein. Im Rahmen einer Corporate-Design-Strategie haben sich architektonische Anliegen mit dem Gesamtfeld eines Unternehmens abzustimmen (Finanzen, Immobilien, Bau, Entwicklung, Marketing, Public Relation, Werbung). Das Berufsfeld des Architekten heute ist die jeweilige Bestimmung seiner Rolle im Prozess der Gestaltwerdung von Objekten.

Architektur-Management

Man sieht an dem bisherigen Szenario sehr deutlich, dass hier traditionelle Strategien der Architektur, ja ihre Autonomie selbst zur Diskussion stehen. Selbst das Star-System ist nicht mehr länger verantwortungsvoll ausübbar, weil die Signatur weltweit agierender Stars zunehmend in Konflikt kommt mit der Zeichenwelt der sie symbolisierenden Unternehmen. Jetzt einen drohenden Verlust zu beklagen, ist ein Glasperlenspiel und verschärft nur die Krise. ==Angesagt ist dagegen eine offensive Strategie, welche die neuen Einflussgrößen benennbar macht, sie in das Programm der Architektur integriert.== Nennen wir diese Strategie einmal Architektur-Management (in diesem Medium kann man sich darauf einigen, dass es sich um eine Tarnung handelt). Denn Tatsache ist, dass architektonische Entscheidungen bei Unternehmen noch immer eine große Symbolkraft besitzen, nicht selten in der Lage sind, ganze Unternehmensphilosophien grundsätzlich zu prägen. Dafür seien einige Beispiele genannt. ==Die ‚alte Strategie'==, obwohl derzeit noch aktuell, wird von Bauherren wie Vitra oder Alessi repräsentiert. Das ist die relativ willkürliche Sammlung von Ikonen der internationalen Architektur. Mag sein, dass daraus einmal ein gewisses touristisches Interesse resultiert, den Ludwig-Schlössern Bayerns entsprechend. ==Die zweite Strategie==, schon wesentlich geschickter als die erste, ist jene von Michael Eisner und der Disney-Corporation. Ihr ist es gelungen, die angeheuerten Stars (Graves, Rossi, Gehry, Isozaki, Stern, Predock etc.) auf ein jeweils vom Unternehmen formuliertes ‚Programm' zu verpflichten, das diese mit Lust und Vergnügen erfüllten. Der Rahmen der ‚Zeichenwelt' und ihrer Rezeption ist vorgegeben, doch einige Realisationen zeigen, dass auch unter diesen Bedingungen beeindruckende architektonische Leistungen möglich sind. ==Die dritte Strategie==, einzig für die Zukunft der Architektur gerüstet, ist bisher nur in Ansätzen erkennbar. Sie dringt ein in die innerste Identität eines Unternehmes und nimmt die Herausforderung der vorhandenen Paradigmen eines Corporate Design an. Dazu gehört, so simpel das zunächst klingen mag, die verbindliche Festlegung eines architektonischen ‚Niveaus', dann die Benennung und Integration aller Schnittstellen der architektonischen Arbeit zu anderen gestaltbildenden Aktivitäten eines Unternehmens (Marketing, Werbung, CI, Imagefaktoren, Produktentwicklung). Die einzelnen Schritte dieses Architektur-Managements sind aus der Entwicklung von CI-Konzepten bekannt (Analyse, Briefing, Konzept, Entwicklung, Richtlinien, Motivation, Durchführung).

The Saints

Several people, especially architects, may now turn away in disgust after these statements, seeing their autonomous artistic identity as architects not only endangered, but even put into question. After so much realism about the theory and practice of future architecture they surely still want to find out something about the "saints" in the end. Principally they have two possibilities. Either to continuously drift into the refusal to draw closer to that effect to the architects among the artists, that they realize their own refuges, financed by they themselves. Donald Judd's *Marfa* is such a fascinating project that he can only realize it as an architectonic manifesto because its cultural-industrial marketing in the art market follows. The other possibility is to find a patron they bow down to, who, step by step, building by building, continuously lets himself be endowed. Then the idealism of the 19th century still prevails in the career planning of the architect: the lonesome artist, whose work and value are misunderstood in the age and will be discovered by history. Saints are obsessive. They produce ideas, concepts. They are far removed from reality. Saints do not know any programmatic realism, they refuse the discourse. The saints are just as necessary for the development of architecture as the Formula 1 is for the development of the automobile industry. Saints are the symbols, the image carriers of practice. Alan Colquhoun, in his 1976 text on realism, determined their fate: "Whatever can be said in defense of such an architecture of polemics, the danger exists that the belief in a purely autoreflexive architecture could lead to a depreciation of the building program and to an architecure that doesn't need to be built any more." As important as this virtual construct of architecture may also be, it always finds its fulfillment in its appearance. Whether the appearance is architecture or not, Sigrid Hauser relatively conclusively fulfilled this sentence of perception: "Architecture makes the imaginary visible and the real conceivable. And the other way around. I don't mean the architecture that is placed down; I mean the architecture as language. And I can find it everywhere, suddenly, coincidentally. Theory is looking on." (Hauser, *Sprache – z.B. Architektur*, Vienna: Löcker, 1998, p. 12)

Ohne diesen Schritten strikt zu folgen, hat eine österreichische Büromöbelfirma dieses einzig zukunftsträchtige Konzept optimal verwirklicht. Dort, bei Bene Büromöbel ist beispielsweise Laurids Ortner als Architekt voll eingebunden in die Produktentwicklung und Unternehmensstrategie, und damit auch voll verantwortlich für das architektonische Erscheinungsbild, in eben jener realistischen Programmatik, die auch theoretisch abgesichert ist. ==Der Architekt als Spieler, als Mitspieler im Reich der Zeichen und Signale.== Wenn er diese Aufgabe erfüllen kann, dann besteht auch keine Bedrängnis der Profession an sich. Er muss nur wissen, dass er nicht der einzige ist, der Zeichen und Räume zu schaffen imstande ist.

Die Heiligen

Einige, Architekten vor allem, mögen sich nun nach diesen Ausführungen angeekelt abwenden, ihre autonome künstlerische Identität als Architekten nicht nur gefährdet, sondern gar infrage gestellt sehen. Nach so viel Realismus über die Theorie und Praxis künftiger Architektur wollen sie sicherlich zum Schluss noch etwas über die ‚Heiligen' erfahren. Sie haben prinzipiell zwei Möglichkeiten. Entweder kontinuierlich in die Verweigerung zu schlittern, sich den Architekten unter den Künstlern dahingehend zu nähern, dass sie eigene, von ihnen selbst finanzierte Refugien realisieren. Donald Judds *Marfa* ist so ein faszinierendes Projekt, das er als architektonisches Manifest nur realisieren kann, weil seine kulturindustrielle Vermarktung am Kunstmarkt erfolgt. Die andere Möglichkeit ist, einen Mäzen zu finden, dem sie sich unterwerfen, der sich Zug um Zug, Bau um Bau kontinuierlich ausstatten lässt. Denn noch immer herrscht der Idealismus des 19. Jahrhunderts in der Berufsvorstellung des Architekten: der einsame Künstler, dessen Werk und Wert in der Zeit unverstanden sind und von der Geschichte entdeckt werden. Heilige sind obsessiv, sie produzieren Ideen, Konzepte. Sie sind weit entfernt von der Wirklichkeit. Heilige kennen keinen programmatischen Realismus, sie verweigern den Diskurs. ==Die Heiligen sind so notwendig für die Entwicklung der Architektur wie die Formel 1 für die Entwicklung der Automobilindustrie.== Heilige sind die Symbole, die Image-Träger der Praxis. Ihr Schicksal hat Alan Colquhoun in seinem Text zum Realismus, 1976, festgelegt: „Was immer sich sagen lässt zur Verteidigung einer solchen Architektur der Polemik, es besteht Gefahr, dass der Glaube an eine rein autoreflexive Architektur zu einer Abwertung des Bauprogrammes und zu einer Architektur führen könnte, die nicht mehr gebaut zu werden braucht." So wichtig dieses virtuelle Konstrukt der Architektur auch sein mag, sie findet ihre Erfüllung immer in ihrer Erscheinung. Ob diese Erscheinung Architektur ist oder nicht, Sigrid Hauser hat diesen Satz der Wahrnehmung relativ endgültig erfüllt: „Architektur macht das Imaginäre sichtbar und das Reale denkbar. Und umgekehrt. Ich meine nicht die Architektur, die hingestellt wird, ich meine die Architektur als Sprache. Und ich kann sie überall finden, plötzlich, zufällig. Theorein ist Zuschauen." [Hauser, *Sprache – z.B. Architektur*, Löcker, Wien 1998, S. 12]

Vierter Tag • Day Four

Sports Resort, Disney World Orlando, 1996. © DS

aus · from

archithese 6_1993
„Es gibt kein Entrinnen"
Translation by Brian Dorsey

There Is No Escape
The Dilemma of Spectacle Architecture

Es gibt kein Entrinnen
Das Dilemma der Erlebnisarchitektur

Warum gerinnt ein Phänomen zum Begriff? Immer dann, wenn ein vage undefinierbares Gefühl, eine Stimmung nur zunächst, kommunikationsfähig wird, Verständigung auf einmal möglich scheint: „Wenn graue Manager glauben, ab nun braune Anzüge tragen zu müssen." (Jacques Herzog) Dann ist nur vordergründig ein Tabu gebrochen, es hat sich auch ein ungewisses Interesse des Allgemeinen verschoben. Denn eine Epoche später ist wieder Braun degoutant und alle bekennen sich, ohne wirklichen Befehl irgendeiner Instanz, wieder zum grauen, gar zum dunklen Anzug, ziehen aber jetzt dunkle Seidenhemden oder auch ein weißes Hemd dazu an, aber beide sind auf einmal nur wirklich richtig ohne Krawatte zu tragen.

Why does a phenomenon solidify into a term? Every time a vague, indefinable feeling, only a mood at first, becomes capable of communicating, understanding suddenly seems possible: "If gray managers believe they have to wear brown suits from now on" (Jacques Herzog). Then a taboo is only broken superficially, and an uncertain interest of the general has also shifted. Because an epoch later brown is disgusting again and everyone commits, without the real command from any kind of authority, to the gray suit again, even to the dark one, but now puts on dark silk shirts or a white shirt to go along with it, but both are suddenly only really to be properly worn without a tie.

No, that has nothing to do with the normal notion of fashion. Because if it were this fashion, one would follow seasonally changing themes of the fashion industry. And therefore the examples from the professional men's world, too, since this reacts, as is well-known, slower, more long-term, more cautious than women's fashion.

Vierter Tag • Day Four

Nein, das hat nichts mit dem normalen Begriff von Mode zu tun. Denn wenn es diese Mode wäre, würde man den saisonal wechselnden Themen der Fashion-Industrie folgen. Und darum auch die Beispiele aus der professionalen Männerwelt, denn diese reagiert bekanntlich langsamer, langfristiger, behutsamer als die Damenmode.

Die Mode ist ein guter Einstieg in ein Thema, ein Phänomen, das auf einmal zum diskutierten Begriff geworden ist. Denn schließlich hat die Mode auch den Zweck, durch Bekleidung der Nacktheit dem Körper Ausdruck zu verleihen, bestimmte Signale zu setzen und zu senden. Das Phänomen heißt schlicht und einfach „Erlebnisarchitektur" und ist akademisch salonfähig geworden. Dies geschah aber nicht plötzlich, wurde auch nicht von einem der normalerweise unbedarft nachhinkenden Trendgurus ausgerufen. Die Konjunktur dieses Begriffs für die Architektur bahnte sich an, zumindest ab den siebziger Jahren.

Seit dieser Zeit entwickelt sich ein janusköpfiges Phänomen – einerseits die zunehmende Hegemonie der Massenmedien, welche die grundsätzlichen Leitlinien, Lebensstile und deren Ausstattung vorgeben und damit alte sozialräumliche Bindungen ablösen; und andererseits, wiederum von der Mediatisierung beschleunigt, die sukzessive Ausdifferenzierung eben dieser Lebensstile in weitgehend autonome Subkulturen. Damit einher geht die Emanzipation dieser Lebensstile zu parallelen Existenzen. Hochkultur und Subkultur werden gleichwertig, und das was in den siebziger Jahren Alternativkultur hieß ist inzwischen zum stabilsten Faktor überhaupt geworden. (Denn die ‚Funktionäre' der Alternativkultur sind im Regelfall seit nunmehr zwanzig Jahren in Amt und Würden, wogegen die Hochkultur beständig Innovationen zu präsentieren hat.)

Es mag sein, dass es für das heutige Phänomen der Erlebnisarchitektur höchst intelligente kunsthistorische Beweisführungen gibt. Wenn es sie gibt, dann greifen sie aber alle zu kurz, weil es sich allzu sehr um ein Phänomen der Alltagskultur einer Kulturindustrie handelt, das nur bedingt mit der historisch-akademischen Nomenklatur zu fassen ist.

Fashion is a good introduction to a theme, a phenomenon that has suddenly become a discussed term. Because fashion also ultimately has the purpose of lending expression to the body by clothing the nakedness, to set and send certain signals. The phenomenon is quite simply called "spectacle architecture" and has become academically respectable. But this didn't happen all of a sudden and was also not proclaimed by one of the trend gurus who normally lags behind without a clue. The boom of this term for architecture was in the offing, at least from the seventies onwards.

Since this time a Janus-faced phenomenon has been developing—on one side, the rising hegemony of the mass media, which predetermine the basic guidelines, lifestyles and their accoutrements, and thereby remove old social-spatial ties; and, on the other side, accelerated in turn by the mediatization, the successive differentiation of precisely these lifestyle into by and large autonomous subcultures. The emancipation of these lifestyles into parallel existences goes along with it. High culture and subculture become equal, and what was called alternative culture in the seventies has meanwhile become the most stable factor altogether. (Because the 'functionaries' of alternative culture have, as a rule, been in office for twenty years now, whereas high culture constantly has to present innovations.)

It may be that there are highly intelligent art-historical lines of argumentation for the present-day phenomenon of spectacle architecture. If they exist, then they all fall too short, because it has all too much to do with a phenomenon of the everyday culture of a culture industry that is only conditionally to be comprehended with the historical-academic nomenclature.

Heinrich Klotz, Gründungsdirektor des Deutschen Architekturmuseums in Frankfurt, eröffnet die deutsche Diskussion für Alltagsästhetik, Buchcover, 1977 · Heinrich Klotz, founding director of the German Architecture Museum in Frankfurt, opens the German discussion on everyday aesthetics, book cover, 1977

„Sputnik"-Briefmarke · Sputnik stamp. © shutterstock

Die heutige Ideologie und Tendenz der Erlebnisarchitektur kommt ganz tief und ganz deutlich ‚von unten'. Erlebnisarchitektur ist die Vermarktung eines ungedeckten Bedürfnisses. Da müssen wir schon den Stier bei den Hörnern packen, kräftig und respektlos, um zu erkennen, dass es doch wieder die Kunsthistoriker und Philosophen waren, wie Heinrich Klotz, Umberto Eco, Giovanni Klaus Koenig, die einstmals in die Phänomene der Alltagskultur emigrierten. So erinnern wir uns vage an die *röhrenden Hirsche der Architektur,* des respektablen Kunsthistorikers Heinrich Klotz polemisches Werk über die bundesdeutsche Ibiza-Sehnsucht. Er wagte die vermaledeite These, dass kaum ein Unterschied bestehe zwischen den neobarocken Sehnsüchten der europäischen Herrscherhäuser der Jahrhundertwende und den popularisierten Nobilitierungen mit ruralen Insignien der Neureichen heutzutage.

Dass sich die akademische Welt mit Kitsch und Prunk, mit den Wünschen der Neureichen nach schwülstigen Stilen beschäftigte, hatte wiederum zu tun mit dem ab Mitte der sechziger Jahre akut gewordenen Thema der ‚Kreativität'. Die Schüler und Menschen der westlichen Hemisphäre sollten auf einmal nicht

The present-day ideology and tendency of spectacle architecture comes very deeply and quite distinctly 'from below.' Spectacle architecture is the marketing of an unmet need. We have to grab the bull by the horns here, powerfully and disrespectfully, in order to realize that it was again art historians and philosophers after all, such as Heinrich Klotz, Umberto Eco and Giovanni Klaus Koenig, who once emigrated into the phenomenon of everyday culture. Therefore, we vaguely recall the "belling stags of architecture" of the respectable art historian Heinrich Klotz, a polemic work about the German longing for Ibiza. He dared to make the accursed assumption that hardly any difference exists between the neo-baroque yearnings of the European dynasties of the fin-de-siècle and the popularized nobilitations with rural insignias of the nouvelle riche today.

The fact that the academic world concerned itself with kitsch and pomp, with the desires of the nouvelle riche for overblown styles, had to do in turn with the topic of 'creativity,' which became acute as of the mid-sixties. The disciples and people of the Western Hemisphere were to suddenly no longer merely function and consume. They were to have ideas, were to discover new ways and new forms, were to be individually creative. But that was, at this point in time, no movement 'from below,' was initially no need of the masses. The generally decreed 'creativity' was, at the beginning and above all, the Western response to the 'Sputnik shock.' As the Soviets were namely the first to shoot a capsule into space, the Western world asked itself why it hadn't already come upon this absurd idea beforehand, and acknowledged lacking 'creativity.'

mehr nur funktionieren und konsumieren. Sie sollten Ideen haben, sollten neue Wege und neue Formen entdecken, sollten individuell kreativ sein. Das war aber zu diesem Zeitpunkt keine Bewegung ‚von unten', war zunächst kein Bedürfnis der Massen. Die allgemein verordnete ‚Kreativität' war am Beginn und vor allem die westliche Antwort auf den „Sputnik-Schock". Als nämlich die Sowjets als erste eine Kapsel in den Weltraum schossen, fragte sich die westliche Welt, warum nicht sie schon zuvor auf diese absurde Idee gekommen war, und konstatierte fehlende ‚Kreativität'.

Damit begann, ganz im Sinne der Politik des Kalten Krieges, die Befreiung der Kultur von den Fesseln der etablierten Hochkultur und deren altkluger Rezeption. Alle mussten aktiv und kreativ werden und alles war ab nun erlaubt. Kulturgrenzen, auf Kenntnissen beruhend, fielen, Kriterien der Qualität wurden aufgehoben, jeder durfte, ja musste irgendwie kreativ sein.

Diese neue Ästhetik, diese Ästhetik von unten, kam eindeutig nicht von unten, sondern wurde als Recht postuliert. Verschönerung, individuelle noch dazu, verbunden mit Selbstverwirklichung sollte die ‚Zerstörungen' der Nachkriegszeit heilen. Gartenzwerge gab es immer, aber ab nun waren sie außer Streit gestellt. Ja mehr noch. Waren die Gartenzwerge bis dahin eine liebenswert verschämte Subkultur, wurde das Recht auf Gartenzwerge im metaphorischen Sinn nun zum Bannerträger der Boulevard-Medien. Kitsch war nun nicht mehr eine harmlose und eigentlich heimlich gelebte und geliebte Abartigkeit. Kitsch war ‚Kreativität', und die Mehrheit liebte Kitsch, war deshalb ‚kreativ' und war im Recht.

Kulturindustrie

Auf dieser Basis etablierte sich die Kulturindustrie, die sukzessive alle Sparten kulturellen Schaffens erfasste. ‚Schaffen', welch altmodisches Wort für die Industrialisierung der kulturellen Wunschproduktion und -befriedigung. Lange Zeit gebräuchlich war in der sich emanzipatorisch fühlenden ‚linken' Terminologie der siebziger Jahre dieser Terminus der „Kulturschaffenden". Und hinkte so schon seiner Zeit und ihren Bedingungen hoffnungslos hinterher. Denn alles ‚Schaffen', auch das ‚kreative', wurde ‚industriell', verlangte nach

Thus began, entirely in the sense of Cold War politics, the liberation of culture from the bonds of the established high culture and its precocious reception. Everyone had to become active and creative and everything was allowed from that point onwards. Cultural borders, based on knowledge, fell, quality criteria were abolished, everyone was allowed to, indeed had to somehow be creative.

Broadcast in German-speaking countries, the TV program Wünsch dir was (Make a Wish), for instance, can be seen today as one of the many responses to the creativity paradigm following the Sputnik shock. A true milestone of European everyday culture. Because Wünsch dir was gathered millions of viewers in Germany, Austria and Switzerland around the same screen with the basic messages: 'Join in,' 'Break all taboos' (the see-through blouse!), 'Your judgment carries weight.' Among all these shows and games, which made everyone into an expert, was one that can be labeled as symbolic for the development of what we today refer to as spectacle architecture. It was the legendary "Hundertwasser Action." The Viennese artist demanded a "façade right for all" and a crooked ecological city as a populist answer to the austere chamber of modernism. Interesting was the reaction of the 'game families' back then to the proposals of the 'treeministration' of the city and the demand for creativity for everyone. More green in the city, hominess and coziness, this found undivided acceptance. But the demand for the creative self-painting of one's own house, even if is an apartment building, was still seen as an anarchistic act against the powers of property management and the preservers of a public appearance of the building: "What will the others say about it?"

This new aesthetic, this aesthetic from below, clearly did not come from below, but was postulated as law. Beautification, individual at that, combined with self-realization was to heal the 'destructions' of the post-war era. Garden gnomes always existed, but from that point on they were placed beyond dispute. And even more. If

Marketing und Verkauf, nach Öffentlichkeit und öffentlichen Medien, nach Publikum und Resonanz. Die gesamte Kulturindustrie hatte gar keine andere Chance als eine Markenartikelindustrie zu werden.

Ob Beatles, Beuys und Beethoven, ob Rothko, Rothenburg und Rolling Stones – sie und alle anderen wurden Markenartikel, die sich im Namedropping der öffentlichen Aufmerksamkeit zu bewähren hatten. Kulturelle Ereignisse, Veranstaltungen, Museen, ganze Städte – sie mussten und müssen heute mehr denn je ihre schiere Existenz mit einer ‚Sensation', einem ‚Star' legitimieren, um sich verkaufen zu können.

Und die Industrie der Kultur würde nicht ihren eigenen strukturellen Bedingungen folgen, wenn sie nicht sukzessive alle Disziplinen der Kultur unterwerfen würde. Dabei spielt es längst keine Rolle mehr, ob die Kulturindustrie primär unter privatwirtschaftlichen Rahmenbedingungen wie die U-Musik, unter staatli-

the garden gnomes were an endearingly bashful subculture up until then, the right to garden gnomes in the metaphoric sense then became the standard bearer of the tabloid press. Kitsch was no longer a harmless and actually secretly lived and loved kinkiness. Kitsch was 'creativity' and the majority loved kitsch, was therefore 'creative' and was in the right.

Culture Industry

The culture industry established itself on this basis, and successively laid hold of all sectors of cultural creative work. 'Creative work,' what an old-fashioned word for the industrialization of cultural desire production and gratification. The term 'cultural worker' was commonly used for a long time in the emancipatory-feeling 'left-wing' terminology of the seventies. And thus already lagged hopelessly behind its time and its conditions. Because all 'creative work' became 'industrial,' called for marketing and sales, for publicity and public media, for an audience and resonance. The entire culture industry had no other chance than to become a branded goods industry.

Whether Beatles, Beuys and Beethoven, whether Rothko, Rothenburg and Rolling Stones—they and all others became branded products that had to prove themselves in the namedropping of public attention. Cultural happenings, events, museums, entire cities—they had to and have to legitimize their very existence today more than ever with a 'sensation,' a 'star,' in order to sell themselves.

And the industry of culture would not follow its own structural conditions if did not successively subjugate itself to all disciplines of culture. It has long not played any role whether the culture industry acts primarily under commercial framework conditions like popular music, under public framework conditions like the German-language theaters and museums, or under

Gartenzwerg · Garden gnome. © Tom Kussin

Sports Resort, Disney World Orlando, 1996. © DS

chen Rahmenbedingungen wie die deutschsprachigen Theater und Museen oder unter gemischtwirtschaftlichen (private Gewinne und öffentliche Verluste) Rahmenbedingungen wie die E-Musik und Oper agiert. Der Erfolgsdruck des Ereignisses, des Events, ist über Rendite oder Frequenz überall gleich gegeben.

So war es nur eine Frage der Zeit, bis auch die Architektur, die sich eben auch – in Teilbereichen – als kulturelle Produktion versteht, denselben kulturindustriellen Bedingungen unterworfen wurde. Dabei kann ich meine seit Jahren vertretene These nicht unterdrücken, dass dieser kulturindustrielle ‚Sündenfall' der Architektur bei der postmodernen Biennale 1980 mit der „Strada novissima" in unübersehbarer Deutlichkeit erfolgt ist: Es war dabei nicht mehr entscheidend, ‚was' der jeweils eingeladene Architekt als seinen Fassadenabschnitt präsentierte, sondern nur mehr ‚wer' überhaupt dafür ausgewählt und eingeladen wurde.

mixed-economy (private profits and public losses) framework conditions like serious music and opera. The pressure for the happening, the event, to succeed through return or frequency is the same everywhere.

So it was only a question of time until architecture, which actually also sees itself—in subareas—as cultural production, was subject to the same cultural-industrial conditions. I cannot thereby suppress the thesis I've been advocating for years that this cultural-industrial "fall" of architecture occurred at the postmodern Biennale in 1980 with the "Strada novissima" in unmistakable clarity: It was no longer decisive 'what' the respective invited architect presented as his façade section, but only 'who' was even chosen and invited for it.

One should, however, not forget thereby that the architectonic avant-garde of the late-seventies (Archigram, Antfarm, Archizoom, Superstudio, HausRucker-Co, Coop Himmelblau, Missing Link, etc.) resorted to consistently popular means of mediation (flyers, actions) and their strength precisely consisted in using the instruments of mass media attention through provocation.

Dabei sollte man aber nicht vergessen, dass schon die architektonische Avantgarde der späten sechziger Jahre (Archigram, Antfarm, Archizoom, Superstudio, HausRucker-Co, Coop Himmelblau, Missing Link etc.) zu durchwegs populären Mitteln der Vermittlung griff (Flugblätter, Aktionen) und ihre Stärke gerade darin bestand, durch Provokation die Instrumente massenmedialer Aufmerksamkeit zu benutzen.

Vor dem Hintergrund der Kulturindustrie gilt letztlich nur der Wert öffentlicher Aufmerksamkeit und Resonanz. Und dabei ist es relativ egal, was der jeweilige Star-Architekt macht, so er zu einem solchen erklärt worden ist. Alles, worauf er zu achten hat, ist eine ‚Meldung' zu produzieren oder zu provozieren. Womit wir wieder beim Problem der Kreativität, dem News-Wert, und damit der massenmedialen Verwertung gelandet sind. Womit auch die feine, aber wesentliche Differenz zur ‚Erlebnis'-Architektur benannt ist. Denn das innerarchitektonische Star-System hat vielmehr ‚Ereignis'-Architektur für die mediale Verwertung geschaffen, die ‚Erlebnisse' – sie sind nicht als Ausgangspunkt und Anlass des Werks eingeplante Absichten.

Therme Vals, Peter Zumthor. © Architekturzentrum Wien, Sammlung · Collection, Margherita Spiluttini

Against the background of the culture industry, only the value of public attention and resonance is ultimately valid. And it is relatively unimportant what the respective star architect does, as long as he has been declared as such. All he has to look out for is to produce or provoke a 'report.' Whereby we have also landed again at the problem of creativity, the news value and hence the mass media exploitation. Whereby the fine, but crucial difference to 'spectacle' architecture is also named. Because the inner-architectonic star system has instead created 'event' architecture for media exploitation, the 'spectacles'—they are nothing other than planned intentions of the starting point and occasion of the work.

Disney World

"We are thinking," said the Mövenpick architect in front of a live television camera, "of the customers and not of the critical artists and intellectuals when we design a venue. And there is naturally," he continued, "a limit where kitsch becomes unbearable." But he doesn't say where this limit lies.

We are hence in the middle of the phenomenon of spectacle architecture, which has apparently disconnected from the inner-architectonic considerations and precisely knows what causes an effect, what has to be staged in order to lure and satisfy the customers.

The quintessence of spectacle architecture is the concept of Disney World. Disney World is not simply only an amusement park but, for American standards, an urban biotope of a pretend city that doesn't have any real analogy anymore. That is the European view of this phenomenon. To study perfectly thereby is how, through 'spectacles,' a sophisticated system of urban management functions at Disney, one that ranges from

Disney World

„Wir denken", sagte der Mövenpick-Architekt vor laufender Fernsehkamera, „an den Kunden und nicht an die kritischen Künstler und Intellektuellen, wenn wir ein Lokal gestalten. Und es gibt natürlich", sagte er weiter, „eine Grenze, wo der Kitsch unerträglich wird." Er sagt aber nicht, wo diese Grenze liegt.

Damit sind wir mitten drin im Phänomen der Erlebnisarchitektur, die sich scheinbar abgekoppelt hat von den innerarchitektonischen Überlegungen und ganz genau weiß, was wirkt, was inszeniert werden muss, um die Kunden zu locken und zu befriedigen.

Die Quintessenz der Erlebnisarchitektur ist das Konzept von Disney World. Disney World ist nicht einfach nur ein Vergnügungspark, sondern für amerikanische Verhältnisse ein urbanes Biotop einer gespielten Stadt, die keine reale Entsprechung mehr hat. Das ist der europäische Blick auf dieses Phänomen. Perfekt dabei zu studieren ist, wie über ‚Erlebnisse' ein ausgeklügeltes System von Urban Management bei Disney funktioniert, das sich von der emotionalen Verkürzung von Wartezeiten über exakt angeordnete Kauf- und Konsumpunkte bis zur Abwicklung der Transporte erstreckt. Ein durch und durch intelligentes System, das die Bequemlichkeit des Kunden in das Konzept eines möglichst friktionsfreien Besuches integriert.

Kritische (Ostküsten-)Amerikaner wie Michael Sorkin oder Richard Sennett, mögen darunter nur die Vermarktung und den totalen Ausverkauf des Städtischen an sich erkennen, weil sie sehnsuchtsvoll nach der vermeintlichen Authentizität europäischer Tradition blicken. Als Europäer und authentischer Bewohner einer authentisch alten Stadt mit authentischer Urbanität weiß man um die inzwischen erfolgte touristische Inszenierung eben dieser Authentizität.

Dabei, im direkten Vergleich der Erlebnisarchitekturen, zwischen Disney World und beispielsweise Wien, wirkt Disney World inzwischen viel authentischer und

---

Whether this withdrawal into the pure temple is really a way out remains questionable at any rate.

---

the emotional shortening of the waiting times, to the exactly arranged buying and consumption points, all the way up to the processing of transports. An out-and-out intelligent system that integrates the comfort of the customer into the concept of a visit that is as frictionless as possible.

Critical (East Coast) Americans like Michael Sorkin or Richard Sennett may only recognize the marketing and the total sell-out of urbanity per se below it, because they longingly look to the alleged authenticity of European tradition. As a European and an authentic inhabitant of an authentic old city with authentic urbanity, one knows the touristic staging of this very authenticity that has meanwhile taken place.

Though in direct comparison of spectacle architectures, between Disney World and, for example, Vienna, Disney World seems to be much more authentic and honest than Vienna in the meantime. Disney World doesn't claim at all to be reality. All of the actors there are employed and are paid for the optimal selling of the surrogate 'city.' In an authentic old city like Vienna, by contrast, all of those living here are obligated, unpaid and emotionally, to spread out the cultural-industrial uniqueness in front of the 'strangers.' No one who visits a still authentic old city is interested in its cracks and contradictions. He wants spectacle, spectacle architecture, in the sugarcoated and smoothed continuity of cultural-industrial consumers interested in highlights.

ehrlicher als Wien. Disney World behauptet gar nicht Realität zu sein. Alle Akteure dort sind angestellt und werden bezahlt für den optimalen Verkauf des Surrogats ‚Stadt'. In einer authentisch alten Stadt wie Wien werden hingegen alle hier Lebenden unbezahlt emotional dazu verpflichtet, vor den ‚Fremden' die kulturindustrielle Einzigartigkeit auszubreiten. Niemand, der eine nach wie vor authentische alte Stadt besucht, ist interessiert an ihren Brüchen und Widersprüchen. Er will Erlebnis, Erlebnisarchitektur, in der geschönten und geglätteten Kontinuität der an Highlights interessierten kulturindustriellen Konsumenten.

Die Wiener Künstlerhäuser

In diese kulturelle Hegemonie des Kitsches gehört auch der Erfolg der „Wiener Künstlerhäuser". Längst kein Einzelphänomen wie das Hundertwasser-Haus mehr, sind die ‚Künstlerhäuser' inzwischen ein ästhetisch kanonisierter Stil. Denn abgesehen von Hundertwasser selbst, dessen Agentur inzwischen höchst erfolgreich als europaweiter Developer für Verschönerungen durch den Meister agiert, hat sich inzwischen eine ganze Gruppe von Malern dem Baugeschehen gewidmet. Das Verwunderliche daran ist, dass sie allesamt ähnlich gestaltet sind. Man könnte es ‚phantastisch' nennen, bunt und quallig sind sie, (bewusst?) linkisch.

Sie drücken damit eine Form von selbsttätiger ‚Kreativität' aus, auf den ersten Blick erkennbar ist, dass hier ein fingerfertiger Handwerker eine ‚Traumwelt' zu schaffen versuchte, unter dem Anspruch einer ‚Verschönerung' des ach so tristen Alltags. Das ist sie also wieder, die Kreativität des befreiten Gartenzwerges, professionell vermarktet. Denn es gehört zum erklärten Programm des Wiener Tourismusverbandes, mit den ‚Künstlerhäusern' offensiv international um Besucher zu werben – für jenes Marktsegment, das nicht nur an der habsburgisch-historischen Erlebnisarchitektur, sondern auch an zeitgenössischen Erlebnissen interessiert ist.

Hundertwasserhaus, Wien · Vienna, Friedensreich Hundertwasser, Joseph Krawina, 1986. © PID

The Viennese Artists' Houses

The success of the "Viennese Artists' Houses" also belongs in this cultural hegemony of kitsch. Long not an isolated phenomenon like the Hundertwasser House anymore, the "Artists' Houses" are meanwhile an aesthetically canonized style. Because apart from Hundertwasser himself, whose agency has in the meantime operated highly successfully as a European-wide developer for beautifications by the master, a whole group of painters have meanwhile devoted themselves to building activity. What is surprising about it is that they are all designed similarly. One could call it 'fantastic,' they are colorful and jellyfish-like, (consciously?) awkward.

Erlebnisarchitektur?

Erlebnisarchitektur hat also mit einer bestimmten Form von ‚Kreativität', mit Originalität und auch mit einfacher Verständlichkeit und Kommunizierbarkeit von etwas ‚Besonderem' zu tun. Erlebnisarchitektur will keine Erfahrungen, sondern Bestätigungen. Und wenn derartige Produktionen unzweifelhaft auch Wirkung zeigen, bestimmtes Verhalten evozieren, dann wird es Zeit, diese Wirkungen auch zu instrumentalisieren.

Dies geschieht auch zuhauf, bei Kaufhäusern und Einkaufspassagen und -parks. Vor allem die Konsumindustrie versucht den Wirkungsgesetzen von Erlebnisarchitektur zu folgen. Wer aber mit diesem Metier der Beratung Kontakt hatte, staunt nur über die architektonische und ästhetische Hilflosigkeit, mit der hier Milliardenbeträge von Investoren mit angeblichen Patentrezepten in den Sand gesetzt werden.

Zulange haben Architekten diesen Bereich des ökonomischen ‚Erfolgs von Architektur' zugunsten der ‚reinen Lehre' aus ihrer Arbeit und ihrer Argumentation auch ausgeblendet. Man kann auch in diesem Metier beobachten, dass überwiegend nur die schlechten Architekten, selbst ästhetisch unsicher, verkrampfte Architekturen mit erlebnishaften alltagstauglichen Argumenten entschuldigen und argumentieren.

Die kunsthistorischen Entgrenzungsversuche mit der Nobilitierung beispielsweise von John Portmans oder Morris Lapidus' Hotelbauten und ihrer kalkulierten Erlebnisästhetik waren nur von kurzer Dauer, und nur für die semiotische und dann für die postmoderne Periode relevant.

Überlebt hat diese Tendenz der Ereignisarchitektur der Postmoderne noch besonders pikant im Dekonstruktivismus und seiner hemmungslosen Einforderung von Originalität und Einzigartigkeit. Pikant daran ist, dass gerade die Protagonisten und die Bauten des Dekonstruktivismus eine subjektivistisch künstlerische Erkenntnisattitude vor sich hertragen und eben darum besonders tauglich sind für den massenmedialen Verwertungsmechanismus einer oberflächlichen Origina-

They thereby express a form of self-acting 'creativity'; it is noticeable at first glance that a nimble-fingered craftsman attempted to create a 'dream world' here, under the claim of a 'beautification' of the ever so drab everyday world. So that is it again, the creativity of the liberated garden gnome, professionally marketed. Because it belongs to the declared program of the Vienna Tourism Association to offensively advertise internationally in order to compete for visitors—for that market segment that is not only interested in the Habsburg-historic spectacle architecture, but also in contemporary spectacles.

Spectacle Architecture?

Spectacle architecture thus has something to do with a certain form of 'creativity,' with originality and also with the simple intelligibility and communicability of something 'special.' Spectacle architecture doesn't want any experiences, but confirmations. And if such productions undoubtedly show an effect as well, evoke a certain behavior, then it is time to instrumentalize these effects, too.

This also happens frequently, in department stores and shopping arcades. Particularly the consumption industry tries to follow the laws of effect of spectacle architecture. Who, however, had contact with this métier of consultation is only astonished by the architectonic and aesthetic helplessness with which investors' billions are wasted here with alleged patent remedies.

Architects have also faded this area of the economic 'success of architecture' out of their work as well as their argumentation for too long in favor of the 'pure doctrine.' One can also observe in this métier that predominantly only the bad architects, themselves aesthetically insecure, excuse and reason inhibited architectures with spectacle-like, everyday life-suitable arguments.

The art-historical attempts at dissolving boundaries with the ennoblement, for instance, of John Portman's or Morris Lapidus' hotel buildings and their calculated spectacle aesthetic were only short-lived, and only relevant for the semiotic period and then for the postmodern period.

lität der ‚reinen Ablenkung'. Verweisend auf ein ‚Problem' erzeugen sie eben dieses. Wie der Tourismus insgesamt, und letztlich jedes Werk, das im Sinne der Verbesserung der Umstände und der Bekämpfung des Chaos Originalität einfordert und damit das Chaos erst erzeugt.

So ist es nur verständlich, dass sich die zeitgenössische Architektur verzweifelt bemüht, sich aus den Interpretationen von ‚Ereignis' und ‚Erlebnis' mit einer neuen Stille, Rigidität und Unauffälligkeit zu absentieren. Die Macht der Erlebnisarchitektur der touristisch entleibten historischen Zentren, und des vom Heimatschutz getarnten Landes, die Macht der Erlebnisarchitektur der Konsumtempel, die Macht der Erlebnisarchitektur jedweder origineller postmodern-dekonstruktivistischer Inszenierung ist unter den allgegenwärtigen kulturindustriellen Bedingungen so groß und unbestimmbar geworden, dass anscheinend nur mehr der totale Rückzug in eine hermetische, technologisch und funktional begründete ‚Verschwiegenheit' eine Rettung der Architektenseele erlaubt. Ob dieser Rückzug in den reinen Tempel ein wirklicher Ausweg ist, bleibt zumindest fraglich.

Denn entweder ist diese neue Rigidität wieder mediales ‚Ereignis', genug um in den Markt integriert zu werden, oder das ganze ‚Feld der konkurrierenden Zeichen' wird kampflos den Erlebnisstrategen überlassen. Man kann sich den kalkulierten Strategien der Erlebnisarchitektur verweigern, aber Architektur zu produzieren, die zumindest kein ‚Ereignis' mehr ist, das wird sich jeder ernstzunehmende Architekt verbieten. Womit auch für ihn, den letzten selbsternannten Dissidenten, die Falle der kulturindustriellen Verwertung zuschnappt. Unausweichlich.

This tendency of postmodern spectacle architecture survived in a particularly piquant manner in deconstructivism and its unrestrained demand of originality and uniqueness. What is piquant about it is that precisely the protagonists and the structures of deconstructivism carry a subjectivistically artistic awareness attitude before them and are especially suitable for the mass media exploitation mechanism of a superficial originality of 'pure distraction' exactly for that reason. By pointing to a 'problem,' they precisely create one. Like tourism altogether and ultimately every work that demands originality in the sense of improving the circumstances and fighting chaos and thus creates the chaos in the first place.

Therefore, it is only understandable that contemporary architecture desperately endeavors to remove itself from the interpretations of 'event' and 'spectacle' with a new silence, rigidity and inconspicuousness. The power of the spectacle architecture of touristically disembodied historical centers and the countryside camouflaged by monument protection, the power of the spectacle architecture of the consumption temples in any original postmodern-deconstructivist staging whatsoever has become so big and indeterminable under the omnipresent cultural-industrial conditions that only the total withdrawal into a hermetically, technologically and functionally reasoned 'reticence' allows a salvation of the architect's soul. Whether this withdrawal into the pure temple is really a way out remains questionable at any rate.

Because this new rigidity is either again enough of a media 'event' in order to be integrated into the market or the whole 'field of competing signs' will be left to the spectacle strategists without a fight. One can deny oneself the calculated strategies of spectacle architecture, but to produce architecture that at least isn't an 'event' anymore is out of the question for every serious architect. Whereby for him, the last self-proclaimed dissident, the trap of cultural-industrial exploitation also snaps shut. Inescapably.

aus · from

Ausstellungskatalog · Exhibition Catalog
Hans Hollein, Wien Museum, 1995
Translation by Brian Dorsey

HOLLEIN – Die Skizze eines Namens

Hans Hollein – Die erwartete Wiener Einführung

Drei Säulen, als Zäsur zwischen Stephansplatz und Stock-im-Eisen Platz derzeit wieder neu angedacht, sind in Holleins Werksverzeichnis das 333. Projekt. Das Werksverzeichnis beginnt mit einem Projekt für ein Einfamilienhaus in Wels im Jahr 1960. Daraus ergibt sich ein Projektschnitt von 9,7 pro Jahr. Dieser Schnitt entspricht exakt dem von Holleins Lehrer Clemens Holzmeister, der es auf 673 Projekte insgesamt brachte. Auch Holzmeister hatte einen Schnitt von 9,7 Projekten pro Jahr. Gleichklang herrscht auch bei ihrem jeweils ersten Auftrag, den beide im zarten Alter von 26 Jahren realisierten. Diese selbstverständlich unmaßgebliche, zufällige und lächerliche Rechnung soll hier nur verdeutlichen, dass Hans Hollein jetzt ziemlich genau in der Mitte seines Werkes angelangt sein dürfte und dass deshalb noch einiges zu erwarten ist. Grund

HOLLEIN – The Sketch of a Name

Hans Hollein – The Anticipated Viennese Introduction

Three columns, currently intended again as a caesura between Stephansplatz and Stock-im-Eisen Platz, are Project No. 333 in Hans Hollein's catalog of works. It begins with a project for a single-family house in Wels in the year 1960. What results is a project average of 9.7 per year. This average corresponds exactly to that of Hollein's teacher Clemens Holzmeister, who tallied 673 projects in total. Holzmeister also had an average of 9.7 projects a year. Consonance prevails as well in their respective first commission, which both realized at the tender age of 26. This naturally non-authoritative, coincidental and ridiculous calculation shall only illustrate here that Hans Hollein may now have precisely reached the middle of his oeuvre and that plenty more is still to be expected. Reason enough to once again elucidate the starting position, here in Vienna as well. Who is Hans Hollein and why is he so famous, so significant, so important?

genug, noch einmal die Ausgangsposition, auch hier in Wien, zu verdeutlichen. Wer ist Hans Hollein und warum ist er so berühmt, so bedeutend, so wichtig?

Die These: Hans Hollein gehört zu den ‚Top Ten' der weltweit wichtigsten internationalen Architekten der zweiten Hälfte dieses Jahrhunderts.

Die Antithese: Hans Hollein ist der bedeutendste österreichische Architekt der zweiten Hälfte dieses Jahrhunderts.

Die Wiener Synthese: Die These schließt die Antithese aus, und umgekehrt. Sollte ein lebender Wiener Mitbürger international wichtig sein, so darf er nicht auch in Österreich bedeutend sein.

Zum Beispiel Hans Hollein: Schon seit Mitte der sechziger Jahre gehört Hans Hollein zur anerkannten internationalen Avantgarde der Architektur – und blieb dennoch in Wien lange Zeit ein unbedeutender Angehöriger der kulturellen Minderheit einer damals hierzulande offiziell nicht vorhandenen Architektur. So bekannte er anlässlich der Verleihung des Preises der Stadt Wien für Architektur (1974), dass er zwar „zum Ansehen, aber nicht zum Aussehen diese Stadt beitragen" dürfe. Hollein hatte einige engagierte private Auftraggeber, die öffentliche Hand aber vermied damals jedwede intensivere, in einem realisierten Bau mündende Berührung. Nur jenseits der Wiener Stadtgrenze, in Perchtoldsdorf, konnte Hollein das Rathaus (1975–76) ein wenig umbauen.

Erst die sich beharrlich öffnende Kulturpolitik im Wien der achtziger Jahre bot Hollein repräsentativere Möglichkeiten. Dafür durfte er zuerst die Wiener Vergangenheit erfolgreich mit den Ausstellungen *Die Türken vor Wien* (1983) und *Traum und Wirklichkeit* (1985) verklären, um, spät aber doch, vor allem durch die völlig neue inhaltliche und architektonische Dimension und die gewaltigen Erfolge dieser Ausstellungen, auch politisch und gesellschaftlich anerkannt zu werden. Die Rache folgte auf dem Fuß: „Er wollte doch immer ein internationaler Architekt werden, warum muss er dann unbedingt in Wien bauen" – so oder ähnlich dröhnte es

„Die Türken vor Wien" · *The Turks at the Gates of Vienna*, Ausstellung · exhibition Künstlerhaus, Wien · Vienna, 1983. Archive DS

The thesis: Hans Hollein belongs to the 'Top Ten' of the world's most important international architects of the second half of this century.

The antithesis: Hans Hollein is the most significant Austrian architect of the second half of this century.

The Viennese synthesis: The thesis excludes the antithesis, and vice versa. Should a living fellow Viennese be internationally important, he is not allowed to be important in Austria, too.

For example, Hans Hollein: Since the mid-sixties Hans Hollein has belonged to the acknowledged international avant-garde of architecture—and nonetheless remained for a long time in Vienna an unimportant member of a cultural minority of an architecture that officially did not exist in this country back then. So he admitted at the awarding ceremony of the City of Vienna Architecture Prize (1974) that he was indeed allowed to "contribute to the reputation of this city, but not to its appearance." Hollein had several committed private clients, but the public sector avoided any more intensive contact back then that led to a realized building. Only beyond the Vienna city limits, in Perchtoldsdorf, was Hollein able to convert the City Hall (1975–76) a bit.

Sollte ein lebender Wiener Mitbürger international wichtig sein, so darf er nicht auch in Österreich bedeutend sein.

Rathaussaal · Council chamber Perchtoldsdorf, 1975–76. Archive DS

von den Stammtischen des staatlich geförderten Widerstands, als einige Jahre später die Haas-Haus-Debatte langsam zur Stadt- und Staatsgroteske wurde.

Heute also, ziemlich genau dreißig Jahre (!) nach seinem internationalen Durchbruch, bewundert und fürchtet die sogenannte Wiener Gesellschaft Hans Hollein gleichermaßen. Oder besser: Sie bewundert ihn, aus Selbstschutz, weil sie ihn fürchtet. Und sie fürchtet ihn, weil er eine andere Dimension oder eine Dimension der anderen Art für sie repräsentiert. Natürlich hat Hollein eine Vielzahl von Bewunderern, auch in dieser Stadt. Und natürlich sind Hollein und sein Werk nicht unumstritten, sie provozieren und verstören. Was man schmerzlich vermisst, das ist ein offenes und unverkrampftes Verhältnis, eine sachlich fundierte Auseinandersetzung mit seiner Person und seinem Werk.

Dass an dieser fehlenden Sachlichkeit das Werk und Hollein als Person auch selbst schuld sind, wird niemand bestreiten, der jemals mit ihm zu tun hatte. So komplex und kompliziert wie sein Werk, ist Hollein auch als Person.

First the persistently opening cultural policy in Vienna of the eighties offered Hollein more representative opportunities. But he was initially allowed to successfully glorify the Viennese past with the exhibition *Die Türken vor Wien* (1983) and *Traum und Wirklichkeit* (1985), in order to, better late than never, also become politically and socially recognized especially through the completely new contextual and architectonic dimension and the huge successes of these exhibitions. The revenge closely followed: "He always wanted to become an international architect after all. Why does he have to build in Vienna, of all places?"—something like that droned from the regulars' tables of the government-funded resistance, when several years later the Haas Haus debate slowly became an urban and national grotesque.

So today, almost exactly thirty years (!) after his international breakthrough, the so-called Viennese society admires and fears Hans Hollein in equal measure. Or better: It admires him, out of self-protection, because it is afraid of him. And it is afraid of him because for it he represents a different dimension or a dimension with a difference. Naturally, Hollein has a large number of admirers, also in this city. And Hollein and his work are, of course, not uncontroversial; they provoke and disturb. What one painfully misses is an open and relaxed relationship, a factually well-founded engagement with his character and his work.

No one who ever had anything to do with him will deny that the work and Hollein as a person are also to blame for this missing objectivity. As a person, Hollein is also just as complex and complicated as his work.

Hans Hollein – Der Wiener Star?

Hollein ist ein österreichischer Architekt, Hollein ist ein Wiener Architekt, aber vor allem, und da hat die bestimmte Wiener Kritik schon recht: Hollein ist ein internationaler Architekt. Eine Internationalität, die zunächst in den sechziger Jahren mit der Wiener Befindlichkeit auf eine völlig neue Art kollidierte. Wir wissen aus der Wiener Nachkriegsgeschichte der Architektur, dass es im Dunstkreis der Holzmeister-Schule an der Akademie der bildenden Künste in den fünfziger Jahren eine erste Generation des aufklärenden Widerstands gab. Widerstand gegen die nachwirkenden Konventionen und Ideologien nationalsozialistischen Bauens, und aufklärend die Wurzeln der österreichischen Architektur der Moderne suchend. Mit Achleitner, Gsteu, Holzbauer, Kurrent, Lackner, Peichl, Puchhammer, Schweighofer, Spalt, Uhl, Wawrik, und vielen anderen ist diese Generation grob benannt. Und ihre Verdienste um eine Rekreation der Wurzeln einer österreichischen Architektur können heute vor dem Hintergrund einer schon damals kunstgeschichtlich akademischen Ignoranz nicht hoch genug eingeschätzt werden.

Verdienste, die auch Hans Hollein für sich beanspruchen kann. Und dennoch war es bei ihm schon mehr und anders. Er war damals, Ende der fünfziger Jahre, der jüngste unter den neugierigen Architekten, er gehörte bereits einer anderen Generation an. Er ging nach Schweden und in die USA. Und dies nicht nur mangels entsprechender Arbeitsmöglichkeiten in Österreich, sondern auch um beispielsweise am IIT in Chicago die Konfrontation mit dem Städtebau Hilberseimers zu suchen und in Kalifornien als erster die Spuren Rudolph M. Schindlers freizulegen.

Man müsste demnach Hans Hollein als den ersten eigentlichen österreichischen ‚Nachkriegsarchitekten' bezeichnen. Was bedeutet das? Er beginnt sein Studium bei Holzmeister, als die meisten anderen bereits diplomieren; dennoch ist der Generationsbruch, der durch Hollein erfolgte, nicht so sehr auf das Alter bezo-

Hans Hollein – The Viennese Star?

Hollein is an Austrian architect; Hollein is a Viennese architect, but above all, and the certain Viennese criticism is right: Hollein is an international architect. An internationality that initially collided with the Viennese state of mind in a completely new way in the sixties. We knew from the Viennese postwar history of architecture that there was a first generation of enlightening resistance in the circle of the Holzmeister School at the Academy of Fine Arts in the fifties. Resistance against the lasting conventions and ideologies of National Socialist building, and enlighteningly searching for the roots of the Austrian architecture of the modern period. This generation is roughly named with Achleitner, Gsteu, Holzbauer, Kurrent, Lackner, Peichl, Puchhammer, Schweighofer, Spalt, Uhl, Wawrik and many others. And their merits for recreating the roots of an Austrian architecture cannot be appreciated highly enough against the background of an art-historical, academic ignorance that already existed back then.

Merits that Hans Hollein can also claim for himself. And yet it was already more and different with him. At that time, in the late-fifties, he was the youngest of the curious architects; he already belonged to a different generation. He went to Sweden and to the US. And he did this not only for lack of appropriate employment opportunities in Austria, but also, for instance, to seek the confrontation with Hilberseimer's urban planning at IIT in Chicago and to be the first to uncover Rudolph M. Schindler's traces in California.

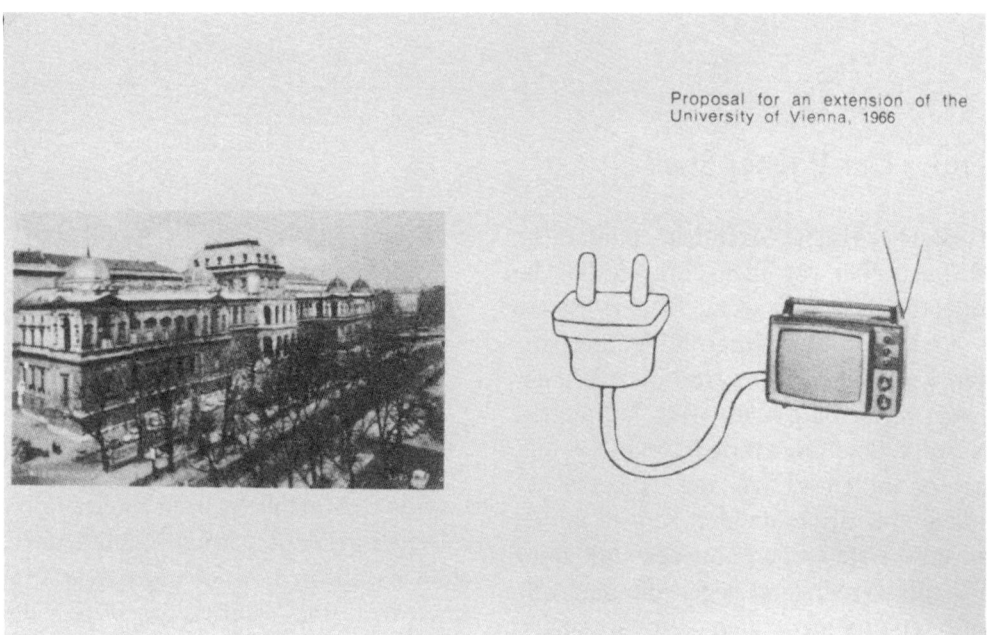

Erweiterung der Universität · Expansion of the university Wien · Vienna, 1966. Archive DS

gen, als auf eine neue Art der kulturellen Position und Reflexion. Kunst und Alltagskultur, technologische Entwicklungen und gesellschaftliche Veränderungen, historische Forschungen und Zukunftsfragen – breit und doch präzise waren die Felder, denen sich Hollein von Beginn an widmete. Man könnte Hans Hollein in dieser kulturellen Situation vielleicht mit Peter Handke vergleichen. So wie Handke die Aufarbeitungssentimentalität der Gruppe 47 attackierte und neue Sprachformen etablierte, so hat auch Hollein die Architektur dieser Zeit um neue Dimensionen der Aufmerksamkeit und Wahrnehmung erweitert. So wie Handke damals neue Bedeutungen in vorhandenen Wörtern suchte und erkannte, dass deren vorgeprägter Inhalt sich nur verändern ließ, wenn sie in neue Zusammenhänge gezwungen werden, sind auch viele damalige Versuche Holleins zu sehen, den Begriff der Architektur zu erweitern, Grenzformen auf der ‚Suche nach neuen Räumen' auszuloten.

Dem anbrechenden Zeitalter der totalen Mediatisierung entsprechend, stilisierte Handke sein Gesicht zur Ikone, legendär der Fotoautomaten-Streifen – Wuschelkopf mit Sonnenbrille – auf dem Buchrücken der ersten Suhrkamp-Gesamtausgabe von 1969. Und auch

According to this, one would have to declare Hans Hollein as the first actual Austrian 'postwar architect.' What does that mean? He begins his study with Holzmeister, when most of the others are already graduating; nonetheless, the generational break that ensued through Hollein was not so much based on age as on a new type of cultural position and reflection. Art and everyday culture, technological developments and social changes, historic research and questions about the future—the fields that Hollein devoted himself to from the start were broad and yet precise. One could compare Hans Hollein in this cultural situation perhaps with Peter Handke. Just like Handke attacked the reappraisal sentimentality of Gruppe 47 and established new language forms, Hollein also expanded the architecture of this time by new dimensions of attention and perception. Just as Handke searched for new meanings in existing words back then and recognized that their pre-shaped content could only be changed if they are forced into new contexts, many of Hollein's attempts at that time to expand the notion of architecture, to sound out fringe forms on the 'quest for new spaces,' are also to be seen.

Hollein ist als Person, als Bild der Person, präsent. In den sechziger Jahren erschien in der Tageszeitung *Kurier* eine Homestory über Hollein, wo seine attraktive Frau als ‚Modeschülerin' vorgestellt wurde. Naheliegend war damit auch die Verbindung zum Kultfilm von 1966: Die Assoziation mit *Blow up* versteht jeder, der sich an diese Zeit erinnern kann. (Warum sonst sollte ich damals, in dieser Zeit, Hollein in der Seilbahngondel in Bad Hofgastein erkannt haben können? Er war übrigens mit dem legendären schwarz-silbernen *Fischer President* ausgestattet, aber dafür nicht gerade schnell bei der Schiabfahrt unterwegs.) Dass man natürlich auch einen Vergleich der narrativen Obsession in den Werken von Handke und Hollein – übrigens bis heute – anstellen könnte, sei den Theoretikern der ästhetischen Werkanalyse als interessante Arbeitshypothese ans Herz gelegt.

Und noch ein Hinweis auf Holleins untrügliches Gefühl für Anlass und Wirkung und den entsprechenden Einsatz architektonischer Mittel: Vor rund zehn Jahren veranstaltete die Internationale Bauausstellung in Berlin eine Ausstellung der beteiligten Architekten. Die Bauten der IBA, daran muss heute erinnert werden, sind das gebaute internationale Architekturmuseum der siebziger und achtziger Jahre. Die Ausstellung fand in der Ruine eines alten Kaufhauses in der Friedrichstadt statt. Leere Fenster, jeder Architekt durfte eines dieser Löcher zur Welt zur Selbstdarstellung benutzen. Viele sahen die Funktion dieses Fensters von innen, für den Besucher der Ausstellung. Sie drapierten kleine ästhetische Modelle oder wortreiche Statements. Von außen – die ganze Fassade wurde gleichsam zu einem Plakat der Architektur – sah man dann nur ein undefinierbares Patchwork von Strichen und Farben. Bis auf ein Fenster. Und das war Holleins Fenster. Denn in Holleins Fenster sah man nur die Buchstaben H-O-L-L-E-I-N, groß und deutlich, und von Weitem lesbar. So als ob nur ein Name, der Name Hollein, für die ganze Aktion stünde, denn andere Namen waren nicht zu lesen. Hollein hat mit diesem Streich die gesamte in den Fenstern vertretene Weltarchitektur ‚signiert'.

In keeping with the dawning age of total mediatization, Handke stylized his face into an icon; legendary are the photo booth strips—curly-head with sun glasses—on the back cover of the first Suhrkamp collected works edition from 1969. And as a person, as the image of a person, Hollein is also present. In the sixties a home story about Hollein appeared in the daily newspaper *Kurier*, where his attractive wife was introduced as a "fashion school pupil." The connection to the cult film of 1966 was also obvious: Everyone who can remember this era understands the association with *Blow-Up*. (How else was I to have been able to recognize Hollein back then in the cable car cabin in Bad Hofgastein? Incidentally, he was equipped with the legendary black-silver *Fischer President* skis, but was not particularly fast while going downhill.) The fact that one could, of course, also draw a comparison of the narrative obsession in the works of Handke and Hollein—up to today, by the way—is warmly recommended to the theorists of the aesthetic works analysis as an interesting working hypothesis.

And another indication of Hollein's infallible feeling for occasion and effect, and the appropriate use of architectonic means: About ten years ago the International Building Exhibition in Berlin held an exhibition of the participating architects. The buildings of the IBA, one must be reminded of that today, are the constructed international architecture museum of the seventies and eighties. The exhibition took place in the ruin of a department store in the Friedrichstadt district. Empty windows, each architect was allowed to use one of these holes to the world as self-presentation. Many saw the function of this window from within, for the visitor of the exhibition. They draped small aesthetic models or verbose statements. From outside—the entire façade became quasi a poster of the architecture—one then saw only an undefined patchwork of lines and colors. Except for one window. And that was Hollein's window. Because one only saw the letters H-O-L-L-E-I-N, large and clear, in Hollein's window, readable from a distance. So as if only a name, the name Hollein, would stand for the whole action, because other names were not to be read. With this prank, Hollein 'signed' the entire world architecture represented in the windows.

Hans Hollein – der postmoderne Star?

Hans Hollein ist angeblich ein Superstar der Postmoderne. Das ist sein Schicksal, und dieses ist eben ein postmodernes. Beginnend mit Charles Jencks und seiner *Language of Post-Modern Architecture* hat sich eine Legion internationaler Kritiker, Theoretiker und Philosophen auf Holleins Werk zur Legitimation postmoderner Positionen gestürzt. Hans Hollein hat sich gegen diese postmoderne Zuschreibung immer gewehrt, wie auch fast alle anderen Architekten, deren Werk als Beleg für dieses stilistische Konstrukt genannt wurde. Inzwischen ist diese Debatte und sind ihre Positionen für viele heute schon wieder Geschichte, abgehakt im hektischen Wechsel der Zeitstile und Moden.

Tatsache bleibt, dass die Kritik an der architektonischen Moderne, das Verzagen an ihren kanonisierten Möglichkeiten bereits ab den fünfziger Jahren evident war. Philip Johnsons Schriften aus dieser Zeit erklären dies ebenso hinreichend wie die Kritik der Moderne, die ihr eigentlich von Anfang an, seit den zwanziger Jahren immanent war (Josef Frank, Hugo Häring u.a.).

Tatsache bleibt, dass ab den sechziger Jahren eine Aufsplitterung architektonischer Positionen stattfand. Dass dem rationalen technologischen Fortschrittsglauben und der medialen Entgrenzung der architektonischen Disziplin eine Rückversicherung im allgemein Historischen ebenso wie eine Überprüfung der Wurzeln der Moderne selbst bis hin in archaische Grundmuster gegenüberstand. Es gab nur eine Gruppe, die das nicht zur Kenntnis nehmen wollte: die akademischen Architekten, welche das ungebrochene Fortschreiben der simplifizierten Positionen einer vermeintlich einheitlichen Moderne zur Konvention des Berufs erklärten. Sie litten, und leiden bis heute, an der Marginalität ihres Berufsbildes, glauben an ihre besondere ständische Kompetenz, die aber heute niemanden mehr interessiert.

Hans Hollein – The Postmodern Star?

Hans Hollein is supposedly a superstar of postmodernism. That is his fate, and this is precisely a postmodern one. Beginning with Charles Jencks and his *Language of Post-Modern Architecture*, a legion of international critics, theorists and philosophers pounced on Hollein's work for the legitimization of postmodern positions. Hans Hollein has always defended himself against this postmodern ascription, like nearly all other architects as well, whose work was named as proof of this stylistic construct. In the meantime, this debate and its positions are once again history for many people today, checked off in the hectic shift of period styles and fashions.

The fact remains that the criticism of architectural modernism, the despair about its canonized possibilities, was already evident from the fifties onwards. Philip Johnson's writings from this era explain this just as sufficiently as the criticism of modernism, which was actually inherent in it from the beginning, since the twenties (Josef Frank, Hugo Häring, among others).

The fact remains that as of the sixties, a fragmentation of architectonic positions occurred. That the rational, technological belief in progress and the media-related dissolution of the boundaries of the architectonic discipline were confronted with a reassurance in the generally historical realm as well as an examination of the roots of modernism itself right up into archaic patterns. There was only one group that did not want to take note of this: the academic architects who declared the uninterrupted extrapolating of the simplified positions of an allegedly uniform modernism to be a convention of the profession. They suffered, and have been suffering up to today, from the marginality of their occupational profile, and believe in their special corporative competence which, however, nobody is interested in anymore today.

Tatsache bleibt, dass die Postmoderne kein architektonischer Stil, sondern ein kultureller Zustand ist, der alle Beteiligten – Künstler, Produzenten und Publikum – umfasst. Dass die aufgefächerten und parallelen Architekturen der letzten Jahrzehnte so oft zum Zeugen eines ‚postmodernen Stiles' aufgerufen wurden, hat mehr mit ihrer medialen Präsenz als mit ihrem innerarchitektonischen Zustand zu tun. Warum eine in Subkulturen aufgesplitterte Gesellschaft gerade von der Architektur ein geschlossenes und einheitliches Bild der Modernität verlangen dürfte, ist mehr als fraglich, wenn nicht gar bedenklich.

Hans Hollein hat die akademischen Grenzen der Architektur schon in den sechziger Jahren, jedenfalls lange vor der Konjunktur der Postmoderne, gesprengt. Er beobachtete aufmerksam die internationalen Entwicklungen der Architektur und Kunst und fand zu einer beide äußerst befruchtenden Zusammenarbeit mit Walter Pichler. Die gemeinsame Ausstellung in der Galerie St. Stephan 1963 war von heute gesehen sicherlich ein Wendepunkt – zumindest der österreichischen Architekturdebatte.

Hans Hollein wurde international populär durch seinen bis heute zitierten Satz: „Alles ist Architektur". Dieser Satz war nicht besonders originell, aber er passte in die Zeit. Gerhard Rühm sagte damals „Alles ist Literatur", und John Cage „Alles ist Musik", und irgendwer, möglicherweise Peter Brook, könnte damals auch gesagt haben „Alles ist Theater", und hätte damit wahrscheinlich wiederum nur Max Reinhardt oder William Shakespeare zitiert. Gemeint war mit diesem ‚Alles ist'-Satz von Hollein, Rühm oder Cage, dass sich die kulturellen Traditionen kontinuierlich den Grenzen der einzelnen Disziplinen entzogen.

Wir erlebten dann in den sechziger und siebziger Jahren prononcierte Positionen zu den aufgefächerten Themen einer neuen Architektur. Verkürzt und vereinfacht gesagt und nur als Beispiele erwähnt: Aldo Rossi entdeckt die Permanenz der europäischen Stadt und rekonstruiert die Grundformen urbaner europäischer Typologien; Robert Venturi entdeckt den Alltag der Symbolisierung durch Architektur und trennt die gesellschaftliche Botschaft von der architektonischen

The fact remains that postmodernism is no architectonic style, but a cultural condition that encompasses all of involved parties—artists, producers and the public. The fact that the fanned-out and parallel architectures of the last decades were so often called on as a witness of a 'postmodern style' has more to do with their media presence than with their inner-architectonic condition. Why a society fragmented into subcultures would be allowed to demand a closed and unified image of modernism precisely from architecture is more than questionable, if not downright alarming.

Hans Hollein already burst the academic limits of architecture in the sixties, in any case long before the boom of postmodernism. He attentively observed the international developments of architecture and art and began collaborating with Walter Pichler, which was extremely fruitful for both. From a present-day perspective, the joint exhibition in the Galerie St. Stephan in 1963 was a turning point—at least in the Austrian architectural debate.

Hans Hollein became internationally popular though his sentence, which is quoted up to today: "Everything is architecture." This sentence wasn't particularly original, but it fit to the times. Gerhard Rühm said back then "Everything is literature," and John Cage "Everything is music," and someone, possibly Peter Brook, could have also said "Everything is theater" and probably would have only quoted, in turn, Max Reinhardt or William Shakespeare. What was meant by this 'Everything is' sentence of Hollein, Rühm or Cage was that the cultural traditions continuously eluded the limits of the individual disciplines.

In the sixties and seventies, then, we experienced pronounced positions on the expanded themes of a new architecture. Shortly and simply said and only mentioned as examples: Aldo Rossi discovers the permanence of the European city and reconstructs the basic forms of urban European typologies; Robert Venturi discovers the daily routine of symbolizing through architecture and separates the social message from the architectonic substance; Peter Eisenman discovers the artificial construct of modernism, O. M. Ungers the archaic patterns of classical composition and Rem Koolhaas the everyday myths and dynamism of pop culture

Substanz; Peter Eisenman entdeckt das artifizielle Konstrukt der Moderne, O. M. Ungers die archaischen Grundmuster der klassischen Komposition und Rem Koolhaas die alltäglichen Mythen und die Dynamik der Pop-Kultur als Muster architektonischen Materials. Einzig Hans Hollein, und das ist wirklich international bedeutsam und wird auch so rezipiert, ist in dieser Zeit in der Lage, praktisch alle diese Positionen zu amalgamieren.

Deshalb auch ist seine Position nicht wirklich zu fassen und zu verkürzen. Viele der neuen, von Mendini so bezeichneten „kleinen Meister" retardierten ab Mitte der achtziger Jahre zu einem immer gleichen Personalstil, zu einer „Signature Architecture", einer Architektur mit dem großen ‚A'. Hans Hollein ist nicht so einfach zu definieren. Obwohl auch in seinem Werk immer wiederkehrende Themen zu finden sind, verfügt er über ein nahezu unerschöpfliches Repertoire der Montage und der Komposition. Hans Hollein war und ist in diesem Sinne der erste wirkliche, pragmatisch wie theoretisch wirksame Kommunikationstheoretiker der Architektur der zweiten Hälfte dieses Jahrhunderts. Hans Hollein hat sich nie nur auf Architektur beschränkt, verstand sich von Anfang an als umfassender ‚Gestalter' und hat deshalb auch die Kraft der Bilder und die Macht der Massenmedien begriffen. Er etablierte seine Arbeiten als sprechende, als kommunizierende ‚Medien'. Mit dieser Methode ist Hollein in der Lage, praktisch grenzenlos Material in alle Richtungen an- und umzuverwandeln: von der Geschichte zum Kitsch, von der Kunst zum Kommerz, und umgekehrt.

In einer der wenigen theoretisch profunden österreichischen Analysen zu Holleins Werk: Otto Kapfinger, Adolf Krischanitz, „Schöne Kollisionen – Versuch über die Semantik in der Architektur von Hans Hollein" in UM BAU 8, findet sich zunächst das Eingeständnis, dass Holleins Werk trotz aller Analysen auf seine eigentliche Analyse erst noch warten muss, es findet sich aber auch die lapidare Feststellung: „Es gelingt ihm, enorm viel Assoziationsenergie in Bewegung zu setzen." Was be-

Haas-Haus · Haas House, Wien · Vienna, 1985–90. Archive DS

as the pattern of architectonic material. Solely Hans Hollein, and that is really internationally significant and will also be received that way, is able at this time to amalgamate practically all of these positions.

That is also why his position is also not really to grasp or to abridge. Many of the new "little masters," as Mendini called them, retarded as of the mid-eighties to a personal style that is always the same, to a "Signature Architecture," an architecture with a capital 'A.' Hans Hollein is not so easy to define. Although the constantly recurring themes are also to be found in his work, he has a nearly inexhaustible repertoire of montage and composition at his command. Hans Hollein was and is, in this sense, the first real, pragmatically as well as theoretically effective communication theorist of the architecture of the second half of this century. Hans Hollein has never limited himself solely to architecture, saw himself from the beginning as an encompassing 'framer' and also therefore understood the force of the images and the power of the mass media. He established his works as speaking, communicating 'media.' With this method Hollein is able to appropriate and transform material in all directions in a practically limitless manner: from history to kitsch, from art to commerce, and the other way around.

deutet das? Zunächst setzt jedwede Wahrnehmung von Welt Assoziationsenergie frei. Warum fällt das bei Holleins Werken besonders auf? Wahrscheinlich beruht dies auf der Komplexität und Mehrschichtigkeit seiner Arbeiten. Dabei ist es nicht, wie viele beim Haas-Haus kritisierten, die Menge und Vielfalt an Formen und Materialien. Es sind vermutlich die präzis kalkulierten Wirkungen, die für die jeweilige Aufgabe und den jeweiligen Einsatz sehr situationistisch verwendeten Materialien, Raumfiguren, Formen und Symbole.

Wie ist es aber dann zu verstehen, wenn Hollein – von Tzonis und Lefaivre – eine besondere Fähigkeit zur Schaffung einer narrativen Architektur zugesprochen wird, eine Fähigkeit Geschichten zu erzählen bis hin zur Geschwätzigkeit, und sich gleichzeitig der „Suche nach dem reinen Raum" zu widmen?

Eine Dichotomie, die hervorragend an zwei Beispielen der letzten Zeit nachvollzogen werden kann: Einerseits das Haas-Haus, der Versuch einer ‚großen Erzählung' – gemeint im Sinne Lyotards, die eben deshalb eigentlich nicht mehr erzählt werden kann –, der sich einer akademischen Architekturdebatte entzieht und mehr sagt über das psychische Verhältnis Wiens zu sich selbst, somit eine ‚Wiener Erklärung' Holleins mit mnemonischer Kraft komprimiert. Außer Streit müsste die richtige städtebauliche Lösung sein. Aber dass sich an der Bildhaftigkeit und Opulenz der Fassade die Kritik so rieb, hat mit ihrer ‚spiegelnden' Wahrheit und Erzählkraft zu tun. Ein interessantes historisches Beispiel dieser Methodik lieferte schon Plečnik mit der Krypta der Kirche in der Herbststraße, die als dramatischer katholischer Comicstrip gelesen werden kann. Dass vielen diese Hollein'sche Bilderkraft – vor allem gegenüber einem Dom, der aus heutiger Wahrnehmung auch vor allem ‚erzählt' – herätisch scheint, da sich die ‚Baukunst' doch einer populären und sinnlichen Verständlichkeit zu enthalten habe, das gemahnt an Zeiten, die das Lesen von Micky-Maus-Heften mit Buße belegten.

In one of the few theoretically profound Austrian analyses of Hollein's work (Otto Kapfinger, Adolf Krischanitz: „Schöne Kollisionen – Versuch über die Semantik in der Architektur von Hans Hollein" in *UM BAU* 8), the admission that Hollein's work, despite all analyses, has to still wait for its actual analysis is first found, as is the succinct statement: "He succeeded in setting an enormous amount of associative energy into motion." What does that mean? Any sophisticated perception initially sets associative energy free. Why does that especially stand out in Hollein's works? This is probably due to the complexity and multiple layers of his works. But it is not, as many criticized in the Haas Haus, the quantity and variety of shapes and materials. It is allegedly the precisely calculated effects, the materials, spatial figures, shapes and symbols that are applied in a very situationistic manner for the respective task and the respective usage.

How is it to be understood, then, if a special ability to create a narrative architecture is ascribed to Hollein—by Tzonis and Lefaivre—, an ability to tell stories to the point of garrulity, and to devote himself at the same time to the "quest for the pure space?"

A dichotomy that can be excellently understood through two recent examples: On one hand, the Haas Haus, the attempt of a "grand narrative"—meant in Lyotard's sense, which, precisely for that reason, actually can no longer be told—, which evades an academic architectural debate and says more about Vienna's psychological relationship to itself, and is thus a 'Viennese explanation' of Hollein's, compressed with mnemonic power. The proper urban planning solution would have to be beyond dispute. But the fact that the criticism chafed at the vividness and opulence of the façade has to do with its 'mirroring' truth and narrative force. Plečnik already provided an interesting historical example of this methodology with the crypt of the church on Herbststrasse, which can be read as a dramatic Catholic comic strip. The fact that this Holleinic pictorial power—particularly with respect to a cathedral

Ganz im scheinbaren Gegensatz zur ‚Erzählung' des Haas-Hauses steht ein gigantisch eindrucksvoller Raum: die neue Halle des Banco Santander in Madrid. Unbelastet von Wiener Rosenkranz-Betern und öffentlicher Debatte schuf Hollein einen ‚reinen Raum', einprägsam, klar und offen. Durch keine ‚Wörter' belastet, verbleibt die Assoziation zunächst im einfachen Staunen und bietet dann doch Anknüpfungspunkte in Holleins Werkgenese zu frühen Arbeiten wie dem Entwurf für eine Zentralsparkasse-Filiale und zu jüngeren, wie den Salzburger oder Wiener Guggenheim-Entwürfen.

Gestehen wir doch, angesichts dieser beiden Beispiele, Hans Hollein eine besondere Fähigkeit zu: das Zusammendenken von Widersprüchlichem, das seiner Methodik immer inhärent war und ist. Holleins Architektur beruht geradezu auf Gegensatzpaaren: auf Komposition und Auflösung, auf anorganisch und organisch. Das ‚reine' Quadrat beispielsweise, von einer ‚wilden' Linie zerstört. Oder der umgekehrte Schichtenaufbau – ‚älteres' Material umschließt ‚jüngeres' –, auf den Achleitner beim Haas-Haus hingewiesen hat.

Hans Hollein – der Künstler als Seismograph

„Begrenzte Begriffsbestimmungen und traditionelle Definitionen über was Architektur ist und welches ihre Mittel sind, haben heute weitgehend ihre Gültigkeit verloren. Heute wird gewissermaßen alles Architektur. Dem ‚environment' als Gesamtheit gilt unser Interesse und unsere Anstrengungen und den Medien, die es bestimmen. Dem Kleid, der durch die Straßen gehenden Frau ebenso wie dem künstlich geschaffenen Klima, der Fernsehsendung wie der Behausung. Nicht als Objekte für ‚künstlerische' Betätigung, sondern als Erweiterung unserer Mittel und des menschlichen Bereiches." – Das schrieb Hollein 1966 im Editorial der Zeitschrift *Bau*. Eine Zeitschrift übrigens, die von 1964–70 ein wesentliches Medium der Theorie und Kritik der zeitgenössischen Kunst und Architektur war. Zu dieser Zeit redaktionell geleitet von Hollein, Oberhuber, Peichl und Pichler. Ohne *Bau*, könnte man behaupten, hätte es das vielgerühmte „Austrian Phenomenon" (Peter Cook) der späten sechziger Jahre nicht gegeben.

that, from today's perception, also primarily 'narrates'—appears heretical to many, since 'building art' is to contain a popular and sensual comprehensibility after all, a cathedral which reminds us of times when the reading of Mickey Mouse comic books was an act of contrition.

A gigantic, impressive space stands totally in apparent contrast to the 'narrative' of the Haas Haus: the new hall of the Banco Santander in Madrid. Unburdened by Viennese rosary prayers and public debate, Hollein created a 'pure space,' memorable, clear and open. Not burdened by any 'words,' the association first remains in simple astonishment and then nonetheless offers points of contact to earlier works in Hollein's work genesis, such as the design for a Zentralsparkasse branch bank and to more recent ones, such as the Salzburg or Vienna Guggenheim designs.

Let us concede after all, in light of these two examples, a special ability to Hans Hollein: the intellectual combination of the contradictory that always was and is inherent in his methodology. Hollein's architecture literally rests upon contrastive pairs: upon composition and decomposition, upon inorganic and organic. The 'pure' square, for instance, destroyed by a 'wild' line. Or the reverse layer structure—'older' material encloses 'younger' material—, which Achleitner pointed out in the Haas Haus.

Hans Hollein – The Artist as Seismographer

"Limited and traditional definitions of architecture and its means have lost their validity. Today everything is architecture to a certain extent. The environment as a whole is the goal of our activities—and all the media of its determination. The dress of the woman walking through the streets as well as the artificially created climate, the TV broadcast as well as shelter. Not as objects for 'artistic pursuit,' but as the extension of our means and the human sphere." Hollein wrote that in 1966 in

Baustellenverkleidung · Construction site covering Retti, Wien · Vienna, 1965. Archive DS

An Holleins Zitat ist wesentlich, dass es ihm damals schon um eine ‚Entgrenzung' der Disziplin der Architektur ging, um neue und erweiterte Mittel der menschlichen Fähigkeiten und ihrer Darstellung. Der Architekt, der Künstler, nicht als ‚Welterschaffer', sondern als Seismograph neuer Entwicklungen. Mit dieser Position kann Hollein niemals unaktuell sein. Seine Kunst ist nicht an Formen, sondern an Phänomenen orientiert. Ein typisches Beispiel dafür war sein Szenario und Manual für die Verkehrsbüro-Filialen (1976–78). Die Bilder der Realisierungen gingen um die Welt, als eindrucksvolle Zeugnisse postmoderner Architektur. Schließlich hatte Hollein hier jede Menge ‚Zitate' und Zeichen aus der Welt des Reisens und der Sehnsucht nach fernen Ländern arrangiert. In Wahrheit ging es bei diesem Programm aber um mehr. Es war die Einschaltung des Architekten in ein komplexes Programm der Corporate Identity eines Reiseunternehmens. Als ein Mitspieler in der Zeichen erzeugenden Darstellung eines Unternehmens. Dass dem einsamen Architekten

an editorial of the magazine *Bau*. Incidentally, a magazine that was a crucial medium of the theory and criticism of contemporary art and architecture from 1964–70. Editorially led by Hollein, Oberhuber, Peichl and Pichler at that time. Without *Bau*, one could maintain, there wouldn't have been the much-vaunted "Austrian Phenomenon" (Peter Cook) of the late sixties.

What is essential about Hollein's quote is that for him it was question of a 'dissolution of the boundaries' of the discipline of architecture, of a new and expanded means of human abilities and their presentation. The architect, the artist, not as a 'creator of worlds,' but as a seismographer of new developments. Hollein can never be "uncurrent" with this position. His art is not oriented to forms, but to phenomena. A typical example of this was his scenario and manual for the Verkehrsbüro branches (1976–78). The images of the realization went around the world as impressive attestations of postmodern architecture. Hollein had ultimately arranged a host of 'quotes' and signs from the world of travel and the longing for distant lands here. In reality, however, this program was about more than that. It was the calling in of the architect into a complex program of the corporate identity of a travel organization. As a fellow player in the sign-creating presentation of an enter-

Vierter Tag • Day Four

Cover *Bau* 2/3_1969. Archive DS

Juweliergeschäft · Jewelry shop Schullin II, Wien · Vienna, 1981–82. Archive DS

letztlich im Unternehmen die Mitspieler abhanden kamen, kann nicht seinem Programm angelastet werden. Wichtig war, dass Hollein die ‚Schrift' und die ‚Elemente' des Unternehmens entwarf. Die Unternehmung ‚Reisen' hatte eine bildwirksame Identität gefunden, dass die Firma dies nicht verstand, ist ihr Schicksal.

Die seismographische Position erklärt die Symbolkraft im Werk von Hans Hollein, die künstlerische Verdichtung, die viele, sozusagen in der Luft liegende kulturelle Zeichen immer wieder genau auf den Punkt bringt. Besonders auffallend ist diese Fähigkeit Holleins bei den frühen Läden, die alle eine sehr klare Aussage über ihr allgemein kulturelles Umfeld bilden, und dabei die schon erwähnte Assoziationsenergie sehr konzentriert freisetzen. Das legendäre Retti (1964–65) war eben nicht nur jahrelang die Ikone Holleins selbst, war nicht nur eine Loos-Paraphrase, war nicht nur ein funktional damals neuer Geschäftstyp, der durch Sakralität und Enge eine besondere Atmosphäre schuf. Das Retti ist auch eine Aussage zur Zeit von Barbarella, zum Raumanzug, zum Versprechen einer aluminiumglänzenden Zukunftsgläubigkeit. Walter Pichlers Aluminium-Fauteuil sollte dabei ebenfalls nicht vergessen werden.

prise. The fact that the lonely architect ultimately lost his teammates in the company cannot be blamed on his program. What was important was that Hollein designed the 'typeface' and the 'elements' of the organization. The undertaking 'travel' had found an image-effective identity; the fact that the company didn't understand this is its fate.

The seismographic position explains the symbolic power in Hans Hollein's work, the artistic densification that precisely gets to the heart of the many cultural signs, lying in the air so to say, again and again. This ability of Hollein's is particularly noticeable in the early shops that all form a very clear statement about their generally cultural environment and thereby unleash the aforementioned associative energy in a very concentrated way. The legendary Retti (1964–65) was not only the icon of Hollein himself for years, was not only a Loos paraphrase, was not only a functional, at that time new shop type that created a special atmosphere through sacrality and narrowness. The Retti shop is also a statement at the time of Barbarella, of the space suit, of the promise of a gleaming aluminum belief in the future. Walter Pichler's aluminum fauteuil should likewise not be forgotten in the process,

The Schullin I (1972–74) was not only the elegant room-in-room box of noble jewelry, the celebration of desire right up to the noble façade. Schullin I not only showed a consistent theme of Hollein's in a geometric-organic manner, it already interpreted the fragility of the previous values of the unconditional belief in

Das Schullin I (1972–74) war nicht nur die elegante Raum-im-Raum-Box edler Juwelen, die Zelebration des Begehrens bis zur edlen Fassade. Das Schullin I zeigte nicht nur ein durchgehendes Thema Holleins, geometrisch-organisch, es interpretierte bereits auch die Brüchigkeit der bisherigen Werte unbedingter Fortschrittsgläubigkeit, die Sprengung der bisherigen Ordnung, den beginnenden Paradigmenwechsel, die Grenzen des Wachstums, den Ölschock. Eine andere Zeit repräsentiert dann Schullin II (1981–83). Im Inneren nun nicht mehr die vom Raum isolierte Box, sondern eine Auseinandersetzung mit der vorhandenen Substanz. Ein Reagieren durch Ein- und Umbauten. Eine souveräne Antwort auf die damalige Wiener „little architecture", mit ihren Material-, Detail- und Formverfremdungen. Aber das Schullin II ging noch einen Schritt weiter, weiter in die Populär- und Alltagskultur. Ratlos standen viele damals vor dem provokanten ‚Beil' über dem Eingang, dem martialischen Schild. Ratlos waren aber nur jene, die die neuen Science-fiction- und Fantasy-Filme wie *Blade Runner* oder *Conan der Barbar* nicht gesehen hatten.

Immer wieder also bietet Hollein die Möglichkeit auch für alltägliche Assoziationen, jenseits akademischer Debatten und kunsthistorischer Etüden. Womit auch die Zeithaltigkeit von Holleins Werken auf der Ebene der Zeichen und Formen vorhanden ist. Ein Besuch des Museums von Mönchengladbach heute, der Entwurf stammt aus dem Jahr 1972, die Eröffnung fand 1982 statt, beweist, dass Holleins Interpretation des Ortes und die Matrix der Raumorganisation heute nach wie vor gültigen architektonischen Wert besitzt. (Daran ändert auch nichts, dass der Betrieb des Museums selbst heute ein wenig vernachlässigt wirkt.)

Nach Mönchengladbach sollte man jetzt noch Holleins Museum moderner Kunst in Frankfurt besprechen, welches das darauffolgende Jahrzehnt (1982–91) beanspruchte. Eine Dekade später weigert sich Hollein, mit seiner Architektur ‚nur' Matrix und Hintergrund zu sein, ‚nur' die städtebauliche Aufgabe konsequent und eindeutig zu lösen. Er interpretiert das ganze Jahrzehnt, die achtziger Jahre, als die Jahre der Ausstattung, der Instrumentalisierung von Kunst – „Design oder Nicht-Sein" –, um gegen den autonomen Willen der kunstinternen Debatte, der isolierten Kunst, der ‚künstlerischen Ausstattung' diese ihre Rolle in dieser Zeit auch zuzuweisen.

progress, the demolition of the earlier order, the beginning paradigm shift, the limits of growth, the Oil Crisis. Schullin II (1981–83) represented a different era. No longer the box isolated by space on the inside, but rather an engagement with the existing substance. A reacting through installations and conversions. A sovereign response to the Viennese "little architecture" of the day, with its alienations of material, detail and shape. But Schullin II even went one step farther, farther into popular culture and everyday culture. Many stood perplexedly in front of the provocative 'guillotine' above the entrance, the martial sign. Only those who had not yet seen the new science fiction and fantasy films such as *Blade Runner* or *Conan the Barbarian*, however, were perplexed.

Hollein thus repeatedly provides the possibility for everyday associations beyond academic debates and art-historical exercises. Wherewith the ability of Hollein's works to keep up with the times on the levels of signs and shapes is also existent. A visit to Museum Abteiberg in Mönchengladbach today, the design dates from 1972, the opening took place in 1982, proves that Hollein's interpretation of the location and the matrix of the spatial organization still possesses a valid architectonic value nowadays. (But that doesn't change anything about the fact that the operation of the museum seems a little neglected even today.)

After Mönchengladbach, one ought to now discuss Hollein's Museum of Modern Art in Frankfurt, which took up the following decade (1982–91). A decade later Hollein refuses to 'merely' be matrix and background with his architecture, to 'merely' solve the urban planning task consequently and clearly. He interprets the entire decade, the eighties, as the years of the endowment and instrumentalization of art, "Design oder Nicht-Sein" ("To design or not to be"), in order to also allot it its role at this time against the autonomous will of the internal art debate, of isolated art, of 'artistic endowment.'

Collage Kopenhagen buried, 1969. Archive DS

Hans Hollein – Ein Besuch

Es ist unmöglich, Holleins Obsession zu verstehen, ohne seine alltägliche Lebensumgebung und Lebensumstände zu kennen. Ich kenne keine internationalen Kritiker oder Journalisten, die nicht, nach einem Atelierbesuch bei Hollein, förmlich am Boden zerstört ihre Eindrücke schilderten und vollkommen desillusioniert den ‚Star-Architekten' fast liebevoll mitleidig betrachteten. Star-Architekt Hollein hat keine Villen und Latifundien, keine großartigen Bürolofts in selbst renovierten Gebäuden. Metastasenartig verbreitet sich seit Jahrzehnten das ‚Atelier' im Miethaus in der Argenti-

Hans Hollein – A Visit

It is impossible to understand Hollein's obsession without knowing his everyday living environment and life circumstances. I know no international critics or journalists who, after visiting Hollein in his studio, shared their impressions, nearly devastated and, completely disillusioned, viewed the 'star architect' in an almost affectionately pitying manner. The star architect Hollein does not have any villas or weekend homes, no spacious office lofts in self-renovated buildings. The 'studio' in the apartment building on Argentinierstrasse in Vienna has been spreading out, metastasis-like, for decades.

nierstraße in Wien. Man stolpert von einem Raum in den nächsten. Überall sitzen bis spät in die Nacht Mitarbeiter zwischen einer Unmenge von Arbeitsmodellen, Studien und Skizzen. Längst könnte Hollein, wie viele postmoderne Star-Kollegen eine weltweit agierende Firma sein, die ihre Signaturen abwirft. Aber noch immer nimmt Hollein an chancenlosen öffentlichen Wettbewerben teil, weil ihn das Thema interessiert: Beispiel Konzerthalle in Kopenhagen. Noch immer verkrampft sich Hollein in kleinliche lokale Angelegenheiten. Ob Hochschule oder Wettbewerbsjurys – wenn er sich mit einer Sache beschäftigt, dann nimmt er sie ernst, todernst, verbeißt sich wie ein Hyperbürokrat in eine ordnungsgemäße Abwicklung.

Befragt nach der spezifischen Qualität der österreichischen Architektur, und damit auch seiner Werke, antwortet er sehr rasch mit einer immateriellen Fähigkeit, mit dem Erzeugen von Stimmungen, mit dem Gefühl für Atmosphären.

Als Künstler kommentiert er mit seinen Installationen die einfache Frage von Leben und Tod. Aber das Rationale kann heute ebenso wie das Irrationale nicht mehr ‚wahr' sein; das Archaische ist ebenso gespielte Attitude wie das funktionell und technisch Aktuelle nicht mehr nur fortschrittlich sein kann. Damit wird er selbst, der Künstler, die Person, die doch vor allem ‚Signatur' ist, nichts weiter als eine Schaltstelle, ein Relais des beständigen Flusses der Assoziationen, der verdeckten Triebe und lautstarken Hoffnungen. Seine Identität ist es, nicht identisch zu sein.

Es bleibt ein einziger Halt. Die Beschäftigung mit der eigenen Biografie und ihren akkumulierten Ideen. Das Forschungsinstitut und Vulkanmuseum für Frankreich erweist sich dann als mögliche Verwirklichung der unterirdischen Städte, der skulpturalen Erlebnisräume aus den sechziger Jahren.

Hans Hollein. Ein Künstler in Wien. Ein weltbekannter internationaler und vielreisender Architekt, der als einziges Statussymbol die Lust an eleganten und teuren Hotels gelten lässt. Und auch die nur, weil sie meist über ein besonders gutes Hotelbriefpapier verfügen, das sich hervorragend für Ideenskizzen eignet.

One stumbles from one room into the next. Staff members sit everywhere until late at night between a vast number of work models, studies and sketches. Like many of his postmodern star colleagues, Hollein could long be a globally active company that cast its signatures about. But Hollein still takes part in chanceless public competitions because the topic interests him: the concert hall in Copenhagen is an example. Hollein still tenses himself up in petty local affairs. Whether the University of Applied Arts or competition juries—if he occupies himself with a matter, then he takes it seriously, deadly earnestly, gets wound up like a hyper-bureaucrat into an orderly processing.

Asked about the specific quality of Austrian architecture and thus about his work as well, he replies very quickly with an immaterial ability, with the creation of moods, with the feeling for atmospheres.

As an artist he comments on the simple question of life and death with his installations. But the rational can, just like the irrational, no longer be 'true' today; the archaic is just as much a played attitude as the functionally and technically current can no longer be only progressive. In this way he himself, the artist, the person, who is mainly a 'signature' after all, is nothing more than a switching point, a relay of the steady flow of associations, of hidden drives and strident hopes. It is his identity to not be identical.

A single foothold remains. The occupation with one's own biography and its accumulated ideas. The research institute and volcano museum for France then proves to be a possible realization of subterranean cities, of sculptural experience spaces from the sixties.

Hans Hollein. An artist in Vienna. A world-famous, international and frequently travelling architect, who admits, as the lone status symbol, to delighting in elegant and expensive hotels. And only because they have particularly good hotel stationery that is excellently suited for idea sketches.

Vierter Tag • Day Four

Team Disney Building, Orlando, Arata Isozaki, 1987–91. © DS
Einer der konzeptionell und architektonisch besten Bauten von Star-Architekten für Disney. Dennoch soll Isozaki das fertige Gebäude nie besucht haben. · One of the conceptually and architectonically best buildings by star architects for Disney. Nevertheless, Isozaki is said to have never visited the completed structure.

aus • from

domus 787, 1996
"A Diary of Disney's Celebration"

Ein Tagebuch des Disney Jubiläums

A Diary of Disney's Celebration

1996 might be seen as an historic date in the history of architecture. This is true for at least one protagonist: the Walt Disney Company. First of all, this international concern was presented at the Architecture Biennale in Venice as the official contribution of the USA, and heralded as a patron of architecture, commissioning important architects. This is incidentally the first time that a 'developer' has been nominated as the official national contribution at the Architecture Biennale. For many observers this represented the Biennale's fall from grace, but Disney—under the wing of no one less than Thomas Krens, director of the Solomon R. Guggenheim Foundation—made a great effort in Venice to present the history of the company and its commitment to architecture in a reserved way and a manner that made its significance for the history of architecture very clear.

Das Jahr 1996 könnte als ein historisches Datum der Architekturgeschichte bezeichnet werden. Zumindest auf einen Akteur trifft dies zu: The Walt Disney Company. Zunächst wurde der Weltkonzern in seiner Funktion als Auftraggeber bedeutender Architekten und *patron of architecture* als offizieller Beitrag der USA bei der Architektur Biennale in Venedig präsentiert. Übrigens das erste Mal, dass solch ein offizieller Länderbeitrag einem ‚Bauherrn' gewidmet war. Für viele Beobachter war dies der Sündenfall der Biennale, doch Disney – kuratiert von niemand Geringerem als Thomas Krens, dem Direktor der Guggenheim-Museen – bemühte sich redlich, Geschichte und Engagement von Disney für die Architektur zurückhaltend und kunsthistorisch klar in Venedig zu präsentieren.

Vierter Tag • Day Four

Das zweite Ereignis, das die Aktivitäten der Disney Company in die Architekturgeschichte einschreibt, findet derzeit in Florida statt: Disney plant und baut eine kleine Stadt, wo echte Menschen richtig wohnen werden. Die Stadt heißt Celebration, befindet sich nahe von Orlando und in unmittelbarer Nähe des Disney-Imperiums mit seinen Themenparks und Hotelanlagen. Celebration wurde am 2. Oktober 1996 vorläufig und informell mit einer *walking tour* eröffnet – ein Tag nach den Feierlichkeiten, mit denen der 25. Jahrestag von Disney World Florida zelebriert wurde.

Viele Gründe also, Disneys Architekturaktivitäten ein eigenes Heft von *domus* zu widmen und nach der Architektur Biennale in Venedig nun in Orlando die Situation selbst zu besichtigen – nicht als einsamer Forscher oder spezieller Gast, sondern als weitgehend anonymer offizieller Teilnehmer der Medienaktivitäten, die Disney zu diesen Ereignissen veranstaltete.

Vorbereitung

Wir beginnen im Sommer für *domus* die Recherche für das vorliegende Heft. Briefe und Faxe werden geschickt und werden mit allgemeinen Pressemappen und Info-Material beantwortet. Keine Antworten erfolgen auf den Wunsch nach detaillierteren Informationen. Erst bei der Eröffnung der Architektur Biennale finden persönliche Kontakte mit tatsächlich verantwortlichen Personen des Konzerns statt, die Zusendung von Publikationsmaterial wird zugesagt. Die Vorbereitung der Reise selbst gestaltet sich schwierig. Veranstaltungsprogramme und Zeitpläne sind nur nach heftigem Nachfragen zu bekommen, über die vorgesehene Unterbringung gibt es keine Auskünfte. Wir bekommen den Eindruck, dass Disney eigentlich keine Organisation, keine Firma mehr ist, sondern bereits ein eigener Staat mit hochentwickelter Bürokratie. Eine Vermutung, die sich während des Besuchs noch bestätigen sollte.

The second event will ensure that the activities of the Disney Company will be written in annals of architectural history is currently taking place in Florida: Disney is planning and building a real small town in which real people will actually live. The town is called Celebration and is near Orlando, right next to the Disney Empire with its theme parks and hotel complexes. Celebration was provisionally and informally opened with a walking tour on 2 October 1996: the day after the festivities to celebrate the 25th anniversary of Disney World Florida.

So there are many reasons to dedicate an issue of domus to Disney's architectural activities and to follow the Architecture Biennale in Venice with a visit to Orlando to look at the "real thing"—not as a lonely explorer or special guest, but as an anonymous official participant in the media activities organised by Disney for these events.

Preparation

In the summer we began research for this issue of domus. Letters and faxes were sent and answered with general press folders and information material. There was no response to our request for more precise and detailed information. Not until the opening of the Architecture Biennale were the first personal contacts made with the responsible people of the company, who assured us that material for publication will be sent. The preparation of the trip proved difficult. The programme of events and schedules were sent only after repeated requests and there was no information to be had about our accommodation. We had the impression that Disney is no longer an organisation, no longer a company, but has turned into an independent state with a highly evolved bureaucracy: a suspicion which was confirmed during our visit.

Dolphin and Swan Hotel, Disney World Orlando, Michael Graves, 1990. © DS

Montag, 30.09., der erste Tag

Flug nach Florida. Es ist keine Reise in ein unbekanntes Land. Ich war vor einigen Jahren das letzte Mal hier und habe Disney World mit all seinen Theme-Parks ausführlich studiert. Die besondere artifizielle Urbanität, die Disney zu erzeugen imstande ist, war mir damals schon eindrücklich klar geworden. Disney World bietet in einem Amerika der totalen urbanen Dispersion den Besuchern ein kontrolliertes, sauberes und sicheres ‚Stadterlebnis'. Die innere Verwandtschaft zu vielen historisch geschützten urbanen Zentren Europas ist naheliegend, denn auch deren Nutzung ist heutzutage ausschließlich touristisch geprägt. Durch diese ‚Macht der Nutzung' verschwindet die Frage der historischen Authentizität hinter der touristischen Fassade. Der ‚reale' Markusplatz von Venedig wird in Wahrheit von den Besuchern nicht anders konsumiert als der ‚künstliche' Markusplatz in Disney Worlds *Epcot Center*. Die touristische Erwartung wird in Disney World nur perfekter bedient, weil keine Störung durch wirkliches Leben von echten Bewohnern erfolgt. Die Simulation bestätigt somit die touristische Erwartungshaltung stärker als das Original.

Zum anderen ist mir ein zweites Element des Erfolgs von Disney in Erinnerung: das pragmatisch klare Verhältnis von Preis und Leistung. Es gibt bei Disney nichts umsonst. Man zahlt für Eintritt und Hotels wahrlich keine Discount-Preise, aber dem entspricht immer auch das Angebot. Regelrecht ‚asiatisch' ist das Überangebot an omnipräsenten helfenden Mitarbeitern. An die 40.000 hat Disney derzeit weltweit, und angeworben werden sie in Orlando für – laut Zeitungsanzeige – 5,95 US-Dollar die Stunde, mit freiem Parkplatz und Discount auf alle Disney Merchandising Produkte…

Monday, 30.9. The First Day

Leave Europe for Florida. It is not a trip to an unknown country. The last time I was here was a few years ago when I studied Disney World and all its theme parks. The special, artificial urbanity, which Disney is capable of creating, made a strong impression on me at the time. In an America of total urban dispersion, Disney World offers its visitors a controlled, clean and safe 'urban experience.' The innate similarity to many historically protected urban centres in Europe is obvious; their function nowadays is also almost solely based on tourism. This 'power of the function' makes the question as to historical authenticity vanish behind the touristic façade. The 'real' Saint Mark's Square in Venice

is in reality not consumed any differently from the 'artificial' Saint Mark's Square in Disney World's EPCOT Center. The only difference is that the tourists' needs are better served in Disney World because they are not disturbed by the real life of real people who live there. The simulation thus fulfils the tourists' expectations better than the original.

The other thing I recall is a second element of Disney's success: the clear pragmatic relationship between price and quality. Nothing at Disney is for free. Entrance and hotel accommodation are in no way at discount prices, but what is on offer is commensurate with the price. The overabundance of helpful staff wherever you go is reminiscent of Asia. About 40,000 people currently work for Disney throughout the world and in Orlando they are hired—so the newspaper advert said—for 5.95 dollars an hour, plus free car parking and discount on all Disney merchandising products.

Evidence of the renewed architectural commitment can be seen in the first architecturally interesting landmarks to be built in Disney World—the Dolphin Hotel and the Swan Hotel, designed by Michael Graves. They are convincing contemporary interpretations of the turn-of-the-century 'Grand Hotel.' The spaciousness and elegance of the Dolphin can compete anytime, for instance, with the Excelsior on Lido.

The Disney Company as a town planner, the Disney Company as a touristic innovator of new architectural programmes and 'types'—those were the questions I wanted to look at during the trip and try to answer by visiting the place itself.

Arrival at Orlando Airport. It seems to have been built for (or maybe by?) Disney. Clean, up-market and spacious. Marble, palms, large atria. In the baggage hall there are many busy Disney staff, asking people's names, checking lists, taking people to buses. The buses went their way through no man's land by night until, in the middle of the highway, decorative gateways symbolically announce the entry into Disney World. And yet the countryside and milieu seem to remain the same, it is just that the street names and signposts now point to the individual theme parks and hotel complexes of Disney World.

Den Neubeginn architektonischen Engagements bezeugen die ersten, auch architektonisch interessanten Landmarks, die in Disney World errichtet wurden: das *Dolphin* und das *Swan* Hotel von Michael Graves. Überzeugende zeitgenössische typologische Neuinterpretationen des Grandhotels der vorigen Jahrhundertwende. Die Weitläufigkeit und Eleganz des *Dolphin* kann sich beispielsweise jederzeit mit dem *Excelsior* am Lido messen.

Die Disney Company als Stadtplaner, als touristischer Innovator neuer architektonischer Programme und ‚Typen' – das waren meine Fragen während der Reise, die ich durch die Besichtigung vor Ort überprüfen und beantworten wollte.

Ankunft am Flughafen in Orlando. Er scheint schon für – oder von? – Disney gebaut zu sein. Sauber, wertvoll, großzügig. Marmor, Palmen, große Atrien. Im Baggage Claim finden sich viele geschäftige Disney-Mitarbeiter, fragen nach Namen, kontrollieren Listen, leiten zu wartenden Bussen. Diese fahren durch nächtliches Niemandsland, bis mitten auf dem Highway dekorative Tore den Eintritt in Disney World symbolisieren. Dennoch ändern sich Landschaft und Umgebung nicht, nur die Straßen- und Hinweisschilder verweisen nun auf die einzelnen Themenparks und Hotelanlagen von Disney.

Ich lande im neuen Hotel-Resort *Boardwalk* von Robert A. M. Stern. Es ergänzt das Hotel-Ensemble am Rande des *Epcot Center* mit den *Swan* und *Dolphin*-Grandhotels und dem Beach-Resort. Sein Name ist sein architektonisches Programm: der Boardwalk aus Holz am Hafen, begrenzt von Hotels und Pensionen, von Geschäften und Lokalen, alles im Stil der dreißiger Jahre. Das Zimmer, ein eigenes kleines Appartement mit Kühlschrank, Kaffeemaschine, Mikrowellen-Herd. Gedacht für einen längeren Ferienaufenthalt. Überraschend nur, dass im Zimmer-TV nicht einmal ein Dutzend Programme zu empfangen sind, die sich jedoch fast alle als Disney-Programme entpuppen.

Ein Tagebuch des Disney Jubiläums • A Diary of Disney's Celebration

Hillary Clinton und · and Michael Eisner am Weg zum Festakt 25 Jahre · on the way to the ceremony marking the 25th anniversary of Disney World Orlando, 1996. © DS

Dienstag, 01.10., der zweite Tag

Die Feierlichkeiten zum 25. Jahresjubiläum finden im *Magic Kingdom* statt, dem historischen Gründungsort von Disney World. Die künstliche Mainstreet ist großräumig für normale Besucher abgesperrt, nur Ehrengäste und rund 11.000 Journalisten und TV-Teams aus der ganzen Welt haben Zutritt. Das Ereignis braucht kein richtiges Publikum, das mediale Auge der weltweiten Verkündigung ist genug. So sind die Ereignisse des Festakts selbst eher bescheiden, eine Streetparade mit Musikkapellen, ein Kinderchor und als dieser die Hymne *When You Wish Upon A Star* beendet hat, fliegt auf die Sekunde genau eine Düsenjägerstaffel der US Navy aus dem Nebel der Regenwolken in donnerndem Tiefflug über die Gäste hinweg. That's timing!

I end up at the new hotel resort, the Boardwalk by Robert A. M. Stern. It completes the ensemble of hotels on the edge of the EPCOT Center which includes the Swan and the Dolphin Grand Hotels and the beach resort. Its name reflects its architectural programme: the wooden boardwalk at the harbour, surrounded by hotels and guest houses, shops and restaurants—all in the style of the 30s. The room, a small apartment, with refrigerator, coffee-maker, microwave. Designed for a longer stay. The only surprise is that the television does not receive more than a dozen stations which all turn out to be Disney stations.

Vierter Tag • Day Four

Tuesday, 1.10. The Second Day

The celebrations for the 25th anniversary take place in the Magic Kingdom, the historical place at the beginning of Disney World. A large area around the artificial Main Street is cordoned off to normal visitors; only guests of honour and some 11,000 journalists and TV crews from around the world have access. The event does not need any real spectators, the eye of the media ensuring worldwide coverage is enough. And so the celebratory events themselves are quite modest: a street parade with bands playing music, a children's choir, and the very second the choir finishes the hymn "When dreams come true", a US Navy jet fighter squadron appears out of the mist of rain clouds in a thunderous flyover above the heads of the guests. That's timing!

It is remarkable that both Michael Eisner, Disney's successful chairman and the First Lady, Hillary Clinton, talk in their speeches of their first visits to Disney World and point out the contribution Disney has made and its significance for the 'education' of the American nation. Hillary Clinton also talks about the family's visit with their daughter Chelsea to Donald Duck's 50th birthday: "This is a place where all of the characters that we all grew up with touch our hearts and for a moment let us all forget our cares." Disney, it is clear from that, is not just a simple holiday and entertainment business. Dis-

Bemerkenswert ist, dass sowohl Michael Eisner, Disneys erfolgreicher Chairman, als auch die First Lady, Hillary Clinton, in ihren Reden ihren ersten Besuch in Disney World beschwören und auf den Beitrag und die Bedeutung hinweisen, die Disney zur ‚Erziehung' der amerikanischen Nation leistet. Hillary Clinton erzählt in ihrer Festansprache auch vom Familienbesuch mit Tochter Chelsea zu Donald Ducks 50. Geburtstag: „This is a place where all of the characters, that we all grew up with, touch our hearts and for a moment let us all forget our cares." Disney, das folgt daraus, ist nicht einfach nur ein erfolgreiches Ferien- und Unterhaltungsunternehmen. Disney ist die moralische Schule der ganzen amerikanischen Nation. Oder wie Frank Rich in einem Kommentar in der New York Times polemisch formuliert: „Disney is the mouse that swallowed American culture – with culture being defined not just by the media of movies, TV, and journalism but by the aestethics or our national life."

Diese Tendenz äußert sich auch bei der folgenden Besichtigung der Baustelle des Walt Disney's Wide World of Sports Complex. Dieser soll die größte und umfassendste Sportanlage der Welt werden. Da stellt sich nur noch die Frage, ob nicht, nach der Erfahrung des aufdringlichen ‚Geschäfts' der Olympischen Spiele in Atlanta, die ‚geschwungene Linie' des Coca-Cola-Logos in Zukunft eine Verbindung der fünf Olympischen Ringe mit dem Logo der ‚drei Kreise', der stilisierten Micky-Maus, herstellen wird und die Olympischen Spiele in Orlando ihre endgültige Heimstatt finden werden.

Partnerschaften mit anderen Weltkonzernen einzugehen ist Disney nicht abgeneigt, wie in der neu erbauten Hotelanlage des Disney's All-Star Sports Resort deutlich erkennbar wird. Im unteren Preissegment angesiedelt, liegen spartanische dreigeschossige Hotelkästen strategisch wohldurchdacht in der Landschaft. Ihre Unterscheidbarkeit wird einzig durch ‚Superzeichen' verschiedener Sportarten an den Stiegenanlagen

Celebration in Bau · under construction, 1996. © DS

ney is the moral school of the American nation. Or as Frank Rich put it dramatically in his comment in *The New York Times*: "Disney is the mouse that swallowed American culture—with culture being defined not just by the media of movies, TV and journalism, but by the aesthetics of our national life."

This tendency can also be seen in the building site for Walt Disney's World Sports Complex, which we go on to visit. This will become the largest and most comprehensive sports complex in the world. The only question to be asked is whether, after the experience of the obtrusive 'business' of the Olympic Games in Atlanta, the unity of the five Olympic rings will be replaced by the logo of 'three rings'—a stylised Mickey Mouse—and whether the Olympic Games will find their permanent home here.

Disney is not averse to partnerships with other international concerns, as can be clearly seen in the newly-built—by Arquitectonica, Laurinda Spear and Bernardo Fort-Brescia—hotel complex at Disney's All-Star Sports Resorts. In the lower price range, Spartan-looking, three-storey hotel boxes are scattered around, strategically well-thought-out. 'Supersigns' on their ramps representing different sports make it possible to tell them apart. Gigantic tennis balls, over-sized Coca-Cola beakers clad the stairs. Linked to the All-Star Sports Resort is the All-Star Music Resort and everything is camouflaged by carefully thought-out imagineering elements. What is striking is that a figure of Goofy tops the swimming pool in the hotel wing dedicated to baseball. And with him is a fountain that does not flow continually, but ejects little balls of water at irregular intervals. In front of the block of rooms dedicated to surfing one has to admire the attention Disney has paid to the surfacing of the paths. Everywhere there are only easy-to-clean, fine concrete paths. But here in front of the over-sized surfboards the concrete path has a wood-like pattern impregnated into it.

gewährleistet. Gigantische Tennisbälle mit deutlicher ‚Spalding'-Schrift, überdimensionierte Coca-Cola-Becher als Stiegenverkleidung. Verbunden mit dem All-Star Sports Resort ist das All-Star Music Resort, und alle sind mit sorgfältig durchdachten Imagineering-Elementen getarnt. Auffallend: Beim dem Baseball gewidmeten Hoteltrakt krönt eine Goofy-Figur das Schwimmbecken. Mit einem Springbrunnen, der nicht kontinuierlich fließt, sondern in unregelmäßigen Abständen kleine ‚Wasserbälle' abschießt. Vor dem dem Surfen zugedachten Zimmertrakt ist die besondere Aufmerksamkeit Disneys zu bewundern, die den Oberflächen der Wege entgegengebracht wird. Es gibt überall nur leicht zu reinigende, fein geglättete Betonwege. Hier, vor den überdimensionalen Surfbrettern, hat der Betonweg eine eingefärbte Holzstruktur.

Mittwoch, 02.10. Der dritte Tag

Die Besichtigung der werdenden Stadt Celebration. Was aber ist Celebration? Disney baut hier in Orlando eine kleine Stadt für 20.000 Einwohner. Warum? Weil das Land der Company gehörte, und vor der Entscheidung, dieses zu verkaufen – an wen, so knapp neben Disneys ‚Weltreich'? – oder zu verwerten, startete man das Wagnis, diesmal keinen weiteren Themenpark, kein x-tes Ferienresort zu errichten, sondern die Methode und die Grundsätze von Disney einmal an der Wirklichkeit eines realen Lebensprojekts zu erproben. Das Projekt war innerhalb der Company heftig umstritten. Das Risiko, aus dem angestammten Bereich der Unterhaltung von Besuchern hin zur Versorgung alltäglicher Bedürfnisse zu schreiten, schien vielen zu groß. Disney im neuen Feld allgemeiner ‚Developer'? Warum sich mit dem Alltag messen, wenn man doch für das besondere Erlebnis die Weltkompetenz errungen hat?

Vierter Tag • Day Four

Mit Image-Produkten für die neue Stadt Celebration von Disney wurden alle Eröffnungsgäste ausgestattet, auch Micheal Eisner, CEO von Disney und Architekt Robert A. M. Stern, einer der Masterplaner der Stadt · All opening ceremony guests, including Disney CEO Michael Eisner and one of the master planners of the city, architect Robert A. M. Stern, were equipped with image products for the new Disney city of Celebration, Florida, 1996. © DS, © Tom Kussin

Wednesday, 2.10. The Third Day

A visit to the budding new town Celebration. But what is Celebration? Disney are building here in Orlando, on their own grounds, a small town of their own for 20,000 inhabitants. Why? Because the land belongs to the company and faced with the decision to sell it—to whom, so close to Disney's 'world kingdom'?—or to use it, they decided to strike out on a bold venture: instead of building a theme park or holiday resort they would test the Disney principles and methods against reality with a real live project. The project was initially viewed with scepticism within the company. The risk of moving out of the traditional field of entertaining visitors and into fulfilling the daily needs of inhabitants seemed too great. Disney in the new role of general developer? Why measure one's strength against ordinary reality when they had reached the top rung of the ladder in creating the extraordinary experience?

Eine befriedigende Antwort darauf, warum Disney dieses Experiment, diese Herausforderung seiner Fähigkeiten startete, gab es im Verlauf des Besuchs nicht. Bekräftigt wurde diese unbeantwortete Frage durch das Bekenntnis, dass Celebration nur ein einmaliges Experiment sei und Disney keineswegs daran denke, nun einen neuen Geschäftszweig als Developer zu eröffnen.

Dies alles als Vorbemerkung. Es beginnt die Besichtigung. Wir werden versorgt, nicht nur mit Celebration-Pressemappen, Plänen und Folders, auch mit Celebration-T-Shirts und -Kappen. Wir, die Journalisten, sind bereits Teil von Celebration. Vor einer improvisierten Medien-Tribüne am Platz der Market Street – die TV-Kameras sind positioniert – bekennt Michael Eisner, dass Celebration schon jetzt, im Rohzustand der Idee, ein totaler Medienerfolg sei. Celebration sei der Gipfel des Engagements von Disney für ‚Architektur'. Hatte man bisher einige berühmte Architekten mit einzelnen isolierten Bauten beauftragt, so sei jetzt der Punkt erreicht, wo mit all den Erfahrungen der zeitgenössischen Architektur und Stadtplanung endlich ein Musterbeispiel für eine kleine Stadt der Zukunft real errichtet werden könne – „I think, it's the most gratifying thing of the Disney company", sagt Eisner zu Celebration; Disney habe inzwischen doch sehr viel für Architektur getan. Für Wirtschaftsleute, Investoren und Developer sei heute in Amerika, dank Disney die Situation erreicht, dass es gesellschaftsfähig geworden sei, „to invite an architect to dinner".

Der Kern der Stadt steht schon. Die Main Street und die Main Buildings sind schon errichtet, im Stil des südostamerikanischen Gefühls von karibisch-kolonialistischem Klassizismus. Klar symbolisch deutbar sind das Bankgebäude von Venturi und das Postamt von Michael Graves. Die Townhall von Philip Johnson stößt auf allgemeines Unverständnis, weil hier im Südosten Amerikas niemand versteht, dass der alte Fuchs Johnson Tessenows legendäres Projekt – die Festhalle auf Rügen, 1936 – zitiert hat, das den Wald der Säulen mit dem gemeinschaftlichen Symbol des deutschen Waldes

During our visit we never heard a satisfactory answer as to why Disney decided to test its abilities. The unanswered question was strengthened by the confession that Celebration was a one-off experiment and that Disney was in no way thinking of opening up a new line of business as town planner and developer.

The tour begins. We are given not only Celebration press folders and maps but also Celebration T-shirts and Celebration caps. We the journalists have already become part of Celebration. In front of an improvised media platform on Market Street Square, where the TV cameras are in position, Michael Eisner admits that Celebration is already a total media success. Celebration is the height of Disney's commitment to 'architecture'. While in the past a few famous architects had been commissioned to design individual buildings, the point has now been reached where a prime example of the small town of the future can be built using all the experiences of contemporary architecture and town planning. "I think the most gratifying thing of the Disney Company" says Eisner on Celebration—and Disney has done a lot for architecture in the past—"is that a situation has been achieved in America thanks to Disney where it is socially acceptable for business people, investors and developers to invite an architect to dinner".

The core of the town is already complete. Main Street and the principal buildings have been built in a style that gives a South-Eastern flavour, a mix of Caribbean Colonial and Classical Revival. The symbolism of Venturi's bank and Michael Graves' post office is easy to interpret. Philip Johnson's town hall, on the other hand, meets with incomprehension. Because in America's South-East no one understands that Johnson, the old fox, is quoting Heinrich Tessenow's legendary project for a festival hall on Rügen (1936) which made the forest of columns—the German forest being a powerful symbol for the entire community—into an architectural expression of late Modernism. César Pelli's small cinema palace is also there, quoting the style of the American thirties.

Johnson and Pelli, along with Charles Moore & Arthur Andersson with their eclectic Preview Center, have created the three buildings which clearly step out of the stringent canon of the regulated building design of the new town of Celebration.

The rest of the buildings, and in particular the general development plan by Robert A. M. Stern and Jaquelin Robertson, all follow a romanticised historical idea: "grandma's apple pie town". This can be seen in the corporate design developed by Pentagram, in the logo which has a girl with a pony tail riding a bicycle, followed by a little dog and sheltered by an apple tree.

But let us follow the plan of the new town. There is a 'place of arrival,' a town centre, the square around which the most important public buildings are grouped. Then there is a proper downtown area with a Main Street; there are shops on the ground floors of the buildings and flats or small law firms on the upper floors. There are no underground car parks, the cars are parked in the backyards. The downtown area is oriented towards the 'harbour' of the small lake where a cinema and restaurants offer urban leisure opportunities. In the other direction the axis of the main street is extended and follows an urban waterway with a green boulevard, which ends at the club house of the golf course. To the left and right of it are residential areas interrupted by small parks. Adjacent to the downtown area is the school district, deliberately situated close to the centre of town to facilitate a functional exchange.

There are four types of houses in Celebration: "estate lots" are the largest houses with prestigious rooms and living quarters for staff, "village lots" are comparable to an expensive European villa, "cottage lots" are modest single-family homes and "townhome lots" are more economical terraced houses. All the houses are available in six 'styles': Classical, Victorian, Colonial Revival, Coastal, Mediterranean, and French. There is also a

zu einem architektonischen Ausdruck der späten Moderne brachte. Mit dabei ist auch César Pelli mit einem kleinen Kinopalast, der den Stil der amerikanischen dreißiger Jahre beschwören darf.

Johnson und Pelli, und auch Charles Moore & Arthur Andersson mit ihren skurril eklektischen Preview-Center, formulieren jene drei Gebäude, die aus dem stringenten Kanon der geregelten Baugestalt der neuen Stadt Celebration heraustreten.

Der Rest, und dazu gehört auch und vor allem der generelle Siedlungsplan von Robert A. M. Stern und Jaquelin T. Robertson, folgt einem romantischen Plan. Das ist ‚Grand-Ma's Apple Pie Town'. Das zeigt schon das von Pentagram entwickelte Corporate Design mit seinem Logo: Mädchen mit Ponyschwanz auf Fahrrad, gefolgt von einem kleinen Hund und beschützt vom Apfelbaum.

Aber folgen wir dem ‚Rezept' der neuen Stadt: Es gibt einen ‚Ort des Ankommens', ein Zentrum – der Platz, um den die wichtigsten öffentlichen Gebäude situiert sind. Daran folgt ein richtiges Down-Town mit Hauptstraße, Geschäften in der Erdgeschoßzone und Wohnungen oder kleinen Kanzleien in den Obergeschossen. Es gibt hier keine Tiefgarage, die Autos parken in den Hinterhöfen. Down-Town orientiert sich zum ‚Hafen' am See, mit Kino und Restaurants als urbanem Freizeitangebot. In der anderen Richtung verlängert sich die Achse der Hauptstraße in einen urbanen Kanal und Grün-Boulevard, der beim Golf-Clubhaus mündet. Links und rechts davon sind die Wohnquartiere, unterbrochen von kleinen städtischen Parks. Seitlich an Down-Town anschließend der Schulbezirk, bewusst nah am Zentrum, damit hier ein funktionaler Austausch stattfinden kann.

Die Wohnhäuser von Celebration sind in vier Typen gegliedert: „Estate Lots" – die größten Häuser mit repräsentativem Raumangebot, Hausangestellte eingeschlossen; „Village Lots" – in etwa einer teuren europäischen Villa vergleichbar; „Cottage Lots" – ein bescheidenes Einfamilienhaus; „Townhome Lots" – einfache Reihenhäuser. Alle Häuser werden in sechs Stilen angeboten: classical, Victorian, colonial revival, coastal, Mediterranean und French. Zusätzlich existiert für die gesamte Stadt ein *Celebration Pattern Book*, das grund-

Celebration Pattern Book that lays down basic architectural and community rules for the entire town. This pattern book, which is the operator's bible and is not available to the public, is intended to define and control the town's identity.

The town of Celebration is a 'normal, public town'; it has no borders, no fence and the public services (police, refuse collection etc.) are the responsibility of the normal authorities. And yet it is not designed to grow indefinitely at will, but is delimited by the large golf course surrounding it. Within the town and behind the romantic, historical façades of its houses lies a high-tech network. All the buildings are linked by glass fibre cables and are connected to the Internet and electronically networked security systems. Each house is actually a fully electronic, multimedia, interactive piece of equipment. The 'bodywork' of each of the historically styled buildings is stuffed full of the most advanced technology; it is as if Henry Ford's Tin Lizzy were driven from computer screens by an automatic pilot. To install the equipment Disney formed 'strategic alliances' with telephone, cable, electronics and security companies who will try out their latest developments in and for Celebration.

Outside Celebration a new health and hospital centre is being built by Robert A. M Stern and a business district has also been earmarked, where the first buildings designed by Aldo Rossi have already been built.

The first phase of the new town of Celebration will be completed this year. And the marketing strategy for Celebration is typical Disney: even the name Celebration is a guarantee for the excellent quality of the product called 'town'. And even before the houses themselves are built all the public spaces have been laid out to perfection. The parks are green, the trees have been planted, the benches are in place. Anyone who knows how to organize the public will tell us that the 'framework', the 'idea' first of all has to be conveyed to our senses before the reality of individual destiny can find a space.

sätzliche architektonische und gemeinschaftliche Regeln festlegt. Dieses Pattern Book als ‚Bibel' der Betreiber soll die Identität der Stadt kontrollieren und festschreiben, ist aber der Öffentlichkeit nicht zugänglich.

Die Stadt Celebration ist eine ‚normale, öffentliche Stadt', hat keine Grenzen und keinen Zaun, die kommunalen Dienste (Polizei, Müllabfuhr etc.) werden von den zuständigen Behörden wahrgenommen. Und dennoch ist sie nicht auf unkontrolliertes Wachstum angelegt, sondern wird mittels eines großen Golf-Kurses vom umgebenden Land abgegrenzt. Innerhalb der Stadt und hinter den romantisch-historisierenden Fassaden seiner Häuser existiert eine hochtechnologische Vernetzung. Alle Bauten sind mit Glasfaserkabeln verbunden, haben Internet-Anschluss, elektronisch vernetzte Sicherheitssysteme. Jedes Haus ist ein vollelektronisches multimediales und interaktives Gerät. Jede der historisch gestylten ‚Karosserien' eines Gebäudes ist mit der avanciertesten Technologie vollgestopft, als würde Henry Fords *Tin Lizzy* mit einem Autopiloten über Computerscreens gesteuert werden. Für die Installierung dieser Ausstattung hat Disney sogenannte ‚strategische Allianzen' mit Telefon-, Kabel-, Elektronik-, Sicherheits-Gesellschaften vereinbart, die alle in und für Celebration ihre neuesten Entwicklungen erproben sollen.

Außerhalb von und in Ergänzung zu Celebration wird derzeit noch ein großer Gesundheits- und Spitalskomplex – von Robert A. M. Stern – errichtet, und es ist ein eigener Business-District ausgewiesen, wo einige von Aldo Rossi entworfene Gebäude bereits errichtet sind.

Die erste Ausbaustufe der neuen Stadt Celebration wird noch in diesem Jahr abgeschlossen sein. Und die Marketing-Strategie ist typisch Disney: Der Name allein bürgt schon für fürsorgliche Qualität des Produktes ‚Stadt'. So sind auch vor den Häusern selbst alle öffentlichen Räume bereits perfekt gestaltet. Die Parks sind grün, die Bänke aufgestellt. Disney weiß, wie ‚Öffentlichkeit' organisiert werden muss, und lehrt uns, dass der ‚Rahmen', die ‚Idee' tatsächlich sinnlich realisiert werden muss, bevor noch das Faktum des individuellen Schicksals verwirklicht ist.

Donnerstag, 03.10., der vierte Tag

Das Architektur-Symposion verspricht, unter dem ehrgeizigen Titel über „Models of Patronage in Architecture" zu diskutieren. Es behandelt natürlich nur die Rolle von Disney und ist nichts als eine für europäische Verhältnisse unkritische Werbeveranstaltung. Bemerkenswert ist eine klare Aussage von Michael Eisner: Wenn Disney baut, dann kostet das 15 Prozent mehr als normalerweise für vergleichbare Bauten kalkuliert wird. Diese 15 Prozent investiert Disney in die ‚Gestaltung', unabhängig ob diese vom Imagineering-Department oder von Architekten erbracht wird. Und Disney weiß, dass diese 15 Prozent als Erfolg vom Publikum honoriert werden und sich damit auch bezahlt machen.

Das Symposion findet im neuerbauten *Disney Institute* statt – eine Urlaubsanlage mit Lernprogramm. Hier sind die Gäste ‚Studenten', können Kurse für Film, Theater, Sport und Kunst buchen. So fügt sich das Programm des Instituts zum Programm von Celebration. Disney zelebriert in Orlando paradigmatisch ein totales Lebensprogramm.

Die Architektur ist dabei nur ein Instrument unter vielen anderen der medialen und emotionalen Strategien. Es ist kein Zufall, dass dabei jede avantgardistische Irritation ausgespart ist. Die architektonisch wirklich interessanten Projekte – von Gehry, Venturi, Rossi, Isozaki – sind in Wahrheit nur abseitigen, publikumsfremden Bereichen zugeordnet.

Celebration ist der Gipfel, die Inkarnation der architektonischen Ideologie von Disney. Wir, die ‚architektonische Debatte', sollten darüber nachdenken, mit welchen Botschaften hier dieses urbanistische Modell proklamiert wird. Celebration ist ‚populistisch' wie alle

Thursday, 3.10. The Last Day

The architecture symposium organised by Disney has set the ambitious task of discussing "Models of Patronage in Architecture". Of course, it only looks at the role of Disney and, by European standards, is in the main an uncritical advertising event. What is remarkable is Michael Eisner's clear statement: when Disney builds it costs 15% more than is normally calculated for comparable buildings. Disney invests these 15% in the 'design,' independent of whether that is done by the imagineering department or by the architects. And Disney knows that these 15% are honoured as a success by the public and are therefore worth spending.

The symposium takes place in the newly-constructed Disney Institute, a hotel complex with study facilities. Here the guests are 'students' and can book courses in film, theatre, sport and art. The Disney Institute program thus fits into the program of Celebration. Disney is celebrating with it in Orlando a program of living that is all-encompassing.

The architecture is only one instrument amongst many other business, media and emotional strategies. It is no coincidence that any avant-garde irritation has largely been excluded. The really interesting projects architecturally speaking—by Gehry, Venturi, Rossi or Isozaki—are mainly in internal areas or service areas not accessible to the public.

Celebration is the climax, the incarnation of Disney's architectural ideology. We, the 'architectural debate' should think about what messages and social know-how this urban model is proclaiming. Celebration is 'popular' like everything that Disney offers but it makes

Ein Tagebuch des Disney Jubiläums • A Diary of Disney's Celebration

Historische Typologie der Südstaaten erzeugt Heimat · Historical typologies of the American South create a sense of home, Celebration in Bau · under construction, 1996. © DS

Angebote von Disney, aber es verwirklicht reale Träume und Wünsche der Menschen. Es ist eben nicht nur einfach eine neue kleine Stadt, sondern ein qualitativer Quantensprung. Ein Unternehmen – eben Disney – beherrscht die Technik der Träume, Wünsche und Hoffnungen der Menschen perfekt und hat eine Idee und ein Modell einer ‚Stadt der Zukunft' entwickelt und realisiert. Diese Stadt, Celebration, wird keine normale Stadt werden. Es wird ein weiterer Themenpark von Disney World, ein Laboratorium für reales Leben sein.

Offen bleibt die Frage, ob die Inszenierung der Realität diese eigentlich erst erzeugt.

people's real dreams and desires come true. Celebration is not just a new small town. Celebration is a quantum leap in terms of quality. A company—Disney in this case—that perfectly masters the technique of people's dreams, wishes and hopes has developed and built a model for a 'town of the future.' This town, Celebration, will not be a normal town. It will be another theme park in Disney World, but this time a laboratory for real life.

The question whether the staging of reality actually first creates it remains open.

5th DAY The 2000s

Bei der Preisverleihung des Mies van der Rohe Pavillon Preises 2005 in Barcelona für die Niederländische Botschaft in Berlin fragt mich Rem Koolhaas, frustriert von den politischen Zeremonien, ob ich nicht nächste Woche zur Voreröffnung der Casa da Musica nach Porto kommen könnte. Es gibt ein Konzert von Lou Reed, und er will einige Freunde einladen. Auf dem verfremdeten Bild sind Muccia Prada und Patrizio Bertelli identifizierbar.
During the award presentation of the Mies van der Rohe Pavilion Award in 2005 in Barcelona for the Dutch Embassy in Berlin, Rem Koolhaas, frustrated by the political ceremonies, asked me whether I could come to Porto the following week for the pre-opening of the Casa da Musica. There is a concert by Lou Reed and he wants to invite several friends. Muccia Prada and Patrizio Bertelli can be identified in the abstracted image, 14.05.2005. © DS

This decade is shaped by the political and bureaucratic problems surrounding the development of the Az W, which opens with new spaces in 2001 upon completion of the MuseumsQuartier (MQ) after nearly 10 years on the construction site. – +++ – It is pure chaos; MQ management fights the activities of all the users, including those of the Az W, for a decade. No cultural-political will that would have corresponded to our new meaning as an "Austrian architectural museum" exists. Nonetheless, the Az W develops content-wise and organizationally into a leading institution in an international comparison. – +++ – As the Austrian Commissioner of the 2002 Architecture Biennale in Venice I can present important, unknown positions with Gerngross, Turnovský, Köberl … – +++ – Guest professorship in Barcelona – +++ – Global star architecture becomes the absolute media hype. But at the fringes the new "bottom-up" movement is already attracting attention with social responsibility. I discover the Rural Studio in Alabama. The exhibition at Az W provokes comparable developments emanating from Vienna in South Africa and becomes a global movement. – +++ – In collaboration with the CCCB in Barcelona the "European Prize for Urban Public Space" recognizes a main task of future European urbanity. – +++ – Many successful consultations and moderations: Fronius' "Welder's Café" (eichinger oder knechtl), KPMG Vienna company headquarters (Gangoly), Loisium (Holl), Liaunig Museum (querkraft) …

5. TAG Die 2000er

Cover des Katalogs *Integrazione* zum Österreich-Beitrag zur Architektur Biennale Venedig 2002 von Tom Kussin, Projektleitung und Redaktion: Katharina Ritter · Cover of the catalog *Integrazione* on the Austrian contribution to the 2002 Architecture Biennale in Venice, by Tom Kussin, project management and editing: Katharina Ritter

Dieses Jahrzehnt ist von den politischen und bürokratischen Problemen der Entwicklung des Az W geprägt, das 2001 mit der Fertigstellung des Museumsquartiers nach fast zehn Jahren auf der Baustelle mit neuen Räumlichkeiten eröffnet – +++ – Es ist Chaos pur, die Verwaltung des MQ bekämpft ein Jahrzehnt lang die Aktivitäten aller Nutzer, auch die des Az W. Es ist kein kulturpolitischer Wille vorhanden, der unserer neuen Bedeutung als „österreichisches Architekturmuseum" entsprochen hätte. Dennoch entwickelt sich das Az W inhaltlich und organisatorisch zu einer führenden Institution im internationalen Vergleich – +++ – Als Österreichs Kommissär der Architekturbiennale Venedig 2002 kann ich mit Gerngross, Turnovský, Köberl … wichtige unbekannte Positionen präsentieren – +++ – Gastprofessur in Barcelona – +++ – Die globale Star-Architektur wird zum absoluten Medien-Hype. Doch am Rande macht sich bereits die neue ‚Bottom-up'-Bewegung mit sozialer Verantwortung bemerkbar. Ich entdecke das „rural studio" in Alabama. Die Ausstellung im Az W provoziert vergleichbare Entwicklungen von Wien ausgehend in Südafrika und wird zur globalen Bewegung – +++ – In Zusammenarbeit mit dem CCCB in Barcelona würdigt der „European Prize for Urban Public Space" eine zentrale Aufgabe künftiger europäischer Urbanität – +++ – Viele erfolgreiche Beratungen und Moderationen: Fronius Schweißercafé (eichinger oder knechtl), KPMG Wien Firmenzentrale (Gangoly), Loisium (Holl), Liaunig Museum (querkraft) …

Fünfter Tag • Day Five

aus · from

Falter 38_2001
„Learning from New York"
Translation by Brian Dorsey

9/11

Modell der Twin-Towers des World Trade Center
mit Architekten · Model of the Twin Towers of the World
Trade Center with the architects. Archive DS

9/11

"The World Trade Center should, because of its importance, become a living representation of man's belief in humanity, his need for individual dignity, his belief in the cooperation of men, and through this cooperation his ability to find greatness."

Architect Minoru Yamasaki
on the idea of the project

„Das World Trade Center wird aufgrund seiner Bedeutung eine zeitgenössische Verkörperung des menschlichen Glaubens an die Humanität werden, sein Streben nach einzigartiger Erhabenheit, sein Vertrauen in die Zusammenarbeit von Menschen, findet sich im gemeinsamen Willen zur Größe."

Architekt Minoru Yamasaki
zur Idee seines Projekts

Angeblich leben wir längst schon in medial vernetzten virtuellen Welten. Angeblich bedürfen wir keiner gebauten Symbole mehr. In geradezu apokalyptischer Dimension hat uns der 11. September 2001 das Gegenteil bewiesen. Die gezielten Angriffe der Terroristen auf das Pentagon und das World Trade Center erfolgten definitiv mit dem Ziel, die gebauten Symbole der militärischen Macht der Vereinigten Staaten und des globalen westlichen Kapitalismus zu zerstören. Alle Kommentatoren sind sich einig, dass mit diesem Ereignis eine neue Dimension des Terrorismus erreicht wurde.

Irgendwo, auf irgendeinem Kanal im TV, läuft, nicht zufällig jetzt, eine Dokumentation der Hintergründe der Entführung der *Landshut*, der Mogadischu-Befreiung, der Schleyer-Entführung und Ermordung, der Selbstmorde der RAF-Terroristen in Stammheim. Der Bericht kreist um Personen und Ziele. Die Orte der Aktionen sind zufällig, der Ortsname Landshut bezieht sich auf den Namen des Lufthansa-Flugzeugs. Der Terrorismus damals, im Deutschen Herbst des Jahres 1977, war auch medial ein bis heute prägendes Ereignis. Es war ein Terrorismus der deklarierten Programme und Ziele, Urheber und Forderungen waren bekannt. Das System beruhte auf Gewalt und Erpressung in einem zeitlich fixierten, aber ortsunabhängigen Verhältnis.

Der neue Terrorismus des 11. September 2001 ist dagegen trotz seiner schrecklichen realen Konsequenzen, abstrakt. Niemand wagt es mehr sich dazu zu bekennen. Keine konkreten politischen Ziele werden formuliert, keine Forderungen erhoben. Die Menschen und handelnden Personen sind unbekannt. Unauffällige Akteure, jederzeit austauschbar, nur die Aufgabe, das Programm und die Vollziehung zählt. Die Tat allein und der Ort sind das Symbol. Pentagon und WTC sind Orte, die als Symbole bezeichnet werden. Unabhängig von ihrer konkreten architektonischen Gestalt. Es wird ihnen die Funktion zugeschrieben, Zentralen der Macht zu sein. Monumente wurden sie, vor allem das WTC, aber erst durch diese schreckliche Tat. Ein bekannter psychologischer Reflex auf Zerstörung wird damit freigesetzt: Erst der Verlust erzeugt die Bedeutung.

Supposedly we have already long been living in a media-interconnected virtual world. Supposedly we don't need any built symbols any longer. In an almost apocalyptic dimension the 11th of September 2001 has proven the opposite. The targeted attacks of the terrorists on the Pentagon and the World Trade Center definitely occurred with the aim to destroy the constructed symbols of the military power of the United States and global Western capitalism. All of the commentators agree that a new dimension of terrorism was reached with this incident.

Somewhere, on some TV channel, a documentary about the backgrounds of the hijacking of the *Landshut*, the rescue in Mogadishu, the Schleyer kidnapping and murder, the suicides of the RAF terrorists in Stammheim is running, not by chance, now. The report revolves around persons and targets. The locations of the actions are coincidental, the town name Landshut refers to the name of the Lufthansa plane. The terrorism at that time, in the German Autumn of the year 1977, remains a formative experience in the media up to today. It was the terrorism of the declared programs and goals; the initiators and demands were known. The system was based upon violence and extortion in a temporally fixed, but location-independent relationship.

Despite its terrible real consequences, the new terrorism of September 11th, 2001 is, in contrast, abstract. No one dares anymore to own up to it. No concrete political goals were formulated, no demands raised. The people and acting persons are unknown. Inconspicuous actors, replaceable at any time; only the task, the program and the execution count. The deed alone and the location are the symbol. The Pentagon and the WTC are the locations that are referred to as symbols. Irrespective of their concrete architectonic form. They are ascribed the function of being the centers of power. They—and particularly the WTC—first became monuments, however, through this ghastly deed. A known psychological reflex to destruction is thus unleashed: It is first the loss that creates the meaning.

Wenn dem Terrorismus der siebziger Jahre noch der romantische Geruch individueller Schicksale mit sektiererischen Zielen zugeordnet werden konnte, so ist ab nun eine neue Dimension einer globalen Bedrohung erreicht. Das Schicksal der zivilisierten Menschheit steht auf dem Spiel, ist die Meinung vieler Politiker und Kommentatoren. Sind also jene, die nicht dem Erfolgsmodell der westlichen Demokratie und des globalen Marktes folgen, unzivilisiert? Sind sie deshalb alle Feinde? Und sind dann nicht, im Umkehrschluss, die gewählten Ziele und deren Zerstörung eine inhaltlich richtige Entscheidung? Nein. Alle diese und andere Einschätzungen der Ursachen und Konsequenzen zum derzeitigen Zeitpunkt verbieten sich. Jetzt ist Nachdenken angesagt, Analysen und neue Einschätzungen von gesellschaftlichen, kulturellen und politischen Wertordnungen sind gefordert, um Auswege zu finden.

Es mag angesichts des Todes von vermutlich tausenden Menschen für viele zynisch erscheinen, aber mit diesem Akt hat der Terrorismus eine urbanistische und gesellschaftliche Ebene erreicht, deren Konsequenzen für die realen Lebensumstände der westlichen Welt absehbar sind. Dazu gibt es gleich die erste Enttäuschung. Obwohl der Angriff auf Gebäude erfolgte, wird er zunächst praktisch keine Auswirkungen auf die Zukunft des Gebauten haben.

Die generelle urbanistische Hybris der Skyscraper an sich hat mit dem Anschlag nichts zu tun. Angegriffen wurde das Symbol World Trade Center, weitgehend unabhängig von seiner Baugestalt. Das World Trade Center in New York ist, wie der Name schon sagt, das Symbol des Welthandels, der globalisierten Wirtschaft. Die Botschaft der Terroristen wäre fast genauso symbolisch wirksam gewesen, wenn sich das WTC als weiträumiger, flacher Business-Park am Stadtrand befunden hätte. Nur ein Zusatz, allerdings ein wesentlicher, war deren Rolle als höchste Gebäude von Manhattan, als deutliches und weithin sichtbares Zeichen der Skyline.

> Although the attack was carried out on buildings, it will initially not have practically any impacts on the future of built structures.

If the terrorism of the seventies could still be associated with the romantic air of individual fates with sectarian goals, a new dimension of a global threat has been reached as of now. Many politicians and commentators believe that the destiny of civilized humanity is at stake. Are those who do not follow the success model of Western democracy and the global market therefore uncivilized? Are they all enemies because of that? And then aren't the chosen targets and their destruction, by implication, a contextually correct decision? No. All of these and other estimations of the causes are, at this current point in time, out of the question. Contemplation is now called for; analyses and new assessments of social, cultural and political orders of values are required in order to find ways out.

It may appear cynical to many in the face of the death of presumably thousands of people, but with this act, terrorism has reached an urbanistic and social level whose consequences for the real life circumstances of the Western world are foreseeable. And there is immediately the first disappointment. Although the attack was carried out on buildings, it will initially not have practically any impacts on the future of built structures.

The general urbanistic hubris of the skyscraper per se has nothing to do with the assault. The World Trade Center, as a symbol, was attacked, largely irrespective of its building design. The World Trade Center in New York is, as the name already says, the symbol of world

Der amerikanische Architekt Minoru Yamasaki mit dem Büro Emery Roth & Sons, beide bewährte amerikanische Business-Architekturfirmen mit architektonischem Anspruch, erhielten 1970 den Auftrag für ihre Twin Tower-Lösung. Auftraggeber war die Port Authority of New York und New Jersey. Yamasaki vertrat auch in anderen Bauten einen ornamentalen Spät-Modernismus, der sich im Falle des WTC in einem engen Fassadenraster mit neogotisch wirkender Basis manifestierte. Ihre minimalistische Eleganz trug erheblich zur markanten Wirkung bei, die allerdings zum Zeitpunkt der Entstehung der Türme in Lower Manhattan am Ufer des Hudson noch ziemlich verloren wirkte. Noch vor zehn Jahren hat der New Yorker Kritiker Paul Goldberger die WTC-Türme als architektonisch rückschrittliche, langweilige Architektur bezeichnet: „Die Türme selbst übernahmen das Prädikat der höchsten Bauten Manhattans, aber trugen mit Ausnahme der reinen Höhe nichts zur Verschönerung der Skyline bei."

Erst durch das Battery Park-Projekt von César Pelli, mit dem auf mehrere Bauten aufgeteilten World Finance Center, erhielt das WTC ab 1980 eine entsprechend aufwertende urbanistische Fassung. Die WTC-Türme waren mit ihren 110 Geschossen und 412 Metern Höhe das Zentrum einer ziemlich rudimentären urbanistischen Lösung mit einer großen Plaza, zusätzlichen Gebäuden und einem Hotel. Bemerkenswert war damals vor allem die Konstruktion. Sie war statisch innovativ und auf der Höhe der Zeit. Ein Außen- und Innenring aus eng gestellten Stahlstützen formte eine Art vertikale Röhre, durch die Decken ausgesteift. Diese neuartige „tube construction" war standfest und dynamisch genug, um Windgeschwindigkeiten von 240 kmh aufzufangen. Neuartig war auch das geteilte Aufzugssystem. Mit großen Expresskabinen wurden die Menschen zu Sky Lobbies gebracht und dort mit kürzeren lokalen Liften weiterverteilt.

commerce, the globalized economy. The message of the terrorists would have nearly been as symbolically effective if the WTC had stood as a spacious, flat business park on the city outskirts. Only one addition, however an essential one, was its role as Manhattan's highest building, as the distinct and widely visible sign of the skyline.

The American architect Minoru Yamasaki, with the office of Emery Roth & Sons, both proven American business architecture firms with architectonic aspirations, secured the order for their twin tower solution in 1970. The client was the Port Authority of New York and New Jersey. Yamasaki also represented an ornamental late modernism in other buildings, which, in the case of the WTC, manifested itself in a narrow façade grid with a neo-Gothic-seeming basis. Its minimalistic elegance significantly contributed to the distinctive impact, which, at the time of the emergence of the towers in Lower Manhattan on the banks of the Hudson, however, still seemed rather lost. Even ten years ago, the New Yorker critic Paul Goldberger described the WTC towers as architectonically retrogressive, boring architecture: "The towers themselves took on the title of Manhattan's highest buildings, but with the exception of the sheer height, contributed nothing to the beautification of the skyline."

The WTC first received an appropriately valorizing urbanistic setting in 1980 through the Battery Park City project of César Pelli, with the World Finance Center, which is distributed among several buildings. With their 110 floors and 412 meter height, the WTC towers were the center of a rather rudimentary urbanistic solution with a large plaza, additional buildings and a hotel. Especially remarkable at that time was the construction. It was statically innovative and state-of-the-art. An outer and inner ring of closely placed steel columns formed a type of vertical pipe, braced by the ceilings. This innovative "tube construction" was stable and dynamic enough to absorb wind speeds of 240 kilometers per hour. The divided elevator system was also novel. The people were brought to the Sky Lobbies in express elevators and further distributed there with shorter local elevators.

Fünfter Tag • Day Five

Es ist eine geradezu groteske Ironie der Geschichte, dass mit dem WTC in New York ein zweites Werk von Yamasaki nicht durch seine Existenz, sondern durch seine Zerstörung zu einem Symbol wurde. Zwanzig Jahre vor dem WTC realisierte Yamasaki mit Joseph Leinweber und George Hellmuth 1950 bis 1954 die damals moderne und auf der Höhe der Zeit befindliche Wohnanlage Pruitt-Igoe in St. Louis. Sie wurde am 15. Juli 1972 aufgrund enormer sozialer Probleme als Symbol eines verfehlten Massenwohnbaus gesprengt. Diese Tatsache und das Bild der Sprengung nahm Charles Jencks zum Anlass, um dieses Symbol des Scheiterns einer ätherisch abgehobenen Moderne zur propagandistischen Geburtsstunde der architektonischen Postmoderne zu erklären. Das Bild der Sprengung von Pruitt-Igoe wurde so zu einem kunsthistorischen Datum und Symbol, wie jetzt die Zerstörung von Yamasakis WTC eine bisher geltende Weltordnung in den Grundfesten erschüttert.

Der fliegenden Bombe eines mit Kerosin prall gefüllten Verkehrsflugzeugs hält kein Bauwerk stand. Höchstens Stahlbetonbunker würden einer derart explosiven Brandlast länger standhalten als ein Stahlskelett wie das WTC. Rein technisch also, sind Hochhäuser nicht mehr gefährdet als andere Bauten auch. Das hat ja auch der erfolgreiche Angriff auf das bestens gesicherte, und nur fünfgeschossige Pentagon gezeigt. Dennoch hatte die kriegerische Gefahr aus der Luft schon einmal zu planerischen Konsequenzen geführt. Bekanntlich berechneten die Planer der Wiener Flaktürme die Stärke der Betondecken äquivalent zu den Stärken der erwartbaren Bomben der Alliierten. Fünf Meter Deckenstärke sollte 500 kg-Bomben standhalten. Allein daran erkennt man, dass es keine statisch-technischen Lösungen gibt, um Angriffen wie jenen auf das WTC zu widerstehen.

It is an almost grotesque irony of history that with the WTC in New York a second work of Yamasaki became a symbol not through its existence, but through its destruction. Twenty years before the WTC, from 1950 to 1954, Yamasaki, Joseph Leinweber and George Hellmuth realized the Pruitt-Igoe housing estate in St. Louis, which was modern and state-of-the-art back then. On July 15, 1972 it was demolished on account of enormous social problems as a symbol of failed mass housing. Charles Jencks used this fact and the image of the demolition as an opportunity to declare this symbol of the failure of ethereally aloof modernism as the propagandistic birth of architectonic postmodernism. The image of the demolition of Pruitt-Igoe thus became an art-historical date and symbol, like now the destruction of Yamasaki's WTC is shaking the very foundations of a world order which had been valid up to that point.

No structure withstands the flying bomb of a commercial aircraft filled to capacity with kerosene. At best, reinforced concrete bunkers would have been able to withstand such an explosive fire load longer than a steel skeleton like the WTC. In a purely technical sense, therefore, skyscrapers are no more endangered than other buildings, too. The successful attack on the optimally secured and only five-story Pentagon also showed that. Nevertheless, the war-like danger from the sky had already led to planning consequences once before. As is well-known, the planners of the Vienna flak towers calculated the thickness of the concrete ceilings equivalently to the strengths of the expectable bombs of the Allies. Five-meter ceiling thicknesses were to withstand 500-kilogram bombs. From that alone one recognizes that there are no statical-technical solutions to withstand attacks like those on the WTC.

The urban planners of National Socialism developed a different solution. In the final war years thought was given to city models for reconstruction, where the destruction through carpet bombing could be minimized. Paradoxically, the ideals of modernism, from the gar-

Eine andere Lösung haben die Stadtplaner des Nationalsozialismus erarbeitet. In den letzten Kriegsjahren wurde intensiv über Stadtmodelle für den Wiederaufbau nachgedacht, bei denen die Zerstörung durch Flächenbombardements minimiert werden könnte. Dabei fügten sich paradoxerweise die Ideale der Moderne, von der Gartenstadtbewegung bis zum Bauhaus perfekt in ein gesamtgesellschaftliches nationalsozialistisches Begehren nach niedrig gebauten dörflichen Gemeinschaften. Zusammengefasst erschienen diese damals ab 1943 getätigten Forschungen für den Wiederaufbau 1957 in dem Buch von Johannes Göderitz, Roland Rainer, Hubert Hoffmann *Die gegliederte und aufgelockerte Stadt*. Diese im nationalsozialistischen Auftrag entwickelte urbanistische Position wurde in der Nachkriegszeit in Europa tatsächlich vollzogen und ab den siebziger Jahren ideologisch als stadtzerstörend revidiert. Ab nun galt wieder die dichte Stadt, die Konzentration von Bebauungen als zivilisatorisch gewünschtes Dogma.

Wer also die Stadt als dichtes Konglomerat intensiver Nähe und Kommunikation anstrebt, muss mit einem höheren Zerstörungspotenzial bei Angriffen oder auch Naturkatastrophen rechnen. Kann eine Welt, die inzwischen global diesem Konzept der dichten Verstädterung folgt, unter dem Eindruck dieser Katastrophe eine urbanistische Kehrtwendung vollziehen? Theoretisch wäre dies möglich. Wenn die urbanistischen Ideen des Zweiten Weltkriegs einer „gegliederten und aufgelockerten Stadt" sich mit jenen avantgardistischen urbanistischen Überlegungen verbündeten, die eine weltumspannende Verschmelzung von Stadt und Landschaft voraussehen. Diese Ideen, populistisch und plakativ verkürzt, würden den Erdmantel anheben, die Natur darauf erhalten und darunter alle urbanen Funktionen zum Überleben auf großen Flächen verstreuen.

Eine Vision, welche die hochtechnologisch zivilisierte Welt jener der zurzeit genannten Feinde annähert. Denn auf den Bildern, die das Fernsehen jetzt vom wahrscheinlichen Ort des Rückschlags der westlichen

den city movement to Bauhaus, fit perfectly into a National Socialist longing, in society as a whole, for low-built, village-like communities. This research, conducted as of 1943 for reconstruction purposes, appeared in a summarized fashion in 1957 in the book by Johannes Göderitz, Roland Rainer and Hubert Hoffmann entitled *Die gegliederte und aufgelockerte Stadt (The Structured and Low-Density City)*. Developed by National Socialist order, this urbanistic position was actually executed during the postwar period in Europe and ideologically revised as of the seventies because it was considered as destructive to the city. From then on, the dense city, the concentration of developments, prevailed again as a dogma desired by civilization.

Whoever strives for the city as a dense conglomerate of intensive proximity and communication has to reckon with a higher destruction potential when attacks or natural catastrophes occur. Can a world that meanwhile follows this concept of dense urbanization on a global scale carry out an urbanistic turnaround under the impression of this catastrophe? This would be theoretically possible. If the urbanistic ideas from the Second World War of a "structured and low-density city" would coalesce with those avant-garde urbanistic considerations, which foresee a worldwide amalgamation of city and landscape. These ideas, abridged in a populist and bold manner, would lift the Earth's mantle, preserve the nature on top and scatter all urban functions for survival onto to large areas below.

A vision which approaches the high-tech, civilized world of that of the currently named enemies. Because only barren hills and deserts, in whose valley and caves the camps of the enemy are hidden, are to be seen on the images that TV is now showing of the probable location of the Western world's retaliation, Afghanistan, for example. A topographic and geopolitical situation that dooms any hope of a conventionally war-like "eradication of terror," as the American defense secretary Rumsfeld formulates as the goal, to failure.

Fünfter Tag • Day Five

> That includes the control and restriction of mobility, of public space as such.

Welt zeigt, Afghanistan zum Beispiel, sind nur unwirtliche Hügel und Wüsten zu sehen, in deren Tälern und Höhlen sich die Lager der Feinde verbergen. Nicht ortbar, nicht auffindbar, nicht wirklich angreifbar. Eine topografische und geopolitische Situation, die jede Hoffnung auf eine konventionell kriegerische „Ausrottung des Terrors", wie sie der amerikanische Verteidigungsminister Rumsfeld als Ziel formuliert, zum Scheitern verurteilt

Ob wir es wollen oder nicht, die Auswirkungen auf die Zukunft der westlichen Zivilisation werden schon bald ganz reale Veränderungen des Alltags mit sich bringen. Das ist die Kontrolle und Beschränkung der Mobilität, damit des öffentlichen Raums schlechthin. Jeder Wechsel von einer kontrollierten Sozietät in eine andere wird mit restriktiven Kontrollen rechnen müssen. Schon der Weg von der Wohnung zum Arbeitsplatz wird ein überwachter sein. Das Modell des Fürstentums Monaco, das Land mit der höchsten Polizeidichte der Welt, wo alle Straßen von Videokameras mit Zoomfunktion zur Fahrzeugidentifikation überwacht werden, wird uns bald als Vorbild der sicherheitstechnischen Aufrüstung des öffentlichen Raums verordnet werden.

Whether we want it or not, the impacts on the future of Western civilization will soon bring quite real changes to everyday life. That includes the control and restriction of mobility, of public space as such. Every change from a controlled branch of society into a different one will have to expect restrictive controls. Even the way from the apartment to the working place will be a monitored one. The model of the Principality of Monaco, the country with highest police-population ratio in the world, where all streets are monitored by video cameras with a zoom function for identifying vehicles, will soon be prescribed for us as the model of the security technology upgrading of public space.

Higher security standards in air traffic are now being demanded on all TV channels and in all media. An optimal model is the prisoner transport flights taking place in the United States. Each passenger is searched naked, given a uniform track suit to wear and tied onto the seat without hand luggage. The flight crew is situated in a closed, armored unit. Intermediate stages to this doomsday scenario will probably be realized in the near future. Hours-long security checks, like those that have long been common at the airport in Tel Aviv, will in any case soon become a daily routine.

As traumatizingly apocalyptic the images of destruction in Manhattan also are, the first aim of the airplane bombers, nevertheless, was not to murder as many people as possible in one fell swoop. Because they would have chosen other targets such as a fully occupied Superdome during a sports event. It was definitively about symbols, about constructed symbols. We now have to think about that. There are probably no places that tell no stories. Every place, every building is a functionary of power and hence of symbolic messages. They are often not originally conceived and designed as such, but can be attributed as such.

A growing number of people are calling for a reconstruction of the WTC towers that replicates the originals. Such a development only exists if all rational criteria are invalidated, if the projection of desire is ascribed a symbolic meaning, if the collective pain is so large that it also hopes to be healed through the most banal, constructed substance. The World Trade Center has only now become a symbol of the strength of the United States.

Auf allen Kanälen und in allen Medien werden jetzt auch höhere Sicherheits-Standards im Flugverkehr verlangt. Optimales Vorbild sind die mit Flugzeugen erfolgenden Gefangenentransporte in den Vereinigten Staaten. Jeder Passagier wird nackt durchsucht, bekommt einen Einheitstrainingsanzug und wird ohne Handgepäck am Sitzplatz gefesselt. Das Flugpersonal befindet sich in einer abgeschlossenen, gepanzerten Einheit. Zwischenstufen zu diesem Endzeit-Szenario werden wohl demnächst verwirklicht werden. Stundenlange Sicherheits-Checks, wie sie seit langem schon am Flughafen von Tel Aviv üblich sind, werden aber auf jeden Fall bald Alltag werden.

So traumatisierend apokalyptisch die Bilder der Zerstörung in Manhattan auch sind, das erste Ziel der Attentäter war dennoch nicht, auf einen Schlag möglichst viele Menschen zu ermorden. Dann hätten sie sich andere Ziele, wie einen vollbesetzten Superdome während einer Sportveranstaltung, ausgewählt. Es ging definitiv um Symbole, um gebaute Symbole. Darüber haben wir jetzt nachzudenken. Wahrscheinlich gibt es keine Orte, die keine Geschichten erzählen. Jeder Ort, jedes Gebäude ist ein Funktionsträger von Macht und damit von symbolischen Botschaften. Sie sind als solche oftmals nicht ursächlich konzipiert und angelegt, sondern können zugeschrieben werden.

Es mehren sich derzeit die Stimmen, die einen originalgetreuen Wiederaufbau der WTC-Türme fordern. Eine derartige Entwicklung gibt es nur, wenn alle rationalen Kriterien außer Kraft gesetzt sind, wenn der Wunschprojektion eine symbolische Bedeutung zugeschrieben wird, wenn der kollektive Schmerz so groß ist, dass er auch durch die banalste gebaute Substanz geheilt zu werden hofft. Das World Trade Center ist erst jetzt zum Symbol der Stärke der Vereinigten Staaten geworden.

Zerstörung des World Trade Centers · Destruction of the World Trade Center. © NIST Robert Miller – International Center for 9/11 Studies, gemeinfrei, commons.wikimedia.org

aus · from

Architectural Design 25_2000
"Promotional Architecture"

Architektur als Werbung

Kathedrale, Museum, Geschäft?

Erstes Bild: New York 1998, Museum Guggenheim–SoHo. Es findet eine große Ausstellung französischer Kunst der Nachkriegszeit statt. Zur Kassa des Museums gelangt man nur nach Überwindung des großen und berühmten Guggenheim Museums-Shops. Ein Shop von solchem Ausmaß, dass er nur von seinem Sortiment her unterscheidbar ist vom Delikatessen-Laden Dean & Deluca schräg gegenüber. Im Vorbereich zur Eingangskontrolle beginnt bereits die Ausstellung mit Kleinplastiken. Kleine Objekte sind auf hüfthohen Sockeln präsentiert. An der Shop-Kassa herrscht Aufregung. Ein Kunde des Shops, oder war er doch Besucher des Museums, hatte plötzlich eine dieser Kleinplastiken, ein Ausstellungstück, vom Sockel geholt und will es kaufen. Er wird über seinen Irrtum aufgeklärt, das Kunstwerk mit einem Shop-Gegenstand verwechselt zu haben.

———

Zweites Bild: Nicht weit entfernt von Guggenheim–SoHo befindet sich der New Yorker Shop des Modedesigners Helmut Lang. Im Inneren eine Rauminstallation aus seriell hermetischen Kuben. Sie könnten vom Künstler Donald Judd stammen. Die Rückseiten sind offen, ausgewählte Kleidungsstücke sind wie Kunstwer-

Promotional Architecture

Is it a cathedral, a museum, or a shop?

Scene one: New York 1998, Museum Guggenheim SoHo. There is a large exhibition of French post-war art. The till of the museum can only be reached after having passed the big and famous Guggenheim museum shop. A shop which is so big that it can only be distinguished by its assortment from the Dean & DeLuca delicatessen situated diagonally opposite. An exhibition showing small sculptures already starts in the entrance lobby. Small objects are presented on waist-high pedestals. There is excitement at the cash desk. A customer of the shop, or maybe he was a visitor of the museum, suddenly had taken one of the small sculptures, an exhibit, from the pedestal and wants to buy it. His mistake of having confused a work of art with an article of the museum shop is explained to him.

———

Scene two: Not far away from the Guggenheim SoHo, there is the New York shop of the fashion designer Helmut Lang. In the interior – a room installation consisting of serial hermetic cubes. They could come from the artist Donald Judd. The backs are open, selected clothes are presented like works of art. Next to the cash desk there is a digital display of moving words. It looks like an installation of Jenny Holzer, but it should be, next to the cash desk (!), advertising for and by Helmut Lang. Disappointment or confusion? The installation which is supposed to be advertising for Helmut Lang has actually been created by Jenny Holzer.

Scene three: New York 2000, Museum Guggenheim SoHo. The Guggenheim Museum shop still exists. But the exhibition spaces have already been rented out to the fashion firm Prada.

———

These are scenes observed in the world of architecture, the arts, and the world of fashion. Scenes with no clear-cut dividing lines, scenes of changing assignments of values. The only important issue is that during the past decade an equally strange as interesting cultural shift has taken place. We remember: The 'museum' has been the ultimate building task in the post-modern development. Then, the museums were characterised as the new cathedrals of society. They were based on the theatrical power of architecture. Frank O. Gehry says that the Guggenheim Museum in Bilbao never would have come into being if the Abteiberg Museum in Mönchengladbach of Hans Hollein had not released the power of the spectacle in the 70s. Since that time there has been the possibility that works of art can be portrayed by architecture, that they can be staged by architecture.

But haven't the museums themselves, by virtue of their architectonic conciseness, become places where lifestyles are staged? Today the evaluations are different; see the scenes in the beginning. The potential of portrayal has been extended from the field of the arts and the museum to the field of fashion and advertising.

We know now that it is difficult, while visiting a museum, to make a difference between a museum and a department store. In the underground entrance floor of the Louvre there is latterly a security control between the otherwise not distinguishable areas of the museum and the shopping mall. For the whole architectonic design of the entrance floor, in its appearance and materiality, shows no difference between the areas of cultural and commercial use.

While visiting a temple of fashion, on the contrary, you have to be sunk in silent humility of cultural devotion. The British minimalist architect John Pawson for instance has developed a nearly sacred architectural ambience for the Calvin Klein flagship stores (Tokyo, Seoul, New York, Paris), which makes of each act of

Calvin Klein Shop, New York, John Pawson, 1993–95,
© Christoph Kicherer

ke aufgebahrt. Neben der Kassa ist eine Laufschrift-Installation. Sie sieht aus wie eine Installation von Jenny Holzer, müsste aber – neben der Kassa (!) – Werbung für und von Helmut Lang sein. Enttäuschung oder Irritation? Die vermeintliche Werbung für Helmut Lang ist tatsächlich eine Installation von Jenny Holzer.

―――――

DRITTES BILD: New York 2000, Museum Guggenheim–SoHo. Den Guggenheim Museums-Shop gibt es immer noch. Aber die Ausstellungsräume sind bereits an die Mode-Firma Prada vermietet.

―――――

Dies sind beobachtete Szenen aus der Welt der Architektur, der Kunst, der Mode. Szenen von fließenden Grenzen, von wechselnden Zuweisungen von Werten. Wichtig ist dabei nur, dass im Laufe des letzten Jahrzehnts eine ebenso merkwürdige wie interessante kulturelle Verschiebung stattgefunden hat. Wir erinnern uns: Das ‚Museum' war in den vergangenen Jahrzehnten die ultimative Bauaufgabe der postmodernen Entwicklung. Als neue Kathedralen der Gesellschaft wurden die Museen damals bezeichnet. Sie beruhten auf der inszenatorischen Kraft der Architektur. Das Guggenheim-Museum in Bilbao, sagt Frank O. Gehry, hätte nie so entstehen können, hätte da nicht in den siebziger Jahren das Museum Abteiberg Mönchengladbach von Hans Hollein die Macht der Inszenierung befreit. Seit damals wurde die Möglichkeit eröffnet, dass Kunst von der Architektur dargestellt, inszeniert werden kann.

Fünfter Tag • Day Five

Aber sind nicht gerade, in diesen letzten Jahrzehnten, die Museen kraft ihrer architektonischen Prägnanz selbst zu Orten der Inszenierung von Lebensstilen geworden? Heute, siehe die Szenen am Beginn, haben sich die Wertungen verschoben. Das Darstellungspotenzial der Architektur hat sich vom Bereich der Kunst und des Museums zur Mode und Werbung hin erweitert.

Man weiß inzwischen, dass beim Museumsbesuch die Unterscheidung zum Kaufhaus schwerfällt. Im unterirdischen Eingangsgeschoss des Louvre trennt neuerdings nur eine Sicherheitskontrolle die ansonsten nicht unterscheidbaren Bereiche von Museum und Shopping-Mall. Denn die gesamte architektonische Gestaltung des Eingangsgeschosses, in seiner Materialität und Erscheinung, macht keinen Unterschied zwischen den Bereichen der kulturellen und der kommerziellen Nutzung.

Ganz im Gegensatz dazu hat man für den Besuch eines Modetempels in schweigender Demut kultureller Andacht zu verharren. Beispielsweise hat der britische Architektur-Minimalist John Pawson für die Flagship-Stores (Tokio, Seoul, New York, Paris) von Calvin Klein ein geradezu heiliges architektonisches Ambiente entwickelt, das jeden Kaufakt zu einer Beichte mit anschließender Erlösung stilisiert. Die VerkäuferInnen sind unberührbar asketische PriesterInnen und die huldvolle Rückgabe der Kreditkarte nach getätigtem Kauf gleicht der erleichterten Annahme der Hostie nach getätigter Wandlung und bekräftigt die Zugehörigkeit zur Glaubensgemeinschaft.

Die Boutique als Kapelle des Konsumismus. Die Mode als Objekt der Anbetung. Das Museum als Kaufhaus. Die Begriffe beginnen zu wandern, die Funktionen verändern sich. Und drängend stellt sich dabei die Frage nach der Rolle der Architektur.

buying a confession with a following redemption. The shop assistants are untouchable ascetic priestesses and the gracious return of the credit card after the purchase resembles the relieved taking of the host after the consecration and enforces the sense of belonging to the brothers in faith.

The boutique as a chapel of consumerism. Fashion as an object of worship. The museum as department store. The definitions begin to shift, the functions are changing. The question arises of what the role of architecture is in this process?

First of all, one myth of modernism has to be questioned. Modernism, but also every other 'style' prior to it, in its time, has always been an expression of lifestyle and fashion. It had to be like that, because otherwise no agreements and codes of society could have been connected with it. Le Corbusier selected carefully the appropriate car models which formed the foreground for the photographs of his houses. Of course, in the Bauhaus and also at the WChUTEMAS in the Soviet Union architecture, art, design and fashion were brought into a culturally-aesthetic context. Only when the architectural history of modernism was infiltrated by the categories of history of art, the term 'fashion' became unacceptable and architecture had to document the striving for truth and honesty, for progress and enlightenment. Therefore, only very rarely the architectural achievements were seen in a cultural context, which, naturally, would have had to comprise fashion and everyday life.

The break of this taboo was allegedly produced by the post-modern age. Not in the references of architectural history, but because of the openness towards phenomena of everyday life. Venturi / Scott Brown / Izenour with *Learning from Las Vegas* opened the views of architecture as well as the rediscovery of effect aesthetics of the American shops and the hotels by Morris Lapidus. The avant-garde of the 60s, however, had left the internal architectural discussion before and fo-

Piazza d'Italia, New Orleans, Charles Moore, 1978. © By Colros, CC BY 2.0

Architektur als Werbung • Promotional Architecture

Hotel Fontainebleau, Morris Lapidus, 1952. © Gottscho-Schleisner, aus · from Heinrich Klotz / John W. Cook, *Architektur im Widerspruch*, Zürich, 1974 „Diese Treppe führt eigentlich nirgends hin. Ich habe hier also diese großartige Treppe, und dort oben ist wirklich nichts." · "This staircase actually leads nowhere. So here I have this grand staircase and up there is really nothing." M.L.

cussed on pop culture. Archigram, Coop Himmelblau, HausRucker Co. and others were the first to intentionally use the marketing instruments of the mass media to communicate their architecture. But it was always about the architectural creation of atmosphere, appropriate ambience, the creation of products and symbols, which could compete with a general 'world of goods'.

In the 80s and 90s there were a lot of signs for a new 'dialogue' between architecture and market or rather between architecture and lifestyle. The set of the film *9½ Weeks* had already assembled numerous 'pictures' in 1986, which should influence architecture later on. The cool atmosphere of lofts with their venetian blinds and stylish lighting. Finally Kim Basinger and Mickey Rourke hung around Rei Kawakubo's Comme des Garçon boutique in Manhattan and shocked bourgeois places in Manhattan like the department store Bergdorf Goodman. Later the opening sequence in the film *Big Easy* became a legend, where a corpse was found in the basin of Charles Moore's "Piazza d'Italia" in New Orleans. Dennis Quaid, as a detective, concluded with incredible logic that a murder which happened at a place with such a name could only have been a mafia murder, what turned out to be, by the way, a wrong conclusion. A classic product placement of architecture like at the end of the same film, when, completely unnecessary and apparently useless, a small Apple Macintosh SE sits on the desk in a rather decorating manner.

Zunächst einmal muss ein Mythos der Moderne infrage gestellt werden. Die Moderne, aber auch jeder ‚Stil' zuvor war auch, in seiner Zeit, ein Ausdruck von Lebensstilen und von Moden. Ja, er musste dies sogar sein, da sonst keinerlei gesellschaftliche Übereinkünfte und Codes damit verbunden werden konnten. Le Corbusier suchte sorgfältig die passenden Automodelle aus, die den Vordergrund für die Fotografien seiner Häuser bildeten. Selbstverständlich waren im Bauhaus ebenso wie bei Wchutemas in der Sowjetunion Architektur, bildende Kunst, Design und Mode in einen kulturell-ästhetischen Zusammenhang gebracht. Erst als die Architekturgeschichte der Moderne von den Kategorien der Kunstgeschichte infiltriert wurde, wurde der Begriff ‚Mode' verwerflich und die Architektur musste fortan als Stil das Streben nach Wahrheit und Ehrlichkeit, nach Fortschritt und Aufklärung dokumentieren. Und nur mehr sehr selten wurden deshalb die architektonischen Leistungen in einen gesamtkulturellen Zusammenhang gestellt, der selbstverständlich auch Mode und Alltag umfassen müsste.

Den Bruch dieses Tabus brachte angeblich die Postmoderne. Nicht in ihren architekturhistorischen Referenzen, sondern in ihrer Öffnung hin zu Alltagsphänomenen. Venturi/Scott Brown/Izenour öffneten mit *Learning from Las Vegas* die Sicht der Architektur ebenso wie die Wiederentdeckung der Wirkungsästhetik der amerikanischen Läden und Hotels von Morris Lapidus. Aber schon zuvor hat die Avantgarde der sechziger Jahre den innerarchitektonischen Diskurs in Richtung Pop-Kultur verlassen. Archigram, Coop Himmelblau, HausRucker-Co und andere haben bewusst erstmals die Marketing-Instrumente der Massenmedien verwendet, um ihre Architektur zu kommunizieren. Immer ging es aber auch um die architektonische Schaffung von Atmosphären, von Stimmungen, von passenden Ambientes, von Produkten und Zeichen, die mit einer allgemeinen ‚Warenwelt' konkurrieren könnten.

Die achtziger und neunziger Jahre zeigten dann eine Fülle von Indizien des neuen ‚Gesprächs' zwischen Architektur und Markt, oder besser, Architektur und Lifestyle. Die Ausstattung des Films *9 1/2 Wochen* versammelte bereits 1986 eine Vielzahl von ‚Bildern', die erst später auch die Architektur beeinflussten. Die Loft-Atmosphäre mit ihrer Coolness, den Jalousien und der raffinierten Beleuchtung. Schließlich trieben sich Mickey Rourke und Kim Basinger auch in Rei Kawakubos Comme des Garçon-Boutique in Manhattan herum, und schockten die bürgerlichen Shopping-Orte Manhattans wie das Kaufhaus Bergdorf Goodman. Legendär war auch später die Eröffnungssequenz des Films *Big Easy*, wo eine Leiche im Becken von Charles Moores Piazza d'Italia in New Orleans gefunden wurde. Messerscharf zog Dennis Quaid als Detective den – übrigens falschen – Schluss, an einem Ort dieses Namens kann es sich nur um einen Mord der Mafia handeln. Ein klassisches Product Placement von Architektur, so wie in der Schlussszene desselben Films völlig unnötig und scheinbar überflüssig ein kleiner Apple-MacIntosh SE den Schreibtisch ziert.

Wenn schon die Filmindustrie die Orte der neuen Architektur bildsprachlich benennt, dann ist der Schritt zur Glorifizierung der Architekten selbst nicht mehr weit. Die zunehmende Verbreitung des Phänomens Star-Architekt machte die Personen selbst bekannt genug und reif für andere Einsatzzwecke. Lord Norman Foster wirbt in Anzeigen für Rolex-Uhren und Michael Graves für gute Schuhe, „fast wie handgemacht". Das war der Zeitpunkt, als auch Disney die Kraft der Star-Architektur – Aldo Rossi, Michael Graves, Arata Isozaki, Robert A. M. Stern, Frank O. Gehry etc. – erkannte und als Marketing-Instrument verwendete, allerdings nur in den Erwachsenen-Bereichen, für Hotels, Bürogebäude etc. Alle anderen Bereiche werden weiterhin und bewährt von Disneys ‚Imagineering'-Department entwickelt und geplant.

Heute hat sich die Business-Architektur in diverse Identitäten aufgesplittert, die dann als Signale der Unternehmen überall auf der Welt ident auftauchen. Nicht nur das Erscheinungsbild von McDonald's ist weltweit gleich und repräsentiert damit für Laurie Anderson, wie die Pop-Künstlerin einmal sagte, überall „Heimat".

If even the film industry names the places of new architecture by means of pictures, the glorification of architects themselves is not far away. The increasing phenomenon of the 'star architect' makes the individuals rather famous and ready for other fields of activity. Lord Norman Foster advertises Rolex watches, Michael Graves good shoes, "nearly like hand-made". At that time also Disney discovered the power of star architecture – Aldo Rossi, Michael Graves, Arata Isozaki, Robert A. M. Stern, Frank O. Gehry, etc. – and used it as a marketing instrument. However, only in the areas for grown-ups, for hotels, office buildings etc. All other areas are still developed and planned by Disney's 'Imagineering' Department.

Today, business architecture has split up into various identities, which turn up similarly everywhere in the world as signals of the corporations. Not only the appearance of McDonalds is identical throughout the world and represents, as Laurie Anderson once put it, everywhere a feeling of home. Big chain stores like Benetton, Body Shop, Esprit etc. have created a new pattern of orientation with their corporate designs at all centres of the world for a long time already. In the meantime also the design and equipment of car salons follows the strict directions of stage design, documented in the corporations' thick and secret manuals.

The fashion empires as well have extended into a corporate culture. They have become lifestyle producers and are in a position to deliver a complete equipment. However, it is interesting that consumers very rarely buy everything from one firm, never stick to one trademark, but happily mix different brands. Therefore the fashion firms, especially in Milan, have become active in the field of urban development. They take up Donna Karan's idea, who created with her gigantic DKNY firewall one of the most important and most frequently photographed landmarks in Manhattan. In Milan, Missoni and Armani started to advertise on gigantic billboards which showed beaming artificial models, which, surprisingly, offer more orientation within the city than any brilliant architecture.

Architektur als Werbung • Promotional Architecture

Werbewand der Mode-Firma · Ad billboard of the fashion company
Donna Karan in SoHo, New York. © Donna Karan

Große Ladenketten wie Benetton, Body Shop, Esprit etc., haben mit ihrem ausgearbeiteten Corporate Design längst schon in alle Zentren der Welt ein neues Muster der Orientierung gelegt. Gleichzeitig folgt auch die Gestaltung und Ausstattung von Autosalons peniblen Regieanweisungen des Stage-Designs, festgehalten in ebenso dicken wie geheimen Manuals der Konzerne.

Ausgeweitet in eine Corporate Culture haben sich auch die Modekonzerne. Sie sind Lifestyle-Produzenten geworden und sind so in der Lage, richtige Komplettausstattungen zu liefern. Interessant ist dennoch, dass die Konsumenten kaum jemals bei ihrer Konsumausstattung bei einem Ausstatter, einer Marke bleiben, sondern fröhlich mixen. Dafür sind die Modekonzerne, vor allem in Milano, auch städtebaulich aktiv geworden. Sie folgen dem Beispiel Donna Karans, die mit ihrer gewaltigen DKNY Feuermauer im New Yorker SoHo eine der wichtigsten und meistfotografierten Landmarks Manhattans geschaffen hat. In Milano begannen zunächst Missoni und dann Armani mit strahlenden artifiziellen Models auf ähnlichen hausgroßen Plakaten zu werben, die überraschenderweise einen größeren Orientierungswert innerhalb der Stadt besitzen, als jede noch so strahlende neue Architektur.

Was bleibt in dieser sich permanent ausweitenden Welt von Corporate Culture und Corporate Design noch übrig für die Architektur? Da gibt es doch immerhin – zumindest in Europa – noch den Wohnungsbau oder auch einzelne Bildungs- oder Kulturbauten. Doch Achtung. Für den sogenannten ‚öffentlichen' oder ‚sozialen' Wohnungsbau ist auch in Europa eine Liberalisierung und Marktöffnung zu erwarten. Dies wird verstärkt eine populäre Komponente erzeugen, die dann bald auf das US-amerikanische Modell des New Urbanism regredieren wird. Und Bildungs- und Kulturbauten sind nur mehr scheinbar architektonisch autonom. Sie folgen nur auf einer sozusagen höheren Stufe den medialen Marktgesetzen der öffentlichen Aufmerksamkeit. Stolz wird aus Bilbao vermeldet, dass sich durch die touristischen Mehreinnahmen und ein dadurch erhöhtes Steueraufkommen die Investition in Frank O. Gehrys Guggenheim-Museum schon nach

What is left over in such a permanently expanding world of corporate culture and corporate design for architecture? There is, at least in Europe, the sector of housing, or several educational or cultural buildings. But one has to be careful. The so-called 'public' or 'social' housing is expected to undergo a liberalisation and opening of markets. This will increasingly produce a popular component not unlike the American model of the new urbanism. Educational and cultural buildings only seem to be architecturally autonomous. They only follow the media market laws of public attention on a higher level. There is a proud report from Bilbao that the additional revenues earned in the tourism industry and the thus increased tax revenue already paid off the costs for Frank O. Gehry's Guggenheim Museum for the Basque government after three years. Therefore this building, which was not built to last forever, could follow the rules of the tourism industry and be left to fall into ruins after its economic return on capital. The trustees of the Tugendhat villa by Mies van der Rohe in Brno want to achieve the opposite effect. The villa serves as a location for TV spots. Presently two spots are on television, one for an insurance company and the other for a brewery. They are meant to finance the necessary renovation.

drei Jahren für die Regierung des Baskenlandes amortisiert hat. Damit könnte der nicht sehr dauerhaft errichtete Bau den Regeln der Tourismusindustrie folgen und nach seiner ökonomischen Rendite jetzt langsam dem selbständigen Verfall überlassen werden. Den gegenteiligen Effekt wollen die Verwalter der Tugendhat-Villa von Mies van der Rohe in Brno erzielen. Die Verwendung als Location für TV-Werbespots – derzeit laufen zwei, für eine Versicherung bzw. eine Bierfirma – soll die notwendige Sanierung finanzieren.

Selbstverständlich ist das Guggenheim-Bilbao – mit dem Signal ‚Spektakel' – für verschiedene Werbekampagnen von Autos und Konsumartikeln als Location verwendet worden. Wer aber hätte gedacht, dass sich bei einem entlegenen, schweigsamen Gebäude wie Peter Zumthors Therme in Vals ein ähnlicher Effekt einstellt? Mode-Shootings, Music-Clips, Werbung – für all diese Zwecke dient es als Hintergrund, um eine besondere, eine ‚spirituelle' Atmosphäre zu vermitteln und um gleichzeitig, ähnlich wie bei Disneys Engagement für Star-Architekten, dem Lifestyle-Kunden gewisse Kenntnisse der Architektur mitzuvermitteln. Warum sonst hätten sich all die Werbeteams der beschwerlichen Fahrt in die Schweizer Berge unterzogen, wo die Bürger auf ihrer schmalen und gefährlichen Straße bestehen, damit nicht zu viele Touristen ihren idyllischen Ort entdecken. Die Werbeleute rechnen damit, dass die potenziellen Käufer der Jeans vor Zumthors Steinwänden auch wissen, von wem diese Wände sind. Trotz dieses gesellschaftlichen und kulturellen Gebrauchs seines Objekts, oder gerade deswegen, kann sich Zumthor weiterhin als der einsame Mönch aus den Bergen stilisieren. Damit unterstreicht er auch ein Selbst-Marketing, das dem des scheuen Helmut Lang nicht unähnlich ist. Vielleicht ist Zumthor, so wie Lang in der Mode, in der Architektur auf der Suche nach dem einzigen und ewig gültigen T-Shirt.

Of course, the Guggenheim Museum – signalling 'spectacle' – has been used as a location in several advertising campaigns for cars and consumer articles. But who would have expected that a remote and quiet building like Peter Zumthor's bath in Vals would have a similar effect? It is used as background for fashion shootings, music clips and advertising in order to create a special 'spiritual' atmosphere and at the same time to communicate a certain knowledge about architecture to the lifestyle customer, similar as in the case of Disney's commitment for star-architects. For what other reasons should the advertising teams have taken on the trouble of the burdensome journey to the Swiss mountains, where the citizens insist on their narrow and dangerous street in order to keep the tourists away from their beautiful village. The advertising agencies reckon that the potential buyers of the jeans shot in front of Zumthor's stone walls also know who the architect is. Despite the social and cultural use of his object or maybe because of it, Zumthor can continue to live as a lonely monk from the mountains. With his lifestyle he emphasises a self-marketing which is not unsimilar from that of the shy Helmut Lang. Maybe Zumthor is searching, like Lang in the field of fashion, for the only and eternally valid T-shirt in the field of architecture.

But there has already taken place an intellectual penetration with this new use of architecture. Rem Koolhaas and Jacques Herzog, two star architects of the second generation, definitely are no longer interested in the strategy of the signature buildings of the first generation of star architects. They don't see the picture, but the structure. They want to establish their achieved fame in a way that the 'firm' is more important than the design. This becomes obvious in the names of the firms OMA and HdM. As a well-calculated marketing strategy they announced the formation of a joint firm for the construction of a new hotel in Manhattan. The announcement for itself has an effect and draws the attention to the firm; even a failure would be secondary. Both offices refer to the strategies of the fashion indus-

Gemeinsames Projekt von OMA und Herzog & de Meuron des Astor-Plaza Hotels für Ian Schrager in New York, 2000–01, unrealisiert · Joint project of OMA and Herzog & de Meuron of the Astor Plaza Hotel for Ian Schrager in New York, 2000–01, never realized. Archive DS

try, where branding and marketing power are essential. Creative power grows nearly anonymous within the group, even though especially the fashion industry attaches importance to the fact that the 'creatives', hired per season, are well-known at least to insiders. OMA and HdM expect that through the conjunction of the two brands there will be the chance to get access to bigger commissions and markets.

In my analytic-resignative text "Superfluous Architecture" (1994) I still attributed architecture in this environment of total commercialisation with roles and qualities like research, the laboratory or the confession of a new realism. But in the meantime, everything which is marketed as architecture has also become event or entertainment architecture. The question as to whether architecture – as the only discipline among all culture industries – could withstand the world domination of medial consumerism, has been answered. Each cathedral and each museum is a shop. At the moment it seems that OMA's and HdM's strategy is the only one which can, – open-eyed and reflexive – control, question and accelerate this development. The last years in architecture clearly demonstrated that even refusal leads to consumption. Architecture is 'promotional architecture' or it is no architecture at all.

Doch schon regt sich die intellektuelle Durchdringung dieser neuen Verwendung und Verwertung von Architektur. Rem Koolhaas und Jacques Herzog, zwei Star-Architekten der ‚zweiten Generation', sind definitiv nicht mehr an der Strategie der Signature Buildings der ersten Generation interessiert. Sie sehen nicht das Bild, sondern die Struktur. Sie wollen ihren nunmehr errungenen Star-Ruhm soweit festigen, dass die ‚Firma' und nicht mehr der Entwurf im Vordergrund steht. Was sich auch in den bisherigen Firmenbezeichnungen OMA und HdM abbildet. Als wohlkalkulierte Marketing-Strategie verkündeten sie die Gründung eines gemeinsamen Büros zum Bau eines neuen Hotels in Manhattan. Diese Ankündigung allein erzielt schon genügend Wirkung und Aufmerksamkeit, selbst ein Scheitern dieses Projekts ist dann nur mehr zweitrangig. Beide verweisen dabei auf die Strategien der Modeindustrie, wo Branding und Marketing-Power entscheidend sind, die kreative Leistung hingegen aus der Gruppe selbst fast anonym erwächst, obwohl gerade die Modeindustrie Wert darauf legt, dass ihre je nach Saison zugekauften ‚Kreativen' zumindest Insidern bekannt sind. OMA und HdM sehen in der Verbindung der beiden ‚Marken' jedenfalls auch die Möglichkeit, einen Zugang zu größeren Aufträgen und Märkten zu bekommen.

In meinem analytisch-resignativen Text „Superfluous Architecture" (1994) wies ich der Architektur in diesem neuen Umfeld der totalen Vermarktung noch die Rolle der Forschung, des Labors, des Bekenntnisses zu einem neuen Realismus zu. Inzwischen ist alles, was als Architektur vermarktet wird, auch zur Event- oder Entertainment-Architektur geworden. Die Frage, ob sich die Architektur – als einzige unter allen Kulturindustrien – der Weltherrschaft des medialen Konsumismus verweigern könnte, ist entschieden. Jede Kathedrale, jedes Museum ist ein Shop. Und derzeit scheint es so zu sein, dass die Strategie von OMA und HdM die einzige ist, die sehendes Auges und reflexiv diese Entwicklung gleichzeitig auffangen, hinterfragen und beschleunigen kann. Denn eines haben die letzten Jahre der Architektur eindeutig gezeigt: Selbst die Verweigerung führt zur Vereinnahmung. Alle Architektur ist ‚Promotional Architecture' oder sie ist keine Architektur.

aus · from

domus 828_2000
"Tate Modern: Interview Jacques Herzog"

Conversation with Jacques Herzog

Interview mit Jacques Herzog

DMS: Jacques, we already met here once in London. At a lecture series about *Emerging European Architecture* at the Architectural Association School. What has changed for you since that time and what role does the Tate Modern play in the process?

JH: Yes, 1983. That was important back then and also freer and more open. Today the whole day is divided into ten-minute interviews, from *Der Spiegel* to the *New York Times*, and I can't speak with anyone in detail anymore. We ought to sit together again sometime quietly and in old friendship.

DMS: Before that, however, I want to verify a rumour about a global player. Are Herzog & de Meuron supposed to do the new shops for Prada together with Rem Koolhaas?

JH: That's not right. We're doing a great project for Prada in Tokyo and Rem is doing something for Prada in the US. But we together—OMA and HdM—are doing a hotel for Ian Schrager in Manhattan. Up to now he had been looking for old objects and then converts them according to his special ideas with the designer Philippe Starck. He always says, 'I'm not in the hotel business, I'm in the entertainment business.'

DMS: Jacques, wir haben uns hier in London schon einmal getroffen. Bei einer Vorlesungsreihe über *Emerging European Architecture* an der Architectural Association School. Was hat sich für euch seit damals verändert, und welche Rolle spielt die Tate Modern dabei?

JH: Ja, 1983. Das war wichtig damals und auch freier und offener. Heute ist der ganze Tag in Zehn-Minuten-Interviews unterteilt, vom *Spiegel* bis zur *New York Times* und ich kann mit niemandem mehr ausführlich sprechen. Wir sollten wieder einmal in Ruhe und alter Freundschaft zusammensitzen.

DMS: Davor aber will ich ein Gerücht zum Global Player verifizieren. Herzog & de Meuron sollen gemeinsam mit Rem Koolhaas die neuen Shops für Prada machen?

JH: Das stimmt nicht. Wir machen ein großartiges Projekt für Prada in Tokio, und Rem macht etwas für Prada in den USA. Aber wir machen zusammen – OMA und HdM – ein Hotel für Ian Schrager in Manhattan. Der hatte sich bisher immer alte Objekte gesucht und diese dann mit dem Designer Philippe Starck nach seinen speziellen Vorstellungen umgebaut. Er sagt ja immer, „I'm not in the hotel business, I'm in the entertainment business".

DMS: Und du und Rem macht jetzt gemeinsam einen Neubau?

JH: Ja. In der Planungsphase bleiben wir zwei *autonomous entities*, das führen wir dann zusammen, und die weitere Planung wird dann von einem gemeinsamen Büro, an dem wir je 50 Prozent Anteil haben, gemacht. Das Hotel in New York machen wir mit Rem Koolhaas zusammen, so wie wir das auch im Büro Herzog, de Meuron und Partner machen, zusammen mit Harry Gugger, Christine Binswanger und anderen. Wir haben mit OMA schon seit fünf oder sechs Jahren über so eine Möglichkeit gesprochen.

DMS: Diese Variante der freiwilligen Kooperation von Star-Architekten in einem konkreten Projekt widerspricht ja der Idee der Signature Architecture. Das markiert ja einen grundsätzlichen Unterschied zur älteren Star-Generation wie Botta, Gehry oder Richard Meier, die Wert darauf legen, dass ihre Architektur überall als die ihre erkannt wird. Für euch gilt stärker ein Forschungsansatz, immer neue Dimensionen der Architektur auszuloten und zu entwickeln, nicht festlegbar zu sein.

JH: Das ist ganz wichtig, sonst könnten wir nicht überleben. Das behalten wir natürlich bei und treiben es weiter. Da arbeiten wir auch intensiv mit der Industrie zusammen, um neue Dinge zu entwickeln. Du hast doch bei uns in Basel vor Jahren diese Versuche mit Beschichtungen mit Pflanzen und Algen gesehen. Jetzt arbeiten wir mit der Glasindustrie an Fragen der Verformbarkeit, Lichtbrechungen etc. Das ist einfach die Art, wie wir arbeiten. Andere Architekten vor uns haben eben dagegen diese *corporate labels* gehabt. Das ist auch gut so und ist auch heute noch eine Strategie, um schnell in den Markt zu kommen, und die Leute können sich schnell entscheiden, ob sie das mögen oder nicht. Aber wenn man anders arbeitet, so wie wir, dann ist die Anzahl der Projekte natürlich limitiert.

DMS: And you and Rem are now doing a new building together?

JH: Yes. We remain two autonomous entities in the planning phase, then we merge that and the further planning is then done by a joint office that we have a 50 percent share in. We are doing the hotel in New York together with Rem Koolhaas, just like we are also doing it at the Herzog, de Meuron and Partner office, together with Harry Gugger, Christine Binswanger and others. We've been talking about such a possibility with OMA for five or six years already.

DMS: This variation of voluntary cooperation of star architects in a concrete project indeed contradicts the idea of signature architecture. This marks a fundamental difference to older star generations such as Botta, Gehry or Richard Meier, who place importance on the fact that their architecture is recognised everywhere as being theirs. A research approach, always sounding out and developing new dimensions of architecture, not being definable, applies more strongly for you.

JH: That's very important; otherwise we couldn't survive. Naturally we keep that up and drive it further. We are also intensively working together with industry in order to develop new things. Years ago you saw our attempts with coverings made of plants and algae in Basel. Now we are working with the glass industry on questions of formability, light refractions, etc. That is simply the way we work. Other architects before us have precisely had these corporate labels, in contrast. And that's a good thing, too, and is still a strategy today to come into the market fast, and the people can decide quickly whether they like it or not. But if one works differently, like we do, then the number of projects is certainly limited.

Fünfter Tag • Day Five

Tate Modern, London, Herzog & de Meuron, 1994–2000.
Archive DS, Margherita Spiluttini

DMS: Is that really true? You now have around one hundred people, working simultaneously on twenty to thirty projects worldwide. That is just about the magnitude of Gehry's office. What distinguishes you there from the old stars?

JH: I think that we are organised differently. We are actually more a group in the offices, and even if most things converge with Pierre and myself—that is, I already know every project and each of them is inspired by me—it is nonetheless the case that more responsibility goes to other people, to Harry, Christine, as well as to the associates. But either way it is hard to become so big and I don't know whether we can still get bigger. You will still recall how we began. Whereby, the work itself is okay. The problem is rather that the increased media attention requires enormous energy. You have to play along, because something will be written in any case and you also profit from it again, because architecture has simply become a matter that the media is more interested in today than ten or twenty years ago. And I always wanted that, too, because I am also a representative of this generation of the medialisation of architecture. But I'm also suffering from that at the moment. Because I simply spend too much time with it and would actually need more time for the projects. That still interests me more.

DMS: Shouldn't you adopt the conventions of Hollywood stars who simply distribute prepared interviews through media agencies?

JH: Compared to architects, film stars have a huge advantage. They do a film, have an intensive phase in return and afterwards they stand in the media and do nothing

DMS: Stimmt das wirklich? Ihr habt jetzt circa einhundert Leute, arbeitet an zwanzig bis dreißig Projekten weltweit gleichzeitig. Das ist in etwa auch die Größenordnung von Gehrys Büro. Was unterscheidet euch da von den alten Stars?

JH: Ich denke, dass wir anders organisiert sind. Wir sind tatsächlich mehr eine Gruppe im Büro, und auch wenn das meiste bei Pierre und mir zusammenläuft – also ich kenne schon jedes Projekt, und es ist auch jedes von mir inspiriert –, ist es doch so, dass mehr Verantwortung an andere Leute geht, an Harry, Christine und auch an die Associates. Aber so oder so ist es schwierig, so groß zu werden, und ich weiß nicht, ob wir noch größer werden können. Du wirst dich noch daran erinnern, wie wir begonnen haben. Wobei, die Arbeit selbst ist okay. Das Problem ist eher, dass die zunehmende mediale Aufmerksamkeit enorme Energie fordert. Du musst da mitspielen, weil es wird auf jeden Fall was geschrieben, und davon profitierst du auch wieder, weil Architektur einfach eine Sache geworden ist, die die Medien heute mehr interessiert als noch vor zehn oder zwanzig Jahren. Und das habe ich ja immer auch gewollt, weil ich bin ja ein Vertreter dieser Generation der Medialisierung von Architektur. Im Moment leide ich aber auch darunter. Weil ich einfach zu viel Zeit damit verbringe und eigentlich mehr Zeit für die Projekte benötigen würde. Das interessiert mich immer noch mehr.

DMS: Solltet ihr da nicht die Konventionen der Hollywood-Stars annehmen, die einfach fertige Interviews über Medien-Agenturen verbreiten?

JH: Filmstars haben gegenüber Architekten einen gewaltigen Vorteil. Die machen einen Film, haben dafür eine intensive Phase und danach stehen sie in den Medien und haben daneben gar nichts. In diesem Sinne wäre ich natürlich lieber ein Filmstar. Denn diese Phase fehlt mir sehr – die Zeit, wo nichts geschieht. Wo ich einfach nur schauen kann und staunen und nichts machen muss. Weil dieses Staunen, wo man auftanken kann, das ist das A und O für alle Menschen. Und als Architekt, wo du kreative und künstlerische Arbeit machst, da brauchst du einfach diese Pausen, diese Löcher in deiner Biografie, um wieder produktiv werden zu können.

PR-AGENTIN: You have to stop the interview. We are running out of time. The next journalist is waiting.

JH: Give us ten minutes more. We just started to discuss an interesting subject. They can wait.

DMS: Okay. Brechen wir hier ab und kommen wir zur Tate Modern. Es war eine weltweite Sensation, als ihr damals diesen Wettbewerb gewonnen habt. Das erste nicht-britische Architekturbüro, das einen großen öffentlichen Auftrag in England gewinnen konnte.

JH: Angeblich seit Jahrhunderten, seit der Westminster Abbey. Ich wusste zunächst gar nicht, dass hier in England so lange kein Ausländer bauen konnte. Aber das spürt man dann schnell, es ist schon eine eigene, andere Gesellschaft. London ist zwar eine *global city*, wahrscheinlich die wichtigste Stadt in Europa, in der Welt im Moment, so unglaublich dynamisch. Die andere Seite ist tatsächlich so eine Art Abgeschlossenheit der Architektur, so *straight forward* modern in der Tradition der Gotik. Architektur, so meint man hier, muss immer diese technische Seite expressiv ausdrücken. Das haben wir hier immer wieder im Prozess des Bauens – als kulturelle Auseinandersetzung – erfahren. Aber das war für uns spannend. Du kommst aus einem kleinen Land, aus der Schweiz, ähn-

at all on the side. In this sense I would naturally prefer to be a movie star. Because I'm really missing this phase—the time where nothing happens. Where I can simply just look and be amazed and don't have to do anything. Because this amazement, where one can recharge one's batteries, is essential for all people. And as an architect, where you do creative and artistic work, you simply need these breaks, these gaps in your biography, in order to be able to become productive again.

PR AGENT: You have to stop the interview. We are running out of time. The next journalist is waiting.

JH: Give us ten minutes more. We just started to discuss an interesting subject. They can wait.

DMS: Ok, let's stop here and talk about the Tate Modern. It was a worldwide sensation when you won the competition back then. You were the first non-British architects' office to win a major public commission in England.

JH: Allegedly for centuries, since Westminster Abbey. I didn't realise at first that here in England it was impossible for foreigners to build. But you get to feel that very quickly, it's a different society all of its own. London may be a global city, probably the most important city in Europe, in the world at the moment, it's so incredibly dynamic. The other side of the coin is a kind of architectural isolation, all straightforward modern in the Gothic tradition. Architecture, they think here, always has to give expression to the technical side. We found that out time and time again in the form of a cultural confrontation during the building phase. But it was exciting for us. We come from a small country, from Switzerland, that's like Austria, but unlike you Austrians, the Swiss don't have a national culture with global and imperial charisma. Wherever we go, we're foreign. But England is certainly something different from Germany or France or the USA. In this way, the experience with the Tate has helped us to get work all over the world. The Tate was the international breakthrough for us, sure, and that's because we've learned to make quite a different appearance on the international stage, to cope with quite different problems.

DMS: To the Tate project itself. For a neutral observer, who didn't know how you worked, the jury's decision back then came as pretty much of a surprise. In the case of your project, people wondered what was actually architecturally new about it.

JH: That's right. No one saw anything. Even now, when they look at the building, many people think: 'What have they actually done?' Because they don't know that actually there was nothing there—it was full up with machinery. A large part of our work was basically a type of clearing up. And then we actually invented the building as a museum. But this invention of the building always kept close to what was actually there. For whenever we departed—in the dialectically anticipatory sense—from what was there, that always became in a sense quite ridiculous, because the existing fabric was always stronger. And that's why the architecture now plays with a subtle, subversive strategy. And this in turn has something English about it, and that in turn accords with our way of doing architecture.

DMS: Excuse me, but what do you mean by that? Your architecture for the Tate is non-English, but then English as well?

JH: Yes, that's a contradiction. Because the Tate is after all different from what the English architectural scene would have made of it. It's not high-tech, in the way the older generation—Foster, Grimshaw or Rogers—would do it, nor is it modernistic or minimalist, à la Chipperfield or Tony Fretton. We have laid a different track here, certainly. We have discovered a different dimension of English culture, the traditional dimension that suddenly turns out to be something quite different. We accepted that, because we also had to accept this building in many ways, because it is so massive, and then we did turn it into something else after all. This is something I discovered in England, this parallelism of contradictions, which I also feel as liberating. This is also something which Hitchcock celebrated in exemplary fashion. No clear contrasts, the beautiful and the ugly, good and evil, but everything is together in one thing, directly. And that is a central element of our work, which you know too, and now it has simply grown clearer.

lich wie Österreich, aber im Gegensatz zu euch haben die Schweizer nicht so eine nationale Kultur mit globaler und imperialer Ausstrahlung. Wir sind überall fremd, wo wir hingehen. Aber England ist sicherlich etwas ganz anderes als Deutschland oder Frankreich oder die USA. So hat uns diese Erfahrung mit der Tate wirklich geholfen, überall auf der Welt tätig zu sein. Die Tate war für uns der internationale Durchbruch, das ist klar, weil wir gelernt haben, auch international ganz anders aufzutreten, mit ganz anderen Problemen fertigzuwerden.

DMS: Zum Projekt der Tate selbst. Für einen neutralen Beobachter, der nicht wusste, wie ihr arbeitet, war die Juryentscheidung damals ziemlich überraschend. Man hat sich bei eurem Projekt gefragt, was geschieht hier eigentlich architektonisch Neues.

JH: Stimmt, man hat ja gar nichts gesehen. Auch jetzt, wenn man das Gebäude anschaut, denken viele, was haben die eigentlich gemacht. Weil man nicht weiß, dass eigentlich gar nichts da war, es war mit Maschinen gefüllt. Ein großer Teil unserer Arbeit war im Grunde eine Art Aufräumen. Und dann haben wir das Gebäude als Museum eigentlich erst erfunden. Aber dieses Erfinden des Gebäudes war immer ganz nah dran an dem, was da war. Denn immer wenn wir weggingen – so in einem dialektischen antizipierenden Sinn – von dem was da war, wurde das in einem gewissen Sinn lächerlich, weil die bestehende Substanz immer stärker war. Und deshalb spielt jetzt die Architektur mit einer subtilen, subversiven Strategie. Und die hat wiederum auch etwas Englisches, und das entspricht ja wiederum unserer Art, Architektur zu machen.

DMS: Entschuldige, aber was heißt das? Eure Architektur der Tate ist nicht-englisch, aber dann doch auch?

JH: Ja das ist ein Widerspruch. Weil die Tate ist ja anders, als die englische Architekturszene das machen würde. Es ist ja nicht high-tech, wie es die ältere Generation von Foster, Grimshaw oder Rogers machen würde, und es ist nicht modernistisch oder minimalistisch, wie es Chipperfield oder Tony Fretton machen würden. Es ist schon eine andere Spur, die hier gelegt ist. Wir haben eine andere Dimension der englischen Kultur entdeckt, dieses traditionelle, das sich plötzlich als etwas ganz anderes entpuppt. Das haben wir akzeptiert, weil wir dieses Gebäude in vielem auch akzeptieren müssen, weil es so mächtig ist, und dann doch in etwas anderes kippt. Das habe ich in England entdeckt, diese Parallelität

von Widersprüchen, die ich auch als befreiend empfinde. Das ist ja auch etwas, was Hitchcock exemplarisch zelebriert. Keine klaren Gegensätze, das Schöne und das Hässliche, das Gute und das Böse, sondern das alles ist gleichzeitig in einem Ding drin, ganz unmittelbar. Und das ist ein zentrales Element unserer Arbeit, die du auch kennst, und jetzt ist es einfach deutlicher geworden.

DMS: Die Architektur als Interpretation eines allgemein kulturellen Zustands?

JH: Ja vielleicht. Schau dir doch den Engländer an, in seinem Nadelstreifanzug, den ich wirklich toll finde, und dann zeigt er sein Gilet, das ist plötzlich pink, und die Unterhose ist geblümt. Auf den ersten Blick ist es pervers, und eigentlich findet er nichts dabei und ist ganz normal. Er ist gar nicht pervers, sondern findet das ganz normal und hat diesen Widerspruch ganz gern. Diese Sachen sind das eigentlich Spannende an der Architektur. Denn Architektur ist eigentlich eine unwichtige Sache. Sie ist ja nur ein Psychogramm für das, was die Menschen sind, was die Städte, was die Kulturen sind. Als solches ist die Architektur interessant – und nicht autonom für sich betrachtet. Weil all die Dinge, die man in der Architektur findet und analysieren kann, findet man auch in anderen Bereichen unserer Kultur.

DMS: Diesen Zusammenhang von Kleidung, von Alltagskultur und Architektur hast du ja schon vor zehn Jahren einmal thematisiert, in einem Artikel über die grauen Nachkriegsmanager, die dann zu braunen Schnürlsamt-Anzügen wechselten und welche Auswirkung das auf die Architektur der siebziger Jahre hatte.

JH: Das war damals ein wenig naiv, aber es hat immer noch Wichtigkeit. Und Künstler wie Gilbert & George haben das immer wieder thematisiert.

DMS: Diese Materialität der Bekleidung kommt ja in der Tate sehr stark zum Tragen. Die rohen industriellen Böden mit den gusseisernen Lüftungsgittern, die wären eigentlich von einem englischen Architekten unvorstellbar.

JH: Ja, undenkbar.

Tate Modern, London, Herzog & de Meuron, 1994–2000. Archive DS, Margherita Spiluttini

DMS: Architecture as the interpretation of a general cultural situation?

JH: Yes, perhaps. Look at the English, in their pin-stripe suits, which I find really great. And then they show you their waistcoat—suddenly it's pink, and they're wearing floral underpants. At first sight it's perverted, but the Englishman thinks nothing of it. He's not perverted at all, he finds it quite normal, and he likes this contradiction. These are the things that make architecture exciting. Architecture is actually something of no importance. It's only a psychogram of what people are, what cities are, what cultures are. That's what makes architecture interesting, not architecture in itself. Because all the things that you can discover and analyse in architecture can also be found in other areas of our civilisation.

DMS: You talked about this connexion between clothing, everyday culture and architecture once before, about ten years ago, in an article about the grey post-war managers who changed to brown corduroy suits, and what changes that brought about in the architecture of the 1970s.

JH: Yes. That was a little naive, but it was important all the same. And artists like Gilbert & George have continued the same theme.

DMS: This materiality of clothing comes across very strongly in the Tate. The rough industrial floor, with the cast-iron ventilation grills—you can't imagine an English architect doing that.

JH: Indeed not.

Fünfter Tag • Day Five

DeYoung Museum, San Francisco,
Herzog & de Meuron, 1999–2005. © DS

DMS: But these rough, untreated oak floors continue to speak this industrial language. They come across as though they were already there, and yet they are the perverted floral underwear being exposed to public gaze.

JH: Precisely. The building has, first of all, this roughness. That's why we took these grilles. Without creating industrial architecture in the strict sense. There's more at issue here than just moods. We're back with the very first topics that we two always discussed together: I'm not an atmosphere fanatic, but architecture does have to do with atmospheres and images. If I have smooth aluminium grilles, for example, then I want to demonstrate that we have a ventilation system which contrasts with the stuffy old industrial building. And with these cast-iron grilles, I blur this question of old and new, I don't even ask it. Because it isn't important to me. The sequence of rooms, the hollowing out, was more important than attaching a time label.

DMS: You two have always built museums and art buildings. The Goetz Collection Museum in Munich, Rémy Zaugg's studio, the little Comic Museum in Basel. Has the Tate changed your relationship to museum building?

JH: Yes, certainly. We have only now properly understood what a museum actually is. And we have become far freer. It's not the case that we only represent this gallery type that we've created here. Later projects, like the De Young Museum in San Francisco—that's much freer; in its layout too, because it's a quite different collection, a quite different place. And that's an important discovery, namely that perception is dependent on the place and not on the collection culture. We don't think that the white box is the be-all and-end-all. For a building like the Tate a highly restrained language is the only correct one.

DMS: Aber die rohen unbehandelten Eichenböden sprechen ja diese industrielle Sprache weiter. Sie wirken, als ob sie schon da gewesen wären, und sind doch die perverse geblümte Unterhose, die öffentlich gezeigt wird.

JH: Genau. Das Gebäude hat zunächst diese Rohheit. Deshalb haben wir auch diese Grills genommen. Ohne im eigentlichen Sinn Industriearchitektur zu machen. Es geht uns hier mehr um Stimmungen. Da sind wir wieder bei den ganz ersten Themen, die auch wir beide immer zusammen besprochen haben. Ich bin zwar kein Stimmungsfanatiker, aber Architektur hat eben auch mit Stimmungen und Bildern zu tun. Wenn ich beispielsweise glatte Aluminiumgrills mache, dann will ich zeigen, hier ist jetzt eine Lüftung drin, und steht im Kontrast zu dem dumpfen alten Industriebau. Und mit diesen Grills aus Gusseisen verwische ich die Frage von alt und neu, ich stelle sie gar nicht. Weil mir das nicht wichtig ist. Die Sequenz der Räume, das Aushöhlen ist mir wichtiger gewesen als das zeitliche Kennzeichen.

DMS: Ihr habt immer wieder Museums- und Kunstbauten gemacht. Das Museum der Sammlung Goetz in München, Remy Zauggs Atelier, das kleine Cartoonmuseum in Basel. Hat sich mit der Tate euer Verhältnis zum Museumsbau insgesamt geändert?

JH: Ja sicher. Wir haben erst jetzt richtig verstanden, was das eigentlich ist, ein Museum. Und wir sind auch viel freier geworden. Es ist ja nicht so, dass wir nur diesen Gallery-Typ vertreten, den wir hier realisiert haben. Neuere Projekte wie das De Young Museum in San Francisco – das ist viel freier, auch im Layout, weil das eine ganz andere Sammlung ist, ein ganz anderer Ort. Und auch das ist eine wichtige Erfahrung, dass die Wahrnehmung abhängig ist vom Ort und auch von der Sammlungskultur. Wir glauben nicht, dass die *white box* die einzig wahre Sache ist. Nur für ein Gebäude wie die Tate ist die sehr zurückhaltende Sprache die einzig richtige.

TEA – Tenerife Espacio de las Artes, Santa Cruz de Tenerife,
Herzog & de Meuron, 1999–2008. © DS

Tate Modern, London, Herzog & de Meuron, 1994–2000.
Archive DS, Margherita Spiluttini

DMS: Die prinzipielle Frage ist ja immer, wie weit kann und darf die skulpturale Autonomie der Architektur bei einem Museum gehen?

JH: Ich führe da keinen Glaubenskrieg. Die Räume dürfen eine gewisse skulpturale Qualität aufweisen. Aber es ist absurd, wenn ein ganzes Museum auf dieser skulpturalen Haltung aufbaut, weil das zu sehr eine autonome Position einnimmt. Wir machen jetzt ein Museum auf Teneriffa, mit Decken die sehr unregelmäßig sind, und wir verwenden immer unregelmäßigere Formen, weil wir die auch ausloten wollen, weil es so viele Sachen gibt, die es noch zu erkunden gibt und die mir wichtiger sind, als mich auf eine Position festzulegen. So wird jedes neue Projekt auch ein vergangenes wieder neu erscheinen lassen. Weil ich überzeugt bin, dass niemand so stark wie wir derzeit diese Erforschung der Architektur betreibt. Diese Unstetigkeit, dieses Abtasten der Welt, was daraus Architektur werden kann. Sie muss einfach einer komplexen Wahrnehmung auch standhalten können. Dann ist Architektur etwas wunderbares, wie die alten Tempel, wie die arabischen Moscheen. Das ist es, was mich am meisten interessiert. Und nicht, wie kann sich Herzog & de Meuron von Rem Koolhaas oder Frank O. Gehry unterscheiden. Schließlich wollen wir alle ähnliches, haben aber vielleicht einen verschiedenen Zugang dazu.

PR-AGENTIN: Now you really have to stop. The next interview is waiting. You have lunch with the US-press. You have the meeting with Rem for the Manhattan project in the office and than the dinner with the sponsors of the museum.

JH: Entschuldige, ich muss weg, es ist nicht Arroganz, aber reden wir doch bald einmal mehr über unsere alten, immer neuen Geschichten: warum sich die Architektur wohin entwickelt. – Where do I have to go now? Swiss-TV?

DMS: The basic question is always how far can and may the sculptural autonomy of architecture go in the case of a museum?

JH: I'm not fighting a religious war: The rooms may certainly evince a certain sculptural quality. But it's absurd when a whole museum is constructed on this sculptural attitude, because that takes too much of an autonomous position. We're currently building a museum in Tenerife, with very irregular ceilings, and we're using more and more irregular forms, because we want to try them out, because there are so many things that we still have to find out, and which are more important to me than nailing myself down to one position. So every new project will bring back an old one again in a new guise. Because I am convinced that nobody at the moment is pursuing this exploration of architecture as strongly as we are. This changeability, this palpating of the world, what can be made into architecture from it. It must simply be able to stand up to a complex perception. Then architecture is something wonderful, like the ancient temples, like the Arab mosques. That's what most interests me. And not: How can Herzog & de Meuron set themselves apart from Rem Koolhaas or Frank O. Gehry. After all, we all want something similar, but maybe have a different way of approaching it.

PR AGENT: Now you really have to stop. The next interview is waiting. You have lunch with the US press. You have the meeting with Rem for the Manhattan project in the office and then the dinner with the sponsors of the museum.

JH: Excuse me, I have to go, it is not arrogance, but let's talk soon again about our old, always new stories: why architecture is developing where to. – Where do I have to go now? Swiss TV?

kultur

In den neuen Prada-Stores, designt von Rem Koolhaas und seiner Firma OMA, überlagern sich virtuelle und reale Welten.

aus · from

profil 32_2001
„Architekten haben keine Macht"
Translation by Brian Dorsey

„Architekten haber

Er ist hager, hoch gewachsen und betont unauffällig gekleidet. Keine jener Persönlichkeiten, deren pure Anwesenheit schon den Raum füllt und dominiert. Er scheint eher schattenhaft vorbeizuschweben, nicht greifbar, still und freundlich, fast schüchtern – wäre da nicht diese ununterdrückbare Grundmotorik. Den magischen Moment der Ruhe kennt er wohl nicht. Es schleudert ihn förmlich durch die Welt, und er saugt jeden beliebigen Ort, jede noch so belanglose Situation gierig in sich auf. Einen Beobachter des Alltags könnte man ihn nennen, wenn er nicht den Anspruch und die Fähigkeit hätte, diesen Alltag auch produktiv zu interpretieren.

Rem Koolhaas ist derzeit sicherlich der einflussreichste Architekt der Welt. Mehr noch als seine Bauten prägen jedoch seine urbanen Strategien, seine Forschungen, Texte und Publikationen die Entwicklung der zeitgenössischen Architektur. Der 57-jährige Holländer lebt in London, hat sein Büro aber in Rotterdam, weil die Stadt nicht von der Arbeit ablenkt und die Büromieten billig sind.

Koolhaas repräsentiert die „zweite Generation" der Star-Architekten. Stilistisch nicht eindeutig festlegbar, unterscheidet sie sich von den prominenten „Signature"-Architekten der achtziger Jahre – Frank

Koolhaas-Kultbuch „S, M, L, XL"
Mit über 100.000 Exemplaren die meistverkaufte Architekturmonografie des 20. Jahrhunderts.

O. Gehry, Richard Meier oder Mario Botta – durch ihr Misstrauen gegenüber eingefahrenen Denk- und Arbeitsmustern. So gründete Koolhaas mit den diesjährigen Schweizer Pritzker-Preis-Trägern Herzog + DeMeuron ein Büro für ein Hotelprojekt in New York. Wichtig war beiden dabei das kulturindustrielle „branding" einer gemeinsamen Marke: Die Synergie zweier Firmen soll gleichsam eine neue Trademark schaffen. Vor wenigen Wochen allerdings hat der Auftraggeber Ian Schrager, der Pate der New Yorker Designerhotels (Paramount, Royalton, Hudson), Angst vor der geballten Innovationskraft seiner Auftragnehmer bekommen und das Projekt abgesagt.

Rem Koolhaas, der Architekt, versteckt sich hinter der Firmenbezeichnung Office of Metropolitan Architecture (OMA). Ge-

Expositur der Eremitage St. Petersburg im „Venetian"-Hotel in Las Vegas. Auf rohen Stahlwänden hängen die Bilder an Magneten.

OMAs neuer Konzertpalast für Porto inszeniert seinen Ort als vielgestaltigen Kristall mit dramatischen Öffnungen zur Außenwelt.

Interview. Rem Koolhaas gilt als der einflussreichste Architekt der Gegenwart. Seine Visionen gehen über das reine Bauen weit hinaus, und seine Arbeit für die Weltmarken Prada und Guggenheim setzt neue Maßstäbe im Zusammenspiel von Kultur und Konsum. Dietmar Steiner hat den öffentlichkeitsscheuen Star getroffen.

keine Macht!"

gründet wurde OMA vor rund 25 Jahren von Koolhaas und seinem damaligen Partner Elia Zenghelis, die beide zu Beginn der siebziger Jahre an der Londoner Architectural Association School studierten, dem Think Tank der heutigen Architektur. Rem Koolhaas ging nach New York und schrieb das legendäre Buch „Delirious New York" mit dem bezeichnenden Untertitel „A Retroactive Manifesto for Manhattan": eine Polemik gegen die Werte der akademischen Architektur und eine Ode an die Gestaltungskraft des Alltäglichen.

1980 kam die große Wende mit der so genannten „postmodernen" Architektur-Biennale in Venedig. Paolo Porthogesi inszenierte die „strada novissima" in den Arsenale, indem er 19 Architekten einlud, ihre Präsentationen mit je einer „Fassade" zu gestalten. Alle entdeckten zu dieser Zeit die Geschichte der Architektur und deren Neuinterpretation. Nur OMA überraschte mit einer abstrakt konstruktivistischen Darstellung, mit der Deklaration „Our New Sobriety" („Die Neue Nüchternheit") und provozierte im Katalog mit dem Foto einer amerikanischen Gefängnis-Popband.

Die postmodernen achtziger Jahre waren erwartungsgemäß nicht die große Zeit von OMA. Die begann 1994 mit Koolhaas' Masterplan für „Euralille": Die kleine französische Industriestadt Lille wurde einem radikalen Redesign unterzogen. Inzwischen ist OMA eine fixe Größe in der neueren Architekturgeschichte. Viele heutige Stars wie Zaha Hadid, Ben van Berkel oder Winy Maas (MVRDV) kommen aus dem Laboratorium von OMA.

1995 erschien die OMA-Monografie „S, M, L, XL", eine verwirrende Text-Bild-Grafik-Kombination. Das Buch setzte völlig neue Maßstäbe für die grafische Vermittlung sperriger Theorien, durchpflügte den Markt der klassischen Architekturpublikation radikal und wurde zur Insider-Bibel. Über 100.000-mal verkauft, ist „S, M, L, XL" trotz ihrer 1346 Seiten die erfolgreichste Architekturmonografie des 20. Jahrhunderts.

Koolhaas war damit endgültig als Star etabliert – der er eigentlich nie sein wollte und bis heute nicht sein will. Interviews gibt er äußerst selten, und auch dem internationalen Vortragszirkus verweigert er sich konsequent. An Veranstaltungen nimmt er nur teil, wenn er selbst etwas davon hat.

kultur

Prada
Die neue Einkaufswelt von Prada inszeniert Koolhaas als erweiterten öffentlichen Raum mit unterschiedlichen Raumstimmungen. Jeder Prada-Shop ist eine kleine Stadt in der Stadt. Diese Bühne des Lebens soll Orte für alle möglichen Zielgruppen bieten.

„Wir waren immer sehr vorsichtig, in der Architektur keine abgeschlossene Identität zu bekommen und dann vom Druck dieser Identität in eine immer gleiche Arbeit gezwungen zu werden. Das Modelabel Prada funktioniert da sehr ähnlich, will auch nicht auf ein bestimmtes Bild festgelegt werden. Wir suchen nach Strategien, um Identitäten zu multiplizieren"

profil: Nach dem Pritzker-Preis im Jahr 2000, sozusagen dem Nobelpreis für Architektur, arbeiten Sie an mehr Projekten als je zuvor. Ist Ihre Firma OMA nach Jahren der Polemiken und der verlorenen Wettbewerbe nun doch ein richtiges Architekturbüro geworden?
Koolhaas: Stimmt, wir betreuen zurzeit sehr viele Projekte: mehrere Museen, den Konzertsaal in Porto, ein Kongresszentrum in Córdoba, die IIT University in Chicago, die Public Library in Seattle, die niederländische Botschaft in Berlin. Aber wir machen auch viele Dinge, die nicht Architektur sind.
profil: Kann man bei so vielen Projekten überhaupt noch andere Aktivitäten entwickeln?
Koolhaas: Das ist nicht wirklich ein Widerspruch. Das beste Beispiel dafür ist unsere Arbeit für Prada. Wir machen die neuen Flagship Stores in New York, San Francisco und Los Angeles. Wir denken über die Entwicklung der Marke nach, entwickeln neue Lösungen für den Verkauf, und wir konzipieren und gestalten die Prada-Website. Das alles stellt die Architektur an sich in ein sehr viel weiteres Spektrum. Und genau das ist es, woran ich wirklich interessiert bin. Es gibt so viele Möglichkeiten der Äußerung von Architektur, notwendige und überflüssige. Deshalb wird Architektur für mich besser definiert, wenn nur das gebaut wird, was auf keine andere Art vermittelt werden kann. Alle anderen Aufgabenbereiche von Architektur sollen von anderen Medien übernommen werden.
profil: OMA ist eine sehr starke Marke in der Architektur, Prada in der Mode. Gibt es keinen Konflikt zwischen diesen beiden Identitäten?
Koolhaas: Wir waren immer sehr vorsichtig, in der Architektur keine abgeschlossene Identität zu bekommen und dann vom Druck dieser Identität in eine immer gleiche Arbeit gezwungen zu werden. Prada funktioniert da sehr ähnlich, will auch

„Jeder spricht über Architektur, jeder denkt über Architektur nach – aber keiner meint mehr Gebäude damit"

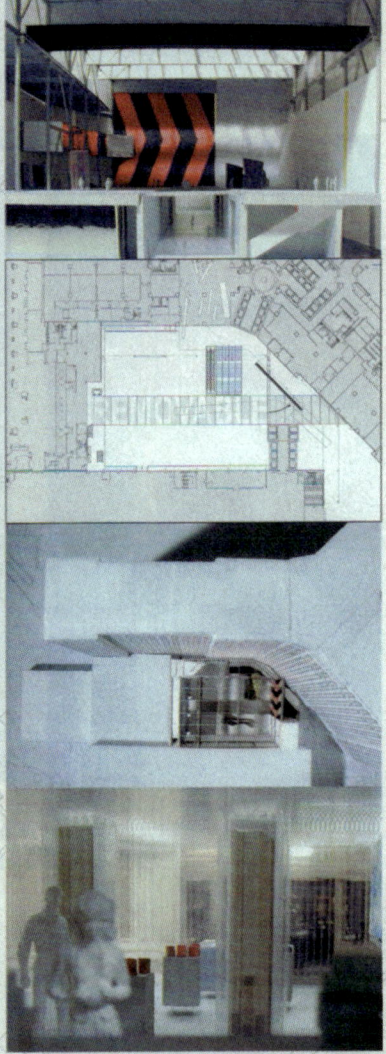

Guggenheim Las Vegas
Der plüschigen Atmosphäre des „Venetian"-Hotelcasinos in Las Vegas pflanzt Koolhaas eine riesige Industriehalle mit Laufkran in die Seite. Darin hätte sogar das New Yorker Guggenheim-Mutterhaus Platz.

nicht auf ein bestimmtes Bild festgelegt werden. Das ist die Basis der Affinität zwischen Prada und OMA. Wir suchen beide nach Strategien, um Identitäten zu multiplizieren und nicht zu konzentrieren.
profil: Es gibt also keinen Bruch zwischen Mode und Architektur?
Koolhaas: Warum sollte hier ein Bruch bestehen? Prada ist in die gemeinsamen Entwicklungen sehr stark involviert. Intern besteht kein Wettbewerb zwischen Kreativen, sondern eine Zusammenarbeit. Das wird bei der Architektur immer vergessen: Ohne Auftraggeber gibt es keine Architektur. Wir versuchen, mit jedem einzelnen Klienten, ob es die Flick-Foundation, Prada oder Guggenheim ist, die unterschiedlichen Probleme und Fragen sehr gründlich zu bearbeiten.
profil: Die Architektur ist also nicht wichtiger oder stärker als die Mode?
Koolhaas: Mächtige Architektur ist ein Widerspruch in sich selbst. Architekten haben keine Macht. Sie sind vielleicht intelligent, aber sie haben keine Macht. Keine ökonomische Macht und keine politische. Deshalb haben wir uns entschlossen, mit einem kreativen Unternehmen wie Prada zusammenzuarbeiten, das interessante Dinge mit einem klaren Auftrag macht: Kreativität mit Marketing zu positionieren. Wir könnten beispielsweise niemals dasselbe für Armani machen.
profil: Für Prada und andere Klienten arbeitet jetzt eine weitere Firma von OMA, die sich AMO nennt. Was hat man sich darunter vorzustellen?
Koolhaas: Das ist ein Büro für Forschung, das über alles nachdenkt, was mit Architektur zu tun hat, aber keine Architektur macht. AMO arbeitet zum Beispiel mit Ove Arup, mit Microsoft, mit Harvard Research, mit Talenten aus allen möglichen Bereichen. Heute wird in allen Bereichen über „Architektur" gesprochen, aber immer über die Architektur von Systemen. So ist Architektur zu einer dominanten ▶

kultur

Koolhaas-Konzertpalast in Porto
Das neue architektonische Superzeichen der portugiesischen Hafenstadt wirkt im Inneren durch die räumlichen Verdichtungen wie ein ausgehöhlter Monolith. Bilbao bekommt Konkurrenz!

„Architektur ist fürchterlich langsam. Man braucht mindestens zwei Jahre, um etwas zu realisieren. Aber in unserer heutigen Gesellschaft bleibt nichts zwei Jahre lang gleich"

Metapher geworden: Jeder spricht über Architektur, jeder denkt über Architektur nach, aber keiner meint mehr Gebäude damit. Es geht um ein architektonisches Denken, das auf verschiedene Gebiete angewandt wird. Ich glaube, es ist heute wirklich notwendig, darüber nachzudenken, wie sich bestimmte Einheiten, auch Firmen, in Verbindung zu anderen definieren und wie Themen sich ausbreiten.

profil: Hat die Arbeit mit AMO Rückwirkungen auf die Architektur von OMA?
Koolhaas: Unbedingt. Denn so, wie Architektur heute definiert wird, wirkt sie extrem limitiert. Man entwickelt als Architekt eine wiedererkennbare Identität, man wird damit vielleicht sogar berühmt, und dann erwarten alle, dass man immer macht, was sie schon kennen. Das wollen wir aufbrechen. Architektur ist fürchterlich langsam: Man braucht mindestens zwei Jahre, um etwas zu realisieren. Aber in unserer heutigen Gesellschaft bleibt nichts zwei Jahre lang gleich. Deshalb ist die Architektur ein schlechtes Medium, um all diese Veränderungen einzufangen. Ich suche nach schnelleren Reaktionen auf offene Situationen.

profil: In Harvard betreiben Sie ein „Research Project", in dem Sie jedes Jahr mit den Studenten ein bestimmtes Thema aufarbeiten. Teile davon wurden in Ausstellungen gezeigt, unter anderem auf der documenta X. Haben Sie nicht schon genug am Hals?
Koolhaas: Harvard gibt mir eine Forschungseinheit, die es mir erlaubt, jene Themen zu bearbeiten, von denen ich glaube, dass sie in Zukunft wichtig sein werden. Hier bin ich von keinem Bauherrn abhängig. Wir haben zum Beispiel die Entwicklung Chinas anhand des Pearl-River-Deltas analysiert – aber auch Themen wie Shopping, Afrika oder, jetzt gerade, den Kommunismus. Wir haben über das Römische Reich als Beispiel einer frühen Globalisierung nachgedacht und daraus ein Computer-Manual entwickelt, mit dem jeder seine eigene römische Stadt bauen kann. Bücher zu all diesen Projekten sollen im Herbst erscheinen.

profil: Es gibt Koolhaas, den Architekten, Denker und Forscher. Aber es gibt auch Koolhaas, den Schriftsteller und Publizisten mit seinen polemischen Essays, die die Architekturwelt regelmäßig in Aufregung versetzen. „generic city" hat Legionen von Studenten mit dem Gedanken der „unkontrollierbaren Verflüssigung" der herkömmlichen Stadtstrukturen infiziert. Ihr neuer Text „junk space" klingt dagegen wie ein trauriger Abgesang auf die Segnungen der modernen Zivilisation.

Koolhaas: Als Schriftsteller interessieren mich die Wirkungen des Geschriebenen. Meine Texte sind keine objektiven Reportagen, vielmehr eine Form der Manipulation. Als ich „generic city" schrieb, waren die Leser entsetzt über meinen Zynismus und meine Gefühlskälte. Mit „junk space" wollte ich deshalb einmal Gefühl und Betroffenheit zeigen. Aber es sind nicht meine wirklichen Gefühle, ich habe damit nur meine Lust am Schreiben ausgelebt. Es ist doch dumm zu glauben, dass alles, was jemand sagt oder schreibt, ein einzigartiger Ausdruck seines Seins zu sein habe. Deshalb war „generic city" unglaublich zynisch, und deshalb ist „junk space" unglaublich feierlich. Wahrscheinlich hat das Schreiben eine der Architektur vergleichbare polemische Kraft.

Kongresszentrum in Córdoba
Selbst die geschichtstrunkene Stadt schmückt sich mit einem gewaltigen liegenden Flügel aus der Rotterdamer Zukunftswerkstätte.

Hotel Astor-Place in Manhattan
Vor dem Mut des Gemeinschaftsprojekts von OMA und Herzog + DeMeuron bekam der Auftraggeber Ian Schrager weiche Knie: Projekt abgeblasen.

Public Library in Seattle
Koolhaas hat einen „gefalteten Raum" mit fließenden Verbindungen erfunden. Die perforierte Haut macht die Innenwelt der Medienmaschine präsent.

„Die Kunstwelt hat in bestimmten Bereichen die Entwicklung vollkommen verschlafen"

profil: Neben Ihrer Arbeit für Prada betreuen Sie derzeit viele Kulturprojekte, zum Beispiel Museen. Im Herbst wird Guggenheim Las Vegas eröffnet, direkt in das Hotelcasino „Venetian" integriert. Wachsen Konsum und Kultur endgültig zusammen?

Koolhaas: Das ist doch schon längst geschehen, es gibt den totalen Wechsel von der Kultur zum Konsum. Man muss sich nur einmal die Dimensionen vor Augen halten. Es werden derzeit mehr Museen als jemals zuvor gebaut. Allein Guggenheim Las Vegas ist zehnmal so groß wie das Mutterhaus in New York. Und durch die Erweiterung des Whitney-Museums in New York, die wir betreuen, werden die bestehenden Flächen verdoppelt.

profil: Aber ist OMAs Guggenheim in Las Vegas nicht eigentlich eine Provokation der Fake-Umgebung des „Venetian"-Hotels? Der Museumstrakt liegt direkt hinter den Slot-Maschinen des Casinos: eine riesige Industriehalle mit Laufkran an der Decke.

Koolhaas: Guggenheim-Chef Thomas Krens ist sehr intelligent und weiß, dass er provozieren muss. Man kann eine architektonische Strategie auch nicht mehr separiert von der „electronic economy" sehen. Deshalb arbeitet Krens intensiv an *Guggenheim dot.com:* Er will eine der dominierenden kulturellen Präsenzen im Internet werden.

profil: Kommt damit die totale Verschmelzung aller ästhetischen Medien und Präsentationsformen?

Koolhaas: Die Kunstwelt hat in bestimmten Bereichen die Entwicklung vollkommen verschlafen. Sie hat hartnäckig die Position der moralischen Integrität perpetuiert, obwohl längst klar war, dass diese an allen Fronten zusammenbricht. Sie war nicht bereit, das Konzept des Museums zu modernisieren – immer mit demselben Argument: eine spezifische geistige Erfahrung zu konservieren. Aber inzwischen sind die Museen die Opfer ihres eigenen Erfolgs. Sie werden von Besuchern so unkontrollierbar gestürmt, dass die zentrale Aufgabe eines Museums, die Konfrontation des einzelnen Individuums mit dem Kunstwerk, gefährdet ist. Deshalb müssen wir andere Strategien der Vermittlung finden. Wir müssen den kurzen, schnellen Besuch berücksichtigen, aber wir müssen auch die konkrete individuelle Konfrontation retten. Das alles ist die Aufgabe von Architektur, aber Architekten allein können diese Aufgabe nicht mehr bewältigen. ∎

Dietmar M. Steiner ist Leiter des Architektur Zentrum Wien und profil-Autor.

„Ich habe schon oft versucht, mein Cholesterin zu senken. Mit becel pro·activ ist es mir gelungen."

7 von 10 Österreichern haben – oft ohne es zu wissen – einen erhöhten Cholesterinspiegel. Mit der neuen becel pro·activ können Sie, bei einer insgesamt cholesterinbewußten Ernährung, Ihr LDL-Cholesterin schon innerhalb von 3 Wochen um 10 - 15 % senken. Denn becel pro·activ enthält hochwirksame Pflanzensterine, die im Körper die Aufnahme von Cholesterin vermindern. Das wurde durch wissenschaftliche Studien Tests bestätig

Translation by Brian Dorsey

"Architects Have No Power", 2001

Interview. Rem Koolhaas is regarded as the most influential architect of the present. His visions go far beyond pure building and his work for the world brands Prada and Guggenheim set new standards in the interplay between culture and consumption. Dietmar Steiner met the publicity-shy star.

He is lean, tall and dressed without ostentation. Not one of those personalities whose sheer presence already fills the room and dominates. He rather seems to float by shadow-like, not graspable, quiet and friendly, almost shy—if it wasn't for this insuppressible basic motor activity. He probably doesn't know the magical moment of calm. He is literally hurtled through the world and he eagerly soaks in every arbitrary place, any still so insignificant situation. One could call him an observer of everyday life if he wouldn't have the aspiration and ability to interpret this everyday world productively as well.
Rem Koolhaas is undoubtedly the most influential architect in the world right now. More than his buildings, however, his urban strategies, his research, texts and publications characterize the development of contemporary architecture. The 57-year-old Dutchman lives in London, but has his office in Rotterdam, because the city doesn't distract him from his work and office rentals are cheap. Koolhaas represents the "second generation" of star architects. Not clearly definable in a stylistic sense, they differ from the prominent "signature" architects of the 1980s— Frank O. Gehry, Richard Meier or Mario Botta—through their mistrust of retracted patterns of thinking and working. Koolhaas therefore established an office with this year's Swiss Pritzker Prize winners Herzog & de Meuron for a hotel project in New York. The cultural-industrial "branding" of a joint brand was important in the course of this: The synergy of two companies is to create a new trademark, so to speak. A few weeks ago, however, the client Ian Schrager, the godfather of New York designer hotels (Paramount, Royalton, Hudson), got scared of the concentrated innovative power of his contractors and cancelled the project. Rem Koolhaas, the architect, hides behind the trade name Office of Metropolitan Architecture (OMA). Around 25 years ago OMA was founded by Koolhaas and his partner at that time Elia Zenghelis, who both studied at the beginning of the 1970s at the Architectural Association School in London, the think-tank of present-day architecture. Rem Koolhaas went to New York and wrote the legendary book *Delirious New York*, with the distinctive subtitle *A Retroactive Manifesto for Manhattan*: a polemic against the values of academic architecture and an ode to the creative power of the commonplace.
In 1980 the big turning point came with the so-called "postmodern" Architecture Biennale in Venice. Paolo Portoghesi staged the Strada Novissima in the Arsenale by inviting 19 architects to design their presentations with one "façade" each. All of them were discovering the history of architecture and its reinterpretation at this time. Only OMA surprised people with an abstractly constructivist presentation with the declaration "Our New Sobriety" and provoked in the catalog with the photo of an American pop band made up of prisoners. As expected, the postmodern 1980s were not the grand era of OMA. This began in 1994 with Koolhaas' master plan for "Euralille": The small French industrial city of Lille underwent a radical redesign. Since that time OMA has been an outstanding figure in more recent architectural history. Many of today's stars like Zaha Hadid, Ben van Berkel or Winy Maas (MVRDV) come from the OMA laboratory.
The OMA monograph *S, M, L, XL*, a dizzying text-image-graphics combination, appeared in 1995. The book set completely new standards for graphically conveying cumbersome theories, radically plowed through the market of the classical architectural publication and became an insiders' Bible. Despite its 1,346 pages, *S, M, L, XL* sold over 100,000 copies and is the most successful architectural monograph of the 20th century. Koolhaas was definitively established as a star—who he actually never wanted to be and doesn't want to be today. He very rarely gives interviews and also consequently rejects the international lecture circus. Moreover, he only takes part in events if he gains something from them for himself.

PROFIL: After the Pritzker Prize in the year 2000, the Nobel Prize of architecture so to say, you have been working on more architecture projects than ever before. Has your company OMA become a proper architect's office after years of polemics and the lost competitions?

REM KOOLHAAS: That's right. We are currently working on an incredible amount of projects. Several museums, the concert hall in Porto, a congress center in Córdoba, the McCormick Tribune Campus Center at the Illinois Institute of Technology in Chicago, the Public Library in Seattle, the Dutch Embassy in Berlin. But we are also doing many things that aren't architecture.

PROFIL: With all these projects can other activities still be developed at all?

REM KOOLHAAS: That isn't really a contradiction. The best example for this is our work for Prada. We're doing the new flagship stores in New York, San Francisco and Los Angeles. We're thinking about the development of the brand, developing new solutions for sales and we're designing and conceptualizing the Prada website. All of that places architecture per se in a very much wider spectrum. And that is exactly what I am really interested in. There are so many possibilities of expressing architecture, necessary ones and superfluous ones. That's why architecture is better defined for me if only that which cannot be communicated in any other manner will be built. All of architecture's other areas of responsibility shall be taken over by other media.

PROFIL: OMA is a very strong brand in architecture, Prada in fashion. Is there no conflict between these two identities?

REM KOOLHAAS: We were always very careful not get any closed identity in architecture and then be forced into always the same work by the pressure of this identity. And Prada is very similar in that respect. They are also very careful to not get defined by one image alone. That is the basis of this affinity between Prada and OMA. We both look for strategies to multiply identities and not to concentrate them.

PROFIL: So there is no breach and no difference between fashion and architecture?

REM KOOLHAAS: Why should a breach exist here? Prada is heavily involved in the joint developments. Internally there is no competition between creatives, but rather collaboration. That is what people always forget in architecture: Without a client and without a contract there is no architecture. With every single client, whether this is the Flick Foundation, Prada or Guggenheim, we attempt to work on the different problems and questions very thoroughly.

Informelle Liste der Begegnungen mit · Informal list of encounters with Rem Koolhaas, ohne Datum · undated. Archive DS

PROFIL: Architecture is therefore not more important or stronger than fashion?

REM KOOLHAAS: Powerful architecture is a contradiction in itself. Architects have no power. They are perhaps intelligent, but they have no power. No economic power and no political power. That's why we have decided to work together with a creative enterprise like Prada, which does interesting things with a clear mandate: to position creativity with marketing. We could never do the same things, for instance, for Armani.

PROFIL: A further OMA company, called AMO, is now working for Prada and other clients. What can one imagine that to be?

REM KOOLHAAS: It is an office that does research and thinks about everything related to architecture, but doesn't do architecture. AMO works, for example, with Ove Arup, with Microsoft, with Harvard Research, with talented people from the most diverse fields. "Architecture" is being discussed in every area today, but it is always about the architecture of systems. So architecture has become a dominant metaphor: Everybody is talking about architecture, everybody is thinking about architecture, but no one means buildings anymore. It is about an architectonic thinking that is applied to different areas. I believe it is really necessary today everywhere in the world to contemplate how certain entities, also companies, define themselves in connection to others and how themes spread.

PROFIL: Does the work with AMO have retroactive effects on the architecture of OMA?

REM KOOLHAAS:: Absolutely. Because the way architecture is being defined now, it is extremely limited. As an architect you develop a recognizable identity. Perhaps you even become famous with it and then everyone expects you to always do what they already know. We want to break that open. Architecture is terribly slow: You need at least two years to realize anything. But in today's society nothing stays the same for two years. That's why architecture is a terrible medium to capture all these changes. I'm looking for quicker reactions to open situations.

PROFIL: At Harvard you conduct a research project where you investigate a certain topic with the students every year. Parts of this were shown in exhibitions, among others, at the *documenta X*. Don't you have enough on your plate already?

REM KOOLHAAS: Harvard gives me a research unit that allows me to work on those themes that I believe will be important in the future. Here I am not dependent on any builder. We analyzed, for instance, the development of China on the basis of the Pearl River Delta—but also other issues like shopping, Africa and now communism. We thought about the Roman Empire, as an example of an early globalization, and developed a computer manual which enables everyone to build their own Roman city. Books on all these projects are to appear in the fall.

PROFIL: There is Koolhaas the architect, thinker and researcher. But there is also Koolhaas the writer and publicist with his polemic essays, which regularly throw the architectural world into a proper dither. "The Generic City" infected legions of students with the thought of the "uncontrollable liquefaction" of conventional city structures. Your new text, "Junk Space," in contrast, sounds like a sad farewell to the blessings of modern civilization.

REM KOOLHAAS: As a writer I am interested in the impacts of what has been written. My texts are not objective reportages, but a form of manipulation instead. When I wrote "The Generic City," the readers were appalled by my cynicism, my callousness. So with "Junk Space" I wanted to show emotion and dismay for once. But these are not my true feelings; I only lived out my delight in writing. After all, it is terribly stupid to believe that everything you say and write has to be a unique expression of your being. That's why "The Generic City" was incredibly cynical and why "Junk Space" is incredibly solemn. Writing probably has a polemic power that is comparable to architecture.

PROFIL: In addition to your work with Prada there are very many cultural projects, for example, museums. Guggenheim Las Vegas will be opened in the fall, directly integrated into the Venetian Hotel Casino. Are culture and consumption growing together?

REM KOOLHAAS: That already happened a long time ago. There is the total shift from culture to consumption. Take a look just once at the dimensions. More museums are currently being built than ever before. Guggenheim Las Vegas alone is ten times as big as the mother house in New York. Then we're doing an extension of the Whitney Museum in New York. The existing areas are going to be doubled there.

PROFIL: But isn't OMA's Guggenheim Las Vegas actually a provocation of the fake surroundings of the Venetian Hotel Casino? The Guggenheim wing lies directly behind the slot machines as a giant factory building with a travelling crane on the ceiling.

REM KOOLHAAS: Guggenheim head Tom Krens is very intelligent and knows that he has to provoke. But you can no longer see an architectonic strategy separately from the electronic economy. That's why Krens is working intensively on guggenheim.com. He wants to become one of the domineering cultural presences in the Internet.

PROFIL: Does the total melding of all aesthetic media and presentation forms come with it?

REM KOOLHAAS: In certain areas the art world has completely missed out on the developments. It quite simply perpetuated the position of moral integrity, although it was long obvious that this would break apart at all corners. It was not prepared to modernize the concept of the museum—always with the same argument: to conserve a specific spiritual experience. Meanwhile, however, the museums have been the victims of their success. Today they are being stormed uncontrollably by visitors to the extent that the main task of a museum, the confrontation of the single individual with the artwork, is endangered. Therefore, we have to find other strategies of mediation. We have to consider the brief, quick visit, but we also have to save the concrete individual confrontation. All of that is the task of architecture, but architecture alone can no longer manage this task.

Rem Koolhaas in der Casa da Musica in Porto, staunend über das gelungene Werk, das er seiner großartigen Projektarchitektin Ellen van Loon zu verdanken hat. · Rem Koolhaas in the Casa de Musica in Porto, amazed at the successful work that he owes to his fabulous project architect Ellen van Loon, 2005. © DS

aus · from

2 G 21_2001
"From the Role of Critic to That of Client"
Translation by Rory O'Donovan

Lacaton & Vassal: Türkisches Café

Dies ist eine heutige Geschichte eines Kritikers, der Architekten entdeckte und dann zum Bauherrn wurde. Ganz nebenbei erfährt man auch etwas darüber, wie die Architektur und deren Medien heute funktionieren.

Es muss irgendwann im Jahr 1996 gewesen sein. In der Redaktions-Baracke von *domus* an Mailands südlicher Peripherie stapeln sich die Dokumente neuer Architekturen. Aufwendige Ektachromes von Fotografen, Portfolios von Architekten, Monografien und Kataloge, die Newsletter der großen Architekturfirmen. Die Sichtung ist redaktioneller Alltag, seit ich Ende 1995 vom damals neuen *domus*-Direktor François Burkhardt engagiert wurde, die Redaktion der Architektur zu leiten.

Lacaton & Vassal: Turkish Café

This is the modern story of a critic who discovered architects and then became a building client. In the process, one also learns how architecture and its various media function today.

It must have been some time in 1996. In the editorial offices of *domus*—a container on the southern outskirts of Milan—documents about new architecture were piling up: lavish Ektachromes from photographers, portfolios from architects, monographs and catalogues, and the newsletters of big architectural offices. Sifting through this material was one of my everyday tasks since I had been appointed head of the editorial team at the end of 1995 by François Burkhardt, the new director of the journal at that time.

In those days, in the mid-90s, I pursued a twofold editorial strategy for architecture at *domus*. First of all, I was constantly in touch with the so-called 'important' architects in the world in order to obtain advance information about significant new projects. Secondly, I also kept an eye open for new and undiscovered buildings by architects who were relatively unknown internationally. I was assisted in this by an extensive network of informed contacts throughout the world. Each issue of the journal focused on a specific topic and presented

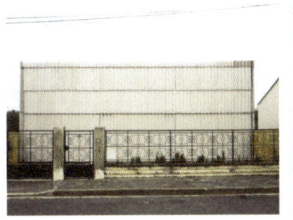

Maison Latapie, Floirac, Lacaton & Vassal, 1993. © Philippe Ruault

Als redaktionelle Strategie der Architektur in *domus* verfolgte ich damals, Mitte der neunziger Jahre, im Wesentlichen zwei Wege. Einerseits hielt ich beständig Kontakt mit den sogenannten bedeutenden Architekten, um rechtzeitig über wichtige neue Bauten informiert zu sein, andererseits suchte ich aber gleichzeitig ständig nach neuen, bisher wenig bekannten Bauten von bislang international unbekannten Architekten. Ein großes Netzwerk von Informanten und Kennern der Szenen aus der ganzen Welt half dabei mit. Gleichzeitig musste jedes Heft einem vorbestimmten Thema zu folgen versuchen. In jedem Heft wurden vier bis sechs Bauten präsentiert. Deren letztendliche Auswahl war also wesentlich von innerredaktionellen Überlegungen bestimmt: Ergibt die Summe der Bauten eine stimmige ‚Geschichte' und kann damit Neugier und Aufmerksamkeit erzielt werden? Die Gratwanderung von *domus*, als weltgrößte Architektur- und Designzeitschrift, bestand darin, einen Weg zu finden zwischen Akzeptanz des Marktes und der Reputation im innerarchitektonischen Diskurs. Schon damals spielte der News-Wert eines Projekts die entscheidende Rolle. Belegt allerdings, durch Kriterien der Entwicklung und Debatte der Architektur.

between four and six buildings. The final selection of projects was largely determined by ideas and suggestions put forward by the editorial team. The overall choice of buildings was meant to ensure that the journal presented a coherent argument that would attract the attention of readers and arouse their curiosity. The balancing act performed by *domus*, the world's largest journal for architecture and design, consisted of finding a path between market acceptance and upholding the reputation it enjoyed as a contributor to architectural debate. Even in those days, the decisive factor was the newsworthiness of a project, combined with other criteria such as the ongoing development of architecture and general discussions within this discipline.

In the midst of all this, back then in 1996, I suddenly found a tiny brochure on the table with photos of landscapes and nature by the French architectural photographer Philippe Ruault. Why had they been sent to *domus*? Among the photos were a few pictures of a house: corrugated plastic, corrugated fiber-cement sheeting, a steel framework and cheap furniture. I no longer remember whether the architects of this house were even mentioned in the brochure; but this form of anti-propaganda was surprising and aroused my curiosity.

Fünfter Tag • Day Five

Mitten in diesem Betrieb, damals im Jahr 1996, lag auf einmal eine winzig kleine Broschüre auf dem Tisch. Landschafts- und Naturfotos des französischen Architekturfotografen Philippe Ruault. Warum bei *domus*? Doch dazwischen eingestreut ein paar Fotos eines Hauses. Wellplastik, Welleternit, ein Stahlgerüst, billige Möbel. Ich weiß heute nicht mehr, ob die Architekten dieses Hauses in dieser Broschüre überhaupt erwähnt waren. Aber diese Form der Anti-Propaganda überraschte und machte neugierig.

Ich animierte bei *domus* Rita Capezzuto zu recherchieren, und sie fand Anne Lacaton und Jean Philippe Vassal in Bordeaux als Architekten des Hauses, das hinter den Bildern steckte. Inzwischen fand ich kleine, rudimentäre Präsentationen des Hauses in französischen Architekturzeitschriften. Verblüffend erschienen die raffinierte materielle Simplizität und die lapidare Auseinandersetzung mit dem Alltag ohne ästhetisierende Attitude. Das Thema des *domus*-Heftes im März 1997 lautete „Peripherie". Das war die Chance, dieses Haus – inzwischen wussten wir, es war das Haus Latapie in Bordeaux – zu publizieren. Warum? Weil wir damals bei *domus* im Bereich der Architektur versuchten, die vorgegebenen Themen sehr metaphorisch zu interpretieren. Und peripher waren die Mittel, die zum Bau dieses Hauses verwendet wurden, peripher war die Architektur, die nicht geeignet schien, repräsentative zentrale Aufgaben wahrzunehmen. Gleichzeitig arbeiteten wir im Architekturzentrum Wien an einer Ausstellung mit dem Titel *Standardhäuser*. Auch in diese Präsentation wollten wir das Haus Latapie mitaufnehmen. Im Juni 1997 hielten Lacaton & Vassal dann einen faszinierend bescheidenen Vortrag an der Technischen Universität in Wien. Fast eine Underground-Veranstaltung. Es war die erste Gelegenheit der realen Begegnung – mit nachhaltiger Wirkung.

Im Februar 1998 trafen wir uns in Bordeaux anlässlich der Ausstellungseröffnung von *Reading–Living*, der von Michel Jacques vom Arc en Rêve entwickelten Ausstellung von Rem Koolhaas und Bruce Mau. OMA's Haus in Bordeaux war noch nicht fertig, aber alle angereisten Kritiker und Journalisten besichtigten ebenso

> The amazing thing about this house was its subtle material simplicity and the concise dialectic it conducted with everyday things, without adopting an aesthetic pose.

At *domus*, I encouraged Rita Capezzuto to do some research, and she found out that Anne Lacaton and Jean-Philippe Vassal in Bordeaux were the architects of the house shown in the pictures. In the meantime I had also discovered small, rudimentary presentations of the building in French architectural magazines. The amazing thing about this house was its subtle material simplicity and the concise dialectic it conducted with everyday things, without adopting an aesthetic pose. The theme of the March 1997 issue of *domus* was "periphery," and this gave us an opportunity to publish the project. By then we had found out that it was the Latapie House in Bordeaux. Why did we wish to publish it? At *domus*, in those days, we sought to interpret the given architectural topics in a very metaphorical way—and the means used to build this house were indeed peripheral, as was the architecture itself, which seemed wholly unsuited for any situation where prestige might play a role.

Sie wollten einen „osmanischen Himmel aus Fliesen",
als ob die Türken doch Wien erobert hätten, zeichneten aber ein
marokkanisches Muster. Der Irrtum konnte aufgeklärt werden.
Entwurfsskizze des Cafés des Az W · They wanted an "Ottoman sky
made of tiles," as if the Turks had conquered Vienna after all,
but drew a Moroccan pattern instead. The error could be clarified.
Design sketch of the Az W café, Lacaton & Vassal, 1999,
© Archive Az W

Lacaton & Vassal Maison Latapie in Floirac. Ich hatte es geahnt. Das real gebaute Haus erfüllte seine bis dahin nur medial elaborierten Vorstellungen und Interpretationen vollkommen. Die Maison à Saint-Pardoux konnte ich dann im April 1998 in *domus* publizieren, im Oktober dieses Jahres sah ich die Maison Latapie wieder in der großen Frankreich-Ausstellung im So-Ho-Guggenheim in New York. Und im November desselben Jahres hielten Lacaton & Vassal dann einen in Wien vielbeachteten Vortrag beim Wiener Architekturkongress des Architekturzentrum Wien zum Thema „Wohnen".

At the same time, we were preparing an exhibition on the subject of "standard houses" at the Architekturzentrum in Vienna, and we were also presenting the Latapie House in this context. In June 1997 Lacaton & Vassal gave a modest yet fascinating lecture at the Technische Universität in Vienna. This almost underground event provided the first opportunity for a live encounter—and it had a lasting effect.

In February 1998 we met in Bordeaux on the occasion of the opening of the exhibition *Reading–Living*, curated by Michel Jacques of Arc en Rêve on the subject of Rem Koolhaas and Bruce Mau. The OMA building in Bordeaux had not been completed, however, and all the critics and journalists who turned up also paid a visit to Lacaton & Vassal's Latapie House in Floriac. Just as I had thought, the house as realized on site fully lived up to the expectations aroused by interpretations in the media. I was able to publish the House in Saint-Pardoux-

Mein Interesse an der Arbeit von Lacaton & Vassal hatte nun bereits eine Geschichte. Faszinierend für mich war, dass es ihnen mit wenigen Bauten und Projekten gelungen war, die zeitgenössische Architektur um eine neue Dimension zu erweitern. Sie durchbrachen in all diesen Projekten radikal die Erwartungshaltungen der Medienindustrie. Nichts an ihren Bauten war glatt und fotogen. Nichts schien sichtbar neu und überraschend. Es war nicht leicht, sie bei *domus* gegen den Direktor durchzusetzen. Ihr ‚dirty realism' resultierte dagegen vielmehr aus einer radikalen Thematisierung des Sachverhalts des Bauens. Sie wollten immer minimale Baukosten, nutzten dafür alle gegebenen bauindustriellen Bedingungen und schufen dennoch eine ebenso intensive wie lapidare Ästhetik, die Substanz genug hatte, um gleichzeitig offen für den Gebrauch zu sein. Für mich war ihre Architektur sehr ‚wienerisch'. In ihrer undogmatischen Leichtigkeit erfüllten sie die Forderung von Josef Frank, das Material der Architektur sei all der „Ungeschmack unserer Zeit".

Anfang des Jahres 1999 vollzog sich der Umbau und die Adaptierung der künftigen Räumlichkeiten des neuen und größeren Architekturzentrum Wien. Wir kämpften bei der Renovierung unserer Räume gegen die Planung der Architekten des Museumsquartiers. Diese wollten unsere Räumlichkeiten in den Bauteilen des 19. Jahrhunderts denkmalgerecht renovieren, mit teuren Steinböden und viel Putz und Stuck. Wir hingegen wollten möglichst rohe Räume, benutzbar, angreifbar. Das war keine ästhetische, sondern eine kulturelle Absicht. Die neuen Räume des Architekturzentrum Wien sollten Architektur zeigen und ausstellen. Verschiedene Architektur. Dafür mussten alle Ausstellungsräume als Hintergrund möglichst neutral sein.

la-Rivière in *domus* in April 1998. The following October, I saw the Latapie House again in a big French exhibition held at the SoHo Guggenheim in New York; and in November of the same year, Lacaton & Vassal held a much acclaimed lecture on "housing" at the architectural congress in the Architekturzentrum in Vienna.

There was now a certain history to my interest in the work of Lacaton & Vassal. What fascinated me was the fact that, on the basis of only a few buildings and projects, they had succeeded in adding a new dimension to modern architecture. In all their projects, they had radically confounded the standard expectations of the media industry. Nothing about their buildings was smooth or photogenic. Nothing seemed evidently new or surprising. It was not easy to overcome the resistance of the director of *domus* and publish them in the journal. Their 'dirty realism,' however, was the outcome of a radical exposition of the circumstances surrounding construction. They sought to minimize building costs, exploiting all available industrial resources to do so. Nevertheless, they created an aesthetic that was as intense as it was concise and that had sufficient substance to make it open to use as well. For me, their architecture was extremely 'Viennese': in their undogmatic lightness and case, they confirmed Josef Frank's claim that the substance of architecture was all the "bad taste of our time."

At the beginning of 1999 work began on the conversion and adaptation of the rooms for the new, enlarged Architekturzentrum in Vienna. As far as the renovation of our own accommodation was concerned, we had to fight against the planning proposals put forward by the architects for the new Museumsquartier. They wanted to refurbish our rooms—situated in a 19th-century building—in historical style, with expensive stone flooring and a lot of plaster and stuccowork. We, in contrast, wanted tough, raw spaces that would be functional and capable of taking knocks and hard wear. That was a cultural, not an aesthetic, aim. The new spaces in the Architekturzentrum in Vienna were to be used for displaying architecture—different forms of architecture. For that reason, we believed, the exhibition spaces should form as neutral a background as possible.

> The sole exception to this was to be the cafeteria, which was allowed to be "architecture."

Die einzige Ausnahme sollte die Cafeteria sein. Sie durfte und sollte ‚Architektur' sein. Selbstverständlich wünschte sich der Vorstand des Architekturzentrum dafür einen internationalen Star-Architekten. Als deutliches Zeichen der Bedeutung und Kompetenz des neuen Zentrums der Architektur. Nach einigen Diskussionen im Team entschieden wir uns aber für eine andere Strategie. Wir wollten jüngere Architekten, keine Stars, noch nicht so bekannt. Auch Architekten, die zu unserer Philosophie passten, ein Programm zu machen, das Architektur als diskursiven Gegenstand hat.

Lacaton & Vassal waren dabei nicht die einzigen, an die wir dachten, aber letztlich nahm ich doch im Mai 1999 mit ihnen den Kontakt auf. Sie kamen nach Wien, studierten die Situation. Und dann kam nach einigen Wochen ihr Entwurf. Ich gestehe, dass ich noch nie in meinem Leben von einem Entwurf so überrascht und verblüfft wurde. Ich erwartete den Entwurf einer Cafeteria, mit Einrichtung, und bekam den Vorschlag eines leeren Raums mit einer traditionellen orientalischen Fliesendecke im dreischiffigen Gewölbe.

Dies war aber, wie auf den ersten Blick erwartbar, keinesfalls zynisch gemeint, war auch kein postmoderner Kommentar. Lacaton & Vassal waren vom vorhandenen Raum begeistert, das traditionelle Gewölbe, eine schwere Substanz, die leichte Interpretation verlangte. Und sie sahen das gesamte Projekt Museumsquartier Wien mit seinen neuen Museen und der extensiven Renovierung der bestehenden Bauteile auch als eine Disziplinierung des Geländes.

The sole exception to this was to be the cafeteria, which was allowed to be "architecture." The governing body of the Architekturzentrum wanted the services of an international star architect, of course, as a clear expression of the importance and authority of the new center. After a number of discussions within our team, we came out in favor of a different strategy. We wanted younger architects, not stars; people who were not so well known yet; architects who were attuned to our philosophy and would design a program in which architecture would be an object of debate.

Lacaton & Vassal were not the only ones we considered, but in May 1999 I finally contacted them. They came to Vienna, studied the situation, and after a number of weeks, their proposals arrived. I must admit that, in all my life, I have never been as flabbergasted by a design as by this one. I expected proposals for a cafeteria with the relevant furnishings and fittings. What I received was a design for an empty space with a traditional Oriental tiled ceiling in three bays of vaulting.

This was not meant at all cynically, as one might initially have thought. Nor was it intended as a postmodern statement. Lacaton & Vassal were most enthusiastic about the existing space with its traditional vaulting; its heavy substance needed to be interpreted with a light touch. They also regarded the overall project for the Museumsquartier in Vienna, with the creation of museums and an extensive restoration of the existing building fabric, as a measure to impose a certain discipline on the area.

Even though it was still a building site, they could recognize the huge, monumental Museumsquartier that was emerging here, and they warned against it with their design. As this was a warning against something so final and definite, their proposals were light and ephemeral. They did not wish to "address the whole issue of perfection." They were more interested in the Viennese tradition of "little architecture," with its love of detail and spatial narrative.

Fünfter Tag • Day Five

Sie sahen, damals als Baustelle noch, das große monumentale Wiener Museumsquartier kommen, und warnten davor. Warnten mit ihrem Entwurf vor dem Endgültigen und Definitiven, und setzten dem eine Position der Ephemeren und der Leichtigkeit gegenüber. Sie wollten sich „nicht der Frage der Vollendung stellen". Sie beschäftigten sich mit der Tradition der „little architecture" in Wien, deren Detailverliebtheit und räumlichen Erzählungen.

„Letztendlich haben wir das alles als zu kompliziert empfunden, zu designt, zu widersprüchlich, alles war zu eingeschlossen, genau das Gegenteil des Flairs des Architekturzentrum Wien. Wir denken, dass es viel Platz gibt und dass man diesen Platz in der einfachsten und leichtesten Art und Weise auch nützen soll. Dieses Café soll ein ganz besonderer Ort sein und gut ins Museumsquartier und in das Architekturzentrum integriert sein. – Nach all dem Zögern und Zaudern ist uns plötzlich die Idee gekommen, dass wir einfach nur einen großen blauen Himmel brauchen, eine Art große Befremdung, einen Traum", schrieben Lacaton & Vassal dazu.

Den optimalen Plan von Lacaton & Vassal, den leeren Raum und die Küche und Lager der Cafeteria in einem Glashaus im Hof davor, wurde uns vom Museumsquartier nicht gestattet. Jetzt trennt eine rohe Betonsteinwand eine der drei Achsen des Raumes ab, dahinter befinden sich nun die Küche und die Lager und der Zugang zu den Toiletten. Als uns Lacaton & Vassal diese letzte und nun realisierte Version präsentierten, sagte ich spontan: Dies sieht aus als ob in der vormaligen Sowjetunion in Aserbeidschan die örtliche Traktoren-Fabrik ein altes Kloster zugewiesen bekommen und seine hauseigenen Bauarbeiter damit beauftragt hätte, dort eine Kantine einzubauen. „Genau das ist es", antwortete Jean-Philippe, „niemand soll auf die Idee kommen, dass diese Wand von einem Architekten gemacht wurde."

"Ultimately, we found it all too complicated, too designed, too full of contradictions," Lacaton & Vassal wrote. "Everything was too self-contained—the very opposite of the flair of the Viennese Architekturzentrum. We believe there is a lot of space here, and that this space should be used in the simplest and lightest form possible. The café should be a very special place, well integrated into the Museumsquartier and the Architekturzentrum. After a great deal of hesitation and procrastination, we suddenly had the idea that all one needed was a broad blue sky—something to take one aback in a big way, a dream."

The ideal plan drawn up by Lacaton & Vassal—the large empty space, with the kitchen and store for the cafeteria housed in a glasshouse in the adjoining courtyard—was not accepted by the bodies responsible for the Museumsquartier. One bay of the space is now divided off by a rough concrete-block wall, behind which are the kitchen, the store and toilet access. When Lacaton & Vassal presented this final version, which has since been implemented, I remarked spontaneously that it looked as if a local tractor combine in Azerbaijan in the former Soviet Union had been allocated an old monastery and had ordered its own building workers to install a canteen in it. "That's exactly the point," Jean-Philippe replied. "No one should suspect that this wall was planned by an architect."

The implementation of the project began. We had understood Lacaton & Vassal's message: the tiled ceiling was a cultural and historical statement made by the city of Vienna, at the interface between the Catholic West and the Islamic East, from the Hagia Sophia in Istanbul to the Baroque Karl's Church in Vienna. The siege of the city by the Turks in the 17th century created a trauma that lingers on in the Austrian psyche. From today's vantage point, this cultural dialogue may be seen as bold commentary on the debate between the different cultures. That was why we deliberately sought a firm in Turkey that could produce the tiles, and we found one in the Gorbon Company in Istanbul.

Entwurfsskizzen des Cafés des Az W · Design sketch of the Az W café, Lacaton & Vassal 1999. © Archive Az W

Anne LACATON . Jean Philippe VASSAL
Architectes
4 Place Pey-Berland - 33000 Bordeaux
tel: 05 56 79 38 10 - fax: 05 56 81 51 91
Palais de Tokyo
2,Rue de la Manutention - 75016 Paris
tel: 01 47 23 49 09 - fax: 01 47 23 49 17

CAFE IM ARCHITEKTURZENTRUM . VIENNE

kitchen under the same sky with wall

views

date 08.12.2000

Fünfter Tag • Day Five

Nun begann die Realisierung. Wir hatten die kulturelle Botschaft von Lacaton & Vassal verstanden. Die Fliesendecke als kulturhistorische Botschaft Wiens, am Schnittpunkt von katholischem Abendland und islamischem Byzanz. Von der Hagia Sophia in Istanbul zur barocken Karlskirche in Wien. Die Türkenbelagerung Wiens im 17. Jahrhundert. Ein Trauma, das noch immer in der österreichischen Psyche existiert. Dieses kulturelle Gespräch heute gesehen, als offensiven Kommentar zum Gespräch der Kulturen. Deshalb haben wir bewusst eine Firma in der Türkei gesucht, die diese Fliesen produzieren konnte, und in der Firma Gorgon in Istanbul gefunden.

Wir haben dann auch eine türkische Designerin gefunden, Asiye Kolbai-Kafalier, die in Abstimmung mit Lacaton & Vassal das traditonelle Muster entwarf. Küche und Bar wurden in Absprache mit Lacaton & Vassal vom Wiener Architekten Stefan Seehof entworfen. Ebenso das Lichtkonzept, sehr reduziert und intim, mit wenigen Leuchten, von der Decke gehängt und frei verteilten Stehlampen. Die Möbel haben Lacaton & Vassal aus Katalogen österreichischer Firmen ausgewählt, und einfache Kaffeehausmöbel des engagierten Tiroler Tischlers Hussl gefunden.

Schon während der Bauzeit der Cafeteria schlichen Wiener Architekten und Studenten auf der Baustelle herum. Schon vor der Eröffnung verbreitete sich das Gerücht in der ganzen Stadt, dass hier ein ganz eigenartiges Projekt entstünde. Die Medien belagerten uns um Material. Aber wir hatten nichts. Keine opulenten Computer-Renderings, keine tollen Entwürfe. Nur marginale Skizzen. Die Medienwelt reagierte mit zunehmendem Ärger, dass wir sie nicht vor Fertigstellung mit Bildmaterial bedienen konnten. Die Pressereferentin des Architekturzentrum Wien war verzweifelt.

Also wieder, wie schon bei der kleinen Broschüre von Philippe Ruault im Jahr 1996, eine Strategie der medialen Verweigerung. Und es war gut und richtig so.

We also found a Turkish designer, Asiye Kolbai-Kafalier. She created the traditional pattern in consultation with Lacaton & Vassal. Similarly, the kitchen and bar were designed in agreement with the French architects by our own architect Stefan Seehof, who was also responsible for the lighting concept—very restrained and intimate, with only a small number of lamps. The light fittings suspended from the ceiling are combined with a free arrangement of standard lamps. Lacaton & Vassal selected the furnishings from the catalogues of Austrian manufacturers. They chose simple coffee-house furniture by the dedicated Tyrolean cabinetmaker Hussl.

During the construction period, Viennese architects and students were already slipping into the site to see what was going on. Prior to the opening of the cafeteria, the rumor went round the city that a very special project was being realized here. The media bombarded us with requests for material, but we had nothing to offer—neither breathtaking designs, nor opulent computer renderings. All we had were marginal sketches. The media reacted with increasing annoyance that we were unable to provide them with pictorial material before completion of the work. The press officer of the Architekturzentrum in Vienna was desperate.

Once again, there was a strategy of denying the media what it wanted, as with the little brochure by Philippe Ruault in 1996. And that was quite in order. Opening day: 10 October 2001. The new Architekturzentrum Vienna shows the programmatic, self-critical exhibition *Sturm der Ruhe – What Is Architecture?*, a staging of succinct architectural situations that examines the processes at work behind the sensationalizing of architecture through the media: a qualitative, daring presentation that will be either loved or hated. A number of negative criticisms of the exhibition were made in the international media. All these critics must have understood the purpose of the exhibition, however, since they could find a positive expression of these aims solely in the cafeteria by Lacaton & Vassal.

Der Tag der Eröffnung: 10.10.2001. Das neue Architekturzentrum Wien wird mit der programmatisch-selbstkritischen Ausstellung *Sturm der Ruhe – What is Architecture* eröffnet. Eine Inszenierung von lapidaren architektonischen Situationen, die bewusst die Prozesse der plakativen Mediatisierung von Architektur hinterfragt. Eine anspruchsvolle, gewagte Präsentation. Sie wird geliebt oder gehasst. Und es gibt eine Reihe von negativen Kritiken in internationalen Medien zur Ausstellung. Alle diese Kritiker haben aber den Anspruch der Ausstellung soweit verstanden, dass sie ihn einzig in der Cafeteria von Lacaton & Vassal letztlich positiv eingelöst sahen.

Am Eröffnungsabend des 10. Oktober gegen Mitternacht sitze ich erschöpft in einer Ecke der überfüllten Cafeteria. Ich blicke zur prächtig leuchtenden Fliesendecke, der ‚große Himmel', der sich in den großen Scheiben der Fassade unendlich in den Außenraum spiegelnd fortsetzt. Ich blicke zur so selbstverständlich wirkenden rohen Betonsteinwand, die bis heute die Frage von Besuchern nach sich zieht, wann sie denn endlich verputzt wird. Darunter der Betonboden, die informell verteilten Tische und Sessel, ein offener sozialer Ort der Begegnung, alles soll und kann stattfinden unter diesem Himmel, für die Zukunft offen. Jean-Philippe ist zufrieden, das Lokal funktioniert. Ich selbst bin fassungslos und unendlich glücklich. Der Kritiker durfte Bauherr sein und einmal in seinem Leben konnte er einen großartigen, real gebauten Raum ermöglichen.

Lacaton & Vassal haben mir persönlich, dem Architekturzentrum Wien, der Stadt und der Kultur etwas geschenkt: „Das was Dietmar Steiner sich wünscht: Die Dinge roh belassen, so, wie sie sind, ungekünstelt, mit einem Minimum an Ausstattung, so, wie wenn die Baustelle sich nicht ganz auflösen würde, sich nicht die Frage der Vollendung stellen, viel eher zum Ausdruck kommen lassen, was hier wichtig ist: Die aktuellen Architekturthemen, die Ausstellungen, und nicht die herzliche Atmosphäre verlieren, sie sogar weiter ausbauen."

Realisiertes Café im Az W. Als Hans Hollein das Lokal zum ersten Mal betrat und die rohe Betonsteinwand sah, sagte er nur: Café Kabul! · The realized Az W café. When Hans Hollein entered the café for the first time and saw the bare concrete stone wall, he said only one thing: Café Kabul!, 2001. © Hertha Hurnaus

Around midnight on the opening night, I am sitting exhausted in a corner of the overcrowded cafeteria. I look up to the magnificent, shining, tiled ceiling, the 'broad sky' which extends out endlessly into the space outside in the form of reflections in the large panes of façade glazing. I look at the rough concrete-block wall standing there so forthrightly. It still prompts visitors to ask when it will be plastered. At the base is the concrete floor with the informal arrangement of tables and chairs. Here is an open place for social encounter. Anything can and should happen beneath this sky, which is receptive to the future. Jean-Philippe is content. The place functions. I am amazed myself and immensely happy. The critic was allowed to play the client's role, and for once in his life has helped to create a real built space.

Lacaton & Vassal have conferred a gift on us all—on me personally, on the Viennese Architekturzentrum and on the arts in general. "What Dietmar Steiner wishes is to leave things in a raw state, as they are, unadulterated, with a minimum of polish, as if the conditions prevailing on the building site would never quite come to an end; not posing the question of completion, but allowing something to be expressed that is important here: the current themes of architecture, the exhibitions—not sacrificing the warm, heartfelt atmosphere either, but actually extending it."

aus · from

DU 742, 12_2003
„Der völlig normale Mensch
Jon Jerde, Prophet des neuen öffentlichen Raumes."
Translation by Brian Dorsey

Jon Jerde

Jon Jerde is a friendly gentleman in the prime of his life. Wiry, a little bit stocky, with a husky voice. Modest. Not exactly someone who fills a room when he enters it. One could encounter him at a motel desk somewhere in the Texas prairie. But Jon Jerde is not just anybody. Jon Jerde is an architect with an office in Venice, the apparently eternally hip beach district of Los Angeles. And he is an insiders' tip.

Can someone be an insiders' tip if he delights hundreds of thousands of people? Just like that, especially if it has to do with two different cultural spheres of influence, business and art, for instance. Hardly anyone knows the names of the world's largest architecture firms, which are mostly located in the US; and a Swiss man is supposedly building the most skyscrapers in Southeast Asia—Remo Riva is nowhere near being a celebrity because of that.

Presumably no one would know who Jon Jerde is if he hadn't met Rem Koolhaas several years ago during a major planning project for Universal City in Los Angeles. Then the American architecture scene took notice. And the rumor slowly went around that Jerde is the prophet of the new public space in American and Japanese downtowns. The American professional journal *architecture* called him "possibly the most influential architect at the moment."

Jon Jerde

Jon Jerde ist ein freundlicher Herr in den besten Jahren. Drahtig, ein wenig untersetzt, mit einer rauchigen Stimme. Bescheiden. Nicht gerade jemand, der einen Raum ausfüllt, wenn er ihn betritt. Man könnte ihm am Counter eines Motels begegnen, irgendwo in der texanischen Einschicht. Aber Jon Jerde ist nicht irgend jemand. Jon Jerde ist Architekt mit Büro in Venice, dem anscheinend ewig hippen Strandbezirk von Los Angeles. Und er ist ein Geheimtipp.

Kann einer ein Geheimtipp sein, wenn er Hunderttausende begeistert? Ohne weiters, vor allem, wenn es sich dabei um zwei verschiedene kulturelle Interessenssphären handelt, um Business und Kunst beispielsweise. Die weltgrößten Architekturfirmen, die meist in den USA angesiedelt sind, kennt kaum jemand mit Namen; und angeblich baut ein Schweizer im südostasiatischen Raum die meisten Skyscraper – eine Berühmtheit ist Remo Riva deswegen noch lange nicht.

Vermutlich wüsste auch niemand, wer Jon Jerde ist, hätte der nicht vor einigen Jahren anlässlich eines großen Planungsprojekts für Universal City in Los Angeles Rem Koolhaas getroffen. Da wurde die amerikanische Architekturszene aufmerksam. Und langsam machte das Gerücht die Runde, Jerde sei der Prophet des neuen öffentlichen Raums in amerikanischen und japanischen Downtowns. Das amerikanische Fachmagazin *architecture* nannte ihn den „möglicherweise momentan einflussreichsten Architekten".

Fallbeispiel Fremont Street, die Main Street von Downtown Las Vegas: Eine riesige Stahlgitter-Tonne überwölbt die Straße. Am Tag spendet sie Schatten und bei Dunkelheit, zu jeder vollen Stunde, erzeugen zwei Millionen computergesteuerte Lichter und eine Soundanlage mit 540.000 Watt eine überwältigende Schau: Blumen sprießen und Jagdflieger donnern im Himmel der Gittertonne. Fremont Street lässt sich derzeit mit nichts vergleichen, und Jon Jerde hat das dahinserbelnde Downtown zu neuem Leben erweckt. Downtown Las Vegas boomt heute genauso wie der Strip mit seinen neuen Mega-Hotels. Und rechnet sich. Hat man Fremont Street nicht gesehen, war man nicht in Las Vegas. Das hat jetzt nichts mehr mit verschiedenen kulturellen Interessen zu tun.

Jerdes Büro ist in einem alten Lagerhaus in Venice untergebracht, nicht leicht zu finden, obwohl es in der ersten Reihe am Strand liegt. Kaum vorstellbar, dass hier hart gearbeitet wird, mit all den Fun-People vor der Tür. Außen ist das Gebäude unscheinbar, innen mit modernster Technik ausgestattet und sehr elegant. Rund hundert Leute arbeiten hier. Jerde, flankiert von einer repräsentativen Chefsekretärin und einer kompetenten PR-Agentin, führt mich ins ‚Hinterland'. Es geht durch mehrere verwinkelte Gänge, dann landen wir in einem intimen, hohen, ein wenig abgedunkelten Raum, nur ein Fensterband fast oben an der Decke gibt den Blick in den Himmel frei. Nachtblaue Wände, ein rotes Regal, große gemütliche Sofas, Fauteuils, ein riesiger niedriger Wohnzimmertisch. Teppiche auf dem Boden und an den Wänden, marokkanische Vasen und Leuchten und erlesenes maghrebinisches Kunstgewerbe. Wow – ein gemütliches Wohnzimmer als Chefbüro? Es gefalle ihm so, sagt er, er wolle immer für eine angenehme Umgebung sorgen. „Und ich brauche einen großen Tisch, weil ich große Pläne mache und gerne von oben draufschauen will."

Case study Fremont Street, the main street of Downtown Las Vegas: A giant steel grid canopy arches over the street. It provides shade during the day and when it is dark, at every full hour, two million computer-controlled lights and a 540,000-watt sound system create a stunning show: flowers sprout and fighter pilots thunder in the sky of the overhead canopy. Nothing can currently be compared with Fremont Street, and Jon Jerde has made the languishing downtown come alive again. Today Downtown Las Vegas is booming, just like the Strip with its new mega hotels. And is paying off. You haven't been to Las Vegas until you've been to Fremont Street. That now has nothing more to do with the different cultural interests.

Jerde's office is housed in an old warehouse in Venice, not easy to find, although it lies in the first row on the beach. Hardly imaginable that hard work is done here, with all the fun people in front of the door. The building is inconspicuous on the outside, equipped with the most modern technology and very elegant on the inside. Around one hundred people work here. Jerde, flanked by a representative executive secretary and a competent female PR agent, leads me into the 'hinterlands.' Going through several twisting corridors, we finally then land in an intimate, high, somewhat darkened space, only a window strip almost on the top of the ceiling reveals the sky. Night-blue walls, a red shelf, large, comfortable sofas, fauteuils, a giant, low living room table. Carpets on the floor and on the walls, Moroccan vases and light fixtures, and fine Maghrebian arts and crafts. Wow—a cozy living room as the executive's office? He likes it this way, he says, he always wants to provide for a comfortable environment. "And I need a large table, because I make large plans and want to look at them from above."

Fünfter Tag • Day Five

I tell him that I had to effectively discover him and he immediately begins to grumble about the misery of present-day architecture production. He had been a very close with Frank O. Gehry for a long time; Rem Koolhaas called them "the evil twins" back then. "But today," he says, "Frank is completely co-opted by this Valley of Death. After the end of modernism everyone thinks they have to especially keep up their individual celebrity status." Not envy, but rather pity for his former friend resonates here. In fact, an impressive Frank O. Gehry exhibition is currently running at the Museum of Contemporary Art in L. A. Grand models of grand projects are being shown, but they are all modifications of a single language, a single style that is prototypically realized with Guggenheim–Bilbao and is now copied in many variations. The experimental phase of the eighties is over, when Gehry was experimenting with crude materials, with wild collages of shapes, with the whole tastelessness of the era. At that time, however, Gehry and Jerde had presumably been really very close.

Just like the meanwhile nearly 75-year-old Frank O. Gehry, the considerably younger Jon Jerde also belongs to that generation of architects who were shaped in their education by the tenets of modernism, but then, in the sixties, experienced the general uncertainty and consequently had to search for new paths. They found them in quite different ways. Gehry was first able to loosen himself from the restraints of the committed,

Ich erzähle ihm, dass ich ihn richtiggehend entdecken musste, und er beginnt sofort über das Elend der heutigen Architekturproduktion zu räsonieren. Mit Frank O. Gehry sei er lange sehr eng befreundet gewesen, Rem Koolhaas habe sie damals „The evil twins" genannt. „Aber heute", sagt er, „ist Frank vollkommen von diesem Valley of Death vereinnahmt. Nach dem Ende der Moderne meinen ja alle, vor allem ihren individuellen Celebrity-Status aufrechterhalten zu müssen." Nicht Neid, eher Mitleid gegenüber dem ehemaligen Freund klingt hier mit. Tatsächlich läuft gerade eine eindrucksvolle Frank O. Gehry-Ausstellung im Museum of Contemporary Art in L. A. Grandiose Modelle grandioser Projekte werden gezeigt, aber sie sind alle Abwandlungen einer einzigen Sprache, eines einzigen Stils, der prototypisch mit Guggenheim–Bilbao verwirklicht ist und nun variantenreich nachgebaut wird. Vorbei ist die experimentelle Phase der achtziger Jahre, als Gehry mit kruden Materialien, mit wüsten Form-Collagen, mit dem ganzen Ungeschmack der Zeit experimentierte. Damals allerdings dürften sich Gehry und Jerde wirklich sehr nahe gewesen sein.

So wie der inzwischen beinahe 75 Jahre alte Frank O. Gehry gehört auch der wesentlich jüngere Jon Jerde zu jener Generation von Architekten, die in ihrer Ausbildung von den Grundsätzen der Moderne geprägt wurden, dann aber, in den sechziger Jahren, die allgemeine Verunsicherung miterlebten und in der Folge nach neuen Wegen suchen mussten. Sie fanden sie auf ganz unterschiedliche Art und Weise. Gehry konnte sich erst Ende der siebziger Jahre aus der Verspannung des engagierten, modernen Business-Architekten lösen, erst jetzt sich auf die Suche nach neuen Formen machen. Jon Jerde gelang das bereits 1964, auf einer Europa-Reise: „Ich gewann ein Stipendium und konnte ein Jahr tun, was ich wollte. Ich ging nach Europa. Ich besuchte jedes Museum, schaute mir jedes architekturgeschicht-

Jon Jerde in seinem osmanisch-maghrebinisch-asiatisch eingerichteten Privat-Atelier · Jon Jerde in his Ottoman-Maghreb-Asian furnished private studio, Venice Beach in Santa Monica, Los Angeles. © DS

> "In contrast to architects who celebrate their individual signature as a celebrity factor, I believe in and listen to the yearnings of normal people."

lich wichtige Gebäude an. Und dabei entdeckte ich die Essenz der europäischen Stadt. Die wunderbare anonyme Substanz, die Rückseiten der Pantheons sozusagen. Besonders beeindruckte mich die urbanistische Kontinuität italienischer Städte. Und ich erkannte, dass alles, was ich als moderner Architekt gelernt hatte, vollkommen falsch war. Der Plan einer Stadt ist nicht rational, er basiert auf der räumlichen Erfahrung. Die Europareise 1964 ist meine eigentliche Ausbildung."

Die Karriere von Jon Jerde beginnt 1977. Horton Plaza, San Diego, ist das erste große Projekt von Jon Jerde Associates. Downtown San Diego hatte die typischen Probleme amerikanischer Downtowns. Vergammelte alte Bauten, neue Office-Towers, staubige Brachflächen für Parkplätze – das war kein Ort mehr, an dem sich Menschen aufhalten wollen. Die Freeways reichen ins Stadtzentrum hinein und schaufeln abends die Menschen hinaus, in die Suburbs, in die Shopping Malls an der Peripherie. Frank O. Gehry hatte bereits 1974 einen Entwurf gemacht: moderne Skyscraper, die untereinander mit rationalen Skywalks verbunden waren. Jerde nimmt sich nun einen sechs Block großen District vor und plant sein Einkaufszentrum als Stadtlandschaft, als gigantischen dreidimensionalen öffentlichen Raum. 1985 wird Horton Plaza eröffnet, und Downtown San Diego erlebt eine Erfolgsgeschichte des neuen Urbanismus – bis hin zur inzwischen aufgewerteten Hafenzone.

modern business architect at the end of the sixties, and then first begin to search for new forms. Jon Jerde already succeeded in doing that in 1964, on a trip to Europe: "I won a fellowship and could do whatever I wanted for a year. I went to Europe. I visited every museum, I looked at every building important to architectural history. And I thereby discovered the essence of the European city. The wonderful, anonymous substance, the back sides of the Pantheon, so to say. The urbanisitic continuity of Italian cites particularly impressed me. And I recognized that everything I had learned as a modern architect was completely wrong. The plan of a city is not rational; it is based on the spatial experience. The Europe trip in 1964 is my actual training."

Jon Jerde's career begins in 1977. Horton Plaza, San Diego, is the first major project of Jon Jerde Associates. Downtown San Diego had the typical problems of American downtowns. Seedy old buildings, new office towers, dusty wastelands for parking lots—it was no longer a place where people want to linger. The freeways extend into the city center and shovel the people out into the suburbs in the evenings, into the shopping malls on the outskirts. Frank O. Gehry had already made a draft in 1974: modern skyscrapers that were connected to each other with rational skywalks. Jerde now takes a six-block-large district and plans his shopping center as a cityscape, as a gigantic, three-dimensional space. Horton Plaza is opened in 1985 and Downtown San Diego witnesses a success story of new urbanism—all the way to the meanwhile gentrified Port District.

There are no signs to Horton Plaza, but one senses an increasing urban densification in the neighborhood and one almost automatically lands in the multi-story parking garage that belongs to it. The individual stories are well-marked and clearly arranged. And one barely leaves the sober garage floors when one finds oneself in an urban dreamland with clean pathways, surprising bridges, bizarre façades, vulgar shapes, gaudy colors. One can do nothing else but simply stroll, and also two hours later one still has the feeling, even in this well-calculated clarity, of not having walked every path, not having explored every nook.

All the ingredients of a shopping mall are in place. A movie center, a food court with ethnic variety, two large department stores, McDonald's and all of the retail stores that are always and everywhere the same. In between are the pushcarts with the everyday kitsch. The consumption choice is not different than in the boring shopping malls of the suburbs. Important is the spatial, multi-sensory experience, the large variety of materials and surfaces. As a visitor, one has the feeling of moving in a neat environment. The area is open, not covered and not air-conditioned.

If one leaves Horton Plaza, one discovers that the surrounding area has also been re-urbanized. Shops and street cafés are everywhere, and Downtown San Diego has meanwhile become a touristic location, too. "During a TV interview," Jon Jerde relates, "we were standing on a bridge of Horton Plaza and I was explaining what we had done here. The camera was hidden behind an arch; one couldn't see that this conversation was being filmed. Then a young girl came by, listened briefly, and then asked if I was really the guy who had planned everything here. 'God bless you,' she said, 'I hope you'll do a lot more projects still, people love to come here and they spend a beautiful time here. I come here every Sunday with my sisters and we are glad. You've really accomplished something awesome here.' Then the journalist asked if I would have paid for this statement."

Horton Plaza, San Diego, Jerde Partnership, 2003. © DS

Es gibt keine Wegschilder zur Horton Plaza, aber in der Umgebung spürt man eine zunehmende urbane Verdichtung und man landet fast automatisch in der zugehörigen Hochgarage. Die einzelnen Geschosse sind gut gekennzeichnet und übersichtlich. Und kaum verlässt man die nüchternen Garagengeschosse, findet man sich mitten in einem urbanen Traumland mit sauberen Wegen, überraschenden Brücken, skurrilen Fassaden, vulgären Formen, knalligen Farben. Man kann nicht anders, man flaniert einfach, und auch nach zwei Stunden hat man selbst in dieser wohlkalkulierten Unübersichtlichkeit immer noch das Gefühl, noch nicht jeden Weg begangen, nicht jeden Winkel erforscht zu haben.

Dabei sind alle Ingredienzen einer Shopping Mall vorhanden. Ein Kino-Center, ein Food-Court mit ethnischer Varietät, zwei große Kaufhäuser, McDonald's und all die immer und überall gleichen Retail Stores. Dazwischen kleine mobile Verkaufsstände mit dem alltäglichen Kitsch. Das Konsumangebot ist nicht anders als in den langweiligen Shopping Malls der Suburbs.

Wichtig ist der räumliche Erlebnisparcours, die große Varietät von Materialien und Oberflächen. Man hat als Besucher das Gefühl, sich in einer gepflegten Umgebung zu bewegen. Das Gelände ist offen, nicht überdacht und nicht klimatisiert.

Verlässt man Horton Plaza, so entdeckt man, dass sich auch die übrige Umgebung neu urbanisiert hat. Überall sind Geschäfte und Straßencafés, und Downtown San Diego ist inzwischen auch ein touristischer Ort geworden. „Bei einem Fernseh-Interview", erzählt Jon Jerde, „standen wir auf einer Brücke der Horton Plaza und ich erzählte, was wir hier getan haben. Die Kamera war hinter einem Bogen verborgen, man konnte nicht sehen, dass dieses Gespräch gefilmt wurde. Da kam ein junges Mädchen vorbei, sie hörte kurz zu und fragte dann, ob ich wirklich der Typ sei, der das alles hier geplant hätte. God bless you, sagte sie, ich hoffe Sie machen noch viele Projekte, die Menschen kommen gerne hierher und sie verbringen eine schöne Zeit hier. Ich komme mit meinen Schwestern jeden Sonntag und wir freuen uns. Sie haben hier wirklich etwas Großartiges geleistet. Da fragte der Journalist, ob ich für dieses Statement bezahlt hätte."

Die Episode erklärt das Geheimnis von Jon Jerde – Pragmatik jenseits aller intellektueller Reflexionen: „Im Gegensatz zu den Architekten, die ihre individuelle Signatur als Celebrity-Faktor zelebrieren, glaube und höre ich auf die Sehnsüchte der normalen Menschen. Sie werden ausgebeutet, von falschen Versprechungen. Und sie folgen diesen leeren Versprechungen. Genau das sollten wir nicht tun. Wir sollten ihnen im Gegenteil gut zuhören. Dann entstehen außerordentliche Dinge. Deshalb habe ich mich dieser Konsumwelt gewidmet. Normale Shopping Malls in Amerika sind fürchterlich. Aber es sind die Plätze, wo sich Öffentlichkeit entwickelt, wo ein öffentlicher Raum entsteht." In Europa, wende ich ein, wird aber diese Entwicklung sehr kritisch beobachtet. Es findet damit eine Kommerzialisierung und Privatisierung des öffentlichen Raums statt, und abweichendes Verhalten wird von privaten Sicherheitsdiensten kontrolliert. „Das mag auf Europa

This episode explains the secret of Jon Jerde—pragmatism beyond all intellectual reflections: "In contrast to architects who celebrate their individual signature as a celebrity factor, I believe in and listen to the yearnings of normal people. They are exploited, by false promises. And they follow these false promises. That is exactly what we shouldn't do. On the contrary, we should listen to them carefully. Then extraordinary things emerge. That is why I've devoted myself to this consumer world. Normal shopping malls in America are terrible. But these are places where public life develops, where a public space arises." In Europe, however, I argue, this development is observed very critically. A commercialization and privatization of the public space takes place thereby and deviant behavior is controlled by private security services. "That may apply to Europe," the answer goes, "but not to America. In our projects everyone is invited to experience this new and better public space. You don't have to consume anything here. You can be here as long as you want. You can do whatever you want."

Jerde Associates do projects that are always connected with new consumption offers; they develop the public space solely on the basis of consumption. Jerde rejects any criticism: "In every city center, everywhere in the world, the first five meters, the first two stories of all houses are occupied by restaurants, shops, commercial activities. That forms the basis of a city center, and that is the reason why the people are here. Sometimes the people believe that I'm only interested in consumption. But that isn't true. In my projects it is first and foremost about the people who take over a public space for themselves and need the appropriate offer to do so. That is really a difference between Europe and America. Europe has no problem with the public space. The people go on the streets and live their public lives. But in America the people live in the suburbs and you don't find any human being on the street there; suburbs are empty space. At the same time the city centers are dying; I want to bring life back into the city. In America

you already have to be happy if there are still any shops at all in the center. But if people are also there in their free time, the buildings will fairly quickly be used differently again. That is what I learned in Europe. When I came back, I asked myself where the people were and they were all out in the shopping centers on the outskirts. Then I said let's begin here in the center. That was the starting point and I had to seek a way into this industry in return."

Well, typical American pragmatism. There is a problem and one looks for the solution. But Jon Jerde goes a step further: "Essentially, it is not a matter for me to design single objects, but the space in between. Normal shopping malls are linear, one signal follows the other. That's how the shopping world functions. That's how you are guided from one consumption point to the next. We, on the other hand, offer a spatial experience. The public space is the major focus with us. We develop an environment that already is an experience in itself. The normal shopping center is fully air-conditioned and indoor. Can you imagine that, indoor in Southern California? What idiocy!"

Jon Jerde is naturally an architect in times of postmodernism. Nothing applies anymore, all boundaries of taste have fallen, everything is allowed. But historical citations have no place in these urban experiments: "Historic architecture interests me. But not architectural history which is canonized as the heroic story of persons. This history follows the change and the development of sketches, drawings and manifestos, but that is not architecture. Architecture is the search, I'll say it once again, for spatial experience." After perusal of the projects, no rummaging in the treasure trove of historic quotation was to be assumed in any case. Jerde's projects are as brutal and sassy as fantasy comics, as science fiction scenarios. "Oh, yes, it's very much in my nature. For many years I was very good friends with the science fiction author Ray Bradbury. We met each other every week. He is one of my mentors. He always said that he helped me to make the things the way I am making them now. Ray Bradbury was my teacher." Are Jon

zutreffen", lautet die Antwort, „aber nicht auf Amerika. In unseren Projekten ist jeder eingeladen, diesen neuen und besseren öffentlichen Raum zu erleben. Du musst hier nichts konsumieren. Du kannst hier sein, solange du willst. Du kannst machen, was du willst."

Jerde Associates machen Projekte, die immer mit neuen Konsumangeboten verbunden sind, sie entwickeln den öffentlichen Raum nur auf der Basis des Konsums. Kritik daran weist Jerde zurück: „In jedem Stadtzentrum, überall auf der Welt, sind die ersten fünf Meter, die ersten beiden Geschosse aller Häuser mit Restaurants, Geschäften, kommerziellen Aktivitäten belegt. Das bildet die Basis eines Stadtzentrums, und das ist der Grund, warum die Leute hier sind. Manchmal glauben die Leute, ich sei nur an Konsum interessiert. Aber das stimmt nicht. In meinen Projekten geht es in erster Linie um die Menschen, die einen öffentlichen Raum für sich erobern und dafür das entsprechende Angebot brauchen. Das ist wirklich ein Unterschied zwischen Europa und Amerika. Europa hat keine Probleme mit dem öffentlichen Raum. Die Menschen gehen auf die Straße und leben ihr öffentliches Leben. Aber in Amerika leben die Menschen in den Suburbs, und dort findest du kein menschliches Wesen auf der Straße. Suburbs sind leerer Raum. Gleichzeitig sterben die Stadtzentren. Ich will das Leben in die Stadt zurückbringen. In Amerika musst du schon froh sein, wenn überhaupt noch Geschäfte im Zentrum sind. Aber wenn die Leute auch in ihrer Freizeit da sind, dann werden die Gebäude recht schnell wieder anders genutzt. Das ist es, was ich in Europa gelernt habe. Als ich zurückkam, fragte ich mich, wo denn die Leute sind, und alle waren draußen in den Shopping Centers an der Peripherie. Da sagte ich, lasst uns hier im Zentrum beginnen. Das war der Ausgangspunkt, und dafür musste ich einen Weg in diese Industrie suchen."

Typischer amerikanischer Pragmatismus also. Es gibt ein Problem und man sucht die Lösung. Aber Jon Jerde geht einen Schritt weiter: „Im Wesentlichen geht es mir nicht darum, einzelne Objekte zu gestalten, sondern um den Raum dazwischen. Normale Shopping Malls sind linear, ein Signal folgt dem andern. So funktioniert die Einkaufswelt. So wirst du von einem Konsumpunkt zum nächsten geführt. Wir dagegen bieten eine räumliche Erfahrung. Bei uns steht der öffentliche

Raum im Vordergrund. Wir entwickeln eine Umgebung, die an sich schon ein Erlebnis ist. Das normale Shopping Center ist vollklimatisiert und indoor. Kannst du dir vorstellen, indoor in Southern-California? So ein Schwachsinn."

Natürlich ist Jon Jerde ein Architekt in Zeiten der Postmoderne. Nichts gilt mehr, alle Geschmackgrenzen sind gefallen, alles ist erlaubt. Aber historische Zitate haben bei seinen urbanen Experimente nichts verloren: „Mich interessiert die historische Architektur. Aber nicht die Architekturgeschichte, die als Heldengeschichte der Personen kanonisiert ist. Diese Geschichte verfolgt den Wechsel und die Entwicklung von Skizzen, Zeichnungen und Manifesten, aber das ist nicht Architektur. Architektur ist die Suche, ich sag es nochmals, nach räumlicher Erfahrung." Nach Durchsicht der Projekte war ohnehin kein Kramen im historischen Zitatenschatz der Architektur zu vermuten. Jerdes Projekte sind so brutal und frech wie Fantasy-Comics, wie Science-Fiction-Szenarien: „Oh ja, das liegt mir sehr. Ich war viele Jahre sehr gut mit dem Science-Fiction-Autor Ray Bradbury befreundet. Wir haben uns jede Woche getroffen. Er ist einer meiner Mentoren. Er sagte immer, dass er mir dabei geholfen habe, die Dinge so zu machen, wie ich sie jetzt mache. Ray Bradbury war mein Lehrer." Sind also die Projekte von Jon Jerde auch Illustrationen, Ausstattungen? „Das mag stimmen. Ein bestimmter Stil ist dabei nicht wichtig. Alle Projekte sind auf ihre Art Stage-Designs. Wenn du in Hollywood lebst, kannst du dich nicht von der Filmwelt abkoppeln."

Das trifft auch auf das Projekt für die Gesamtgestaltung der Olympischen Spiele in Los Angeles 1984 zu. Der Hintergrund war die damalige Krise der Olympischen Spiele. Nach dem terroristischen Ende der Spiele in München 1972, nach dem finanziellen Desaster von Montreal 1976 und dem Boykott der Moskauer Spiele 1980 wollte sie niemand mehr veranstalten. Los Ange-

Horton Plaza, San Diego, Jerde Partnership, 2003. © DS

Jerde's projects therefore illustrations, furnishings? "That may be true. A certain style is not important thereby. All of the projects are stage designs in their own way. If you live in Hollywood, you cannot disconnect from this film world

That is also the case for the project for the overall design of the 1984 Olympic Games in Los Angeles. The background was the crisis of the Olympic Games back then. After the terrorist end of the 1972 Games in Munich, after the financial disaster of Montreal 1976 and the boycott of the Moscow Games in 1980, no one wanted to hold them anymore. Los Angeles was the only candidate for 1984 and there was a budget of just ten million dollars to give them a creative frame. Jerde developed the concept of the co-creatives out of necessity. He put together a manual of colors and symbols and distributed them to 30 other designers and creatives. "We took garbage, old tubes made of cardboard, coated with plastic, and made them available as symbols for the 130 locations of the Olympic Games. And

Fünfter Tag • Day Five

Kanyon Shopping Mall, Istanbul,
Jerde Partnership mit with Murat Tabanlioglu,
2006. © DS

something wonderful happened. A higher form of creativity emerged out of it." The Los Angeles Olympic Games were the first that provided all of the Olympic venues with a consequent corporate identity, although they were in truth disguised. After the Games finished with a profit, the present-day Olympic business arose out of it.

Jon Jerde celebrated the truly grand and fantastic successes in recent years in Japan. "In Japan the success of Horton Plaza was noticed. I still remember the first contact very well. We were invited and sat at a big conference table, and I asked: 'What can I do for you?' 'We don't know,' the Japanese replied. 'We thought you could explain to us what we have to do.'" A magic moment in the life of an architect. Jerde begins to fantazise and to plan. The projects are called Canal City Hakata, Namba Parks in Osaka, Dentsu Headquarters at Shiodome, Riverwalk Kitakyushu, La Cittadella. Each

les war der einzige Bewerber für 1984, und es gab ein Budget von gerade zehn Millionen Dollar, um ihnen einen gestalterischen Rahmen zu geben. Aus dieser Not hat Jerde das Konzept der Co-Creatives entwickelt. Er hat ein Manual aus Farben und Zeichen zusammengestellt und an 30 andere Designer und Kreative verteilt: „Wir haben Abfall genommen, alte Rohre aus Karton, mit Plastik beschichtet, und sie als Zeichen für die 130 Orte der Olympischen Spiele zur Verfügung gestellt. Und das Wunderbare geschah. Es entstand eine höhere Form der Kreativität daraus." Die Olympischen Spiele Los Angeles waren die ersten, die mit einer konsequenten Corporate Identity alle olympischen Orte umfassten, obwohl sie in Wahrheit nur verkleidet waren. Nachdem die Spiele mit Gewinn abschlossen, entstand daraus das heutige olympische Business.

Die wirklich großen und fantastischen Erfolge feierte Jon Jerde in den letzten Jahren in Japan: „In Japan hat man den Erfolg der Horton Plaza beobachtet. Ich erinnere mich noch gut an den ersten Kontakt. Wir wurden eingeladen, saßen an einem großen Besprechungstisch, und ich fragte: Was kann ich für sie tun? Das wissen wir nicht, antworteten die Japaner, wir dachten, sie könn-

ten uns erklären, was wir tun müssen." Eine Sternstunde im Leben eines Architekten. Jerde beginnt zu fantasieren und zu planen. Die Projekte heißen Canal City Hakata, Namba Parks in Osaka, Dentsu Headquarters at Shiodome, Riverwalk Kitakyushu, La Cittadella. Jedes Projekt umfasst Tausende von Quadratmetern, jedes ist ein neues Stadtzentrum, jedes ein neuer urbaner Erlebnis- und Erfahrungsraum – und Jerde wird immer radikaler. Für Canal City in Fukuoka, das größte private Investment-Projekt in Japan, schiebt er einen echten Kanal durch die Stadt, ein Canyon mit tiefen Schluchten und großen Bühnen. Für das Headquarter von Dentsu, einen japanischen Mediengiganten in Tokio, treibt er die Vereinigung von Kultur und Natur voran. „Natur und Architektur sind dasselbe. Ich sehe keinen Unterschied. Wenn wir Architektur machen, gestalten wir gleichzeitig auch eine neue Natur. Wir sind nicht unabhängig von der Natur. Alles was wir machen ist eine Version künftiger Natur. All meine Ideen und Entwürfe leiten sich formal von Muscheln, Felsblöcken und Gebirgen ab, von den tiefen Spuren der Flüsse. Das sind die Dinge, die mich wirklich inspirieren: Die Canyons von Arizona und New Mexico."

Und warum funktionieren diese wahrlich utopischen Konzepte von Jon Jerde? Denn jedes Projekt ist ein enormer ökonomischer Erfolg: „Eigentlich weiß ich es nicht. Wahrscheinlich weil ich eine starke Affinität zu ganz normalen Menschen habe. Ich kenne ihre Wünsche, weil ich selbst einfach ein völlig normaler Mensch bin. Ich bin in einem Trailer in Texas aufgewachsen. Alle zehn Monate sind wir woandershin gefahren. Mein Vater hat für Ölraffinerien gearbeitet. Ich hatte nie einen Ort, eine Heimat, ich bin im ständig wechselnden Niemandsland aufgewachsen. Deshalb habe ich keine Grenzen in meinem Kopf, ich bin es gewohnt, das Neue und Unbekannte anzunehmen, hinzuschauen, wo Dinge sich ändern."

Und da gibt es nie das Gefühl, von Hollywood aus nicht entsprechend anerkannt und gefeiert zu werden? „Ich habe einmal mit Herbert Muschamp, dem Starkritiker der *New York Times*, über die heutigen Star-Architekten gesprochen. Auf einmal stellt sich im Gespräch heraus, dass eigentlich alle Architekten Star-Architekten sind. Das sagt alles. Mir genügt es, dass ich einfach soviel Spaß an meiner Arbeit habe."

project encompasses thousands of square meters, each is a new city center, each a new urban event and experience space—and Jerde becomes more and more radical. For Canal City in Fukuoka, the largest private investment project in Japan, he pushes a real canal through the city, a canyon with deep gorges and large stages. For the Dentsu Headquarters, a Japanese media giant in Tokyo, he pushes the unification of art and nature forward. "Nature and architecture are the same. I see no difference. If we make architecture, we also design a new nature at the same time. We are not independent from nature. Everything we do is a vision of future nature. All of my ideas and designs are formally derived from shells, boulders and mountains, from the deep traces of rivers. Those are the things that really inspire me: the canyons of Arizona and New Mexico."

And why do these truly utopian concepts of Jon Jerde work? Because each project is an enormous economic success: "Actually I don't know. Probably because I have a strong affinity to entirely normal people. I know their desires, because I myself am simply a completely normal person. I grew up in a trailer in Texas. Every ten months we had to drive somewhere else. My father worked for oil refineries. I never had a place, a home, I grew up in a steadily changing no man's land. That's why I have no borders in my head; I am used to embracing the new and unknown, looking where things are changing."

And is there never the feeling of not being accordingly recognized and celebrated outside of Hollywood? "I once spoke with Herbert Muschamp, the star critic of the *New York Times*, about today's star architects. Suddenly during the conversation it turned out that actually all architects are star architects. That says everything. It's enough for me that I simply have so much fun in my work."

aus · from

Hintergrund 18_2003
„Sweet Home Alabama"
Translation by Brian Dorsey

Sweet Home Alabama.
Protokoll einer Reise

Sweet Home Alabama
Record of a Journey

In the summer of 2002 we attempt to establish contact with the "Rural Studio." It is difficult, because the founder, Samuel Mockbee, died at the end of 2001 and the authority of the successors has not been clarified by Auburn University. But we have to travel there in order to get to know the location and to organize the material for the exhibition. In mid-December we succeed in arranging a visit and material collection in Hale County. I travel to Alabama with Katharina Ritter, who researched beforehand with Johannes Porsch and created an initial exhibition concept.

Wednesday, 11.12.02

Austrian Airlines flight to Washington goes without a hitch and lands on time. Nonetheless, the transfer from Washington to Atlanta was close, but managed with a small United Express plane. Atlanta–Little Rock with Delta was delayed for several hours because a flight attendant was missing. I am dressed much too warmly. The photographer Timothy Hursley is waiting for us at the airport in Little Rock and brings us to the Capitol Hotel. Very tasteful, but located in an abandoned and random aggregation of urbanity. Little Rock has about 200,000 inhabitants, but there is no city.

We have been on the road for 19 hours since out departure in Vienna. I relax still with nightly e-mail correspondence to Vienna.

Im Sommer 2002 versuchen wir, mit dem „Rural Studio" Kontakt aufzunehmen. Es ist schwierig, weil der Gründer, Samuel Mockbee Ende 2001 verstarb und die Zuständigkeit der Nachfolger von der Auburn-University nicht geklärt ist. Aber wir müssen hinfahren, um vor Ort die Situation kennenzulernen und das Material für die Ausstellung zu organisieren. Mitte Dezember gelingt es uns, eine Besichtigung und Materialsammlung in Hale County zu vereinbaren. Ich reise mit Katharina Ritter, die mit Johannes Porsch zuvor recherchiert und ein erstes Ausstellungskonzept erstellt hat, nach Alabama.

Mittwoch, 11.12.02

AUA-Flug nach Washington problemlos und pünktlich. Trotzdem war der Transfer zu Washington–Atlanta knapp, aber mit einer kleinen United-Express-Maschine bewältigt. Atlanta–Little Rock mit Delta hatte mehrere Stunden Verspätung, weil ein Flight-Attendant gefehlt hat. Ich bin viel zu warm angezogen. In Little Rock hat Timothy Hursley, der Fotograf, am Airport auf uns gewartet und bringt uns zum Hotel „The Capitol". Sehr gediegen, aber in einer verlassenen und zufälligen Aggregation von Urbanität. Little Rock hat etwa 200.000 Einwohner, aber eine Stadt gibt es nicht.

19 Stunden waren wir seit unserem Abflug in Wien unterwegs. Ich erhole mich noch beim nächtlichen E-Mail-Verkehr nach Wien.

Thursday, 12.12.02

The Capitol Hotel in Little Rock is one of these dignified old boxes from the railroad pioneer era, but freshly renovated. Everything is perfect. Hursley picks us up at nine o'clock. We drive a short stretch through 'downtown.' I'll never understand cities like Little Rock. Streets, dirt roads, scattered houses, wasteland in between. There is no urban space whatsoever. Old, new, everything jumbled. Just area, lost objects populating the land. Enthroned all alone at the top of a hill, the Capitol of Arkansas. Where Clinton comes from?! We spend the whole day at Hursley's place. Katharina has prepared a detailed project list. Several selected Rural Studio objects and an overview of all projects. Hursley has all the pictures only as Ektachromes. We sift through several hundred of them. His studio is a not uninteresting two-story wooden house on a steep slope. Accessible only straight over a gravel lane, the houses had visibly been there before the road. The house is totally cluttered; there is hardly any place to sit. A secretary between two Macs, the bathroom on the first floor, and a further space where an assistant is sitting at a large Mac. Students are coming by again and again and finishing something. Why is Hursley sitting in Little Rock, although he is an internationally sought-after, professional architectural photographer? His brother is also here, he succinctly replies. He has just photographed the new museum by Tadao Ando in Fort Worth for *Newsweek*. On his last trip to Europe he was supposed to take pictures of the Guggenheim Bilbao for *Architectural Record*.

Donnerstag, 12.12.02

„The Capitol" in Little Rock ist einer dieser würdigen alten Kästen aus der Eisenbahnpionierzeit, aber frisch renoviert. Alles perfekt. Hursley holt uns um neun Uhr ab. Wir fahren eine kurze Strecke durch ‚Downtown'. Städte wie Little Rock werde ich nie verstehen. Straßen, Pisten, versprengte Häuser, Brachland dazwischen. Es gibt keinerlei urbanen Raum. Alt, neu, alles durcheinander. Einfach Gegend, verlorene Objekte das Land besiedelnd. Einsam auf einem Hügel thronend, das Capitol der Hauptstadt von Arkansas. Where Clinton comes from?! Wir verbringen den ganzen Tag bei Hursley. Katharina hat eine detaillierte Projektliste ausgearbeitet. Einige ausgewählte Objekte des Rural Studio und eine Übersicht über alle Projekte. Hursley hat alle Bilder nur als Ektachromes. Wir sichten mehrere Hundert davon. Sein Studio ist ein nicht uninteressantes zweigeschossiges Holzhaus an einem steilen Hang. Nur in der Direttissima über eine Schotterfahrspur erreichbar, es waren sichtlich die Häuser vor den Straßen da. Das Haus ist total vollgeräumt, es gibt kaum einen Platz zum Sitzen. Eine Sekretärin zwischen zwei Macs, im 1. Stock das Bad und ein weiterer Raum, wo ein Assistent an einem großen Mac sitzt. Immer wieder kommen Studenten

Rural Studio, HERO Playground, Greensboro, 1997. © DS

Fünfter Tag • Day Five

Rural Studio, Lewis House, Moundville, 1998. © DS

We take a short ride for lunch in a Mexican restaurant, somewhere on a street in the landscape. Hursley will burn a CD with the chosen pictures, we will make a final selection and he will then make the prints and send them to us. Before that a cost estimate. Apparently he doesn't want any fee for the exhibition, although over one hundred of his pictures will comprise the main part of the show.

Timothy Hursley is aware that the Rural Studio, which he has uniquely accompanied from the very beginning, has become the central theme in his photographic life.

He brings us to the airport in the late afternoon. Again absurd highways through no-man's land. We fly to Atlanta. Two very strict security checks, probably because we are foreigners. The entire luggage is taken apart, shoes taken off. I have collected lighters and matches in my travel bag. All the matches are taken away from me; I am only allowed to take two lighters. But the security people do that with a sense of humor, that's the way it is now. Before 9/11 there were no security controls at all within the US.

We order a Chevrolet Blazer at Avis in Atlanta, because we will ultimately be coming to a rather 'unpaved' area. We leave at around 9 p.m., find the highway without a problem and despite the sometimes heavily pouring rain reach the destination of Newbern at about 1 a.m. In between is no-man's land, night, surrealistic situations. The street is a black ribbon, to the left and right black night. Interrupted by big advertising billboards that leave one to assume that there's always a town behind them, as meager indications of location, Highway 85, Highway 80. In Montgomery, but where is Montgomery?—only recognizable through the concentration of malls, restaurants, lights at the edge, a real city, that is. Somewhere out there we have a quick dinner at the side of the road. Jambalaya: shrimps, vegetables, sausage, rice, stew. Everything is actually empty, but everything is still open. Montgomery? The American South. Somehow I remember that a major event in the

vorbei und erledigen irgendwas. Warum Hursley in Little Rock sitzt, obwohl er ein international gefragter, professioneller Architekturfotograf ist? Sein Bruder sei auch hier, meint er lapidar. Gerade hat er für *Newsweek* das neue Museum von Tadao Ando in Fort Worth fotografiert. Das letzte Mal war er in Europa, als er für *Architectural Record* das Guggenheim-Bilbao fotografieren sollte.

Wir fahren kurz zum Mittagessen in ein mexikanisches Restaurant, irgendwo an einer Straße in der Landschaft. Hursley wird eine CD mit den ausgewählten Bildern machen, wir eine letzte Auswahl, und er macht dann die Prints davon und schickt sie uns. Vorher noch ein Kostenvoranschlag. Anscheinend will er für die Ausstellung kein Honorar, obwohl über hundert Bilder von ihm den Hauptteil bestreiten werden.

Es ist Timothy Hursley bewusst, dass das Rural Studio, das er einzigartig von Anfang an begleitet hat, sein fotografisches Lebensthema geworden ist.

Er bringt uns am späten Nachmittag zum Flughafen. Wieder absurde Highways durch Niemandsland. Wir fliegen nach Atlanta. Zwei penible Security-Checks, wahrscheinlich weil wir Ausländer sind. Das ganze Gepäck wird auseinandergenommen, Schuhe ausziehen. Ich habe in der Reisetasche Feuerzeuge und Zündhölzer angesammelt. Alle Zünder werden mir abgenommen, ich darf nur zwei Feuerzeuge mitnehmen. Aber die Security-Leute machen das mit Schmäh, es ist halt jetzt so. Vor 9/11 gab es innerhalb den US überhaupt keine Security-Kontrollen.

Civil Rights Movement took place here. We continue driving, the traffic gets thinner; we are often alone on the highway for a half hour. In the middle of black nothingness. Now I am happy that I'm not the only one on the road. Suddenly in the middle of Selma, an apparently real city, real houses on the street with upper floors, a real Main Street, with Christmas lights, a gas station with ancient pumps, a black priest explains to me that I have to single-handedly place the lever on the pump in the right position to put gas in the tank. All European pumps have been doing that automatically for decades. From there on comes no-man's land, in Uniontown we are supposed to turn north onto Highway 81, but miles later we take the first street to the north, find our way back to the east and Highway 81 turns out to be Highway 61. According to Katharina's telephone calls, it was called Highway 81, and it is also marked as Highway 81 on the road atlas Hursley gave us, but it is Highway 61 that brings us to Newbern.

Newbern calls itself a city, and has 310 inhabitants. Once along the main road, lined by single Southern houses with 30m² tree lawns and back, we find our Bed & Breakfast house of the Bailey family. We read "no smoking in the house" and sit for a good hour still smoking on the porch, with brochures and folders about Rural Studio, which are available courtesy of the house.

Mrs. Bailey's Bed & Breakfast lives from Rural Studio. We find a photocopied brochure that was put together by students after Mockbee's death. *Tributes to Mockbee.* He must have been a real fool and a daredevil and ritualized his extensive life, 'back to life, back to real experiences.' Somewhat comparable perhaps with Heidulf Gerngross. A myth, surely with an enormous personal presence and charisma.

And now I'm sitting in bed at a Bed & Breakfast House, far from any civilization and nonetheless in the middle of Alabama, and I am happy to be able to bring a new myth into architectural debate. Although Max Protetch, the New York gallery owner, secured the rights to Mockbee's work. We will see what the next days will bring.

To conclude: No mobile network in Newbern. No contact with the world is possible. I can't remember when and where this was the case the last time.

Bei Avis in Atlanta einen Chevrolet-Blazer bestellt, weil wir schließlich in eine ziemlich „unbefestigte" Gegend kommen werden. Wir fahren gegen neun Uhr abends ab. Problemlos den richtigen Highway gefunden, und wir sind trotz teilweise strömenden Regens gegen ein Uhr Nachts am Zielort Newbern. Dazwischen Niemandsland, Nacht, surrealistische Situationen. Die Straße ist ein schwarzes Band, links und rechts davon schwarze Nacht. Unterbrochen von großen Werbetafeln, die immer einen Ort dahinter vermuten lassen, als spärliche Hinweise der Verortung, Highway 85, Highway 80. In Montgomery, aber wo ist Montgomery? – nur erkennbar durch eine Verdichtung von Malls, Restaurants, Lichtern am Rande, also eine richtige Stadt. Irgendwo da draußen nehmen wir am Rande der Straße ein schnelles Abendessen. Jambalaya: Shrimps, Gemüse, Würste, Reis, Eintopf. Eigentlich ist alles leer, aber dennoch ist alles in Betrieb. Montgomery? Der Süden der USA. Irgendwie erinnere ich mich, dass hier eine große Aktion der Bürgerrechtsbewegung war. Wir fahren weiter, der Verkehr wird immer dünner, wir sind oft eine halbe Stunde lang allein auf dem Highway. Mitten im schwarzen Nichts. Jetzt bin ich froh, dass ich nicht allein unterwegs bin. Plötzlich mitten in Selma, einer scheinbar richtigen Stadt, richtige Häuser an der Straße mit Obergeschoss, eine echte Main-Street, weihnachtlich beleuchtet, eine Tankstelle mit uralten Zapfsäulen, ein schwarzer Priester erklärt mir, dass ich zum Tanken den Hebel an der Zapfsäule eigenhändig in die richtige Stellung bringen muss. Alle europäischen Zapfsäulen machen das seit Jahrzehnten automatisch. Ab dann kommt das Niemandsland, in Uniontown sollten wir nach Norden abzweigen, Nr. 81, aber erst Meilen weiter nehmen wir die nächste Straße nach

Fünfter Tag • Day Five

Friday, 13.12.02

Up at 8 a.m., breakfast is ready. Katharina has already been up longer and we only have coffee and a few snacks. Mrs. Bailey has prepared bacon and eggs for an American breakfast in a climate-controlled case. We drive to Morrisette House, the center of Rural Studio. An old mansion, built around the turn of the last century, newly used, rather rundown on the inside. A giant meadow all around; a large roof stands there—the "Supershed"—with the student cabins—the "Pods." Each one different, everything experimental, a little like Venice Beach in L.A. We ask the way and get the day's schedule. As of noon there is a review with a party afterwards; a pig will be roasted over the open fire.

The pig is meanwhile roasting away on an improvised grill, arched over with a wild collection of wood poles, which is covered with a plastic membrane to keep out the rain. Suddenly the pig begins burning, the plastic catches flame and drips onto the pig; an attempt is made to put it out with brackish water. Female students are screaming hysterically. But first the active help of a black local professional calms the situation and the pig continues to roast in the rain without a plastic roof.

We use the time until the review and drive via Greensboro, the 'capital city' of Hale County, to Mason's Bend, where several houses of the Studio are located. We actually only find it reachable over a forest trail; remote spots, rather an incidental clearing where a few mobile homes stand, and then, however, the Butterfly House, the Lucy House, the Community Center, the Bryant House. All of these houses are, in reality, very small; especially the Community Center seems three times as big on the pictures. Hursley did a good job. At least three junked cars stand near each mobile home.

Norden, finden zurück nach Osten, und Nr. 81 stellt sich als Nr. 61 heraus. Katharinas Telefonaten zufolge wurde sie Nr. 81 genannt, auch auf dem Road-Atlas, den uns Hursley schenkte, ist die Nr. 81 verzeichnet, doch es ist die Nr. 61, die uns nach Newbern bringt.

Newbern nennt sich Stadt, und hat 310 Einwohner. Einmal die Hauptstraße, gesäumt von einzelnen Südstaaten-Häusern mit 30m² Vorgarten, durch und zurück und wir finden unser Bed & Breakfast House der Familie Bailey. Wir lesen „no smoking in the house" und sitzen noch eine gute Stunde rauchend auf der Veranda, mit den Broschüren und Mappen über Rural Studio, die freundlicherweise im Haus vorhanden sind.

Mrs. Baileys Bed & Breakfast lebt von Rural Studio. Wir finden eine kopierte Broschüre, die von den StudentInnen nach Mockbees Tod angefertigt wurde. *Tributes to Mockbee*. Er dürfte ein reiner Tor und wilder Hund gewesen sein, hat sein extensives Leben ritualisiert, „back to life, back to real experiences". Ein wenig vergleichbar vielleicht mit Heidulf Gerngross. Ein Mythos, sicherlich mit einer enormen persönlichen Präsenz und Ausstrahlung.

Und ich sitze jetzt im Bett in einem Bed & Breakfast House, fernab jeder Zivilisation und dennoch mitten in Alabama, und freue mich darüber, einen neuen Mythos in die Architekturdebatte bringen zu dürfen. Obwohl sich Max Protetch, der Galerist in N.Y., die Rechte für Mockbees Werk gesichert hat. Wir werden sehen, was die nächsten Tage bringen.

Zum Schluss: Kein Mobile-Netz in Newbern. Kein Kontakt mit der Welt möglich. Ich kann mich nicht erinnern, wann und wo dies das letzte Mal der Fall war.

Rural Studio, Antioch Baptist Church, Perry County, 2002. © DS

Rural Studio, Pods, Newbern, 1999. © DS

On the return journey through Sawyerville we find the Goat House, but we don't really approach it. A property, a farmer, no social project, *be aware of the dogs*. In Greensboro there is a big supermarket, two gas stations, a fairly trashed motel that everybody warned us about, etc. We buy a little car food, water, fruit, snacks. Back in Newbern, the reviews begin. An old, small circus tent is set up in the wet meadow and constantly threatens to collapse under the wind gusts. A group of thesis students are showing their project for a new building on the premises. A strictly symmetrical long house with a long table in the middle, for approx. 40 people, where people can eat together; at one end the Rural Studio library, at the front end of the table a pulpit for the speaker. Very monastic, hierarchal, militaristic, and only worked out in sketches. Professors from Washington University and others serve as critics for the review and deal very gently with the students. They mainly discuss about the position of the building on the lot.

Freitag, 13.12.02

8.00 auf, Frühstück ist angerichtet. Katharina ist schon länger auf und wir nehmen nur Kaffee und ein paar Snacks. In einer Klima-Kiste hat Mrs. Bailey Speck und Eier für ein amerikanisches Frühstück vorbereitet gehabt. Wir fahren zum Morrisette House, der Zentrale des Rural Studio. Eine alte Villa, um die letzte Jahrhundertwende gebaut, neu genutzt, innen ziemlich verkommen. Rundherum eine riesige Wiese, dort steht das große Dach – das „Supershed" – mit den Studentenkabinen – den „Pods". Jedes anders, alles experimentell, ein wenig wie Venice Beach in L.A. Wir fragen uns durch und bekommen einen Tagesplan. Ab Mittag ist Review mit anschließendem Fest, eine Sau wird am offenen Feuer gebraten.

Fünfter Tag • Day Five

A baseball field project is introduced. Possible pieces of land were analyzed for a concrete initiative from Newbern. Then a project was developed, consisting of steel pipe elbows that are not strung as usual with barb wire, but with catfish nets around the playing field, resulting in a protected tunnel for all the facilities. A full-scale model has been set up on the meadow.

We finish off in the "Red Barn"—it is the Rural Studio's work building; things are drawn and developed here—a design for a single-family house for Johnny Parker, a local Rural Studio employee, is being introduced; he is the structural engineering supervisor of Rural Studio, who is fetching the materials with his truck. Andrew Freear (co-director of the Rural Studio) and Jennifer Bonner (Rural Studio assistant) are presenting the project; no students are involved yet.

Then back to Morrisette House. It is always an armada of pickups and SUVs, many parents of students are also here. It is raining, it is cold. All gather around the open fire. We encounter Andrew Freear for the first time. Following Mockbee's death in December 2001, after his partner withdrew into private practice and in the wake of a heart attack suffered by the designated

Suddenly the pig begins burning, the plastic catches flame and drips onto the pig; an attempt is made to put it out with brackish water.

Diese brät inzwischen auf einem improvisierten Rost vor sich hin, mit einem wilden Holzgestänge überwölbt, das mit einer Plastikhaut gegen Regen abgedeckt ist. Auf einmal beginnt die Sau zu brennen, die Plastikhaut fängt Flammen und tropft auf die Sau, mit Brackwasser wird versucht zu löschen. Studentinnen kreischen hysterisch. Aber erst die tatkräftige Hilfe eines schwarzen *local professional* beruhigt die Situation, und die Sau brät nun im Regen ohne Plastikdach weiter.

Wir nutzen die Zeit bis zur Review und fahren über Greensboro, die ‚Hauptstadt' von Hale County nach Mason's Bend, wo sich einige Häuser des Studios befinden. Tatsächlich finden wir diesen nur über einen Waldweg erreichbaren, abgelegenen Flecken, eher eine zufällige Lichtung, wo einige *mobile homes* stehen und dann aber auch das Butterfly House, das Lucy House, das Community Center, das Bryant House. Alle Häuser sind in Wirklichkeit ganz klein, besonders das Community Center wirkt auf den Fotos dreimal so groß. Hursley hat ganze Arbeit geleistet. Bei jedem Mobile Home stehen mindestens drei ausrangierte Autowracks.

Bei der Rückfahrt durch Sawyerville finden wir das Goat House, aber wir nähern uns nicht wirklich an. Eine *property*, ein Farmer, kein Sozialprojekt, *be aware of the dogs*. In Greensboro gibt es einen großen Supermarkt, zwei Tankstellen, ein ziemlich abgefucktes Motel, vor dem uns alle gewarnt hatten etc. Wir kaufen ein wenig Autonahrung ein, Wasser, Obst, Snacks. Zurück in Newbern, die Reviews beginnen. Ein altes kleines

Der gescheiterte Versuch, ein Schwein im Regen zu rösten · The failed attempt at roasting a pig in the rain, 2002. © DS

successor Dennis K. Ruth, he is now the actual head of Rural Studio. We want to arrange a date with him tomorrow, in order to talk about the exhibition. At the moment he is completely busy with the reviews. End of the semester. Moreover, he had been misinformed or not informed at all by Bruce Lindsey, the head of Auburn who is supposed to be here, but cancelled on account of fever. It is impossible to do anything at all for the Viennese exhibition; we can actually forget the whole thing. He's now stuck alone with the Studio, next June a workshop is taking place at a university in Barcelona and in September a big Rural Studio exhibition in Birmingham, Alabama. Since the book appeared and the Rural Studio was at the Whitney Biennale, there has been no end to the inquiries. And there is no one who could take care of public relations. They also have no archive that would have documented the previous work.

All the same, we have Hursley's photos. Jay Sanders, a supervisor of the student projects, wants to help us procure some videos. We stumble around a bit more; there are a few speeches by Freear and Sanders at the open fire; "The Music Man"—he's getting the next single-family house by Rural Studio—says thanks by handing over strange little bottles to all second-year students who made the design; Jennifer Bonner helps us out with copies of a map which the locations of the projects up to now are listed on, and then we decide to flee from the party after all and forego a taste of the pig soaked with PVC and brackish water.

We both urgently want to make contact with Vienna and decide to drive ten miles to the south to Uniontown, where Highway 80 crosses, and then as far back to the west until we receive the signals of a mobile network. We drive around 40 minutes, when the network message shows up on the mobile phones shortly before Selma.

Zirkuszelt ist in der nassen Wiese aufgestellt, droht ständig unter den Windböen einzubrechen. Eine Gruppe von Thesis-Studenten zeigt ihr Projekt für einen Neubau am Gelände. Ein streng symmetrisches langes Haus mit einem langen Tisch in der Mitte, für ca. 40 Personen, wo gemeinsam gegessen werden kann, an einem Ende die Bibliothek des Rural Studio, am Kopfende der Tafel eine Kanzel für den Speaker. Sehr mönchisch, hierarchisch, militärisch. Und nur in Skizzen ausgearbeitet. Professoren der Washington University und andere bilden die *critics* der Review, und gehen sehr sanft mit den Studenten um. Diskutiert wird vor allem die Lage des Gebäudes am Grundstück.

Das Projekt eines Baseball-Fields wird vorgestellt. Für eine konkrete Initiative aus Newbern wurden mögliche Grundstücke analysiert. Dann ein Projekt entwickelt, das aus Stahlrohrbögen besteht, die nicht wie sonst üblich mit Maschendrahtzaun, sondern mit Catfish-Netzen bespannt rund um das Spielfeld einen geschützten Tunnel für alle *facilities* ergeben. Ein 1:1-Modell ist auf der Wiese aufgebaut.

Zum Schluss in der „Red Barn" – es ist das Arbeitsgebäude des Rural Studio, hier wird gezeichnet und entwickelt – wird ein Entwurf für ein Einfamilienhaus für Johnny Parker, einen lokalen Rural Studio Mitarbeiter vorgestellt; er ist bautechnischer Supervisor des Rural Studio, der mit seinem Truck die Materialen zusammenholt. Andrew Freear (Co-Direktor des Rural Studio) und Jennifer Bonner (Mitarbeiterin des Studios) stellen das Projekt vor, derzeit sind dabei noch keine Studenten involviert.

Dann zurück zum Morisette House. Es ist immer eine Armada von Pick-ups und SUVs, viele Eltern von Studenten sind auch hier. Es regnet, es ist kalt. Alle versammeln sich ums offene Feuer. Wir treffen erstmals auf Andrew Freear. Er ist nach dem Tod Mockbees im Dezember 2001, nach dem Rückzug seiner Partner in die private Praxis, und nach dem Herzinfarkt des designierten Nachfolgers Dennis K. Ruth der eigentliche Leiter des Rural Studio. Wir wollen uns mit ihm einen Termin für morgen vereinbaren, um über die Ausstel-

Fünfter Tag • Day Five

Rural Studio, Pods, Newbern, 1999. © DS

Back to Newbern, past the party, the fire's still burning, we fetch a six-pack of Budweiser at the gas station in Greensboro, but are too tired on the way back to still get out into the cold and wetness. We drink a beer at Mrs. Bailey's, the woman student who still lives here comes, too, we chat briefly and soon disappear into our rooms.

So, the First Day of Rural Studio:

The social components are right: architecture students come in direct contact with a world they would otherwise never get to now. Here in Hale County people live, drive cars, eat, drink, love, but where is the work? Why do they live here? It's about recognizing basic needs without any civilizing disturbance. The training is only right to a point: students are students. They first of all have no idea about building, and it is obvious that they had to be helped here by many craftsmen and laborers. They have not designed and then built something according to their technical capability. They were helped, but that also helps nonetheless.

The architecture remains exotic. In the case of the first structures, Mockbee seems to have had a strong influence on the drafts. I presume he set the agenda that was carried out by enthusiastic students. The priest and the monks or a boy and girl scout camp. Intellectually, in the architectonic meaning and the tradition of self-building, nothing is visible here. Go west, dream and build your house, that's it! American pragmatism. Just build it!

lung zu sprechen. Er ist zurzeit völlig beschäftigt mit den Reviews. Semesterende. Zudem ist er von Bruce Lindsey, dem Head von Auburn, der hier sein sollte, aber wegen Fieber abgesagt hat, überhaupt nicht oder falsch informiert worden. Es ist unmöglich, für die Wiener Ausstellung auch nur irgendwas zu machen, wir können eigentlich das Ganze vergessen. Er hat jetzt das Studio allein am Hals, es findet nächsten Juni ein Workshop an einer Universität in Barcelona statt und im September eine große Ausstellung des Rural Studio in Birmingham/Alabama. Seit das Buch erschienen ist und das Rural Studio auf der Whitney-Biennale war, nehmen die Anfragen kein Ende. Und es gibt niemanden, der sich um die Öffentlichkeitsarbeit kümmern könnte. Sie haben auch kein Archiv, das die bisherige Arbeit dokumentiert hätte.

Immerhin haben wir Hursleys Fotos. Jay Sanders, ein Betreuer der Studentenprojekte, wird uns bei der Beschaffung von Videos helfen. Wir stolpern noch etwas herum, es gibt beim Feuer im Freien ein paar Ansprachen von Freears und Sanders, „The Music Man" – er bekommt das nächste Einfamilienhaus vom Rural Studio – bedankt sich mit der Übergabe von seltsamen Fläschchen bei allen Studenten *of the second year*, die den Entwurf gemacht haben, Jennifer Bonner hilft uns mit Kopien einer Karte aus, auf der die Standorte der bisherigen Projekte verzeichnet sind, und dann beschließen wir, nun doch von der Party zu flüchten und auf die Kostproben von der mit PVC und Brackwasser getränkten Sau zu verzichten.

Wir wollen beide dringend mit Wien Kontakt aufnehmen und beschließen, die zehn Meilen nach Süden nach Uniontown zu fahren, wo der Highway 80 quert, und dann soweit zurück nach Westen, bis wir die Signale eines Mobil-Netzes empfangen. Wir fahren ca. 40 Minuten, als kurz vor Selma auf den Handys die Netzmeldung auftaucht.

Zurück nach Newbern, vorbei an der Party, das Feuer brennt noch, wir holen einen Sixpack Budweiser an der Tankstelle in Greensboro, sind aber beim Zurückfahren zu müde, um noch in die Kälte und Nässe auszusteigen. Trinken ein Bier im Quartier bei Mrs. Baileys, die Studentin, die hier noch wohnt ist, kommt auch noch, wir plaudern kurz und verziehen uns bald in unsere Zimmer.

Saturday, 14.12.02

The second day in Newbern. We set out around ten in the morning to find and film Rural Studio houses. First towards Akron in the north. A railroad line, a wild accumulation of houses and mobile homes, somewhat more ordered than in Mason's Bend. Here we find the Boys & Girls Club. A beautiful piece of work. The conversion of an old house. The atmosphere is as equally frightening as it is loose. We stand out, since we are the only white people in the area. Suddenly a young man comes out of the trailer next to the Club and simply begins shooting his pump gun over the heads of the playing children at a wall about ten meters away from us. Then he goes around the mobile home once and back into it again. Without any special excitement. And again there is a conglomeration of car wrecks that are simply overgrown by nature and standing around in the area. We drive to the north and search for the so-called Akron Pavilion. At a forest clearing the Rural Studio built an event plaza. A stage with a roof, next to a group of toilets with walls made of corrugated cardboard, uncompleted and somehow rundown like a lot of other things here, too. The place itself is a wonderful meadow, which turns into a forest, at the edge of a marsh. An obviously private farm property.

Even farther north, despite wrong maps, we find the quite remote Lewis House. Actually a conventional, modern single-family house, with the old trailer still standing next to it. It somehow seems uninhabited. Then back to Greensboro and in a right angle eastwards to Perry County. Peculiar primeval forest landscape, woods, noticeably unmanaged. We are long out of Hale County and simply keep driving on, coming into a real city called Marion, which isn't indicated anywhere; near an industrial conglomeration of catfish ponds we surmise a muddy forest trail, which can only be conquered with 4-wheel drive, and finally reach the Cedar Pavilion. An idyllic forest glade. At the edge of a swamp. The pavilion is nothing but a large roof over a platform where people can eat, drink and celebrate. But interesting nevertheless. The concrete base pulled up, expressively planked with red boards. A special ramp leads up to the platform as a spatial element. One sees how the students slaved away on the issue of vertical and horizontal connections.

Also. First day Rural Studio:

Es stimmt die soziale Komponente: Architekturstudenten kommen in direkten Kontakt mit einer Welt, die sie sonst nie kennenlernen würden. Hier in Hale County leben Menschen, fahren Auto, essen, trinken, lieben, aber wo ist die Arbeit? Warum leben sie hier? Es geht um das Erkennen elementarer Bedürfnisse ohne jede zivilisatorische Störung. Es stimmt die Ausbildung nur bedingt: StudentInnen sind StudentInnen. Sie haben zunächst einmal keine Ahnung vom Bauen, und es ist offensichtlich, dass ihnen hier von vielen Handwerkern und Hilfskräften geholfen werden musste. Sie haben nicht entworfen und dann nach ihrem technischen Vermögen gebaut. Es wurde ihnen geholfen, aber das hilft doch auch.

Die Architektur bleibt exotisch: Mockbee scheint bei den ersten Bauten starken Einfluss auf die Entwürfe gehabt zu haben. Ich vermute, dass er die Linie vorgab, die von begeisterungsfähigen StudentInnen ausgeführt wurde. *The priest and the monks* oder ein Pfadfinderlager. Intellektuell, in der architektonischen Bedeutung und Tradition des Selbstbaus, ist hier nichts sichtbar. *Go west, dream and build your house, that's it!* Amerikanischer Pragmatismus. *Just build it!*

Samstag, 14.12.02

Der zweite Tag in Newbern. Wir fahren gegen zehn Uhr los, um Rural Studio-Häuser zu finden und zu filmen. Zunächst nach Akron im Norden. Eine Bahnlinie, eine wilde Ansammlung von Häusern und Mobile Homes, etwas geordneter als in Mason's Bend. Wir finden hier den Boys & Girls Club. Eine schöne Arbeit. Der Umbau eines alten Hauses. Die Stimmung ist ebenso beängstigend wie locker. Wir fallen auf, sind die einzigen Weißen in der Gegend. Plötzlich kommt aus dem

Fünfter Tag • Day Five

Rural Studio, Pods, Newbern, 1999. © DS

On a different route back to Greensboro over an equally adventurous path we find our way to Antioch Baptist Church, which was just recently completed. Nothing seems experimental or improvised here. Simply an average, modern, small church in a clearing. An old church previously stood here, next to a small cemetery. I find two gravestones from 1866 beside an old oak tree. It is a strange area. Totally uncultivated primeval forest alternates with cultivated farmland. Swamps in between again and again. A plethora of churches on the road. More churches than farm houses at any rate.

Back to Greensboro, we eat sandwiches in the probably only restaurant and back to Bailey's. At 5 p.m. we meet Andrew Freear at Spencer House, which also belongs to Rural Studio, as well as the three professors who we became acquainted with at the review yesterday, and a further Rural Studio professor. We are to

Trailer neben dem Club ein junger Mann heraus, und beginnt einfach mit seiner Pump-Gun über die Köpfe der spielenden Kinder hinweg auf eine Wand zu schießen, rund zehn Meter von uns entfernt. Dann geht er einmal ums Mobile Home herum und wieder hinein. Ohne sonderliche Aufregung. Und wieder gibt es die Ansammlung von Auto-Wracks, die einfach von der Natur überwuchert werden und in der Gegend herumstehen. Wir fahren weiter nach Norden und suchen den sogenannten Akron Pavilion. Auf einer Waldlichtung hat das Rural Studio einen Veranstaltungsplatz gebaut. Eine Bühne mit einem Dach, daneben eine WC-Gruppe mit Wänden aus Wellpappe, unfertig und irgendwie abgefuckt wie vieles andere hier auch. Der Platz selbst ist eine wunderschöne Wiese, geht über in den Wald, am Rande ein Sumpfgebiet. Ein sichtlich privates Farm-Gelände.

Wir sollen zum Dinner mitkommen. Andrew fährt einen Monster-Pickup und rast los, wir hinten nach.

come with them for dinner. Andrew drives a monster pickup and takes off, with us on his tail. Andrew is an Englishman and puts the pedal to the metal. He wants to leave us behind, but he doesn't pull it off. The Blazer is at its limit. We race through on a one-lane dirt road between catfish ponds and scattered houses and land at "Buck's," a restaurant at Lock 5 on the banks of the Black Warrior River. We eat catfish and fries there, and drink Budweiser out of cans. We can briefly talk with Andrew another time about the exhibition. That was the second attempt. Slowly we draw hope that we will get an exhibition after all.

Towards 7 p.m. back to Greensboro, to the opening of an exhibition in an old hall that was converted into a gallery by Rural Studio. 1012 Beacon Street. Prior to that we still drive by a classic hardware store where we pay our room bill for Mrs. Bailey's and then buy the obligatory Budweiser six-pack and land in the gallery, Steve Badanes holds a 2 ½ hour lecture on his architecture. We talk with people and students and stand around the open fire with our beer cans, under the nocturnally cold sky of Alabama. The connections are established.

Another appointment with Andrew and Jay has been arranged for tomorrow, visits to further Rural Studio projects, which Katharina then films, and then back towards Atlanta in the evening. Around midnight we drive back to Newern, for the final night at Mrs. Bailey's Bed & Breakfast

Noch weiter im Norden finden wir trotz falscher Karten das ziemlich abgelegene Lewis House. Eigentlich ein konventionelles, modernes Einfamilienhaus, der alte Trailer steht noch daneben. Es wirkt irgendwie unbewohnt. Dann zurück nach Greensboro und im rechten Winkel ab in den Osten nach Perry County. Eigenartige Urwaldlandschaft, Wälder, sichtlich ohne Bewirtschaftung. Wir sind längst aus Hale County heraus und fahren einfach nur weiter, kommen in eine richtige Stadt namens Marion, die nirgends verzeichnet ist, bei einer industriellen Ansammlung von Catfish-Teichen erahnen wir einen gatschigen Waldweg, der nur mit 4-Wheels zu bewältigen ist, und erreichen schließlich den Cedar Pavilion. Eine idyllische Waldlichtung. Am Rande eines Sumpfes. Der Pavillon ist nichts als ein großes Dach über einer Plattform, wo man essen, trinken und feiern kann. Aber dennoch interessant. Die Beton-Fundamente hochgezogen, mit rohen Brettern expressiv geschalt. Eine spezielle Rampe führt als räumliches Element auf die Plattform. Man sieht, wie die StudentInnen sich am Thema von vertikalen und horizontalen Verbindungen abgearbeitet haben.

Auf einem anderen Weg zurück nach Greensboro finden wir über ebenso abenteuerliche Pfade zur Antioch Baptist Church, die erst kürzlich fertiggestellt wurde. Nichts scheint hier experimentell oder improvisiert. Einfach eine durchschnittlich moderne kleine Kirche auf einer Waldlichtung. Hier stand zuvor eine alte Kirche, daneben ein kleiner Friedhof. Ich finde zwei Grabsteine von 1866, daneben eine alte Eiche. Es ist eine seltsame Gegend. Völlig unbewirtschafteter Urwald wechselt mit gepflegtem Farmland. Dazwischen immer wieder Sümpfe. An der Straße eine Unmenge von Kirchen. Jedenfalls mehr Kirchen als Bauernhäuser.

Impression of the Second Day:

After Mockbee the architecture becomes simple, meanwhile also more professional. It still has to do with the social concern and with the building of students. The situation here is extreme, that's why it also works. Everyone who comes here exposes himself/herself to a one-of-a-kind experience.

SUNDAY, 15.12.02

Morning in Spencer House. Likewise a late 19th-century mansion. The professors and students live and sleep here. Somewhere with sleeping bags in the midst of chaos. Outside on the porch we find a place to finally do the interview with Andrew Freear. He has now thawed out to the point that we find a strategy to collect the material for the Vienna exhibition. He gives an account of the development and change of the Rural Studio. Now less experimentation with new materials is going on in the buildings, the Studio now receives second-hand glass and steel parts directly from companies, which they can fit into their projects. We still take a look through Jay's videos, which we can use for the exhibition.

Rural Studio, Akron Boys & Girls Club, Akron, 2001. © DS

Zurück nach Greensboro, wir essen Sandwiches im wahrscheinlich einzigen Lokal, und zurück ins Bailey's. Um 17 Uhr treffen wir Andrew Freear im Spencer House, das auch zum Rural Studio gehört, die drei Professoren, die wir bei der gestrigen Review kennengelernt haben, und einen weiteren Professor vom Rural Studio. Wir sollen zum Dinner mitkommen. Andrew fährt einen Monster-Pickup und rast los, wir hinten nach. Andrew ist Engländer und fährt Vollgas. Er will uns abhängen, was ihm aber nicht gelingt. Der Blazer ist an seinem Limit. Wir rasen auf einspurigen Pisten zwischen Catfish-Teichen und vereinzelten Häusern durch und landen bei „Buck's", einem Restaurant an Lock 5 am Ufer des Black Warrior River. Essen dort Catfish und Fries, und trinken Budweiser aus Dosen. Kurz können wir nochmals mit Andrew unsere Ausstellung besprechen. Das war der zweite Versuch. Langsam schöpfen wir Hoffnung, dass wir doch eine Ausstellung bekommen werden.

Gegen 19 Uhr zurück nach Greensboro, zur Eröffnung einer Ausstellung in einer vom Rural Studio zur Galerie umgebauten alten Halle. Beacon Street 1012. Wir fahren vorher noch bei einem klassischen Hardware-Store vorbei, wo wir bei Mrs. Bailey unsere Zimmerrechnung bezahlen, kaufen dann noch das obligate Budweiser-Sixpack und landen in der Galerie. Steve Badanes hält einen 2 1/2 Stunden Vortrag über seine Architektur. Wir reden mit Leuten und StudentInnen und stehen mit unseren Bierdosen rund ums offene Feuer, unter dem nächtlich kalten Himmel von Alabama. Die Connections sind hergestellt.

Für morgen nochmals einen Termin mit Andrew und mit Jay vereinbart, weitere Rural Studio-Projekte besichtigen, die Katharina filmt, und abends dann zurück Richtung Atlanta. Gegen Mitternacht fahren wir zurück nach Newbern, zur letzten Nacht in Mrs. Baileys Bed & Breakfast

Eindruck zweiter Tag:

Nach Mockbee wird die Architektur einfacher, inzwischen auch professioneller. Es geht nach wie vor um die sozialen Anliegen und um das Bauen von StudentInnen. Die Situation hier ist extrem, deshalb funktioniert das auch. Jeder, der hierher kommt, setzt sich einer einmaligen Erfahrung aus.

Sonntag, 15.12.02

Vormittag im Spencer House. Ebenfalls eine Villa des ausgehenden 19. Jahrhunderts. Hier leben und schlafen die Professoren und StudentInnen. Irgendwo mit Schlafsäcken mitten im Chaos. Draußen auf der Veranda finden wir einen Platz, um endlich das Interview mit Andrew Freear zu machen. Dabei taut er nun insoweit auf, dass wir eine Strategie finden, um das Material für die Wiener Ausstellung zu sammeln. Er schildert die Entwicklung und Veränderung des Rural Studio. Jetzt wird bei den Bauten weniger mit neuen Materialien experimentiert, das Studio bekommt nun second-hand Glas- und Stahlteile direkt von Firmen, die sie in die Projekte einbauen können. Wir sehen noch die Videos von Jay durch, die wir für die Ausstellung verwenden können.

Abreise. Katharina filmt nochmals das Supershed, das H.E.R.O. Children Center in Greensboro, das Baseball Field in Newbern.

Am Abend zurück nach Atlanta. Noch während der Fahrt überlegen wir, ob wir unterwegs ein Quartier suchen sollen. Wir durchqueren auf dem Weg zurück nach Atlanta auch Auburn, finden aber kein passendes Hotel. Also durch bis Atlanta.

Montag, 16.12.02

Hotel Crown Palace in der Nähe des Flughafens ist eine alte Hütte. Das Abenteuer Alabama ist vorüber. Wir trinken noch unser letztes Budweiser. Um 9.30 Uhr morgens treffen wir uns in der Halle. Wir fahren zu einer Shopping-Mall, Katharina muss Weihnachtsgeschenke für Helene kaufen. Zum Flughafen. Rückgabe des völlig verdreckten Blazer bei Avis. So bleibt der Leistungsbeweis der Reise durch das Niemandsland zurück. Abflug Atlanta–Washington – *next morning* Wien. Die Arbeit an der Ausstellung beginnt.

Mrs. Bailey's Bed & Breakfast, 2002. © DS

Departure. Katharina once again films the Supershed, the HERO Children's Center in Greensboro, the Baseball Club in Newbern.

Back to Atlanta in the evening. During the ride we still ponder whether we ought to look for accommodation. We also traverse Auburn on the way back to Atlanta, but we do not find a suitable hotel. So that means all the way to Atlanta.

Monday, 16.12.02

Hotel Crown Palace near the airport is an old cabin. The Alabama adventure is over. We still drink our last Budweiser. At 9:30 a.m. we meet in the lobby. We drive to a shopping mall. Katharina has to buy Christmas presents for Helene. Off to the airport. Return the totally filthy Blazer to Avis. The proof that we accomplished the journey through no-man's land therefore remains behind. Departure Atlanta–Washington—next morning Vienna. Work on the exhibition begins.

aus · from

domus 893, 6_2006
"Steven Holl. Hotel Winery"

Loisium

Every month, a jewel of contemporary architecture lands somewhere on our planet. The spectacle of architecture has assumed global dimensions. What were celebrated by the media just ten years ago as isolated sensations, the rare realisations of a dream from the world of the former architectural avant-garde, have now become nothing less than everyday events. Even so, they are in demand as individually exciting signatures, unmistakably alien symbols in banal surroundings, symbols which can demonstrate their media sexiness time and time again. The reverse side of the boom in new super-symbols can be seen in the often clearly excessive budgets set by star architects, and in inadequate fitness for the purpose. But another downside of contemporary architecture is represented by clients who, seduced by the media effect, want to buy only the name of the star and are then not prepared to pay for the implementation of the architect's demands in respect of quality.

Loisium

Jeden Monat landet ein Diamant zeitgenössischer Architektur irgendwo auf unserem Planeten. Das Spektakel Architektur hat globale Dimensionen angenommen. Was vor zehn Jahren noch medial als vereinzelte Sensation gefeiert wurde, die seltene Realisierung eines Traums aus der Welt der ehemaligen Architektur-Avantgarde, ist heute zu einem geradezu alltäglichen Ereignis geworden. Gefragt sind sie dennoch als individuell spannende Signaturen, als deutlich fremde Zeichen im banalen Umfeld, die ihre mediale Wirksamkeit immer wieder nachweisen können. Die Kehrseite des Booms der neuen Superzeichen sind oftmals von Stararchitekten deutlich überhöhte Baubudgets und mangelnde Funktionalität. Aber auch Bauherren, die, verführt vom medialen Effekt, nur den Namen des Architektenstars einkaufen möchten und dann nicht bereit sind, die hohen Qualitätsforderungen des Architekten zu ermöglichen, markieren die Schattenseite der zeitgenössischen Architektur.

Besucherzentrum der Loisium Erlebniswelt · Visitor Center at the Loisium World of Wine, Langenlois, Steven Holl, 2003. © DS

But there are projects where all the factors and background conditions are right, allowing a committed and successful new architecture. Often enough it is strangely old-fashioned conditions that ultimately lead to success. One such old-fashioned story is the "Loisium" project in Langenlois, Austria's largest wine-producing district some 70 km from Vienna. No one lusted after spectacle and there were no coldly calculated marketing considerations. Committed clients, the Nidetzky and Steininger families, wanted to create a "world-of-wine" experience for tourists. It was not to be a short-lived shooting star, but a long-term investment with a claim to culture. Steven Holl was the desired architect. But would he, the star from New York, be interested in a small project like this? "If you have a good client, you can do a good job," was his opinion on the matter. The clients and the local authorities in the small town of Langenlois were completely convinced by his first design for the entrance pavilion and the hotel for the world-of-wine experience, presented in July 2001. Of course at the start of the project there was mutual sus-

Aber es gibt auch Projekte, bei denen alle Faktoren und Rahmenbedingungen stimmen und eine engagierte und erfolgreiche neue Architektur ermöglichen. Es sind sehr häufig seltsam altmodische Verhältnisse, die am Ende zum Erfolg führen. Eine derart altmodische Geschichte ist das Projekt „Loisium" in Langenlois, der größten Weinbaugemeinde Österreichs, rund 70 km von Wien entfernt. Keine Gier nach Spektakel, keine knallhart kalkulierten Marketingüberlegungen spielten eine Rolle. Engagierte Bauherren, die Familien Nidetzky und Steininger, wollten eine touristische Weinerlebniswelt schaffen. Kein schnelles, kurzlebiges Spektakel, sondern eine nachhaltige Investition mit kulturellem Anspruch. Steven Holl war der Wunscharchitekt dafür. Aber würde er, der berühmte Architekt aus New York, sich für dieses kleine Projekt engagieren? „If you have a good client, you can do a good job", meinte er dazu. Sein erster Entwurf für den Eingangspavillon und das Hotel der Weinerlebniswelt, im Juli 2001 präsentiert, überzeugte Bauherren und die Politik der kleinen Stadt

Fünfter Tag • Day Five

Loisium Hotel, Langenlois, Steven Holl, 2005. © DS

picion. What necessities even a star architect had to fulfil, and what scope a client had to allow him in order to fulfil them: this had to be discussed at length in an atmosphere of mutual respect. Not least, an important factor was the choice of local architects. The Austrian architects Franz Sam and Irene Ott-Reinisch did sterling work on Steven Holl's design and demands. Together with Christian Wassmann, the project architect in Steven Holl's studio, they managed to guide the project to a sensational success without exceeding the budget and without forfeiting any quality.

In 2003 the entrance pavilion of the "Loisium" world-of-wine experience was opened, at which time it was still not certain whether the planned hotel, included in Steven Holl's concept, could also be realised. The investors were still looking for additional financial backers. But the entrance pavilion, along with the world-of-wine experience, went down well both with the media and among visitors. A further argument in favour of building the hotel was provided by Steven Holl himself in the form of his strategic concept: the world-of-wine experience in the ancient cellars he called "underground", the entrance pavilion was a deliberately tilted cube he called "in the ground", and the final object of this architectural ensemble—the hotel—was to be "over the ground". Thus it was clear to all concerned that the hotel quite simply had to be built in order to complete not only the business plan but also the architectural concept.

Langenlois vollkommen. Natürlich gab es dann am Anfang des Projekts gegenseitiges Mißtrauen – welche Notwendigkeiten eines Programms auch ein Stararchitekt zu erfüllen und welche Möglichkeiten dazu ihm ein Bauherr einzuräumen hat, das muss mit gegenseitigem Respekt ausdiskutiert werden. Und eine wesentliche Rolle spielte die Wahl der lokalen Kontaktarchitekten. Die österreichischen Architekten Franz Sam und Irene Ott-Reinisch leisteten eine kongeniale Arbeit zu Entwurf und inhaltlichem Anspruch von Steven Holl. Gemeinsam mit Christian Wassmann, dem Projektarchitekten in Steven Holls Studio, konnten sie das Projekt zu den gegebenen Kosten ohne Einbußen an Qualitäten zu seinem sensationellen Erfolg führen.

Im Jahr 2003 wurde der Eingangspavillon der „Weinerlebniswelt Loisium" eröffnet, und es war zu diesem Zeitpunkt noch nicht endgültig sicher, ob das geplante und von Steven Holl im Konzept mitentwickelte Hotel auch realisiert werden könnte. Noch suchten die Investoren weitere Geldgeber dafür. Aber der Eingangspavillon und die Weinerlebniswelt waren ein medialer und touristischer Erfolg. Und ein weiteres Argument für die Realisierung des Hotels hat Steven Holl mit seinem strategischen Konzept selbst geliefert. Die Weinerlebniswelt in den alten Kellern nannte er „underground", den bewusst gekippten Würfel des Eingangspavillons bezeichnete er als „in the ground". Und das letzte Objekt dieses architektonischen Weges, das Hotel, sollte „over the ground" sein. Damit war allen klar, dass nicht nur für die Vollendung des unternehmerischen, sondern auch des architektonischen Werks das Hotel gebaut werden musste.

Steven Holls Loisium-Hotel ist kein Designer- oder Boutique-Hotel, wie der neue Gattungsbegriff heißt, der von Philippe Starck und Ian Schrager geschaffen wurde. Es ist mehr als das. Es ist ein bis zur Einrichtung und jedem innenräumlichen Detail, durchgeplantes architektonisches Manifest. „Over the ground" bedeutet zunächst, dass die zwei Geschosse mit 82 Hotelzimmern über einem öffentlichen, großzügig verglasten Raum von 7 m Höhe schweben. In diesem Raum versammeln sich Lobby, Tagungsräume, das exklusive Restaurant und eine einzigartige Erholungslandschaft, ein Spa, das von der Kosmetik-Kultmarke Aveda betrieben

Steven Holl's Loisium Hotel is not a designer hotel or a boutique hotel, to use the term coined by Philippe Starck and Ian Schrager. It is more than that. It is an architectural manifesto thought out and planned to the last detail, including the furnishings and interior design. "Over the ground" means, first of all, that the two storeys with their 82 hotel rooms hover above a generously glazed public space 7 metres in height. This space comprises a lobby, conference rooms, the exclusive restaurant and a unique leisure facility—a spa operated by the cult cosmetic brand Aveda. These functions enclose an intimate interior courtyard with a pool. Visitors will be surprised by the urbanely generous proportions of the rooms, which constitute a positively cosmopolitan island in the provincial rural surroundings. Bold colours and surfaces accompany the tension of the spatial continuum, which is unmistakably reminiscent of the Austrian Surrealist Frederick Kiesler. The newly made Kiesler furniture produced by the Wittmann furniture workshop is in altogether apt surroundings here. Steven Holl has also designed a chair for the hotel, inspired by Kiesler and made by Wittmann: it is sensationally comfortable.

The thoroughgoing logic of the unique design is continued in the corridors and hotel rooms. Subtly structured concrete surfaces, specially designed door-handles, the innovative way in which the bathrooms are integrated into the bedrooms by way of large rotating walls, which Holl first developed for his residential design in Fukuoka. The entire hotel is a unique world of architectural experience in itself, offering architecturally naive guests a rich, surprising ambience while serving up hard-boiled architectural critics food, or rather space, for thought. If Jean Nouvel's Hotel Saint James near Bordeaux was the hotel icon of the last decade, Steven Holl's Hotel Loisium is the ultimate message of the first decade of the new millennium.

Marketing experts can design and build as many boutique hotels as they like wherever they like, and star architects can be assembled to build uninhabitable horror stories or storeys in media-sensation hotels, as recently in Madrid. But Steven Holl's Loisium project is an original and unique total strategy, already a landmark in architectural history, which as we said could only result from an old-fashioned relationship between architect and committed client.

wird. Diese Funktionen umschließen einen intimen Innenhof mit einem Pool. Die Räume überraschen durch ihre urbane Großzügigkeit, bilden eine geradezu weltstädtische Insel im ländlichen Umfeld. Mutige Farben und Oberflächen begleiten das spannende Raumkontinuum, das unverkennbar seine Reminiszenzen an den österreichischen Surrealisten Frederick Kiesler leistet. Die von den Möbelwerkstätten Wittmann neu produzierten Kiesler-Möbel finden hier eine adäquate Umgebung. Steven Holl hat für das Hotel auch einen Stuhl entworfen, von Kiesler inspiriert, von Wittmann produziert, der einen sensationellen, den heute wohl besten Sitzkomfort bietet.

Die Konsequenz der singulären Gestaltung setzt sich bei den Gängen und Zimmern fort. Subtil strukturierte Betonoberflächen, eigens entwickelte Türgriffe, innovative Integrationen der Bäder in die Zimmer mit großen Drehwänden, die Holl schon für seinen Wohnbau in Fukuoka entwickelt hatte. Das ganze Hotel ist eine einzigartige ‚Architekturerlebniswelt', die dem unbefangenen Gast ein reiches, überraschendes Ambiente bietet und dem Architekturkenner einen neuen Gedankenraum eröffnet. War Jean Nouvels Hotel Saint-James bei Bordeaux die Hotel-Ikone des letzten Jahrzehnts, so ist Steven Holls Hotel Loisium die ultimative Botschaft des ersten Jahrzehnts des neuen Jahrtausends für diese Aufgabe.

Da können noch so viele Marketingexperten Boutique-Hotels wo immer auf der Welt konzipieren und errichten, da können Stararchitekten versammelt werden, um unbewohnbare Horroretagen in medialen Sensationshotels, wie kürzlich in Madrid, zu errichten. Steven Holls Loisium-Projekt ist eine originäre und einzigartige Gesamtstrategie, ein heute schon architekturgeschichtliches Landmark, das eben nur aus einer altmodischen Beziehung zwischen engagierten Bauherren und dem Architekten entstehen konnte.

Dietmar Steiner

Landscape of Nonentity

Die Schönheit der spärlich bebauten Leere

aus · from

91° 2_2008
„Die Schönheit der spärlich bebauten Leere"
"Landscape of Noentity"
Translation by Lisa Rosenblatt / Charlotte Eckler
Graphic design: lenz+ büro für visuelle gestaltung

Vorab muss ich bekennen, dass mich in der Pubertät die sozialromantischen Romane des isländischen Nationaldichters Hálldor Laxness mit den eindrucksvollen Schilderungen der Unterdrückung der Isländer durch die Fremdherrschaft von Norwegern und Dänen so sehr beeindruckten, dass ich damals unbedingt nach Island emigrieren wollte. Irgendwie war ich dann doch zu feig dazu, aber der magische Ort am Ende der Welt behielt seine Faszination.

First of all, I have to admit that during puberty, the socio-romantic novels by the Icelandic national bard Hálldor Laxness, with their impressive descriptions of the Icelander's oppression at the hands of the Norwegians and Danes impressed me so much that at the time, I was absolutely determined to immigrate to Iceland. Somehow in the end I couldn't bring myself to do it, but I've still retained my fascination with the magical place at the end of the world.

Elsewhere

Endless countryside, not many people. Iceland, the barren, treeless volcanic island at the Arctic Circle has its own kind of magic. And the architecture waiting to be discovered by Studio Granda and the mysterious "Högna's Houses" fits in with that. All set to the intoxicating sounds of Icelandic pop music.

Dietmar Steiner

Unendliche Landschaft, wenige Menschen. Island, die karge, baumlose Vulkaninsel am Polarkreis hat ihren eigenen Zauber. Darein fügt sich auch die zu entdeckende Architektur von Studio Granda und die geheimnisvollen ‚Högna's Houses'. Alles unterlegt vom berauschenden Klangteppich der isländischen Popmusik.

Landscape of Nonentity

Island, die magische Insel, ein Traumland, wie geschaffen für Fluchtprojektionen eines anderen Lebens. Jeder Island-Urlauber, den man trifft und befragt, kommt ins Schwärmen ob der unvergleichlichen Andersartigkeit dieser eindrucksvollen vulkanischen Landschaft. Die unendliche Weite, die Geysire, die heißen Quellen, die Wasserfälle, die Island-Pferde. Jeder Tourist schwärmt davon, etwas gesehen und erlebt zu haben, das sich nicht in die alltäglichen massentouristischen Muster fügt. Die Frage nach Architektur, sehenswert moderner noch dazu, wird mit erstauntem, ratlosem Blick beantwortet.
Überraschend ist nach ersten Erkundigungen, für wie viele Europäer in den fünfziger und sechziger Jahren des letzten Jahrhunderts Island deshalb zum Begriff wurde, weil sie zu günstigen Tarifen über Reykjavík in die USA fliegen konnten. Die Fluglinie Loftleidir bot Billigstflüge, meist ab Luxemburg, an, weil sie durch die Ausstellung von zwei Tickets – Europa–Island und Island–USA – die damals restriktiven Preisbindungen für Direktflüge unterbot. Internationaler Flugverkehr auf einer abgelegenen Insel im Nordatlantik? Das begann 1940, als zuerst britische und dann amerikanische Truppen Island als geopolitisch strategischen Punkt zwischen den Kontinenten besetzten. 1944 wurde Island, das schon seit 1900 eine relative Eigenständigkeit genoss, nach jahrhundertelanger Herrschaft durch Norwegen und Dänemark ein souveräner Staat.

Dennoch fliegen auch heute noch neben den beiden lokalen Fluggesellschaften Icelandair und Iceland Express nur wenige internationale Fluglinien Island an. Das hat auch klimatische Gründe. Jeder europäische Wetterbericht kennt es: Das berühmte Island-Tief – gibt es wirklich. Wenn man in einer robusten alten Boeing im Sturm eines solchen

Iceland, a magical island, a dreamland, as though created for projections of escape to another life. Every Icelandic tourist that one meets and asks about their trip raves about the incomparable uniqueness of the nature in this impressive volcanic landscape: endless expanses, geysers, hot springs, waterfalls, Icelandic ponies. Every tourist goes into raptures about having seen and experienced something that does not conform to the common pattern of mass tourism. But if you ask about architecture, or for that matter, about modern architecture worth looking at, the answer is an astonished, helpless gaze.
After initial inquiries, it became clear that surprisingly, a great number of Europeans became aware of Iceland in the 1950s and 1960s because they could fly low-fare through Reykjavík to the US. The airline Loftleidir offered cheap flights, usually from Luxembourg, since by issuing two tickets—Europe to Iceland and Iceland to the US—they could undercut the restrictive controlled prices for direct flights. International air traffic on a remote island in the North Atlantic? That began in 1940, when first British and then American troops occupied Iceland as a geopolitical strategic point between the continents. In 1944, Iceland became a sovereign state. It had enjoyed relative autonomy since 1900, after centuries of being ruled by Norway and Denmark.

Nevertheless, nowadays very few international airlines fly to Iceland other than the two local operations: Icelandair and Iceland Express. There are also climatic reasons behind that: Every European weather report talks about the famous Iceland low

Elsewhere

Tiefs am Flughafen Keflavík sitzt, die ganze Maschine schon am Stand mit schwingenden Flügeln zu schlingern beginnt und eigentlich an einen Start unter diesen Bedingungen nicht zu denken ist, ziehen die Piloten von Icelandair den tanzenden Flieger wider alle Kräfte der Natur dennoch in die Höhe und die lokalen Passagiere empfinden diesen Zustand als vollkommen normal. Das erklärt auch die Antwort auf die Frage, warum die alltäglichen Bauten in Island überwiegend mit Wellblech verkleidet sind: Ursprünglich errichteten die Siedler Unterkünfte aus Treibholz, Erde, Steinen, nennenswerten Baumbestand und Ziegel gibt es nicht. Erst das aus England importierte Blech hielt den vor allem winterlichen horizontal anbrechenden Regen- und Schneestürmen stand und erlaubte richtige Häuser mit geraden Wänden.

Wahnsinniges Wetter und regelmäßige Vulkanausbrüche, die geologische Lage an der Bruchlinie zwischen nordamerikanischer und eurasischer Platte, kann nur mit einer Einstellung der ‚positiven Gedankenlosigkeit', wie sie der deutsche Essayist und Island-Kenner Henryk M. Broder bezeichnete, bewältigt werden: ‚Hätten die Isländer vor 100 oder 200 Jahren über ihr Leben gründlich nachgedacht, alle Vor- und Nachteile gegeneinander abgewogen, wären sie zu dem Schluss gekommen: Nichts wie weg von hier!' Dennoch leben rund 300.000 Isländer auf der größten Vulkaninsel der Welt, rund 200.000 davon im Großraum Reykjavík. Und nach dem jahrzehntelangen Ziel eines vorbildlichen skandinavischen Wohlfahrtsstaats mit einer egalitären Gesellschaft, mit einer Ökonomie, die vorwiegend Fischfang und wenig Industrie – vor allem Aluminium aufgrund der günstigen Energiepreise dank geothermischer Verfügbarkeit – als Grundlage hatte, wurde Island

pressure system—well, it really exists. When one sits in a robust old Boeing at Keflavík airport in the storm of such a low and the entire machine begins to rock while still standing, with wings swinging, and a start under such conditions is actually inconceivable, the pilots from Icelandair nonetheless pull the plane into the heights, opposing all of nature's power, and the local passengers consider this an entirely normal situation. That also answers the question of why common buildings in Iceland are covered with corrugated metal: originally, the settlers set up their dwellings from driftwood, earth, and stone. The island has no appreciable tree population and no clay brick. Sheet metal imported from England was the first material capable of withstanding the weather, mainly the horizontally broaching winter rain and snow storms, allowing the Icelandic people to build proper homes with straight walls.

The geological situation on the fault line between North American and Eurasian plates, insane weather and steady volcanic eruptions, can be overcome only with an attitude of "positive thoughtlessness" as the German essayist and Iceland expert Henryk M. Broder calls it: "If, some hundred or two hundred years ago the Icelandic people had thought thoroughly about their lives, weighed out all advantages and disadvantages, they would have come to the conclusion: time to get out of here!" Yet roughly 300,000 Icelandic people live on the world's largest volcanic island, around 200,000 of them in the Reykjavík metropolitan area. And after striving for decades to become a model Scandinavian welfare state with an egalitarian society, an economy based primarily on the fishing industry, and some

Landscape of Nonentity

Dietmar Steiner

Welthistorische Bedeutung. *Typisch für viele Häuser dieser Zeit wurde auch der Wohnsitz des französischen Konsuls Brillouin in Norwegen produziert und 1909 als Fertighaus an der Bucht von Reykjavík montiert. Seit 1968 dient das ‚Höfdi' als repräsentatives Gästehaus für offizielle Empfänge. Reagan und Gorbatschow vereinbarten hier 1986 das Ende des Kalten Krieges.*
World historical significance. *Typical of many houses from this era, French consulate Brillouin's residence was prefabricated in Norway and brought to Reykjavík bay in 1909. Since 1968, Höfdi house has been the site of official receptions. Reagan and Gorbachev agreed to end the Cold war here in 1986.*

Megastau im Niemandsland. *Rund um den kleinstädtischen Stadtkern von Reykjavík wird die weitverstreute Peripherie der neuen Einfamilienhäuser, Shopping-Malls und Business-Parks von gewaltigen Stadtautobahnen erschlossen. Islands Bauboom kann heute nur mit ausländischen Arbeitskräften bewältigt werden.*
Traffic jam in no-man's-land. *Massive urban highways connect the suburban sprawl of single family houses, shopping malls, and business parks surrounding Reykjavík's modest city center. Iceland's current construction boom can be handled only with the help of foreign workers.*

heute in eine postmoderne IT-, Dienstleistungs- und Finanzökonomie katapultiert, die einen ebenso enormen wie für diese Landschaft absurden Wirtschaftsboom erzeugte.

Reykjavík, die Hauptstadt, ist eine nette Kleinstadt, die noch vor hundert Jahren nicht einmal 10.000 Einwohner hatte. Fußläufig hat man in rund einer Stunde den Stadtkern gesehen. Meist ein- bis zweigeschossige Häuser. Sehnsüchtig erwartete man um 1900 den Beton, der die Errichtung der ersten drei- und vierstöckigen Häuser erlaubte. Doch jetzt herrscht ein Immobilienboom, der die international überall gleich grausigen Büro- und Condominium-Türme ins Brachland setzt. Woher wirklich das große Geld und der plötzliche offensichtliche Reichtum kommen, weiß niemand so recht. Jedenfalls hat heute Island Norwegen als teuerstes Land der Welt abgelöst. Nähert man sich der Stadt, glaubt man sich nach Los Angeles versetzt, wenn man auf sechsspurigen Stadtautobahnen eine schier unendlich weitläufige Besiedlung durchquert. Inklusive Megastaus zur Rush-Hour, die nur die Erklärung zulassen, dass jeder Einwohner anscheinend mit mindestens drei Autos gleichzeitig fährt. Eisenbahn gibt es keine, öffentlicher Busverkehr ist nur marginal wahrnehmbar.

Es ist aber diese sonderbare Paradoxie zwischen lokaler, mythenbesetzter Abgeschiedenheit und gleichzeitiger internationalisierter Vernetzung, die auch die zeitgenössische isländische Kultur ins Zentrum der Aufmerksamkeit rückt. Isländische Musiker jenseits von Björk wie Amiina, Múm oder Sigur Rós sind längst kein Geheimtipp mehr. Aber alles begann mit dem Schriftsteller Halldór Laxness. Dass er, mit feiner poetischer Sprache sozialromantische Romane in und über Island

industry,—mainly aluminum, due to low energy costs from available geothermic resources—Iceland has now catapulted into a postmodern IT, service, and finance economy, which has generated an economic boom that is just as large as it is absurd for this landscape.

Reykjavík, the capital, is a nice little city that just one hundred years ago had less than 10,000 inhabitants. It is possible to see the entire city center by foot in about an hour. The buildings are mainly one- and two-story structures. Concrete, which allowed the construction of the first three- and four-story buildings, was eagerly awaited around 1900. Yet nowadays a property boom is underway, erecting in the fallow areas the same ghastly grey office and condominium towers found all over the world. No one really knows exactly where the big money and the sudden, obvious wealth come from. In any case, Iceland has now replaced Norway as the most expensive country in the world. While on the six-lane highway crossing a nearly endlessly rambling settlement approaching the city, one gets the feeling of having been transposed to Los Angeles. At rush hour, thrown in for good measure are the mega traffic jams, for which the only explanation can be that every inhabitant apparently drives three cars simultaneously. Railways are nonexistent and public bus transport is only marginally discernible.

It is this special paradox of local, mythically charged remoteness and simultaneously the internationalized networks that has also shifted Icelandic culture into the limelight. Icelandic musicians other than Björk, such as Amiina, Múm, and Sigur Rós, have no longer been secret tips for quite some time now. Nonetheless, it all

Elsewhere

Magische Orte. Das moderne Wohnhaus des Nationaldichters und Nobelpreisträgers Halldór Laxness ist eine Pilgerstätte. Sein weißer Jaguar steht heute nicht mehr davor. Seit auch der Megakünstler Dieter Roth die Einsamkeit der Insel in seinem Haus in Harnell nutzte, wurde Island zum Kultort der Kreativen.

Magical site. National poet and Nobel Prize winner Halldór Laxness's modern home is a pilgrimage site. His Jaguar no longer parks out front. Star artist Dieter Roth partook of the island's isolation in his house in Harnell and ever since, Iceland has been a cult site for creative people.

schreibend, 1955 den Nobelpreis für Literatur bekam, hatte nicht zuletzt mit dem Kalten Krieg zu tun. Man wollte damit auch auf ein Land aufmerksam machen, das sich außerhalb der Konfliktlinien positionierte und friedfertig ein drittes Gesellschaftsmodell, das des sozialen Ausgleichs, propagierte. Laxness wurde für die Isländer zum Symbol, auch international wahrgenommen zu werden. Man nannte ihn damals den wichtigsten Botschafter Islands. Sein 1945 vom Architekten Ágúst Pálsson gebautes, modernes Haus Gljúfrasteinn ist eine Pilgerstätte, die tiefen Einblick in sein Leben und Schaffen erlaubt. Doch auch ein anderer großer Künstler fokussierte die Aufmerksamkeit auf die lebensfeindliche Insel. Der Schweizer Multi-Künstler Dieter Roth zog 1957 nach Reykjavík zu Sigridur Björnsdóttir, einer isländischen Studentin, die er heiratete. Mitte der sechziger Jahre kaufte er ein norwegisches Fertigteilhaus, das aus nur vier zusammenschraubbaren Teilen bestand. Es stand zuvor beim Kraftwerksbau Burfell und musste 500 km transportiert und wieder aufgebaut werden, was zu erheblichen Kosten führte. Das Haus in Harnell, auf der Halbinsel Snæfellsnes, wurde ein wichtiger Rückzugsort für Roth: ‚Ich schrieb in diesem Haus die meisten der Prosatexte meiner 70er Jahre. Wenn ich allein dort wohnte, konnte ich ziemlich ruhige, auch euphorische Wochen haben...'

Die Tradition, norwegische Fertigteilhäuser als damals modische ‚Schweizer Chalets' oder im Jugendstil Ende des 19. Jahrhunderts nach Island zu importieren, hinterließ auch ein Gebäude des damaligen französischen Konsuls, das heute der isländischen Regierung als Gästehaus dient. Es erlangte welthistorische Bedeutung, weil sich in diesem Haus am 11. und 12. Oktober 1986 Ronald Reagan und Michail Gorbatschow

began with the writer Halldór Laxness. The fact that he was awarded the Nobel Prize for Literature in 1955 for his subtly poetic socio-romantic novels in and about Iceland had to do with the Cold war. The idea at the time was to draw attention to a country that positioned itself outside of the lines of conflict, peacefully propagating a third social model of societal balance. Laxness also became the Icelandic people's symbol of being recognized internationally. At the time, he was called Iceland's most important ambassador. Gljúfrasteinn, his modern house, built in 1945 by the architect Ágúst Pálsson, is a pilgrimage site that allows a profound look into his life and creation. Another great artist also focused attention onto the hostile island. The Swiss artist Dieter Roth moved to Reykjavík in 1957 to be with Sigridur Björnsdóttir, an Icelandic student whom he married. In the 1970s he bought a Norwegian prefabricated house composed of only four parts that could be screwed together. It was located at the Burfell power station and had to be transported 500 kilometers, which led to significant costs. The house in Harnell, on the Snæfellsnes peninsula, became an important retreat for Roth. "In the seventies I wrote most of the prose texts in this house. When I was able to live there alone, I had rather calm, but also euphoric weeks..."

The tradition of importing to Iceland, Norwegian prefabricated houses, fashioned at the time as popular "Swiss Chalets" or late-nineteenth-century Jugendstil, also left behind a building from the former French consulate. Today, the building serves the Icelandic government as a guest house. The structure made its mark in world

Landscape of Nonentity   Dietmar Steiner

trafen, um das Ende des Kalten Krieges zu beschließen, an dessen Höhepunkt der legendäre Sieg Bobby Fischers über Boris Spasski in der Schachweltmeisterschaft 1972 in Reykjavík erfolgt war.

Für euphorische Wochen, besser Nächte, steht heute ‚101 Reykjavík'. So heißt der zentrale Bezirk der Hauptstadt, aber auch der Kultroman von Hallgrímur Helgason, woraus der Regisseur Baltasar Kormakúr einen leichtfüßig skurrilen Szenefilm gedreht und damit auch auf die reiche Filmkultur der Insel aufmerksam gemacht hat. Das verbindet sich nun mit der aktuellen Architektur, weil die Architekten von Studio Granda, Steve Christer und Margrét Hardadóttir, für Kormakúrs Familie ein Wohnhaus gebaut haben. Elegant in die Landschaft komponiert, eröffnet sich das umgebende Panorama mit großen Ausblicken unter einem gefalteten Grasdach. Ganz wesentlich war die Mitwirkung der Bauherrin, Lilja Pálmadóttir, was zu einem kultivierten Haus auf höchstem Niveau geführt hat. Studio Granda ist sicherlich das zur Zeit auch international interessanteste Architekturbüro Islands. Nur zwei Jahre nach ihrem Studium an der Architectural Association in London haben sie 1986 den Wettbewerb für das neue Rathaus in Reykjavík gewonnen. Am Ufer des Tjörnin-Sees im Zentrum der Stadt gelegen, in mehrere Bauteile aufgelöst und von einem öffentlichen Weg geschickt durchwegt, ist der ausgewogen komponierte Betonbau, der auch international erstmals die Aufmerksamkeit auf zeitgenössische isländische Architektur richtete, zum heutigen Wahrzeichen Reykjavíks geworden. Mitte der neunziger Jahre gewann Studio Granda auch den Wettbewerb für den Obersten Gerichtshof. Und auch dieser Bau zeichnet sich durch exzellente Material- und Raumkomposition aus, die sich in der

history when Ronald Reagan and Mikhail Gorbachev met there on 11 and 12 October 1986 to agree on an end to the Cold war. At the peak of the war, the legendary victory of Bobby Fischer against Boris Spasski in the 1972 World Chess Championships occurred in Reykjavík.

Nowadays, it is "101 Reykjavík" that stands for euphoric weeks, or rather, nights. That's the capital city's central district, but also the name of the cult novel by Hallgrímur Helgason from which director Baltasar Kormakúr shot a light-footed, comical film, which also drew attention to the island's rich film culture. That now ties in with contemporary architecture, because the architects from Studio Granda, Steve Christer and Margrét Hardadóttir, built a residential house for the Kormakúr family. Composed elegantly in the countryside, the surrounding panorama opens up in enormous vistas under a folded grass roof. The collaboration with the owner, Lilja Pálmadóttir, was substantial, leading to a cultivated house of the highest standard. Studio Granda is certainly also Iceland's most interesting architectural office internationally. Only two years after studying at the Architectural Association in London, they won the competition for the new city hall in Reykjavík in 1986. The well-balanced concrete building on the shores of Lake Tjörnin at the center of the city, resolved in several building parts and cleverly traversed by a public path, was the first structure to turn international attention to contemporary Icelandic architecture and has now become a Reykjavík landmark. In the mid-1990s, Studio Granda also won the competition for the Supreme Court. And this

Elsewhere

Szenographie der Landschaft. *Im von Studio Granda geplanten Haus wird die enorme Präsenz der Natur inszeniert und im Inneren verdichtet reflektiert.*
Landscape scenography. *Nature's enormous presence is staged and reflected on in condensed form inside the home planned by Studio Granda.*

Neues Wahrzeichen. *Es war ein Glücksfall für die neue Architektur Islands, dass Studio Granda als junge Architekten den Wettbewerb für das Rathaus in Reykjavik gewannen. Die prägnante Komposition mit Einbeziehung des Seeufers, öffentlicher Durchwegung, sorgfältiger Innengestaltung und thematischer Inszenierung lokaler Materialien katapultierte Island auf die Landkarte der internationalen Architektur.*
New symbol. *Pure luck for Iceland's new architecture that Studio Granda won the competition for the city hall in Reykjavík: The composition of shoreline, pathways, precise interior design, and local materials has catapulted Iceland onto the map of international architecture.*

111 ninety-one degrees

Landscape of Nonentity   Dietmar Steiner

Hafnarhús. Ein altes Hafenhaus wurde von Studio Granda zu einem zeitgenössischen Kunstzentrum umgebaut. Die subtilen Interventionen verstärken das vorhandene Potenzial der grandiosen Räume. Ein Kunstort der Weltklasse.
Hafnarhús. Studio Granda redesigned an old harbor house as a contemporary art center. The subtle interventions intensify the existing potential of the fantastical spaces: A world-class art location.

Virtuos. Der Oberste Gerichtshof Islands von Studio Granda zelebriert einmal mehr ihr Talent bei der Interpretation der räumlichen Möglichkeiten eines Ortes und die Sorgfalt bei der Auswahl bedeutungsvoller Materialien und Details.
Virtuoso. Iceland's Supreme Court by Studio Granda once again celebrates their talent in interpreting the spatial possibilities of a site and their care in the selection of meaningful materials and details.

Elsewhere

Staatsarchitekt. *Gudjón Samúelsson hat die moderne Architektur Islands entscheidend geprägt. Er wurde 1937 mit dem Bau der Hallgrímskirche beauftragt, der 1945 begann. Weil Spendengelder für den Bau notwendig waren, erlebte er die Fertigstellung im Jahr 1986 nicht mehr.*
State architect. *Gudjón Samúelsson has decisively influenced Iceland's modern architecture. He was commissioned to build Hallgríms church, and began in 1945. Sponsors were still necessary for the construction: he was no longer around to experience its completion in 1986.*

ungewöhnlich kultivierten inneren Ausgestaltung konsequent fortsetzen. Islands Architektur hatte über Jahrhunderte eine bloß rurale Funktion der Behausung unter widrigsten Bedingungen, die einfach nur Hütten elementarster Form zeitigte. Erst um 1900 entstand die Möglichkeit, mit Betonkonstruktionen an die stilistischen Standards Europas anzuschließen. Gudjón Samúelsson war der erste Staatsarchitekt, der ab nun alle wichtigen Gebäude Islands durch die folgenden Jahrzehnte hindurch in verschiedenen Stilen baute. Vom Symbol Reykjavíks, der Kathedrale Hallgrímskirkja, bis zur Universität und zum Staatstheater. Das ganze 20. Jahrhundert entwerfen weitere Architekten sehr engagiert alle Stile einer skandinavischen Moderne, für Siedlungen, Schulen, Kirchen auf einem hohen pragmatischen Niveau.

Beim Studium des exzellenten, aber leider vergriffenen Architekturführers Islands von Birgit Albrecht und im Gespräch mit dem allwissenden Architekturhistoriker Petúr Ármannsson taucht der Name einer Architektin auf, deren Projekte von eigentümlicher Poesie und Kraft aus der allgemein guten isländischen Moderne herausragen: Högna Sigurdardóttir studierte an der École des Beaux Arts in Paris – die Begegnung mit ihren Häusern wird zur Entdeckung. Auf Grundrissen ausgeklügelter Raumkompositionen errichtete sie in den späten sechziger Jahren einige kontrolliert skulpturale Einfamilienhäuser, die lokale Traditionen des Bauens und der Landschaft aufnahmen und diese Architektin, bislang weitgehend unbekannt, der absoluten Spitze der internationalen Architektur ihrer Zeit zuführen. ‚Högna's Houses' sind sensationelle artifizielle Manifeste, ihr präziser und kreativer Umgang mit rohem Beton ist einzigartig.

building, too, is distinguished by excellent material and spatial compositions, which consistently follow through in extraordinarily cultivated interior design.
For centuries, Iceland's architecture fulfilled a merely rural function of providing an abode under extremely adverse conditions, which simply yielded the most elementary form of cottages. Subscribing to European style standards was first possible in the 1900s through the advent of concrete construction. From this time on, Gudjón Samúelsson, the first state architect, built all of Iceland's important buildings throughout the following decades in various styles: from the symbol of Reykjavík, Hallgrímskirkja Cathedral, through to the university and State Theater. Further highly committed architects delivered highly pragmatic designs in all possible modern Scandinavian styles throughout the entire twentieth century: for housing estates, schools, and churches.

In reviewing the excellent but unfortunately out-of-print architectural guide to Iceland by Birgit Albrecht, and in conversation with the all-knowing architecture historian Petúr Ármannsson, the name of one architect comes up whose projects display a unique poetry and power that elevates them from the generally well-designed Icelandic modern: Högna Sigurdardóttir who studied at the École des Beaux Arts in Paris. Encountering her houses is a discovery. In the late 1960s, she built several controlled, sculptural single family homes on outlines with ingenious spatial compositions, which integrated local building traditions and the landscape, leading the architect, hitherto largely unknown, to the absolute peak of

Landscape of Nonentity   Dietmar Steiner

Högna's Houses. Auf die internationale Entdeckung wartet das Werk der genialen Architektin Högna Sigurdardóttir. Zwei Einfamilienhäuser verstecken sich unter der winterlichen Schneedecke, die allein schon kraft ihrer Architektur in der Liga von Carlo Scarpa, Sverre Fehn oder Jørn Utzon mitspielen können.

Högna's Houses. *The work of the ingenious architect Högna Sigurdardóttir has yet to attain international attention. Two single family homes hide under a winter coat of snow. The power of their architecture alone puts them in the same league as Carlo Scarpa, Sverre Fehn, and Jørn Utzon.*

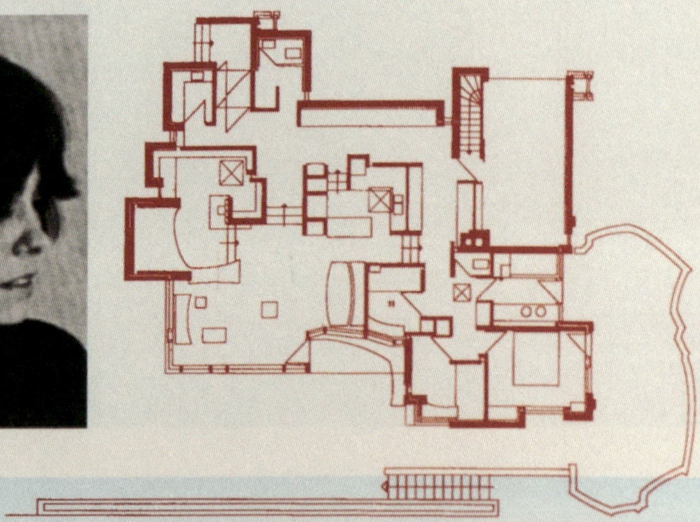

Elsewhere

Überraschend bleibt insgesamt das hohe Niveau vieler moderner Bauten in Island, die unter dem Druck des aktuellen Baubooms zu verschwinden drohen. Da verführen vor allem Studio Grandas und Högna Sigurdardóttirs konzeptionell und materiell virtuose architektonische Verweise auf die Stimmung und Präsenz von Islands einzigartiger Landschaft, eröffnen den unbedingten Wunsch, diese auch erleben zu wollen. Auf ziellos scheinenden Straßen gleitet man dann durch scheinbar unbewohntes Land. Der alles bedeckende Schnee im Winter erinnert an eine Wüstendurchquerung. Ein seltsames autosuggestives Gefühl stellt sich ein, kaum ein anderes Auto, nichts als Landschaft ist zu sehen. Alle paar Stunden versammeln sich einige am Horizont verstreute Schemen von kleinen Häusern und Hütten zu einem Dorf, das sich nur durch eine wenige hundert Meter entlang der Straße erstreckende, völlig irrational wirkende Straßenbeleuchtung als solches zu erkennen gibt. Zur meditativen Vollendung gelangt diese Durchquerung des Niemandslandes, wenn dazu noch die magische Sound-Tapete der wunderbaren zeitgenössischen isländischen Popmusik erklingt, die erst den wirklichen emotionalen Raum dieser so exotischen Welt einer eigentlich unbewohnbaren Insel nahe des Polarkreises eröffnet, die davon lebt, dass sich ihre Bewohner entschlossen hatten, wider alle Vernunft diesem Ort eine nur hier erfahrbare, einzigartige poetische Form der Zivilisation abzuringen.

international architecture of her day. "Högna's Houses" are sensational artificial manifests. Their precise and creative way of dealing with exposed concrete is matchless.

Yet what is surprising as a whole is the high quality of many of the modern structures in Iceland that are threatened with being wiped out under the pressure of the current construction boom. These conceptually and materially virtuoso architectural testimonies to the ambiance and presence of Iceland's unique landscape by Studio Granda and Högna Sigurdardóttir are what primarily tempt us, open up the desire to also want to experience this landscape. One glides on seemingly aimless streets through an apparently uninhabited land. The snow, which blankets everything in winter, makes it seem like a desert crossing. A strange auto-suggestive feeling surfaces, nary a car in sight, nothing to see but countryside. Every few hours, a scattered pattern of diminutive houses and cottages gathers on the horizon to form a village, discernible as such only by the seemingly utterly irrational street lights extending along the road for a few hundred meters. This meditative journey through nowhere land is rendered complete by the magical sounds of Iceland's incredible contemporary pop music, which first opens the emotional space of this highly exotic world on an uninhabitable island near the Arctic Circle. And it persists because its inhabitants have decided, against all rationality, to wrest from this place a tremendously poetic form of civilization that is possible to experience here, alone.

Landscape of Nonentity   Dietmar Steiner

Riesiges Niemandsland. *Die ‚Architektur' versammelt sich im Zentralraum der Hauptstadt Reykjavík. ‚Europäisch' ist die urbane Baukultur der Insel im 20. Jahrhundert, ‚amerikanisch' sind hingegen die räumlichen Dimensionen Islands, erschlossen von unglaublichen 13.000 km Straßen/Pistennetz.*
Enormous No-man's-land. *The "architecture" is gathered in the central space of the capital Reykjavík. The island's urban building culture is European, whereas the spatial dimensions are, in contrast, American: connected by an unbelievable street/runway network of 13,000 km.*

Island Porträt

Wenn auf einer 103.125 Quadratkilometer großen Insel 313.376 Einwohner leben, dann haben die statistischen 3,1 Einwohner pro Quadratkilometer ziemlich viel Fläche und Raum zur Verfügung. Allerdings ist der Großteil der Insel unbewohnbar, Island ist die größte Vulkaninsel der Welt. Sie liegt auf der Reibungsfläche der Nordamerikanischen und Eurasischen Platte, die jährlich zwei Zentimeter auseinander driften. Fischfang war die Basis der Inselökonomie. Aber schon an zweiter Stelle rangiert heute ein heftig zunehmender Tourismus mit über 400.000 Besuchern pro Jahr, der von den Grenzerfahrungen in der einzigartigen Landschaft mit ihren Geysiren, Wasserfällen und Gletschern fasziniert ist. Dieser findet im Sommer statt, denn der Winter ist zwar aufgrund des Golfstroms unerwarteterweise relativ mild, aber die Stürme des Island-Tiefs erlauben nur eine eingeschränkte Mobilität. Nach jahrhundertelanger Unterdrückung durch Dänen und Norweger ist Island seit 1944 eine unabhängige demokratische Republik, der schon ab 1904 von Dänemark eine relative Autonomie gewährt worden war. Island ist zum einen Mitglied der NATO, ohne über eigene Streitkräfte zu verfügen, da es ein Verteidigungsabkommen mit den USA gibt, und zum anderen als Mitglied des Schengener Abkommens, ohne EU-Mitglied zu sein, für Europäer visafrei.
Über neunzig Prozent der Bevölkerung lebt in den Städten der Insel, wobei der Großraum Reykjavíks mit rund 200.000 Einwohnern das Zentrum bildet. In dieser Agglomeration findet seit Jahren eine Suburbanisierung statt, die sich mit mehrspurigen Stadtautobahnen deutlich von der Infrastruktur der restlichen Insel unterscheidet. Eisenbahnen gibt es nicht, rudimentär sind öffentliche Busverbindungen vorhanden. In den letzten Jahren ist Island ein wichtiger Standort für internationale Dienstleistungsunternehmen geworden. Der tertiäre Sektor boomt und erzeugt für die einstmals egalitäre Gesellschaft eine neue Klasse individuellen Reichtums. An Bedeutung gewinnt auch die Energieerzeugung durch Wasserkraft und mit geothermischen Kraftwerken, was Island eine weitgehende Autonomie der Energieversorgung sichert.

Portrait of Iceland

When 313,376 inhabitants live on a 103,125 square-kilometer island, then the statistical 3.1 inhabitants per square kilometer have quite a bit of surface area and space available. Mind you, though, the majority of the island is uninhabitable. Iceland is the largest volcanic island in the world. It lies on the mid-Atlantic ridge separating the North American and Eurasian plates, which drift two centimeters apart every year. Fishing was once the basis of the island's economy. But tourism, which is growing intensely, already ranks second with more than 400,000 visitors per year who are fascinated by the ultimate experience of this unique landscape with its geysers, waterfalls, and glaciers. Tourism takes place in summer; the winter is unexpectedly relatively mild due to the Gulf Stream, but the storms of the Icelandic Low permit limited mobility only. After centuries of oppression by the Danish and Norwegians, Iceland has been an independent democratic republic since 1944, after having already been granted relative autonomy from Denmark in 1904. Iceland is, for one, a member of NATO, but without its own armed forces; it has a defense agreement with the US. For another, as a member of the Schengen Agreement it offers visa-free entry for Europeans, but is not a member of the EU.
More than 90 percent of the population lives in the island's cities. The metropolitan area around Reykjavík, with roughly 200,000 inhabitants, forms the center. A process of suburbanization has been taking place in this agglomeration for years. Its multilane city highways clearly distinguish it from the rest of the island. There is no railway, and public bus connections are rudimentary. In recent years, Iceland has become a key location for international service companies. The tertiary sector is booming, generating a new class of individual wealth in the once egalitarian society. Also gaining in importance is energy production through waterpower and with geothermal power plants, assuring Iceland extensive autonomy in terms of energy supplies.

Elsewhere

Island Architektur

Island hat eine Bautradition, die sich mit keinem anderen Land vergleichen lässt. Erst vor etwas mehr als 1000 Jahren begann die Besiedlung der Insel durch die norwegischen Wikinger. Sie mussten sich mit der elementarsten Form der Behausung zufrieden geben. Erde und Steine wurden aufgeschichtet und auf diese Art sogenannte Langhäuser zum Schutz vor der Witterung errichtet. Ziegel und Holz gab es nicht. Später wurden dann in Skandinavien vorgefertige Holzkonstruktionen importiert, und ab dem 19. Jahrhundert ganze Häuser in verschiedenen Stilen. Einen Fortschritt bildete das aus England importierte Wellblech, das dem isländischen Wetter entsprechenden Widerstand leisten konnte. Der nächste Schritt wurde mit der Verbreitung von Beton eingeleitet. Staatsarchitekt Gudjon Samúelsson entwarf ab 1916 bis in die fünfziger Jahre alle wichtigen Bauten der neuen Periode: Nationaltheater, Universität, die alte Parlamentsstätte und neben dem Wahrzeichen von Reykjavík, der Hallgrímskirche, noch weitere Kirchen, den Nationalfriedhof, einen Leuchtturm und Wasserkraftwerke – alles beseelt von der Suche nach einem Nationalstil. Die Architekturentwicklung des 20. Jahrhunderts folgte der internationalen Moderne mit kultivierten Beispielen. Das Standardwerk über isländische Architektur ist der 2000 erschienene und leider vergriffene ‚Architekturführer Island' von Birgit Albrecht in Isländisch, Deutsch und Englisch. Eine unerschöpfliche Quelle bietet das Archiv von Pétur H. Ármansson, der die leider aufgelöste Architekturabteilung des Museums Kjarvalsstadír leitete. Die isländische Architektenvereinigung hat einen kleinen und handlichen ‚Guide to Icelandic Architecture' herausgebracht. Die derzeitige Alltagsarchitektur unterscheidet sich nicht von der übrigen skandinavischen Businessarchitektur. In den letzten Jahrzehnten sorgten vor allem die Bauten von Studio Granda für internationale Aufmerksamkeit.

Iceland Architecture

Iceland has a building tradition that cannot be compared with that of any other country. The settling of the island first began just over 1,000 years ago by the Norwegian Vikings. They had to be content with the most basic form of dwelling. Turf and stones were piled up, and in this way, so-called long-houses were erected as protection from the elements. Neither bricks nor wood were available. Later, prefabricated wood constructions from Scandinavia were imported, and beginning in the nineteenth century, entire houses in a variety of styles. Progress came with the corrugated sheet metal imported from England, capable of adequately withstanding Icelandic weather. The next step was introduced with the spread of concrete. From 1916 through to the 1950s, State Architect Gudjon Samúelsson designed all important buildings of the new period: national theater, university, the old parliament, the symbol of Reykjavík, Hallgrím's Church, and also other churches, the National Cemetery, a lighthouse and hydroelectric power plants—always animated by the search for an Icelandic national style. Architectural development in the twentieth century followed from International Modernism and offered cultivated examples. The standard work on Icelandic architecture is "Architectural Guide to Iceland" by Birgit Albrecht, in Icelandic, German, and English, published in 2000, unfortunately out of print. An inexhaustible source is the archive of Pétur H. Ármansson who was manager of the—unfortunately, now closed— architectural section at Kjarvalsstadír Museum. The Association of Icelandic Architects has published a small, handy "Guide to Icelandic Architecture." Everyday architecture nowadays does not differ from the rest of Scandinavian business architecture. Over the past decades, the buildings by Studio Granda, first and foremost, have stirred international attention.

6ᵗʰ DAY The 2010s

Fassadenreinigung · Façade Cleaning · Beijing. © DS

New business architecture prevails worldwide. The software and rendering industry eliminates the architect as "author." The star system is obsolete. – +++ – Several trips to China provide me with a deepened understanding for this coming superpower. On the one hand, the Western-influenced apocalyptic urbanization and, on the other hand, the discovery of the huge potency of its autochthonous tradition and history – +++ – The media landscape of architecture has fundamentally changed. The blogs and social media of the Internet now only follow the "attention economy." – +++ – Classic science fiction scenarios are becoming reality: The high-tech world of the rich increasingly finds itself at war against the world of the lost. – +++ – The reflection of postwar modernism, of brutalism, of participation and of postmodernism, sets in. From now on the distance of time is large enough. The theory of architecture is rediscovered. – +++ – The development of the Architecture Biennale in Venice has broken out into a positively critical direction since 2010 and has increasingly broached the issue of the role of the architect and architecture in a world of hardships and needs. – +++ – Nonetheless, I now bid adieu to this market of cultural-historically postmodern and historically neo-modern novelties in which all architects and positions since the year 1959 now fall into each other simultaneously. I am now only interested in the architecture of the future's past ...

6. TAG Die 2010er

Kunstbezirk · Art District · Caochangdi, Ai Wei Wei. © DS

Weltweit setzt sich eine neue Business-Architektur durch. Die Software- und Rendering-Industrie eliminiert den Architekten als ‚Autor'. Das Star-System ist obsolet – +++ – Mehrere China-Reisen eröffnen mir ein vertieftes Verständnis für diese kommende Supermacht. Einerseits die westlich geprägte apokalyptische Urbanisierung und andererseits die Entdeckung der gewaltigen Potenz seiner autochthonen Tradition und Geschichte – +++ – Die Medienlandschaft der Architektur hat sich grundsätzlich verändert. Die Blogs und Social Media des Internet folgen nur mehr der „Ökonomie der Aufmerksamkeit" – +++ – Die klassischen Science-Fiction-Szenarien werden Wirklichkeit: Die hochtechnologisierte Welt der Reichen befindet sich zunehmend im Krieg gegen die Welt der Verlorenen – +++ – Die Reflexion der Nachkriegsmoderne, des Brutalismus, der Partizipation und der Postmoderne setzt ein. Der zeitliche Abstand ist von nun an groß genug. Die Theorie der Architektur wird wiederentdeckt – +++ – Dazu schlägt die Entwicklung der Architektur-Biennale in Venedig seit 2010 eine positiv kritische Richtung ein und thematisiert zunehmend die Rolle des Architekten und der Architektur in einer Welt der Bedrängnisse und Notwendigkeiten – +++ – Dennoch verabschiede mich jetzt von diesem Markt der kulturgeschichtlich postmodernen und historistisch neumodernen Neuigkeiten, in der alle Architekturen und Positionen seit dem Jahre 1959 nunmehr gleichzeitig ineinanderfallen. An der Architektur der Zukunft interessiert mich nur mehr deren Vergangenheit …

Sechster Tag • Day Six

1 Wohnhaus Linke Wienzeile 96, Wien Vienna, 1991-95. © Pez Hejduk

2 Reihenhaussiedlung Othellogasse, Wien Vienna, 1987-93. © Margherita Spiluttini

3 Wohnhausanlage Oberlaa West, Wien Vienna, 2003-05. © Michael Hirner

4 Wohnhaus City X, Wien Vienna, 1999-2003. © Pez Hejduk

5 Wohnhausanlage Attemsgasse 23, Wien Vienna, 2012-15. © cuferteam

6 Wohnhausanlage WMR - Kaltenleutgebner Straße 24, Wien Vienna, 2012-16. © cuferteam

Seit 36 Jahren arbeitet Architektin Margarethe Cufer für den sozialen Wohnbau in Wien.
For 36 years architect Margarethe Cufer has been working for Viennese social housing.

aus · from

Contemporary Vienna / Architecture, Art, Design, Film, Literature, Music, edited by Christoph Thun-Hohenstein, departure, Schlebrügge editor, 2010
"Housing: Architecture for everyone"
Translation by Mark Gilbert

Wiener Wohnbau

Housing in Vienna

The burning issue for Vienna in the 20th century was housing. And this will not change in the new millennium. Not only because housing is the most important constitutive building block of the city; but also because housing is and will always be a central social, cultural and political instrument for urban development in Vienna. And, above and beyond all else, the Viennese project of social housing is legendary, almost larger than life: a highly complex system, which no one outside of Vienna is truly able to comprehend.

Please allow me to explain. For centuries, housing in Vienna was rarely a sphere for the exercise of civil self-determination. During the long years of the monarchy, the emperor wielded the Hofquartierspflicht, which was the legal right of the court to summarily appropriate private residences in order to house its officials. The Church and the various monasteries were the only institutions to receive exemption from this onerous load; they in turn had their own housing endowments, which they allocated amongst the members of their own 'courts.' This sociological and urban typological pecu-

Das für die Stadt Wien zentrale Thema im 20. Jahrhundert war der Wohnungsbau und er wird es auch im neuen Jahrtausend sein. Dies nicht nur deshalb, weil das wichtigste Element für die Gestaltung der Stadt immer der Wohnungsbau sein wird. Dies auch deshalb, weil der Wohnungsbau für die Stadt Wien ein zentrales soziales, kulturelles und politisches Instrument ist und immer war. Darüber hinaus ist der Wiener Wohnbau ein Mythos, ein hochkomplexes System, das außerhalb Wiens niemand versteht.

Ich versuche zumindest eine Erklärung: Wohnen in Wien war über Jahrhunderte hinweg überwiegend keine Sache ziviler Selbstbestimmung. In der Monarchie bestand die so genannte Hofquartierspflicht, die dem Kaiserhaus erlaubte, jederzeit für seine Beamten Wohnungen in privaten Häusern zu akquirieren. Ausgenommen davon waren nur die Besitztümer der Kirche und der Klöster, die selbst wiederum mit ihren „Höfen" über eine eigene Wohnungsversorgung verfügten. Diese soziologische und typologische Eigenart der Wiener

Reumannhof, Hubert Gessner, 1924–26.
© Architekturzentrum Wien, Sammlung · Collection,
Margherita Spiluttini

liarity of Viennese culture is one of the primary reasons that, to this day, the public spaces of the city—the space 'between the courts'—have generally been neglected. Housing in Vienna has always been shaped by relationships of hierarchy and dependency. One didn't acquire housing; metaphorically speaking, housing was 'lent' to its users by their respective masters.

It was from out of this set of circumstances that, upon the collapse of the monarchy, Viennese social democracy assumed a largely unprecedented and wide-ranging obligation for the provision of housing in the city. The breadth of this obligation allowed the social democratic government to build an incomparable program for social housing out of the ashes of the catastrophic urban living conditions that characterized the city's late 19th century Gründerzeit era. It was certainly no coincidence that one of the first large social housing projects produced under the new socialist government—the Reumannhof by Hubert Gessner—resembled a castle. While this result was neither architecturally nor programmatically proscribed, the conceptual

Stadtkultur führte übrigens auch dazu, dass dem öffentlichen Raum der Stadt – dem Raum ‚zwischen den Höfen' – bis heute geringe Aufmerksamkeit geschenkt wird. Das Wohnen in Wien war also immer schon von einer hierarchischen Abhängigkeit gekennzeichnet. Man erwarb eine Wohnung nicht, sie wurde einem vielmehr – metaphorisch gesprochen – von der jeweils herrschenden Macht ‚verliehen'.

Diese Grundstimmung erlaubte der Wiener Sozialdemokratie, nach dem Zusammenbruch der Monarchie die nahezu totale Fürsorgepflicht für das Wohnen in Wien zu übernehmen und sie angesichts der damals herrschenden katastrophalen Wohnverhältnisse im gründerzeitlichen Wohnungsbestand zu einem weltweit einzigartigen Programm auszubauen. Nicht architektonisch programmatisch verordnet, aber doch signifikant in seiner Konzeption, erinnert einer der ersten großen Gemeindebauten, der Reumannhof von Hubert Gessner, nicht zufällig an eine Schlossanlage, Schönbrunn ist in gedanklicher Rufweite. Mit diesem monarchischen Anspruch wurde die Legende vom „Roten Wien" begründet.

underpinnings of this particular form were not without significance—clearly, the Emperor's residence at Schönbrunn was not far from mind. One might even say that the legend of "Red Vienna" was founded on this rather monarchal gesture.

The social housing program of "Red Vienna" lasted from 1922 to 1934, and it was one of the great urban projects of the 20th century. Despite that era's desolate economic situation, more than 60,000 housing units were built. In terms of their construction, the results were quite conventional; architecturally, they were definitely heterogeneous. The program offered little room for Modernism's vision of technological progress. In view of the era's raging unemployment, the utmost priority was for investments in housing to generate as many jobs as possible; and this was better achieved by using traditional building methods than through the application of industrialized processes. Under Austro-Fascism (1934–1938) and National Socialism (1938–1945), the production of new housing came practically to a standstill; during this latter period, 'demand' was largely 'satisfied' through the 'Aryanization' of some 59,000 apartments and homes. Vienna suffered far less damage than other major German cities during the Second World War, yet still 13 per cent of the total housing stock in the city was destroyed, and almost 90,000 housing units were uninhabitable.

Reconstruction began at the end of the 1940s; it assumed the form of a moderate Modernism that was built in accordance to a strict set of standards laid down by municipal authorities. During the 1960s and 70s, the City of Vienna faithfully followed the larger international trend towards prefabrication—which architects themselves lobbied for and promoted—and developed large-format, panel-construction housing systems for its urban periphery. After the Oil Crisis of the early 1970s, urban sprawl began to come under increasing criticism, and the rediscovery of urbanity in the European City made small-scale, participatory processes for

Biberhaufenweg, Heinz Tesar, Carl Pruscha, Otto Häuselmayer, Wafler Architekten. © Architekturzentrum Wien, Sammlung · Collection, Margherita Spiluttini

Der Wiener Gemeindebau des „Roten Wien", von 1922 bis 1934, war eine der größten urbanistischen Leistungen des 20. Jahrhunderts. In dieser wirtschaftlich schwierigen Zeit wurden über 60.000 Wohnungen gebaut. Bautechnisch konventionell und architektonisch durchaus heterogen. Die technologischen Visionen der Moderne fanden dabei kaum Berücksichtigung. Wichtiger war angesichts der großen Arbeitslosigkeit die Beschäftigung von Menschen, die mit arbeitsintensiven traditionellen Bautechniken leichter als mit industrialisierten erfüllbar war. Im Austrofaschismus (ab 1934) und im Nationalsozialismus (ab 1938) kam der Wohnungsbau praktisch zum Erliegen. Der ‚Bedarf' dieser Zeit wurde mit der Arisierung von rund 59.000 Mietwohnungen ‚gedeckt'. Wien war nach dem Ende des Zweiten Weltkriegs weniger zerstört als deutsche Städte. ‚Lediglich' 13 Prozent des gesamten Wiener Wohnhausbestands waren vernichtet, fast 90.000 Wohnungen unbewohnbar.

Der Wiederaufbau erfolgte ab den späten 1940er Jahren in Form einer moderaten Moderne und nach strengen Normen der Dienststellen der Gemeinde Wien. In den 1960er und 70er Jahren folgte die Stadt Wien dem internationalen, auch von Architekten gefor-

Wohnpark Alt-Erlaa, Harry Glück & Partner, Kurt Hlaweniczka, Requat & Reinthaller, 1968–85. Archive DS

urban renewal increasingly important. Nonetheless, Vienna continued to erect new, large-scale housing projects—Am Schöpfwerk, Wohnpark Alt-Erlaa, Wohnen Morgen—which were largely indebted to the metabolistic idea of systematically built, dense urban housing.

The historical groundwork for the present Viennese social housing process was laid in 1984 through the founding of the Viennese Land Allocation and Urban Renewal Fund (WBSF), which, under the name wohnfonds_wien, controls and finances Vienna's social housing program in its entirety. (Since this point in time, by the way, the number of housing units erected directly by the municipality of Vienna has continuously declined; the city's last project was finished in 2004. Today, the City of Vienna manages some 220,000 units of municipal housing.) At that time I declared that the WBSF was an instrument of "enlightened Stalinism." Why? In its first years only the WBSF was allowed to buy those building parcels that were zoned for subsi-

derten Trend und entwickelte Fertigteilsysteme und Großtafelbauweisen für den Wohnbau der Stadterweiterung. Anfang der 1970er Jahre (nach der Ölkrise) setzte aber die Kritik der Stadterweiterung ein, die Wiederentdeckung der urbanen Grundlagen der europäischen Stadt förderte eine kleinteilige und partizipatorische Stadterneuerung. Dennoch wurden in dieser Zeit in Wien noch neue Großanlagen errichtet – Am Schöpfwerk, Wohnpark Alt-Erlaa, Wohnen morgen –, die der metabolistischen Idee verdichteter urbaner Wohnformen verpflichtet waren.

Die historische Grundlage für den heutigen sozialen Wiener Wohnbau wurde 1984 mit der Gründung des Wiener Bodenbereitstellungs- und Stadterneuerungsfonds (WBSF) geschaffen, der unter seinem heutigen Namen als wohnfonds_wien das gesamte soziale Wohnbauprogramm in Wien kontrolliert und finanziert. (Die Gemeinde Wien errichtete ab diesem Zeitpunkt immer weniger Wohnbauten selbst; das letzte Projekt wurde im Jahr 2004 realisiert. Heute verwaltet

dized housing; it would then alone decide which housing developers received these parcels to build. As there was only one buyer for residential building land, the cost of land could be controlled and held at low price levels. Again under the oversight of the WBSF, the developers were responsible for producing and marketing architectural solutions whose quality conformed to the standards set down by Vienna's subsidized housing program.

A number of impressive and innovative projects emerged from out of this 'regime,' such as the Siedlung Biberhaufenweg by the architects Carl Pruscha, Heinz Tesar, Otto Häuselmayer, Franz and Wilfried Wafler; the Siedlung Traviatagasse, based upon Raimund Abraham's master plan, and with contributions by Carl Pruscha, Günter Lautner, Peter Scheifinger and Rudolf Szedenik, Walter Buck and Uta Giencke. Even an early work of the Pritzker Prize winners Jacques Herzog and Pierre de Meuron was realized in this era: the Siedlung Pilotengasse, which was the product of a cooperative, multi-national planning team that also included Adolf Krischanitz (Vienna) and Otto Steidle (Munich). These and many other housing estates from the 1980s and 1990s were remarkable experiments for an urbanistic and typological renewal of Viennese social housing. It was also in this era that other quality architects—Helmut Richter, Johannes Spalt, Friedrich Kurrent, Hermann Czech, Jean Nouvel, Rob Krier, just to name a few—were first allowed break through the housing cooperatives' phalanx of so-called 'house architects' and realize social housing projects on their own.

The 1980s were without a doubt the most innovative decade for housing in Vienna during the second half of the 20th century. Committed architects and developers

Am Schöpfwerk, Viktor Hufnagl mit Eric Bauer, Leo Parenzan, Michael Pribitzer, Fritz Waclawek, Traude und Wolfgang Windbrechtinger, 1976–80. Archive DS

die Stadt Wien rund 220.000 dieser Gemeindebauwohnungen.) Ich nannte den WBSF damals eine Institution des „aufgeklärten Stalinismus". Warum? In den Anfangsjahren durfte nur der WBSF für den geförderten Wohnungsbau gewidmete Grundstücke kaufen und konnte diese dann den Bauträgern zur Verfügung stellen. Indem es für ganz Wien nur einen Käufer von Grundstücken gab, konnten die Grundstückspreise kontrolliert und niedrig gehalten werden. Dann oblag es in der Folge den Bauträgern, wieder unter Kontrolle des WBSF, entsprechend qualitative architektonische Lösungen für den geförderten Wiener Wohnbau anzubieten.

Unter diesem neuen ‚Regime' entstanden in den 1980er Jahren architektonisch beachtliche und innovative Projekte, wie die Siedlung Biberhaufenweg mit den Architekten Carl Pruscha, Heinz Tesar, Otto Häuselmayer, Franz Wafler, die Siedlung Traviatagasse nach dem Masterplan von Raimund Abraham, mit Bauteilen von Carl Pruscha, Günter Lautner, Peter Scheifinger und Rudolf Szedenik, Walter Buck und Uta Giencke. Sogar ein Frühwerk der Pritzker-Preisträger Jacques Herzog und Pierre de Meuron ist darunter: die Siedlung Pilotengasse, die als trinationale Gemeinschaftsarbeit mit Adolf Krischanitz (Wien) und Otto Steidle (München) verwirklicht wurde. Diese und viele andere Siedlungen der 1980er und 90er Jahre waren auch beachtliche experimentelle Versuche einer urbanistisch-typologischen Erneuerung des Wiener Wohnbaus. Aber auch andere Qualitätsarchitekten wie Helmut Richter, Johannes Spalt, Friedrich Kurrent, Hermann Czech, Jean Nouvel, Rob Krier konnten in

Sechster Tag • Day Six

Siedlung Traviatagasse, Raimund Abraham, Walter Buck & Uta Giencke, Günter Lautner & Peter Scheifinger & Rudolf Szedenik, Carl Pruscha, 1987–1991. Archive DS

shared a desire for quality and innovation and were able to capitalize upon the new political freedoms first given to the ÖVP-dominated housing developers by the Vice-Mayor Erhard Busek (1978–87) and then made available after 1984 to the SPÖ-dominated developers by Mayor Helmut Zilk. This historical development brings a particular fact into focus: In Austria, publicly subsidized housing is largely realized by development corporations closely affiliated with either the Socialist (SPÖ) or the conservative Peoples' Party (ÖVP). For it is politics which determines which developer will receive which housing subsidies.

dieser Periode erstmals mit Projekten des sozialen Wohnbaus in Wien betraut werden und brachen damit in die Phalanx der ‚Hausarchitekten' der Wohnbaugenossenschaften ein.

Die 80er Jahre waren zweifellos das innovativste Jahrzehnt im Wiener Wohnbau der zweiten Hälfte des 20. Jahrhunderts. Engagierte Architekten und Bauträger verspürten den Wunsch nach Qualität und Innovation und nutzten die neuen, von der Politik gegebenen Freiheiten, die zunächst unter Vizebürgermeister Erhard Busek (1978–87) für die ÖVP-dominierten Wohnbaugesellschaften und ab 1984 unter Bürgermeister

Nonetheless, Vienna's system of subsidized housing as well as the political mechanisms that guided it were continuously developed further. In 1994, Werner Faymann became the Municipal Councilor for Housing and Urban Renewal as well as the President of the WBSF. (In January 2007, he left Viennese city politics in order to become the Federal Minister for Infrastructure and Development and later on Federal Chancellor of Austria.) In the first year after Faymann's assumption of office in Vienna, the municipal system of subsidized housing was reformed from the ground up. In 1995, Faymann established the so-called Real Estate Advisory Board and revolutionized the allocation of projects through the establishment of the Developers' Competition process. The Board's function was to assess all projects applying for housing subsidies with respect to the three criteria of architecture, ecology and economy. Comprised of a group of independent experts, the board judged each project on the basis of a checklist for project standards; only when these standards are met or exceeded could a project be recommended for realization. Project submissions must display high architectural quality, and demonstrate excellent ecological performance; the quality construction and furnishings must be established and justifiable rent tables for future tenants must be calculated. If a project contains more than 300 housing units, a Developers' Competition must be held. In this case, housing developers compete for the commission on the basis of a fully-formulated project design that has been worked-out in cooperation with an architect. The Advisory Board applies its catalog of qualitative criteria to these project entries as well. Since 1995, this system of cooperative competitions involving both developers and architects has significantly reduced unit costs while simultaneously improving the

Helmut Zilk auch für die SPÖ-dominierten Bauträger gegeben waren. Dieser Hinweis beruht auf der Besonderheit, dass in ganz Österreich der öffentlich geförderte Wohnbau überwiegend von parteinahen Wohnbaugesellschaften – entweder SPÖ oder ÖVP – realisiert wird. Denn es ist die Politik, die darüber entscheidet, welcher Bauträger welche Wohnbauförderungsmittel erhält.

Dennoch wurde in Wien das System des geförderten Wohnbaus mit seinen politischen Instrumenten konsequent weiterentwickelt. Im Jahr 1994 wurde Werner Faymann – der spätere Infrastrukturminister und Bundeskanzler – Stadtrat für Wohnbau und Stadterneuerung und Präsident des WBSF. Schon ein Jahr nach seinem Amtsantritt erfuhr der geförderte Wohnbau eine grundsätzliche Reform. Faymann etablierte 1995 den sogenannten Grundstücksbeirat und revolutionierte die Projektvergabe durch die Bauträgerwettbewerbe. Dieser Beirat beurteilt alle Projekte des geförderten Wohnbaus nach den Kriterien Architektur, Ökologie, Ökonomie – und setzt sich aus unabhängigen Experten zusammen, die alle Projekte des geförderten Wohnbaus

Wohnbau Brunner Straße, 1986–91, Helmut Richter.
© Architekturzentrum Wien, Sammlung · Collection, Margherita Spiluttini

Projekt Sargfabrik, BKK-2, 1994–96. © Architekturzentrum Wien, Sammlung · Collection, Margherita Spiluttini

architectural quality of subsidized housing in Vienna. Since 2010, Michael Ludwig—Werner Faymann's successor as Councilor for Housing and Urban Renewal—expanded the list of project criteria through the inclusion of the so-called fourth pillar of social sustainability, which means that experts in the field of housing and urban research now assess project submissions on the basis of their contribution to social stability and integration as well.

What do the built projects of the last 15 years demonstrate about social housing in Vienna? The fact is no other major city in the world has a system of subsidized housing that is so complex, yet so successfully structured, that affordable, high-quality housing can be offered to all those who want it. The end result is positively paradoxical. By virtue of its extensive systems of quality control and competitive allocation of real and

nach einem Kriterienkatalog begutachten und erst nach Erfüllung dieser Kriterien für eine Förderung empfehlen und freigeben. Dem Beirat müssen architektonische Qualitäten vorgelegt, aber auch ökologische Qualitäten nachgewiesen werden, ebenso wie die Bau- und Ausstattungsqualitäten sowie eine für die künftigen Bewohner leistbare Miethöhe. Die Bauträgerwettbewerbe wiederum müssen ab einem Bauvorhaben von 300 Wohnungen veranstaltet werden. Dazu bewerben sich Bauträger gemeinsam mit Architekten mit dafür ausgearbeiteten Projekten. Auch hier gelten dann die Kriterien des Beirats. Dieses Instrument des Wettbewerbs von Bauträgern und Architekten hat ab 1995 zu einer signifikanten Reduktion der Kosten bei gleichzeitiger Steigerung der Qualität des geförderten Wohnbaus in Wien geführt. Ab 2010 wurden von Michael

financial subsidies, subsidized housing in Vienna can offer quality that exceeds the general standards of market-rate accommodations. Today in Vienna, we develop, plan and build lodgings for the 'socially deserving' at a level of quality that can only be found elsewhere—world wide—in the market-financed, luxury housing sector.

In this context, it is useful to more precisely define what 'socially deserving' means. Tenants with incomes that extend well into the upper middle-class are eligible for subsidized housing in Vienna. This is a conscious political decision; this insures that new housing estates will house a diverse group of mixed-income tenants; the assistant professor actually lives next door to the newly immigrated janitor from Sri Lanka. This process is one of the city's most important means for fighting ghettoization and gentrification. The system of social housing in Vienna rests upon three essential programs for distributing housing subsidies, all of which support the goal of a socially diversified city. First of all are the developers' subsidies, which—as was previously explained—are based upon the fulfillment of a strict catalog of criteria which insure the quality of the finished construction. Then there is the individual housing assistance, which is an additional, direct grant to the tenant; assessed on basis of personal income, this subsidy makes quality housing available to those who couldn't otherwise afford it. Finally, funding is allocated for the maintenance and improvement of existing living quarters; this process is moderated by the City of Vienna's highly successful Neighborhood Assistance program. Through these three different forms of subsidization, Vienna invests a total of some 600 million Euros into social housing every year.

Donaucity im Bau · under construction, 1993–2000. Archive DS

Ludwig, der 2007 Werner Faymann nachfolgte, die Beurteilungskriterien um die so genannte vierte Säule erweitert, die mit ExpertInnen der Wohnbauforschung die soziale Nachhaltigkeit der Projekte beurteilt.

Was beweisen nun aber die gebauten Beispiele des sozialen Wiener Wohnbaus der letzten 15 Jahre? Faktum ist, dass keine andere Großstadt der Welt das System des geförderten Wohnbaus derart komplex strukturiert hat, dass hochqualitative Wohnungen zu einem leistbaren Preis für alle angeboten werden können. Das ergibt die geradezu paradoxe Situation, dass aufgrund des aufwendigen Kontrollsystems und des qualitativ kontrollierten Wettbewerbs des öffentlich geförderten Wohnbaus die Qualität des geförderten weit über jener des frei finanzierten Wohnungsbaus liegt. Wir entwickeln und bauen heute in Wien Wohnungen für die ‚sozial Bedürftigen' in einer Qualität, die anderswo auf der Welt nur im Segment des frei finanzierten Luxuswohnbaus angeboten wird.

Sechster Tag • Day Six

How does subsidized public housing make its presence felt in Vienna's contemporary urban landscape? At first glance, not at all. For new residential construction built anywhere in the city, it is not possible to distinguish between subsidized and market-rate housing just from the façade. This fact is alone insured by the very restrictive nature of the city's municipal planning regulations. Only if one delves deeper into a building does it become possible to recognize the particular traits of subsidized housing. For years now, social housing in Vienna must be fully accessible for the handicapped and its construction must insure low energy usage in the building's operation. Often, new buildings even fulfill the criteria for passive-house construction.

Of course, Vienna's system of social housing reacts to the continuing change in our society. We know today that only about 50 per cent of all housing units need be tailored to the needs of the 'classic' small family. All other residences need to respond to new forms of living; each dwelling must provide each of its inhabitants with a defined, intimate and autonomous space. For example, this rules out children's bedrooms of less than ten square meters, as this room must also be able to

An dieser Stelle muss deshalb der Begriff des ‚sozial Bedürftigen' näher erläutert werden. Die am Einkommen orientierte Berechtigung, eine geförderte Wohnung zu beziehen, reicht in Wien bis in den gehobenen Mittelstand. Das ist bewusste politische Absicht. Denn damit erzielt man in jedem neuen Wohnbau eine soziale Durchmischung. Der Universitätsassistent lebt dann tatsächlich im selben Haus wie die zugewanderte Reinigungskraft aus Sri Lanka. Das ist ein wesentliches stadtpolitisches Instrument gegen Ghettobildung und Gentrifizierung, wie überhaupt das System des sozialen Wohnbaus in Wien auf drei Säulen ruht. Zunächst die Förderung, die der Bauträger zur Errichtung der Wohnbauten bekommt, und die – wie ausführlich dargelegt – nach einem strengen Kriterienkatalog zur Erfüllung der Bauqualität gegliedert ist. Dann die individuellen Wohnbeihilfen, die jeder Mieter zusätzlich bekommt, wenn er sich auf Grund seiner Einkommenssituation die Wohnung sonst nicht leisten könnte. Und drittens jene Mittel, die für die Erhaltung und Verbesserung bestehender Wohnbauten und Quartiere aufgewendet werden, unter Moderation der sehr erfolgreichen Gebietsbetreuungen. Diese drei Säulen ergeben in Summe rund 600 Millionen Euro, die von der Stadt Wien jährlich in den sozialen Wohnbau investiert werden.

Wie macht sich nun der sozial geförderte Wohnungsbau im heutigen Wiener Stadtbild bemerkbar? Zunächst einmal gar nicht. Wird irgendwo in der Stadt ein Wohnbau errichtet, kann man an der Fassade normalerweise nicht unterscheiden ob es sich dabei um einen frei finanzierten oder um einen geförderten Wohnbau handelt. Dafür sorgen die für alle gültigen, restriktiven baubehördlichen Bestimmungen. Erst wenn man sich genauer mit den einzelnen Projekten beschäftigt, erkennt man die besonderen Qualitäten des geförderten Wohnbaus. Jeder geförderte Wohnbau in Wien muss seit Jahren barrierefrei ausgeführt werden und folgt den ökologischen Standards eines Niedrigenergie- oder sogar Passivhauses.

Kabelwerk, Schwalm-Theiss & Bresich, 2002–07. © Hertha Hurnaus

Wiener Wohnbau • Housing in Vienna

Kabelwerk, Hermann & Valentiny, Mascha & Seethaler, pool Architektur, Schwalm-Theiss & Bresich, Werkstatt Wien, Martin Wurnig und • and Branimir Kljajic, 2002–07. Archive DS

function as a single room within a shared-living arrangement, or as a part of an assisted-living apartment. A further principle is that each apartment must have an individual garden, balcony or loggia. And we know that developers must not only be required to equip their housing estates with community rooms that are accessible to all residents; they must also provide for the management and moderation of these spaces as well. In more recent years, project briefs have been developed which target specific residential issues; for instance, the problem of social and ethnic integration has been a subject of abiding interest. "Women's Residences," "Bike-City" or "Car-free City" are topics which have also been attended to. These represent just a few examples of the social and programmatic investigations being addressed by Viennese housing today.

Selbstverständlich reagiert das Wiener Wohnbausystem auch auf soziologische Veränderungen der Gesellschaft. Wir wissen heute, dass nur mehr rund 50 Prozent der Wohnungen von der klassischen Kleinfamilie bewohnt werden. Alle anderen Wohnungen müssen neuen Wohnformen entsprechen können, die in einem Wohnungsverband jedem Bewohner einen intimen und autonomen Raum zugestehen. Das verbietet sogenannte Kinderzimmer unter zehn Quadratmeter, weil sie auch als Einzelzimmer in einer Wohngemeinschaft oder für betreutes Wohnen funktionieren müssen. Als weitere Regel gilt, dass jede Wohnung einen individuellen Freiraum bieten muss, als Garten, Balkon oder Loggia ausgebildet. Zudem wissen wir, dass Gemeinschafts-

Sechster Tag • Day Six

The fact is no other major city in the world has a system of subsidized housing that is so complex, yet so successfully structured, that affordable, high-quality housing can be offered to all those who want it.

Yet, even though it must fulfill this lengthy list of formal and economic preconditions, social housing in Vienna consistently produces high-quality architecture. As an innovative platform for collective living, the Sargfabrik by the architects BKK-2 has attracted worldwide attention; the project not only explored new dimensions in architectural form, but has also established new and paradigmatic directions for forming residential communities. The project began as a grass-roots initiative for collective living which sought and found new ways for re-inhabiting the existing urban fabric. The Mustersiedlung Hadersdorf (also known as "Projekt 9=12") represented another direction for one-off urban housing. Once again—as was the case with the Siedlung Pilotengasse in the 1980s—an international community of architects experimented with a new, compact pattern for settling the outskirts of the city. For this project, Adolf Krischanitz invited Hermann Czech and Heinz Tesar from Austria, Max Dudler, Steidle Architekten, and Hans Kollhoff from Germany, and Marcel Meili Markus Peter Architekten, Peter Märkli,

räume nicht nur angeboten, sondern auch verwaltet und moderiert werden müssen. In den letzten Jahren gibt es auch Intentionen und Projekte für themenbezogenes Wohnen, die beispielsweise besonders auf Integration abgestimmt sind. Thematisiert werden auch „Frauenwohnen", „Bike-City" oder die „Autofreie Stadt"… um nur einige Hinweise auf die typologischen und konzeptionellen Überlegungen, die heute im Wiener Wohnbau angestellt werden, zu geben.

Mit all diesen geschilderten Maßnahmen hält der soziale Wiener Wohnbau sein hohes qualitatives Niveau aufrecht. Internationale Beachtung erlangte das Wohnmodell Sargfabrik der Architekten BKK-2, das nicht nur architektonisch, sondern auch sozial eine neu Dimension aufzeigt. Die Sargfabrik entstand als Basisinitiative, die als Wohngruppe für sich selbst eine neue Wohnform im Bestand realisierte. Ebenso eine Sonderlösung war die Mustersiedlung Hadersdorf, auch als Projekt „9=12" bekannt, wo noch einmal, wie schon bei der Siedlung Pilotengasse, eine internationale Architektengemeinschaft ein neues, verdichtetes Wohnmodell für den Stadtrand erprobte. Adolf Krischanitz versammelte dafür Hermann Czech und Heinz Tesar aus Österreich, Max Dudler, Steidle Architekten und Hans Kollhoff aus Deutschland, und Marcel Meili Markus Peter Architekten, Peter Märkli und Diener & Diener aus der Schweiz, um kleine, typologisch neue Stadtvillen mit innovativen Wohnungsgrundrissen für urban periphere Zonen zu entwickeln, die gleichzeitig besonders innovativ mit dem Baustoff Beton experimentieren sollten. Das Vorzeigeprojekt der Wiener Stadtentwicklung ist aber heute das Projekt Kabelwerk. Hier wurden neue Formen der Flächenwidmung erprobt. Gegeben war eine Gesamtkubatur, die in einem aufwendigen Partizipationsverfahren mit den Bewohnern der Umgebung zu freien neuen Gebäudeformen entwickelt wurde. Entstanden ist ein architektonisch abwechslungsreicher und sozial erfolgreicher neuer Stadtteil, an dem eine Vielzahl von engagierten Architekten beteiligt werden konnte.

and Diener & Diener from Switzerland to develop small, typologically original villas with innovative floor plans for construction on the urban periphery. At the same time, the architects were asked to find unusual and innovative methods for building with poured-in-place concrete. Today's showcase for new urbanism in Vienna is the Kabelwerk project, which explored how inventive uses of zoning can be the engine for progressive urban development. The zoning designated the project's total allowable building volume; through an elaborate process of neighborhood co-planning, this volume was organized into a free composition of sculptural building forms. What arose from this process is an architecturally varied and socially successful, new urban district, and numerous architects were able to contribute to the planning of its ultimate form.

As I put together this highly distilled reappraisal of the phenomenon that is 20th and 21st century Viennese Social Housing, I have repeatedly tried to locate and identify Vienna's lasting contribution to the development of the European City. From this vantage point, however, I can only distinguish singular and exceptional achievements. Housing is a centrally important task for Vienna and is one of the city's most important social and political responsibilities. Yet, in the last decades, social housing in Vienna has primarily produced notable solo performances. With 5,000 or so new subsidized housing units produced each year, remarkable objects of extraordinary social and architectural distinction are being effectively strewn across the city.

Each subsidized public housing project strives to find an original, adequate and contextual solution for its own modest parcel; the difficulty of this undertaking is compounded by the frequently incomprehensible and bureaucratic regulation of development in the city. Unlike in the glorious age of "Red Vienna," social housing is no longer an integral part of a comprehensive vision for the city. Housing in Vienna has become a mimetic political image of an extremely heterogeneous society. It answers this heterotopic challenge with situationistic creativity, and with social responsibility of the highest order.

Mustersiedlung Hadersdorf, Hermann Czech, Roger Diener, Max Dudler, Stefan Kießling (Otto Steidle), Hans Kollhoff, Adolf Krischanitz, Peter Märkli, Marcel Meili + Markus Peter, Heinz Tesar, 2000–07.
© Architekturzentrum Wien, Sammlung · Collection, Margherita Spiluttini

Ich habe im Verlauf dieses Versuchs einer konzentrierten Rekonstruktion des Phänomens des sozialen Wiener Wohnbaus des 20. und 21. Jahrhunderts immer wieder versucht, generelle Fragen seines Beitrags zur Zukunft der europäischen Stadt einzuflechten, konnte sie für die aktuelle Situation aber immer nur mit herausragenden punktuellen Leistungen belegen. Seit Jahrzehnten nun erreicht die für Wien so zentral bedeutsame und mit höchster politischer und sozialer Verantwortung erfüllte Aufgabe des sozialen Wohnungsbaus hochqualitative Einzelleistungen. Mit jährlich rund 5.000 neu gebauten geförderten Wohnungen werden einzelne Objekte mit höchstem sozialen und architektonischen Standard über die Stadt verstreut.

Anders als in der glorreichen Zeit des „Roten Wien" ist der soziale Wohnbau heute nicht mehr in eine umfassende urbane Vision der Stadt eingebunden. Der Wiener Wohnbau ist damit ein getreuliches politisches Abbild einer extrem heterogen gewordenen Gesellschaft. Er beantwortet diese heterotopische Herausforderung mit situationistisch kreativen Leistungen und zugleich sozialer Verantwortung auf höchstem qualitativen Niveau.

aus · from

hunch – the berlage institute report 6/7, Summer 2003
GAM 04, 2008, "Emerging Realities"
oris 46, September 2009
Translation by Susanne Baumann-Cox and
Maria Nievoll of Y'plus

Architektur: Neustart

Architecture: Reset

Man stelle sich vor, es gäbe gar keine Kunst der Architektur und auch nicht ihre Geschichte, keine ArchitektInnen, keine ArchitekturstudentInnen. Würde uns etwas fehlen? Möglicherweise. Möglicherweise aber auch nicht. Eine ganze, sich angeblich mit Architektur beschäftigende akademische Kaste wäre ganz einfach nicht mehr vorhanden. Und auch die Profession der Architekten selbst wäre bloß in ein allgemeines Baugeschehen eingegliedert. Unvorstellbar?

Möglicherweise. Aber dennoch, und davon bin ich überzeugt, würde Architektur entstehen. Denn irgendjemand, der nie von Architektur gehört hat, der das Wort nicht kennt und nicht das Metier, irgendjemand würde etwas bauen, das eben mehr als bauen ist.

Architektur entsteht, irgendwo, irgendwann, und niemand kann sie verhindern. Architektur ist immer da. Aber von Zeit zu Zeit sollte man das Metier, in dem man sich befindet, einfach wieder einmal an den Anfang zurücksetzen. Man macht das ja auch bei den heutigen uns umgebenden Geräten, wenn sie sich vor

Imagine there were no art of architecture, no history of architecture, no architects, no students of architecture. Would we be missing something? Possibly. But possibly not. A whole academic caste, supposedly dealing with architecture, would simply no longer exist. And the architect's profession itself would simply be part of a general building industry. Inconceivable? Possibly. And yet architecture, I am certain, would still be built. Someone or other who had never heard of architecture, who knew neither the word nor the profession, someone or other would build something that would be more than just building.

Architecture gets built, somewhere, at some time, and no one can stop it. Architecture is always there. But from time to time you should reset the profession in which you find yourself. After all, we do this with the appliances that surround us today when, having been programmed ad nauseam, they become lost in an endless loop: we press the 'reset' button. This is a question

lauter Programmierungen in einer wirkungslosen Endlosschleife verlieren: Taste ‚reset' (Neustart) drücken. Das ist eine Frage, die sich jenen, die sich im Metier befinden, nur sehr selten stellt. Denn sie leben ihre Rollen, müssen allein schon zur Rechtfertigung ihrer Existenz an die Existenz von Architektur glauben. Ob überhaupt Architektur eine eigenständige künstlerische Disziplin ist oder sein soll, will ich jetzt einfach als Frage und Behauptung so stehen lassen. Schließlich hatte schon der österreichische Volksschauspieler Hans Moser in *Hallo Dienstmann* den legendären Satz genuschelt: „Auf gebaut kommt's nicht an."

Warum sollten wir nun die Reset-Taste drücken? Weil Architektur eine Konjunktur im öffentlichen, im medialen, im politischen Leben hat wie niemals zuvor. Niemals zuvor in der Geschichte war Architektur populärer als heute. Aber niemals zuvor konnten wir uns darüber so wenig verständigen, was überhaupt zur Architektur gezählt werden soll, wie heute!

Als die Architektur noch Ideologie war

Deshalb ist ein kurzer Rückblick unbedingt nötig, um den Verlust der Gegenwart verstehen zu können. Die Nachkriegszeit in Europa lebte von den Modernitätsversprechungen des Wiederaufbaus. Architektur war ein Mittel zur Überwindung des Faschismus, der gleichgesetzt wurde mit allen formalen Traditionalismen. Architektur war ein Minderheitenprogramm der kulturellen Avantgarde, das sich aber gutgläubig mit der sich entwickelnden Bauindustrie verband. In den 1960er Jahren opponierte dagegen die utopische und politisierte architektonische Avantgarde, schon affirmativ bereit für das massenkulturelle Phänomen der neuen Popkultur. Ein wenig bedenklich vielleicht, dass fast alle Stars von damals es bis heute geblieben sind. Aber Architektur ist eben eine langdauernde Kunst, auch biografisch.

that people in this profession only rarely face, for they live their roles, they must believe in the existence of architecture in order to justify their very existence. I will let both the statement and the question stand as to whether architecture is or should be a stand-alone discipline of art at all. After all, in *Hallo Dienstmann* Austrian actor Hans Moser mumbled those legendary words: "Auf gebaut kommts nicht an" (It's not about how somebody is 'built').

So why should we press the reset button? Because architecture is booming in public life, in the media, and in politics as never before. Never before in history has architecture been as popular as it is today. But never before have we been so unable to agree on what should count as architecture as we are today!

When Architecture Was Still Ideology

That is why it is essential to take a brief look back to understand the present loss. Postwar Europe thrived on the promises of modernity brought by reconstruction. Architecture was a means to overcome Fascism, which was equated with all formal traditionalisms. Architecture was a minority program of the cultural avant-garde that allied itself in good faith with the evolving construction industry. In the sixties, the utopian and politicized architectural avant-garde opposed this, ready for and affirming the mass culture phenomenon of the new pop culture. It is perhaps rather alarming that almost all of the stars of that time have remained stars to this day. But architecture is a long lasting art, also biographically speaking.

Then, at the beginning of the seventies, the oil crisis (1973), the change of paradigm, the break in modernity. The rediscovery of the urban, the regional, and history came hand in hand with post-modernism. The sixties had already paved the way for this with the anal-

Sechster Tag • Day Six

Zapfstellen für Bier in einem spanischen Restaurant als Vorbilder für Skyscraper · Beer taps in a Spanish restaurant as models for skyscrapers. © DS

Dann Anfang der 1970er Jahre die Ölkrise (1973), der Paradigmenwechsel, der Modernitätsbruch. Die Wiederentdeckung des Urbanen, des Regionalen und der Geschichte kam mit der Postmoderne. Dies war vorbereitet schon in den 1960er Jahren mit den Analysen von Jane Jacobs, Robert Venturi und Denise Scott Brown, Aldo Rossi etc. Aber es war auch ein Nachschein der Sehnsucht der Studentenrevolte nach dem wirklichen Leben, die Entdeckung und Verwandlung des Alltäglichen. Die Zukunft blieb auch in den 1980er Jahren gebrochen. Ridley Scotts *Blade Runner* (1982) zeigte uns dann erstmals, dass auch in ferner Zukunft nicht alles neu gebaut sein wird und wurde nicht umsonst zum Kultfilm der Architekturdebatte dieser Zeit. Im Besichtigungsbus der „Internationalen Bauausstellung Berlin" (1984) erzählten Baubeamte des Senats mit säuerlicher Miene von den großen Fortschritten im Zeilenwohnungsbau der 1960er Jahre, als den Menschen Licht, Luft und Sonne geboten wurde, und bedauerten eigentlich, dass nun die internationalen Star-Architekten wieder die alte enge Stadt bauen wollten.

Jawohl, es war schön und spannend, in den 1960er, 1970er und auch noch in den 1980er Jahren. Als mit Argumenten und Verleumdungen um die richtige oder yses of Jane Jacobs, Robert Venturi and Denise Scott Brown, Aldo Rossi, etc. But it was also an afterglow of the yearning of the student revolts for real life, the discovery and transformation of everyday life. The future remained broken in the eighties, too. Ridley Scott's *Blade Runner* (1982) showed us for the first time that, even in the distant future, not everything will be newly built, and it was not without reason that it became the cult film of the architectural debate of the time. On the sightseeing bus of the International Building Exhibition in Berlin (1984), local building officials spoke somewhat sourly of the great advances in linear housing development in the sixties, when people were offered light, air and sun, and regretted that international star architects now wanted to build the old narrow city once again.

Yes, it was great and exciting, in the sixties, seventies, and even still in the eighties. When people fought for right or wrong architecture with arguments and defamations. When positions were backed up with theories. The argument about the 'post-modern Biennale' (1980) in Venice, the German museum competitions (e.g. James Stirling, Staatsgalerie Stuttgart, 1979–84). It was great and exciting, but it was a damned insider discussion that probably only a minority of architects and intellectuals in the Western hemisphere were really able to or wanted to follow. An academically disputed, but secretly sworn community that arrogantly ignored the rest of the world.

falsche Architektur gekämpft wurde. Als Positionen mit Theorien belegt wurden. Der Streit um die ‚postmoderne Biennale' (1980) in Venedig, um die deutschen Museumswettbewerbe (z.B. James Stirling, Staatsgalerie Stuttgart, 1979–84). Es war schön und spannend, aber es war eine verdammte Insiderdiskussion, der wahrscheinlich nicht mehr als eine Minderheit von Architekten und Intellektuellen der westlichen Hemisphäre wirklich folgen konnte und wollte. Eine akademisch zerstrittene, aber insgeheim verschworene Gemeinschaft, die den Rest der wirklichen Welt arrogant ignorierte.

Als die Architektur entdeckt wurde

Und auf einmal herrschte große Verwirrung. Im Laufe der letzten zwanzig Jahre lösten sich alle allgemeinverbindlichen innerarchitektonischen Kriterien der Architektur zunehmend auf. Nicht anders als in der Gesellschaft, deren Lebensstile und Kulturen sich zunehmend fragmentierten. Manche wollten noch zwischen einer transnationalen kapitalistischen und einer subalternen lokalen Klasse unterscheiden, obwohl die hybride Existenz zum Daseinsprinzip geworden war. Im Design verschwindet die ‚gute Form' und kommt als saisonaler Lifestyle wieder.

Und auf einmal war die Postmoderne als Stil zumindest im inneren Diskurs der Architektur erstarrt. Sie fand ihr letztes Aufbäumen im Dekonstruktivismus und wurde abgelöst von Computerprogrammen, die zumindest auf den Bildschirmen – und mit viel Bastelei auf den Baustellen – den Colani-Kitsch der 1960er Jahre zum Mainstream einer heutigen Formsprache exhumierten. Wie sagte schon Friedrich Kittler in den 1980er Jahren: Das Werkzeug bestimmt das Sprechen. Und nichts wurde wahrer, als die Prophezeiung von Mary McLeod, die in einem Artikel in *assemblage* meinte, dass der Dekonstruktivismus nur die andere Seite derselben Medaille der Postmoderne war.

When Architecture Was Discovered

And suddenly there was great confusion. Over the past twenty years, all generally binding inner-architectural criteria regarding architecture began to disintegrate. As in society, too, whose lifestyles and cultures were becoming increasingly fragmented. Some still wanted to distinguish between a transnational capitalist and a subordinate local class, although the hybrid existence had become an existential principle. 'Good form' disappears in design and returns as seasonal lifestyle. And all of a sudden post-modernism had become ossified as a style, at least in the inner discourse of architecture. It last reared its head in deconstructivism and was replaced by computer programs that, at least on screen—and with a great deal of tinkering on the building site—exhumed the Colani kitsch of the sixties, turning it into the mainstream of a current language of form. As Friedrich Kittler said back in the eighties: The tool determines the speech. And nothing came to be more true than Mary McLeod's prophecy, who, in an article in *assemblage*, opined that deconstructivism was just the flip side of the same coin of post-modernism.

As a result, today no one can tell whether all the stuff on today's 'market'—i.e. that which decorates the hundred or so most important international architecture magazines—is in fact good or bad architecture, important or unimportant buildings or projects. Everything accelerates the culture industry, is at least a media event or simply does not take place.

Today we are in a phase of transition. But all the pundits tell us that we will be in phases of transition for the rest of the future. Today, phase of transition first of all means a persisting post-modern state. A state that has left behind all the old distinctions between high culture and everyday culture that cannot grant any single ideology the status of exclusiveness.

Die Verschmelzung von Archaik und virtueller Realität ist bereits in *Blade Runner* simuliert · The melding of archaic elements and virtual reality is already simulated in *Blade Runner*. Screenshot DS

So kann heute niemand mehr unterscheiden, ob es sich bei all dem, was heute auf dem sogenannten Markt ist – das heißt, was die rund hundert wichtigsten internationalen Architekturmagazine dekoriert – um gute oder schlechte Architektur, um wichtige oder unwichtige Bauten oder Projekte handelt. Alles beschleunigt den Kulturbetrieb, ist ein zumindest medialer Event oder findet einfach nicht statt.

Wir befinden uns heute in einer Übergangsphase. Aber alle Auguren sagen uns, dass wir uns für die gesamte Zukunft nur mehr in Übergangsphasen befinden werden. Übergangsphase heute bedeutet zunächst einmal einen anhaltend postmodernen Zustand. Ein Zustand, der alle alten Trennungen von Hochkultur und Alltagskultur hinter sich gelassen hat, der keiner einzelnen Ideologie einen Charakter der Ausschließlichkeit zubilligen kann.

Übersetzt auf die Kulturtechnik der Architektur ist die Trennung von kulturell wichtigen Künstlerarchitekten und den marktkonformen Architekturfirmen, die noch in den 1980er Jahren in der Szene klar war, heute aufgehoben. Wenn beispielsweise Peter Cook und Peter Eisenman, die ewigen Avantgardisten, ihre Zukunft als Design-Berater von HOK, einer der weltgrößten Business-Architekturfirmen, sehen, dann sollten wir darin nicht die tragische Selbstaufgabe alter Männer sehen,

Translated into terms of the cultural technology of architecture, the distinction between culturally important artist-architects and market-geared architecture firms, which was still clear-cut in the eighties, has now been annulled. When, for example, Peter Cook and Peter Eisenman, the eternal avantgardists, see their future as design consultants of HOK, one of the world's biggest business architecture firms, then we should not see this as the tragic self-abandonment of old men, but rather as revealing the changed underlying conditions of architecture. And what has become of Daniel Libeskind since winning 9/11 is surprising to the say the least. Currently the distinction between types of architects is completely forgotten, as stated by Richard Saxon of RIBA: He distinguishes between architects as "strong idea" firms and "strong service" firms, coolly observing that service firms need "clients," while idea firms need "patrons."

"Great Attention – Less Seriosity"

"Great attention, less seriosity," scoffed Rem Koolhaas, and he's damn right. The diamonds of star architects are spreading around the globe like spam mail. They all follow the much cited economy of attention; although in many cases they cannot fulfill it due to surfeit. And "Great Attention" has spread and expanded. Speculative leisure landscapes such as the new use of the Zeppelin Hall near Berlin and Formula One track design are already appearing in serious architecture magazines. Michael Eisner's Disney architecture strategy was an example of this in the nineties. Why did Arata Isozaki never view his project for Disney in Orlando in 1991? After all, it is the best building, architecturally speaking. But what would be the opposite of this? Less Attention – Great Seriosity? The list of those calling for a re-

sondern die veränderten Rahmenbedingungen der Architektur erkennen. Und was aus Daniel Libeskind geworden ist, seitdem er „9/11" gewonnen hatte, ist zumindest erstaunlich. Völlig vergessen wird derzeit die Unterscheidung zwischen Typen von Architekten, wie sie Richard Saxon vom RIBA erklärte: Er unterscheidet die Architekten zwischen „strong idea"-firms und „strong service"-firms, und meint sehr cool, dass die „service-firms" „clients" benötigen, die „ideafirms" aber „patrons".

„Great Attention, Less Seriosity"

So spottete Rem Koolhaas und hat verdammt recht damit. Die Diamanten der Star-Architekten verbreiten sich wie Spam-Mails über den Erdball. Sie folgen alle der vielzitierten Ökonomie der Aufmerksamkeit, obwohl sie vielfach diese wegen Übersättigung gar nicht mehr erfüllen können. Und die ‚Great Attention' hat sich ausgebreitet und ausgeweitet. Schon erklimmen spekulative Freizeitlandschaften wie die Neunutzung der Zeppelin-Halle bei Berlin und das Design von Formel 1-Strecken die ernsthaften Architekturmagazine. Michael Eisners Disney-Architektur-Strategie hat das bereits in den 1990er Jahren vorgelebt. Warum wohl hat dann Arata Isozaki sein Projekt für Disney in Orlando von 1991 niemals selbst besichtigt? Immerhin das architektonisch beste Gebäude, das Disney jemals zusammengebracht hat. Aber was wäre das Gegenteil davon? Less Attention, Great Seriosity? Von Prince Charles und den Kriers, den anhaltend stilistisch Postmodernen wie Robert Stern oder Michael Graves bis hin zum amerikanischen New Urbanism und Vittorio Magnago Lampugnanis neuem Konservativismus oder den Berliner Steinbaumeistern reicht die Palette derer, die eine Rückkehr zur Konvention des Bauens fordern. Jawohl, es wäre dann „Baukultur", wenn sie sich durchsetzen könnte. Wir hätten dann wieder verbindliche

Die Stadt 2019: In den Designs für *Blade Runner* von Douglas Trumbull und Syd Mead visioniert · The city of 2019: envisioned in the designs for *Blade Runner* by Douglas Trumbull and Syd Mead. **Screenshot DS**

turn to the convention of building ranges from Prince Charles and the Kriers, the unwaveringly stylistic post-modernists such as Robert Stern and Michael Graves, to American "New Urbanism" and Vittorio Magnago Lampugnani's new conservatism, and Berlin's master stonemasons. Yes sir, this would be "building culture," if it could only catch on.

We would have binding conventions again, we would have harmonious villages and towns again—only on new tracks, and that is important. We would have compensated for the loss of culture. But what culture would we then have? The culture of the *Truman Show,* an artificial idyll, which was coincidentally, but aptly shot in the real New Urbanism pilot project "Seaside" in Florida. That is not exactly the Great Seriosity which is called for. However, a current return of the historical is certainly not modern living in the wrong consciousness, as many die-hard modernists would like to claim. After all, when you consider the complete reconstruction of the Acropolis or the further development of the Sagrada Familia, living in historically staged settings has long since been symbolically decided—and will shape our everyday lives in future.

'Great Attention' has, in any case, brought architecture unprecedented public and media attention. With all the consequences. One of which is the end of expert culture. Criticism and education are either performed

Sechster Tag • Day Six

Die Blob-Architektur der 1990er Jahre · Blob architecture of the 1990s. Archive DS

Dieses Cover des *Time Magazin* etablierte die Star-Architektur · This cover of *TIME* magazine established star architecture. Archive DS

Konventionen, wir hätten dann wieder, in neuen Spuren nur – und das ist wichtig – harmonische Dörfer und Städte. Wir hätten den Verlust der Kultur kompensiert. Aber welche Kultur hätten wir dann? Die Kultur des Films *Die Truman Show*, einer künstlichen Idylle, die zwar zufällig, aber doch treffend im realen New Urbanism-Pilotprojekt „Seaside" in Florida gedreht wurde. Das ist nicht gerade die „Great Seriosity", die gefordert wird. Eine gegenwärtige Wiederkehr des Historischen ist aber sicherlich kein heutiges Leben im falschen Bewusstsein, wie viele der Ewigmodernen gerne behaupten würden. Schließlich ist mit dem kompletten Wiederaufbau der Akropolis oder dem Weiterbau an der Sagrada Família längst auch symbolisch das Leben im historisch Inszenierten beschlossen – und wird in Zukunft unseren Alltag prägen.

in the role of the marketing agent or switched to the parallel texts of 'cultural studies,' where they revolve around the phenomenon of architecture as such. Individual 'critical' assessments of buildings and positions turn out to be what they have long been in other disciplines of art: envious private conditions with the whiff of pontifical dissatisfaction.

This is the logical consequence of the loss of all binding criteria. The combative modernism of architecture reached its completion in the last century. Following no stylistic code, no artistic ideology, out of pure force of habit it continues to build away, largely insensibly, in the global architectural middle class of building industry service providers. Still vested with the authority of the architect's profession, which stands for a promise of a better world. If we were to believe architects, everything would be better if only it were planned by architects.

Provocative counter-question: Would we all want to live in a world created only by 'committed' high-quality architects?

Die „Great Attention" hat jedenfalls der Architektur eine bislang nicht bekannte öffentliche und mediale Aufmerksamkeit gebracht. Mit allen Konsequenzen. Eine davon ist das Ende der Expertenkultur. Kritik und Vermittlung finden sich entweder in der Rolle des Marketing-Agenten wieder oder weichen aus in die Paralleltexte der Cultural Studies, um von dort aus das Phänomen der Architektur an sich zu umkreisen. Individuelle ‚kritische' Wertungen von Bauten und Positionen entpuppen sich als das, was sie seit langem auch in anderen Kulturdisziplinen sind: als neiderfüllte private Befindlichkeiten, mit dem Odeur des pastorenhaft Unbefriedigten behaftet.

Das ist die logische Folge des Verlusts aller verbindlicher Kriterien. Die kämpferische Moderne der Architektur hat sich im letzten Jahrhundert vollendet. Keinem stilistischen Code, keiner künstlerischen Ideologie folgend, aus reiner Gewohnheit baut sie einfach in der weltweiten architektonischen Mittelschicht der Bauindustriedienstleister weitgehend bewusstlos nach wie vor vor sich hin. Noch immer ausgestattet mit der Autorität des Berufsstandes der Architekten, der für das Versprechen auf eine bessere Welt steht. Würden wir den Architekten glauben, dann wäre alles besser, wäre es nur von Architekten geplant.

Provokante Gegenfrage: Würden wir alle in einer Welt leben wollen, die nur von sogenannten engagierten Qualitätsarchitekten geschaffen wurde?

Das infame nackte Leben

Was ist bloß aus der Architektur geworden? Nein. Das ist nicht die Frage. Was ist aus den Architekten geworden? Aus den Architekten, die im westlich zivilisierten Standard der nördlichen Hemisphäre einstmals, Demiurgen gleich, einen gesellschaftlichen Stand bildeten, der Visionen einer allzu menschlichen und dann auch banalisierten Moderne mit guten Honoraren entwarf. Der Architekt, diese Lifestyle-Ikone, wurde jedoch zunehmend in seinem Ruf und seiner Verantwortung gesellschaftlich demontiert.

Odious Bare Life

What has become of architecture? No. That is not the question. What has become of architects? Of the architects who—like demiurges—constituted a social rank in the western civilized standard of the northern hemisphere, drafting visions of an all too human and then banalized modernism for good fees. The reputation and responsibility of the architect, that lifestyle icon, was, however, slowly chipped away by society.

Today we have a flood of students and graduates, throughout Europe, uniformly following in a venerating train, craving the star fame of their star professors, and ending up in tasteless neo-modernist formal experiments.

In June 2002, I—like many others from the illustrious world of architecture—was asked to submit a statement on the future of architecture for *hunch* magazine published by the Berlage Institute in Rotterdam. No problem, I thought, I will do it straightaway. But first there was a lecture to write, that somehow had to do with the topic, and then there was a panel discussion, and another article, and all of a sudden all of my work and subjects had to do with this blasted question, and suddenly I could no longer answer the question because I hoped that every new challenge would finally help me find the answer.

I read the statements on the future of architecture by other architects and theorists, teachers—and, of course, somehow they were all right. I remembered thousands of conversations with architect friends; I started listening more closely during every architect's lecture and self-explanation. And in the end the answers that have meanwhile been written seemed so strangely banal and logical at the same time.

They were answers as they simply have to be formulated, politically correctly, in the community of 'world

Dachausbau in Wien · Attic conversion in Vienna, **Falkestraße, Coop Himmelblau, 1983–88.** Archive DS

Heute haben wir europaweit eine Flut von StudentInnen und AbsolventInnen, die stromlinienförmig im ehrenden Schweif ihrer Star-Professoren nach einem ebensolch vorgelebten Star-Ruhm gieren und in abgeschmackten neomodernistischen Formalversuchen verenden.

Im Juni 2002 wurde ich – wie viele andere aus der illustren Welt der Architektur – angefragt, ein Statement zur Zukunft der Architektur für die Zeitschrift *hunch* abzugeben, die im Berlage-Institut in Rotterdam erscheint. Kein Problem, dachte ich, mache ich sofort. Aber davor war noch ein Vortrag zu schreiben, der irgendwie mit dem Thema zu tun hatte, und dann kam

architecture.' They talked about the necessity of star architects, the media and the culture industry of architecture, the change in the new image of the profession although the old image of the profession still exists. Of course innovation is important, too, more and more new spaces and technologies need to be explored and found. And there is the fact that the profession is always obliged to engage in research that is not paid but should be performed at universities, which are stifled by bureaucracy, and only small, highly committed postgraduate schools such as the Berlage Institute can afford it.

Has anyone noticed that architecture today, or what we call architecture today, would not exist without universities? Once upon a time, thirty or forty years ago, people used to complain about universities and the bad teachers who did not play a cultural role in architectural practice. Today these bad teachers, who simply taught the craft of architecture, have vanished from the universities or died out. The universities are looking for stars, and make sure that the academic discipline is preserved by giving appropriate jobs in this academic undertaking to those architects who engage in architecture as an 'innovative science.' In other words: an 'innovative architect' can hardly survive today without 'university insurance.'

Finally, the question of the architect's responsibility came up. What are the responsibilities of an architect? And that was the crucial point. For there it was again, the old, perennial obligation of the architect of having and wanting to assume responsibility for the world as a whole. That self-imposed obligation of architecture, modern architecture in particular, that has caused the current dilemma. And then I came across the following words: "In today's world, anyone who isn't prepared to build the tower of Babel has no right to be an architect" said Wolf Prix from Coop Himmelb(l)au in 2002.

eine Podiumsdiskussion, und noch ein Artikel, und auf einmal hatten alle Arbeiten und Themen mit dieser verflixten Frage zu tun, und auf einmal konnte ich die Frage nicht mehr beantworten, weil ich von jeder neuen kommenden inhaltlichen Herausforderung endlich Hilfe für die Antwort erwartete.

Ich las die Statements zur Zukunft der Architektur von anderen Architekten und Theoretikern, Lehrern – und sie hatten natürlich alle irgendwie Recht. Ich dachte an tausende von Gesprächen mit Architektenfreunden, ich begann genauer zuzuhören bei jedem Vortrag und jeder Selbsterklärung eines Architekten. Und zum Schluss schienen mir die inzwischen geschriebenen Antworten so seltsam banal und logisch zugleich zu sein.

Es waren Antworten, wie sie ‚political correct' innerhalb der Community der ‚World Architecture' einfach formuliert werden müssen. Da war die Rede von der Notwendigkeit von Star-Architekten, von den Medien und von der Kulturindustrie der Architektur, von der Veränderung des neuen Berufsbildes, obwohl das alte immer noch vorhanden ist. Natürlich ist auch die Innovation wichtig, immer neue Räume und Techniken müssen erforscht und gefunden werden. Und dass der Beruf immer der Forschung verpflichtet ist, die nicht bezahlt wird, aber dafür an den Universitäten geleistet werden sollte, die aber in Bürokratie ersticken und nur kleine engagierte Postgraduate-Schulen, wie eben das Berlage-Institut, dies leisten können.

Ist eigentlich schon jemandem aufgefallen, dass es die Architektur heute oder das, was wir heute als Architektur bezeichnen, ohne die Universitäten gar nicht geben würde? Früher, vor dreißig, vierzig Jahren, schimpfte man über die Universitäten und die schlechten Lehrer dort, die in der Praxis der Architektur keine kulturelle Rolle spielten. Heute sind diese schlechten Lehrer, die einfach nur das Handwerk der Architektur lehrten, von den Universitäten verschwunden oder ausgestorben. Die Universitäten suchen nach den Stars und sorgen dafür, dass die akademische Disziplin erhalten bleibt, indem sie jene Architekten, die Architektur als ‚innovative Wissenschaft' betreiben, mit den entsprechenden Jobs in diesem akademischen Betrieb versorgen. Anders gesagt: Kaum ein ‚innovativer Architekt' kann heute ohne ‚universitäre Versicherung' überleben.

Schließlich kam die Frage der Verantwortung des Architekten. „What are the responsibilities of an archi-

Wonderful! No one has ever summed it up as clearly. Today's 'innovative' architecture therefore follows the 'Babel metaphor' according to which a single architect must be able to give humanity, the era, the world a meaningful monument in the form of a unique masterpiece. That is it. That is what drives it on, the academic rally of academic architecture. The architecture of the little masters, who strive to attract media attention with original arts and crafts, is then just a by-product of the 'Babel metaphor.' I love and admire this world, admire the constant struggle of the grand masters to spread many more faux diamonds around the planet in the name of the Babel metaphor.

But at the same time, I am losing interest in this 'world architecture media business' with its pseudo-theoretical, academically intellectual superstructure. The history of architecture of the second half of the twentieth century is replete with unredeemed edifices of theory that seek to academically justify current and future architecture with a fog (now called spheres and foams) made up of philosophy and sociology, statistics and nanotechnology. Equally academic are the new-old architects, the re-creators of classical orders, who still believe that a building's tectonics automatically create "systematic relations of communication" (Fritz Neumeyer) with the viewer. For these always end in a populist perception or, to put it differently, in Disney World.

Today, on the other hand, we have the great opportunity that millions of young people around the world study architecture, more than ever before in the history of architecture. Everywhere in the world, these students are being taught more or less intelligent strategies for exploring the world. It is time for them to go out into the world and start exploring and testing a new practice of architecture. Before they do, however, they should have learned the entire history of architecture so that they realize that they will not be able to invent anything

tect?" Und das war endgültig nun der kritische Punkt. Denn da war sie also wieder, die alte und ewige Verpflichtung des Architekten, für die Welt als Ganzes die Verantwortung übernehmen zu müssen und zu wollen. Jene Selbstverpflichtung der Architektur, der modernen im Besonderen, die das heutige Dilemma verursacht hat. Und dazu entdeckte ich den Satz: „Wer heute nicht bereit ist, am Turm zu Babel zu bauen, hat kein Recht Architekt zu sein", sagte Wolf Prix von Coop Himmelb(l)au im Jahr 2002.

Wunderbar. So klar hat dies noch niemand sonst formuliert. Die heutige ‚innovative' Architektur folgt also der ‚Babel-Metapher', die besagt, dass ein einziger Architekt in der Lage sein muss, mit einem einzigartigen Meisterwerk der Epoche, der Welt, der Menschheit ein sinnstiftendes Monument zu schenken. Das ist es. Das treibt sie an, die akademische Rallye der akademischen Architektur. Nur ein Abfallprodukt der ‚Babel-Metapher' ist dann die Architektur der kleinen Meister, die sich bemühen, mit originellem Kunstgewerbe jeweils für mediale Aufmerksamkeit zu sorgen. Ich liebe und verehre diese Welt, bewundere den beständigen Kampf der Großmeister, im Namen der ‚Babel-Metapher' viele weitere Glasdiamanten auf dem Planeten zu verstreuen.

Aber gleichzeitig verliere ich das Interesse an diesem ‚World Architecture Media Business' samt seinem pseudo-theoretischen, akademisch-intellektuellem Überbau. Die Architekturgeschichte der zweiten Hälfte des 20. Jahrhunderts ist voll von uneingelösten Theoriegebäuden, die mit einem Nebel (heute Sphären und

that has not already existed. (All the critics are currently moaning about when the kitschy retro 'blobject' fashion will finally be over.) But what will they do then, the future architects—including, hopefully, more and more women architects?

I still believe that among all students of architecture some have a particular interest in culture as a whole. Which is a good thing. That should protect them from unbalanced clarifications and explanations. Twenty years ago, I thought that the self-reflective analysis of the human body and its emotions (body language) might offer a way out. On the other hand, the seemingly direct language of the methods of Mannerism, translated into current massmedia image languages, was also supposed to offer an inexhaustible reservoir at that time. Today, I no longer believe in models of teaching and analyses. Perhaps I no longer believe in architecture?

No, I do. It is still there, that enthusiasm in view of extraordinary contemporary and historical works and buildings. But now I only trust seeing things first-hand, concrete experience. You should refrain from talking about things that you have not experienced for yourself. And, beyond the media machine of world architecture, there are thousands, millions of "situations," anonymous buildings, landscapes, views that create that immediacy of being touched that make you say: this is architecture. (So old Adolf Loos was right, after all.)

Again, then. What should they do today, the aforementioned new thousands of architecture students? They cannot all be stars. (No, dear Jacques, do not pes-

Junge polnische Architekten weisen mit der Umnutzung eines alten Industrieareals frech und beispielhaft in die Zukunft der Architektur · Young Polish architects point brazenly and exemplarily into the future of architecture with the reutilization of an old industrial complex, **Katowicze**. © DS

Santiago Calatravas Konzerthalle auf Tenerifa, kontextualisiert in der urbanen Umgebung · Santiago Calatrava's concert hall on Tenerife, contextualized in the urban setting. © DS

Schäume genannt) aus Philosophie und Soziologie, aus Statistik und Nanotechnik die heutige und zukünftige Architektur akademisch zu begründen versuchen. Ebenso akademisch sind die neu-alten Baumeister, die Re-Kreatoren klassischer Ordnungen, die immer noch glauben, dass sich aus der Tektonik eines Gebäudes „systematische Verständigungsverhältnisse" (Fritz Neumeyer) mit dem Betrachter geradezu zwangsläufig ergeben. Denn diese enden immer in einer populistischen Perzeption, oder anders gesagt: in Disney World.

Demgegenüber haben wir heute die große Chance, dass weltweit Millionen von jungen Menschen Architektur studieren. Mehr als jemals zuvor in der Geschichte der Architektur. Überall auf der Welt werden diesen StudentInnen mehr oder weniger intelligente

ter us with that cheap Warholism that every architect can be a star for fifteen minutes.) Nor do I know how this media marketing will continue—until every backwater has its own Bilbao Museum effect. First, starting in 1980, we had the generation of 'signature stars,' today we have the generation of 'branding stars,' and what comes next? Perhaps the music industry's boy-and-girl groups, who will no longer even do the planning themselves but rather just pose for the media and sell projects drawn—or rather, today, 'rendered'—in cheap planning countries?

Strategien zur Erkundung der Welt vermittelt. Es ist Zeit, dass sie hinausgehen in die Welt und beginnen, eine neue Praxis der Architektur zu erforschen und zu erproben. Davor sollten sie aber jedenfalls die gesamte Geschichte der Architektur gelernt haben, damit sie wissen, dass sie nichts erfinden können, was es nicht schon gegeben hat. (Alle Kritiker stöhnen derzeit, wann denn endlich die kitschige Retro-‚Blobject'-Mode vorüber ist.) Aber was sollen sie dann tun, die zukünftigen Architekten und hoffentlich immer mehr Architektinnen?

Noch immer glaube ich, dass unter allen ArchitekturstudentInnen einige besonders kulturell umfassend interessiert sind. Das ist gut so. Das sollte sie vor einseitigen Klärungen und Erklärungen schützen. Vor zwanzig Jahren glaubte ich, dass in der selbstreflexiven Analyse des menschlichen Körpers und seiner Empfindungen (body language) ein Ausweg zu finden sei. Andererseits sollte die scheinbar unmittelbare Sprachlichkeit von Verfahren des Manierismus, umgelegt auf heutige massenmediale Bildsprachen, damals auch ein unerschöpfliches Reservoir bieten. Heute glaube ich nicht mehr an Lehrmodelle und Analysen. Vielleicht glaube ich auch nicht mehr an Architektur?

Nein, doch. Es gibt sie noch immer, die Begeisterung angesichts außerordentlicher zeitgenössischer und historischer Werke und Bauten. Aber ich vertraue nur mehr der direkten Anschauung, dem konkreten Erleben. Was du nicht selbst erlebt hast, darüber sollst du schweigen. Und es gibt abseits der Medienmaschine ‚World Architecture' Tausende, ja Millionen von ‚Situationen', von anonymen Bauten, Landschaften, Blicken, die jene Unmittelbarkeit von Betroffenheit erzeugen, die einen sagen lassen, das ist Architektur. (Der alte Adolf Loos hatte also doch recht.)

Also nochmals. Was sollen sie tun, heute, die erwähnten neuen tausenden von ArchitekturstudentInnen. Nicht alle können Stars werden. (Nein, lieber Jacques, quäle uns nicht mit diesem billigen Warhol-Verschnitt, dass jeder Architekt für fünfzehn Minuten ein Star sein kann.) Ich weiß auch nicht, wie diese mediale Vermarktung weitergehen wird, bis jedes Kuhdorf

Until that has been cleared up, they should keep swarming out, those thousands of students, out into the real world, the everyday world. I dream of committed, intelligent and pragmatic 'task forces' which intervene in concrete, real situations in real life, which disrupt the everyday run of consumerism, opening up new life-worlds, designing houses or just interventions in the public space, and perhaps even build them with their own hands. Imagine all these masses of architecture students hidden away in overcrowded lecture halls, sitting in front of computer screens around the clock, just waiting to be sucked into the industrial standard of programs that configures them (how about watching that old film *Tron* again?); imagine these masses swarming out into the reality of our cities and villages and landscapes and simply starting to really change concrete situations with real means. Suddenly they start to become a social 'necessity.' That would be architecture.

That is what I replied to *hunch* when asked about the future of architecture in 2002. And I am seeing people set up exactly this kind of task force all over. In Vienna, Johannesburg, Madrid, throughout the world. That also leads to emotional involvement among the actors, above and beyond the gain in knowledge regarding the concrete mechanisms of planning and execution. For no one who has experienced such a situation first-hand will ever be able to engage in academic investor arrogance in their life again without scruples or cynicism. These 'performative interventions' are not academic excursions either, but rather a co-operation with local actors that also leads to 'empowerment.' 'Task forces' set an example regarding solidarity and commitment. They leave behind hope and span out a space of possibilities.

It is by no means sentimental to see a theoretical future of architecture too in such activities. Only with these approaches to working in real situations can we conceive a union of academic, culturally advanced

Verlust der architektonischen Autorschaft an die Rendering-Software. Spektakel aus dem Architekturmagazin *Mark* · Loss of architectonic authorship to rendering software. Spectacle from the architecture magazine *Mark*. Archive DS

seinen Museums-Bilbao-Effekt bekommen hat. Zuerst, ab 1980, hatten wir die Generation von ‚signature stars', heute haben wir die Generation der ‚branding stars', und was kommt dann? Vielleicht die aus der Musikindustrie schon bekannten Boys and Girls Groups, die gar nicht mehr selbst planen, sondern nur mehr medienwirksam posieren und verkaufen, was anderswo, in Billig-Planungsländern gezeichnet oder heute besser gesagt ‚gerendert' wurde?

Bis das geklärt ist, sollen sie ausschwärmen, die Tausenden von StudentInnen, hinaus in die Wirklichkeit, in die Alltäglichkeit. Ich träume von engagierten, intelligenten und pragmatischen ‚task forces', die konkret und real eingreifen in das tatsächliche Leben, die den konsumistischen Alltag stören und neue Lebenswelten eröffnen, Häuser oder auch nur Interventionen im öffentlichen Raum entwerfen und vielleicht gleichzeitig mit eigenen Händen auch bauen. Stellt euch vor, all diese Massen von ArchitekturstudentInnen, die in verstopften Hörsälen versteckt sind, die rund um die Uhr vor ihren Bildschirmen hocken und nur darauf warten, hineingesogen zu werden in den industriellen Standard der Programme, der sie figuriert (schaut euch den alten Film *Tron* wieder einmal an!), stellt euch vor, diese Massen schwärmen aus in die Realität unserer Städte und Dörfer und Landschaften – und beginnen einfach tatsächlich und mit realen Mitteln, konkrete Situationen zu verändern. Sie beginnen auf einmal, gesellschaftlich ‚notwendig' zu werden. Das wäre dann Architektur.

Das habe ich *hunch* auf die Frage nach der Zukunft der Architektur im Jahr 2002 geantwortet. Und genau solche ‚task forces' sehe ich heute überall entstehen. In Wien, Johannesburg, Madrid, ja überall auf der Welt. Da stellt sich bei den Akteuren, über den Erkenntnisgewinn der konkreten Mechanismen von Planung und Realisierung hinaus, auch emotionale Betroffenheit ein. Denn niemand, der eine derartige Situation konkret erlebt hat, wird jemals in seinem Leben wieder ohne Skrupel oder Zynismus eine akademische Investoren-Arroganz ausüben können. Es geht bei diesen

‚performativen Interventionen' auch nicht um akademische Ausflüge, sondern um das Zusammenarbeiten mit den lokal Betroffenen, das auch ein ‚empowerment' zur Folge hat. ‚Task forces' haben Beispielwirkung für Solidarität und Engagement. Es bleibt Hoffnung zurück, ein Möglichkeitsraum wurde aufgespannt.

Es ist absolut nicht sentimental, in Aktionen wie diesen auch eine theoretische Zukunft der Architektur zu erkennen. Nur mit diesen Handlungsansätzen in realen Situationen ist eine Vereinigung von akademischen, kulturell avancierten Ansprüchen der Architektur mit den Notwendigkeiten des Bauens in sozialer und nachhaltiger Verantwortung vorstellbar. Unter der Weltherrschaft des Konsumismus kann sich eine heutige emanzipatorische Architektur nur dem „Archiv der marginalisierten Lebensformen, der Rettung des Übersehenen" (Drehli Robnik) widmen. Diese Architektur dürfte sich nicht an den herrschenden ästhetischen und sozialen Codes orientieren, sondern müsste sich dem infamen nackten Leben widmen. Es geht heute um nicht mehr und nicht weniger als eine zukünftige Begründung der ‚Notwendigkeit' der Architektur. Wer immer das wo immer auch tut.

Das Ende der Aufmerksamkeit

Wir erleben zurzeit wohl die letzten Zuckungen einer Ökonomie der Aufmerksamkeit, bei der die sogenannte Innovationskraft der Architektur noch eine Rolle spielt. Indikator dafür ist die neue Technologie der ‚Renderings'. Denn diese Renderings haben einen verhängnisvollen ästhetischen Effekt. Sie machen die Bilder von allen Projekten gleich, ununterscheidbar. Damit klärt sich die Behauptung, dass es heute keine guten oder schlechten Projekte mehr gibt, denn alle sehen am Ende der Präsentation gleich aus, sprechen eine gemeinsame ästhetische Sprache. Denn die entwickelte Computersoftware der ‚Bilderzeugung' wirkt auf noch verhängnisvollere Art und Weise auf die Projekte der Architektur zurück. Sie suggerieren die leichte Mög-

standards of architecture with the necessity of building with social, sustainable responsibility. Under the world dominion of consumerism, a current emancipatory architecture can only devote itself to "archiving marginalized ways of life and saving what is overlooked" (Drehli Robnik). This architecture could not orient itself to prevailing aesthetic and social codes but rather would have to devote itself to odious bare life today. Today it is no more and no less a matter of the future justification of the 'necessity' of architecture. Whoever does it, and wherever.

The End of Attention

We are currently seeing what are probably the death throes of an economy of attention in which the 'innovative force' of architecture still plays a role. One indicator of this is the new technology of 'rendering.' These renderings have a disastrous aesthetic effect. They make all images of all projects the same, indistinguishable. That explains the claim that there are no longer good or bad projects today, for at the end of the presentation they all look the same and speak the same aesthetic language. Today's 'image creation' computer software has an even more disastrous effect on the architectural projects. They suggest the easy possibility—"at the click of a mouse on the screen"—of creating irregular, free, organic forms of design that convey to the public a kind of uniqueness and spectacularity that is increasingly in demand today. Today, every building client wants to have the most unique, most sensational office tower, the most unique and most sensational museum, or the most unique, most sensational shopping center. More and more client calls for tender and programs today demand that the architect give a project a unique 'symbolic' character. And the software for this purpose is there and it is used.

lichkeit – ‚mit einem Mausklick am Bildschirm' – der Erzeugbarkeit von irregulären, freien, organischen Formen der Gestaltung, die der Öffentlichkeit, eine Form von Einzigartigkeit und Spektakularität vermitteln, die heute mehr und mehr gefragt ist. Jeder Bauherr will heute den einzigartigsten und sensationellsten Büroturm, das einzigartigste und sensationellste Museum oder auch das einzigartigste und sensationellste Einkaufszentrum. So findet sich heute auch in immer mehr Ausschreibungen und Programmen von Bauherren an Architekten die Forderung nach einer singulären ‚Zeichenhaftigkeit' des Projekts. Wofür dann eben auch die entsprechende Software zur Verfügung steht und in Anspruch genommen wird.

Indem also allen Architekten weltweit inzwischen die selben technischen Werkzeuge und Möglichkeiten der Präsentation eines Projekts zur Verfügung stehen, spielt es keine Rolle mehr, ob das Projekt von einem der weltweit gefeierten Stararchitekten oder von einem, sagen wir einmal bei allem Respekt, talentierten chilenischen oder chinesischen Architekturstudenten stammt. Das klingt alles völlig normal, aber dahinter verbirgt sich eben eine dramatische neue Situation der Architektur. Denn ist ein Bauherr mit diesen Bildern unterschiedlichster professioneller Herkunft konfrontiert, kann er nicht unterscheiden und dann auch entscheiden, ob die perfekten, die gewünschte architektonische Sensation suggerierenden Renderings auch tatsächlich baubar sind oder nicht. Intellektueller hat diese Entwicklung schon Alan Colquhoun in seinem Text zum Realismus (1976) kommentiert: „Was immer sich sagen lässt zur Verteidigung einer solchen Architektur der Polemik, es besteht Gefahr, dass der Glaube an eine rein autoreflexive Architektur zu einer Abwertung des Bauprogrammes und zu einer Architektur führen könnte, die nicht mehr gebaut zu werden braucht."

Und die weltweite Erfahrung der letzten Jahre mit diesen spektakulären Projekten, die geboren aus den Möglichkeiten der heute gängigen Computersoftware

Die Architektur des gelenkten Blicks · The architecture of the directed view. © DS

As all architects, the world over, now have the same technical tools and chances to present a project at their disposal, it no longer matters whether the project comes from an internationally celebrated star architect or, let us say, with all due respect, a talented Chilean or Chinese architecture student. That all sounds perfectly normal, but behind it all is a dramatically new situation in architecture. For when a client is faced with these images of very different professional provenance, he can no longer distinguish or decide whether the perfect 'renderings' that suggest the desired architectural sensation are in fact buildable or not. Alan Colquhoun commented on this situation more intellectually in his essay on realism (1976): "Whatever may be said in de-

Sechster Tag • Day Six

unendlich freie Formen zur Baubarkeit bringen wollten, ist ernüchternd. Immer wenn eines dieser weltweit medial gefeierten Gebäude der ‚Spektakularität' medial abgefeiert wurde, verschwieg man die tatsächlichen Kosten. Die Inkunabel dieser neuen Architektur ist das Guggenheim-Museum in Bilbao von Frank Gehry. Dieses Spektakel war nur möglich, weil der Vertrag zwischen Guggenheim und der Landesregierung des Baskenlandes vorsah, dass Guggenheim und Gehry entwerfen konnten, was sie wollten, und die öffentliche Hand des Baskenlandes alle Kosten dafür tragen musste. Der inzwischen sogenannte ‚Guggenheim-Effekt' erzeugte in den letzten Jahren immer mehr Begehrlichkeiten nach vergleichbaren ‚Spektakelbauten' und die Renderings versprachen diese auch. Doch nun setzt eine ‚Götterdämmerung' ein, weil sich einfach viele dieser Entwürfe als nicht baubar oder finanzierbar erweisen. Die ‚Babel-Metapher' von Wolf Prix ‚needs patrons', und praktisch immer sind die Bauten, die sich diesem Anspruch verpflichtet fühlen, nur mit enormen Kostensteigerungen und einmaligen technologischen Verkrampfungen realisierbar, die man oft wahrlich nicht als produktive Entwicklung der Bauindustrie bezeichnen kann.

Deshalb mussten wichtige Proponenten der freien Formen der Spektakularität, wie Greg Lynn, bei einer Konferenz, die am CCA in Montreal (*Devices of Design*, 2004) stattfand, dann auch eingestehen, dass diese Formen über die heutigen Schnittstellen von CAD zu CNC in der Wirklichkeit nur aus kleinen, additiven Teilen zusammengesetzt werden können. Man kann also ruhigen bautechnischen Gewissens behaupten, dass auf absehbare Zeit die heutigen Software-Spektakel der Architektur in ihren Renderings erstarren werden und nur mehr ‚weißes Rauschen' erzeugen.

Demgegenüber wird eine ‚unsichtbare Architektur' wieder an Stellenwert gewinnen, die sich der Nachhaltigkeit und der Minimierung der Baukosten bei gleich-

fense of such an architecture of polemics, there is a risk that faith in a purely auto-reflective architecture could lead to a depreciation of the building program and to an architecture that no longer needs to be built."

And the global experience of recent years with these spectacular projects which, born of the possibilities of today's common computer software, sought to make infinite free forms buildable, is sobering. Whenever one of these buildings of 'spectacularity' was celebrated by the media around the globe, there was no mention of the actual costs involved. The incunabulum of this new architecture is the Guggenheim Museum in Bilbao by Frank Gehry. This spectacle was only possible because the contract between Guggenheim and the provincial government of the Basque region stipulated that Guggenheim and Gehry could design whatever they wanted, and that the Basque government had to pay all the costs. The "Guggenheim effect," as it is now known, has caused more and more people to covet comparable 'spectacular buildings' in recent years, and the renderings promised to deliver just that. But now a *Götterdämmerung* is in the offing, because many of these designs turn out to be simply unbuildable or unaffordable. Wolf Prix's Babel metaphor 'needs patrons,' and the buildings that feel obliged to this standard are almost always only feasible with vast additional costs and unique technological contortions, that often enough can hardly be referred to as a productive development of the building industry.

Therefore, important proponents of free forms of spectacularity such as Greg Lynn were forced to admit at a conference at CCA in Montreal ("Devices of Design," 2004) that these forms can in fact only be assembled from small, additive parts via the current interfaces from CAD to CNC. So with a safe, constructional conscience we can say that the current software spectacle of architecture will, in the foreseeable future, ossify in its renderings and bring forth nothing but 'white noise.'

„add-on" in Wien – temporäre Behausungsinstallation von Peter Fattinger, Michael Rieper und Team. · "add on" in Vienna—temporary housing installation by Peter Fattinger, Michael Rieper and team. Archive DS

zeitigem Gewinn an räumlicher, atmosphärischer und haptisch-sinnlicher Qualität verpflichtet fühlt. Sie beweist sich durch ihren Umgang mit dem Alltag, durch ihre Direktheit, Angemessenheit und Lebenstauglichkeit. Diese Architektur existiert bereits, als derzeit noch abseitige Parallelwelt. Zur Wahrnehmung ihrer Qualitäten müssen wir allerdings noch unsere Sinne kultivieren und schärfen. Wir nähern uns dem Ende des ersten Jahrzehnts eines neuen Jahrtausends. Am Ende des letzten Jahrtausends wagte ich nicht zu hoffen, dass es jenseits der medialen Spektakel wieder einmal Architektur geben wird. Doch inzwischen ist das ‚reset' erfolgt. Wir stehen am Beginn einer neuen Architektur.

Der Essay ist eine Momentaufnahme eines sich anhaltend schreibenden Textes, dessen Thesen und Inhalte sich seit rund fünfzehn Jahren immer wieder erweitern und verändern, und der in verschiedenen Fassungen, in verschiedenen Zusammenhängen Verwendung fand. Es entstand daraus keine Debatte, keine Entgegnung forderte mich heraus. Er ist damit auch ein Beweis für die Sinnlosigkeit des Schreibens über die Architektur in unserer heutigen Zeit. Es könnte aber auch sein, dass diese sich seit fünfzehn Jahren anreichernde Diagnose nur beobachtend die Zeit begleitet und Phänomene benennt, die ohnehin jedem im Feld der Architektur tätigen Akteur präsent sind.

On the other hand, an 'invisible architecture' will gain ground once again, which feels obliged to sustainability and minimizing building costs while increasing physical, atmospheric and haptic-sensorial quality. It proves itself through its handling of everyday life, its immediacy, appropriateness and suitability for life. This architecture already exists, as at present an esoteric parallel world. In order to perceive its qualities, we will, however, have to cultivate and hone our senses. We are nearing the close of the first decade of a new millennium. At the end of the last millennium I dared not hope that architecture would once again exist beyond the media spectacle. But this 'reset' has now taken place. We are at the beginning of a new architecture.

This essay is a snapshot of an ongoing text, the theses and topics of which have been expanding and changing for some fifteen years, it has been used in various versions and different contexts. No debate ensued from this, no retort challenging me. It is thus also proof of the pointlessness of writing about architecture at our present time. However, it may also be that this diagnosis, which has been growing for fifteen years, merely accompanies time as an observer, designating phenomena of which everyone working in the field of architecture is aware anyway.

Sechster Tag · Day Six

Laudatio · Laudation

Erich-Schelling Architekturpreis · Architecture prize 2010
Translation by Brian Dorsey

Amateur Architecture Studio

Amateur Architecture Studio

From the viewpoint of the award jury of the Schelling Prize, the works of the Amateur Architecture Studio, as the architectural office of Wang Shu and Lu Wenyu is called, represent all aspects of an architecture fit for the future. In the shadow of the spectacular global manifestos of China's new architecture, Amateur Architecture Studio is demanding a return to the grand historical tradition of Chinese architecture in its dialog with crafts and landscape. The office is consciously working with local resources and materials and derives its poetic and atmospheric energy out of it.

This attitude is found in the small installations, such as *Tile Gardens*, China's contribution to Architecture Biennale X in Venice is 2006, imposing on account of its material effort, but equally in the large *Xiangshan Campus* for the China Academy of Art in Hangzouh, realized in two phases between 2002 and 2007, or the *Ningbo Museum of Contemporary Art*. The Amateur Architecture Studio has succeeded in realizing its artisanal method of construction, its consideration of local resources and its atmospheric creativity at every scale. Particularly remarkable is the specific experimental approach carried out in the *Five Scattered Houses*, the pavilions in Mingzhou Park or the *Ceramic House*. It is this refreshing curiosity and the unique talent to develop new forms and applications from traditional materials that ascribes this architectural office nothing less than a strategic importance for the future of architecture.

Die Arbeiten des Amateur Architecture Studio genannten Architekturbüros von Wang Shu und Lu Wenyu repräsentieren aus der Sicht des Wahlkuratoriums des Schelling-Preises alle Aspekte einer zukunftsfähigen Architektur. Im Schatten der spektakulären globalen Manifeste der neuen Architektur Chinas fordern sie eine Rückbesinnung auf die große historische Tradition chinesischer Architektur in ihrem Dialog mit Handwerk und Landschaft. In ihren Projekten arbeiten sie bewusst mit den lokalen Ressourcen und Materialien und schöpfen daraus eine hohe poetische und atmosphärische Kraft.

Diese Haltung findet sich bei kleinen Installationen, wie dem ob seiner materiellen Anstrengung imposanten *Tiles Garden*, dem Beitrag Chinas zur X. Architektur Biennale in Venedig 2006, aber ebenso beim riesigen *Xiangshan Campus* für die Kunstakademie in Hangzouh, der in zwei Abschnitten zwischen 2002 und 2007 realisiert wurde, oder dem *Museum für zeitgenössische Kunst von Ningbo*. Dem Amateur Architecture Studio gelingt es, seine handwerkliche Methode des Bauens, seine Berücksichtigung lokaler Ressourcen, seine atmosphärische Kreativität in jedem Maßstab zu realisieren. Besonders bemerkenswert ist der spezifische experimentelle Ansatz, der sich in den *Five Scattered Houses*, den Pavillons im Mingzhou Park oder dem

	Schelling-Foundation Preisträger • Pricewinners
1992	Coop Himmelblau
1994	Zaha Hadid
1996	Peter Zumthor
1998	Sauerbruch-Hutton, Busse+Geitner
2000	Kazuyo Sejima
2004	Benjamin Foerster-Baldenius
2008	Anne Lacaton & Jean-Philippe Vassal
2010	Jan Olaf Jensen & Borre Skodvin
2012	Wang Shu & Lu Wenyu
2014	Al Borde Arquitectos

Der chinesische Beitrag von Amateur Architecture Studio zur Architektur Biennale Venedig 2006 · The Chinese entry of Amateur Architecture Studio to the 2006 Architecture Biennale in Venice. © DS

Ceramic House realisierte. Es ist diese erfrischende Neugier und das einzigartige Talent, aus traditionellen Materialien neue Formen und Anwendungen zu entwickeln, die diesem Architekturbüro eine geradezu strategische Bedeutung für die Zukunft der Architektur zuweisen.

Das Amateur Architecture Studio verweist auf die Notwendigkeit einer philosophischen und konzeptiven Begründung der Architektur, die ihren Ursprung noch vor der Realisierung finden muss. Polemisch behauptet das Studio, dass im spontanen, illegalen, temporären Bauen die professionelle Architektur herausgefordert werden müsse, damit jenseits der gebauten Objekte eine neue Beziehung zur Landschaft und zur vorhandenen urbanen Struktur hergestellt werden könne.

Das Kuratorium der Schelling-Stiftung würdigt und unterstützt mit dieser Würdigung des Amateur Architecture Studios auch eine Entwicklung der Architektur, die – jenseits und nach der fragwürdigen Konjunktur eitler Ikonen einer globalisierten Kultur – wieder dort landet, wo jede Architektur immer schon begonnen hat: bei der Nutzung lokaler Ressourcen und der Aufnahme lokaler Traditionen. Und wenn diese Strategie aus einer solchen Substanz heraus einzigartige architektonische Lösungen der heutigen Zeit entwickelt, dann ist diese in China entwickelte Position Vorbild für jede andere Region der Welt. Es mag paradox erscheinen, dass im Reich jener Weltmacht, die heute am stärksten eine globale Entwicklung beschleunigt, eine derart kraftvolle Gegenposition formuliert wird.

The Amateur Architecture Studio points to the necessity of a philosophical and conceptual rationale of architecture, which has to still find its origin before it is executed. The Studio polemically maintains that professional architecture would have to be challenged in spontaneous, illegal, temporary building so that a new relationship to landscape and to the existent urban structure could be established beyond the constructed object.

With this appraisal of the Amateur Architecture Studio, the Board of Trustees of the Schelling Foundation acknowledges and supports the advancement of architecture, which—beyond and following the global boom of vain icons—returns to the point from which it has always started anew: in the use of local resources and the incorporation of local traditions. And if this strategy develops unique architectonic solutions of the present age from such a substance, then this attitude developed in China is a paradigm for every other region of the world. Perhaps it is a paradox that such a powerful counter position is being formulated in the realm of the very world power which is accelerating global development today.

Sechster Tag • Day Six

"I am just a local architect. I'm not smart enough to be fashionable."

Fußgängerzone in der Altstadt von · Pedestrian zone in the old city of Hangzhou. © DS
Campus der chinesischen Kunstakademie · China Academy of Art campus in Hangzhou. © DS

Amateur Architecture Studio • Schelling Prize

Der „Westsee" in Hangzhou ist ein beeindruckend magischer Ort des alten China · The "West Lake" in Hangzhou is an impressively magic place of old China. © DS

A Day with Brodsky Ein Tag mit Brodsky

Diese Bilder und Texte erzählen von zwei Aufenthalten in Moskau. Am 21. Februar und 12. Mai 2011. Katharina Ritter und Dietmar Steiner arbeiteten mit Alexander Brodsky an der Ausstellung im Az W und besichtigten einige seiner Bauten. Die Bilder entstanden als absichtslose Schnappschüsse mit dokumentarischem Anspruch.

Eine Chronologie der Hintergründe, Rahmenbedingungen und Atmosphären für einige Bauten von Alexander Brodsky – im folgenden AB genannt...

These images and texts tell the story of two stays in Moscow. On February 21 and May 12, 2011, Katharina Ritter and Dietmar Steiner worked with Alexander Brodsky on the exhibition in Az W and visited several of his buildings. The pictures emerged on the road as unintentional snapshots with a documentary aspiration.

A chronology of backgrounds, framework conditions and atmospheres for a number of buildings by Alexander Brodsky—referred to as AB in the following …

1) AB wohnt in einer Wohnanlage, die in den 30er Jahren für Offiziere der Sowjetarmee erbaut wurde. · AB lives in a housing complex that was built in the 1930s for officers of the Soviet Army.

2) Der Lebensraum der Brodskys im ausgebauten Dachgeschoss · The living space of the Brodsky family on the converted attic floor.

3) Teil der Wohnung: Das Atelier von ABs Vater, Architekt und Grafiker. Alles blieb, wie es war. · Part of the apartment: The studio of AB's father, architect and graphic artist. Everything remained like it was.

4) Fotoserie von ABs Installation. · Photo series of AB's installation "Canal Street," New York.

5) Boutique und Café von AB in Moskau. Er ist mit dem Ergebnis nicht zufrieden. · Boutique and café by AB in Moscow. He is not satisfied with the result.

6) Restaurant Uliza OGI von AB. Das Alu-Blech erinnert an eine selbst gebastelte Raumstation. · Restaurant Uliza OGI by AB. The aluminum sheet metal recalls a home-made space station.

7) Fahrt zum Pirogovo Resort, wo die meisten von ABs Bauten zu finden sind. · Trip to the Pirogovo Resort, where most of AB's buildings are to be found.

aus · from
___

Ausstellung · Exhibition
„It still amazes me that I became an Architect", DVD, 2011
Translation by Brian Dorsey

8) Pirogovo Resort. Am Ufer des Kljasminskoe Reservoirs. Befremdlich gespenstische Hütten zufällig verstreut im Wald am Ufer des Sees. · Pirogovo Resort. On the shore of the Klyazma Reservoir. Strange, spooky huts scattered randomly in the forest near the lakeshore.

11) Landseite des Restaurants 95°. ABs erster Bau, 2000 realisiert. · Landward side of the restaurant 95°. AB's first building, realized in 2000.

14) Der Pavillon als Krönung. Ein Belvedere für geschlossene Gesellschaften. · The pavilion as the crowning. A Belvedere for private functions.

9) Mitten im Wald ein öffentliches WC aus Beton-Fertigteilen der Sowjetzeit. AB liebt es. · In the middle of the forest a public toilet made of Soviet-era prefabricated concrete components. AB loves it.

12) Die spontan temporäre Konstruktion überlebte schon zehn russische Winter. · The spontaneous temporary construction has already survived ten Russian winters.

15) Die schiefen Stützen erinnern an die Vergänglichkeit alles Gebauten. · The slanted supports recall the transience of everything that is built.

10) „Bucht der Freude" des Kljasminskoe Reservoirs. · "The Bay of Joy" of the Klyazma Reservoir.

13) Regenrinnen? Wo man doch nur draußen sitzt. Ein Sitzplatz, nur über die Leiter erreichbar. · Rain gutters? Where one somehow sits outside after all. A seat that can only be reached by a ladder.

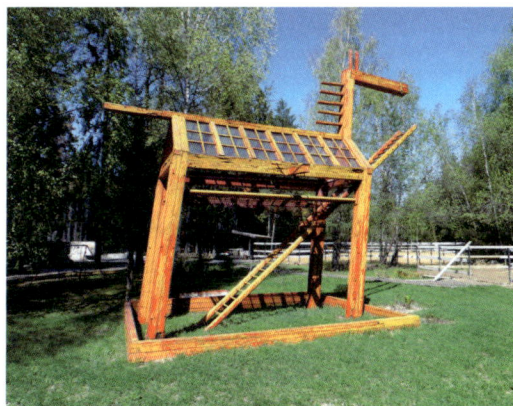
16) Am „Gestüt" dann ein hölzernes Pferd. ABs erste große Skulptur ist ein Kinderspielgerät. · A wooden horse on the stud farm: AB's first large sculpture is a children's playground item.

17) Datschas am Weg von der Bucht der Freude zu Marina und Golfclub. · Dachas on the way from the Bay of Joy to the marina and golf club.

20) Dennoch ist die poetische Stimmung spürbar. · The poetic atmosphere is nonetheless perceptible.

23) Das Haus gehört dem Rockmusiker Andrey Makarevic · The house belongs to the rock musician Andrey Makarevich.

18) ABs legendärer „Pavillon für Wodka-Zeremonien". · AB's legendary "Pavilion for Vodka Ceremonies." 2003

21) Unweit des Pavillons der „Sportplatz" von AB. · Not far from the pavilion is the "Sports Field" by AB. 2004

24) Clubhaus der Driving Range des Golfplatzes von Pirogovo von AB. · Club house of the golf course driving range in Pirogovo by AB. 2006

19) Manche Scheiben fehlen. · Some of the panes are missing.

22) Versteckt, die Tonne vom „Haus am Ufer" von AB, 2003 · Hidden, the buoy of the "House on the Lake Shore" by AB, 2003

26) Schutzdach der Driving Range. · The canopy of the driving range.

27) Das „Haus am 5ten Green" des Golfplatzes war für AB eine Auftragsarbeit ohne Bauherrn. · The "House on the Fifth Green" of the golf course was a commission without a client for AB. 2009

30) Badehaus für die Bewohner der Gemeinde Pirogovo am Ufer des Kljasminskoe Reservoirs. · Bath House for the inhabitants of the community of Pirogovo on the shore of the Klyazma Reservoir. 2002

33) Der zweigeschossige Aufenthaltsraum wird beherrscht von einem Luster aus getrockneten Eichenblättern. · The two-story recreation room is dominated by a chandelier made of dried oak leaves.

28) Für das „Haus im Wald" suchte AB eine Lichtung, um keinen Baum fällen zu müssen. · For the "House in the Forest" AB looked for a clearing in order to not have to cut down a tree. 2003

31) Die Veranda im Obergeschoss. Die Blockwand wird zum Parapet · The veranda on the top floor. The block wall becomes the parapet.

34) Es folgt ein letzter Besuch im Atelier von AB im Moskauer Architekturmuseum. · A final visit to the studio by AB in the Moscow Architecture Museum follows.

29) Wohn- und Essraum sind voll verglast zum Wald und der vorgelagerten Veranda. · Living and dining spaces are fully glazed towards the forest and the veranda in the front.

32) Im Erdgeschoss sind auch die Zwischenwände aus Baumstämmen. · On the ground floor the partitions are also made of tree trunks.

35) Dessen Kontakt mit der Welt ein handgeschriebenes Telefonbuch ist. · His contact with the world is a hand-written telephone book.

Kornati Memorial

The Kornati Memorial

"When we chance upon a mound in the woods, six feet long and three feet wide, arranged with a blade in the shape of a pyramid, we frown and something inside us says: someone is buried here. This is architecture."

ADOLF LOOS, "ARCHITECTURE," 1910

„Wenn wir im walde einen hügel finden, sechs schuh lang und drei schuh breit, mit der schaufel pyramidenförmig aufgerichtet, dann werden wir ernst, und es sagt etwas in uns: Hier liegt jemand begraben. Das ist architektur."

ADOLF LOOS, ARCHITEKTUR, 1910

Kornati Memorial, Nikola Bašić, 2010. © DS

aus · from

oris 66_2010
"Kornati Memorial"

Selten ist das legendäre Zitat von Adolf Loos so treffend wie angesichts des Mahnmals, das Nikola Bašić für die Insel Kornati entworfen und konzipiert hat. Ein Mahnmal für ein Ereignis, das ganz Kroatien berührt und beschäftigt hat. Am 30. August 2007 wurde eine Gruppe junger Feuerwehrleute mit einem Militärhubschrauber zu einem Einsatz auf die Insel geflogen. Nachdem sie abgesetzt worden waren, brach plötzlich ein Feuersturm aus, dem zwölf junge Männer nicht entkommen konnten und verstarben.

Im Jahr darauf wurde ein Wettbewerb für ein Mahnmal dieses tragischen Ereignisses ausgeschrieben, den Nikola Bašić für sich entscheiden konnte. Sein Konzept sah vor, zwölf liegende Kreuze zu errichten, aus Tro-

This legendary quote of Adolf Loos is rarely as appropriate as when looking at the memorial site created by Nikola Bašić in the Kornati archipelago. It marks an event that touched and shocked all of Croatia. On 30 August 2007, a group of young firemen was flown by helicopter to the island to participate in firefighting. After they had landed, a sudden firestorm took the lives of twelve young men. The following year, a competition was launched for the construction of a memorial to these tragic events, and Nikola Bašić won. He planned to build twelve crosses lying on the ground, twelve drystone walls made without machines, built only by the hands of volunteers using stones from the rocky island. There was also to be a "chapel," a round stone wall with a Latin sail as the roof. Contrary to the ideas of Bašić, the Ministry of Culture intended to entrust the works to a professional contractor. But then a small miracle happened. In the village of Kolan on the island of Pag, a man surfing the internet came upon the award-winning project of Nikola Bašić. That man, Ivo Butković, is actually a librarian, but also a fireman and the president of Suhozid, an association dedicated to the preservation of traditional drystone walls. He immediately looked for the telephone number of Nikola Bašić and proposed

ckensteinmauern, ohne Maschinenhilfe, von Freiwilligen nur mit der Hand aus den am Ort vorhandenen Steinen errichtet. Dazu noch eine ‚Kapelle', eine runde Trockensteinmauer mit einem Segel als Dach. Im krassen Widerspruch zu Bašićs Konzept plante das Kulturministerium, die Arbeiten an eine einschlägige Firma zu vergeben. Doch dann geschah ein kleines Wunder.

Zu dieser Zeit surfte im Dorf Kolan auf der Insel Pag ein junger Mann im Internet und stieß auf das preisgekrönte Projekt von Nikola Bašić. Dieser Ivo Butković ist Bibliothekar, aber auch Feuerwehrmann und Präsident der Gesellschaft zur Erhaltung der traditionellen Trockensteinmauern „Suhozid". Spontan suchte er die Telefonnummer von Nikola Bašić und bot ihm an, mit den Mitgliedern seiner Gesellschaft das Mahnmal zu bauen. Noch heute, wenn Nikola Bašić davon erzählt, schwärmt er von diesem geradezu schicksalshaften Moment als grundsätzlichen und eigentlichen Beginn der Idee und des Konzepts, dessen Realisierung nicht er gesucht, das vielmehr ihn gefunden hatte.

Nikola Bašić ist ohne Zweifel eine authentische und singuläre Persönlichkeit der Architektur im adriatischen Raums, stark verwurzelt in der kulturellen Tradition der Küstenregion von Zadar und Šibenik, seiner Heimat. Sein Lebenswerk entwickelte sich entlang der jugoslawischen und kroatischen Moderne, in der er nach all den traumatischen Brüchen konsequent eine kulturelle Kontinuität verfolgte. Und innerhalb dieser

to build the monument together with members of his association. Even now, when Nikola Bašić remembers that telephone conversation, he is enthusiastic about that fateful moment, seeing it as the symbolic and actual start of the implementation of his idea and concept, a start he did not look for, but which found him instead.

Without a doubt, Nikola Bašić is an authentic and singular phenomenon in the architecture of the Adriatic region, firmly rooted in the cultural tradition of the coastal area where he grew up, around Zadar and Šibenik. His life's work has evolved under the auspices of Croatian Modernism, consequently following a cultural continuity even after all the traumatic historical ruptures. Within this Modernism and in light of the great historical tradition of this region, he has deliberately explored the possibilities of transforming both general and local archetypes. We could say that he is still searching for the "soul" of architecture.

This is also the basis of his concept for the memorial park. Bare and jagged, the Kornati Islands are actually picturesque uninhabited hills rising from the Adriatic Sea. Their surface is characterized by the sharp lines of cracks in the rocks covered with vegetation that just barely survives. Not at all suitable for human habitation. Therefore, these surfaces were used only as grazing land for sheep, with untouched territories separated by radically geometric lines of drystone walls, reflecting the abstract grid of cadastral maps. They lie across the natural organic forms of the archipelago like the "square miles" of the settlement of American territories. Bašić intended to continue this tradition with his concept for the memorial park. But he also knew that the protected

Bau des Memorials mit freiwilligen Helfern · Construction of the memorial with volunteers, 2008. © oris

Freiluft-Kapelle des Memorials · Open air chapel of the memorial, 2010. © DS

Moderne selbst suchte er, angesichts der großen historischen Tradition dieser Region, bewusst nach einer Transformation der generellen ebenso wie der lokalen Archetypen. Man könnte auch sagen, er sucht bis heute nach der ‚Seele' der Architektur.

Darauf beruht auch sein Konzept für das Mahnmal. Die nackten, kargen Inseln der Kornaten sind eigentlich nur pittoreske, unbewohnbare Hügel im adriatischen Meer. Die Oberfläche bilden scharfkantige Bruchlinien des Gesteins, nur zaghaft von einer gerade noch überlebensfähigen Pflanzenwelt getarnt. Keine wirtlichen Orte für einen menschlichen Aufenthalt. Deshalb nur genutzt von frei weidenden Schafherden, deren unberührt wirkende Territorien durch radikal geometrisch gesetzte Trockensteinmauern abgegrenzt sind. Sie vollziehen den abstrakten Raster der Katasterpläne, legen sich wie die *square-mile* der amerikanischen Landnahme über die natürlich-organischen For-

islands of the Kornati National Park would never allow any other kind of "structure." Since these walls have no artistic motivation, instead developing from collective needs, Bašić wanted the monument to be built as an expression of a collective effort.

Cue Ivo Butković: with a hundred members of his association for the preservation of drystone walls from the island of Pag, he built the first wall in just three hours. When the media spread the news about their work, more volunteers appeared, and a wave of enthusiasm swept over the country; in 41 days from 23 March to 25 May, 2578 volunteers built twelve crosses 15 m wide, 25 m long, and a "chapel" for this site of collective memory. Today it is described as the greatest act of Croatian solidarity comparable only to the war year of 1991.

Sechster Tag • Day Six

In 41 days from 23 March to 25 May, 2578 volunteers built twelve crosses 15 m wide, 25 m long, and a "chapel" for this site of collective memory.

It completed the idea and concept of Nikola Bašić, it was more than the creation of simple archaic architecture. He wanted the people to re-master the technique of building stone walls, using only stones found on site, moved with hands, roughly worked up with mallets. "You need two people to find the stones, two to transport them, two to put them in place," says Ivo Butković.

This activity, mastering this skill, revives a building culture that had been considered lost, and the collective work is again etched in the collective memory.

The issue of the shape of the monument remains open. Why did Nikola Bašić choose a cross? He could have chosen circles or steles. No. Beyond any Christian meanings, a cross on the ground is primarily the sign of love combined with fear, of anxiety mixed with hope. In the wild rocky landscape, the twelve crosses precisely mark special places, made disturbing by the apparent randomness of their placement. These are not traces of sites, like crumbling walls and foundations of old hous-

men der Inseln. Diese Tradition wollte Bašić mit seinem Konzept für das Mahnmal fortsetzen. Auch weil er wusste, dass vom Nationalpark Kornati keine andere Form eines ‚Bauwerks' auf der geschützten Insel erlaubt worden wäre. Und weil diese Mauern keiner artistischen Gestaltungsabsicht folgten, sondern aus kollektiver Notwendigkeit entwickelt wurden, wollte Bašić demgemäß auch das Mahnmal als kollektive Anstrengung vollzogen wissen.

Da schlug die Stunde von Ivo Butković, und mit 100 Männern seiner Trockensteinmauergesellschaft von der Insel Pag, wurde in drei Stunden die erste Mauer gebaut. Da diese Aktion über die Medien verbreitet wurde, meldeten sich weitere Freiwillige, es setzte eine Welle der Begeisterung im ganzen Land ein, und zwischen 23. März und 25. Mai, in nur 41 Tagen, haben 2578 freiwillige Helfer die zwölf Kreuze mit den Maßen von je 25 mal 15 Metern, und die ‚Kapelle' als Ort des kollektiven Gedenkens, gebaut. Man spricht heute vom größten Akt kroatischer Solidarität.

Damit hat sich das Konzept von Nikola Bašić vollendet, das mehr beinhaltete als einen simplen Akt archaischen Architekturschaffens. Er wollte, dass die Menschen wieder die Technik der Trockensteinmauern erlernten, die nur mit den vor Ort gefundenen Steinen errichtet werden, mit den Händen bewegt, mit dem Hammer grob bearbeitet. „Es braucht zwei Männer, um die Steine zu suchen und vorzubereiten, zwei Männer, um sie zu transportieren, und zwei Männer, um sie zusammenzufügen", sagt Ivo Butković dazu. Dieses Tun, der Erwerb dieser Fertigkeiten, gibt einer verloren geglaubten Baukultur das Leben zurück, die gemeinschaftliche Arbeit gräbt sich wieder ein in die kollektive Erinnerung.

Besprechung des Projekts · Discussion of the project, Nikola Bašić, Dietmar Steiner und Übersetzerin · and translator, 2010. © oris

Es bleibt die Frage nach der Form des Mahnmals. Warum wählte Nikola Bašić die Kreuzform? Es hätten doch auch Kreise oder Stelen sein können? – Nein. Denn das liegende Kreuz ist jenseits seiner christlichen Konnotation zuerst die Verbindung von Liebe und Furcht, von Angst und Hoffnung. In der wilden Felslandschaft liegend markieren die zwölf Kreuze nur präzise den besonderen Ort, in der scheinbaren Zufälligkeit ihrer Verteilung verstörend auch. Sie bilden keine Spuren von Räumen wie die verfallenen Mauerreste und Fundamente alter Gebäude auf den verlassenen Inseln. Um dieses abstrakte Gefühl noch zu verstärken, ist unmerklich fast ein schmaler Weg von der Bucht zum Mahnmal von groben Steinen freigeräumt, der am Beginn des Mahnmalareals beim Rundbau der ‚Kapelle' endet. Die Kapelle darf einen verlassenen Raum markieren, weil dieser durch eine gemeinschaftliche Versammlung des Gedenkens im Kreis wiederersteht. Mit einem runden Stein in der Mitte, an den Mühlstein des Heiligen Florian erinnernd, durch den der Märtyrer zum Heiligen der Feuerwehren wurde.

Ich habe vergessen, nach dem Namen des Mahnmals zu fragen, nicht bei der erlebten Besichtigung und auch nicht im Gespräch mit Nikola Bašić. An den Kreuzen selbst finden sich sparsame Spuren des persönlichen Gedenkens angelagert. Namen, Wörter, Texte, Kerzen, Devotionalien. Aber kein Hinweis auf die Geschichte des Unglücks. Weil eben nur dann ein kollektives Mahnmal aus Gebautem entsteht, wenn das Schicksal des Einzelnen in das Schicksal der Menschheit eingebunden ist, und eben dann eine ‚Architektur' der Ewigkeit, ohne Anfang und Ende und immer schon dagewesen, erfahren werden kann.

es on abandoned islands. In order to intensify this abstract feeling, they subtly removed bigger stones from the narrow path leading from the cove to the beginning of the monument site next to the rounded structure of the chapel. The chapel can mark an abandoned site, since it is recreated by a common gathering and commemoration within its perimeter. The round stone in the middle recalls the millstone of St. Florian, which was instrumental in his becoming the patron saint of firemen.

During my visit to the site and talk with Nikola Bašić, I forgot to ask for the name of the monument. The crosses have some scant traces of personal memories. Names. Words. Texts. Candles. But nothing that would explain the history of the tragedy. A built memorial becomes a collective monument only when the fate of the individual is integrated in the fate of mankind. Only then can we experience the "architecture" of the eternal, without beginning or end, always present.

Sechster Tag · Day Six

Zur Attraktivierung des öffentlichen Busverkehrs im Bregenzerwald wurden die BUS:STOPS entwickelt · The BUS:STOPS were developed to make public bus transportation in the Bregenz Forest region more attractive. © DS

aus · from

Postkarten-Katalog *BUS:STOP Krumbach,*
Verein kultur krumbach, 2014
Translation by Rory O'Donovan

The Miracle of Krumbach

Das Wunder von Krumbach

Why Vorarlberg?
Why the Bregenzerwald?
Why me?

Warum Vorarlberg?
Warum der Bregenzerwald?
Warum ich?

Since the 1970s I have been friendly with many people from Vorarlberg, and with many Vorarlberg architects, a number of whom studied alongside me in Vienna. In the 1980s as a journalist I accompanied what were known as the Baukünstler, and supported their resistance to centralism and the rigid Austrian structure based on chambers for the various professions. Therefore I experienced firsthand the emancipation of Vorarlberg architecture, which initially saw itself in opposition to the established world of building, and was slowly able to get official politics interested as well. Without the intellectual back-up of a university in the province, this was a genuine 'bottom up' movement of architects, clients and craftspeople. There were also a number of particularly committed mayors, without doubt Austria's best local politicians to date. Gradually this groundwork led to a culture of building of high quality.

Seit den 1970er Jahren habe ich freundschaftliche Beziehungen mit vielen Vorarlbergern, vielen Vorarlberger Architekten, einige waren meine Studienkollegen in Wien. In den 1980er Jahren war ich ein publizistischer Begleiter der „Baukünstler", ihren Widerstand gegen Zentralismus und den Kammernstaat unterstützend. So erlebte ich die Emanzipation der Vorarlberger Baukultur mit, die sich zuerst als Opposition zum etablierten Baugeschehen verstand und wie sich langsam auch die offizielle Politik dafür interessierte. Es war, ohne Hochschule mit intellektueller Rückendeckung im Land, eine echte Bottom-up-Bewegung, von Baukünstlern und Bauherren und Handwerkern. Dann fanden sich besonders engagierte Bürgermeister, ohne Zweifel die besten Gemeindepolitiker Österreichs bis heute. So hob diese Basisarbeit langsam zum Höhenflug der Qualität der Baukultur ab.

Sechster Tag • Day Six

Es gibt inzwischen viele Analysen und Publikationen, die alle diesem in Europa einzigartigen Phänomen ihre Dokumentationen und Erklärungen widmeten. Dass es sich hier um eine Provinz im Schrumpfland Österreich handelt, das immer irgendwie anders im heutigen europäischen Umfeld ist. Aber auch vom österreichischen Selbstverständnis aus gesehen ist Vorarlberg anders, und ganz besonders die Region des Bregenzerwaldes, die wiederum eigentlich nichts mit Österreich zu tun hat, sondern zutiefst europäisch im satten Zentrum eines heute prosperierenden Wirtschaftsraums liegt. All diese Situationsbeschreibungen sind bekannt und erklären doch nicht dieses einzigartige Niveau der Alltagskultur, das längst nicht mehr das Bauen allein, sondern Essen, Leben, Arbeiten und die besondere Art und Weise, wie damit umgegangen wird, umfasst.

Im Jahr 1998 war ich Mitglied der Jury des Mies van der Rohe-Preises, des europäischen Preises für Architektur. Die Besonderheit dieses mit großem Aufwand organisierten und wichtigsten europäischen Architekturpreises ist, dass die gesamte Jury die fünf bis sieben Bauten der letzten FinalistInnen in einer konzentrierten Reise vor der Entscheidung besichtigt. Bei dieser Reise fuhren wir mit einem Bus aus der Schweiz nach Vorarlberg zu Peter Zumthors Kunsthaus Bregenz, das letztlich den Preis erhielt. Wir hatten noch ein paar Stunden frei, wollten auch andere Bauten besichtigen. Aber so richtig ‚outstanding' war damals nicht viel zu finden. Viele brave kleine Einfamilienhäuser, alles irgendwie ähnlich. Sehr kultiviert, aber nichts ‚besonders'.

Inzwischen hat sich die Landschaft der Architektur total verändert. Die Vorarlberger Baukultur hat auch

Today there are numerous analyses and international publications that document and explain this phenomenon of "being different" that is unique in Europe. But even looked at from an internal Austrian viewpoint Vorarlberg, and in particular the region of the Bregenzerwald, is different. These areas have little to do with the rest of Austria but, in a highly European way, form part of the centre of a prosperous economic area. All these descriptions of the situation are well-known, yet they cannot entirely explain the unique level of an everyday culture that no longer is confined to building alone but also includes eating, living, working and the particular way in which these aspects of life are addressed.

In 1998 I was a member of the jury for the Mies van der Rohe Award. One particular aspect of this award, the most prestigious and elaborately organized European architecture prize, is that the entire jury makes a concentrated trip to visit the five to seven buildings by the shortlisted finalists. During this journey we travelled by bus from Switzerland to Vorarlberg to visit Peter Zumthor's Kunsthaus Bregenz, which was ultimately awarded the prize. We had a few hours at our disposal and wanted to look at some other buildings. But there was nothing truly 'outstanding' to be found. A number of sound, single family houses, all of them somehow or other similar, very cultivated to be sure, but nothing 'special'.

In the intervening period the architecture landscape has changed completely. The Vorarlberg culture of building has also reached the area of public buildings: museums, schools, kindergartens, local authority offices, and hotels. It has become part of the province's identity. And architecture tourism has also discovered places where it can focus its attentions and bring visitors.

BUS:STOP Glatzegg, Amateur Architecture Studio – Hermann Kaufmann Architekten. © DS

öffentliche Bauten erreicht. Museen, Schulen, Kindergärten, Gemeindehäuser, Hotels. Sie ist zur Identität des Landes geworden. Mittlerweile findet auch der Architekturtourismus seine Orte der Aufmerksamkeit und der Besuchsmöglichkeit.

Viele Kräfte im Land haben dazu beigetragen. Das vai – Vorarlberger Architektur Institut – wurde zum Knotenpunkt der architektonischen Entwicklung und zum Zentrum des Diskurses. Zumthors Kunsthaus, und seinem seit Edelbert Köb mit einer klugen Wahl folgender Direktoren immer hervorragenden Programm ist und bleibt ein Ankerbau für internationales Interesse an der Region. Architektur wurde Gegenstand der Landespolitik, befördert vom individuellen, lokalen Engagement vieler BürgermeisterInnen. Qualitative Architektur in Europa entsteht nur dann, das behaupte ich aus Erfahrung, wenn sie von einem entsprechenden Niveau lokaler Politiker auch erkannt und gefordert wird.

Die verrückte Idee

Ende des Jahres 2011 erreichte mich aus heiterem Himmel eine E-Mail-Anfrage aus Krumbach im Bregenzerwald. Von der anstehenden Erneuerung bestehender Bus-Wartehäuschen war die Rede, und dafür wollte man berühmte internationale Architekten einladen, denen kein Honorar, aber ein Urlaub vor Ort versprochen werden sollte. Das war zunächst einmal nicht ernst zu nehmen. Verrückte Anfragen wie diese, erhalte ich oft. Also antwortete ich höflich, ich würde darüber nachdenken, hätte aber jetzt keine Zeit dazu …

Doch einige Monate später kam die Anfrage noch einmal, insistierend. Ein Treffen mit einem Abgesandten wurde vereinbart. Abverlangt wurde mir die Nominierung von einigen Star-Architekten. Nachdenken setzte ein. Die Antennen wurden aktiviert.

Das Wissen über die rezenten Entwicklungen der Architektur allein hilft aber nur bedingt, wenn es darum geht, für ein bestimmtes Projekt, eine bestimmte Aufgabe mit bestimmten Rahmenbedingungen die

BUS:STOP Kressbad, Rintala Eggertsson Architects – BaumschlagerHutterPartners 2014. © DS

Many different forces in the province have contributed to this situation. The vai Vorarlberger Architektur Institut has become a node of architectural development and a centre of discourse. Zumthor's Kunsthaus, which has had a succession of wisely chosen directors starting with Edelbert Köb, has been and remains an anchor building for international interest in the region. Encouraged by the individual local commitment of many mayors architecture became a theme for regional politics. On the basis of my experience I maintain that in Europe architecture of quality is built only when it is recognized and encouraged by local politicians of the requisite standard.

The Crazy Idea

At the end of 2011 out of the blue I received an email from Krumbach in the Bregenzerwald. It described the upcoming replacement of existing bus shelters and expressed a wish to invite famous international architects to design the new shelters who, instead of a fee, would be offered a holiday in Vorarlberg. Initially I couldn't take this seriously as I often receive crazy enquiries like this. And therefore I answered politely that I would think about it but that at the moment I had little time …

But a few months later the enquiry came again, this time more insistently. A meeting with a representative was arranged. I was asked to name a number of star architects. I began to think about it, the antennae were activated.

Sechster Tag • Day Six

BUS:STOP Bränden, Sou Fujimoto – Bechter Zaffignani
Architekten, 2014. © DS

richtigen ArchitektInnen zu finden. Auch ruht auf meiner Position als ‚Vermittler' die Verantwortung, ob ich dem Ansinnen trauen kann oder ob nur eine weitere der vielen Anfragen nach Architektur mit dem ‚big A' ohne wirkliches Engagement dahintersteht. Man kennt schließlich die Sorgen von Star-ArchitektInnen, die bei jeder Anfrage deren Seriosität zu hinterfragen haben. Will der Klient nur ein Image, dass er medial verwerten und verkaufen kann, oder ist er wirklich an einer inhaltlichen Zusammenarbeit mit der damit verbundenen Verantwortung interessiert?

So verging das Jahr 2012. Immer wieder wurde aus Krumbach nachgefragt, immer wieder nagten meine Zweifel am Projekt. Zu diesem verrückten Projekt konnte ich nur Architekten vorschlagen, die ich kannte, die mich kannten und mir vertrauten. Aber zur Aufgabe einer kleinen Bushaltestelle, noch dazu ohne Honorar? Niemand konnte mir und den von mir vorgeschlagenen Architekten garantieren, dass diese Ideen und Vorschläge dann auch realisiert würden. Und internationale, globale Architekten. Warum sollten sie sich engagieren, Ideen und Projekte entwickeln, für den Gegenwert eines Urlaubs im Bregenzerwald?

However, when you need to find the right architects for a certain project, a specific task, knowledge about recent developments in architecture is only of limited help. My position as mediator also involves responsibility for assessing such matters and discerning whether they are just one of the many demands for architecture with a capital 'A' that lack any real commitment. After all, one is familiar with the worries of star architects who have to question the seriousness of every approach made to them. Is the client only interested in an image that he can exploit in the media and sell, or in collaboration in terms of content after all and willing to assume the responsibility that this involves?

And so the year 2012 passed. Enquiries came regularly from Krumbach, but doubts about the project persisted. For such a crazy project I could only suggest architects whom I knew, who knew me and trusted me. But a commission to build a small bus shelter—without a fee? Nobody could give me and the architects I proposed a guarantee that their ideas and proposals would ultimately be carried out. And why, in the first place, should global architects get involved, develop ideas and projects in return for a holiday in the Bregenzerwald?

Beyond the Stars

At the end of 2012 the project began to really take shape. I recommended the initiators to involve the Vorarlberger Architektur Institut, as, if the project were to be realized, then clearly it would need a local partner to handle the organization.

Before this I was able to convince the people behind the project that international star architects were not appropriate for the situation and the task at hand. But it soon became clear to me that they were not in any case interested in 'big names' but rather in international contributions of architectural quality that could enrich and indeed even provoke the local culture of building.

Beyond the Stars

Ende des Jahres 2012 kam dann Bewegung ins Projekt. Ich hatte den Initiatoren empfohlen, das vai einzubeziehen. Denn wenn dies überhaupt realisiert werden konnte, brauchte es einen organisatorischen lokalen Partner vor Ort.

Davor noch konnte ich die Initiatoren des Projekts davon überzeugen, dass der Wunsch nach international prominenten Star-ArchitektInnen der Situation und der Aufgabe nicht gerecht werden würde. Doch es ging ihnen, das wurde mir inzwischen klar, nicht um ‚big names', sondern um internationale Beiträge einer architektonischen Qualität, welche die lokale Baukultur anreichern, ja vielleicht auch provozieren könnten.

Wie schon eingangs zur globalen Situation der Architektur erläutert, sind die heutigen Star-ArchitektInnen mit ihren egomanischen ikonischen Manifestationen nicht geeignet, in einen kleinmaßstäblichen intimen Dialog mit einer lokalen Baukultur einzutreten. Diese sind inzwischen global agierende Architekturfirmen geworden, mit Hunderten von Mitarbeitern, mit Büros auf der ganzen Welt. Wenn ich sie um eine Beteiligung gebeten hätte, dann hätte sich, wenn überhaupt, ein prekaristischer Praktikant mit dieser kleinen Aufgabe befassen müssen und das Ergebnis wäre eine eiskalte Fingerübung ihrer großen, ikonischen Gebilde geworden, einer Karikatur nahekommen. Peinlich für mich, peinlich für Krumbach. Und lächerlich machen, das wollte ich die von ihrer verrückten Idee enthusiasmierten Krumbacher keinesfalls.

So begann die Recherche nach den erwähnten Architekten der nächsten, der neuen Generation. Wer läuft nicht mit im Mainstream der globalen Business-Architektur und hat inzwischen eine eigenständige künstlerische Position entwickelt? Und welcher interessante Architekt könnte in der Lage sein, einen störenden – manche nennen das innovativen – Beitrag zur Baukultur des Bregenzerwaldes zu leisten?

Ab diesem Zeitpunkt der Auseinandersetzung mit der ‚verrückten Idee' wurde es auch für mich spannend. Erhielt ich doch zunächst einmal eine Carte blanche, wirklich jene ArchitektInnen vorzuschlagen, die noch keine medialen Weltstars sind, aber im inneren Diskurs der Architektur beobachtet werden und anerkannt sind und deren Werk mich bisher einfach fasziniert und beeindruckt hat.

BUS:STOP Unterkrumbach Süd, Architekten de Vylder Vinck Taillieu – Thomas Mennel / memux, 2014. © DS

As explained earlier, today's star architects with their iconic manifestations are not in a position to engage in small-scale, intimate dialogue with a local culture of building. They have become global architectural firms with hundreds of staff and offices throughout the world. If I had asked them to get involved then, if they had agreed at all, they would have entrusted an intern at the start of his or her career with this small project and the result would have been a cold finger exercise based on one of their large iconic formations, almost a caricature. Embarassing for me, embarrassing for Krumbach. And the last thing I wanted to do was make the people of Krumbach, who were so filled with enthusiasm for their crazy idea, to look ridiculous.

And so research into finding architects from the next generation began. This involved identifying those who are part of the mainstream in the global business of architecture but have developed an independent artistic position of their own. And it meant discovering which interesting architects might be in a position to make a disturbing—some would call it an innovative—contribution to the culture of building in the Bregenzerwald.

From this point onward dealing with this 'crazy idea' became an exciting undertaking for me also. After all, I was given a 'carte blanche' to propose precisely those architects who, while not yet world stars, are being watched and are recognized in the internal architecture discourse and whose work simply interested, fascinated and impressed me.

Die Auswahl der ArchitektInnen

Zunächst war die Frage zu klären, ob die Auswahl der ArchitektInnen wirklich global oder doch nur beschränkt auf Europa erfolgen sollte. Heftiger E-Mail-Verkehr mit Marina Hämmerle, der damaligen Leiterin des vai. Namen flogen hin und her. Die globale Szene wurde sozusagen ‚gescreent'.

Ich bringe jene ArchitektInnen in die Auswahl, deren Arbeit mich seit Jahren schon interessiert und die ich für diese Aufgabe mit skulpturalem Anspruch als geeignet empfinde. Auch ArchitektInnen, die sich mit der Zukunft des ländlichen Raums beschäftigten; denen die Verbindung mit Natur, ein neugieriger Respekt vor Geschichte und die Kontextualität und Materialität des Gebauten wichtig sind.

Beginnen wir mit Wang Shu, dem global wohl berühmtesten dieser Auswahl, der mit seiner Frau Lu Wenyu das Büro Amateur Architecture Studio führt – ein Name, der ihren Widerstand zum sogenannten Professionalismus des neuen globalen Urbanismus in China manifestiert. Dass sie 2012 den Pritzker-Preis, den Nobelpreis der Architektur, erhielten, war eine Sensation in der Architekturwelt. Ich kenne Wang Shu seit 2007, als im Architekturzentrum Wien der Wiener Architekturkongress zur Ausstellung *Chinaproduction* stattfand. Diese Ausstellung fand in Zusammenarbeit mit dem MUMOK statt, das eine Ausstellung zur aktuellen Kunst in China veranstaltete. Und es war der damalige Direktor, Edelbert Köb, der mich auf Wang Shu und seine Bauten aufmerksam machte. Der Vortrag,

Selecting the Architects

First of all we had to clarify whether the choice of architects was to be made at a global level or restricted to Europe. Busy email correspondence began with Marina Hämmerle, the head of vai at the time. Names flew back and forth. The global scene was 'screened', so to speak.

I introduced the names of those architects whom I thought suitable for this commission with its sculptural aspirations. These were architects who look at the future of the rural areas, for whom the connection with nature, an enquiring respect for history, and the contextuality and materiality of buildings is important.

Let's start with Wang Shu, perhaps globally the most famous architect in this selection, who with his wife Lu Wenyu set up the office "Amateur Architecture Studio". The name was deliberately chosen to illustrate their resistance to the so-called professionalism of the new global urbanism in China. That they were awarded the Pritzker Prize, architecture's Nobel Prize, in 2012 represented something of a sensation in the architecture world. I have known Wang Shu ever since 2007, when the Vienna Architecture Congress on the exhibition *Chinaproduction* was held in the Architekturzentrum Wien. This exhibition was made in collaboration with MUMOK, which organised an exhibition on contemporary art in China. And it was the MUMOK Director of the time, Edelbert Köb, who drew my attention to Wang Shu and his buildings. The lecture that Wang Shu gave back then received a standing ovation. He expressed an emphatic commitment to developing traditional Chinese building culture further, respect for nature was and is a *leitmotif* of this work. His museums in China, in which he reused old bricks, the building for

BUS:STOP Unterkrumbach Nord, Ensamble Studio – Dietrich | Untertrifaller Architekten, 2014. © DS

den Wang Shu damals hielt, führte zu Standing Ovations. Ein emphatisches Bekenntnis zur Weiterentwicklung der traditionellen chinesischen Baukultur, ein Bekenntnis zum Respekt vor der Natur war und ist das Leitmotiv der Arbeiten des Büros. Dessen Museen in China, bei denen gebrauchte Ziegel wiederverwendet wurden, der Bau der riesigen Kunstuniversität in Hangzouh mit traditionellen Materialien und viele andere Bauten in China zeugen davon, dass Amateur Architecture Studio diese Grundsätze auch in großem Maßstab verwirklichen kann. Immer in enger Zusammenarbeit mit den Handwerkern. Als ich Wang Shu nach der Verleihung des Pritzker-Preises fragte, wie er nun mit den unweigerlich kommenden globalen Aufgaben umgehen würde, wo er doch sosehr auf seine lokalen chinesischen Handwerker angewiesen sei, meinte er noch, dass er dann halt mit diesen Handwerkern im Ausland bauen würde. Gut, er hat sie nun in Krumbach gefunden, wo sein erster dauerhafter Bau außerhalb Chinas realisiert wurde.

In ihrem Zugang zur Architektur vergleichbar sind Sami Rintala und Dagur Eggertsson. Sami stammt aus Finnland und lebt jetzt auf den Lofoten, im Norden Norwegens. Dagur stammt aus Island. Sie sind Künstler, Designer und Architekten und wandern zwischen diesen Welten. Dazu gehören temporäre Installationen, die sich immer um die Definition eines Raumes für Menschen bemühen. Teilnahmen an Kunstbiennalen und -festivals gehören zu ihrem Repertoire. Sie schufen wunderschöne und intelligente Objekte und Aktionen, und langsam wachsen sie in die reale Architektur hinein. Auch Sami Rintalas Projekte verfolge ich seit Jahren. Das Alvar Aalto-Symposion 2009 in Jyväskylä wurde von ihm kuratiert und er präsentierte die schon erwähnten widerständigen Positionen einer lokalen und nachhaltigen Architektur gegenüber dem globalen Professionalismus. Ein Statement von ihm habe ich mir zum Argument gemacht: „Die ganze Welt spricht vom Prozess der Urbanisierung und dass in Zukunft die Hälfte der Menschen in Städten leben wird – mein Interesse gilt der anderen Hälfte …"

Präsentation der Modelle von BUS:STOP im Kunsthaus Bregenz am 10.10.2013. Die Blasmusikkapelle von Krumbach spielte den Song *Bus Stop* von den Hollies · Presentation of the BUS:STOP models in Kunsthaus Bregenz on 10.10.2013. The local Krumbach brass band played the song "Bus Stop" by the Hollies. © DS

the enormous art university in Hangzhou with its traditional materials, and many other buildings in China show that Amateur Architecture Studio can implement these principles at a larger scale also. And always in close collaboration with skilled workers. When I asked Wang Shu after he had been awarded the Pritzker Prize how, given that he was so dependent on his local Chinese craftsmen, he would handle the global commissions that he would certainly now receive, he said that he would build abroad with the same workers. Good, he now found them in Krumbach, where he has carried out his first permanent building outside China.

Sami Rintala and Dagur Eggertsson take a similar approach to architecture. Sami comes from Finland and now lives on the Lofoten, in the north of Norway, Dagur is from Iceland. They are artists, designers and architects and they move between these worlds. This involves temporary installations which repeatedly attempt to define space for people. Participation in art biennales and festivals belong to their repertoire. They created beautiful, intelligent objects and installations and they gradually grew towards real architecture. I have also followed Sami Rintala's projects for many years. He curated the Alvar Aalto Symposium in

Sechster Tag • Day Six

Skizze von • Sketch by Alexander Brodsky
für seinen • for his BUS:STOP. Archive DS

Beim besagten Aalto-Symposion 2009 traf ich endlich auch erstmals Alexander Brodsky. Auch sein Werk erweckte durch Publikationen mein Interesse. Unter allen ArchitektInnen und KünstlerInnen Russlands, bietet er eine provokante eigenständige Position und gilt im Land als der bedeutendste und wichtigste Künstlerarchitekt. Wir wollten ihn für eine Ausstellung im Architekturzentrum Wien gewinnen und versuchten jahrelang mit ihm Kontakt aufzunehmen. Aber damals verweigerte er sich noch der digitalen Kommunikation. Seine Homepage hatte eine italienische Domain, E-Mails druckte sein Assistent Kyrill Ass einmal wöchentlich aus und legte sie ihm zur Beantwortung vor. In Jyväskylä dann das erste Zusammentreffen mit ihm und seiner Familie. Einladung zu einer Ausstellung in Wien, die nach intensiven Vorbereitungen dann 2011

Jyväskylä in 2009 and he presented the positions already referred to that are based on a local and sustainable architecture in contrast to global professionalism. I made one of his statements into an argument: "The entire world speaks about the process of urbanisation and that, in the future, half of humankind will live in cities—I'm interested in the other half ..."

At the Aalto Symposium just referred to in 2009 I finally met Alexander Brodsky for the first time. Illustrations of his work in publications had awakened my interest. Among all the architects and artists in Russia he offered a provocative, independent position and in that country he is regarded as the most significant and important artist-architect. We wanted to exhibit his work in the Architekturzentrum Wien and attempted for years to establish contact with him. But at that time he still refused to engage in digital communication. His homepage had an Italian domain, his assistant Kyrill Ass printed out incoming emails once a week and placed them in front of Brodsky to answer them. In Jyväskylä I then met him and his family for the first time. I invited him to make an exhibition in Vienna which, after intensive preparation work, took place in 2011 and was the sensation of the year. It was a wonderful full-scale space installation accompanied by pictures of his objects and architecture. From this work a Russian friendship developed, and therefore I had reason to hope that he would agree to take part in BUS:STOP Krumbach.

My approach to the person and work of Smiljan Radić was similarly complex. After decades of agony a reawakening of architecture in South America became apparent in the first years of the new millennium. Chile, in particular, attracted international attention with a series of architects and projects. Many architects were then published globally but one architect in particular interested me: Smiljan Radić showed extreme projects, spatial experiments that always explored the boundaries of the material, accompanied by sensitive poetic reflections about architecture, space and the histories that

stattgefunden hat und zur Sensation des Jahres wurde. Es war eine großartige 1:1-Rauminstallation und die Bilder seiner Objekte und Architekturen begleitend. Aus dieser Arbeit war, ich gestehe es, eine russische Freundschaft entstanden, auf seine Beteiligung an BUS:STOP Krumbach durfte ich also hoffen.

Ähnlich komplex war meine Annäherung an Person und Werk von Smiljan Radić. Nach Jahrzehnten der Agonie davor war in den Nuller Jahren ein Wiedererwachen der Architektur Südamerikas erkennbar. Besonders Chile rückte mit einer Reihe von ArchitektInnen und Projekten in die internationale Aufmerksamkeit. Viele Architekten wurden mittlerweile global publiziert, aber ein Architekt erregte meine besondere Aufmerksamkeit. Smiljan Radić zeigte extreme Projekte. Räumliche Experimente, immer die Grenzen der Materialität auslotend. Begleitet mit sensiblen poetischen Reflexionen über Architektur, Raum und den Geschichten, die in den Objekten materialisiert werden konnten. Für mich ein Geheimtipp, war ich überrascht und bestätigt zugleich, als Smiljan 2010 von Kazuyo Sejima mit einer großen Installation zur Architektur Biennale in Venedig eingeladen und 2014, für die Fachwelt überraschend, mit dem prestigeträchtigen Serpentine-Pavillon in London beauftragt wurde.

Eine Großmacht der zeitgenössischen Architektur ist seit dem Ende der Franco-Diktatur in den 1970er Jahren Spanien. Unter den jüngeren Architekten fiel besonders Antón Garcia Abril auf, der sich nun mit seiner Frau Débora Mesa und dem Tragwerksplaner Javier Cuesta „Ensamble Studio" nennt. Aufgefallen ist das Studio mit wahrlich extremen Projekten, Experimenten mit Statik und Material, die immer eindrucksvolle Skulpturen zeitigten.

Die derzeit spannendste Architekturszene Europas hat Belgien. Wahrscheinlich befördert durch die Heterogenität des kleinen Landes, an vielen kulturellen Schnittmengen beteiligt. De Vylder, Vinck, Taillieu sind durch geradezu literarische Projekte aufgefallen, die nach Jahren allgemeiner Entwicklung zu modernistischer Schweigsamkeit wieder ein hochkomplexes Spiel mit Raum, Material und Atmosphären entfachen.

could be materialized in the buildings. For me he was an insider's tip, and therefore I was both surprised and confirmed when in 2010 Kazuyo Sejima invited Smiljan to take part in the Venice architecture biennale with a large installation and in 2014, to the surprise of the expert world, he was commissioned to design the prestigious Serpentine Pavilion in London

Since the end of Franco's dictatorship in the 1970s Spain has been a major power in the world of contemporary architecture. Among the younger architects Antón García Abril in particular stood out who with his wife Débora Mesa and the structural designer Javier Cuesta now call themselves "Ensamble Studio". The Studio is remarkable for truly extreme projects: experiments with structural design and material that always produce impressive sculptures.

Belgium currently has Europe's most exciting architecture scene. This is probably encouraged by the cultural heterogeneity of the small country. De Vylder, Vinck, Taillieu attracted attention by their almost literary projects which, following years in which the general development was in the direction of modernist taciturnity, again started off a highly complex game with space, material and atmospheres.

All that remained was the selection of the seventh samurai, who, naturally, could only come from Japan, the contemporary architectural world power. The awarding of the Pritzker Prize in recent years alone

BUS:STOP Oberkrumbach, Alexander Brodsky – Hugo Dworzak / Architekturwerkstatt, 2014. © DS

Verbleibt die Auswahl des siebten Samurai, der nun natürlich nur aus Japan – der zeitgenössischen Architekturweltmacht– sein konnte. Allein die Pritzker Preise der letzten Jahre machen dies deutlich: 2010 Kazuyo Sejima & Ryue Nishizawa, 2013 Toyo Ito und 2014 Shigeru Ban. Unter der jungen Generation ist Sou Fujimoto einer der radikalsten und konsequentesten. Die Versöhnung von Architektur und Natur treibt ihn zu ungeahnter Radikalität, jenseits einer Architektur zur Erhaltung der Körperwärme.

Die Reaktionen

Ich habe die Namen und Adressen der ArchitektInnen an den Kulturverein Krumbach zunächst einfach erwartungslos weitergeleitet. Aber ich war zufrieden. Ich hatte mit Marina Hämmerle eine Liste von Architekten erarbeitet, deren Werk interessant und faszinierend ist und deren Haltung zur Architektur mir ganz generell für die Zukunft der Architektur wichtig erscheint.

Doch ich konnte mir einfach nicht vorstellen, dass diese ArchitektInnen auf ein solches verrücktes Angebot reagieren würden. Eine kleine Busstation irgendwo in der Landschaft, kein Honorar, warum sollte man sich das als Architekt antun? Umso mehr überraschten mich die Reaktionen und sofortigen Zusagen von allen Eingeladenen.

makes this clear: 2010 Kazuyo Sejima & Ryue Nishizawa, 2013 Toyo Ito and 2014 Shigeru Ban. Among the younger generation Sou Fujimoto is one of the most radical and consistent. The reconciliation of nature and architecture drives him to an unsuspected radicalism, beyond an architecture intended just to conserve body heat.

The Reactions

I simply sent the names and addresses of the architects to the Kulturverein Krumbach without any great expectations. But I was satisfied. Together with Marina Hämmerle I had put together a list of architects whose work personally interested and fascinated me and whose approach to architecture in general was and is important for the future of the discipline.

But I could not imagine that these architects would respond to this crazy offer. A small bus shelter somewhere in the landscape, no fee—why would an architect agree to take that on? Therefore I found the responses and immediate willingness of all those invited to take part all the more surprising.

Naturally, I later asked all of them, also during their site visits in spring 2013, why they had agreed. The most important reason was the relatively unrestricted challenge to their analysis and creativity—the craziness of the whole idea, if you like. Then there was the content of the commission itself. All were aware of the social and ecological dimension of the task and that their building would give public transport in the rural area greater prominence. And, in the end, they were also convinced by the selection of the other architects. Naturally, they knew that they would have to prove themselves able—also in terms of content—to play in this special 'division'. This led to the so called 'school class effect': the high regard for the other architects and the challenge to match them in terms of both content and architecture.

BUS:STOP Zwing, Smiljan Radić – Bernardo Bader, 2014. © DS

Die Kinder von Krumbach singen im BUS:STOP von Smiljan Radić, bei der Präsentation im Kunsthaus Bregenz: „Wir fahren mit dem Landbus wohl in die weite Welt hinaus ...". · The children of Krumbach singing in Smiljan Radić's BUS:STOP during the presentation in Kunsthaus Bregenz: "We are riding on the country bus out into the big wide world ...". © DS

Ich habe selbstverständlich dann bei allen nachgefragt, auch bei den Ortsbesichtigungen im Frühjahr 2013. Der wichtigste Grund für ihre Teilnahme war die relativ freie Herausforderung für ihre Analyse und Kreativität. Ja, das Verrückte an der Idee. Dann kam aber schnell der Inhalt der Aufgabe selbst. Alle verstanden, dass es nicht um ein privates Projekt ging, sondern um die öffentliche Infrastruktur. Allen war die soziale und ökologische Aufgabe bewusst, dass ihre Objekte dem öffentlichen Nahverkehr im ländlichen Raum erhöhte Aufmerksamkeit schenken würden. Und zum Schluss überzeugte sie unsere Auswahl der jeweils anderen ArchitektInnen. Natürlich kannten sie deren bisherigen und wussten dass sie sich inhaltlich in einer ‚Spielklasse' zu beweisen haben würden. Damit trat der sogenannte Schulklassen-Effekt ein: Die Wertschätzung der jeweils anderen und die Herausforderung, vor diesen anderen inhaltlich und architektonisch bestehen zu können.

The Implementation and the Results

At the very start of the visits we were confronted with a major problem. The seven architects had been found, the seven locations for the BUS:STOPS had been determined. But who would design and build where? The allocation of the sites took place quickly and, ultimately, without conflict. Only the most famous participants, Wang Shu and Lu Wenyu, had to be satisfied with the last remaining site. They were the only ones unable to make a site visit. This had been scheduled for their trip to Vienna to serve on a competition jury but proved impossible due to a lack of geographical knowledge shared by many visitors from China and also from the

Die Umsetzung und das Ergebnis

Gleich am Beginn der Besichtigungen standen wir vor einem großen Problem. Die sieben ArchitektInnen waren gefunden, die sieben Orte der BUS:STOPS fixiert. Doch wer entwirft und baut wo? Die Zuteilung der Orte erfolgte dann doch spontan und letztlich konfliktfrei. Einzig die berühmtesten, Wang Shu und Lu Wenyu, mussten sich mit dem letzten verbliebenen Bauplatz begnügen. Sie waren auch die einzigen ohne Ortsbesichtigung. Diese war zwar geplant, als sie sich zu einer Jury in Wien aufhielten. Scheiterte aber am geographischen Missverständnis, das viele Besucher aus China und auch den USA auszeichnet. Sie befinden sich in Wien, und denken dass sie an einem Nachmittag schnell Vorarlberg besichtigen können, und am Abend aus Wien wieder wegfliegen. Ich habe Wang Shu und Lu Wenyu in Wien mit allen Unterlagen und Daten versorgt, und sie haben dann sehr präzise auf den landschaftlichen Wert des Ortes reagiert.

Im Sommer 2013 langten dann alle Entwürfe bei den Vorarlberger KontaktarchitektInnen ein, die sich auf Augenhöhe mit den internationalen KollegInnen befanden. Das war ein wichtiger Teil des auch geplanten kulturellen und architektonischen Austauschs, der zwischen den lokalen und den internationalen ArchitektInnen stattfinden sollte. Am 10. Oktober 2013 fand die öffentliche Präsentation des Projekts im Kunsthaus Bregenz statt. Mit phantastischen Modellen aller Projekte, mit einem 1:1-Modell des BUS:STOPS von Smiljan Radić, und einem Workshop der Kinder von Krumbach. Über den Winter bis zum Frühjahr wurden die Objekte konkretisiert und gebaut. Alles lief professionell und perfekt, einzig beim Projekt von Fujimoto mussten die Vorstellungen von seinem Büro in Tokio immer wieder mit der Wirklichkeit eines gebauten Objekts im Gebrauch abgeglichen werden.

BUS:STOP Krumbach has already written architectural history.

USA. When they were in Vienna they thought that in the space of an afternoon it would be possible to make a quick visit to Vorarlberg and on the evening of the same day leave Vienna by plane. I provided Wang Shu and Lu Wenyu with all the documents and data and they responded to the landscape of the place and its value in a very precise way.

In summer 2013 all the designs arrived at the offices of Vorarlberg contact architects who worked as equal partners with the international architects. This was an important part of the cultural and architectural exchange that was intended to take place between the local and the international architects. On 10.10.2013 the public presentation of the project took place in the Kunsthaus Bregenz. With fantastic models of all projects, with a 1:1 scale model of the BUS:STOP by Smiljan Radić, and a workshop for the children of Krumbach. Over the winter until springtime the designs were detailed and then built. Everything ran professionally and smoothly, only in the case of Fujimoto's project was it necessary to repeatedly reconcile the ideas of his office in Tokyo with the reality of how the built shelter was to be used.

However, with regard to one intention of this project I failed. In the last twenty years the culture of building in Vorarlberg has developed such a sophisticated qual-

Doch mit einer inhaltlichen Intention bin ich bei diesem Projekt gescheitert. In den letzten zwanzig Jahren hat sich die Vorarlberger Baukultur in eine derart raffinierte Qualität und Authentizität vorgearbeitet – Peter Zumthor hat ihr mit dem Werkraumhaus auch den entsprechenden ‚Tempel' gewidmet –, dass eine zumindest ästhetische Störung durch ArchitektInnen aus anderen Kulturkreisen durchaus von mir beabsichtigt war. Doch das Gegenteil trat ein. Die ausländischen ArchitektInnen waren von der Präzision und Sorgfalt der Handwerkskultur des Bregenzerwaldes derart beeindruckt, dass sie bisher in ihrem Werk unbekannte Dimensionen der Präzision eröffnet fanden. Nicht der Bregenzerwald hat also von der Welt gelernt, sondern die Welt vom Bregenzerwald.

Wenn jetzt die BUS:STOPS in Krumbach eröffnet werden, die Ausstellung die wunderbare Geschichte dieses Projekts erzählt, dann darf eines nicht vergessen werden: Es war letztlich nur möglich mit einem einzigartigen Engagement des Kulturvereins Krumbach und des Bürgermeisters Arnold Hirschbühl. Sie haben rund um die Uhr – mein E-Mail-Verkehr beweist dies – dafür gearbeitet. Niemals zuvor habe ich auch ein derartiges Engagement von Handwerks- und Gastronomiebetrieben einer Region erlebt. Bei ihnen habe auch ich mich zu bedanken. Sie haben mir die Mitwirkung beim schönsten und größten Projekt meines Lebens ermöglicht. BUS:STOP Krumbach hat jetzt schon Architekturgeschichte geschrieben.

BUS:STOP Trips, Tischler Markus Faißt, Marina Hämmerle, Sou Fujimoto.
© Adolf Bereuter

ity and authenticity—with his Werkraumhaus Peter Zumthor has devoted an appropriate 'temple' to it—that introducing a certain aesthetic disturbance by architects from other cultural circles was very much part of my intention. But the opposite occurred. The foreign architects were so impressed by the precision and attention to detail shown by the culture of handcraft in the Bregenzerwald region that they revealed previously unknown dimensions of precision in their work; it was not the Bregenzerwald that learned from the world but the world from the Bregenzerwald.

Now that the BUS:STOPS in Krumbach are being inaugurated and the exhibition tells the amazing story of this project, one thing should not be forgotten. This was all possible thanks only to the unique commitment of the Kulturverein Krumbach and the mayor Arnold Hirschbühl. They worked all around the clock—as my email correspondence shows—to carry out the project. Never before have I encountered such a level of commitment from craft and restaurant businesses in a region. And I must express my thanks to them. They made it possible for me to take part in the loveliest and greatest project of my life. BUS:STOP Krumbach has already written architectural history.

7th DAY Sunday

Der „Monolith" von Jean Nouvel für die The "Monolith" by Jean Nouvel for
Swiss Expo, Murtensee, 2002. © DS

7. TAG Sonntag

Siebenter Tag • Day Seven

By the Wayside

Am Wegesrand

Meine ersten Begegnungen mit „Architektur" fanden durch die Ausbildung in der technischen Mittelschule für Hochbau statt. Da lernten wir von einem begnadeten Professor Baudetails von Prouvé, Gropius, Mies etc. Aber war das schon „Architektur"? Ich begann meinen Blick zu schärfen und versuchte meine Umgebung in gut oder schlecht Gebautes abzutasten und einzuteilen. Kriterien dafür gab es zunächst keine, jedenfalls spielte groß oder klein dabei keine Rolle. Also begann ich mit Gartenhütten und erkannte, dass es entweder ruhige, bescheiden klassische, ohne jede scheinbare Ambition gab oder besonders originelle und persönliche. Welche davon die architektonisch besseren Gartenhütten waren, konnte ich nicht entscheiden, und kann es bis heute nicht. Aber es gab welche ‚dazwischen', und die waren einfach wirklich schlecht.

Erst später las ich die Schriften von Adolf Loos, und erkannte, dass es auf groß und bedeutend nicht ankommt, sondern dass die wahren Monumente eben am Wegesrand liegen: „Wenn wir im walde einen hügel finden, sechs schuh lang und drei schuh breit, mit der schaufel pyramidenförmig aufgerichtet, dann werden wir ernst, und es sagt etwas in uns: Hier liegt jemand begraben. *Das ist architektur.*" Das schrieb der große

My first encounters with "architecture" took place during my education at the Higher Technical College for Civil Engineering. A gifted professor taught us about construction details by Prouvé, Gropius, Mies, etc. But was that already "architecture?" I began to sharpen my view and tried to sense and divide my surroundings into well- or badly-built structures. No criteria for this initially existed, but in any case large and small played no role. So I began with garden sheds and recognized that there were either sedate, modestly classic ones without any apparent ambition, or particularly original and personal ones. I couldn't decide which of these were the architectonically better garden sheds and I cannot do it up to today. But there were some 'in-between,' and these were simply really bad.

I first read later in the writings of Adolf Loos that it did not depend on large and important, but that the true monuments lay precisely by the wayside: "If we find a mound in the forest, six feet long and three feet wide, raised by a shovel to form a pyramid, we become serious and something within us says, 'someone lies

Adolf Loos in seinem Aufsatz *Architektur* 1910. Er verwahrte sich darin einer unendlichen architektonischen Sucht nach Originalität und gebauter Einzigartigkeit, hinterfragte das Geplante und Gebaute nach ihren „Stimmungen", die sie im Benutzer und Betrachter auslösen. Und wenn wir diese Stimmungen suchen, dann finden wir sie nicht selten weit abseits jener spektakulären Objekte, die heute dem Markt der üblichen Aufmerksamkeit der medialen Verwertung von Architektur ausgesetzt sind. Es sind dann die Objekte „am Wegesrand", mit architektonischer Ambition gestaltet, oder auch nur irgendwie geschehen, von ewig unbekannt bleibenden Autoren geschaffen. Oft unbedeutende Objekte, die sich einschreiben, in jede Biografie jedes individuell gelebten Lebens, als Orientierungspunkte und Merkmale, nur selten bewusst. Die Architekten sind dafür Experten, und wissen um diese geheime Architekturgeschichte. Ich kenne keinen intellektuell reflektierten und bedeutenden Architekten, der nicht zu später Stunde, beim dritten Glas Wein, von der Faszination von ihm entdeckter beiläufiger Objekte „am Wegesrand" erzählen würde.

Das allein ist keine neue Entwicklung. Schon immer hat sich die Architektur von der Beobachtung und Einverleibung des Alltäglichen und des Ruralen genährt. Die Spannweite reicht hier von den Untersuchungen, die der amerikanische Urbanist Kevin Lynch schon in den 60er Jahren des letzten Jahrhunderts anstellte und erkannte, dass sich die Menschen im Alltag am Nebensächlichen und nicht am architektonisch Bedeutenden orientieren: der Briefkasten an der Hausecke, die Parkbank, die Bushaltestelle. Bis hin zu den Forschungen und Erkundungen von Bernard Rudofsky, der im All-

Die Hütte am Kitzbüheler Horn, wo Margarethe Cufer alle Ferien ihrer Kindheit verbrachte · The "Hut" on Kitzbüheler Horn, where Margarethe Cufer spent all the holidays of her childhood. © Franz Huber

buried there.' *That is architecture*." That is what the great Adolf Loos wrote in his 1910 essay "Architecture." He kept an endless architectonic craving for originality and constructed uniqueness within it for himself, questioning the planned and the built about the "moods" they evoke in the user and beholder. And if we search for these moods, we will quite often find them far away from those spectacular objects that are exposed today to the market of the usual attention of architecture's media exploitation. These are then the objects "by the wayside," designed with architectonic ambition, or also only happening somehow, created by authors who will remain unknown for eternity. Often insignificant objects that inscribe themselves into every biography of every individually lived life, as points of reference and distinguishing marks, very rarely in a conscious way. The architects are experts for that and have knowledge of this secret architectural history. I know no intellectually reflecting and important architect who, at a late hour, drinking the third glass of wine, would not talk of the fascination of incidental objects he discovered "by the wayside."

Siebenter Tag • Day Seven

täglichen ruraler Gesellschaften den wahren Quell für neue ‚Lebensweisen' entdeckte und in Publikationen und Ausstellungen thematisierte: *Architecture without Architects* sei nur als Slogan dafür genannt.

Nun sind wir wieder einmal an einem Wendepunkt der Architekturgeschichte angelangt. Angesichts der Inflation des Spektakulären, die den Fortschritt der Architektur nur mehr in immer neuen und immer exaltierteren Formen der Rendering-Software zu generieren glaubte, schlägt nun das Pendel zurück in die Beobachtung des Alltäglichen unserer Konsumgesellschaft, in die produktive Wahrnehmung des scheinbar Unerheblichen. So erinnere ich mich an die Architektur Biennale 2002 in Venedig, als inmitten der anstrengt ambitionierten Präsentationen aller Länder, Estland mit gebotener Selbstironie die morphologische Vielfalt individuell gebauter ‚Scheißhäuser' präsentierte. Und wir im Architekturzentrum Wien wenig später eine Studie über estnische Buswartehäuschen mit unerwartet großem Erfolg zeigen konnten. All dieses Nebensächliche bekam seine Bedeutung durch das sanfte Lächeln, die stille Freude, die sich in den Mienen der Besucher breit machte. Eine seltsame Form der Entspannung von all den sonst sich so bedeutsam gebenden erratischen Diamanten von Star-Architekten.

Immer schon hat der Architektur hier die Kunst diese Richtung der Wahrnehmung gezeigt. Nicht nur dass Duchamps *Flaschentrockner* bereits 1914 eine bis heute anhaltende Richtung des Dialogs von Kunst und Wirklichkeit etablierte, sind es auch heute Künstler, die durch ihre Installationen der Architektur den Weg in die Wirklichkeit weisen können. Nur als Beispiel dafür, haben Michael Elmgreen und Ingar Dragset 2005 eine gefakte „Prada"-Boutique in Marfa, Texas, gebaut – an

That alone is no new development. Architecture has always lived on the observation and incorporation of the everyday and the rural. The span ranges here from the investigations that the American urbanist Kevin Lynch already undertook in the 1960s, realizing that people orient themselves in everyday life on the trivial and not on the architectonically meaningful: the mailbox on the house corner, the park bench, the bus stop. This goes all the way to the research and explorations of Bernard Rudofsky, who discovered the true source for new 'styles of living' in the everyday world of rural societies and made it a subject of discussion in publications and exhibitions: *Architecture without Architects* is merely named as a slogan for it.

Now we have once again reached a turning point of architectural history. In view of the inflation of the spectacular, which believed to generate the progress of architecture only in always newer and more exalted forms of rendering software, the pendulum is now swinging back to the observation of the everyday world of our consumer society, to the productive perception of the apparently trivial. I therefore recall the 2002 Architecture Biennale in Venice when, in the middle of the intensely ambitious presentation of all countries, Estonia presented with due self-irony the morphological diversity of individually built 'outhouses.' And we were able to show a study of Estonia bus shelters shortly afterwards at the Architekturzentrum Wien with unexpectedly great success. All of this trivia acquired its meaning through the soft smile, the quiet joy spreading in the faces of the visitors. A rare form of relaxation from the otherwise so important seeming, erratic diamonds of star architects.

Architecture has always shown the art of this perceptive direction here. Not only did Duchamp's *Bottle Dryer* already establish a course of dialog between art and reality in 1914 that has persisted to this day, but artists are also the ones today who can point architecture's way

Tankstelle von · Gas station by Mies van der Rohe in Montreal. © DS

dem magischen Ort, den sich Donald Judd auserkoren hatte, um dieses Niemandsland mit seinen Spuren zu tränken. Und insgesamt hat die „Kunst im öffentlichen Raum" unsere Wahrnehmung für das Nebensächliche geschärft. Ihre Interventionen sind meist nur durch die Schärfung und Verschiebung der Wahrnehmung überhaupt als künstlerischer Eingriff zu erkennen. Das ist gut so. Denn nur so werden wir wieder eine Architektur ‚vom Anfang an' denken können, wenn wir das Alltägliche, das sogenannte Anonyme, die verlorenen Objekte am Wegesrand, als ernsthaften, weil existierenden Beitrag zur gestalteten Umwelt und damit auch als Material der Anverwandlung erkennen können. Übrigens, um doch von großer Architektur zu reden. Wissen Sie, welches das schönste und bedeutendste Gebäude von Montreal ist: Eine Tankstelle von Mies van der Rohe aus dem Jahr 1968.

into reality through their installations. Just to take an example, Michael Elmgreen and Ingar Dragset built a faked Prada boutique in Marfa, Texas in 2005, at that magic place Donald Judd had chosen to saturate this no-man's land with his traces. And "art in public space" has sharpened our awareness for the trivial altogether. Most of the time its interventions are only to be recognized as artistic interventions at all by the sharpening and shifting of perception. And that is a good thing. Since only in this way will we be able to think an architecture again 'from the beginning,' if we can recognize the everyday, the so-called anonymous, the lost object by the wayside, as the serious contribution to the designed environment for the simple reason that it exists, and therefore as a material of adaptation, too. Do you know what Montréal's most beautiful and significant building is? A gas station by Mies van der Rohe from 1968.

Auf der Fahrt · On The Road Bishkek – Almaty, 23.10.2010. © DS

The End: Anna Heringer and Dietmar Steiner on August 11, 2016 in Laufen

DS: After your contribution to the Architecture Biennale in Venice, realized with a gigantic time input, you have reached your physical limit. How are you doing now?

AH: Together with Martin Rauch and Andres Lepik we worked intensively for three months here and in Venice in order to realize the entry. Since every hand was needed at the building site, a lot of work piled up in the office and that simply became too much. I had to take time out.

DS: That is altogether a mystery to me how you manage it all. Lectures and projects around the globe, child and family here in idyllic Laufen in Bavaria.

AH: The profession of the female architect doesn't make it exactly easy to arrange with family life, and most of the time only those who have no children make it to the top. One is either a diva or a man. I have the feeling of running with a giant carriage against race horses. An incredible feat, but it is nonetheless worth it.

DS: A woman cannot do the job without a nanny. Hélène Jourda had four children and it is usual in France to have a nanny.

AH: But in Bavaria the social pressure in terms of the mother role is still big. I am often the only mother who is not at a family event. That gives one a guilty conscience. Nevertheless, we continue to do a lot of projects. My big advantage is that I design very quickly. I've learned to tap into my intuition well, and I have a small, but terrific team backing me up.

Ende: Anna Heringer und Dietmar Steiner am 11.08.2016 in Laufen

DS: Nach deinem mit zeitlichem Rieseneinsatz verwirklichten Beitrag bei der Architektur Biennale in Venedig bist du an deinem körperlichen Limit angelangt. Wie gehts dir jetzt?

AH: Gemeinsam mit Martin Rauch und Andres Lepik haben wir drei Monate intensiv hier und in Venedig gearbeitet, um den Beitrag zu verwirklichen. Weil jede Hand auf der Baustelle gebraucht wurde, hat sich im Büro eine Menge Arbeit angehäuft und das wurde dann einfach zu viel. Ich musste eine Auszeit nehmen.

DS: Das ist mir insgesamt ein Rätsel, wie du das alles schaffst. Vorlesungen und Projekte rund um den Globus, Kind und Familie hier im idyllischen Laufen, in Bayern.

AH: Der Beruf der Architektin lässt sich mit einer Familie nicht gerade leicht vereinbaren und es kommen meist nur diejenigen nach oben, die keine Kinder haben. Entweder ist man eine Diva oder ein Mann. Ich habe das Gefühl, mit einer riesigen Kutsche gegen Rennpferde anzutreten. Ein unglaublicher Kraftakt, aber wert ist er es trotzdem.

DS: Ohne Nanny ist für eine Frau der Job nicht zu machen. Hélène Jourda hatte vier Kinder und in Frankreich ist es üblich, eine Nanny zu haben.

AH: Aber in Bayern ist der gesellschaftliche Druck, was die Mutterrolle anbelangt, immer noch groß. Ich bin oft die einzige Mutter, die nicht bei einer Familien-Veranstaltung dabei ist. Das macht ein schlechtes Gewissen. Nichtsdestotrotz machen wir weiterhin noch viele Projekte. Mein großer Vorteil ist, dass ich sehr schnell entwerfe. Ich habe gelernt, meine Intuition gut anzuzapfen, und ich habe ein kleines, aber tolles Team im Rücken.

Anna Heringer • Dietmar Steiner

DS: Let's get to the reason for our conversation. At the beginning of this book I wanted a dialog with Jacques Herzog, since the exchange about architecture with him has accompanied me my whole architectural life, also because we share the experiences of the same generation. And at the end, a conversation with a young woman architect who I especially value in her potential for the future of architecture. I have observed your development, but if I recall correctly we first met each other in Jyväskylä, Finland, at the 2009 Aalto Symposium curated by Sami Rintala.

AH: That's right, but you already had importance for me before that. I began writing my diploma thesis in 2003 and back then the topic of the 'global south' practically didn't exist.

DS: How did you come upon the topic?

AH: At the age of 19 I went to Bangladesh and lived there for a year as a development learner. During this time I not only built up a passion for developmental cooperation, but also for architecture. Back then it wasn't clear to me how both subject areas could be linked together. But I then succeeded with the material of clay. That was the 'missing link' which made it possible for me to combine design and aesthetics with ecological and social aspects, right up to political issues. It was very surprising for me and also fascinating that the connection of the two areas succeeded through the material level.
The clay workshops with Martin Rauch also brought me additional clarity that my diploma thesis should be carried out in Bangladesh, but I nonetheless felt very

DS: Kommen wir zum Anlass für unser Gespräch. Ich wollte am Beginn dieses Buches ein Gespräch mit Jacques Herzog, da der Austausch über Architektur mit ihm mein ganzes Architekturleben begleitet hat, auch weil wir die Erfahrungen derselben Generation teilen. Und am Ende ein Gespräch mit einer jungen Architektin, die ich in ihrem Potenzial für die Zukunft der Architektur besonders schätze. Ich habe deine Entwicklung beobachtet, aber wir haben uns, wenn ich mich recht entsinne, in Jyväskylä, in Finnland, bei dem von Sami Rintala kuratierten Aalto-Symposium 2009 zum ersten Mal getroffen.

AH: Das ist richtig, aber du hattest schon davor Bedeutung für mich. Ich habe 2003 mit dem Diplom begonnen und damals war der Themenkreis „globaler Süden" praktisch nicht vorhanden.

DS: Wie bist du auf das Thema gestoßen?

AH: Ich bin mit 19 Jahren nach Bangladesch gegangen und habe dort ein Jahr lang als Entwicklungslernerin gelebt. In dieser Zeit hat sich sowohl eine Leidenschaft für die Entwicklungszusammenarbeit als auch für die Architektur aufgebaut. Damals war mir nicht klar, wie ich die beiden Themenbereiche in Verbindung bringen könnte. Mit dem Material Lehm ist es mir dann gelungen. Das war das ‚missing link', welches es mir möglich machte, die Gestaltung und die Ästhetik mit dem Ökologischen und Sozialen bis hin zum Politischen zu verknüpfen. Es war für mich sehr überraschend und auch faszinierend, dass die Verknüpfung der beiden Bereiche über die Materialebene gelang.
Auch die Lehm-Workshops bei Martin Rauch brachten mir zusätzliche Klarheit, dass meine Diplomarbeit in Bangladesch umgesetzt werden sollte, aber ich habe mich trotzdem mit meiner Idee sehr alleine gefühlt. Ich war mir nicht sicher, ob sich das Thema sinnvoll umsetzen lässt. In dieser Zeit sind dann bei uns an der Kunstuni Linz über Roland Gnaiger erste Texte von dir aufgetaucht und es war ein Gefühl großer Erleichterung zu wissen, dass Dietmar Steiner diese Ideen für richtig und wichtig hält. Es war wie ein Befreiungsschlag – nach dem Motto ‚die Richtung stimmt'. Das Bewusstsein, dass es an der Zeit ist, sogar zeitrichtig ist, als Europäer Wissen in diesen Ländern einzubringen. Und mit „BASEhabitat – architecture for development" ist parallel sogar eine Bewegung entstanden. Und du hast die intellektuelle Unterfütterung geliefert.

alone with my idea. I wasn't sure whether the theme lets itself be implemented meaningfully. At this time, then, texts by you first turned up by us over at the University of Art and Industrial Design in Linz through Roland Gnaiger and it was a feeling of great relief to know that Dietmar Steiner regarded these ideas as right and important. It was like an act of liberation—according to the motto 'The direction is right.' The awareness that the time has come, that it is even the right time, as a European to bring knowledge into these countries. And with 'BASEhabitat – Architecture for Development' a movement even emerged concurrently. And you supplied the intellectual underpinning.

DS: If you are talking about my texts, we have to find a temporal correspondence. When did you complete the school in Bangladesh?

AH: I finished the diploma thesis in 2004. I spent a year collecting money and in 2005 we could begin with construction in the team with Eike Rosweg; the completion followed in March 2006.

DS: So we are coming closer. In 2002 I saw photos of very unique buildings at the Whitney Biennale in New York and asked myself what place this type of architecture has at an art biennale. At the same time a book about Rural Studio appeared. I was able to fill the Az W team with enthusiasm for the idea of making an exhibition about it. It was very difficult back then to establish contact with the Rural Studio, but after initial obstacles we succeeded in contacting Andrew Freear. The Az W then held the first exhibition about this office in Europe. During the preparations we also made contact with the Austrian universities about whether comparable activities would be conceivable in Austria. We got in touch with Peter Fattinger, who had already initiated the design.build projects, and Christoph Chorherr was also very interested in these developments and consequently founded 'S²arch – Social Sustainable Architecture.' The projects of Rural Studio left a lasting impression on me, but when I saw the pictures of your school in Bangladesh, I thought: Look, it also works with good, new architecture. A real alternative to the egocentric, technoid star architecture of this era.

DS: Wenn du von meinen Texten sprichst, müssen wir eine zeitliche Übereinstimmung finden. Wann hast du die Schule in Bangladesch fertiggestellt?

AH: 2004 habe ich die Diplomarbeit beendet. Ein Jahr lang war ich beschäftigt, Geld zu sammeln und 2005 konnte im Team mit Eike Rosweg mit dem Bau begonnen werden, die Fertigstellung erfolgte im März 2006.

DS: So kommen wir uns näher. 2002 habe ich in New York auf der Whitney-Biennale Fotos von sehr eigenartigen Bauten gesehen und mich gefragt, was diese Art der Architektur auf einer Kunstbiennale zu suchen hat. Zeitgleich ist dazu auch ein Buch über das Rural Studio erschienen. Ich konnte dann das Az W-Team für die Idee begeistern, eine Ausstellung darüber zu machen. Es war damals sehr schwierig, Kontakt mit dem Rural Studio aufzunehmen, aber es ist uns nach anfänglichen Schwierigkeiten gelungen, Andrew Freear zu kontaktieren. Das Az W hat dann die erste Ausstellung über dieses Büro in Europa gezeigt. Während der Vorbereitungen haben wir auch mit den österreichischen Universitäten Kontakt aufgenommen, ob nicht vergleichbare Aktivitäten in Österreich denkbar wären. Wir haben Peter Fattinger, der bereits Design Built!-Projekte initiiert hatte, kontaktiert und auch Christoph Chorherr war sehr an diesen Entwicklungen interessiert und er hat in Folge „S²arch – Social Sustainable Architecture" gegründet. Für mich waren die Projekte des Rural Studio nachhaltig beeindruckend, aber als ich die Bilder deiner Schule in Bangladesch gesehen habe, habe ich mir gedacht: Schau, es geht auch mit guter neuer Architektur. Eine echte Alternative zur egozentrischen technoiden Star-Architektur dieser Zeit.

AH: Dein Appell an eine Architektur als Notwendigkeit, Architektur als Lebensmittel. Das war für meine Generation eine Vision. Diese Vision hat mich über all die Jahre begleitet und bringt meine Intention auf den Punkt. Diese Vision hat wie eine Bombe eingeschlagen, dieser Leitsatz war prägend für mich. Architekturtexte sind oft intellektuell komplex und schwer zugänglich. Du hast die Gabe, mit deinen Architekturtexten komplexe Dinge mit gesundem Menschenverstand direkt auf den Punkt zu bringen. Auch sprachlich wird die essenzielle Notwendigkeit, um die es geht, wieder nachvollziehbar. Deshalb waren deine Texte so bestärkend für mich, weil sie mich in meiner Intuition bestärkt haben.

Anna Heringer und · and Dietmar Steiner. © Stefano Mori

AH: Your appeal for an architecture as necessity, architecture as food. This was a vision for my generation. This vision accompanied me throughout the years and gets to the heart of my intention. This vision hit like a bomb, this guiding principle was defining for me. Architecture texts are often intellectually complicated and difficult to access. You have the gift with your architectural writings of boiling complex things down directly to the essence with healthy human understanding. Linguistically as well, the essential necessity it has to do with becomes comprehensible again. That's why your texts were so strengthening for me, because they fortified me in my intuition.

DS: Although I never really saw myself as an architectural theorist, more as a journalist and observer. In the period after the 1970s, from postmodern deconstructivism onwards, an esoteric architectural theory which had removed itself from building, ensuing from the academic American debate in the 1990s and 2000s, developed. Today I assume that these incomprehensible exegeses simply tried to legitimize the individualistic, neo-liberal affectations of artist-architects in the succession of postmodern deconstructivism. That reminds me of an analysis of city planning theories of the 1960s, when the attempt was made to make city developments assessable. With the most complicated formulas and calculation methods that only panned out if one made at least three coincidental assumptions. Anyway, an intellectual game likewise far removed from any reality.

AH: For us architecture students these positions were extremely confusing and elusive. We had lost sight of the concrete goal, the question as to where the way leads us. The message 'architecture as necessity, architecture as food' was again a goal for me, the way there was then found automatically.

DS: Obwohl ich mich ja nie wirklich als Architekturtheoretiker verstanden habe, mehr als Journalist und Beobachter. In der Zeit nach 1970er Jahren, ab dem postmodernen Dekonstruktivismus, hat sich in den 1990er und 2000er Jahren, ausgehend von der akademischen amerikanischen Debatte, eine esoterische Architekturtheorie entwickelt, die sich vom Bauen selbst entfernt hatte. Heute vermute ich, dass diese unverständlichen Exegesen einfach versuchten, die individualistischen neoliberalen Allüren von Künstlerarchitekten in der Nachfolge des postmodernen Dekonstruktivismus zu legitimieren. Das erinnert mich an eine Analyse der Städtebautheorien der 1960er Jahre, als versucht wurde, die Stadtentwicklungen berechenbar zu machen. Mit kompliziertesten Formeln und Berechnungsmethoden, die nur aufgingen, wenn man mindestens drei zufällige Annahmen machte. Also ebenfalls ein von jeder Realität weit entferntes intellektuelles Spiel.

AH: Für uns Architekturstudierende waren diese Positionen extrem verwirrend und schwer nachvollziehbar. Wir hatten das konkrete Ziel, die Frage, wohin der Weg geht, aus den Augen verloren. Die Botschaft ‚Architektur als Notwendigkeit, Architektur als Lebensmittel' war für mich wieder ein Ziel, der Weg dorthin fand sich dann von selbst.

DS: Diese Formphantasien der Architekten waren nur aufgrund von technischen Entwicklungen und der Bauindustrie möglich. Die Architekten entwickeln Formen am Computer, simulieren diese (Bildwirksamkeit der Architektur und Fortschritt der Rendering-Software) und dann müssen sie sich auf Techniker und Statiker verlassen, dass diese den Entwurf umsetzen. Das sehe ich

DS: These design fantasies of architects were only possible thanks to the technical advancements and the construction industry. The architects develop forms on the computer, simulate these (pictorial effectiveness of the architecture and progress of the rendering software) and then have to leave it up to the technicians and structural engineers to implement the design. I don't see this as progress for architecture. Harry Gugger said in an interview that it is becoming increasingly more difficult to communicate with the clients or the builders because the renderings of the structures meanwhile look like the built reality. As a consequence, in a development process, which always depicts the construction, it is now only very difficult to let changes and developments flow in. The rendered image is passed on to the construction industry and the question then arises about where the architect is and if he/she is still needed at all.

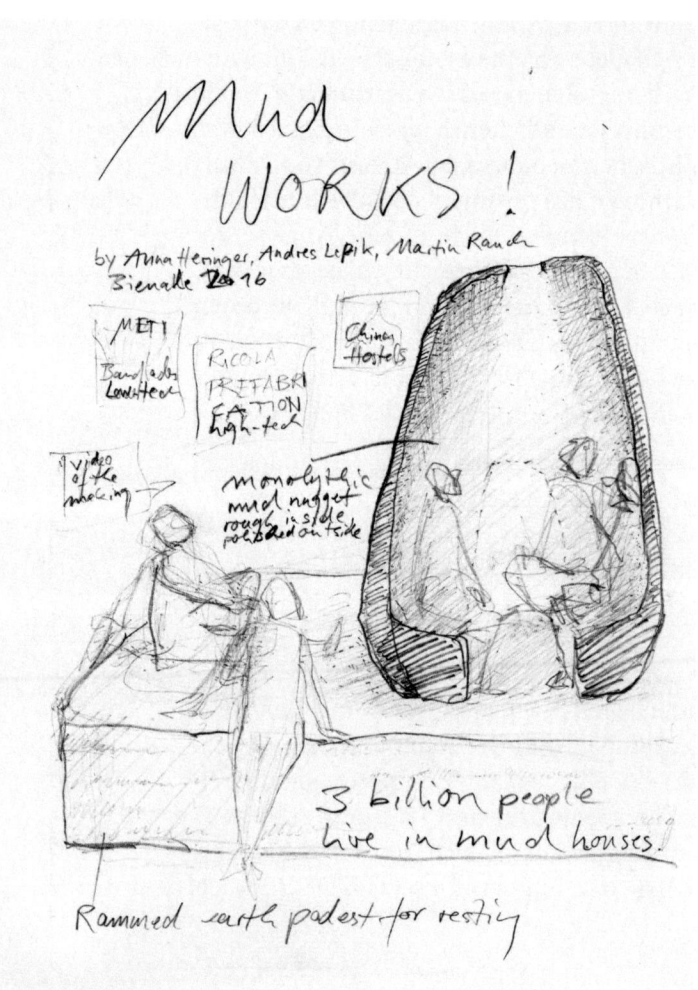

nicht als Fortschritt für die Architektur. In einem Interview sagte Harry Gugger, dass es immer schwieriger wird, mit den Klienten oder den Bauherren zu kommunizieren, weil die Renderings der Bauten mittlerweile wie die gebaute Wirklichkeit aussehen. Somit kann man in einem Entwicklungsprozess, welcher das Bauen immer darstellt, nur mehr sehr schwer Änderungen und Entwicklungen einfließen lassen. Das Rendering-Bild wird der Bauindustrie übergeben und es stellt sich dann die Frage, wo ist der Architekt, und braucht es ihn überhaupt noch.

AH: Es gibt immer mehr Kontrolle und immer weniger Vertrauen. Und Partizipation ist nur dann möglich, wenn Vertrauen und ein gewisser Respekt vorhanden sind und es muss ein gewisses Maß an Unperfektheit möglich sein. Ich merke dies an meinen Gebäuden. Wenn das Konzept stimmig ist, dann ist es völlig egal, wenn eine Ecke nicht ganz meinen Vorstellungen entspricht. Als ich das DESI-Gebäude in Bangladesch realisierte, wurde in meiner Abwesenheit eine Wand von den Arbeitern schief aufgestellt, weil sie dies für gut befanden. Da habe ich mir die Frage gestellt, was ist wichtiger, dass die Arbeiter Eigeninitiative zeigen oder dass eine Wand, die eigentlich nebensächlich ist, schief ist, und ich habe mich für die Eigeninitiative entschieden, weil ein gutes Gesamtkonzept dies aushalten muss. Es zeigt sich für mich, dass durch diesen Perfektionswahn das Kreative, das Spielerische verlorengeht, und dies ist sehr schade. Der Beruf des Architekten wird so zwänglerisch und es geht die Freude am Gestalten verloren. Für die Zukunft wünsche ich mir, dass der Beruf wieder mehr Freude macht, dass die Kreativität aus dem Bauch heraus genügend Raum erhält, um sich zu entfalten. Wenn der Architekt die Basisbedürfnisse der Menschen wieder wahrnimmt, seiner Intuition vertraut, das Projekt am Modell entwickelt, dann gelingen Entwürfe wieder stimmiger.

DS: Das ist ein interessanter Punkt. Das heißt, du siehst einen Zusammenhang zwischen Perfektion, Technologie, Standardisierung, Regulierung, Normen, Vorschriften etc. und dem Traum der Moderne von der Industrialisierung. Diese Form der Industrialisierung funktioniert zwar bei vielen Geräten wie z.B. bei Autos oder Fotoapparaten, aber bei einem Bau, der den menschlichen Körper umgibt, passt es nicht.

Skizze · Sketch, „Mud Works", Biennale Venedig · Venice 2016.
© Anna Heringer, Andres Lepik, Martin Rauch

"Mud Works", Architektur · Architecture Biennale Venedig · Venice, 2016.
© Stefano Mori

AH: There are more and more controls and less and less trust. And participation is only then possible if trust and a certain respect exist and a certain measure of imperfectness has to be possible. I notice this on my buildings. If the concept is consistent, then it doesn't matter at all if a corner doesn't quite correspond to my imagination. When I was building the DESI building in Bangladesh, in my absence a wall was set up crookedly by the workers, because they thought it was good. So I asked myself the question of what is more important: that the workers show their own initiative or that a wall, which is actually incidental, is not straight, and I decided for the self-initiative, because a good overall concept has to withstand this. It showed me that the creative, the playful, gets lost through this perfection mania, and this is a great pity. The occupation of the architect becomes so obsessive-compulsive and the joy of designing disappears. For the future I wish that the profession gives me more pleasure again, that intuitive creativity is provided enough space to unfold itself. If the architect perceives the basic needs of humans again, trusts his/her intuition, develops the project on the model, then designs succeed more coherently again.

DS: That is an interesting point. This means you see a correlation between perfection, technology, standardization, regulation, standards, provisions, etc., and the modernist dream of industrialization. This form of industrialization indeed functions with many devices, such as with cars or photo cameras, but it doesn't fit in the case of a building that surrounds the human body.

AH: I totally agree with you. Together with Martin Rauch we developed the method of clay-storming. The students are given a large quantity of clay, which they knead. Through this physical activity the student is to get familiar with the self-lost, but concentrated way of working. Exercises follow afterwards, which have to be carried out quickly, in order to then be scrapped again. It is about getting into the flow, into the activity. Especially when urban planning exercises were on the agenda, it was extremely interesting to observe what types of lively forms (reminiscent of a Moroccan old city) evolved.

AH: Da bin ich ganz bei dir. Gemeinsam mit Martin Rauch haben wir die Methode Clay-Storming entwickelt. Die Studierenden erhalten eine große Menge Ton, die sie kneten. Durch diese physische Tätigkeit soll der Student in das selbstverlorene, aber konzentrierte Arbeiten hineinkommen. Danach folgen Übungen, die rasch umgesetzt werden, um dann wieder verworfen zu werden. Es geht darum, in den Fluss, ins Tun zu kommen. Gerade wenn städtebauliche Übungen auf dem Plan waren, war es äußerst interessant zu beobachten, was für lebendige Formen (erinnern an eine marokkanische Altstadt) entstanden sind.

Wenn am Computer ein städtebaulicher Plan entwickelt wird, unterliegt dieser immer einem Raster. Ich habe mir dann die Frage gestellt, ob wir diese Raster wirklich brauchen. Brauchen wir sie, um uns daran festzuhalten, weil wir den Kontakt zu unserer Intuition verloren haben. Müssen wir nicht beide Fähigkeiten trainieren? Ich mache bei jedem Projekt eine Analyse der Ressourcen, kläre die Potenziale, auf denen aufgesetzt werden kann. Aber wir können ja die Informationen, die auf uns einströmen, mit dem Verstand nicht mehr zur Gänze erfassen. Und letztendlich ist die Entscheidung beliebig, ob man diese oder jene Parameter verwendet. Nach meiner Erfahrung kommt man schneller zu einem lebendigen Ergebnis, wenn man die Analysen beiseite schiebt und das Wissen wirken lässt, einfach schaut, was sich aus dem Arbeiten, aus dem Tun mit dem Ton entwickelt. Das Arbeiten mit Ton erlaubt viel Kreativität. Beim Modellbau mit Styrocut muss die Idee bereits im Kopf sein und wenn man etwas weggeschnitten hat, dann bleibt es auch meistens weg. Beim Ton ist der Entwurfsprozess ständig am Fließen. Man nimmt Ton weg, man fügt Ton hinzu. Auch beim gemeinsamen Entwerfen im Team zeigt sich dann nicht mehr die individuelle Handschrift. Es fließen alle Ideen

Siebenter Tag • Day Seven

Bau des Beitrags zur Architektur Biennale Venedig · Construction of the contribution to the Architecture Biennale in Venice, 2016. © Stefano Mori

If an urban construction plan is developed on a computer, it is always subject to a grid. I then asked myself the question whether we really need this grid. Do we need it to cling onto because we've lost the contact to our intuition? Don't we have to train both skills? During every project I make an analysis of the resources, clarify the potentials that can be built upon. But we can no longer register the information streaming into us entirely with the mind. And the decision is ultimately arbitrary whether one uses this or that parameter. According to my experience, one reaches a lively result quicker if one pushes the analyses aside and lets knowledge take effect, simply looks at what develops out of the work, out of the activity with the clay. Working with clay allows a lot of creativity. When building models with Styrocut, the idea already has to be in your head, and if you cut something away, then it usually also remains away. With clay the design process is constantly flowing. You take clay away, you add it. Also when jointly designing in a team, the individual handwriting is no longer apparent. In the end it is 'one' design and this is very satisfying for the teamwork. When I design with Martin Rauch, we have noticed that it is better if we do not speak with each other during the design process, but simply work on the model. Because the thoughts don't have to be collected in advance, while the hand follows a direct impulse, meaning it does not unconditionally act in a rational manner.

DS: Your story reminds me of Steven Holl, who told me that he paints his 'watercolors'—his watercolor pictures—before breakfast. He goes to the office with them, they are scanned there, and then the further design process first begins. He holds the view that there is a direct connection of head to hand, on a pre-linguistic level.

AH: Or from stomach to hand.

DS: Heinz Tesar also begins the design process with his watercolors.

AH: One notices more and more that cities have arisen out of information. The color design is left up to advertising; don't dare show any emotion, only standard dimensions, nothing can be wrong there, because it is logical.

DS: Carlo Baumschlager implemented an interesting project with a builder in Vorarlberg, where the builder treated the new house like an older building, where the building stock also had to be taken over. This led to a situation where all of companies didn't have to take liability premiums any longer into account, which then resulted in the building being able to built around one-third cheaper. If the risk and liability premiums are dropped, we can return to cheaper construction. If we manage a building process on equal footing, in mutual trust, where everyone respects the other's effort and everyone does their best at a fair price, then we will come again to a better quality and a reasonable price.

AH: Yes, we have to get back there again. However, the bigger the systems become, the harder it will get. Trust needs a certain smallness in order to function.
I'm happy that I have a small office, because I can keep contact to my clients in this way. Because trust doesn't come immediately, one has to build it up, and this requires a certain amount of time.

ein. Es wird am Ende ‚ein' Entwurf und dies ist für die Zusammenarbeit sehr befriedigend. Wenn ich mit Martin Rauch entwerfe, haben wir festgestellt, dass es besser ist, wenn wir während des Entwurfsprozesses nicht miteinander reden, sondern einfach am Modell arbeiten. Denn die Gedanken müssen vorab gefasst werden, während die Hand einem direkten Impuls folgt, also nicht unbedingt kopfgesteuert agiert.

DS: Deine Erzählung erinnert mich an Steven Holl, der mir gesagt hat, dass er vor dem Frühstück seine ‚Watercolors' – seine Wasserfarbenbilder – malt. Mit diesen geht er dann ins Büro, dort werden sie eingescannt und erst dann beginnt der weitere Entwurfsprozess. Er vertritt die Ansicht, dass es eine direkte Verbindung vom Kopf zur Hand gibt, auf einer vorsprachlichen Ebene.

AH: Oder vom Bauch zur Hand.

DS: Auch Heinz Tesar beginnt den Entwurfsprozess mit seinen Aquarellen.

AH: Man sieht den Städten immer mehr an, dass sie aus der Information heraus entstanden sind. Die Farbgestaltung überlässt man der Werbung, nur ja keine Emotionen zeigen, nur Standardmaße, da kann nichts falsch sein, weil logisch.

DS: Carlo Baumschlager hat ein interessantes Projekt mit einem Bauträger in Vorarlberg umgesetzt, bei dem der Bauträger das neue Haus wie einen Altbau, bei dem ja auch der Bestand übernommen werden muss, behandelt hat. Dies hat dazu geführt, dass alle Firmen keine Haftungszuschläge mehr berücksichtigen mussten, was dann zur Folge hatte, dass der Bau um ein Drittel billiger umgesetzt werden konnte. Wenn der Risiko- und Haftungsaufschlag wegfällt, kommen wir wieder zu einem günstigeren Bauen. Wenn wir es schaffen, einen Bauprozess auf Augenhöhe, auf gegenseitigem Vertrauen, wo jeder die Leistung des anderen respektiert und jeder das Beste zu einem fairen Preis macht, dann kommen wir wieder zu einer besseren Qualität und einem vernünftigen Preis.

AH: Ja, da müssen wir wieder hinkommen. Doch, je größer die Systeme werden, umso schwieriger wird es. Vertrauen braucht eine gewisse Kleinheit, um zu funktionieren. Ich bin froh, dass ich ein kleines Büro habe, weil ich so den Kontakt zu meinen Bauherren halten kann. Denn Vertrauen kommt nicht sofort, man muss es aufbauen und dies erfordert eine gewisse Zeit.

Siebenter Tag • Day Seven

METI Schule · METI School, Rudrapur,
Realisierung mit · realization with Eike Roswag, 2005-06.
© Anna Heringer

DS: And where is the road taking you next?

AH: I would also like to apply the gained experiences that I collected in Bangladesh and also in Africa here. What could an implementation in Europe actually look like? The Rauch House is the only example for me where the 'clay hut' was implemented at a European standard. Local resources were used; the material from the building pit was used for construction, processed by hand, but taking a very high living standard into account. I'm interested in the question of how I, for example, can build social housing in a participatory manner by involving the users. That a community already arises during the construction process, that one can already feel at home at this stage. I also see this potential with public buildings. Imagine that, for example, the refugees here contribute to constructing a clay building. If they return to their home country, then they can take this knowledge with them and apply it advantageously when rebuilding on site. The structural

DS: Und wo geht es als nächstes hin?

AH: Ich möchte gerne die gewonnenen Erfahrungen, die ich in Bangladesch und auch in Afrika gesammelt habe, auch hier anwenden. Wie könnte eine Umsetzung in Europa tatsächlich aussehen? Das Haus Rauch ist für mich das einzige Beispiel, wo die ‚Lehmhütte' auf europäischem Standard umgesetzt wurde. Es wurden die lokalen Ressourcen genutzt, das Material aus der Baugrube zum Bau verwendet, mit den eigenen Händen bearbeitet, aber einen sehr hohen Lebensstandard berücksichtigend. Mich interessiert die Frage, wie kann ich zum Beispiel Sozialbauten partizipativ durch die Einbindung der Nutzer errichten. Dass schon während des Bauprozesses eine Gemeinschaft entsteht, dass man sich schon zu diesem Zeitpunkt zuhause fühlt. Auch bei öffentlichen Bauten sehe ich dieses Potenzial. Stell dir vor, dass zum Beispiel die Flüchtlinge hier bei einem Lehmbau mitwirken. Wenn sie wieder zurückkehren in ihre Heimat, dann können sie dieses Wissen mitnehmen und beim Wiederaufbau vor Ort gewinnbringend einsetzen. Die baulichen und menschlichen Ressourcen wären vorhanden, es fehlt nur an Know-how. Arbeiten mit Lehm kann auch ungelernte Arbeitskräfte auffangen und es wäre möglich, eine große Zahl von Personen zu integrieren.

DS: Solche Projekte würden das vorhandene Regelsystem in Frage stellen. Gerade bei den Flüchtlingsunterkünften ist unklar, was als Quartier genehmigt, wie mit eventuellen Risiken verfahren wird. Das Abschieben von Verantwortung auf Gesetze ist hinderlich.

AH: Dass bei uns der Lehmbau teurer als der Betonbau ist, ist unglaublich. Hier fordere ich von den Politikern ein, dass sie für Materialien wie Beton, die weder den Menschen noch der Umwelt guttun, CO2-Steuern einfordern.

DS: Und warum ist der Lehmbau teurer?

AH: Der Faktor der menschlichen Arbeitskraft ist hoch. Aber auf der Welt leben 7 Milliarden Menschen, diese Ressource wäre vorhanden und die Baubranche ist in der Lage, sinnvolle Arbeit anzubieten. Dabeizusein, wenn etwas entsteht, hebt das Selbstwertgefühl.

and human resources would be available; the only thing missing is know-how. Unskilled workers can also pick up working with clay and it would be possible to integrate a large number of people.

DS: Such projects would challenge the existing system of rules. Precisely in the case of refugee housing it is unclear what is approved as accommodation, how to proceed with possible risks. The shifting of responsibility to laws is obstructive.

AH: It is incredible that clay construction is more expensive in our country than concrete construction. I demand here from the politicians to call for a CO2 tax for materials like concrete, which neither benefit people nor the environment.

DS: And why is clay construction more expensive?

AH: The factor of manpower is high. But seven billion people live in the world; this resource would be available, and the construction industry is capable of offering meaningful work. Being present when something is created boosts the feeling of self-esteem.

DS: That's true. I don't know any foreman who doesn't proudly explain that this or that building was put up by him and he took the responsibility. But you are actually demanding a reversal of the political economy. You say let human manpower be worth something again and let us reduce the technical effort.

AH: That's right. Besides, it is important for me with my buildings that the aesthetic of the material also comes into effect with the sustainability, that the design is palpable. And that, like with the material of clay, for instance, enough of it is available, or with bamboo, that this grows back again within a year.

Siebenter Tag • Day Seven

DS: An incredible perversion of the term 'sustainability' has occurred. Houses that have been standing for centuries are sustainable. Those are the empirical facts of sustainability. And we want to replace this knowledge, which has been amassed over centuries, with technology today?

AH: Manual design is sustainable. Austria has a special role here with Vorarlberg and the Bregenz Forest.

DS: I would transfer this to every region in the world.

AH: It is no longer the custom that architecture students come into contact with a skilled trade.

DS: We already thought about reforming the study of architecture in the 1970s and I've always demanded that building practice ought to be performed in the scope of the study. Students should work in the summer on a construction site. I add my favorite sentence: The person who never sat in a trench doesn't know shit! If architects can also do manual skills again, then they are respected in an entirely different way on a building site.

AH: In Bangladesh we as architects did all the work—also the grunt work—on the construction site in order to break up the hierarchies. It was then first clear to me how strenuous certain activities were and afterwards I was able to estimate much better how much time an activity requires. That was a very important experience. What was your first construction site, then?

DS: I dug a trench for an exhibition pavilion on the Wels Fairgrounds.

DS: Stimmt, ich kenne keinen Polier, der nicht stolz erzählt, dass dieses oder jenes Gebäude von ihm hochgezogen und verantwortet wurde. Aber du verlangst eigentlich eine Umkehrung der Volkswirtschaft. Du sagst, lass uns die menschliche Arbeitskraft wieder etwas wert sein und reduzieren wir den technischen Aufwand.

AH: Das stimmt. Außerdem ist es mir bei meinen Gebäuden wichtig, dass bei der Nachhaltigkeit auch die Ästhetik des Materials zum Tragen kommt, dass die Gestaltung spürbar ist. Und dass, wie zum Beispiel beim Material Lehm, genügend davon vorhanden ist, oder beim Bambus, dass dieser innerhalb eines Jahres wieder nachwächst.

DS: Es hat eine unglaubliche Perversion des Begriffs Nachhaltigkeit stattgefunden. Nachhaltig sind Häuser, die seit hunderten von Jahren stehen. Das sind die empirischen Tatsachen der Nachhaltigkeit. Und dieses Wissen, das über Jahrhunderte zusammengetragen wurde, wollen wir heute durch Technik ersetzen?

AH: Die handwerkliche Gestaltung ist nachhaltig. Österreich hat hier eine besondere Rolle mit Vorarlberg und dem Bregenzerwald.

DS: Ich würde dies auf jede Region auf der Welt übertragen.

AH: Dass Architekturstudierende mit einem Handwerk in Berührung kommen, ist nicht mehr Usus.

DS: Wir haben schon in den 70er Jahren über eine Reform des Architekturstudiums nachgedacht und ich habe immer schon verlangt, dass im Rahmen des Studiums eine Baupraxis geleistet werden soll. Studenten sollten im Sommer auf einer Baustelle arbeiten. Dazu mein Lieblingssatz: Wer nie in einer Künette saß, der waaß an Schaß! Wenn auch Architekten wieder das Handwerkliche können, dann werden sie ganz anders auf einer Baustelle respektiert.

AH: Wir haben in Bangladesch als Architekten alle Arbeiten – auch die niedrigen – auf der Baustelle erledigt, um die Hierarchien aufzubrechen. Erst dann war mir klar, wie anstrengend gewisse Tätigkeiten waren und ich konnte im Nachhinein viel besser abschätzen, wieviel Zeit eine Tätigkeit in Anspruch nimmt. Eine sehr wichtige Erfahrung.
Was war denn deine erste Baustelle?

DS: Ich habe eine Künette für einen Ausstellungspavillon auf dem Welser Messegelände gegraben.

Biography Biografie

Dietmar Steiner. © Peter Rigaud

Geboren am 31. 12. 1951 in Wels +++ Realgymnasium Wels +++ HTL Krems +++ Akademie der bildenden Künste Wien: Studium der Architektur in Wien bei Ernst A. Plischke, später bei Gustav Peichl; Mitarbeit im Büro von Rob Krier +++ Generalsekretär der ÖGfA – Österreichische Gesellschaft für Architektur (1980–1982) +++ Hochschule für angewandte Kunst Wien: Lehrauftrag und Mitarbeit am Archiv „Österreichische Architektur des 20. Jahrhunderts" von Friedrich Achleitner (bis 1989) +++ Eigenes Büro für Architekturberatung (ab 1989) mit Aufträgen national und international +++ Gründung (1993) und Leitung des Architekturzentrum Wien (bis 2016) mit reger Ausstellungs-, Vermittlungs- und Sammeltätigkeit (Bibliothek, Archiv, Sammlung, Baubesuche, Architekturreisen, internationale Übernahmen und Kooperationen, eigene Produktionen mit Weitervermittlung an internationale Ausstellungshäuser)

Im In- und Ausland umfangreiche Vortrags- und Publikationstätigkeit, Ausstellungskurator, Jurymitglied, Redakteurs- und Herausgebertätigkeit. Unter anderem verantwortlicher Autor der Architekturseite in *Die Presse – spectrum* (alternierend mit Otto Kapfinger); in den 1980er Jahren Chefredakteur Architektur bei *domus*; in den 1990er Jahren Mitglied des Advisory Committee des „European Union Prize for Contemporary Architecture – Mies van der Rohe Award" (1996–2014); Österreichischer Kommissär bei der 8. Architektur Biennale Venedig (2002); Präsident des Weltverbandes der Architekturmuseen ICAM (2006–14).

Vorträge und Lehre (Auswahl):
Barcelona, Basel, Belgrad, Berlin, Biel, Boston (Harvard, MIT), Bregenz, Bukarest, Buenos Aires, Delft, Düsseldorf, Edinburgh, Eindhoven, Frankfurt, Gävle, Gelsenkirchen, Graz, Grenoble, Hangzhou, Helsinki, Kaiserslautern, Kassel, Karlsruhe, Liechtenstein, Linz, Ljubljana, London, Los Angeles, Lugano, Mendrisio, Milano, Montreal, München, New York, Nürnberg, Ottawa, Oslo, Paris, Piran, Potsdam, Rom, Rotterdam, Santiago de Compostela, Shenzhen, Skopje, Split, Stockholm, Trondheim, Usedom, Warschau, Wien, Zagreb, Zürich …

Born on December 31, 1951 in Wels +++ Realgymnasium (grammar school with emphasis on natural sciences), Wels +++ Higher Technical College for Civil Engineering, Krems +++ Academy of Fine Arts Vienna: Architecture study in Vienna in the masterschool of Ernst A. Plischke, later with Gustav Peichl; assistant at Rob Krier's office +++ General Secretary of the Austrian Society for Architecture (ÖGfA) (1980–1982) University of Applied Arts Vienna: Teaching assignment and collaboration in Friedrich Achleitner's archive "Austrian Architecture of the 20th Century" (until 1989) +++ Own office for architectural consulting (as of 1989) with national and international commissions +++ Founding (1993) and management of the Architekturzentrum Wien (until 2016) with considerable exhibition, mediation and collection activities (library, archive, collection, site visits, architectural journeys, international transfers and cooperation, own productions with further distribution to international exhibition venues)

Extensive lecture and publication activity at home and abroad, exhibition curator, jury member, editing and publishing activity. Among other things: Responsible author of the architecture page in *Die Presse – spectrum* (alternating with Otto Kapfinger in the 1980s); Chief Architecture Editor at *domus* in the 1990s; Member of the Advisory Committee of the "European Union Prize for Contemporary Architecture – Mies van der Rohe Award" (1996–2014); Austrian Commissioner at the 8th Architecture Biennale in Venice (2002); President of the International Confederation of Architecture Museums (ICAM) (2006–14).

Teaching and Lectures (selected):
Barcelona, Basel, Belgrad, Berlin, Biel, Boston (Harvard, MIT), Bregenz, Bukarest, Buenos Aires, Delft, Düsseldorf, Edinburgh, Eindhoven, Frankfurt, Gävle, Gelsenkirchen, Graz, Grenoble, Hangzhou, Helsinki, Kaiserslautern, Kassel, Karlsruhe, Liechtenstein, Linz, Ljubljana, London, Los Angeles, Lugano, Mendrisio, Milano, Montreal, München, New York, Nürnberg, Ottawa, Oslo, Paris, Piran, Potsdam, Rom, Rotterdam, Santiago de Compostela, Shenzhen, Skopje, Split, Stockholm, Trondheim, Usedom, Warschau, Wien, Zagreb, Zürich, …

Index Personenregister

Aalto, Alvar 137, 367f, 383
Abraham, Raimund 13, 30, 32, 115, 141, 319, 320
Abril, Antón Garvia 369
Achenbach, Helge 164f
Achleitner, Friedrich 7, 70, 86f, 90f, 98, 100, 135, 164f, 197, 204, 393
Albrecht, Birgit 307, 311
Amateur Architecture Studio 346–349, 362, 366f
Anderson, Laurie 238
Antfarm 36f, 188f
Appelt, Werner 60–63, 67f
Arakeljan, H. 54f
Aranas, Uwe 52
Archigram 36f, 43, 188f, 237
Archizoom 36f, 43, 188
Arets, Wiel 75, 77, 79
Ármansson, Pétur H. 311
Artmann, H.C. 31, 34
Arup, Ove 252
Ass, Kyrill 368

Badanes, Steve 291f
Baller, Hinrich und Inken 115
Ban, Shigeru 370
Banfi, Gian Luigi 51
Bangle, Chris 46
Bašić, Nikola 355–359
Basinger, Kim 237f
Batteríið Architects 83
Bauer, Eric 319
Baumann, Atelier 41f
Bayer, Konrad 30f, 32f
BBPR 51f
Beatles 37f, 187
Beethoven 187
Behnisch und Partner 112, 113
Behnisch, Günther 18
Behrens, Peter 94
Belgiojoso, Ludovico 51
Belz, Walter 112, 113
Bentmann/Müller 174f
Bertelli, Patricio 224
Bétrix, Marie-Claude 72
Beuys, Joseph 187
Binswanger, Christine 243
Björnsdóttir, Sigridur 303
Blau, Luigi 12, 60–64, 67, 69, 98f
BKK-2 322
Bofill, Ricardo 131f, 144
Boga, Thomas 160, 163
Bogart, Humphrey 109
Bogdanović, Bogdan 21f

Bohigas, Oriol 77
Bonell, Esteve 79, 82
Bonner, Jennifer 286ff
Botta, Mario 61, 67, 70f, 168f, 243, 250, 256
Bradbury, Ray 276f
Braghieri, Gianni 122, 123125
Broder, Henryk M. 301
Brodsky, Alexander 350–353, 368f
Brook, Peter 201
Budilowskyj, M. 55
Burckhardt, Lucius 14ff, 164f
Burdett, Ricky 14f, 80, 81
Burkhardt, François 164f, 260
Burroughs, William S. 31, 33
Buck & Giencke 320
Busek, Erhard 13, 320
Butković, Ivo 355–358
BWM Architekten 10

Cage, John 31, 33, 201
Cagney, James 109
Calamai, Clara 133f
Campi, Mario 72f
Capezzuto, Rita 262
Cervelló, Marta 73f
Chachola Schmal, Peter 80, 81
Chamberlin, Powell and Bon 54
Chipperfield, David 76, 79f, 83, 246
Chorherr, Christoph 384
Christer, Steve 304
Chu, Karl S. 47
CIAM 26f
Clinton, Bill 281
Clinton, Hillary 215, 216
Coates, Nigel 170f
Colani, Luigi 331
Colquhoun, Alan 180f, 343
Consolascio, Eraldo 72
Cook, John W. 237
Cook, Peter 29, 30, 33, 36f, 96f, 204f, 332
Coop Himmelblau 20, 22, 26f, 36–46, 144f, 171, 188f, 237, 336, 347
Cuesta, Javier (s. a. Ensamble) 369
Cufer, Margarethe 21, 57, 314, 377
Czech, Hermann 12, 14f, 21, 61–66, 67ff, 96–107, 133, 144, 319, 326, 327

Davies, John 115
de Meuron, Pierre (s. a. Herzog & de Meuron) 128, 319
de Vylder Vinck Taillieu 365, 369
Deplazes, Andrea 163
Dibelius, Ulrich 172–175

Diener, Roger 327
Disney 144f, 178f, 182, 188, 189ff, 210, 211–222, 238, 240, 332f, 337f
Diwnow, W. 54
Dorsey, Brian 9
Dragset, Ingar 378f
Dschalagania, Z. 54
Duchamp, Marcel 378
Dudler, Max 372

Eco, Umberto 185
Eggertsson, Dagur 363, 367
eichinger oder knechtl 90f, 158, 224f
Eisenman, Peter 75, 86, 115, 164f, 168f, 201f, 332
Eisner, Michael 178f, 215f, 218, 219, 222, 332f
Eliasson, Olafur 83
Elmgreen, Michael 378f
Emery Roth & Sons 229
Ensamble Studio, 366f

Faloci, Pierre-Louis 76
Fattinger, Peter 345, 384
Fehn, Sverre 76, 308
Feininger, Lyonel 59, 66
Feireiss, Kristin 79
Fernández Galiano, Luis 79ff
Feuerstein, Günther 30f, 32, 97
Florian, Friedrich St. 30, 32
Fonatti, Franco 33
Ford, Henry 221
Foster, Norman 82, 144f, 168f, 174f, 238, 246
Frank, Heinz 86
Frank, Josef 61, 67, 100f, 200, 264
Fretton, Tony 246
Frischmuth, Barbara 118, 119
Fujimoto, Sou 364, 370, 372, 373

Galí, Beth 81
Galliano, Luis Fernandez 79, 81
Gangoly, Hans 224f
García-Abril, Antón (s. a. Ensamble) 369
Gaudí, Antoni 73
Gausa, Manuel 73f
Gehry, Frank 92f, 157, 168f, 235, 238f, 249, 250, 256, 272f, 344
Gerngross, Heidulf 63, 65, 68f, 224f, 283f
Gessner, Hubert 316
Giedion, Sigfried 30, 32
Gigon & Guyer 77
Gilbert & George 247
Gilliam, Terry 144
Ginsburg, Moisei 95
Glück, Harry 318
Gnaiger, Roland 7, 8f, 383f
Godard, Jean-Luc 132f
Göderitz, Johannes 231
Goldberger, Paul 229
Golossow, Ilja 95
Götz, Bettina 80f
Grabowska-Hawrylak, Jadwiga 55
Gramsci, Antonio 14f
Grassi, Giorgio 115
Graves, Michael 113, 178f, 213, 214, 219, 238, 333
Gray, Diane 76, 80
Greenberg, Allan 93, 113
Grimshaw, Nicholas 82, 246
Gropius, Walter 26f, 60, 66, 102f, 376
Gsteu, Johann, Georg 98, 100, 197
Guallart, Vicente 73f
Gugger, Harry 243, 386
Guttmann, Eva 9

Hadid, Zaha 13ff, 75, 79f, 83, 110, 111, 251, 256, 347
Haerdtl Oswald 59, 69
Hafner, Bernhard 33
Halbwachs, Maurice 130
Hämmerle, Marina 366, 370, 373
Hardadóttir, Margrét 304
Häring, Hugo 200
Harrap, Julian 83
Häuselmayer, Otto 13, 317, 319
Hauser, Sigrid 180f
HausRucker-Co (s. a. Ortner) 26f, 32, 36–49, 188f, 237
Hejduk, John 115, 141, 152
Hejduk, Pez 314
Helgason, Hallgrimur 304
Heller, Gerhard 56
Hellmuth, George 230
Heringer, Anna 382–391
Hermann & Valentiny 325
Herzog & de Meuron 74, 122, 123, 124f128, 133, 136, 139, 241, 242–249, 250, 255, 256

Herzog, Jacques 11–25, 74, 128, 183, 240f, 242–249, 319, 383
Hild, Andreas 163
Hirner, Michael 314
Hirschbühl, Arnold 373
Hlaweniczka, Kurt 318
Hoffmann, Ernst 87
Hoffmann, Hubert 231
Hoffmann, Josef 30, 32
Holl, Steven 12, 17, 224f, 294–297, 389
Hollein, Hans 20, 22, 26f, 30f, 32ff, 62, 68, 93, 97, 103f, 105ff, 115, 117, 133, 157, 194–209, 235, 269
Holzbauer, Wilhelm 30, 32, 115, 197
Holzer, Jenny 164, 234f
Holzmeister, Clemens 26f, 98, 194, 197f
Horowitz, Michael 36
Hortet, Lluís 80
Hrausky, Andrej 76f
Huber, Franz 377
Hufnagl, Viktor 319
Hummel 62, 67, 106
Hundertwasser, Friedensreich 30, 32, 191
Hunte, Otto 109
Hursley, Timothy 280–288
Hussl 268

Isozaki, Arata 75, 114, 178f, 210, 222, 238, 332f
Ito, Toyo 76, 370
Izenour, Steven 236f

Jacobs, Jane 330
Jacques, Michel 262f
Jahn, Helmut 157
Jencks, Charles 200, 230,
Jerde, Jon 270–279
Johnson, Philip 89147, 200, 219f
Judd, Donald 180f, 234, 379
Juen, Wolfgang 123, 124

Kaiser, Gabriele 7, 9f
Kammerer, Hans 112, 113
Kannonier, Reinhard 9
Kapfinger, Otto 12, 62–66, 68f, 86f, 90f, 132f, 202f, 393
Karan, Donna 238f
Kawakubo, Rei 237f
Kerez, Christian 163
Kerouac, Jack 31, 33
Kesler, L. 54
Kettelhut, Erich 109
Khomeini, Ruhollah 89
Kiesler, Frederick 30, 32, 47, 297
Kießling, Stefan 327
Kimberg, W. 54
Kittler, Friedrich 331
Kleihues, Josef Paul 73, 92
Kljajic, Branimir 325
Klotz, Heinrich 185, 237
Kneissl, Franz Eberhard 60–65, 67f, 132f
Köb, Edelbert 363, 366
Köberl, Rainer 224f
Koenig, Giovanni Klaus 185
Kolbai-Kafalier, Asiye 268
Kollhoff, Hans 170f, 173, 326, 327
Kolomijez, W. 55
Konstantinovsky, G. 55
Koolhaas, Rem 83, 111, 115, 144, 170f, 201f, 224, 240f, 242f, 249, 250ff, 256–259, 262f, 270, 272, 332f
Kormakúr, Baltasar 304
Kostin, W. 55
Kotschar, G. 54
Krasnoff, Sarah 118, 120
Krawina, Joseph 191
Krens, Thomas 211, 255, 258
Krier, Léon 14f, 93, 101f, 131, 144
Krier, Rob 56f, 84–87, 101f, 115, 131, 144f, 147f, 174f, 319, 333, 393
Krischanitz, Adolf 12f, 62–65, 68f, 86f, 132f, 135, 137, 202f, 319, 326, 327
Kubelka, Peter 107
Kubrick, Stanley 151
Kurrent, Friedrich 197, 319
Kussin, Thomas 9, 26, 198, 110, 187, 218, 225

Lacaton & Vassal 79f, 260–269, 347
Lackner, Josef 197
Landyj, W. 55
Lang, Fritz 109
Lang, Helmut 234f, 240
Lapidus, Morris 192, 236f
Larsen, Henning 78f, 83
Lautner & Scheifinger & Szedenik 320
Laxness, Halldór 302f
Le Corbusier 113, 117, 236f
Leary, Timothy 31, 33, 39
Ledoux, Claude-Nicolas 29, 30
Lefaivre, Liane 170f, 203
Leinweber, Joseph 230
Leonidov, Ivan 111
Leontjew, D. 55
Lepik, Andres 382, 386
Libeskind, Daniel 77, 141, 143, 147f, 152f, 332f
Lindsey, Bruce 287f
Löcker 63, 68, 96, 98, 100f
Loos, Adolf 12, 14f, 31, 34, 59f, 65, 69, 91, 206, 338, 340, 354f, 376f
Lucan, Jacques 74, 76
Lukács, Georg 86f
Lynch, Kevin A. 24f, 377f
Lynn, Greg 47, 344
Lyotard, Jean-François 118, 121, 203

Maas, Winy 251
Märkli, Peter 327
Magnago Lampugnani, Vittorio 77, 79, 333
Mahrer, Alois 26f
Mansilla + Tuñón 79f, 83
Mao Zedong 89
Marinetti, Filippo Tommaso 111
Marukow, W. 55
MAscha & Seethaler 325
Mateo, Josep Lluís 73f
Mau, Bruce 262f
Mauer, Otto 30, 32
Mauthe, Jörg 13
Mayer, Karoline 7, 10
Mazanek, Claudia 9
McLeod, Mary 331
McLuhan, Marshall 31, 33
Mead, Syd 109, 333
Meier, Richard 157, 168f, 243, 250, 256
Meili Peter Architekten 327
Melnikow, Konstantin 63, 68, 94
Melnytschenko, W. 54
Mesa, Débora 369
Mesa, Débora (s. a. Ensamble) 369

Mies van der Rohe 21f, 26f, 40f, 76, 78, 80f, 82, 164f, 224, 239f, 362, 376, 379, 393
Milezkyj, A. 54
Milinis, Ignaty 95
Mironowitsch, W. 55
Missing Link 26f, 33f, 98f, 101f, 188f
Mistelbauer, Wolfgang 100f
Mockbee, Samuel 280, 283f, 286–289, 292
Moneo, Rafael 78f, 83
Monina, O. 55
Moore, Charles 92, 113, 220, 236ff
Morrison, Jasper 149
Mostafavi, Mohsen 80f
Muschamp, Herbert 279
Mušić, V. 55
Navarro Baldeweg, Juan 78
Nervi, Pier Luigi 52
Nestroy, Johann 31, 33
Netschurin, A. 55
Neumann, Heinz 87
New York Five 100f
Ngo, Anh-Linh 10
Nishizawa, Ryue 370
Norberg-Schulz, Christian 118, 121
Norri, Marja-Riitta 76f
Nouvel, Jean 78f, 170–173, 297, 319, 374
NOX 47

Oberhuber, Oswald 204f
Olgiati, Rudolf 116, 117
OMA 77, 83, 92f, 111, 131f, 240–243, 250ff, 256–259, 262f
Ortner, Laurids 36–49, 170f, 178, 181
Ortner, Manfred 36f
Ott-Reinisch, Irene 296

Pahlavi, Reza Schah 89
Pálsson, Águst 303
Parenzan, Leo 319
Parkinson, John + Donald 109
Pasterk, Ursula 165
Pawson, John 235f
Peichl, Gustav 56f, 115, 197, 204f, 393
Pelli, César 219f, 229
Pentagram 220
Peressutti, Enrico 51
Perrault, Dominique 76f, 79, 82
Piano, Renzo 77
Pichler, Walter 30, 32, 38f, 97, 201, 204, 206
Pinter, Klaus 36f
Pisarik, Sonja 7, 10
Plečnik, Josef 203
Plischke, Ernst A. 56f, 393
Podrecca, Boris 64f, 69, 99f
Polanski, Roman 132f
Ponti, Gio 51ff
pool Architektur 325
Porsch, Johannes 280
Portoghesi, Paolo 92, 131f, 256, 378f
Prada 234f, 242, 252f, 256ff, 378f
Prada, Muccia 224
Prader+Fehringer 34
Predock, Antoine 178f
Pribitzer, Michael 319
Prince Charles 333, (399)
Prix, Wolf D. 36–49, 74, 168, 171, 336, 338, 344
Prochazka, Elsa 60–65, 67f
Protetch, Max 283f
Prouvé, Jean 26f, 376
Pruscha, Carl 13, 317, 319, 320
Puchhammer, Hans 98, 100, 197
Purini+Thermes 93

Quaid, Dennis 237f
querkraft 224f

Radić, Ivo 55
Radić, Smiljan 368f, 370
Rainer, Roland
Rambert, Francis
Rauch, Martin 382f, 386–389
Reagan, Ronald 89
Reed, Lou 224
Reichlin, Bruno 70f, 72, 130
Reinhardt, Max 201
Reinhart, Fabio 70f, 72, 161
Requat & Reinthaller 318
Ricciotti, Rudy 79f
Rich, Frank 216f
Richter, Helmut 13, 63, 65, 68f, 319, 321

Rieper, Michael 345
Rintala, Sami 363, 367, 383
Ritter, Katharina 7, 10, 225, 280
Rius, Francesc 82
Riva, Remo 270
Robertson, Jaquelin T. 220
Robnik, Drehli 342
Rogers, Ernesto N. 51ff
Rogers, Richard 111, 246
Rolling Stones 31, 33, 37f, 187
Rossi, Aldo 12, 14ff, 56f, 60, 66, 71, 72ff, 85f, 100f, 122, 123, 125, 130, 133f, 144, 168f, 178f, 201, 221ff, 238, 330
Rosweg, Eike 384
Roth, Dieter 303
Rothko, Mark 187
Rourke, Mickey 237f
Ruault, Philippe 261f, 268
Rudofsky, Bernard 26f, 377f
Rühm, Gerhard 201
Rural Studio 224f, 280–293, 384
Rybatschuk, A. 54

Sacks, Herman 109
Safdie, Moshe 54
Salz der Erde 34, 96f
Sam, Franz 296
Samuelsson, Gudjón 307, 311
Sanders, Jay 287f
Saxon, Richard 332f
Scarpa, Carlo 308
Schadrin, I. 55
Schiele, Egon 113
Schindler, Rudolph M. 30, 32, 197
Schinkel, Friedrich 113
Schmid, Peter 26f
Scholten, Rudolf 165
Schönberg, Arnold 172f
Schrager, Ian 241, 242, 250, 256, 296f
Schtolko, W. 55
Schwalm-Teiss & Bresich 325
Schweighofer, Anton 115, 197

Schwetschenko, W. 55
Scolari, Massimo 93
Scott Brown, Denise 236f, 330
Scott, Ridley 89, 109, 330
Seehof, Stefan 268
Segal, L. 55
Sejima, Kazuyo 347, 369f
Semper, Gottfried 63, 68, 157ff
Sennett, Richard 190
Shu, Wang 346f
Sigurdardóttir, Högna 307, 309
Šik, Miroslav 74, 160, 161, 163
Siza Vieira, Álvaro 82, 115
Slogozka, N. 55
Snozzi, Luigi 70f
Solà-Morales, Ignasi y 168f
Sorkin, Michael 190
Spalt, Johannes 197, 319
Spiluttini, Margherita 77, 85, 95, 103, 105f, 127, 189, 244, 247, 249, 314, 316f, 321f, 327
Springsteen, Bruce 118, 123, 125
Spuybroek, Lars 47
Starck, Philippe 242, 296f
Stefantschuk, J. 54
Steidle, Otto 13, 135, 138, 319, 326, 327
Steiner, Eric 87
Steinmann, Martin 118, 119, 131–135,
Stern, Robert A. M. 93, 178f, 214f, 218, 220f, 238333
Stirling, James 18, 113, 115330f
Strehler, Giorgio 50
Studio Granda 300, 304ff, 309, 311
Studio Grau 93
Superstudio 36f, 43, 188f
Swiczinsky, Helmut 36ff
Swoboda, Hannes 165
Szeemann, Harald 56f

Tabanlioglu, Murat 278
Tarragó Cid, Salvador 72f
Tchilawa, T. 54
Tendenza 12, 56f, 70
Tesar, Heinz 13, 34, 60, 66, 98ff, 317, 319, 326, 327, 389
Tessenow, Heinrich 219
Thatcher, Margaret 89
The Doors 47
Thun, Matteo 145f, 155ff
Tito 21, 23
Trumbull, Douglas 109, 333

Tschachawa, G. 54
Tschumi, Bernard 170f
Turnovský, Jan 224f
Tzonis, Alexander 170f, 203

Uhl, Ottokar 30, 32, 135, 197
UN Studio 80
Ungers, Oswald Matthias 147, 157, 168f, 201f
Utzon, Jørn 308

Vacchini, Livio 71
van Berkel, Ben 80, 81, 251, 256
van Doesburg 30, 32
van Loon, Ellen 80, 81, 83, 259
Venezia, Francesco
Venturi, Robert 56f, 85f, 130, 132f, 149, 201, 219, 222, 236f, 330
Vesnin (brothers) 94
Virilio, Paul 118, 120, 122, 123
Vitruv 152f
Voggenhuber, Johannes 90f
Vollbrecht, Karl 109

Wachsmann, Konrad 26f, 30, 32, 60, 63, 66, 68, 102–105
Waclawek, Fritz 319
Wafler Architekten 317
Wagner, Otto 12, 20f, 29, 30, 61, 67, 101f
Wang, Wilfried 14f, 77
Wassmann, Christian 296
Wasylewskyj, I. 54
Wawrik, Gunther 98, 100, 197
Weaver, Sigourney 89
Welzenbacher, Lois 135ff
Wenders, Wim 118, 119
Wenyu, Lu 346f
Werkstatt Wien 325
Wesnin (Brüder) 94
Wiener Gruppe 31, 34
Wiener, Oswald 31, 33
Windbrechtinger, Traude & Wolfgang 319
Wittgenstein, Hermine 60, 66
Wittgenstein, Ludwig 59f, 66f, 69, 172f
Wright, Frank Lloyd 109, 113
Wurnig, Marin 325
Wyman, George 109

Yamasaki, Minora 226, 229f

Zamp Kelp, Günter 36f
Zanuso, Marco 50
Zaugg, Remy 248
Zenghelis, Elia 76f, 79, 111, 251256
Zilk, Helmut 104, 320f
Zumthor, Peter 76f, 82, 189, 240347, 362f, 373

About the Photographs

Zu den Abbildungen

Nach einer Hochblüte der professionellen Architekturfotografie in den 1950er und 1960er Jahren begannen in den späten 1970er Jahren die Architekten selbst ihre Bauten zu fotografieren. Von Antonionis Blow up befördert, kauften sie sich Hasselblad Kameras, wurden kreativ und glaubten, auf professionelle ArchitekturfotografInnen verzichten zu können.

Bis dahin zeichneten sich Architekturmagazine überwiegend durch drucktechnische Bleiwüsten aus, mit Plänen und abgesoffenen Schwarz-Weiß-Fotografien. Die Autorschaft von Bildern war kein Thema. Für Vorträge und Publikationen erhielt ich von den Architekten Fotos ihrer Bauten ohne Hinweis auf die Urheberschaft. Viele dieser Bilder wurden hier verwendet. Die dafür verantwortlichen FotografInnen mögen mir verzeihen, dass mir davon keine Kenntnis übermittelt wurde.

Mitte der 1980er Jahre kam es zu einem neuen Aufschwung der Architekturfotografie. Die Magazine konnten nun kostengünstig in full color drucken. Es waren die professionellen ArchitekturfotografInnen, die den Architekturzeitschriften die neuen Projekte der ArchitektInnen anboten und so zu den maßgeblichen Agenten des Architektur-Marketings wurden.

Inzwischen hat sich der Markt nochmals weiterentwickelt. Von jedem Projekt, von jedem Bauwerk findet man im Internet Bilder, die frei verfügbar sind und eine ernsthafte Konkurrenz für ArchitektInnen wie für ArchitekturfotografInnen darstellen.

Ich habe deshalb versucht, die Herkunft aller Fotografien in diesem Buch – durch Kennzeichnung beim jeweiligen Bild – deutlich zu machen.

Der Großteil stammt von mir selbst: © DS.

Jene Fotografien, die mir für Artikel und Vorträge ohne Nennung der Urheberschaft zur Verfügung gestellt oder die aus Publikationen, in denen der Urheber nicht genannt wird, reproduziert wurden, tragen die Kennzeichnung: Archiv DS.

Following the heyday of professional architectural photography in the 1950s and 1960s, architects began to photograph their buildings themselves in the late 1970s. Promoted by Antonioni's Blowup, they bought Hasselblad cameras, became creative and thought they were able to do without architectural photographers.

Up to then, architecture magazines were overwhelmingly characterized by typographically gray deserts, with blueprints and oversaturated black-and-white photographs. The authorship of images was not an issue. For lectures and publications I received pictures from architects of their buildings without any indication of the originator. Many of these images were used here. May the responsible photographers forgive me for the fact that no knowledge of authorship was conveyed to me.

A new upswing of architectural photography came about in the mid-1980s. The magazines were now able to print in full color affordably. It was the professional photographers who offered the architecture magazines the new projects of architects and thus became the essential agents of architectural marketing.

In the meantime, the market has advanced once again. Freely available pictures of every project, every structure, can be found on the Internet and pose serious competition to architects, as well as to architectural photographers.

I have therefore attempted to make the source of all photographs in this book clear—through the labeling of each picture.

Most of them originate from me personally: © DS.

Those photographs that were made available to me for articles and lectures without any mention of the authorship or were reproduced from publications in which the originators were not named carry the identification: Archive DS.

Thanks

Dank

Steiner's Diary is my very personal synopsis of goings-on in the architectural world during the past decades. Therefore, it is a matter of course for me that this book is funded without any grants from my employer, the Architekturzentrum Wien, and without public subsidies.

I am especially grateful to the editor and all the sponsors from the private sector who have made the production of this book possible through their terrific commitment.

Steiner's Diary ist meine ganz persönliche Zusammenschau über das Architekturgeschehen der vergangenen Jahrzehnte. Daher ist es für mich selbstverständlich, dass dieses Buch ohne Zuwendungen meines bisherigen Arbeitgebers, des Architekturzentrum Wien, und ohne Förderungen öffentlicher Subventionsgeber finanziert wird.

Dem Herausgeber und all den Sponsoren aus der Privatwirtschaft bin ich ganz besonders dankbar, dass sie durch ihr großartiges Engagement die Produktion dieses Buches ermöglicht haben.

Universität für künstlerische und industrielle Gestaltung Linz

Eternit Werke Ludwig Hatschek GmbH
Kallco Development GmbH
Gesiba – Gemeinnützige Siedlungs- und Bauaktiengesellschaft
wertinvest

ÖSW – Österreichisches Siedlungswerk, Gemeinnützige Wohnungsaktiengesellschaft
Wien 3420 Aspern Development AG
WBV-GPA – Wohnbauvereinigung für Privatangestellte GmbH
Neues Leben – Gemeinnützige Bau-, Wohn- und Siedlungsgenossenschaft Reg.Gen.m.b.H.
MIGRA Gemeinnützige Wohnungsges.m.b.H.
WOGEM – Gemeinnützige Wohn-, Bau- und Siedlungsgesellschaft für Gemeindebedienstete GesmbH

Strabag
Sozialbau AG
Wittmann Möbelwerkstätten GmbH

Herausgeber / Editor: Linzer Vorlesungen Kunstuniversität Linz,
Roland Gnaiger | die architektur

Lektorat (Deutsch) / Copy Editing (German): Claudia Mazanek
Übersetzung und Lektorat (Englisch) /
Translation and Copy Editing (English): Brian Dorsey

Buchgestaltung / Graphic Design:
Thomas Kussin / Silvia Druml, Rosi Ladner, Andreas Posselt, buero8

 Papier / Paper: Eos Werkdruck von Salzer 100g / 2,0 Vol.
Schrift / Typeface: Apex Serif, Fago, Museo Sans, Minion Pro
Druck / Printing: Holzhausen Druck GmbH, Wolkersdorf

© 2016 Dietmar Steiner, Vienna, and Park Books, Zurich

Park Books AG
Niederdorfstrasse 54
8001 Zurich, Switzerland
www.park-books.com

Alle Rechte vorbehalten; kein Teil dieses Werks darf in irgendeiner Form ohne vorherige schriftliche Genehmigung des Verlags reproduziert oder unter Verwendung elektronischer Systeme verarbeitet, vervielfältigt oder verbreitet werden.
All rights reserved; no part of this publication may be reproduced, stored in a retrieval system or transmitted in any form or by any means, electronic, mechanical, photocopying, recording or otherwise, without the prior written consent of the publisher.

ISBN 978-3-03860-032-9

kunstuniversität linz
Universität für künstlerische und industrielle Gestaltung
www.ufg.at

Bilder / Credits:
Cover: Dietmar Steiner at the Sori Rossii (Sunrise of Russia) Sanatorium, Crimea,
W. Zhylin, O. Ivanov, H. Kostomarov, Je. Perchenkov, 1985
© Simona Rota, 29.04.2012

Enviromental Reproductions:
© Elmar Bertsch, Hand-Modell: Fanny Wilder

Dank an: Katrin Ecker, Architekturzentrum Wien,
Sammlung · Collection, Margherita Spiluttini

Last of all: Visit in the new city of Poundbury ...
Zu allerletzt: Besuch in der neuen Stadt Poundbury ...